THE BOOK OF FILM NOIR

OF RELATED INTEREST FROM

CONTINUUM

For more information on these and other titles on the arts, write to:

Continuum
370 Lexington Avenue
New York, NY 10017

The Book of

FILM NOIR

edited by Ian Cameron

CONTINUUM • NEW YORK

1993

The Continuum Publishing Company
370 Lexington Avenue, New York, NY 10017

Produced by Cameron Books
PO Box 1, Moffat, Dumfriesshire DG10 9SU, Scotland

Printed in Great Britain

Designed by Ian Cameron

Library of Congress Cataloging-in-Publication Data

The Book of film noir / edited by Ian Cameron
      p.   cm.
   Includes bibliographical references and index.
   ISBN 0-8264-0589-4
   1. Film noir—United States—History and criticism.   I. Cameron,
Ian Alexander, 1937–   .
PN1995.9.F54B66 1993   93—2128
791.43'655—dc20   CIP

Stills reproduced by courtesy of British Film Institute Education
Department, Columbia, National Film Archive, New Realm, Orion,
Paramount, PRC, Rank, RKO Radio, Twentieth Century-Fox, United
Artists, Universal, Warner Brothers

CONTENTS

FOREWORD

For a cycle of films that began some fifty years ago and was significant for only about fifteen years, *film noir* still has a remarkable appeal. Its more obvious conventions and stylistic features have become part of the cinematic vocabulary, drawn on by even the most unambitious of film-makers and recognised by the reviewers, whose sense of what characterised *film noir* may be somewhat diffuse. There was clearly more to *film noir* than contrasty lighting, wet streets and *femmes fatales*. Yet even at the most rudimentary level of recognition, *noir* almost invariably has positive connotations: as a descriptive (or evocative) term, *film noir* carries an undertone of almost automatic approbation that, say, western or musical do not.

This book arose from the feeling that, although the fashion for *film noir* was attended from the 'seventies onwards by quite a wide literature, most of the books were very general surveys of the field that lacked thorough treatment of the individual films. The combination of general articles and detailed analyses of a selection of films here is designed to cover *film noir* in both breadth and depth.

The contents were to a large extent worked out, as regards both topics and films to be covered, through a consensus of the *Movie* editorial board, although inevitably the choice has been modified by factors such as the availability of prints. The only areas that have been deliberately excluded – notably the topic of women in *film noir* and the films *Gilda* and *Mildred Pierce* – are those covered in the British Film Institute publication *Women in Film Noir* (1978), edited by E. Ann Kaplan, which is still in print as this book goes to press. The extended coverage of Robert Siodmak as a *film noir* director was prompted both by the lack of anything substantial on him in the English language and by his importance to the cycle – three or four of the films dealt with at length in the article would otherwise have merited individual treatment. In all, twenty *films noirs* of the 'forties and 'fifties are covered in detail.

The focus of this book is on American *film noir*. However, an article is included on French antecedents, mainly from the 'thirties, when many of the German directors who ended up in Hollywood in the 'forties – Fritz Lang, Robert Siodmak, Billy Wilder, Max Ophuls and Curtis Bernhardt, not to mention the French Jacques Tourneur – were working in France. It does not deal with British or European films made during the late 'forties and the 'fifties that could be said to have features in common with the American cycle. (A short article, 'British Film Noir' by William K. Everson, published in *Films in Review*, June/July 1987, includes a useful list of titles.) Finally, the story of American *film noir* is brought up to date with articles on the revival that started in the late 'sixties with *Harper* in 1966 and *Point Blank* in 1967.

None of the articles has appeared before in book form, and the majority have been specially written for this volume. All of the five articles that have been published before have been re-edited. Three of them appeared in a special issue of *CineAction* devoted to film noir (No.13-14, Summer 1988): Florence Jacobowitz's 'The Man's Melodrama', Deborah Thomas's 'How Hollywood Deals with the Deviant Male' and Michael Walker's 'The Big Sleep' (which appears in an amended form). Richard Maltby's 'The Politics of the Maladjusted Text' first appeared in *Journal of American Studies* 18 (Cambridge University Press, 1984) and Jonathan Buchsbaum's 'Tame Wolves and Phoney Claims' was in *Persistence of Vision* 3/4 (Summer 1986). I am grateful to the editors, editorial boards and publishers of these journals for permission to reprint the articles.

Ian Cameron
September 1992

My thanks are due to those members of the *Movie* editorial board – Andrew Britton, Edward Gallafent, Jim Hillier, V.F. Perkins, Douglas Pye and Deborah Thomas – who have been involved to a greater or lesser degree in discussions about the content of this volume and in reading the various articles. In particular, I wish to acknowledge the contribution of Michael Walker, who has been involved at all stages of the book's preparation and took on the difficult task of writing the introduction, helped in the drafting by useful contributions from Bob Baker, Edward Gallafent, V.F Perkins, Douglas Pye and Deborah Thomas.

REFERENCES

The following list includes books and articles on *film noir* referred to in the text, where they are cited by author/editor and date. Other references are given in full on their first citation in any article.

Borde, Raymond, & Chaumeton, Etienne *Panorama du Film Noir Americain, 1941-1953*, Éditions du Minuit, Paris, 1955

Buchsbaum, Jonathan 'Tame Wolves and Phoney Claims: Paranoia and Film Noir' in *Persistence of Vision* 3/4, Summer 1986, reprinted in this volume

Cozarinsky, Edgardo 'American Film Noir' in Richard Roud, ed. *Cinema – A Critical Dictionary*, Secker & Warburg, London, 1980

Damico, James 'Film Noir: A Modest Proposal' in *Film Reader* 3, 1978

Durgnat, Raymond 'Paint It Black: The Family Tree of Film Noir' in *Cinema* (UK) 6/7, August 1970

Dyer, Richard 'Homosexuality and Film Noir' in *Jump Cut* 16, November 1977

Dyer, Richard 'Resistance through Charisma: Rita Hayworth and *Gilda*' in Kaplan, 1978

Gledhill, Christine '*Klute* 1: A Contemporary Film Noir and Feminist Criticism' in Kaplan, 1978

Gregory, Charles 'Living Life Sideways' in *Journal of Popular Film*, vol.5, nos.3-4, 1976

Harvey, Sylvia 'Woman's Place: the Absent Family in Film Noir' in Kaplan, 1978

Hirsch, Foster *Film Noir: The Dark Side of the Screen*, Da Capo, New York, 1980

Johnston, Claire '*Double Indemnity*' in Kaplan, 1978

Kaplan, E. Ann, ed. *Women in Film Noir*, British Film Institute, London, 1978

Kerr, Paul 'Out of What Past?' Notes on the B Film Noir' in *Screen Education* 32/33, reprinted in Paul Kerr, ed. *The Hollywood Film Industry*, British Film Institute, London, 1986

Krutnik, Frank *In a Lonely Street: Film Noir, Genre, Masculinity*, Routledge, London, 1991

McArthur, Colin *Underworld USA*, Secker & Warburg, London, 1972

Maltby, Richard 'Film Noir: The Politics of the Maladjusted Text' in *Journal of American Studies* 18, Cambridge University Press, 1984, reprinted in this volume

Ottoson, Robert *A Reference Guide to the American Film Noir*, Scarecrow Press, Metuchen, N.J., 1981

Place, J.A., & Peterson, L.S. 'The Visual Style of Film Noir' in *Film Comment*, January/February 1974

Place, Janey 'Women in Film Noir' in Kaplan, 1978

Schrader, Paul 'Notes on Film Noir' in *Film Comment*, Spring 1972, reprinted in Kevin Jackson, ed. *Schrader on Schrader*, Faber & Faber, London, 1990

Silver, Alain, & Ward, Elizabeth, eds. *Film Noir: An Encyclopedic Reference to the American Style*, Overlook Press, New York, 1979, Secker & Warburg, London, 1980

Telotte, J.P. *Voices in the Dark: The Narrative Patterns of Film Noir*, University of Illinois Press, 1989

FILM NOIR

Introduction

Michael Walker

The cycle of 'forties and 'fifties Hollywood films that retrospectively became known as *films noirs* seems at first sight to be rather too diverse a group to be constituted with any precision as a generic category. Nevertheless, various critics have sought different unifying features: motif and tone (Durgnat, 1970), social background and artistic/cultural influences (Schrader, 1971), iconography, mood and characterisation (McArthur, 1972), visual style (Place & Peterson, 1974), the 'hard-boiled' tradition (Gregory, 1976), narrative and iconography (Dyer, 1977), representation and ideology (Kaplan, 1978), a master plot paradigm (Damico, 1978), conditions of production (Kerr, 1979), paranoia (Buchsbaum, 1986, reprinted in this book) and patterns of narration (Telotte, 1989). Each of these approaches is productive, and one could construct a pretty good overview of the cycle by judiciously combining them – which is essentially Edgardo Cozarinsky's approach (1980) and Foster Hirsch's in his 1981 book. Finally, Frank Krutnik's 1991 book (published after this introduction was drafted) suggests another approach, combining psychoanalysis with a concern with ideology and representation, and complementing Kaplan by focusing primarily on the 'crisis in masculinity' found in *film noir*. In the interests of conciseness, I will not discuss these earlier expositions of the *noir* form (for such an exercise, *see* Jane Root's entry on *Film Noir* in Pam Cook, ed., *The Cinema Book*, British Film Institute, 1985), but will incorporate and summarise as seems appropriate.

The 'forties/'fifties *noir* cycle has traditionally been seen as stretching from *The Maltese Falcon* (John Huston, 1941) to *Touch of Evil* (Orson Welles, 1958), peaking between 1946 and 1950. The dates are somewhat fluid: a hitherto obscure B movie, *Stranger on the Third Floor* (Boris Ingster, 1940) is now generally taken to be the first film of the cycle, and there were few significant contributions after 1956. First labelled *films noirs* at the end of the war by French critics – who linked the films with the series of crime novels (including American novels in translation) known as *Série Noire* – the films mark a distinct break with the generic groupings of the 'thirties. Although almost always concerned with crime, they differ from earlier crime films in the hero's entanglement in the passions of the criminal world. Although usually located in an urban milieu, they differ from the gangster movies in the types of criminal activity involved and their focus on a lone, often introverted hero. And, although featuring heroes who are frequently victims of a hostile world, they differ from the social problem films in their shift from a political to a personal perpective, a perspective that is often informed by popular psychology. Characteristically, the mood of the films is downbeat and pessimistic.

However, *film noir* is not simply a certain type of crime movie, but also a generic field: a set of elements and features which may be found in a range of different sorts of film. The generic labelling of films adopted by the Hollywood studios for their own purposes (casting, production, marketing, etc.) does not do justice to the complex interaction of determinants – including generic elements – in any given film. *Pursued* (Raoul Walsh, 1947), for example, is primarily a western, but it is also part *film noir* and part psychological melodrama, and all three generic fields are crucial to its meaning. Undoubtedly there are problematical areas: the question of the transmission of generic influence, the complex synthesis of multiple determinants in a given film, the elusiveness of the concept of genre itself. But, as Cozarinsky cogently points out, 'the notion of genre is a theoretical tool, not a "natural" fact: to consider any group of works as a genre is to choose some traits as pertinent, others as irrelevant' (Cozarinsky, 1980, p.58). As a generic field, *film noir* combines a number of elements in a way which makes it peculiarly complex and interesting: a distinctive and exciting visual style, an unusual narrative complexity, a generally more critical and subversive view of American ideology than the norm. For these and other reasons – the films' lack of sentimentality, their willingness to probe the darker areas of sexuality, their richly suggestive subtexts, the emotional force of the downbeat – *film noir* as a phenomenon continues to fascinate. The other essays in this volume address specific issues around the *noir* phenomenon and the particular pleasures of certain texts. What follows here is a summary of, on the one hand, the set of influences, determinants and factors which produced this particular cycle of films and, on the other, what seem to me to be its key features. Apart from certain exceptions which will become apparent, I have broadly followed the consensus listings of *films noirs* as included, for example, in Silver and Ward (1980) and Telotte (1989). Further discussion of the extent to which individual works possess *noir* elements may be found in the other essays in this book.

Narrative and Character Types

To a large extent, the typical *film noir* character types and narrative can be traced back to literary crime fiction of the 'thirties and 'forties. There seem to be three main strands of influence: Dashiell Hammett/Raymond Chandler, James M. Cain and Cornell Woolrich, although, inevitably, some films combine material from more than one.

Dashiell Hammett and Raymond Chandler: the 'hard-boiled' private eye.

Both Hammett and Chandler began by writing short stories for *Black Mask* magazine: Hammett in the 'twenties, Chandler in the 'thirties. John Cawelti (in *Adventure, Mystery and Romance*, University of Chicago Press, 1976) has discussed how Hammett's stories, and his subsequent novels – the latter published between 1929 and 1934 – introduced a new formula into the detective story, focusing on 'the hard-boiled hero', with his 'mixture of toughness and sentimentality, of cynical understatement and eloquence' (p.163). He summarises the story's differences from the 'classical detective story' as 'the subordination of the drama of solution to the detective's quest for . . . justice; and the substitution of a pattern of intimidation and temptation of the hero for . . . what Northrop Frye calls "the wavering finger of suspicion" passing across a series of potential suspects' (p.142). He also notes 'a greater personal involvement on the part of the hard-boiled detective. Since he becomes emotionally and morally committed to some of the persons involved, or because the crime poses some basic crisis in his image of himself, the hard-boiled detective remains unfulfilled until he has taken a personal moral stance towards the criminal' (p.143). Of the nature of the world the detective investigates, Cawelti writes, 'As the . . . action develops, the rich, the powerful, and the beautiful attempt to draw the detective into their world and use him for their own corrupt purposes. He in turn finds that the process of solving the crime involves him in the violence, deceit and corruption that lies beneath the surface of the respectable world' (p.145). Above all, the hard-boiled detective novel placed the emphasis on a tough detective in an urban milieu, moving firmly away from the classical 'whodunnit' tradition (Edgar Allan Poe, Arthur Conan Doyle, Agatha Christie, Dorothy Sayers, S.S Van Dine *et al.*) of a refined, ratiocinative detective in a frequently upper middle-class milieu.

Although there was an early version of *The Maltese Falcon* (Roy Del Ruth, 1930) which was relatively faithful to the 1930 novel, it did not set a trend. Hollywood detective films of the 'thirties – particularly after 1934, when the Production Code was rigorously enforced – tended to be 'comedy-thrillers'. When Hammett went to Hollywood as a screenwriter, it was the success of his *The Thin Man* (W.S. Van Dyke, 1934), flip and light-hearted, which dictated the tone of most of his work there, including follow-up *Thin Man* screen stories. Such films are very different from *films noirs*, which depict a far darker view of the underworld of American crime and in which – apart from the occasional cynical/defensive/barbed wisecrack – humour fits uneasily. When *The Maltese Falcon* was remade as *Satan Met a Lady* (William Dieterle, 1936), it moved much further from the original story, becoming not just light-hearted, but positively camp.

Nevertheless, Hammett is crucial to *film noir* as an influence. It was Huston's 1941 version of *The Maltese Falcon*, which stuck very closely to the novel, that effectively launched the private-eye *film noir*, to be developed – in its first phase – over the next fifteen years or so. *The Glass Key* (novel, 1931/film, Stuart Heisler, 1942), the only other Hammett novel to be made into a *film noir*, includes a murder investigation, but is more concerned with the violence and corruption of local politics. Nevertheless, the novel and film introduced what was to become a recurrent *noir* situation: the bloody beating-up of the hero by a sadistic thug.

Hammett ceased publishing in book form in the early 'thirties; his mantle was taken up by Raymond Chandler. Chandler's work was first published in *Black Mask* in 1933; then, in a series of novels beginning with *The Big Sleep* in 1939, he created Philip Marlowe, soon to become *film noir*'s most enduring private eye. However, the first two film adaptations of Marlowe novels – *The Falcon Takes Over* (Irving Reis, 1942) from *Farewell, My Lovely* (1940) and *Time to Kill* (Herbert I. Leeds, 1942) from *The High Window* (1942) – both reprocessed the stories to fit into already established B movie series with already established detectives: George Sanders's Falcon and Lloyd Nolan's Michael Shayne. Despite *The Maltese Falcon*, the detective movie still had to emerge from the low-budget series format, popularised in the 'thirties by the likes of Charlie Chan, Mr Moto and Bulldog Drummond.

In 1943, Chandler was employed as a screenwriter by Paramount. His first project was to assist Billy Wilder (who was also to direct the film) in adapting James M. Cain's *Double Indemnity*, which had been serialised in *Liberty* magazine in 1936. The success of the film of *Double Indemnity* (1944) was followed by film adaptations of the first four Marlowe novels which kept Marlowe as the hero. However, each of the novels was bought by a different studio, resulting in four very different films with four very different Marlowes: RKO's *Murder My Sweet* (Edward Dmytryk, 1944), with Dick Powell (from *Farewell My Lovely*; the original title was retained in the

UK); Warners' *The Big Sleep* (Howard Hawks, 1946), with Humphrey Bogart; MGM's *The Lady in the Lake* (novel 1943/film 1946), the notorious subjective camera film, in which Robert Montgomery both directs and 'plays' Marlowe; and Twentieth Century-Fox's *The Brasher Doubloon* (John Brahm, 1947), with George Montgomery (from *The High Window*). (Later novels were filmed in the second *noir* cycle; *see* Edward Gallafent, 'Film Noir in the 'Seventies'.) Although the quality of these films seems to me to vary enormously, the two obvious successes, *Murder My Sweet* and *The Big Sleep*, developed the formula established by *The Maltese Falcon* and set the tone for subsequent private-eye *films noirs*.

In effect, Hammett and Chandler established the format of the first type of *noir* story. The novels and the films made from them influenced a range of subsequent films with an investigative structure, whether private-eye or not, e.g. *Phantom Lady* (Robert Siodmak, 1944), with its investigative heroine, *Deadline at Dawn* (Harold Clurman, 1946), *Somewhere in the Night* (Joseph L. Mankiewicz, 1946), *The Killers* (Siodmak, 1946), *Dead Reckoning* (John Cromwell, 1946) – much of which is modelled on *The Big Sleep* – *Calcutta* (John Farrow, 1947), *Out of the Past/Build My Gallows High* (Jacques Tourneur, 1947), *The Big Heat* (Fritz Lang, 1953), *Kiss Me, Deadly* (Robert Aldrich, 1955), *The Big Combo* (Joseph H. Lewis, 1955). By contrast, *Laura* (Otto Preminger, 1944) still possesses much of the structure of the classical whodunnit detective story.

These may be termed seeker-hero *films noirs*: a major *noir* category. In these films, the hero's investigation takes the form of a quest into a dangerous and threatening world, the *noir* world. This *noir* world has two facets. On the one hand, it is an underworld of crime, vice and murder; on the other, it frequently lies behind what Cawelti calls the 'respectable world', the world of bourgeois order and propriety. It is a world of duplicity and dissimulation: the hero doesn't know who to trust and is confused about what's going on. The characters he encounters are indeed rarely trustworthy, but tend to be variously corrupt, perverse, threatening or violent. His quest may even assume mythical overtones: a descent into an underworld where, *à la Propp* (V. Propp, *Morphology of the Folktale*, University of Texas Press, 1968, pp.39-42), he is repeatedly 'tested, interrogated, attacked, etc.,' not so much to prepare him for the receipt of a magical agent or helper as to test his wits, perseverance and integrity. As he unravels the often labyrinthine plot and uncovers the layers of deception, it is as much his incorruptibility as his intelligence which enables him, finally, to emerge safely.

The seeker hero is protected further by a generally cynical view of people's motivations and a frequently misogynistic attitude towards women. A particular danger is the *femme fatale* using her

Still: The Maltese Falcon. *The misogynistic private eye – Spade (Humphrey Bogart) is amused by Iva Archer's (Gladys George's) tears.*

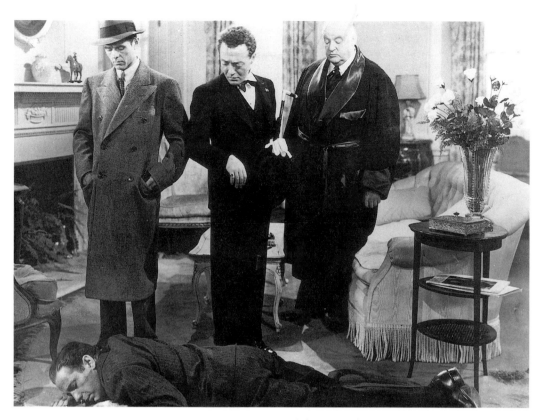

Still: The Maltese Falcon. *The trials of a seeker hero – Spade drugged by Wilmer (Elisha Cook Jr), Cairo (Peter Lorre) and Gutman (Sydney Greenstreet).*

sexuality to get what *she* wants as well as being implicated in murder: *The Maltese Falcon, Murder My Sweet, The Killers, Dead Reckoning, Calcutta, Out of The Past.* Christine Gledhill has argued that the films may indeed displace 'solution of the crime as the object of the plot' to concentrate rather on investigation of the woman (Gledhill, 1978). The seeker hero strives to bring order to the *noir* world, an order which is often linked to the control of transgressive female sexuality.

Other character types in these films include those populating the criminal and night worlds of the city: small-time crooks, grifters, blackmailers, hoods, gamblers, and the women who try to survive in the same worlds: nightclub singers, showgirls, taxi-dancers, bar-girls, mistresses, prostitutes. There are also figures from the opposite end of the social scale: the decadent rich, who live in huge mansions and spawn wayward offspring; powerful, corrupt politicians and nightclub/casino owners. The films' representations of law officers vary. Where the hero is himself a cop, he is typically a loner, pursuing his obsessive quest against the orders of the department (*The Big Heat*; *The Big Combo*). Other cops vary from nuisances who get in the hero's way (the usual situation in Hammett and Chandler) to figures who offer useful assistance, which, untypically of Siodmak, they do in *Phantom Lady* and *The Killers*. Usually, however, the

noir hero stands at an oblique angle to authority, and his relationship with the cops is frequently a crucial indicator of this. A film may even contrive an otherwise redundant scene in which the hero and the cops are in conflict: late in *Dead Reckoning*, Lieutenant Kincaid (Charles Cane) blunders into the apartment of Coral (Lizabeth Scott) simply so that Rip (Humphrey Bogart) can tie him up and lock him in a cupboard. Finally, and especially associated with *film noir*, there are the figures who represent a marked deviance from the norms of society: grotesques such as Moose Malloy (Mike Mazurki) in *Murder My Sweet*; sadists such as Jeff (William Bendix) in *The Glass Key*,

Still: Dead Reckoning. *The bumbling cop – Rip (Humphrey Bogart) and Coral (Lizabeth Scott) stick up Lt Kincaid (Charles Cane).*

Canino (Bob Steele) in *The Big Sleep* and Krause (Marvin Miller) in *Dead Reckoning*; sexual 'deviants' such as Gutman (Sydney Greenstreet) and Cairo (Peter Lorre) in *The Maltese Falcon*.

It is the nature of the *noir* world and the hero's interaction with it which seems to me the essence of the seeker-hero *films noirs*. The moral certainties of the classical detective story are absent: even though the *noir* seeker hero solves the case, there is usually the sense at the end that little good will come of this or that the cost has been absurdly high (a regular feature of these narratives is the number of dead bodies the hero encounters during his investigation.) It is this that distinguishes him from the complacent and invincible series detectives, who are not scarred by their investigations in the same way. Nevertheless, in the seeker-hero films, the hero tends to survive the dangers of the *noir* world. In other types of *film noir*, his survival is much more at risk.

James M. Cain: The femme fatale as destroyer.

Unlike Hammett and Chandler, Cain was employed as a screenwriter before he wrote the novels that made him famous: he joined Paramount in 1931 and subsequently went to Columbia. And, although his screenwriting credits are negligible, three of the novels he went on to write were made into particularly famous *films noirs*: *Double Indemnity*, *The Postman Always Rings Twice* (novel 1934/film Tay Garnett, 1945), and *Mildred Pierce* (1941/Michael Curtiz, 1945). (A later film from a Cain novel, *Slightly Scarlet*, Allan Dwan, 1956 – from *Love's Lovely Counterfeit*, 1942 – is a rare example of a colour film which is nevertheless accepted as part of the first *noir* cycle.) No less hard-boiled than Hammett and Chandler, and arguably even more cynical and misogynistic, Cain introduced a very different type of story. In *The Postman Always Rings Twice* and *Double Indemnity*, the hero becomes so obsessed sexually by a woman that he is persuaded to murder her husband, and the *noir* world which he enters is psychological rather than physical, characterised above all by corrosive guilt and the fear of discovery. The importance of Cain's contribution to the cycle may be seen in the way in which Damico's master plot for *film noir* (quoted in Root and in Krutnik, 1991) is clearly based on the Cain story.

I would like to take the Cain story as a paradigm in a slightly different way from Damico, concentrating on the way i) the *femme fatale* becomes the key figure who lures/tempts/seduces the hero into the *noir* world and ii) the hero becomes a 'victim' of his own desires. As in the Russian fairytales analysed by Propp, these victim heroes are structurally quite distinct from seeker heroes. Apart from the paradigm movies – *Double Indemnity* and *The Postman Always Rings Twice* – examples would include *The Woman in the Window* (Lang, 1944), *Scarlet Street* (Lang, 1945), *The Locket* (Brahm, 1946), *The Lady*

from Shanghai (Welles, 1947), *Pitfall* (Andre de Toth, 1948), *Criss Cross* (Siodmak, 1949), *The File on Thelma Jordon* (Siodmak, 1949), *The Woman on Pier 13* (Robert Stevenson, 1949), *Where Danger Lives* (Farrow, 1950), *Sunset Boulevard* (Wilder, 1951), *Angel Face* (Preminger, 1952) and *Human Desire* (Lang, 1954). In addition, there are films which contain both sorts of hero: in *The Killers*, Reardon (Edmond O'Brien) is a seeker hero, the Swede (Burt Lancaster) a victim hero; in *Out of the Past*, the seeker hero becomes a victim hero when he is seduced by the *femme fatale*. The deadliness of the *femme fatale* varies, from Barbara Stanwyck's Phyllis Dietrichson in *Double Indemnity*, who is a ruthless killer, to an essentially sympathetic figure such as Lizabeth Scott's Mona in *Pitfall*. But her role is dramatically crucial: like the villain in 19th century melodrama, she gets the plot moving. Apart from the Cain movies, it is only occasionally in these films that the hero is driven to murder, but the power of the *femme fatale* is such that he has only about even chances of surviving the film. And, when he does, he often ends as a broken man: *Scarlet Street*, *Pitfall*, *The File on Thelma Jordon*. Related films – in which the central female figure is not a *femme fatale*, but in which the hero, desiring her, commits murder – include *Conflict* (Curtis Bernhardt, 1945), *The Suspect* (Siodmak, 1945), *711 Ocean Drive* (Joseph M Newman, 1950) and *The Prowler* (Joseph Losey, 1951).

A third feature of these films – that the *femme fatale* is already in the possession of another man – is more complicated. First, there is the question of the relationship between the *femme fatale* and this male figure. He may be a wealthy husband, in which case it is usually implied that she has used him to seek money and security, as in the Cain movies, *The Lady from Shanghai* and others. However, the crucial point is that he possesses some sort of proprietorial claim on the *femme fatale*. Accordingly, his presence is blatantly ideological: an entirely independent, sexually dangerous woman being rather more than Hollywood could countenance. This can be seen in the films where the male figure is seemingly absent or weak. In *The Woman on Pier 13*, the figure has been replaced by the Communist Party which, through the agency of master-villain Vanning (Thomas Gomez), explicitly attempts to control the *femme fatale's* sexuality. Max (Erich von Stroheim) in *Sunset Boulevard* seems to be only the butler, but Joe (William Holden) subsequently discovers not only that he is the ex-husband of Norma (Gloria Swanson), but also that he actually writes her fan mail, keeping alive her fantasy that she is still a star. In other words, he exercises considerable control over her. *Nightmare Alley* (Edmund Goulding, 1947) provides a complementary instance. Helen Walker's 'consulting psychologist' is indeed independent, but while she joins forces with the hero and then betrays him, her power over him is not sexual, i.e she is not a *femme fatale* in the usual sense of the term.

Still: Pitfall. *The obsessed heavy - MacDonald (Raymond Burr, left) comes to watch Mona (Lizabeth Scott) modelling.*

Second, the representation of this proprietorial male figure relates strongly to the type of hero involved. Where the latter is single, and (also usually) relatively young and virile, the figure is typically older and economically more powerful, i.e. the films possess an implicit Oedipal structure. (This can occur, too, when the heroine is not a *femme fatale*: 711 Ocean Drive and *The Prowler*.) By contrast, where the hero is married, and also usually middle-aged and non-virile, the male figure, if not always younger, is usually more potent: *The Woman in the Window, Scarlet Street, Pitfall, The File on Thelma Jordon*. These films tend to deal centrally with the hero as a 'castrated' figure: only in *Pitfall* does the film's coding imply that the hero actually manages to have sex with the *femme fatale*.

Clearly, some of these victim heroes are victims of their own villainy. But they, too, enter a *noir* world. And, because it is desire that has motivated them to step outside the normal, 'safe' world, this *noir* world differs from that of the seeker heroes in being more associated with a dissolution of the self, with a surrender to dangerous and disturbing passions. As a corollary of this, a victim hero is more likely to suffer the fear of discovery and punishment, not just in the films in which he is driven to murder, but when he has knowingly desired and possessed another man's woman, as in *The Killers, Out of the Past, Pitfall* and *Criss Cross*. Like the seeker hero, the victim hero also enters a network of relationships of which the true nature is masked, and which are

frequently highly dangerous in their deceptiveness. He, too, struggles towards understanding which, in his case, is usually achieved too late. The most famous example of the impenetrability of the *noir* world in these films is probably *The Lady from Shanghai*, but all of them have elements of the impenetrablility which may extend to the enigma of the *femme fatale*: what does she want? Again, the dangers of the *noir* world function in part as a 'test': is the hero capable of surviving them or not? But he has less control – particularly over the potentially threatening women – than the seeker hero: far from bringing order to the *noir* world, he is more likely to be engulfed by it.

A character type more frequent in these movies than in the seeker-hero examples is the domestic woman: a wife or girlfriend who is in opposition to the *femme fatale*, associated with the home and offering the hero love, understanding and nurturing (the two types are discussed at length by Place, 1978). Just as the heroine in the woman's film is regularly pulled between the lover figure and the husband figure, so the hero in these films is equally often pulled between these two similarly ideologically determined character types, and suffers equally disastrous consequences if the lure of the sexual figure proves too strong. In both generic triangles, one can see the persistence of puritanical nineteenth-century thought: sex is dangerous and destructive, and the figures who are defined as sexual, however alluring and exciting, are ultimately discredited. The same principle applies with the many female figures who are not *femmes fatales* but are, nevertheless, defined as 'sexual' as opposed to 'domestic': e.g. Gloria Grahame's taxi-dancer in *Crossfire* (Dmytryk, 1947) and her gangster's

13

moll in *The Big Heat*; Rita Johnson's mistress in *The Big Clock* (Farrow, 1947); Hazel Brooks's good-time girl in *Body and Soul* (Robert Rossen, 1947); Shelley Winters's waitress in *A Double Life* (George Cukor, 1947). For want of a better collective term, I will refer to such figures as 'sexual women'. The *femme fatale* represents a particular elaboration of the sexual woman, one in which she is dominant in the (sexual) relationship and is seeking to get from it what she wants, whereas these figures are less deadly in their impact on the hero. Of course, no clear dividing line can be drawn between the two – is it fair to call Alice in *The Woman in the Window* or Mona in *Pitfall* a *femme fatale* at all? – but it is important to establish that, even in *film noir*, not all sexual women are necessarily *femmes fatales*, as can be seen in *The Big Sleep*.

Cain also introduced the *noir* 'confessional mode': the sense of the protagonist narrating his story out of an inner need to confess. The films take this further: in the novel of *The Postman Always Rings Twice*, Frank writes his story down for a priest to read, but in the film he actually narrates it – and it is only at the end that we discover he's been talking to a priest. Cain has said in an interview (with Peter Brunette and Gerald Peary, reprinted in Pat McGilligan, ed., *Backstory*, University of California Press, 1986, p.125) that, if he'd thought of it, he would himself have used Wilder's solution to the problem of the first person narrative of *Double Indemnity*: Walter narrating into a dictaphone as a 'confession' to his father-figure Keyes.

In their book on the effects of the Production Code, Leonard J. Leff and Jerold L. Simmons argue that it was Joseph Breen's sanctioning of a treatment of *Double Indemnity* in September 1943 that led to the Hays Office being 'flooded with murder and eros' (*The Dame in the Kimono*, Weidenfeld & Nicolson, London, 1990). In other words, it was Wilder and Chandler's skills at adaptation and Breen's more relaxed attitude to subjects he had hitherto considered unfilmable that enabled the *noir* cycle to develop into something substantial: *The Big Sleep*, *Mildred Pierce* and *The Postman Always Rings Twice* (this last vetoed for ten years) all received Breen's approval in the wake of the *Double Indemnity* decision. At the same time, the 'lurid and sensational' material in the novels still had to be appropriately 'toned down' to be acceptable to Breen (for an exemplary case *see* 'The Big Sleep' in this book). In particular, screenwriters sought to find ways within the restrictions of the Production Code of dealing with non-romantic sexuality; in which desire rather than affection is at stake. Again, *Double Indemnity* is the benchmark film: it is patently sex, not love, that attracts Walter to Phyllis, and it is after *Double Indemnity* that the twin *noir* concerns of murder and desire become focused as in the film adaptation of *Mildred Pierce*. Cain's novel (his least typical) has no murder, but the film begins with the murder of Monte

Still: Mildred Pierce – *Monte (Zachary Scott) about to become a victim of Veda (Ann Blyth).*

(Zachary Scott), and an important thread to its narrative is the question of whodunnit. And when the murderer is finally identified, the film may readily be recast as – in part – another *femme fatale film noir*, in which Monte becomes the victim of his passion for Veda (Ann Blyth), the *femme fatale*.

Cornell Woolrich: the paranoid noir story

Geoffrey O'Brien has written: 'In mystery and hardboiled fiction, the transition from the 'thirties to the 'forties is unmistakable. Cain and Hammett and (Horace) McCoy deal in a clear unblinking light . . . Then, with the 'forties, comes the Great Fear. The light is shadowed over; for ten years the key words will be "night" and "dark". The hardboiled wry grimace will be replaced by abject terror, by a sense of ultimate impotence in a world suddenly full of danger, of nothing but danger' (Geoffrey O'Brien, *Hardboiled America*, Van Nostrand Reinhold, New York, 1981, p.88). He goes on to cite David Goodis, Dorothy B. Hughes and, above all, Cornell Woolrich.

Around a dozen of Woolrich's novels and short stories were made into *films noirs*, mostly B movies. Among the novels were *The Black Curtain* (1941), which became *Street of Chance* (Jack Hively, 1942), *Phantom Lady* (1942/film 1944), *The Black Angel* (1943/Roy William Neill, 1946), *Deadline at Dawn* (1944/1946), *Night Has a Thousand Eyes* (1945/Farrow, 1947); among the short stories, 'Nightmare' was twice made into a *film noir* by Maxwell Shane, as *Fear in the Night* (1947) and as *Nightmare* (1956); 'The Boy Cried Murder' became *The Window* (Ted Tetzlaff, 1949). (Famous non-*noir* Woolrich adaptations include Hitchcock's *Rear Window*, 1954, and François Truffaut's *La Mariée était en noir*, 1967, and *La Sirène du Mississippi*, 1969; for a full list of Woolrich's works and of films made from them, *see Monthly Film Bulletin*, May 1978.) The contributions of Goodis and Hughes to *film noir* were rather more modest, but nevertheless significant. *Dark Passage* (novel 1946/film Delmer Daves, 1947), *Nightfall* (1947/Tourneur, 1956) and *The Burglar* (1953/Paul Wendkos, 1957) – together with Truffaut's *hommage, Tirez sur le pianiste* (1960) from *Down There* (1956) – were made from Goodis's novels (Goodis also wrote the screenplay for *The Burglar*); *The Fallen Sparrow* (1942/Richard Wallace, 1943), *Ride The Pink Horse* (1946/Robert Montgomery, 1947) and *In a Lonely Place* (1947/Nicholas Ray, 1950) were made from Hughes's.

In the narratives of Woolrich, Goodis, Hughes and others, further types of *noir* story are developed. The dominant one is that of a man who becomes a victim of a violent and hostile world and who lives in fear. Typically, he is an ordinary man who becomes involved in a situation which threatens his life, whether as a result of 'fate', as in *Detour* (Edgar G. Ulmer, 1945) and *Deadline at Dawn*; of another's murderousness as in *Desperate* (Anthony Mann, 1947), and *Nightfall*; or both, as in *D.O.A.* (Rudolph Maté, 1950) and *Night and the City* (Jules Dassin, 1950). Sometimes he is being framed: *I Wake Up Screaming/Hot Spot* (H. Bruce Humberstone, 1942), *Phantom Lady*, *The Big Clock*, *The Web* (Michael Gordon, 1947). Sometimes he is doubly victimised: having already been framed and jailed, he is no sooner out of jail than he is once more threatened with murder or being framed for murder: *Dark Passage*, *The Dark Corner* (Henry Hathaway, 1946), *Raw Deal* (Mann, 1948). In *The Fallen Sparrow*, not only does he suffer from psychological trauma as a result of having been tortured by the Nazis in a Spanish jail, but he finds that his torturers have followed him to America to continue the persecution. *Fear in the Night* and *Whirlpool* (Preminger, 1949) feature a villain powerful enough to use hypnosis to implicate the hero (or, in the Preminger, the heroine) in murder. *The Window* provides another variant on the paranoid framework. The central character is an eleven-year-old boy who witnesses a murder, but is not believed by his parents. Then the murderers discover that he was a witness and set out to dispose of him.

Other 'paranoid' *films noirs* are those in which the hero becomes caught up in crime in such a way that this leads, through a steadily mounting sequence of events, to his death: *They Live By Night* (Ray, 1948), *Try and Get Me* (UK title, *The Sound of Fury*, Cy Endfield, 1950), *Roadblock* (Harold Daniels, 1951). Such films are *noir* in the nature of the escalation of events: involved with criminal figures more ruthless and powerful than he, the hero becomes enmeshed in events beyond his control. Related to these are two films, *Nora Prentiss* (Vincent Sherman, 1947) and *They Won't Believe Me* (Irving Pichel, 1947), in which the hero, seeking to escape from his marriage, takes advantage of a freak accident in which he is able to use a dead body to make in the one case himself, in the other his wife, 'disappear'. Again, however, events conspire against

him to such an extent that, eventually, he is arrested for murder.

Also developed by Woolrich *et al.* is the *noir* version of the story about a psychologically unstable or disturbed hero. In *Street of Chance, Black Angel, Somewhere in the Night* and *The High Wall* (Bernhardt, 1947), he suffers from amnesia, which is one of the means whereby the notion of an *alter ego* can be suggested, as in *Black Angel*, where the hero finally discovers that he himself is the murderer for whom he has been searching. In Hitchcock's *Spellbound* (1945), too, the hero is amnesiac, but in this case the focus is more explicitly psychoanalytical. Indeed, *Spellbound* announces itself as a film about psychoanalysis and it initiated a cycle of films which I have termed psychological melodramas (*see Movie* 29/30, p.21 and *Movie* 34/35, pp.16-18). In these films, the psychologically disturbed character is more often female than male, and there is an explicit concern, usually channelled through a psychoanalyst or psychiatrist, with the aetiology of the disturbance.

However, this cycle may be related closely to *film noir*. First, a correlation may be drawn between the *noir* world and that produced by the psychological disturbance: in effect, the *noir* world has moved *inside* the disturbed protagonist. Sometimes, as in the *noir* amnesiac films, the narrative emphasises this, and we experience events primarily from the point of view of the disturbed protagonist: *Possessed* (Bernhardt, 1947), *The Snake Pit* (Anatole Litvak, 1948). In others, we experience events more from the point of view of those subjected to the dangers of the disturbed character: *The Locket, The Dark Mirror* (Siodmak, 1946), *Secret Beyond the Door* (Lang, 1948). In *Spellbound*, our identification is divided between the psychologically disturbed hero and the psychoanalyst heroine. Second, some of the films contain other generic material which is typically *noir. The Locket* has, indeed, a highly characteristic *noir* narrative in which, because of her unsuspected illness, Nancy (Laraine Day) becomes in effect a *femme fatale* for a series of men. In both this film and *Possessed*, the heroine's illness leads to her killing someone. A similar situation occurs in *A Double Life*, in which the actor hero's overidentification with Othello takes him into a psychotic nightmare of jealousy and murder.

But *A Double Life* belongs to another group of films, in which the central character is or becomes so psychotic that he is beyond cure: *So Dark the Night* (Joseph H. Lewis, 1946), *White Heat* (Walsh, 1949), *M* (Losey, 1951). This takes these films firmly back into *noir* territory; indeed Hirsch isolates them as a distinct *noir* subgroup: 'The psychopath is the dark underside of the *noir* victim – far gone before the film opens, he remains trapped in an ongoing nightmare' (Hirsch, 1980, p.167). But, where the films invite our sympathy for the psychotic character – which would exclude films where he is the villain, such as *Born to Kill* (Robert Wise, 1947) – I

Still: Night and the City. *Death of a* noir *hero – Strangler (Mike Mazurki) throws the body of Harry (Richard Widmark) into the Thames.*

would see him more as an extreme version of the *noir* victim. The *noir* world has moved inescapably inside him, and so he is inevitably doomed. The same is true of *Night Has a Thousand Eyes*, in which the hero's ability to foresee the future is like a curse which destroys him.

Dix (Humphrey Bogart) in *In a Lonely Place* is a more complex example. In Hughes's novel, he is psychotic: a serial killer. In the film, he is not a murderer, but he is suspected by the police of being one. However, the sense of threat which this creates is exacerbated by Dix's own paranoid and self-destructive violence, which I would argue is the ultimate cause of the breakdown of his relationship with Laurel (Gloria Grahame). He relates to the *noir* cops who are psychologically flawed by a tendency to excessive violence, as in *Where the Sidewalk Ends* (Preminger, 1950), *On Dangerous Ground* (Ray, 1951), *Detective Story* (William Wyler, 1952). Significantly, both the Preminger and the Wyler locate the source of the violence in an attempt by the hero to live down his father's criminal past: his hatred of crooks is a hatred of what he fears in himself.

In the 'paranoid' *films noirs*, a *femme fatale* is no longer the figure who causes the hero's destruction. The hero may encounter an attractive woman who is duplicitous, as in *Street of Chance* and *The Fallen Sparrow*, but she is less a sexual threat than an aspect of the deceptiveness of the *noir* world. Far more often, however, the central female character seeks to help the victimised hero: to provide him with comfort and sustenance through his ordeal, and even, as in *Phantom Lady*, *Spellbound*, *The Dark Corner* and *Deadline at Dawn*, help with the detective work to save him. The representations of this character tend to cover a broader range than those of domestic woman in the Cain paradigm movies: she is more likely to have a job (as in these four films) and more likely to be capable and determined, and thus actively useful to the hero in his predicament.

Nevertheless, in the examples I have listed, the hero's chances of survival are again only about even. These are the true victim heroes, and they constitute by far the largest *noir* category. The *noir* world into which they are plunged may be likened to the chaos world that Robin Wood has identified as the antithesis to the world of order in Hitchcock's films. The world is often like a nightmare, a nightmare from which the hero will usually escape only at great cost, if at all. Films such as *Detour, Nightmare Alley, D.O.A., Night and the City* (and, from the Cain paradigm group, *Scarlet Street*) end with a bleakness that is surely without parallel in other genres – at least, of the era – taking the hero on a downward path to a miserable death or annihilating despair.

Hitchcock and film noir: the heroine and the noir world

The link between the Hitchcock chaos world and the *noir* world suggests that Hitchcock is more of a *noir* director than has generally been recognised, a position held by Foster Hirsch. My feeling is that the issue is rather more complicated. Hitchcock is so strong an *auteur* that his films tend to be seminal – like *Spellbound* – rather than derivative and they have far more connections with one another than with any particular cycle or genre. As a genre director – e.g. with the thriller – Hitchcock completely dominates the field: other films are measured in relation to his. Nevertheless, a good case can be put for certain Hitchcock films as *films noirs*, and this merits discussion.

Using *Shadow of a Doubt* (1943) as her example in 'Psychoanalysis and Film Noir', Deborah Thomas argues that point of view in Hitchcock films is frequently divided between male and female protagonists, and that this distinguishes those of his films which have been labelled *films noirs* from the more conventional male-centred examples. I would substantially share this position, but push it a little further: it seems to me that Hitchcock tends to make the chaos world more threatening (more *noir*) when it is the *heroine* who is its victim rather than the hero. For all

Still: Strangers on a Train – *Bruno (Robert Walker) strangles Miriam (Laura Elliott).*

that *Shadow of a Doubt* begins with Uncle Charlie (Joseph Cotten) as a typically tormented *noir* figure, it is only a matter of time before he becomes explicitly the villain, creating the *noir* world which threatens the life of Charlie (Teresa Wright). And this *noir* world seems to me to be more dangerous, for example, than that experienced by Guy (Farley Granger) in *Strangers on a Train* (1951), another Hitchcock film which is seen as a *film noir*.

The point may be clarified by reference back to Patricia Highsmith's 1950 novel, *Strangers on a Train*. The novel is strongly *noir*: in it Guy becomes embroiled in Bruno's machinations to the point where he does indeed kill Bruno's father which, of course, dooms him. However in the film Guy resists Bruno (Robert Walker) and, eventually, extricates himself from the chaos world. Morally, he 'passes the test'. But a consequence is that, so far as Guy is concerned, the tone of the film does not have the bleakness of the novel. Although the film has a number of distinctively *noir* scenes – the murder of Miriam (Laura Elliott), Guy's wife; Guy joining Bruno behind the railings outside his apartment; Guy's visit to Bruno's house – the climactic struggle on the runaway merry-go-round has, rather, a sense of play and dizzying excitement, which is crucially at odds with the nightmare of the *noir* world. It seems significant that the first draft of the script was by Chandler, but that Hitchcock rejected it. In effect, the Hitchcock authorial discourse lightens the *noir* discourse of the novel, a change which can be seen far more dramatically in the way Hitchcock transforms Victor Canning's bleak and pessimistic novel *The Rainbird Pattern* (1972) into the light-hearted thriller *Family Plot* (1976).

The Hitchcock film that seems most strongly *noir* is *The Wrong Man* (1956), in which Manny (Henry Fonda) is plunged into a nightmare when he is wrongly identified as a robber. But Rose (Vera Miles), his wife, suffers far more drastically than he the consequences of this, having a breakdown from which she does not recover until some years after the mistaken identification has been rectified.

The Hitchcock sense of the chaos world as more dangerous and engulfing for heroines than for heroes finds particular focus in the persecuted-wife cycle. Initiated by Hitchcock's *Rebecca* (1940) and *Suspicion* (1942) – and Thorold Dickinson's British film of Patrick Hamilton's play *Gaslight* (1940) – the cycle runs in parallel with *film noir*, taking off after Cukor's Hollywood version of *Gaslight* (1944), which had the same sort of seminal impact as *Double Indemnity* (made the same year) had on *film noir*. These films include *Experiment Perilous* (Tourneur, 1944), *Dragonwyck* (Mankiewicz, 1946), *Notorious* (Hitchcock, 1946), *Undercurrent* (Vincente Minnelli, 1946), *The Two Mrs Carrolls* (Peter Godfrey, 1947), *Sleep, My Love* (Douglas Sirk, 1947), *Sorry, Wrong Number* (Litvak, 1948), *Secret Beyond the Door, Caught* (Max Ophuls, 1949), *Whirlpool* and *Sudden Fear* (David Miller, 1952). Andrea Walsh characterises these and other allied films as *noir* woman's films: 'films of suspicion and distrust' in which '*noir* cinematography, by its eerie and unsettling contrasts, spells paranoia and menace' (*Women's Film and Female Experience*, Praeger, New York, 1984, p.29). In these films the *noir* atmosphere of claustrophobia, entrapment and threat is focused on a heroine with whom we closely identify. Here the male is the dangerous enigma and the heroine's experience of him is the structural equivalent of the hero's experience of the *femme fatale* in *film noir*. But, whereas the hero's desire for the *femme fatale* is transgressive, the heroine's marriage is of course socially sanctioned. And so, when the frequently insane and/or sadistic husband turns the *home* into the *noir* world, the Production Code edict that 'the sanctity of the institution of marriage and the home shall be upheld' is clearly threatened. Like *film noir*, the persecuted-wife films carry a subversive charge (I discuss the cycle in my article on *Secret Beyond the Door* in *Movie* 34/35.)

The home as the *noir* world appears equally in other allied films in which the heroine is the identification figure and victim: *Jane Eyre* (Stevenson, 1944), *Dark Waters* (De Toth, 1944), *The Unseen* (Lewis Allen, 1945, co-scripted by Chandler), *My Name Is Julia Ross* (Lewis, 1945), *The Spiral Staircase* (Siodmak, 1945) and *The Dark Mirror*. Whereas, in the persecuted-wife films, the heroine is disadvantaged legally by her marriage, in these films, she tends to be disadvantaged in other ways: either by her position as a servant in the house or by a physical disability. The fact that she is disadvantaged not

only exacerbates the tension and suspense, but acts as a commentary on the oppression of women under patriarchy. Equally, although her plight is structurally equivalent to that of the *noir* victim hero, she is generally more 'innocent' than he. Indeed, most of the heroines in these films are entirely innocent; their only flaw is trusting too much.

Andrea Walsh's designation of these as '*noir* woman's films' seems apt. It draws attention to the way in which the *noir* generic field interacts with that of the woman's film, rather than subsuming it. This would seem to be a general feature of films in which the heroine, rather than the hero, enters the *noir* world, even when the film is taken from a novel by such a *noir* specialist as Woolrich, as with *No Man of her Own* (Mitchell Leisen, 1950), closely based on Woolrich's *I Married a Dead Man* (1948). This is not to say that the experiences of the heroine in such films are any less intense or dangerous than those of the *noir* hero (although it is, of course, rare for such a heroine to die) but that the films are more like generic hybrids. This can make them more complicated – generically speaking – than 'conventional' *films noirs*. Both *Possessed* and *A Double Life*, for example, deal with a protagonist who suffers a mental breakdown and murders her/his lover, but in *Possessed* Louise (Joan Crawford)

Still: Sorry, Wrong Number. *The flashback of Evans (Harold Vermilyea, in white hat) – Stevenson (Burt Lancaster, seated) is pressured by the gangster Moreno (William Conrad, right) into killing his wife for the insurance money.*

Still: The Reckless Moment – *Lucia ((Joan Bennett) finds the body of her daughter's blackmailing boyfriend, Darby (Sheppherd Strudwick).*

is caught up in a far more complex network of relationships than those in the hero-centred *A Double Life.*

Just as it is her husband who precipitates the heroine into the *noir* world in the persecuted-wife films, so in other heroine-centred films it is usually an event connected with her family. In *Mildred Pierce*, Mildred (Joan Crawford) is plunged into the *noir* world when her daughter Veda (Ann Blyth) shoots her husband, Monte (Zachary Scott). But the structure of the film masks her experience of this from the audience: because the identity of the killer is withheld until the end, we don't know what Mildred is going through. The *noir* narrative centring on Mildred as victim is suppressed: of the three flashbacks she narrates, the two main ones belong to the woman's film discourse. In other words, the *noir* narrative is not articulated through the heroine: it takes place in the present-tense scenes outside the flashbacks and in the third flashback, when the detective forces Mildred to tell the truth about Monte's murder. In *The Reckless Moment* (Max Ophuls, 1949), by contrast, although again it is a 'family problem' that takes Lucia (Joan Bennett) into the *noir* world – her daughter's accidental killing of a gigolo boyfriend – we follow in detail Lucia's attempts to protect her family. Here the heroine's experience of the nightmare of the *noir* world is not suppressed. More rarely, a heroine enters the *noir* world in the same manner as a hero, as in *Phantom Lady*. Another example would be *Born to Kill*, which shows the heroine falling for a psychopathic

man in exactly the same way as the *noir* hero falls for the *femme fatale*, and eventually suffering a similar fate.

The films do, however, show a strong resistance to the idea of a seeker heroine. In *Stranger on the Third Floor* and *Phantom Lady*, the man the heroine loves is jailed for murder, which leads to her pursuing her own investigation and finding the real murderer. However, even in these films, her powers are limited (*see Phantom Lady* in 'Robert Siodmak' in this book). And other examples of seeker heroines are rare. There are some films in the persecuted-wife cycle – notably *Secret Beyond the Door* and *Sudden Fear* – in which the heroine investigates her husband. Under certain circumstances – most obviously, when he seems to threaten her with murder – this would seem to be a permitted area for a woman to investigate. When her investigation is related to a political rather than a personal matter, as in *Notorious*, she requires the assistance of the hero. *Spellbound* is another example in which, although the heroine again uncovers the real murderer, the scope of her investigation is heavily circumscribed: her main evidence is a Freudian interpretation of the hero's dream. *Sorry, Wrong Number* is a good example of the problem for a film when a woman pursues the investigation. Through a series of phone calls, the bed-ridden Leona (Barbara Stanwyck) gradually uncovers

evidence that her husband is planning to kill her. But her character is such that she has a powerful resistance to accepting anything unusual: she is utterly useless as an investigative figure. This is balanced to an extent by the actions of Sally (Ann Richards), who is quite skilled in her investigation of *her* husband's suspicious activities, but who has a much smaller role.

In this discussion I have not mentioned British novelists such as Graham Greene and Eric Ambler. Some of their novels were made into films which have been included within the *noir* cycle: *This Gun for Hire* (Frank Tuttle, 1942), *Ministry of Fear* (Lang, 1944) and *Confidential Agent* (Herman Shumlin, 1945) from Greene; *Journey into Fear* (Norman Foster, 1943) and *Mask of Dimitrios* (Jean Negulesco, 1944) from Ambler. However, despite the *noir* feel of these works, they are all – with the exception of *This Gun for Hire* – marginal to the cycle because they are more concerned with espionage and international intrigue. (*This Gun for Hire* is also about espionage, but that isn't its dominant feature.) And, although a correlation may undoubtedly be drawn between the *noir* world and that produced by dangerous spy networks, as in *The Fallen Sparrow*, the concern with international conspiracies makes the spy movie technically a distinct sub-genre.

The seeker-hero/victim-hero distinction (along with its rather rarer female counterparts) is useful in mapping the *noir* field. Some films, like *The Killers*, possess both types of hero, e.g.

Crossfire and *Act of Violence* (Fred Zinnemann, 1948). (*Phantom Lady*, like *Spellbound*, has a victim hero and a seeker heroine.) *Crossfire* shows the two types particularly clearly: Finley (Robert Young), the seeker hero, is calm, probing, authoritative; Mitchell (George Cooper), the victim hero, is lost, confused, helpless. *Act of Violence* is darker, with the two in a mutually destructive relationship: the seeker hero relentlessly hunting down the victim hero to exact revenge for a wartime betrayal.

In other films, the hero plays out both sorts of role, as in *Out of the Past*. Indeed, Tourneur's movie incorporates material from all three of the *noir* narrative strands of influence – when Jeff (Robert Mitchum) returns to San Francisco, he is being framed by Whit (Kirk Douglas), a frame from which he is ultimately unable to extricate himself – which is a clear indication of its centrality to the cycle. In *D.O.A.*, the hero is simultaneously a seeker and a victim hero: fatally poisoned from the beginning of the film, he desperately hunts down his poisoner. Similarly, George Taylor (John Hodiak) in *Somewhere in the Night* is a seeker hero in his investigation into his past, but a victim hero in the amnesia which motivates the investigation. Bradford Galt (Mark Stevens) in *The Dark Corner* is ostensibly a private eye, but he is so weak in the role – and so comprehensively victimised by both the police and the villains – that the victim-hero aspect is dominant: the oft-quoted 'I'm backed up in a dark corner and I don't know who's hitting me.' But Galt is also an example of a hero who is being framed/hunted for murder and who, to clear his name, has himself to seek out the real murderer. As Martha Wolfenstein and Nathan Leites point out in *Movies: A Psychological Study* (The Free Press, Glencoe, Ill., 1950, Chapter 3), this is a common plot of the era, also found, for example, in *The Blue Dahlia* (George Marshall, 1945, from an original screenplay by Chandler), *The High Wall*, *The Big Clock* and *99 River Street* (Phil Karlson, 1953). In all these films, the victim hero is forced to become a seeker hero. This situation is dramatised particularly effectively in *The Big Clock*, in which the hero, who is being framed for murder by the villain (his boss), is obliged to conduct a double investigation: one in public, which is leading inexorably to the identification of himself as the murderer, the other in private to capture the real murderer.

Because *film noir* is ultimately a generic field rather than a category to which films may or may not belong, there are also films which, like *Pursued*, show a clear mixture of generic elements. *The Strange Love of Martha Ivers* (Lewis Milestone, 1946) begins as a melodrama, with the three main characters, Martha, Sam and Walter, as teenagers. It then moves forward eighteen years as Sam (Van Heflin), recently demobilised,

Stills: The Unsuspected. *Right – Matilda (Joan Caulfield) arrives home to find Steven Howard (Michael North) posing as her husband. Below – Althea (Audrey Totter) says nothing about hearing a murder over the telephone.*

finds himself back in the small town he left as a boy. Walter (Kirk Douglas) is now the District Attorney, Martha (Barbara Stanwyck) is his wife. It is Walter's paranoid conviction that Sam is out for blackmail that takes the film into *noir* territory. He himself blackmails Toni (Lizabeth Scott), Sam's girl, into setting Sam up and then has the latter viciously beaten up and dumped outside town. Only after this – some two-thirds of the way through the movie – does the familiar *noir* structure of the Cain paradigm take over: Martha setting out to seduce Sam and to persuade him to murder Walter.

Equally, other films blend the *noir* elements in unusual ways. *The Unsuspected* (Curtiz, 1947) is not only visually one of the most brilliant films of the cycle, but it has a highly intriguing narrative. It begins with a murder and the (albeit fleeting) identification of the murderer. But it is some time before one is able to identify a seeker hero – posing as the heroine's husband, the figure seems

at first decidedly suspicious – and it is even longer before the film introduces another familiar pattern: that of the heroine being menaced in the home by a man she loves and trusts. The film is suspenseful not only in its own right, but in terms of how it develops the generic features. One feels strongly that these are generic features with which Charlotte Armstrong, the novelist, and Ranald MacDougall, the scriptwriter, would have been perfectly familiar. It is this sense that the writers would have seen themselves as working within a generic tradition – whatever it was called – that provides a strong case for *noir* as a genre.

The *noir* world and the hero or heroine's interaction with it are central to what is distinctive about *film noir*. At the beginning of the story, the protagonist is leading a safe, ordinary life in the 'respectable world'. Partial exceptions are the private eyes, whose lives tend to be somewhat more adventurous than those of most *noir* heroes. Then, as the result of a chance meeting or event, or an act of villainy, or – in the private-eye films – a seemingly simple commission, he/she is plunged into the dangers of the *noir* world. The latter could be seen to illustrate the sense of existentialism which has often been identified in the films: it embodies in an acute form the unheeding randomness of a world in which the only certainty is death (*see* Robert G. Porfirio, 'No Way Out: Existential Motifs in *Film Noir*', *Sight & Sound*, Autumn 1976).

Although the path taken through the *noir* world seems to me to be rather different for the two types of hero or heroine, each protagonist struggles towards a clarity of vision, which may be achieved imperfectly or too late. The spectator, too, is implicated in the struggle: Richard Dyer has characterised the *noir* narrative 'as like a labyrinth with the hero as the thread running through it' (Dyer, 1977), and it may be consciously misleading, even to the extent of a lying flashback, as in *Crossfire*. The spectator's confusion could then be seen as a condition produced by the slipperiness and deceptiveness of the *noir* world. For *noir* heroes, the interaction with the *noir* world also frequently reveals a fundamental crisis in male control and, behind this, in Dyer's words, 'an anxiety over the existence and definition of masculinity and normality' (Dyer, 1978). Foregrounded in the victim-hero *films noirs*, the feature is by no means absent from the seeker-hero examples, appearing, for instance, in the incapacitated state of Dick Powell's Marlowe at the beginning of *Murder My Sweet*. The *noir* world may be a relatively fluid concept; I have suggested a number of different characteristics in the different types of *film noir*. But, like the monster in the horror movie – another relatively fluid concept – it is crucial in conveying the sense of threat and danger which invades the lives of the protagonists. The difficulty they have in extricating themselves from these dangers and the frequently enormous cost of this bear testament to its power.

Still: The Locket. *Flashback within a flashback – Norman (Robert Mitchum) chats up Nancy (Laraine Day).*

I have concentrated on novelists rather than scriptwriters, because it was the former who first created the characteristic *noir* narratives and character types, and who gave early expression to the *noir* moods of pessimism and despair. The novelists in turn influenced the scriptwriters; indeed, some of them, like Hammett and Chandler, went to Hollywood themselves. Others were more significant as scriptwriters than as novelists. Horace McCoy has considerably more film scripts credited to his name than novels, and only one of his novels, *Kiss Tomorrow Goodbye* (1948/Gordon Douglas, 1950) was made into a *film noir* during the first cycle (*see* 'Horace McCoy' in *Film Dope* 37). Similarly, Jonathan Latimer – a 'thirties crime writer who went to Hollywood and scripted, *inter alia*, *The Glass Key*, *They Won't Believe Me*, *The Big Clock* and *Night Has a Thousand Eyes* – virtually ceased publishing when he became a scriptwriter (*see* 'Jonathan Latimer' in *Film Dope* 33), and Daniel Mainwaring – both author and scriptwriter of *Build My Gallows High/Out of the Past* – had a particularly successful career as a scriptwriter (*see* 'Daniel Mainwaring' in *Film Dope* 38). Krutnik provides a very useful tabulation of the overall impact of the hardboiled writers on Hollywood, citing both novels adapted and scripts worked on between 1940 and 1950 (Krutnik, 1991, pp.182-187).

One vital contribution of the scriptwriters was the use of flashbacks with subjective voice-over to recreate the effect of the first-person narrative of the novels. Subjective voice-over was employed very rarely in 'thirties feature films – it seems to have been associated too closely with the 'objective' voice-over of documentaries – but was used, to great effect, in Ford's *How Green Was My Valley* (1941), which won the Academy Award for Best Picture. *Citizen Kane* (Welles, 1941) has, of course, a flashback structure, but it does not use the voice-over: the moment each flashback begins, the narrator's voice fades out. The difference is crucial: the subjective voice-over personalises the experience of the recollected past in a very direct way, contributing both thoughts and feelings to the narrative, as in the first-person novel. In addition, in its sense of looking back at events, the technique ties in with the mood of fatalism of *film noir*, as in *Double Indemnity*, where Walter is steadily bleeding away as he narrates the events leading up to his current state. In this and other films – whether the hero is 'confessing' or simply telling his story in a desperate attempt to understand – the *noir* world is reinflected, through the flashback structure, as a *personal* nightmare. This leads to irony in a film such as *The Locket*, which has three layers of flashbacks, through which runs the motif of the narrator of each successive flashback not being believed.

Character Relationships

A number of key *films noirs* show a particular configuration of three interlocking sexual triangles. Five character types are involved, linked together:

husband/older male   hero   respectable man

femme fatale   domestic woman

In other words, all three central characters – *femme fatale*, hero and domestic woman – are between alternative partners. First seen in *Double Indemnity*, where Lola as domestic woman is underdeveloped as an alternative to Phyllis as *femme fatale*, the structure finds its most complete expression in *Out of the Past*, another reason why the film seems so central to the *noir* cycle. The structure can be seen with only minor variations in *films noirs* as diverse as *The Killers*, *The Woman on Pier 13*, *Night and the City*, *Sunset Boulevard* and *Angel Face*. The husband/older male is the same as the 'proprietorial male figure'

Still: Pitfall. *The Powell hero as victim – John Forbes (Dick Powell) cared for by his wife (Jane Wyatt) and son (Jimmy Hunt) after being beaten up.*

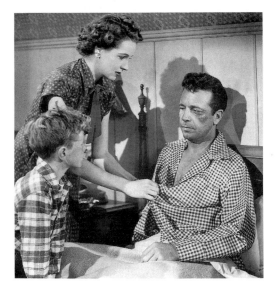

from the Cain paradigm movies, and here the Oedipal overtones may be pronounced: in *Angel Face*, this figure is the *femme fatale*'s father; in *Sunset Boulevard*, the *femme fatale* is twenty years older than the hero. In *The Killers*, the hero abandons the domestic woman when he meets the *femme fatale*; more often, he seeks to escape from the power of the *femme fatale* with the domestic woman. (In *Angel Face*, he is pulled between the two of them.) But he is doomed to die – in most cases, along with the *femme fatale* and the husband/older male – hence the ideological requirement for the domestic woman to have a safe, conventional man she can turn to. Except in the case of *Double Indemnity*, however, this man is seen by the domestic woman as second best: she really loves the hero.

Many groups of films possess two sexual triangles; thus, the persecuted-wife films often have a variation on the paradigm established by Charlotte Brontë's *Jane Eyre*:

previous wife – hero – heroine – asexual man

But the three interlocking sexual triangles seem to present a specifically *noir* configuration, and hence to merit further discussion.

1) The structure emphasises both the sexualisation of relationships in *film noir* and the ensuing repression of this, with the overtly sexual figures almost invariably killed off. Order is restored – however unconvincingly – through the non-*noir* figures of the domestic woman and the respectable man.

2) The model is essentially for victim heroes. However, certain of the films (*Double Indemnity*, *The Killers* and *Out of the Past*) also possess an investigative figure. And here, too, Christine Gledhill's notion that *film noir* is frequently preoccupied with 'investigating the woman' is found: the culpability of the *femme fatale* – both sexual and criminal – may be seen as the implicit subject of his investigation. This is shown doubly in *Out of the Past*. After Jeff's own investigation of Kathie (Jane Greer) has been neutralised by his seduction and the two of them run away together, his partner Fisher (Steve Brodie) is despatched to find them. And he turns up at their secret romantic rendezvous, as if signalling that the implicit purpose of his investigation is their sexual relationship.

3) The model is useful as a paradigm. Many other *films noirs* show simple variations on it, e.g. when the hero does not die, and so the alternative man is unnecessary, for example in *Murder My Sweet*, *The Strange Love of Martha Ivers*, *Johnny O'Clock* (Robert Rossen, 1947), *Pitfall*, *The File on Thelma Jordon*, *Where Danger Lives* and *Human Desire*. The three Dick Powell films here introduce their own particular inflection: although Powell as hero does not die, he ends up temporarily blinded and just released from custody (*Murder My Sweet*), wounded and in custody (*Johnny O'Clock*), and haunted with guilt and

just released from custody (*Pitfall*). In other words, his physical or psychological state bears testament to the dangers of the *noir* world.

4) Similarly, the model can throw into relief the character relationships in films that relate to it more eccentrically. In *Mildred Pierce*, Veda as *femme fatale*, Monte as 'hero', Mildred as 'domestic woman', and Bert (Bruce Bennett) as respectable man may be approximately fitted to the model, but Mildred is also located as the figure who (officially) regulates the *femme fatale's* sexuality, in this case, as her mother. The complexity of the relationships around Louise in *Possessed* may be illustrated by the fact that these can be related to the model in different ways. If David (Van Heflin) is taken as the hero, and Louise as the *femme fatale* – after all, she does kill him – then all the character types are present except the respectable man for Carol (Geraldine Brooks). With David, her lover, dead, she is left unattached at the end, which is most unusual (and signals the film's lack of closure). However, if Louise is placed at the structural centre (i.e. in the position of the hero), the three triangles fall into place, but with the male and female characters reversed: wife (Pauline) – domestic man (Dean/Raymond Massey) – heroine (Louise) – *homme fatal* (David) – respectable woman (Carol).

5) The representations of the *femme fatale* and the domestic woman may be differently inflected in the individual films, but they nevertheless represent crucial moral/ideological alternatives for the hero. This is evident even in *Night and the City*, where Helen (Googie Withers) is not really a *femme fatale* at all, but simply a woman who desperately seeks independence from her nauseating husband, Nosseross (Francis L. Sullivan), and Mary (Gene Tierney) works as a nightclub singer in Nosseross's club. The heroes have a lot in common: they seem rootless, without a stable home or a stable job (or, like Walter Neff or Jeff as a private eye in *Out of the Past*, in a peripatetic job) and many are seduced, not simply by the *femme fatale*, but also by the lure of the big break, the easy money. Jeff is the only one of these heroes who is essentially indifferent to money, which makes him the most romantic figure amongst them.

6) The seven films I mentioned as illustrations of the paradigm may be divided into two basic groups. In one group, there are underworld associations and the husband/older man also acts as the hero's boss: *The Killers*, *Out of the Past*, *Night and the City*. *The Woman on Pier 13* also belongs in this group: the commies are clearly represented as being like gangsters and Vanning acts as if he's Brad's (Robert Ryan's) boss. In these films, the hero becomes involved in crime or transgression, seeks to escape by flight, but is

Still: Johnny O'Clock. *Hardboiled hero, phlegmatic cop, future victim – Johnny (Dick Powell), Inspector Koch (Lee J. Cobb), Ellen (Nina Foch).*

inexorably pursued by underworld figures whose powers of vengeance are magnified by the potency and ruthlessness of the boss. (In *Night and the City*, there is a displacement from this structure, the powerful gangster Kristo, Herbert Lom, taking over from Nosseross the role of the vengeful figure.) The other group – *Double Indemnity*, *Sunset Boulevard* and *Angel Face* – represents the middle-class version of the paradigm: the hero is in 'respectable' employment, and the narrative tends to centre round the *femme fatale*'s luxurious mansion. (In '*Angel Face*', Edward Gallafent discusses the links between *Angel Face* and *Double Indemnity*.) A good case can be made for these two groups – respectively the underworld and the bourgeois versions of the three interlocking sexual triangles – as the generic heart of *film noir*.

7) *The Woman on Pier 13* is included to show how readily the structure may be appropriated for the purposes of propaganda: the film is one of the most notorious of the anti-communist films of the period. Here the function of Christine (Janis Carter) as the *femme fatale* is to seduce men into communism, which stands in structurally for the lure of riches in the other movies. That they are so readily seduced – her success with Brad in the past is echoed in her success

Still: Night and the City – *Helen (Googie Withers) and her husband Nosseross (Francis L. Sullivan).*

with Don (John Agar), Brad's brother-in-law, in the present – suggests one of a number of ways in which the film subverts itself. Finally, since Vanning is acting for the Communist Party in the way he seeks to control Christine's sexuality, he collapses the functions of proprietorial husband and pimp.

8) Whilst I cannot pretend to comprehensiveness, I have been able to locate the structure in only one non-*noir* film, *Great Day in the Morning* (1956), a western directed by the same director as *Out of the Past*, Jacques Tourneur. These two films also possess another character in common: a boy, who is/has been adopted by the hero. One could discover a great deal about the ideological similarities and differences between the two genres by juxtaposing the two films: although *Great Day in the Morning* is a bleak, even subversive western, the hero does not die.

Visual Style and Iconography

The distinctiveness of the stylistic elements in *film noir* is frequently cited: the use of low-key lighting to create unusual shadows and chiaroscuro

effects, a high proportion of night scenes, off-angle camera compositions, deep-focus shots framing characters in cluttered, claustrophobic interiors, a greater or lesser sense of expressionist distortion, and so on. This is not to claim that all films that show a preponderance of such stylistic features are necessarily *films noirs*. A number of horror films possess them: *Son of Frankenstein* (Rowland V. Lee, 1939) is one of the most expressionist of all Hollywood movies. Nor, in order to be considered a *film noir*, would a film necessarily have to possess all or most of such features: *The Big Sleep* most certainly does not. Nevertheless, these features are important in a large number of the films, interacting with the *noir* narratives in a highly productive manner. Place and Peterson illustrate their article on *noir* visual style with a number of representative frames from the films, and, although they neglect to point out that each specific image will be located in a narrative which is simultaneously contributing to the tone and mood of the scene, their argument that visual style is a unifying feature of a sometimes rather disparate set of films is often convincing (Place & Peterson, 1974).

In particular, critics have sought to relate the *noir* visual style to the imagery of the German Expressionist movement of the 'twenties. Some of the directors who contributed most impressively to *film noir* were Austrian or German Jewish refugees from the Nazis who had had a direct or indirect association with the Expressionist movement: Fritz Lang, Robert Siodmak, Otto Preminger, Billy Wilder. Michael Curtiz, too, had made films in

Still: Stranger on the Third Floor. *Expressionist lighting as Mike Ward (John McGuire) catches a glimpse of the stranger (Peter Lorre).*

Germany in the 'twenties, and John Brahm had worked in the theatre in Vienna and Berlin. Although the degree of expressionism in these and other *noir* directors' films varies considerably, elements of the expressionist tradition may be traced through the *noir* cycle from the highly stylised fantasy sequence in *Stranger on the Third Floor* to the harsh, slashing lighting and off-beat camera angles of *Touch of Evil*.

Obviously I am using expressionism here in a wider sense than that suggested by *The Cabinet of Dr Caligari* (Robert Wiene, 1919). Expressionism serves as a convenient shorthand for the notion of the outer world expressing the inner world of the characters, and it occurs across the arts. It is a 'heightened' form, bringing into play exaggeration, distortion, the grotesque and the nightmarish, and it may be found in a literary form in some of the *noir* writers, notably Woolrich, no less than in a visual form in the films themselves (for example, Woolrich's description of the jazz cellar sequence in *Phantom Lady*).

However, there is a strong correlation between the mood of German Expressionism – bleak, fatalistic, claustrophobic, with overtones of madness and despair – and that of many *films noirs*. A similar correlation – in terms of fatalism and the sense of destiny – has been noted with the late 'thirties/early 'forties French 'poetic realist' films of directors like Marcel Carné and

Julien Duvivier (*see* Ginette Vincendeau's article). And, just as the German Expressionist movement expressed fears and anxieties whose relevance to 'twenties Germany has been much discussed (notably by Siegfried Kracauer in *From Caligari to Hitler*, Princeton University Press, 1947, and Lotte Eisner in *The Haunted Screen*, Thames & Hudson, London, 1969), so *film noir* can be seen as an equivalent – if more heavily disguised – barometer of fears and anxieties in 'forties America.

The fantasy sequence in *Stranger on the Third Floor* illustrates Hollywood expressionism at its most feverishly exaggerated. The sequence begins with fantasised figures surrounding the journalist hero and accusing him of murder. Unlike a similar effect towards the end of Fritz Lang's *Fury* (1936), the figures here are not ghost-like, but as 'real' as the hero. It continues with a series of short scenes, in which decor, props and acting are all heavily stylised. Against a painted backdrop of skyscrapers, the heroine reads a newspaper report of the hero's arrest and histrionically throws up her hands; fellow journalists gloat behind newspapers in which the word MURDER covers the front page in huge letters. The hero's jail cell is visualised as the size of a hall, with huge diagonal bar-like shadows on the walls and floor; this space then transforms into the court-room with even larger zigzag shadows on the walls. With the camera shifting between high angles emphasising the hero's helplessness and low angles emphasising the power of the judicial process, the hero is accused by witnesses, repeatedly silenced by the judge, and he pleads his innocence to a sleeping jury. They rouse themselves to chorus a verdict of guilty and, when the sentence of death is passed, we see, from the hero's point of view (another low angle), the judge transformed into a statue which combines the figure of justice with that of the grim reaper: scales of justice in one hand; scythe in the other.

Given Boris Ingster's obscurity, it is difficult to assess his importance to *Stranger on the Third Floor*. However, the sets were designed by Albert S. D'Agostino, later to make his name as the art director on the Val Lewton series of B horror movies, and the film was photographed by Nicholas Musuraca, later to become one of *film noir*'s most distinguished cameramen. This draws attention to the extremely important contribution of such personnel to the stylistic features of *film noir*. Although few *films noirs* have sequences as overtly expressionist as the one I have described, such creative personnel would work with the director to express in visual terms the sense of nightmare of the *noir* world, and to create a repertoire of stylistic effects which have their roots in this type of expressionism. (The same could be said for the horror movie: Musuraca, too, worked on the Lewton horror movies.) Other cameramen who contributed in a highly distinctive way to *film noir* include John Alton (especially in his films with Anthony Mann),

Woody Bredell (especially in his films with Siomak), John F. Seitz at Paramount, Burnett Guffey at Columbia and Joseph MacDonald and Joseph LaShelle at Twentieth Century-Fox.

Another influence on the visual style of the films was the development of camera and lighting technology in the late 'thirties: faster film stock, coated lenses (which significantly increased the light transmission) and more powerful lights. Together with the more extensive use of the wide-angle lens, these developments facilitated both depth-of-field photography and the need for fewer light sources (*see* David Bordwell, Janet Staiger & Kristin Thompson, *The Classical Hollywood Cinema*, Routledge, London, 1985, Chapter 27). James Wong Howe, another master cameraman, argued that the lower lighting levels of 'forties films were an improvement because they enabled a cameraman to move towards 'the actual room-illumination levels whose effects we are trying to duplicate'. He traced the 'hard, undiffused' look of the films back to the influence of picture magazines such as *Life* and *Look*, and photographic journals such as *U.S. Camera* and *Popular Photography*: 'The public has seen the stark realism of the newspicture reporters . . . and wants something of that type of realism . . . in its movies' (*American Cinematographer*, July, 1941).

There seems little doubt that most good cameramen rose to the challenge of lighting scenes to create the dramatic play of light and dark typical of the films. Equally, the more visually sophisticated directors would encourage cameramen to produce exciting images: a comparison of Harry J. Wild's work for Dmytryk on *Murder My Sweet* with his work for the more pedestrian Irving Pichel on *They Won't Believe Me* is highly instructive in this regard. In autumn 1942, the War Production Board imposed a ceiling of $5,000 on new materials for set construction, and ways of economising included using lighting techniques which minimised the limitations of the sets. (Perry Ferguson – the art director on *Citizen Kane* – put forward a number of suggestions to cope with the restrictions, *see American Cinematographer*, September 1942). In addition, cameramen have acknowledged that they examined one another's films, looking for particularly striking solutions to lighting and filming problems, and *American Cinematographer* regularly ran articles on innovative practices. Wong Howe was interviewed in its series, 'Aces of the Camera', which began in January 1941 and featured a different cameraman each month. Nevertheless, in another series, on the making of individual films, the magazine did not really discuss low-key photography in the context of a film we would now call a *film noir* until it covered Siodmak and Bredell's work on *The Killers* in December 1946. (Joe Valentine discussed the making of *Shadow of a Doubt* in 1942, but that was in the context of filming on location in Santa Rosa.) It was not until 1948 that a whole series of articles appeared (monthly between February and August) on the making of

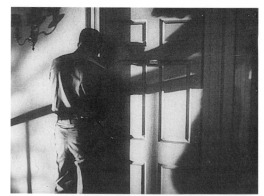

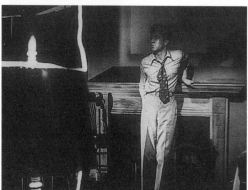

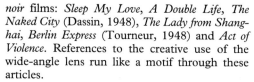

noir films: *Sleep My Love*, *A Double Life*, *The Naked City* (Dassin, 1948), *The Lady from Shanghai*, *Berlin Express* (Tourneur, 1948) and *Act of Violence*. References to the creative use of the wide-angle lens run like a motif through these articles.

A film which illustrates both the expressionist influence on *film noir* and the use of wide-angle lenses is *Crossfire*. It begins with one man beating another to death. For narrative purposes, the killer is not shown, and the opening shot shows the action through exaggerated shadows of the men thrown on an apartment wall, the distortion an expression of the violence of the scene (frame 1). A similar shadow-effect occurs later, when Montgomery (Robert Ryan), the killer, is shown arriving at the apartment of Samuels (Sam Levene), the victim, and his accompanying shadow is so distorted it seems to hint at the

Frames: Crossfire – *the numbers in the text read from left to right across the double spread.*

monster within him (frame 2). A specific motif of German Expressionism, the staircase (*see* Eisner), is visually emphasised in a number of scenes, creating a cage-like effect around Mitchell (George Cooper), the victim hero, early in the film (frame 3), and Montgomery towards the end (frame 4). Both these shots also show the distorting effect of the wide-angle lens. The terror of Bowers (Steve Brodie), Montgomery's buddy who witnessed the murder, is conveyed in one scene through a deep-focus shot in which a fore-grounded lampshade is used to hem him in (frame 5) and, in close shot, by the harsh light from the lamp highlighting his frightened, sub-missive posture (frame 6). Most of the events of the film take place during the course of one

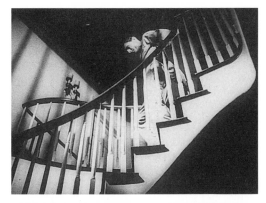

night, during which Mitchell is associated with two women: Ginny (Gloria Grahame), a sympathetic taxi-dancer, and Mary (Jacqueline White), his wife. The two are lit and photographed in a way which distinguishes between them in characteristic terms: Ginny – the 'sexual woman' – in harsh, undiffused light (frame 7); Mary – the domestic woman – in soft lighting, as in her introduction, when she is caught in the light from the projection booth in a smoke-filled cinema (frame 8). When Mitchell wakes in Ginny's apartment and encounters an enigmatic character referred to in the credits as 'the man' (Paul Kelly), the ensuing scene is played out in semi-darkness, mirroring the sense of the man as one of the 'lost souls' of *film noir*, wandering in the dark (frames 9 – 11). Finally when, at the end of this scene, Mitchell decides to go back to Keeley (Robert Mitchum), a foregrounded coffee-pot,

which bubbles over, hints – along with other details in the film – at a suppressed gay subtext, which is a feature of so many *films noirs* (frame 12). The subtext has a particular relevance to *Crossfire*, since in Richard Brooks's original novel, *The Brick Foxhole*, the killer was anti-gay, which had to be changed in the film to anti-Semitic in order to satisfy Breen. As in *The Big Sleep*, this trace of the novel has been left in the subtext.

In the TV series 'The RKO Story', Edward Dmytryk has recounted how the distinctively *noir* style of *Crossfire* was achieved. Because the three stars had been relatively expensive, he had to shoot the film on a tight schedule of twenty days. And so, seeking to reverse the standard 4:1 time ratio for setting up as against filming a scene, he wanted simple high-contrast lighting: 'it was a lot faster to light the people and then throw a couple of big shadows on the wall. In the old days, if they were to light a wall, every fixture would be lit . . . with three point lighting. But we didn't have the time . . .' He also used a succession of wide-angle lenses of decreasing focal length to suggest Montgomery's increasing abnormality: 'I started out with a 50 mm lens, because I wanted him to be perfectly normal. As we went along, I went from a 40 to a 35 and in the last third of the picture everything I shot with him was [with] a 25, to [give] that slight, subliminal distortion which made him a different kind of character.'

Dmytryk's creative use of *noir* conventions may also be seen in his earlier *Murder My Sweet*. In particular, two scenes in the film exemplify the correlation between *noir* expressionism and inner anxieties. In Marlowe's office at the beginning of the film, the first appearance of Moose – reflected in the window and looming over him like a giant – occurs at the precise moment that Marlowe lays aside his gun. It is as if, temporarily 'unmanned', Marlowe is promptly confronted with the phallic monster. The hallucinatory sequence which expresses Marlowe's drug-induced nightmare at the clinic is even more explicit. Before being overpowered by the villains and pumped full of drugs, Marlowe had again been relieved of his gun. And, in his nightmare, he is being pursued by a man in a white coat with a hypodermic, with the needle massively emphasised at the moment of penetration. Freud has written, 'In the anxiety dreams of girls, being followed by a man with a knife or a firearm plays a large part' (Sigmund Freud, *Introductory Lectures on Psychoanalysis*, Penguin, Harmondsworth, 1973, p.188). It seems that even Marlowe, that *noir* icon of seeker heroes, is implicated in the anxiety about masculinity: here, rather pointedly, the fear of being raped.

Iconography

Although *noir* iconography is by no means as comprehensive or precise as that of the gangster movie, a few comments are in order. In Woolrich's novel *Deadline at Dawn*, the city (New York) is explicitly the villain: the heroine never ceases to see it as a sentient, malevolent force, deliberately setting out to sabotage any plans for happiness or escape. Although few of the films are quite as explicit as this, *film noir* nevertheless took over from nineteenth-century melodrama the sense of the city as a dangerous, hostile place. The films may range through some of the same settings as the gangster movie – downtown bars, classy nightclubs, seedy hotel rooms, precinct stations, the city at night – but the emphasis is crucially different. In the gangster movie, the city may be dangerous, but it's also exciting, and the hero moves through its settings with a breezy confidence and sociability; in *film noir*, it is, rather, bleak and isolating, and the hero tends to take to the streets uneasily, aware of himself as an outsider. If the city may be taken as an image of capitalism, the gangster movie

dwells on its luxuries and spoils in a way which captures something of their allure; but in *film noir* the focus is on the seedy underside of the city: the casualties or crooks of capitalism. Where the glamour and glitter are shown, there is typically a sense of alienation. At the beginning of *Murder My Sweet*, as the narrative moves into flashback, the camera dollies from Marlowe narrating to look out of the window at the city at night. We see the neon-lit glitter, but Marlowe's downbeat voice-over mediates the imagery for us; the overall effect is of the city as alien and unwelcoming. Alfred Newman's theme from *Street Scene* (King Vidor, 1931), played over the credits and end titles of virtually all Fox's city-based films of the 'forties, strikes an equivalent, mournful, note.

A setting which has different connotations in *film noir* and in the gangster movie is the casino. In *Smart Money* (Alfred E. Green, 1931) and *The Roaring Twenties* (Walsh, 1939), it is associated with the gangster hero himself: a symbol of his dynamic climb to power. But, in *film noir*, it is invariably run by a powerful criminal who is a threat to the hero, as in *The Big Sleep*, *Gilda* (Charles Vidor, 1946), *Dead Reckoning* and *Johnny O'Clock*. Usually, the casino owner is a sexual rival, and the woman who is between the two men features in public performances in the casino in a way which potentially threatens the hero with the owner's greater power. But it is a corrupt power, founded on blackmail and murder.

The archetypal *noir* image is of a man, alone at night in an unlit office or hotel room, whilst outside a flashing neon sign rhythmically but only dimly lights up the room. This is how we first see Marlowe in the flashback in *Murder My Sweet*, setting the scene for the spectacular materialisation of Moose, how Fritz Lang visualises the descent into madness of Chris Cross towards the end of *Scarlet Street* and how Press (Jack Lambert), a murderer, is first seen in *The Unsuspected*. This last is a particularly ingenious use of the motif: Grandison (Claude Rains), who knows about Press's crime, is speaking over the radio about the guilt an unsuspected murderer carries inside himself, whilst the flashing hotel sign is so framed by the window that, as Press looks out, it spells 'KILL . . . KILL' – a visualisation of the crime that haunts him.

In *Scarlet Street*, the scene is even more expressionist. Chris's descent into madness is marked by his hallucinating the voices of Kitty, whom he killed, and Johnny, who he ensured was sent to the chair for the crime. The voices taunt him with their lovers' reunion in the afterlife. The flashing sign suggests not only that the electricity which killed Johnny has returned here to haunt Chris, but also that Chris is metaphorically in hell. He cannot sleep – as soon as he sinks on his bed, the voices rouse him – and he cannot even find oblivion in death. Tormented beyond endurance, he attempts to hang himself, but is rescued. The voices continue.

Still: Dead Reckoning. *Martinelli's Sanctuary Club – Coral (Lizabeth Scott) sings 'Either it's love or it isn't' to Rip (Humphrey Bogart).*

Settings in *film noir* frequently become charged with such expressionist associations. A famous expressionist setting is the fairground: its association with madness, and with the granting of wishes in a nightmarish form, goes back to *The Cabinet of Dr Caligari* and forward to *Something Wicked This Way Comes* (Jack Clayton, 1982). It has similar associations, too, in *film noir*. In *Nightmare Alley*, which is based around a travelling carnival, Stan (Tyrone Power) gets his wish to become the partner of Zeena (Joan Blondell) in a fake mind-reading act when he accidentally kills her husband and current partner; at the end of the film, degraded to the level of the animal-like 'geek', Stan runs berserk. In *Strangers on a Train*, Bruno appears to Miriam as the most exciting 'attraction' the fair has to offer – and he kills her (a murder which Hitchcock films as a distorted reflection in Miriam's glasses: a consciously expressionist effect). When Michael (Orson Welles) finds himself precipitated into a fairground 'Crazy House' at the end of *The Lady from Shanghai*, the decor actually seems to be modelled on that of *The Cabinet of Dr Caligari*, a visual tour de force which ironises the rushed explanation of the plot in the voice-over. Another nightmarish setting in *film noir* is the border town and, beyond that, the border itself. Ideologically viewed as the outer reaches of the 'civilised' (American) world, the border town tends to be presented as peculiarly dangerous and threatening, as in *Where Danger Lives* or *Touch of Evil*. In *Border Incident* (Anthony Mann, 1949), not only are those who cross the border illegally likely to be killed by bandits, but the terrrain itself is so dangerous that both the hero and his buddy are almost sucked into a swamp.

Other settings may 'comment on' their owners. General Sternwood's greenhouse in *The Big Sleep*, with its oppressive hothouse atmosphere and its orchids ('their perfume has the rotten sweetness of corruption'), acts as a metaphor for his family's 'corrupt blood'. The mansion of the similarly wealthy Mr Grayle (Miles Mander) in *Murder My Sweet* has echoing marble halls which suggest a museum. In *The Dark Corner*, the place where Hardy Cathcart (Clifton Webb) spends most of his time is actually a museum (or rather an art gallery), in the vault of which he keeps the Raphael which stands in for a portrait of his wife Mari (Cathy Downs), expressing how he wishes to keep her. Each of these sites bears testament to the impotence of the elderly patriarchal figure who presides over it; sex is accordingly displaced to other sites, notably Geiger's house in *The Big Sleep* and the beachhouse in *Murder My Sweet*. But, like other such locations in movies of the era – the boathouse in *Rebecca* and *The Reckless Moment*, the beachhouse in *Mildred Pierce*, the cabin in *Out of the Past* – these sites are not only associated with illicit desire, but with murder. Especially in *film noir*, a safe haven for illicit sexuality simply does not exist, and the explosiveness of the sexuality is registered in the violence which terminates it.

Geoffrey O'Brien's survey of the American paperback market, *Hardboiled America*, shows how paperbacks took off in the early 'forties. A particularly successful line – the subject of O'Brien's book – was the sort of hard-boiled crime fiction which would find its cinematic home in *film noir*: Hammett, Cain and McCoy were reprinted, and virtually all the novels subsequently filmed as *films noirs* were published during this paperback boom. Their illustrated covers were an important sales feature, and (apart from novels published as movie tie-ins, which tended to have rather conservative covers emphasising the stars) many of the covers were fairly lurid, suggesting sex and violence. A favourite subject was a woman with a gun, usually threatening a man. This image, too, can probably be claimed for *noir* iconography: Mrs Grayle (Claire Trevor) drawing a gun on Marlowe in the beachhouse climax of *Murder My Sweet*; Veda emptying a gun into Monte in another beachhouse climax in *Mildred Pierce*; Mari doing the same to her husband at the entrance to the vault in *The Dark Corner* – these are only a few of the many manifestations of the motif. In *film noir*, women possess sufficient phallic power to be shown regularly wielding – and frequently firing – such weapons; and, as can be seen from these few examples, *where* a woman produces the gun can be a crucial element in the film's symbolic system.

Iconographically, the two most visually distinctive *noir* figures are the *femme fatale*, glamorously dressed in revealing gowns and coolly enigmatic, and the private eye, sloppily dressed in trench-coat and fedora, and suitably hard-boiled. Richard Dyer has also drawn attention to the make-up (dark lips; long, flowing hair) of the former, in which 'artifice and sensuality' are emphasised (Dyer, 1977). Both have iconic antecedents: the *femme fatale* in Marlene Dietrich as she appeared in 'thirties Josef von Sternberg movies, the private eye in the gangster-movie hoodlum. Both smoke extensively; indeed, the proffering and lighting of cigarettes is a highly convenient device, in films of the era, for establishing contact and smoothing intercourse. Equally, both feature prominently on posters for the movies. The *femme fatale* on these was rarely given a gun (as she was on the book covers), but was nevertheless clearly the main attraction, as is indicated by her positioning and posture, and the rhetoric of the ad lines. Sometimes, in lieu of a gun, she was given a smoking cigarette, as on the American poster for *Murder My Sweet* and *Out of the Past*.

The other characters of *film noir* may be vivid enough, but they are signalled in the transgeneric way typical of Hollywood movies: plug-ugly heavies, butch masseuses, dandified gays (e.g. Cairo in *The Maltese Falcon*), tuxedo-clad socialites, leggy showgirls, etc. Colin McArthur has suggested that 'in *film noir* the physical qualities of the villains are used as visual shorthand to suggest depths of evil. Hence obesity – Sydney Greenstreet in *The Maltese Falcon* and Laird Cregar in *Hot Spot* – and hence the sinister, babyish Peter Lorre, and Elisha Cook's tormented eyes' (McArthur, 1972, p.44). But although certain actors may evoke the genre – Elisha Cook Jr's gallery of petty hoods and victims certainly has a privileged place in *noir* iconography – all character actors were typed by their appearance for certain sorts of role; this is not specifically a *noir* feature.

Social and Industrial Determinants

The evolution of film noir
The time lag between the publication of the *noir* novels of Hammett, Cain and Chandler and their translation into *films noirs* was no doubt the result of a number of factors, but the most significant was the Production Code, which was rigorously enforced from June 1934. Before that date, it was possible for films to be relatively uncompromising in their depiction of the darker side of American life. Several hard-hitting cycles belong to the early sound era: 1) the gangster film: e.g. *Little Caesar* (Mervyn LeRoy, 1930), *Public Enemy* (William Wellman, 1931), *Scarface* (Hawks, 1932); 2) films dealing with shyster lawyers and

Still: Women without Names – *the brief meeting between Joyce (Ellen Drew) and Fred (Robert Paige) before his scheduled execution.*

politicians: e.g. *Lawyer Man* (Dieterle, 1932), *State's Attorney* (George Archainbaud, 1932), *Washington Masquerade* (Charles Brabin, 1932); 3) a prison cycle: e.g. *The Big House* (George Hill, 1930), *The Criminal Code* (Hawks, 1930), *20,000 Years in Sing Sing* (Curtiz, 1932). (For a discussion of the cycles, *see* Andrew Bergman, *We're in the Money*, Harper & Row, New York, 1971.)

In their concern with social issues of the day, such films reflect the general politicisation of the culture during the Depression. This concern found particular focus in the 'social problem film'. The most powerful and *noir* of these was *I Am a Fugitive from a Chain Gang* (LeRoy, 1932), from Robert E. Burns's autobiographical story. Indeed, the film's bleakness and pessimism suggests that, but for Code clampdown, *noir* narratives might have been a regular feature during the Depression. But, with the enforcement of the Code, it became far more difficult to make ideologically challenging films. Nevertheless, it was in the social problem films that a *noir* sense of revealing something of the underside of American life could, on occasion, be found: lynch mobs (*Fury*; *They Won't Forget*, LeRoy, 1937); the Ku Klux Klan (*Black Legion*, Archie Mayo, 1937); victimisation of the ex-convict (*You Only Live Once*, Lang, 1937) or racial minorities (*Massacre*, Alan Crosland, 1934; *Bordertown*, Mayo, 1935). (Peter Roffman & Jim Purdy in *The Hollywood Social Problem Film*, Indiana University Press, 1981, deal comprehensively with this area.)

Women without Names (Robert Florey, 1940), a B movie co-scripted by Horace McCoy, illustrates how the social problem film can blend into *film noir*. Although owing much to *You Only Live Once*, it is more explicitly political, showing the hero and heroine – arrested, tried and convicted for a murder they did commit – as pawns in a legal system governed by the electoral ambitions of its practitioners rather than a concern for justice. At one point, even a newspaper photographer – a hardbitten breed – protests about a ploy in which the couple's plight is cynically manipulated by one side seeking to gain political advantage over the other. And, even when he hears the belated confession of the real woman in the case, the assistant DA who conducted the successful prosecution refuses to accept it: it would spoil his election chances. Equally, the film takes the hero and heroine into a *noir* world of remarkable bleakness: most of the action is set in the jail – which has both male and female wings – in the weeks before the hero's execution. It also has a brilliant jury sequence which goes, more plausibly than *Twelve Angry Men* (Sidney Lumet, 1957), in precisely the opposite direction to this illustrious successor: the one juror who is convinced of the couple's innocence is worn down by the impatience of the others.

Clearly, the *noir* ethos didn't spring out of nowhere in 1940: it would be more accurate to say it had been suppressed during the 'thirties, only finding the occasional outlet – primarily in the social problem film. No doubt a thorough investigation of 'thirties crime movies would produce more proto-*noir* films – I would nominate *Nancy Steele Is Missing* (Marshall, 1936) as a strong candidate – but it was not until the end of the decade that a genuinely *noir* mood began to be felt across a whole range of movies: *The Hunchback of Notre Dame* (Dieterle, 1939), *Of Mice and Men* (Milestone, 1939), *The Letter* (Wyler, 1940), *The Grapes of Wrath* (John Ford, 1940), *City for Conquest* (Litvak, 1940), *The Sea Wolf* (Curtiz, 1941) and *Kings Row* (Sam Wood, 1941). *Citizen Kane*, by contrast, is not *noir* in mood, although its use of the investigative flashback structure, and of high-contrast/deep-focus photography had a lasting influence on 'forties Hollywood cinema in general and the *noir* cycle in particular.

Throughout the 'thirties, Joseph Breen had been firm over 'morally dubious' properties: his vetoing of *The Postman Always Rings Twice*, even though MGM had bought the screen rights in 1934, was characteristic. Towards the end of the decade, responding to pressure from both the Hollywood majors and independent producers, he began to permit a greater degree of licence. Huston's *The Maltese Falcon* was made in this climate. However, the film is less ideologically threatening than later *films noirs*: Spade's control over the *noir* world is never really in doubt and the villains enter the USA from abroad, and are coded as foreign: Brigid's (Mary Astor) name is Irish and her accent, like Gutman's, is English; Cairo, with his three passports (one of them British) is of indeterminate nationality (he's called the Levantine in the novel). In other words, the film possesses an ideological equivalent to that noted of the 'thirties Hollywood horror film by Robin Wood: 'horror exists, but is unAmerican'

('The Return of the Repressed', *Film Comment*, July/August 1978, p.29). A fundamentally rather reactionary film, it has nothing of the darkness of *The Grapes of Wrath* or *Kings Row*.

America's entry into World War II in December 1941 introduced a different set of priorities. In April 1942, the Office of War Information set up a Hollywood office with a brief to encourage the studios to produce films which would help the war effort (*see* Clayton R. Koppes & Gregory D. Black, *Hollywood Goes to War*, The Free Press, New York, 1987, pp.58-72). Patently, films which reflected on the darker side of American life did not chime with such propaganda impulses, nor did they fit safely into the area of 'escapist entertainment'. Under the circumstances, it is perhaps surprising that the *noir* cycle did begin in earnest during the war, even though it did not really take off until the end of the war.

Another factor that militated against the earlier development of the *noir* cycle was economics. Studios already had their own brands of crime movie in production, and the proliferation of the series detectives indicates the films' lowly status. Crime movies were B movies, and although some of the early 'forties examples, like *Stranger on the Third Floor*, may seem in retrospect unmistakably *noir*, they would not at the time have exerted the same sort of influence as successful A movies. For example, *The Falcon Takes Over* has distinctive low-key lighting, but its cameraman, George Robinson, is not a well-known figure, even though he also photographed *Son of Frankenstein* and other visually distinguished movies.

It was not until 1944, the year of (in release date order) *Phantom Lady*, *Gaslight*, *Christmas Holiday*, *Double Indemnity*, *Laura* and *Murder My Sweet* (all of them either A movies or, in the case of *Phantom Lady*, a high-grade B movie) that a substantial body of films was made in what we would now term the *noir* style, and that the influence of the films can be documented. *Phantom Lady* was an unexpected critical success and was broadcast as a radio play in Cecil B. DeMille's 'Lux Radio Theatre' as early as March 1944, whilst the film was still on release. *Gaslight* and *Double Indemnity* were major critical successes and both received Academy Award nominations including Best Picture and Best Actress (Ingrid Bergman won in the latter category). In addition, *Double Indemnity* not only changed the climate of censorship, but caused producer Jerry Wald to say, 'From now on, every picture I make will be done in flashback', (quoted in Albert La Valley's introduction to the published script of *Mildred Pierce*, University of Wisconsin Press, 1980, p.29). *Laura* won LaShelle an Academy Award for his cinematography. Finally, *Murder My Sweet* – with its flashback and voice-over, and its distinctively *noir* visual style – was far more influential in establishing the mood and manner of subsequent investigative thrillers than *The Maltese Falcon* had been.

Despite the fact that the better-known examples tend to be A movies, *film noir* also flourished in B movies from *Stranger on the Third Floor* onwards. For economic reasons, B movies enjoyed a boom between 1940 and the mid 'fifties, from the beginning of the US Government's anti-trust action against the majors to its completion (*see* Kerr, 1979). B movies were usually made on tight shooting schedules in terms of days, but with long hours per day, so that night-time filming was a natural part of the schedule. Underlighting sets was not only economical, as Dmytryk stresses, but could also help build atmosphere and conceal design limitations. B movies often have complicated or elliptical narratives as a result of hurried scripting or failure to shoot all the scenes. In other words, the conditions under which B movies were produced were suitable for *films noirs*, just as they were for horror movies. B movies were also subject to less Front Office supervision, and directors would often use the relative freedom this gave them to experiment more. Some directors, most famously Edgar G. Ulmer, who directed *Detour*, preferred to remain B directors because of this freedom.

Freud

A further important contribution to *film noir* came with America's discovery of Sigmund Freud, and the gradual absorption of his theories into popular culture. It was not until the 'forties that Hollywood films – no doubt prompted in part by the number of refugee psychoanalysts who settled in Los Angeles – became widely influenced by Freudian thought, which was registered in a number of different ways. First, there was a general shift towards seeking to understand the psychology of sexuality, human development, family relationships, dreams, the emotions, repression, etc. Films such as *Kings Row, Now, Voyager* (Irving Rapper, 1942) and *Lady in the Dark* (Leisen, 1944) explicitly invoke Freudian concepts to explore such areas. Second, 'forties films tended to be less inhibited about the use of Freudian symbolism, which was one of a number of mechanisms for implying the forbidden. A film such as *Secret Beyond the Door* is saturated with such symbolism and there seems little doubt that most of this was consciously intended by Lang (*see* article in *Movie 34/35*). Third, as films moved to explore the darker areas of the human psyche, they entered into specifically Freudian territory. *The Woman in the Window* – which begins with a lecture on Freud – merely makes explicit a general awareness in *film noir* that characters are often subject to inner forces over which they have limited control. This is also relevant to the persecuted-wife cycle, with its sense of paranoia and its focus on sadism and masochism (in *Sorry, Wrong Number*, it is explicit that the wife's illness is psychosomatic), and is foregrounded in the psychological melodramas. In sum, one could say that 'forties narratives – but particularly those dealing, like *film noir*, with

crime and desire – became Freudianised, both consciously and unconsciously. Freud's theories contributed in a variety of ways to the representation of sexual obsession, sexual anxieties (both male and female), criminal impulses and 'the perverse'. This last has a particular significance for *film noir*, since the films regularly deal – in a necessarily coded form – with 'deviant' sexuality. Richard Dyer (1977) has discussed some of the many gay characters in *film noir*, but his examples are restricted to the more overtly signalled instances. There are many more which are suggested subtextually in the narratives.

Representation and contemporary fears

The ways in which *noir* narratives relate to the social unrest in post-war USA are discussed in general terms by Richard Maltby. A specific link is commonly made between the negative view of female sexuality in *film noir* and contemporary male fears about the greater independence women achieved during the war, notably economic independence as a result of working in more highly paid men's jobs. The argument is convincing, but the *femmes fatales* go back to the hard-boiled novels of the 'thirties and owe much to that tradition of writing. In Hammett, Chandler and, above all, Cain, women are not to be trusted, and if the private-eye hero manages to survive the narrative by maintaining a suitable detachment, a typical Cain hero is destroyed by his obsession with a woman. If Cain's view of women is bad enough, he is even more neurotically hostile to what he considers 'deviance' (foreigners, socialists) and, in *Serenade* (1937), where a homosexual occupies the position of the *femme fatale*, he presents the character with a loathing which has to be read to be believed. (When a film was finally made of the novel, directed by Anthony Mann in 1956, the character was inevitably made into a woman, and one can see traces of Cain's hysterical homophobia in the excessiveness of her ruthlessness and heartlessness.) The nadir of this trend is, of course, Mickey Spillane, who is also, disturbingly, the most popular novelist in the hard-boiled tradition.

Nevertheless, the fact that *film noir* took off so strongly at the end of the war, and that the most influential films very often possess suitably dangerous *femmes fatales*, suggests that there is a correlation with contemporary male fears. As Andrea Walsh points out in *Women's Film and Female Experience* (pp.183–185), the persecuted-wife cycle expresses the same sorts of fear for women, although the films typically deal with the fears by displacement: to upper-class and/or foreign settings, and to the past. With both the male-centred and the female-centred narratives, it is relatively rare for the fears to be made explicit, e.g. for a man to return from the services and find out that his wife has been unfaithful during his absence, as in *The Blue Dahlia, Desire Me* (Cukor/LeRoy, 1947) and *The Unfaithful* (Vincent Sherman, 1947), or for the man's violence

towards the woman to be linked in some way to the war, as in *In a Lonely Place*.

The Unfaithful is a particularly interesting example of a film which self-consciously reflects contemporary fears and concerns; it even begins with a documentary-style voice-over, announcing, 'The problem with which it deals belongs not to any one city, town or country, but is of our times.' Although the film's script is credited solely to David Goodis (his first screenwriting credit) and James Dunn, it is in fact a reworking of that of *The Letter*, a common Warner practice: plots were regularly recycled in different contexts and genres. Nevertheless, the reworking is substantial, relating the film explicitly to the problem of wartime separations, which often, as here, occurred after a whirlwind courtship and marriage. Whereas the unfaithful wife in the Chandler-scripted *Blue Dahlia* is presented unsympathetically and soon murdered, the situation of the wife here is viewed with great sympathy. It is Chris (Ann Sheridan), not her husband Bob (Zachary Scott), who is plunged into the *noir* world at the beginning of the movie, when her discarded lover forces his way into her house one night and attacks her – and she kills him. But the *noir* discourse (guilt, blackmail, arrest and trial for murder) is balanced by a woman's film discourse, in which, through the figure of his cousin (the indispensable Eve Arden) Bob is made to see his responsibility: sweeping Chris off her feet, 'making with the uniform and the "today we live" routine' – 'You didn't marry her – you took an option out on her.'

A number of *films noirs* depict the plight of the returning veteran in terms of amnesia: *Spellbound, Somewhere in the Night, The High Wall.* This is another example of the psychological thread that runs through the films: where 'twenties and 'thirties films about veterans of the

Still: The Unfaithful – *Chris Hunter (Ann Sheridan) is blackmailed by Barrow (Steven Geray).*

World War I tended to stress physical rather than psychological damage, films about World War II veterans focused on the 'problems of readjustment', a psychological slant on their reintegration into country, society and family. *The Best Years of Our Lives* (Wyler, 1946) depicts this in the framework of melodrama; *Crossfire* shows it in the context of *film noir*. Each of the soldiers in *Crossfire* has a problem with returning home: Keeley seems markedly reluctant to return to his wife, preferring the company of his army buddies; Mitchell spends the first half of the film drifting aimlessly from one downtown location to another; Montgomery is a psychopath, who marks his return to America by beating a man to death simply for being Jewish; Bowers is pathetically dependent on Montgomery, who ultimately kills him, too. Set in Washington DC, the film – through its visual intimation of the city as nightmare – suggests that the heart of America is the *noir* world. Whereas *The Best Years of Our Lives* moves towards the rehabilitation of its three veterans, *Crossfire* has a very different ending. Montgomery, of necessity, is killed. Although Mitchell is – tentatively – reunited with his wife, the other soldiers remain in the city. In place of Mitchell as kid-brother figure, Keeley adopts LeRoy (William Phipps), the young soldier who proved himself by facing up to Montgomery. The film ends with the two of them going off for a cup of coffee, a stark contrast to the home-directed endings of melodrama, encapsulated in the familiar last line, 'Let's go home'.

Whether it takes the form, as here, of returning veterans showing uneasiness about returning home, or of all those men who feel trapped in marriage and family, or the more general form of the rootlessness and restlessness of so many of the heroes of the era, domesticity almost invariably poses a threat to the *noir* hero. This, too, would seem to be a very specific reflection of contemporary male fears. Whereas melodrama tends to be focused on the home, the action in *film noir* is nearly always centrifugally away from the home: even when the *noir* hero seeks domesticity, it becomes an ideal which he cannot realise – as in *Out of The Past*, *The Locket* and *Criss Cross* – or which is violently destroyed, as in *The Big Heat*. Overall, the films register a profound sense of alienation from family, society and roots: it is symptomatic that, when a *noir* hero returns 'home' after many years, he should be driven out of the house again within minutes (*The Blue Dahlia*) or violently ejected from the town (*The Strange Love of Martha Ivers*). *Human Desire* – which begins with the hero coming back from Korea – is an obvious exception in this respect, and goes some way towards balancing the pessimism of Lang's earlier *The Big Heat*. Significantly, it finds a way of accommodating the inherent restlessness of the returning veteran in the hero's job as a train engineer: his long journeys to and from the small town where he lives are the exact equivalent of, for example, the hero's restless journeys to and from Los Angeles in *The Blue Dahlia*.

Very occasionally – *Deadline at Dawn* and *Fallen Angel* (Preminger, 1945) are two examples – a *film noir* will use the 'Let's go home' ending. But, far more frequently, a *noir* 'happy ending' has something tentative or uncertain or problematic about it. At the end of *Pitfall*, the husband and wife are driving home, but the most positive statement they can come up with is that they'll try to preserve the marriage. At the end of *Mildred Pierce*, Mildred and Bert walk off into the sunrise side by side, but we are fully aware what a compromise this is for Mildred, and the rhetoric of the happy ending is consciously undermined by the presence in the image of women scrubbing the floor. A genuinely happy *noir* ending is more likely to focus on the couple escaping: *The Strange Love of Martha Ivers*, *Dark Passage*. This, too, is the real point of the *Deadline at Dawn* ending: they're escaping from the city. Finally, *The Dark Corner* has a very unusual *noir* happy ending: the hero and heroine going off to be married.

Using *Out of the Past* as his example, and concentrating on Jeff as a *noir* hero who has been unable to escape his past, Richard Maltby suggests two different metaphorical readings of the film. In one, the past is viewed as 'like' that of an ex-communist, with Jeff required to purge himself of 'past dubious . . . allegiances with people and organisations working against the social order'. (This reading gains strength when one considers how *The Woman on Pier 13* structurally resembles *Out of the Past*). In the other, the past is 'like' that of a military veteran, who now seeks

to settle down, but is prevented from doing so by 'the guilt and obsessive neuroses he has acquired during his period of absence from society.'

I would like to take both notions and elaborate on them slightly differently from Maltby. With reference to the *noir* cycle overall, chronologically the second of them is the earlier feature: indeed, Maltby considers that 'the central male protagonist in *films noirs* of 1946-48 is almost invariably marked as a veteran by one means or another,' either explicitly or metaphorically. On this reading, the war is the 'traumatic event' which lies behind many *noir* narratives, making its presence felt textually in a variety of ways. It may feature directly in the narrative. In *The Locket*, the breakdown of Harry (Brian Aherne) – the moment when he is plunged into the *noir* world – occurs when he realises that Nancy, his wife, really is the thief (and hence murderess), Norman (Robert Mitchum), her earlier boyfriend, had claimed. But the film visualises Harry at this moment as a shell-shocked war victim, standing amidst the bombed ruins of his London flat. In other words, the devastation caused by the war acts as a metaphor for the *noir* world. Alternatively, the war as 'traumatic event' may echo through the narrative. In *Angel Face*, a wartime air-raid when Diane was ten not only killed her mother, but led to Charles, her father, marrying the hated Catherine. In Frank's case, his military service ended when he was shot out of a tank. The violence of these two separate wartime traumas is then echoed in the two extremely violent car crashes in the movie: the first kills both Catherine and Charles, the second both Frank and Diane. Here it is as if the trauma of the war has generated symptoms

Still: Night and the City – *the hunted* noir *hero, Harry Fabian (Richard Widmark).*

which are re-enacted, compulsively, in the text: both crashes are so devastating that it looks as if a bomb has hit the car. Finally, the general sense of the *noir* hero as a man haunted by a violent past which is only rarely attributed to the war suggests, as Maltby implies, that the films – like those in the persecuted-wife cycle – are operating by displacement. Consider how often a war veteran returns home only to be subjected to a bloody beating up by thugs: *The Blue Dahlia*, *The Strange Love of Martha Ivers*, *Dead Reckoning*. This last takes the connection a step further: the thug's name, Krause, is obviously German.

The relationship of the films to the growing anti-communist witchhunts is more problematic. Gordon Kahn has argued in *Hollywood on Trial* (Boni & Gaer, New York, 1948, p.105) that Dmytryk and Adrian Scott, the director and producer of *Crossfire*, were summoned to appear before the House Un-American Activities Committee *because* they had made the film, which attacks anti-Semitism. In other words, the members of HUAC were so racist themselves that they considered a film such as *Crossfire* threatening. And the success of HUAC – Maltby mentions the notorious Waldorf Statement, which in effect initiated the blacklist – gradually had an effect on the types of film made. By 1950-51 – when Senator McCarthy began his much more virulent anti-communist campaign, the Hollywood Ten (including Dmytryk and Scott) finally went to jail and the second round of HUAC hearings got under way – one can discern a clear shift away from the radicalism of the late 'forties. The social problem film virtually disappeared, and the crime film in general became more conservative: the forces of law and order were now more likely to be shown as worthy of esteem than criticised. By the time of the second round of hearings, the atmosphere in Hollywood was much more bitter; not least because a number of people – among them Dmytryk – caved in to the Committee and 'named names'. Those who refused were blacklisted, and many talented directors, writers and actors were unable to find work.

For a significant number of left-wing figures, persecution during these years was very real, and it would only be natural for some of the films to register this in a disguised form. Although the attribution of the generalised sense of paranoia in *film noir* to anti-communist persecution seems rather facile, there are films where one feels that the analogy is relevant. A good example is Dassin's brilliant *Night and the City*, made in London the year before he was named as a member of the Communist Party by Dmytryk and forced into long-term exile. From its dynamic opening – Harry Fabian (Richard Widmark) pursued through the alleyways and bomb-site rubble around St Paul's Cathedral – it shows a man who seems to be always on the run. Eventually, as even those whom he had taken to be his friends betray him (a radical departure from Gerald Kersh's novel), and he is hunted down remorselessly by what seems to be the whole of London's underworld, the sense of paranoia becomes all-pervading.

The semi-documentary and location filming

Although location-filming had increased during the war – it was one of the ways that the wartime restrictions on set-building costs could be surmounted – the end of the war brought a more general shift to such filming. In part, this was a consequence of the success of a cycle of films pioneered by producer Louis de Rochement (previously the producer of the 'March of Time' newsreels) called semi-documentaries. Although some critics have subsumed this cycle into *film noir*, the films are materially different, and it is crucial to distinguish between the two groups. The first of the semi-documentaries, *The House on 92nd Street* (Hathaway, 1945) established the format. A reconstruction of a real-life espionage case, it was filmed on 'the actual locations' and used some of 'the actual participants' of the original case, and included a detailing of FBI techniques and procedures. In addition, it was overlaid with a documentary-style voice-over. Later films which used essentially the same format include the de Rochement-produced *Boomerang* (Elia Kazan, 1947), the Mark Hellinger-produced *The Naked City* (Dassin, 1948) and *The Street with No Name* (William Keighley, 1948).

The semi-documentaries are a good example of the shift away from the radicalism of *film noir*. Ideologically, they are the polar opposite to *films noirs*: they celebrate the efficacy of the American crime-fighting institutions that *film noir* views with such suspicion. (The celebration may indeed be strident: each time the narrative of *The House on 92nd Street* or *The Street with No Name* returns to FBI headquarters, stirring martial music surges up on the sound-track.) They marginalise or discredit characters who would be sympathetically viewed as victim heroes in *film noir*. And their use of the voice-over – the authoritative 'voice of God' of the documentary – is completely foreign to the highly subjective, frequently painful use of flashback and voice-over in *film noir*.

The semi-documentaries also exerted a strong ideological influence over other post-war crime movies, particularly those concerned with the crime-busting activities of the police. In effect, they set up a discourse (realist/reactionary/reassuring/authoritative/upbeat) which is in opposition to that of *film noir* (expressionist/subversive/disturbing/confusing/downbeat). The two discourses frequently interact in the same film: *Kiss of Death* (Hathaway, 1947) has a *noir*-like defeatism built into a crime-busting narrative; *T-Men* (1947) combines a semi-documentary script (based on the exploits of the Treasury service) with a vigorously *noir mise-en-scène*, courtesy of director Anthony Mann and cameraman John Alton. *Call Northside 777* (Hathaway, 1948) is also more of a hybrid. Although it seems like a typical semi-documentary (based on a real-life case, with 'voice of God' introduction) and has some of the more obvious trappings of the cycle (e.g. a ponderous exposition of how a lie detector works), it also has a journalist hero who, for the first half of the film, is as cynical as any embittered *noir* hero. More crucially, its narrative drive is primarily directed *against* the law and order establishment rather than setting out to validate it: the story concerns a miscarriage of justice – and the police are extremely hostile to a journalist looking into the case. In addition, it has a strikingly *noir* sequence in which, in the pursuit of his investigation, the hero (James Stewart) goes into the seedy night-time world of the Polish quarter of Chicago. Throughout, *noir* elements have more of a purchase on the film than on other semi-documentaries. In *Cry of the City*, the influence goes the other way: the reactionary elements of the semi-documentary cycle tending to suppress the *noir* discourse (*see* 'Cry of the City' in 'Robert Siodmak').

The conservative influence of the semi-documentaries may be seen in particular in the B movie sector. *Undercover Man* (Joseph H. Lewis, 1949), *Armoured Car Robbery* (Richard Fleischer, 1950), *Mystery Street* (John Sturges, 1950) and *Union Station* (Maté, 1950) are all included in Silver and Ward (1980) as *films noirs*, but *noir* elements in the films are for the most part displaced and marginalised: the films are all primarily concerned with the efficacy of police/treasury agent procedures and have suitably nasty villains. As for *The Racket* (Cromwell, 1951), it seems to me positively unpleasant in its right-wing crime-busting rhetoric. There were, however, still plenty of radical *films noirs* being made in the early 'fifties – Lewis, in particular, went on to direct one of the *noir* masterpieces, *The Big Combo*.

The issue of whether the *noir* cycle constitutes a genre is not very interesting: it all depends on how genre is defined, and the fact that it was not a genre for the Hollywood studios and filmmakers at the time is not a valid argument against its being considered one in retrospect. In 'The RKO Story', Dmytryk tells how a student informed him that he was one of the founders of *film noir*, and in his book *On Screen Directing* (Focal Press, London, 1984, p.81) he writes about *noir* techniques as if that were now the natural way to speak of them. Certainly, for filmmakers today, *film noir* constitutes a genre: the films in the current *noir* cycle – which began, in effect, as long ago as *Harper/The Moving Target* (Jack Smight, 1966) – make conscious reference to the conventions established in the films of the 'forties/'fifties cycle.

Furthermore, as a generic field, *film noir* was extremely pervasive: *noir* elements can be found in almost all mainstream genres in the late 'forties and early 'fifties. *Noir* hybrids with melodrama and the woman's film have already been discussed; equally there are hybrids with the gangster movie – e.g. *White Heat, Kiss Tomorrow Goodbye*

and *The Enforcer*, (Bretaigne Windust/Walsh, 1951), the western, e.g. *Pursued, Blood on the Moon*, Wise, 1948, and *The Furies* (Anthony Mann, 1950) and the period thriller, e.g. *The Lodger* (Brahm, 1944), *The Suspect* (Siodmak, 1945) and *Reign of Terror/The Black Book* (Mann, 1949). In particular, the *noir* influence may be seen in films dealing with contemporary issues, from *The Lost Weekend* (Wilder, 1945), a film about alcoholism, to *Brute Force* (Dassin, 1947), a prison movie. But *noir* elements also occurred in less likely genres. For example, *Unfaithfully Yours* (1948), one of Preston Sturges's funniest comedies, contains a distinctly *noir* sequence in which Rex Harrison's hero fantasises about murdering his wife, a sequence that strikingly anticipates its equivalent in *Sudden Fear*, when Joan Crawford fantasises murdering her husband. The pervasiveness of *film noir* in the late 'forties was such that certain types of movie were effectively subsumed into it: *Crossfire* as a social problem movie is an excellent example. This occurred in particular with the boxing movie, which had been around in the 'thirties, but became much bleaker in the 'forties. *Body and Soul* (Rossen, 1947) not only deals with boxing corruption, but incorporates such mainstream *noir* elements as the 'sexual woman'/domestic woman choice, a corruptible hero who is seduced by the lure of riches, and magnificent low-key photography from James Wong Howe.

Like all Hollywood films of the era, *films noirs* were policed by the Production Code Administration, which obviously limited the extent to which they could be openly critical of American ideology. Nevertheless, viewed collectively, they can be seen to re-inflect the familiar Hollywood discourses about romance, the family, sexuality, the law and so on in a manner which is not a little subversive. In *films noirs*, sex, greed and power tend to displace love as the motivating feature of 'romantic relationships', marriages tend to be bleak and unfulfilling, and the family is viewed in a consistently negative light. The films probe the darker areas of the psyche (obsession and neurosis are common preoccupations) and focus in particular on male sexual anxieties and on the pathology of male violence. Their view of the legal system is frequently highly critical, and figures of the establishment are often shown as corrupt. Overall, they portray a society in which the American dream of success is inverted, alienation and fatalistic helplessness being the dominant moods, and failure the most frequent outcome. In this, they show the accommodation of a 'European' sensibility which is also reflected visually in the films' expressionistic *mise-en-scène*. Finally, the quality of the movies as a group is unusually high, and they possess some extremely provocative subtexts. The *noir* cycle was a particularly fertile period of Hollywood's history, and its influence is still being felt today, both as a rich source of inspiration to modern film-makers and as a highly rewarding field of interest to film students.

THE POLITICS OF THE MALADJUSTED TEXT

Richard Maltby

I

This article aims to explore the relations of metaphor and coincidence between a group of films released between 1946 and 1949 (dubbed by the industry variously as 'Detective-Mystery Melodramas', 'Social Problem Crime Films' and 'Psychological Dramas',[1] and including, but not exclusively, those movies now commonly identified as *films noirs*), the postwar disillusionment of liberal intellectuals concerned with the mass media, and the development of Cold War sentiments in American domestic politics in the same period. Since its plot will be as convoluted as those of the movies it discusses, it should perhaps imitate its subject by beginning with the kind of coincidental encounter that determines narrative development.

Jacques Tourneur's *Out of the Past* (whatever *film noir* is, *Out of the Past* is undoubtedly *film noir*) opened its New York run at the Palace Theatre on Broadway on Tuesday, 25th November 1947, a few blocks away from the Waldorf Astoria Hotel where, a couple of hours earlier, the Association of Motion Picture Producers had concluded a two-day meeting by releasing the first document of the entertainment industry blacklist, the Waldorf Statement.[2] It announced that the industry would forthwith discharge from its employment the ten 'unfriendly' witnesses who had refused to answer the House Un-American Activities Committee's questions about their membership of the Communist Party.

The plot of *Out of the Past* might be metaphorically reconstructed as a sympathetic portrayal of Robert Mitchum as an ex-Communist witness before HUAC – Whittaker Chambers, perhaps, or Elizabeth Bentley. A man with a shady past, trying to live a normal life as a well-adjusted American, is propelled by a combination of circumstance and conscience to justify his citizenship not on the basis of his present activities, but by accounting for his past dubious connections and allegiances with people and organisations working against the social order. The account he produces is not in itself sufficient expiation. He has also to perform an act of exorcism to demonstrate his independence from those past allegiances and redress the social imbalance his earlier conduct created. That act, although providing a somewhat ambiguous moral redemption, may

not be sufficient to permit his re-integration back into the society he originally betrayed. Everything he does takes place in the framework of the knowledge that, at the end, his social permit may remain withdrawn.

Two features, at least, of this metaphor fit fairly convincingly. The first is the requirement placed upon the central male protagonist to account for his past, a past containing dark and menacing secrets that can no longer remain hidden, but must surface and find resolution. The second is the narrative form in which that explanation takes place. 'I think I'm in a frame,' declares Mitchum at one point, 'I'm going in there to look at the picture.' The investigative narrative dominates the crime film of the 1940s, in both *films noirs* and the stylistically and thematically related private-eye and semi-documentary films, and it was virtually a new form for the decade. Where previous crime films had relied on a conventional linear structure, depicting, for example, the chronological rise and fall of a gangster figure or the equally linear deductive process of the Thin Man or Charlie Chan, the investigative narrative provided a much more intricate and less stable surface, looking back into the past of the film to an event whose explanation would provide a motor or a resolution for the narrative.

The hero of these films, who was not always the central protagonist, was the investigator, the man assigned the task of making sense of the web of coincidence, flashback and unexplained circumstance that made up the plot. Uncertainly adrift in a world of treachery and shifting loyalties, the investigator of the *noir* movie was himself less than perfect, frequently neurotic, sometimes paranoid, and often managed to re-establish a stable world in the film only by imposing an arbitrary resolution on the other characters. At the end of *The Big Sleep* (Howard Hawks, 1946), Humphrey Bogart as Marlowe presents three explanations of the plot to the gambler Eddie Mars, and imposes his own preferred solution by shooting three times. If it seems too large an imaginative step from Bogart to Robert

1) 'Feature-Length Films, 1944, 1945 and 1946', *Hollywood Quarterly*, vol.2, no.3, 1947, pp.306-307.

2) Larry Ceplair & Steven Englund, *The Inquisition in Hollywood*, Anchor Press/Doubleday, New York, 1980, p.445.

Stripling, chief investigator for HUAC, it may perhaps be mediated through the semi-documentary films of the immediate postwar period, such as *The House on 92nd Street* (Henry Hathaway, 1945), which presented a largely anonymous, corporate hero in the form of FBI agents investigating Nazi atom spies, 'photographed, wherever possible, in the actual place where the original incident occurred,' as the opening credits put it, and featuring real FBI agents playing themselves. Hollywood's wartime obsession with spies and sabotage had been no less rampant than HUAC's. Of the 64 movies dealing with the enemy released in 1942, all but two were stories of espionage and sabotage.[3] As I have argued elsewhere,[4] Hollywood's production of melodramatic fictions where the villains were enemy agents and the heroes were investigators at least provided an ideological soil in which the Committee's melodramatic fantasies could take root.

II

By coincidence, Hollywood itself was the subject of much investigation in late 1947. The Supreme Court was preparing to hear the Department of Justice's nine-year-old anti-trust suit against the eight major companies, and two other House Committees had recently completed inquiries into the jurisdictional disputes among Hollywood unions and local recommendations for a censorship plan for the District of Columbia.[5] A wide assortment of other bodies was also investigating Hollywood in November 1947. The Institute of Industrial Relations at UCLA was undertaking an extensive study of motion picture economics.[6] The Commission on Freedom of the Press had just published Ruth Inglis's *Freedom of the Movies*, an examination of Hollywood's practices of self-regulation.[7] Hortense Powdermaker was then conducting the second major anthropological inquiry into the mores and products of Hollywood.[8] Martha Wolfenstein and Nathan Leites had begun their psychological study of the movies in the Columbia University Research in Contemporary Cultures.[9] Paul Lazarsfeld's Bureau of Applied Social Research was conducting a number of investigations into the effects of motion pictures on audience attitudes,[10] while separate research projects were being carried out at the University of Pittsburgh and New York University into the impact on public opinion of two films dealing with anti-Semitism, *Gentleman's Agreement* and *Crossfire*.[11] Reports from some of these inquiries appeared in the November 1947 volume of the *Annals of the American Academy of Political and Social Science*, which was devoted to a study of the motion picture industry.[12]

There was, then, a climate of concern about the effects of movies on their audiences, and about the social responsibility of the industry in representing America to itself and to the rest of the world. Although Terry Ramsaye, conservative

editor of the *Motion Picture Herald*, the most influential exhibition trade paper, maintained that the movie audience had no interest in these controversies,[13] concern was not limited to legislators and academics. It had percolated down at least to the readership of major periodicals in a spate of articles about the extent of the motion picture's harmful influence.[14] It is, however, important to note that the nature of this concern was no longer directed primarily against the movies' overtly dubious moral content, as the Legion of Decency's campaign in 1934 had been. It seemed to be generally agreed that in that department the Hays Code had done its job. The *Woman's Home Companion* in 1947 found that only 8% of its readership felt there should be a campaign for cleaner motion pictures.[15]

The main concern was rather with what Franklin Fearing described as 'the question of the cultural values in our society which films express and the extent to which films communicate these values.'[16] Even Martin Quigley, co-author of the Hays Code and perhaps the supreme proponent of the 'pure entertainment' movie with no message,[17] would not have been out of sympathy with Hortense Powdermaker's suggestion

3) Dorothy B. Jones, 'The Hollywood War Film: 1942-1944', *Hollywood Quarterly*, vol.1, no.1, 1945, p.5.

4) Richard Maltby, 'Made For Each Other: the Melodrama of Hollywood and the House Committee on Un-American Activities, 1947', in Philip Davies & Brian Neve (eds), *Cinema, Politics and Society in America*, Manchester University Press, 1981, pp.82-84.

5) *Motion Picture Herald*, 28th June 1947, p.13.

6) Anthony H. Dawson, 'Motion Picture Economics', *Hollywood Quarterly*, vol.3, no.3, 1948, pp.217-240.

7) Ruth A. Inglis, *Freedom of the Movies: A Report on Self-Regulation from the Commission on Freedom of the Press*, University of Chicago Press, 1947.

8) Hortense Powdermaker, *Hollywood the Dream Factory: An Anthropologist Looks at Hollywood*, Little, Brown, Boston, 1950.

9) Martha Wolfenstein & Nathan Leites, *Movies: A Psychological Study*, The Free Press, Glencoe, Ill., 1950.

10) Paul F. Lazarsfeld, 'Audience Research in the Movie Field', *Annals of the American Academy of Political and Social Science* 254, 1947, pp.160-168.

11) Irwin C. Rosen, 'The Effect of the Motion Picture *Gentleman's Agreement* on Attitudes towards Jews', *The Journal of Psychology* 26, 1948, pp.525-536; Louis E. Raths & Frank N. Trager, 'Public Opinion and *Crossfire*', *Journal of Educational Sociology* 21, 1948, pp.345-368.

12) *Annals of the American Academy of Political and Social Science* 254, November 1947, hereafter referred to as *Annals*.

13) Terry Ramsaye, 'The Rise and Place of the Motion Picture', *Annals*, p.9.

14) *See, for example*, Siegfried Kracauer, 'Those Movies with a Message', *Harper's* 196, June 1948, pp.567-572; Gordon Kahn, 'One Psychological Moment, Please', *Atlantic Monthly*, vol.178, no.4, October 1946, pp.135-137; John Houseman, *Vogue*, 15th January 1947.

15) Geoffrey Shurlock, 'The Motion Picture Production Code', *Annals*, p.145.

16) Franklin Fearing, 'Influence of the Movies on Attitudes and Behaviour', *Annals*, p.71.

17) Martin Quigley, 'Importance of the Entertainment Film', *Annals*, pp.65-69.

that the issues now under discussion required different considerations:

'Part of the problem has been so oversimplified as to lose validity. Would-be reformers, looking for easy solutions, regard the movies as a prime cause of delinquency, crime and drunkenness. But these are symptoms of social and individual pathology, with a complex history. As anthropologists, we are more interested in the normal than the pathological. What is the effect of the movies on the vast audience who are not criminals, delinquents, or drunkards? How do movies influence their concepts of human relations, their value systems, their notions of reality?'[18]

Whether Quigley would have been quite so happy with the way Powdermaker developed her argument is another matter.

'Movies have a number of functions. They are one of several forms of mass communication, functioning primarily through their production of daydreams. They are entertainment, which of course, in any form, is never "pure", but always has hidden or open psychological and educational subfunctions.'[19]

Her 'hidden psychological and educational subfunctions' were not very far away from HUAC's concern with subversive Communist propaganda, slipped undetectably, according to Chairman J. Parnell Thomas, into at least 20 or 25 movies by the legions of Communist scriptwriters working to undermine democracy and the American way from their comfortable sanctuary in Hollywood.[20] The liberal producer John Houseman expressed comparable reservations about a new kind of postwar crime film he described as the 'tough' movie, taking as his examples *The Big Sleep* and *The Postman Always Rings Twice* (Tay Garnett, 1946).

'What is significant and repugnant about our contemporary "tough" films is their absolute lack of moral energy, their listless, fatalistic despair . . .'[21]

'One wonders what impression people will get of contemporary life if *The Postman Always Rings Twice* is run in a projection room twenty years hence. They will deduce, I believe, that the United States of America in the year following the end of the Second World War was a land of enervated, frightened people with spasms of high vitality but a low moral sense – a hung-over people with confused objectives groping their way through a twilight of insecurity and corruption.'[22]

And that, indeed, is very much what critics have done with the movies. From Raymond Borde and Etienne Chaumeton[23] to Foster Hirsch,[24] they have identified a *noir* sensibility, traced it across a body of films, and then sought to attach it to a general American cultural condition of 'postwar malaise'.

'The unstable universe depicted in so many noir films is a continual reflection of the tremendous cultural apprehension focused on both the "Red menace" and the chances of nuclear devastation.'[25]

Such statements, and such criticism, articulate a *Zeitgeist* theory of film as cultural history, which is based more on critical ingenuity in textual interpretation than on any precise location of movies within the historical circumstances of their production and consumption. Its method, essentially, is first to establish correlations among texts through the identification of recurrent pictorial and thematic motifs, and then to find ways of reading these motifs as metaphors for what Siegfried Kracauer called 'psychological dispositions – those deep layers of collective mentality which extend more or less below the dimensions of consciousness.[26] It deals in generalisations made convincing by their critical neatness, and as criticism it is often highly revealing. As history, however, it is notoriously difficult to substantiate, since it is inevitably dependent on the selective presentation of its evidence. For example, in the same two months that saw the release of *Out of the Past* (November and December, 1947), its producers, RKO, also released *Magic Town*, a Robert Riskin/James Stewart comedy about a small town which is discovered to reflect exactly the opinions of the entire nation, *The Bishop's Wife*, a Sam Goldwyn production featuring the unlikely combination of Cary Grant as an angel and David Niven as a bishop, a three-hour version of *Mourning Becomes Electra*, a Tim Holt western called *Wild Horse Mesa* and a John Wayne box-office disaster called *Tycoon*.[27] To my knowledge not a word has been written about any of these movies' relation to the *Zeitgeist*, nor have those critics who have written of *film noir*'s depiction of a postwar malaise suggested why *Out of the Past* should be seen as more *zeitgeistig* than the rest. What is involved in such criticism is a process of historical distortion which comes about from the practice of generic identification, and has the effect of imposing an artificial ideological homogeneity on Hollywood production.

18) Hortense Powdermaker, 'An Anthropologist Looks at the Movies', *Annals*, p.81.

19) Powdermaker, *Annals*, p.81.

20) *Motion Picture Herald*, 1st November 1947, p.13.

21) John Houseman, 'Today's Hero: A Review', *Hollywood Quarterly*, vol.2, no.2, 1947, p.163.

22) John Houseman, *Vogue*, 15th January 1947, quoted in Lester Asheim, 'The Film and the Zeitgeist', *Hollywood Quarterly*, vol.2, no.4, 1947, p.416.

23) Borde & Chaumeton, 1955.

24) Hirsch, 1981.

25) Silver & Ward, 1979.

26) Siegfried Kracauer, *From Caligari to Hitler: A Psychological History of the German Film*, Princeton University Press, 1947, p.6.

27) *Motion Picture Herald*, 22nd November 1947, pp.39-42; Richard B. Jewell & Vernon Harbin, *The RKO Story*, Octopus Books, London, 1982.

In a rebuttal of Houseman's argument, Lester Asheim noted that the most popular movies of 1946, according to *Variety* and Dr Gallup, had been *The Bells of St Mary's*, *Leave Her to Heaven*, *Blue Skies*, *Road to Utopia*, *Spellbound*, *The Green Years*, *Easy to Wed*, *State Fair*, *Night and Day*, *Anna and the King of Siam*, *Rhapsody in Blue* and *Love Letters*.[28] Questioning the selective sampling that Houseman was using as a method, and which the *Zeitgeist* critics have followed, he suggested that if an audience in twenty years' time 'see *The Razor's Edge*, they will deduce that our generation was an intensely earnest group of mystical philosophers who gladly renounced the usual pleasures of this world in order to find spiritual peace. From *State Fair* they can conjure up a nation of simple agrarians whose major problems centred around the prize hog and spiked mincemeat. And what would they make of a generation reflected in *Road to Utopia*?'[29]

What was at issue was a divergence between two approaches to the analysis of the movies, and the social and cultural significance of mass communication. When Houseman replied to Asheim, he suggested that the latter's proposal for an analysis of the whole body of Hollywood production 'might be sociologically valuable, but critically it would be negligible.'[30] Kracauer, whose 'psychological study of the German film under Weimar', *From Caligari to Hitler*, was published in 1947, shared Houseman's concern with the psychological veracity of what he was arguing rather than with its quantification.

'What counts is not so much the statistically measurable popularity of films as the popularity of their pictorial and narrative motifs. Persistent reiteration of these motifs marks them as outward projections of inner urges.'[31]

At the same time that these writers were arguing for a distinction between critical and sociological approaches to the cinema, they were, in their claim that the 'tough' movies of the period embodied a particularly virulent form of postwar malaise, establishing a tradition within which *film noir* has continued to be interpreted. The less mythological and more answerable question is not whether these films did by some unexplained osmosis embody a *Zeitgeist*, but why they were taken to do so by liberal critics of the period. It is with the liberal imagination of a postwar malaise, rather than with any such condition that there might have been, that we are concerned. Houseman and Kracauer's analyses of the 'tough' movies are evidence of that imagination, which has proved crucial to the critical history of *film noir*. Their arguments, reinforced by Wolfenstein and Leites and Barbara Deming,[32] gave rise to the traditional mode of interpreting *film noir* as particularly revealing of its historical moment – whatever that interpretation might be. The reasons for this are partly to be found in the nature of the movies as texts, and partly in the directions that academic and critical investigations

of the cinema were taking in the postwar period.

Like German Expressionism, *film noir* has always been prone to what Parker Tyler called 'psychoanalytic-mythological' criticism,[33] because of the nature of its narratives and its evident use of visual motifs, lighting codes and camera techniques to signify individual emotional states. Such movies provided ideal material for those students of mass communication who wished to use the metaphor of movie as dream as the basis for a psychoanalytic interpretation of American culture through its shared daydreams. Texts which made themselves available to such an analysis achieved a greater critical prominence than their industrial status merited precisely because of that availability. They have maintained that prominence because film criticism has historically paid more attention to revising the opinions of earlier critics about a relatively small number of texts than it has to the commercial considerations of Hollywood.

If Houseman and Kracauer were representative of a critical movement which sought to employ psychoanalytic and anthropological insights into the study of culture, Asheim's dissenting position reflected the attitudes of another group of academics. At the same time that Kracauer, Wolfenstein and Leites were exploring the cinema as a fertile field for the psychological study of culture, more statistically oriented sociologists were gradually coming to the conclusion that their earlier assumptions about the pervasive effects of mass communication had been much exaggerated. Asheim's rebuttal of Houseman's claims reflected that attitude, but, in the clash of their approaches, there was more at stake than Houseman's oversimplified split between sociology and criticism. In order to elucidate the fundamental disagreement over methods of studying the media which emerged in the postwar period, the investigative narrative I am constructing requires a flashback to the 1930s.

28) Asheim, 1947, p.415.

29) Asheim, 1947, p. 416.

30) John Houseman, 'Houseman Replies to Asheim', *Hollywood Quarterly*, vol.3, no.1, p.89.

31) Kracauer, 1949, p.8.

32) Barbara Deming, *Running Away from Myself: A Dream Portrait of America Drawn from the Films of the 'Forties*, Grossman Publishers, New York, 1969. The book was written in 1950, and portions of it were published in the magazine *City Lights*, 1953-55.

33) Parker Tyler, *Magic and Myth of the Movies*, Secker & Warburg, London, 1971, p. 31.

34) William Henry Chamberlain, 'The American "Discovery" of European Totalitarianism', in Robert Allen Skotheim & Michael McGiffert (eds), *American Social Thought: Sources and Interpretations*, Addison-Wesley, Reading, Mass., vol.2, p.318.

35) Hans Gerth, 'Public Opinion and Propaganda', in Joseph Bensman, Arthur J. Vidich & Nabuko Gerth (eds), *Politics, Character and Culture: Perspectives from Hans Gerth*, Greenwood Press, Westport, Conn., 1982, p.63.

III

What William Henry Chamberlain referred to as 'the American "Discovery" of European Totalitarianism'[34] in the second half of the 1930s provided the impetus for the rapid development of empirical inquiries into the effects of mass communications. America became, in Hans Gerth's phrase, 'propaganda-conscious',[35] and an academic discipline came into existence concerned with research into the effects of the mass media, in which the principal establishments were the Institute for Propaganda Analysis and Paul Lazarsfeld's Bureau of Applied Social Research at Columbia. In tandem with these academic activities an industry was developing in opinion testing, poll taking and market research, to provide services for politicians, manufacturers and advertisers; its leading light was Dr George Gallup. What the academic and commercial practices shared was a belief in the measurability of public opinion, and the efficacy of their quantitative methods. The war expanded this research with the Army's inquiries into the effectiveness of films as instruments for training and indoctrination,[36] and in the circumstances it was hardly surprising that Hollywood was duly recruited into the war effort.[37]

It was in large part the belief in the cinema's potential propaganda value that had caused the industry so scrupulously to avoid political subjects during the 1930s. The self-denying ordinance that was the Hays Code was designed to produce an anodyne product which would offend as few as possible as little as possible, disguising corporate self-interest as civic responsibility.[38] The war, however, changed that obligation, and the movies, under the direction of the Office of War Information (OWI), joined the propaganda effort.[39]

But by the outbreak of war, in part as a result of the widespread diffusion of psychiatric practice in the second half of the 1930s, another dimension was added, one which suggested that the study of media effects might need a more complex methodological apparatus than that provided by content analysis and questionnaire. Hans Gerth told his students at Madison:

'We have devised methods of measuring attitudes towards newspaper contents and methods of measuring the content of radio programs, films and newsreels . . . Yet we realise more and more that rational consciousness is only one factor in determining human behaviour and that reason is not always, in fact is seldom, the strongest factor. The development of psychology, especially the psychology of unconscious motivations coupled with social psychology, makes it possible to understand more of the mechanisms of attitude formation.'[40]

Such ideas had penetrated Hollywood, too. Walter Wanger called in 1943 for the establishment of an advisory 'board of theoretical psychologists'[41] to assess Hollywood's output and suggest ways of enhancing its propaganda effectiveness. Although that never came about, it was at least an indication of an atmosphere which would encourage the studios to turn to market research techniques as a normal mechanism for pre-testing their product. For their benefit, Dr Gallup constructed such strange devices as the 'preview profile', the 'penetration index' and the 'want-to-see graph', devices which became increasingly important to the industry's decision-making, on every level from plot development to release pattern, during the 1940s.[42]

The American discovery of European totalitarianism provided the impetus for other investigations besides those of Lazarsfeld and Leo Lowenthal. In 1938, it led Congressman Samuel Dickstein to propose the establishment of the House Un-American Activities Committee, and it prompted other Americans, perhaps more positively, to try to define what Americanism might be. The onset of war made the articulation of an American ideology even more urgent, and one formulation involved the recourse to a revised theory of national character as a way of explaining social behaviour. The phrenology and scientific racism of previous approaches was discarded in favour of a broadly anthropological method which borrowed creatively from psychoanalysis. This new sociological entity, which Geoffrey Gorer called 'psycho-cultural' study,[43] was a child reared by Margaret Mead, and both its claims to science and its ideological intention were made explicit in its first important text, her 1942 book, *And Keep Your Powder Dry*.[44]

'Here, we are going to discuss what are the strengths and weaknesses of the American character – the psychological equipment with which we can win the war. To do this we have got to get clearly in mind just what that American character is. The clearest way I know of to do that, is to describe how it is made.'[45]

36) Garth Jowett, *Film: The Democratic Art*, Little, Brown, Boston, 1976, p.321.

37) 'Hollywood in Uniform', *Fortune* 25, April 1942, pp.92-95, 130-138; Herman Lowe, 'Washington Discovers Hollywood', *American Mercury*, April 1945, pp.407-414.

38) Richard Maltby, *Harmless Entertainment: Hollywood and the Ideology of Consensus*, Scarecrow Press, Metuchen, N.J., 1983, pp.102-105.

39) Cedric Larsen, 'The Domestic Motion Picture Work of the Office of War Information', *Hollywood Quarterly*, vol.3, no.4, 1948, pp.434-443.

40) Gerth, p. 66.

41) Walter Wanger, 'OWI and Motion Pictures', *Public Opinion Quarterly*, vol.7. no.1, 1943, p.108.

42) Leo A. Handel, *Hollywood Looks at its Audience: A Report of Film Audience Research*, University of Illinois Press, 1950.

43) Geoffrey Gorer, *The Americans: A Study in National Character*, The Cresset Press, London, 1948, p.8.

44) Margaret Mead, *The American Character*, Penguin Books, Harmondsworth, 1944; originally published in the USA under the title *And Keep Your Powder Dry*, 1942.

45) Mead, p.25.

What Mead and her followers – Gorer, Riesman, Wolfenstein and Leites – were seeking to do was to identify what she called 'a consistent and specific American inconsistency.'[46] Crucial to her project was a wartime rhetoric of liberal internationalism. The penultimate chapter of her book was called 'Building the World New', and the world in question was Wendell Wilkie's One World.

'The lesson that the world is now one . . . must be held clearly before us. When we talk of policing the world, this is meant to be a transition from armies to police, from seeing the world as a set of warring national entities to seeing it as one civic unity.'[47]

She was echoing the liberal spirit of the OWI's propaganda, which saw the war as an opportunity to unify America as well as the world. As one internal OWI memo put it, 'By making this a people's war for freedom, we can help clear up the alien problem, the negro problem, the anti-Semitic problem.'[48]

IV

An element in the propaganda rhetoric of common purpose, and also an underlying assumption in the writings of Mead and her followers, was the idea of the normal. A notion of the norm was inherent in the source of much of their statistical information, which came both from the polling procedures of Gallup and his ilk and from the empirical and quantitative tradition of American social science. Statistics produced norms, but the idea of the normal was intensified by the psychoanalytic dimension the cultural anthropologists added to it. Mead's account of the American character, with its claim that 'We Are All Third Generation,'[49] depends strongly on the argument that the heterogeneous and rapidly changing society she describes produces in its people a strong desire to conform. 'Outward conformity made possible by economic success – these are the marks that one is a good American.'[50] In Mead's analysis, but even more clearly in Gorer's, the drive to outward conformity is motivated by a neurotic anxiety, initially communicated from mother to child and resulting, according to Gorer, 'in psychological symptoms which are technically known as compulsive,'[51] as variable as breast fetishism in popular culture and the 'quite excessive anxiety induced by an unbalanced national budget.'[52] Gorer's account of the normal as neurotic, which extended as far as to describe loneliness as 'intolerable to well-adjusted Americans,'[53] was of course only one contribution among many to the pervasive growth of psychiatric and psychoanalytic writing intended for a popular audience, but it is a significant one in the way that it applies a psychoanalytical procedure to the analysis of the culture as a whole. It is itself both a description and a symptom of that culture's discovery and pursuit of neurosis,

a pursuit which proceeded with some rapidity in the war and immediate postwar period, fuelled not only by Mead and her followers, but also by the publication of material derived from the large-scale psychiatric and psychological testing programmes carried out by the armed services on recruits.[54] These programmes were designed to discover the well-adjusted recruit and weed out the maladjusted, and the statistics derived from this research provided psychological definitions of normality and abnormality. In their popularisation,[55] the academic niceties of the notion that neurosis could be normal tended to get lost, and were replaced by an increasingly anxious concern about problems of what was defined as the psychological readjustment of returning veterans.

Psychiatric studies represented the war as a traumatic experience for its participants. That description, no less than the idea of 'the people's war,' was an ideological necessity to the liberal internationalists who wanted to police Wilkie's postwar One World. It proposed that the normal soldier would undoubtedly return from the war maladjusted and confronted with an array of psychological problems in relocating himself in a peacetime society. Newspapers and popular magazines inundated families with advice about how to deal with readjustment, a problem they presented as being of at least equal magnitude to the difficulties of economic reorganisation that the country would face.[56] The solution arrived at dealt with both the psychological and the economic aspects of readjustment; normality would be re-established by reversing a number of wartime social trends. Women war-workers should give their jobs back to the returning soldiers, marry and buy the plethora of consumer durables which would replace the war materiel, abandoning their economic independence for a role as providers of well-adjusted homes for their husbands and children – the Levittown ideal of conformist suburban living. It was a solution reiterated in the half dozen movies which dealt explicitly with the situation of the returning veteran

46) Mead, p.53.

47) Mead, p.155.

48) Quoted in Richard Polenberg, *One Nation Divisible: Class, Race and Ethnicity in the United States since 1938*, Penguin Books, Harmondsworth, 1980, p.47.

49) Mead, p.27.

50) Mead, p.126.

51) Gorer, p.53.

52) Gorer, p.56.

53) Gorer, p.80.

54) *See, for example*, Roy R. Grinker & John P. Spiegel, *Men Under Stress*, Blakiston, Philadelphia, 1945.

55) *See* Edward R. Strecker, *Their Mothers' Sons*, Lippincott, New York, 1946.

56) William Manchester, *The Glory and the Dream: A Narrative History of America, 1932- 1972*, Michael Joseph, London, 1973, p.425.

in 1945 and 1946. Their archetype was *Pride of the Marines* (Delmer Daves, 1945), in which an embittered and blinded John Garfield is gradually cured of his neurotic disillusionment by the love of a good domesticated woman (Eleanor Parker), whose powers of healing seem to extend miraculously, at the end of the film, to restoring Garfield's sight.

V

Hollywood's ostensible acquisition from its wartime involvement with the government propaganda machine was an apparently changed attitude to what the movies should be doing for their public. The press releases of the Motion Picture Association and the studio heads bristled with statements of high postwar intentions to consolidate their wartime image of social responsibility. Even Louis B. Mayer was proclaiming in July 1947:

'The screen, in common with the newspapers and radio, fights the battle for freedom of speech . . . A motion picture should not only afford entertainment, but be of educational value. It can portray fairly and honestly the American way of life and can be a powerful influence in the lives of millions in other countries who are either denied access to our way of life, or who have never had the opportunity of experiencing it.'[57]

That statement, one of many such comments, made its subtext rather clearer than most. When Mayer talked of education, he was clearly thinking of the education of foreigners, and the continued use of the movies as an instrument of propaganda abroad, not the production of social reformist liberal texts for home consumption. Hollywood's postwar interest in the ideologically underprivileged was not entirely altruistic, either. In 1945 the industry established the Motion Picture Export Association to operate as a legally empowered cartel acting as the sole negotiating body for the industry in all its dealings with foreign governments.[58] The doubling of production costs during the 1940s made the industry increasingly dependent for its profitability on foreign sales, and it wanted State Department assistance in negotiating favourable arrangements over quotas and tariffs in foreign markets in exchange for its good works in selling the American Way of Life, and American goods, abroad.[59]

In many respects, this foreign responsibility was a hindrance to Hollywood's development of a social conscience, for the primary obligation it imposed was one of providing an optimistic portrayal of the American way of life. Newspapers carried reports that the Russians had been showing *The Grapes of Wrath* as a documentary account of what ordinary life in the United States was like, and the MPEA determined that movies such as *The Grapes of Wrath* and *Tobacco Road* were not suitable material for export.[60] A lack of access to foreign markets inevitably discouraged the production of such 'controversial' movies, since it impaired their profitability. As early as September 1945 American exhibitors were expressing their lack of enthusiasm for movies dealing with any aspect of the war. E.C. Rhoden, of the Fox Midwest Amusement Corporation in Kansas City, told the *Motion Picture Herald*,

'The first function of the screen is to entertain, no matter what the period. Comedy, romance, action and adventure should be emphasised in fictional films, leaving sociological problems and the promotion of various ideologies to other mediums.'[61]

The inclination to avoid any examination of social problems was widespread. Sam Goldwyn met considerable resistance from his bankers when he announced his intention of making *The Best Years of Our Lives* (William Wyler, 1946), and Darryl Zanuck had to face a deputation from Hollywood's Jewish elite who tried to dissuade him from making *Gentlemen's Agreement* (Elia Kazan, 1947).[62] Objections came from less likely sources, too. The American Jewish Association was highly critical of Dore Schary's plans to make *Crossfire* (Edward Dmytryk, 1947), on the grounds that it might very well have the opposite effect to that intended. The AJA's criticism, orchestrated by Elliot Cohen, editor of *Commentary*, centred on the fact that the anti-Semite in the movie was a psychopath. An effective cinematic critique of anti-Semitism, he argued, would need to show 'a normal anti-Semite and a normal Jew.'[63] If that remark makes little sense, it does at least indicate the pervasiveness of a vocabulary of normality, as well as the widespread concern about both how Hollywood did, and how Hollywood should, represent a postwar America which had so conspicuously failed to realise the liberals' domestic dreams. Race riots and the wave of postwar strikes seemed to indicate that wartime unity had been no more than a temporary illusion, and the 1946 Wanna-Go-Home riots in Germany, Paris and Manila[64]

57) *Motion Picture Herald*, 12th July 1947, p.27.

58) Maltby, 1983, p.78.

59) Thomas Guback, *The International Film Industry: Western Europe and America since 1945*, Indiana University Press, 1969, pp.121-141.

60) Leo C. Rosten, 'Movies and Propaganda', *Annals*, p.119.

61) *Motion Picture Herald*, 1st September 1945, p.14.

62) K.R.M. Short, 'Hollywood Fights Anti-Semitism', in K.R.M. Short (ed.), *Feature Films as History*, Croom Helm, London, 1981, p.174.

63) Short, p.173.

64) Manchester, pp.405-409.

suggested that there was, indeed, a maladjusted Army about to return, which just might be full of psychopaths like Robert Ryan in *Crossfire*.

According to Alain Silver and Elizabeth Ward,[65] *Crossfire* is a *film noir*, whereas the other anti-anti-Semitic movie of 1947, *Gentleman's Agreement*, is not. *Gentleman's Agreement* won three Oscars at the 1947 ceremonies, while *Crossfire*, although it received five nominations, won none.[66] That may well have had something to do with the fact that its producer and director, Adrian Scott and Edward Dmytryk, were both members of the Hollywood Ten, awaiting trial for contempt of Congress, but it is also the case that no *film noir* catalogued by Silver and Ward won any of the major Academy Awards in the period under discussion.[67] That had principally to do with their relative status as Hollywood products, something designated by their trade description as melodramas rather than dramas, and largely determined by the size of their budgets and the audiences at which they were directed. Describing different kinds of movie theatre in a 1947 article on 'The Exhibitor', Charles P. Skouras mentions as his last category, 'the grind house, a small theater along a busy downtown street catering to transients, [which] does its biggest business with action melodramas like *The Killers*.'[68] The *film noir*, in other words, was a low-status product, playing predominantly to the bottom end of the urban market, to exactly that part of the market which reformers, liberal or otherwise, always worried about most. Conservatives were concerned with the question of 'Communist infiltration of the motion picture industry'; disillusioned liberals like Houseman were directing their concern elsewhere, at the 'tough' movie and the horror film. What they seemed to see in *film noir* in particular was their own worst nightmare enacted on the screen for the casual titillation of the urban transient audience: the maladjusted veteran in full, paranoid flight from the broken wartime dream of liberal rationalism, the movies' equivalent of the contemporary newspaper sensation stories headlined 'Crazed Vet Runs Amok.'[69]

VI

The central male protagonist in *films noirs* of 1946-48 is almost invariably marked as a veteran by one means or another. Frequently, he is actually identified as such in the plot – in *Dead Reckoning* (John Cromwell, 1946) and *Boomerang!* (Elia Kazan, 1947), for example. Elsewhere, he is regularly played by an actor whose career at that stage was firmly identified with military roles. Mitchum's career, for instance, had taken off with his nominations for Best Supporting Actor for his part in *The Story of G.I. Joe* (William Wellman, 1945), and since then he had played veterans in *Till the End of Time* (Dmytryk, 1946) and *Crossfire*. Important as this persistent source of identification for audiences

is, the narrative structure common to the majority of *films noirs* of this period is one in which the protagonist has to account for a missing period of his life, when he was outside the world in which the film is set, and in which things happened to him which set him at a distance from that world and its inhabitants. It is possible to see *Out of the Past* as providing a narrative metaphor for the veteran, Mitchum, seeking readjustment to a normal America by settling down with an ordinary job and the domestic idyll of Virginia Huston, but prevented from doing so by the guilt and the obsessive neuroses he has acquired during his period of absence from society.

In *films noirs* and the related crime melodramas of the postwar period, the trajectory of the central male figure is either towards recuperation or death – either towards a re-integration into a normal society with the demonstration of his innocence (*The Big Clock*, John Farrow, 1947), or towards fatal retribution for past guilt (*Out of the Past*). No place is provided in these fictions for the survival of the separate heroic figure, the embodiment of the American individualist heroic tradition. The central protagonist of these movies is not marked as a figure of difference by the conventional signs of heroism – the possession of exceptional abilities or a dynamic moral certainty. Rather, he is average, conventional particularly in his ambitions, and his capacity to survive the fiction is above all determined by whether he can manage to re-establish a normality which has been disrupted at the start of the movie. That disruption invariably has a psychological dimension; the protagonist of these movies is Hollywood's neurotic personality *par excellence*, afflicted with one or another form of compulsive behaviour, psychosis, identity crisis, guilt complex, amnesia or general paranoia.

He is the unstable occupant of a paranoid world, in which objects are not what they appear to be, people are likely to change their identities, and the plot is capable of going off at an unexpected tangent in a world thrown out of joint. He occupies a position of neurosis in the plot. where his place is commonly pervaded by guilt, either through an accusation of which he is innocent, or through his sense of an obligation to atone for some guilty event in his past. His attitude to the past takes one of two forms:

65) Silver & Ward, 1979, p.73.

66) Roy Pickard, *The Oscar Movies from A-Z*, Hamlyn, London, 1978, p.55.

67) Joan Crawford's Best Actress Award in 1945 for her performance in *Mildred Pierce* might be regarded as an exception; it does not, however, fall strictly within the period I am discussing, and the movie's status as a *film noir* is at least debatable.

68) Charles P. Skouras, 'The Exhibitor', *Annals*, p.29.

69) Manchester, p.426.

either a resigned fatalism like that of Burt Lancaster in *The Killers*, who waits unresisting for his assassins because, he says, 'I did something wrong, once,' or the investigator's obligations to explain the past, and to reveal why and how it is the source of his psychoneuroses. This process often takes the form of a narration, telling a story to a largely silent witness, who is intermittently referred to during the narration and who is also commonly the figure of redemption in the narrative. The telling of the story is a form of psychotherapy, and the place of the analyst is taken not only by a character in the story but also by the audience. We are watching a character whose emotional stability is in question, a male figure who for the first time in the American cinema can no longer occupy frame centre with assurance, who provides us with no guarantees of his reliability either as a narrator or as an ethical being. Our only hope of understanding him is through the psychoanalytic investigation that the movie's narrative conducts.

What differentiates *film noir* from other psychological crime and social problem films of this period is that through the use of flashbacks, subjective camera and other visual and narrative analogues for his disturbed mental state, the controlling perception in *films noirs* is that of the maladjusted protagonist, whose world we enter in the often forlorn hope that he will find a way to leave it. These movies are about maladjustment, but more than that, they are themselves maladjusted texts, what David Riesman called 'Tales of Abnorm',[70] representing the failure of readjustment where Hollywood's musicals, comedies and romances of the period represented its own return to normality and, indeed, its proselytising for the re-establishment of the ideology of pure and harmless entertainment in a conformist society. Given their existence as psychological narrative investigations, it is hardly surprising that the films have themselves come in for so much psychoanalytically based criticism. The appearance of such texts at the same time as the apparatus for a psychoanalytic cultural criticism was being developed may be coincidence or synchronicity, but it has certainly had a determining effect on the way the movies have subsequently been understood and analysed. The interpretation initially made of them is also revealing of a cultural climate, at least among liberal intellectuals. The fact that that they paid any attention at all to such low-rent material as *The Killers* and *The Dark Corner* (Henry Hathaway, 1946) was noteworthy in itself,[71] and is at least partly (and speculatively) explained by the way in which the liberal critics took the movies as being symptomatic of a social condition they themselves were desperately in need of discovering. The movies themselves are excessive representations of the normal as neurotic, providing confirmation, for anyone seeking it, that maladjustment was a normal response to postwar America.

VII

Very little in the postwar world went as the liberal intellectuals had planned. Even the psychological problems of readjustment did not appear as they had been expecting, and that, in its own way, was as disillusioning to their construction of the American character as the closing of the Iron Curtain was to Wilkie's One World or, in a different arena, Hollywood's enthusiastic return to escapist fantasy by the end of the war. In November 1947, Irving Pichel, one of the Hollywood Nineteen, complained,

'Today we find ourselves limited in the use of our great medium for the depiction, even in the most objective terms, of those sources of strain and conflict which have the greatest contemporary interest for us.'[72]

While Pichel, not surprisingly, laid the blame for this at the feet of the HUAC and its ilk, the failure of Hollywood's wartime liberal vision had set in two or more years earlier. Another of the Hollywood Nineteen, Abraham Polonsky, expressed the disillusionment most pointedly in his critique of *The Best Years of Our Lives*, charging it with failing adequately to depict the social problems of the returning soldiers and for sentimentalising them. 'Here at home,' he concluded, 'we have returned to cynicism from our betters, sharpened social conflicts, and a mood of vulgar despair among the artists.'[73] One aspect of that 'vulgar despair' was *film noir*'s abnormal tales of a maladjustment that hadn't happened, on which many of Hollywood's younger generation of radicals and liberals, including Polonsky himself, worked. Another aspect was the liberal acceptance of the defeat of reason, as prevalent in Hollywood as it was elsewhere.

Kracauer, in an analysis of 'Those Movies with a Message'[74] such as *Crossfire*, *Gentleman's Agreement* and *Boomerang!*, saw them as revealing 'the profound weakness of the very cause for which they try to enlist sympathy.' Their liberal spokesmen, he suggested, seemed 'to be overwhelmed by a mood of resignation, as though [they] had discovered that the struggle for enlightenment is a Sisyphean task.'[75] And they also featured as:

'the recipient of the liberal gospel . . . an ex-G.I. in a state of complete bewilderment . . . Visionless,

70) David Riesman, *The Lonely Crowd, A Study of the Changing American Character*, Yale University Press, 1950, p.87.

71) Siegfried Kracauer, 'Hollywood's Terror Films: Do They Reflect an American State of Mind?', *Commentary* 2, 1946, pp.132-136.

72) Irving Pichel, 'Areas of Silence', *Hollywood Quarterly*, vol.3, no.1, 1947, p.52.

73) Abraham Polonsky, 'The Best Years of Our Lives: A Review', *Hollywood Quarterly*, vol.2, no.3, 1947, p.260.

74) Kracauer, 1948, pp.567-572.

75) Kracauer, 1948, p.569.

at the mercy of any wind, benumbed even in their love-making, they drift about in a state bordering on stupor . . . Significantly, these characters place little confidence in reason. They are not only impervious to ideas but instinctively shun them as sources of suffering rather than as means of redemption . . . In sum, our postwar films present a common man reluctant to heed the voice of reason and a liberal spokesman unable to run the emotional blockade around him.'[76]

His description of the ex-G.I. common man could also stand as a description of Mitchum in *Out of the Past*, whose performance James Agee described as having 'a curious languor, which suggests Bing Crosby supersaturated with barbiturates.'[77]

With a weariness that echoed his subjects, Kracauer continued,

'The world has become one world indeed. In it the average individual feels completely at sea. Situations that seemed controllable in prewar days now seem confused by developments beyond his reach. Unable to orient himself, he instinctively shuts his eyes, like a man overwhelmed by dizziness on the edge of an abyss . . . The apathy of this country today might be called ideological fatigue, a fatigue which in part accounts for the present vogue of psychiatry, with its emphasis on psychological relations rather than social meaning.'[78]

Yet while Kracauer was criticising the retreat into psychiatry as an escape from the political he was himself encouraging it by pursuing his psychoanalytically based critical method. The movie's preoccupation with psychoanalysis was readily enough explained in conventional, commercial terms, as a topical ingredient which could be readily incorporated into the standardised structures of Hollywood's individualist narratives. By dwelling on the alienated individual, psychoanalytical criticism tended to obscure the ideological drift of Hollywood's postwar productions at the same time that it observed the movies' failure to endorse wartime liberal dreams.

As documents in a cultural history, it is difficult to regard the postwar *films noirs* as expressions of a liberal existentialism. Their rhetoric of paranoia, however much their liberal critics psychoanalysed it, was more closely attached to an alternative political tendency. The beneficiaries of the apathy that Kracauer described and the disillusionment with rationality that accompanied it were the anti-Communists, with their rhetoric of a new melodramatic politics of emotion. Norman Woelfel, in an article on 'The American Mind and the Motion Picture,' asked,

'Can America lift itself by its bootstraps and overcome the inertia of things as they are? Where can the necessary spiritual might and the necessary will and energy to achieve socially and culturally in peacetime be obtained? Quite obviously, if these things are to come, they must come by way of popular leaders who can express what the masses of Americans deep in their hearts really feel.'[79]

The masses of Americans got, at least, a new definition of their national character. 'McCarthyism,' the man himself said in 1950, 'is Americanism with its sleeves rolled.'[80] From Hollywood, in 1948, they got the first of a wave of anti-Communist movies, the majority of which employed the mannerisms of *film noir*, fixing a positive political charge to a style whose previous ideological meaning had been defined only by negatives. The *femme fatale* revealed herself, at last, as a Commie Sex Trap, and the protagonist's neurosis, in *My Son John* (Leo McCarey, 1952) or *I Was A Communist for the FBI* (Gordon Douglas, 1951), could now be seen to have been induced by the Communist Conspiracy. It was not Joe McCarthy, but Geoffrey Gorer who had explained that 'The lure of Soviet power has an insidious appeal for those who are humiliated by their own weakness or frustrated by their own insecurities.'[81]

Gorer had described at length an American condition he called the 'panic-fear of homosexuality.'[82] Its symptoms were replicated in the anti-Communist persecutions which revealed a similar need not merely to ostracise its victims as unclean but to expose them as maladjusted and sick. In many respects, Truman's Federal Loyalty Program, designed to eliminate subversives from the Government, was a displaced extension of the Army's psychological testing procedures designed, at least according to Gorer,[83] to eliminate homosexuals from the armed forces. Not for the first time in American cultural history, a tool of liberal analysis found itself displaced and perverted into an instrument of political repression. If liberal concern with the ideological implications of *film noir* turned out, in the event, to be well placed if somewhat misdirected, the convoluted mechanisms which led to their disillusioned anxieties, and indeed to the movies' psychological representation of a maladjusted postwar world, were in large part creatures of their own devising.

76) Kracauer, 1948, pp.570-571.

77) James Agee, review of *Out of the Past*, *Time*, 15th December 1947.

78) Kracauer, 1948, p.572.

79) Norman Woelfel, 'The American Mind and the Motion Picture', *Annals*, p.91.

80) Quoted in Colin Shindler, *Hollywood Goes to War: Films and American Society, 1939-1952*, Routledge & Kegan Paul, London, 1979, p.127.

81) Gorer, 1948, p.187.

82) Gorer, 1948, p.91.

NOIR IS ALSO A FRENCH WORD

The French Antecedents of Film Noir

Ginette Vincendeau

In their classic pioneering study published in 1955, Raymond Borde and Etienne Chaumeton dismissed the European influence on American *film noir* as 'feeble' and the French as especially insignificant. Reluctantly they conceded that Julien Duvivier, Jean Renoir and Marcel Carné created a certain '*noir* realism', but, they asked rhetorically, 'did *Pépé le Moko, Quai des brumes, La Bête humaine* foreshadow the American *film noir*? We don't think so.' (p.27). The analysis on which they base this judgment is, in some respects, unarguable: French cinema is on the whole a realist cinema, lacking the sense of the dream-like and the uncanny often found in *film noir*. In French films, action is steeped in a well-defined social milieu, and violence tends to be motivated, not gratuitous. Though they concede a certain lineage in the French emphasis on 'the

poetry of wet cobblestones, of nights in the faubourgs and of bleak dawns' (p.28), Borde and Chaumeton clearly don't see this as important. This should not surprise us, for these two writers' views are typical of 1950s French critics' eagerness to dismiss their national cinema in order to valorise American film (the year before their book came out, François Truffaut had led the way with his famous attack in *Cahiers du Cinéma* 31st January 1954, on 'a certain tendency of the French cinema').

Subsequent writing on *film noir* has accepted these views without much comment. 'Poetic Realism' is sometimes mentioned as a source, but without further probing (Raymond Durgnat

Still: Pièges, *the last film Robert Siodmak made in France, with Marie Déa.*

49

does mention the connection in *Jean Renoir*, University of California Press, Berkeley, 1974). However, a less biased and more thorough look at the French cinema of the 1930s reveals strong intertextual links with American *film noir*, via film-makers' careers, filmic reworkings and more diffuse cultural references. I should say at this point that I shall use 'American *film noir*' in its most common sense to cover a body of films made in Hollywood in the 1940s and 1950s, often based on crime literature, pervaded by a sense of gloom, and characterised by visual motifs of dark, low-key lighting, strong shadows, and unusual compositions.

Berlin-Paris-Hollywood

Borde and Chaumeton's final evidence that French cinema had no influence on American *film noir* was that it was simply not known in Hollywood: 'Nothing proves that John Huston or Howard Hawks had seen a single French film of that time.' (Borde & Chaumeton, 1955, p.28). This may well be true, but, on the other hand, other major exponents of *film noir* – Robert Siodmak, Fritz Lang, Billy Wilder, Max Ophuls, Jacques Tourneur and Curtis Bernhardt – had seen plenty of French films of the 1930s. Not only that, they had actually been *making* them. Before they went to Hollywood, these directors spent time working in the French studios. Most had been sent there by the political circumstances of the Nazi regime but also by the increased internationalisation of the film industry.

The 'French' film industry of the early 1930s was a multinational affair, comprising practitioners from Germany, Russia, Italy and the USA alongside indigenous personnel. The influx of émigrés from the Berlin studios in

Still: a very French mélange of genres - Siodmak's Mollenard, with Harry Baur and Marcel Dalio.

1933 only confirmed this trend. Some, like Lang and Wilder, only stayed one year and made one film, while others, like Ophuls and Siodmak, built careers that lasted almost a decade. (For accounts of the German émigrés' careers in French, *see* Thomas Elsaesser & Ginette Vincendeau, *Les Cinéastes allemands en France, Les années trente*, Goethe-Institut, Paris, 1983; Ginette Vincendeau '*Des Portes ouvertes seulement à contrecoeur*', *Positif*, January 1988; Heike Hurst & Heine Gasser, eds, *Tendres ennemies, cent ans du cinéma entre la France et l'Allemagne*, L'Harmattan, Paris, 1991). Their stay in France was not easy as the French film industry was economically in the doldrums, unemployment was high and xenophobia rampant. Despite their recognised artistic and technical virtuosity, the émigrés had to put up with a lot, from snide anti-Semitism to overt hostility. The passage through Paris was thus an (unwelcome) exercise in adaptation and survival, often a taste of things to come in Hollywood. Beyond this, two questions need to be asked, the answers to which will define the scope of this article: what did the émigrés' stay in France contribute to the making of their American films? And outside this direct connection, what features of American *film noir* can be related to those of French cinema?

Hitherto, on the rare occasions when the French films of the German émigrés have been granted attention, they have been studied either from an auteurist perspective (and found lacking compared to each director's German and American work) or for their *difference* from French cinema. Thomas Elsaesser, for example, has pointed out how the German fascination with technique and objects contrasted and occasionally clashed with the importance given in French films to social setting, dialogue and performances (*see* Thomas Elsaesser, 'Pathos and Leave-taking', *Sight & Sound*, vol.53, no.4, Autumn 1984). Hence the qualifications of 'hybrid', 'heterogeneous' or even 'incoherent' attached to the émigrés' films. This is not entirely inappropriate. Lang's *Liliom* (1934) veers between populist realism and the fantastic, Ophuls's *La Tendre Ennemie* (1936) alternates between comedy and fantasy. Siodmak's *Mollenard* (1937) goes from exotic sleaze in Shanghai to a satire of the provincial bourgeoisie of Dunkerque; his *Pièges* (1939) shifts from menacing dark street scenes to Maurice Chevalier singing a comic ditty. In *La Crise est finie* (Siodmak, 1934), characters and situations from pure French vaudeville collide with a Warner-Brothers-style backstage musical (there is even an allusion to Busby Berkeley's 'forgotten man' number from *Gold Diggers of 1933*). In Bernhardt's *Carrefour* (1938), a scene with Jules Berry and Suzy Prim addressing their audience – as was their habit – as if they were on a French boulevard stage, is embedded in a glossy cabaret episode featuring a jazz band with a black American singer. It would be wrong, however, to see this just as an example of cultural mismatching

or a curiosity. This melange of genres was itself a feature of the French cinema of the 1930s: when Maurice Chevalier started singing in *Pièges*, this came as no surprise to the French audience, not only because they would expect him to sing, but also because this practice could be seen in countless other French films of the period. Directors like Siodmak and Bernhardt not only adapted to harsh new working conditions, but they also successfully integrated French generic practices, something which, again, would come in useful in Hollywood. Bernhardt was invited there on the strength of *Carrefour*, and Siodmak took a copy of *Pièges* on his transatlantic journey.

Apart from taking their own French work in their suitcases, the émigrés also carried as baggage a more diffuse sense of the dominant features of the French cinema to which they had been exposed for several years. As Borde and Chaumeton recognised in passing, some French films of the 1930s were remade in Hollywood, or were the original versions of examples of American *film noir*. Significantly, most were directed by émigré film-makers, some of whom had worked in France. Thus *La Chienne* (Renoir, 1931) was remade as *Scarlet Street* (Lang, 1946), *La Bête humaine* (Renoir, 1938) as *Human Desire* (Lang, 1954), *Pépé le Moko* (Duvivier, 1936) as *Algiers* (John Cromwell, 1938) and *Casbah* (John Berry, 1948), *Le Jour se lève* (Carné, 1939) as *The Long Night* (Anatole Litvak, 1947), *Pièges* (Siodmak, 1939) as *Lured/Personal Column* (Douglas Sirk, 1947), *Le Dernier Tournant* (Pierre Chenal, 1939)

as *The Postman Always Rings Twice* (Tay Garnett, 1946) and *Le Corbeau* (Clouzot, 1943) as *The Thirteenth Letter* (Otto Preminger, 1950). (Let us not forget that in the 1940s, Renoir, Duvivier and Siodmak were themselves in Hollywood, and their output included some *films noirs*, for instance Renoir's *Woman on the Beach*, 1947.) Jacques Tourneur's transatlantic career is also relevant here. His *Out of the Past* (1947) ranks as a classic *film noir* (and is hailed by Leslie Halliwell of all people in *Halliwell's Film Guide*, (Granada, London, 1977) as 'a moody *film noir*, with Hollywood imitating French models'), but he also worked in France in the early 1930s. Although the films he himself directed there were comedies, he also had a thorough training as an editor on the films of his father, Maurice Tourneur, most of which were crime stories: *Accusée, levez-vous!* (1930), *Au nom de la loi* (1931), and *Partir* (1931) – the last, in its combination of crime and doomed love, almost a blueprint for *film noir*.

It is striking that in both their French and their American films, Lang, Siodmak, Sirk, Bernhardt and Tourneur chose plots, themes and locations that were very close to – or based on – the Poetic Realist tradition (populist-realist might be a more accurate label, but this is not the place to question such a well-established historical category). The expression, originally applied to literature, was first used in the cinema for Pierre Chenal's *La Rue sans nom* (1933); it describes a genre of

urban drama, often set among the Paris prole-
tariat or lower middle classes, with romantic/
criminal narratives emphasising doom and
despair. In these films, 'poetry' and mystery are
found in everyday objects and settings – hence
the proletarian milieu (see Dudley Andrew,
'Poetic Realism' in Mary-Lea Bundy, ed., *Redis-
covering French Film*, Museum of Modern Art,
New York, 1983). Archetypal examples are the
films directed by Marcel Carné and scripted by
Jacques Prévert, for instance *Quai des brumes*
(1938) and *Le Jour se lève* (1939). Poetic Realism was, of course, only one French film genre
among many others (comedies, for example,
were more numerous and often more popular),
but it has gained the highest critical appraisal
and as a result had the greatest international
impact. The few French films that were known
in the USA in the 1930s and 1940s were more
than likely to be Poetic Realist films.

Poetic Realism into Film Noir

While the distorted camera-angles and strong
contrasts of light and shadow in German
Expressionist films of the 1920s are always cited
as a source of *film noir*, the impact of Poetic
Realism has been underestimated. Yet that
'poetry of wet cobblestones, of nights in the
faubourgs and of bleak dawns', mentioned by
Borde and Chaumeton as defining Poetic Realism, found a strong after-echo in US *film noir*, as
Joel Greenberg and Charles Higham evocatively
described it: 'a dark street in the early morning
hours, splashed with a sudden downpour' (quoted
in Place & Peterson, 1974).

From a very early sound film like René Clair's
Sous les toits de Paris (1930), to Carné's *Le Jour
se lève* and Siodmak's *Pièges*, both made on the
eve of World War II, the pre-*noir* tradition of
1930s French film is defined by its romantic/
pessimist narratives, by the visual motifs of night-
time city streets bathed in strong shadows and
pools of light from street lamps, of patterned
lighting on characters' faces and bodies, and of
sleazy locations, of which the night club or bar –
occasionally in exotic colonial locations – is the
epitome. Apart from the films just mentioned,
the locus classicus of Poetic Realism comprises
Renoir's *La Bête humaine*, Carné's *Quai des
brumes*, Duvivier's *La Belle Équipe* (1936) and
Pépé le Moko, Jacques Feyder's *Le Grand Jeu*
(1933) and Jean Grémillon's *Remorques* (1940);
less well-known examples include Pierre Chenal's
La Rue sans nom, *L'Alibi* (1937) and *Le Dernier
Tournant* (1939), Raymond Bernard's *Faubourg-
Montmartre* (1931), Henri Decoin's *Abus de confiance* (1937), Jeff Musso's *Le Puritain* (1937)
and *Dernière Jeunesse* (1939), Roger Richebé's
Prisons de femmes (1938) and Albert Valentin's
L'Entraîneuse (1938).

The tradition continues in some wartime films
like Henri-Georges Clouzot's *Le Corbeau* (1943)
and postwar ones such as Maurice Tourneur's

*Still: the world-weary Françoise Rosay in the
colonial bar of Jacques Feyder's* Le Grand Jeu.

Impasse des Deux-Anges (1948), Clouzot's *Quai
des Orfèvres* (1947), and Carné's *Les Portes de la
nuit* (1946). (See Ginette Vincendeau, 'Melodramatic Realism', *Screen*, vol.3, no.3, Summer
1989.) One unarguable common feature of these
films is their darkness: in 'atmosphere', narrative
trajectory and *mise-en-scène*. Compared with
bright vaudeville farces, glittering costume dramas or
Marcel Pagnol's Southern comedies, these films
were not just dark, they were, indeed, black.

It has been argued that Poetic Realism was
itself a 'German' aesthetic – from Fascist writers
like Maurice Bardèche and Robert Brasillach,
who saw the gloom and despair of *Le Jour se lève*
or *Quai des brumes* as 'Judeo-German', to less
ideologically-biased critics who point to the fact
that the look of Poetic Realism was to a large
extent not French, but bore the marks of German
cameramen (Eugen Schüfftan and Kurt Courant,
as well as Otto Heller and Franz Planer) or
French assistants enamoured with their style
(Henri Alekan), as well as Russian or Central
European set designers (Serge Pimenov or Lazare
Meerson, the latter particularly influential on
two other important emigres, Alexandre Trauner
and Georges Wakhévitch (see Philippe Roger
'*L'Obscure Clarté – la lumière allemande du cinéma*

français' in Hurst & Gassin). Undoubtedly, the contrasty lighting used to outline and shape characters and objects was part of the training of UFA cameramen, who, given their impact on French films, can claim some authorial credit.

However, they also had to adapt, first of all to the fact that the French cinema was dedicated to a representation of communities and to the showcasing of actors' performances, as opposed to the more abstract German approach in which actors tended to become part of abstract compositions (the argument in Elsaesser, 1984). Jean Renoir telling Kurt Courant on the set of *La Bête humaine* to stop 'getting on the actors' nerves with [his] UFA photography' (Philippe Roger) would seem to bear witness to this cultural clash. They also had to adapt their lighting to different sets. Though stylised, French sets designed by Meerson, Wakhévitch, Trauner and others had solidity, giving a sense of volume and depth of space, as opposed to the flatter, more abstract German ones (typified, at its most excessive, by *The Cabinet of Doctor Caligari*, Robert Wiene, 1920).

One reason for the more concrete aspect of the French sets was the narrative requirement of recreating a community; another was their evocation of Paris, a real city with an unusually high iconic status, as, for instance, in Clair's *Sous les*

Still: the continuation of prewar tradition in Henri-Georges Clouzot's Le Corbeau, *with Ginette Leclerc and, right, Pierre Fresnay.*

Still: UFA photography, French icons – Jean Gabin and Simone Simon in Jean Renoir's La Bête humaine.

toits de Paris or *Quatorze Juillet* (1932) and Renoir's *Le Crime de Monsieur Lange* (1936). Several films not set in Paris, such as *Le Jour se lève* still make use of the Parisian iconography. This is, again, significantly different from the abstract city of German films. Although the city in American *film noir* also tends to be non-specific, it is still meant to be emblematic of a 'real' or at least plausible city rather than an abstract one. By proposing a more physically concrete environment while retaining some German stylisation, Poetic Realism realises a synthesis closer to the classic realist American cinema than the German cinema did. Raymond Durgnat's argument that

Poetic Realism could be considered to 'fill the gap between impressionism in painting and realism in literature' (Durgnat, 1974, p.79) could be recast as saying that it 'filled the gap' between German Expressionism and classical Hollywood cinema.

Visual Motifs: the City

Both American *film noir* and Poetic Realism are predominantly urban genres. The *noir* city of films like *Double Indemnity* (Billy Wilder, 1944), *Out of the Past*, or *The Big Sleep* (Howard Hawks, 1946) is darkness itself, but it is a darkness defined by light. The sharp edges of objects and structures are used to reflect skilfully applied lighting, as they were in the French films of the 1930s. The gloom of the Poetic Realist city is illuminated by shiny cobblestones and pierced by gleaming neon signs welcoming passers-by to dance halls and gambling clubs: the 'bal' of *Sous les toits de Paris*, 'Le Tabarin' of *Quai des brumes*, 'La Dame de coeur' of *L'Entraîneuse*, or the flashing letters of 'Chez Michèle' in *Carrefour*. Though these signs are less ubiquitous and frantic than in American *film noir*, they nevertheless mark the Poetic Realist films as precursors of the American genre's 'Alphabet city', to use Guido Fink's evocative term (quoted in Pam Cook's report on Mystfest, *Sight & Sound*, vol.58, no.4, Autumn 1989, p.221).

The places labelled by the neon signs are, by definition, night spots, which function as the reverse of the daytime working-class cafe. Whereas the latter is the surrogate home where the (male) community asserts its unity, the night-spots are spaces of conflict, of 'dangerous' gender, class and sometimes racial mix. They are the stage where the lure of the 'working and dangerous classes' so central to French culture can be fully represented, often emphasised by the presence of mesmerised bourgeois onlookers (as in *Sous les toits de Paris*). They are also a perfect *mise-en-abîme* of the 'social voyeurism' that has informed French popular art since the early nineteenth

Still: L'Entraîneuse – a French precursor to the noir 'Alphabet city'.

century, from Emile Zola to the 'proletarian' and populist literature of the 1920s (Eugène Dabit, Francis Carco, Marcel Aymé, Pierre MacOrlan), to the poems of Jacques Prévert and the photography of Brassaï. In *Carrefour*, the respectable M. de Vétheuil (Charles Vanel) meets Michèle (Suzy Prim), the woman from his shady past, in her own nightclub. Vétheuil's male companion says, 'Let's go, this is not a place for us', but the two stay, irresistibly drawn to the sleaze they profess to hate – a neat metaphor for the attraction of both Poetic Realism and *film noir*. Roger Richebé's *Prisons de femmes* is entirely organised around the opposition between the bourgeois and the working-criminal class, the latter visualised in a nightclub, the two worlds linked by author Francis Carco playing himself.

In terms of *mise-en-scène*, the nightclub is a gift for the scope it gives to effects in lighting, music and costumes. The cabaret scene in *Carrefour* is a riot of criss-cross patterns in the sets, the lighting and costumes (down to Jules Berry's tie). This scene is also representative in its soundtrack use of jazz, acknowledging the impact of American popular culture and again anticipating what would be developed in *film noir*. A more detailed study would chart the struggles for cultural identity waged through the soundtracks of the dance hall and cabaret scenes, the accordion vying with jazz trumpets; this struggle is symbolised in the narrative of *Zouzou* (Marc Allegret, 1934), in which Jean Gabin sings an archetypal accordeon-backed 'java' and is 'half-brother' to Josephine Baker, who naturally ends up on an Anglo-Americanised music-hall stage. In a stereotypically racist way, jazz in some Poetic Realist films is also sometimes called upon to connote exoticism, danger, or sexual allure/obsession, foreshadowing both the frenzy of *Phantom Lady* (Robert Siodmak, 1944) and French *films noirs* of the 1950s such as *Du Rififi chez les hommes* (Jules Dassin, 1955) and *Razzia sur la chnouf* (Henri Decoin, 1955).

The inhabitants and objects of the Poetic Realist city, like those of *film noir*, participate in this iconography – not only the cobblestones glisten, so do the cars and even the characters. When Joan Bennett appears to Edward G. Robinson in *Scarlet Street*, she is clad in a shiny transparent raincoat, not actually worn by Lulu in Renoir's original, *La Chienne* (1931). However, a number of late 1930s French films featured heroines wearing similar garb, often complemented by a beret to make up the uniform of the 'lost girl' – for instance Danielle Darrieux in *Abus de confiance*, Jacqueline Delubac in *Dernière Jeunesse*, Simone Simon in *La Bête humaine*, and Michele Morgan in *Quai des brumes*. Metonymically transferring the night-time street – in its dark and 'wet' look – on to the body of the woman, the raincoat is ideal for picking up complex lighting arrangements. Blackness and rain, two key elements of *film noir*, are repeatedly inscribed in Poetic Realist films through this motif.

Visual Motifs: Livid Faces

One ubiquitous visual motif of *film noir* consists of 'strange highlights . . . often on the faces of the sinister or demented' (Place & Peterson, 1974 p.31). Generally, lighting patterns on actors' faces signal disturbed or intense psychological states: fear, division, deep introspection, madness (Burt Lancaster's face in *The Killers*, Robert Siodmak, 1946; Joan Crawford's in *Mildred Pierce*, Michael Curtiz, 1945). If this motif is present in German Expressionist films (Lang's *M*, 1931 for instance), it is found systematically adorning the face of the most iconic of Poetic realist actors, Jean Gabin. Though lit by a variety of cameramen (French: Christian Matras, Claude Renoir, Jules Krüger; German: Kurt Courant, Eugen Schüfftan, Günther Rittau; Russian: Fédote Bourgassoff), Gabin's face from *La Bandera* (Julien Duvivier) in 1935 to *Remorques* in 1940 is consistently highlighted in this particular way. Central to Borde and Chaumeton's argument against French cinema's influence on *film noir* was the fact that 'there is no trace of gratuitous violence . . . Jean Gabin kills, but he is a sentimental criminal, an ordinary man who sees red' (Borde & Chaumeton 1955, p.27). However, the lighting on Gabin's face, and particularly on his eyes, always marks out his 'otherness', setting him apart from his proletarian colleagues and environment. Typical examples would be the scenes after Séverine's murder in *La Bête humaine*, before Madeleine's murder in *Gueule d'amour*, or before his suicide in *Le Jour se lève*. Gabin's violence may not be 'gratuitous', but the visual effect ascribes transcendent causes to it. During these moments, Gabin leaves the working-class suburb to attain a mythical realm, and the doomed fate of the *noir* character is encapsulated in this visual motif. We find an echo of it, naturally, on Henry Fonda's face in *The Long Night*, but also on countless others – compare, for instance, Gabin's visual treatment in *Le Jour se lève* with Burt Lancaster's at the beginning of *The Killers*.

Both *film noir* of the 1940s and 1950s and Poetic Realism in the 1930s, then, exist in a visual dialectic between gleaming lights and sharply highlighted faces, and a darkness that threatens to engulf characters, technically produced by low-key lighting and night-for-night shooting (Place & Peterson, 1974, p.31). I can find no better illustration of this than in Carné's *Quai des brumes*, where Gabin emerges into the fiction literally out of the dark, to return to it at the end when he is shot down; in the meantime he wanders through the black, wet streets of Le Havre, from bleak quayside to down-and-out café. Among the many connotations of the word *noir* in French (like black in English) is pessimism, an attribute as often applied to Poetic Realism as to *film noir*. Henri Agel, in a polemical essay on Duvivier, Chenal, and the *noir* tendency in French 1930s cinema, summed it up as follows:

Frame: Le Jour se lève – *the lighting on Jean Gabin's face marks out his 'otherness'.*

'The pessimism which oozed out of Duvivier's films became one of the shameful diseases of French cinema' (*Miroirs de l'insolite dans le cinéma français*, Editions du Cerf, Paris, 1958, p.14. 'Shameful diseases' – *maladies honteuses* – has the connotation of venereal disease).

No Future

This pessimism is a direct link between Poetic Realism and *film noir*. If 'post-war disillusion' is often quoted as a determinant of *film noir*, then 'prewar lack of illusion' is a determinant of Poetic Realism. Poetic Realist films are often seen as mirroring the anxiety felt at the rise of fascism and looming war, even though such pessimism considerably antedates the prewar years, being a pervasive aspect of French culture, affecting literature – both learned and popular – and popular song, particularly the *'chanson réaliste'*.

Hollywood directors – and in particular the émigrés – were repeatedly drawn to the French films, not just visually but also in terms of their pessimistic narratives and themes, either directly (in the remakes) or indirectly. The sense of hopelessness, of destructive forces not outside but within the (male) characters that pervades American *film noir* also characterises Poetic Realism. One example is the myth of escape – from country, identity or circumstances – and the attraction of exoticism, which we find in *Mauvaise Graine* (Wilder, 1934), *Sans lendemain* (Ophuls, 1940), *Mollenard, Mademoiselle Docteur* (G.W. Pabst, 1936), *Le Drame de Shanghaï* as well as *La Chienne, Faubourg Montmartre, La Bête humaine, Pépé le Moko, Quai des brumes* and many others. In these films, as in American *film noir*, the dream of escape is thwarted. Endeavours are doomed and heroes will be destroyed.

There is no future in Poetic Realist films, something which Paul Schrader has also isolated as an overriding theme of *film noir*: 'In *Out of the Past*, Robert Mitchum relates his history with such pathetic relish that it is obvious there is no hope for any future: one can only take pleasure in reliving a doomed past' (Schrader, 1972). Similarly, the heroes and heroines of *Jenny* (Carné, 1936), of *Carrefour*, of *La Bête humaine*, *Pépé le Moko* and *Le Jour se lève*, and many others, are forever thrown back to their past: 'For us, the future is blocked,' says Simone Simon to Jean Gabin in *La Bête humaine*. *Le Jour se lève*, of course, inscribed this most forcefully in its innovative flashback structure. The 'claustrophobic framing devices, such as doors, windows, staircases' (Place & Peterson, 1974, p.31) that pervade *film noir* also characterise Poetic Realism. The most striking visual image of Jean Gabin – from one film to another – is that of his face trapped behind a window. In an early scene in *La Bandera*, this is even underlined by what became a cliché of *film noir*: his face is crossed by the diagonal shadows of a Venetian blind. Poetic Realism found poetry in the quotidian, the banal everyday world of modest characters and environments. Its major preoccupation, as seen in the films of Jacques Feyder, Carné, Duvivier, Chenal and Renoir, was the exploration of the rapport between characters and environments – hence the concentration on the relationship between actors and decor. If the 'meaning' of Poetic Realist films derives from this interaction, so does that of *film noir*. As Place

and Peterson proposed, the 'interaction between man and the forces represented by that *noir* environment is always clearly visible' (Place & Peterson, 1974, p.31); as an illustration of this point, we can compare Gabin trapped in his bedroom in *Le Jour se lève*, and Burt Lancaster equally imprisoned in his in *The Killers*.

While the directors of American *film noir* greatly emphasised the violence inherent in this relationship between character and environment, they played down the social context. The remakes provide us with convenient points of comparison: contrast, for instance, *Scarlet Street* and *La Chienne*, *La Bête humaine* and *Human Desire*, or *Le Jour se lève* and *The Long Night*. In the last of these, class identity is reduced to being 'from the wrong side of the tracks' and class oppression is 'universalised' into war trauma. Some of the narrative streamlining had to do with censorship. Whereas the narrative logic of *Le Jour se lève*, as well as Gabin's star persona, dictated that he must die, Henry Fonda's in *The Long Night* pulled through. The same went for Gabin in *La Bête humaine*, and Glenn Ford in *Human Desire*. The conclusion of *Scarlet Street*, while closer to that of *La Chienne*, nevertheless greatly attenuated its cynical force. Legrand's (Michel Simon's) murder of Lulu goes unpunished. Dédé instead goes to the guillotine and Legrand happily becomes a tramp. Chris Cross

(Edward G. Robinson) on the other hand goes 'mad'. As Lotte Eisner put it, the cynicism of *La Chienne*'s ending was 'only possible in France' (*Fritz Lang*, Secker & Warburg, London, 1976). Similarly, Charles Boyer does not kill himself at the end of *Algiers*, as Gabin does in *Pépé le Moko*, but is shot by a policeman. While *Scarlet Street* and *Human Desire* are still violent and bleak narratives, in the sense of the depiction of a social and moral universe, French Poetic Realist films are actually more *noir* than *film noir*.

Noir Crime

Crime is as much a pervasive element of Poetic Realism as it is of *film noir*. It is not, however, crime examined in its psychopathic dimension as in 1920s German cinema. French cinema is not interested in serial killers, maniacs or sadistic brutes, and in this respect Weimar cinema is one of the more obvious sources of inspiration for the Gothic strand (e.g. *Gaslight*, George Cukor, 1944) or the studies of brutal crime (e.g. *Kiss Me, Deadly*, Robert Aldrich, 1955) in *film noir*. The criminal activity found in Poetic Realist films, including the Gabin films, is embedded in everyday life. Gabin's heroes attain a mythical dimension, but that myth is connected to their 'ordinariness' as characters and to their class identity. This is understandable in view of the literary heritage of Poetic Realism. The literary genres on which it drew were in the realist-naturalistic mode, with a strong pessimistic streak. *Noir* elements were already present in Zola and Guy de Maupassant in the nineteenth century, as well as in other twentieth-century writers already mentioned. When French writers started to develop a separate genre of crime literature, they drew on the factual memoirs of Vidocq (convict turned chief of police) and the adventure-melodramatic novel. They were also inspired by the British crime writers – Arthur Conan Doyle, Agatha Christie – who were adept at placing their narratives within clear class parameters, though the class was different. Allain and Souvestre, authors of the more fantastic *Fantômas*, still placed their hero in a very recognisable Paris. The 1930s saw the first work of the master of sociological detail and realistic 'atmosphere': Georges Simenon. Simenon's narratives were ideally suited to the French cinema, and his first cinematic adaptation, Jean Renoir's *La Nuit du carrefour* ('Night at the Crossroads', an emblematic *noir* title) is a model of visually created *noir* atmosphere: shiny black cars with semi-visible occupants travelling down lonely roads to a forlorn cafe. Some critics thought the film too dark to watch and the plot similarly obscure. Maigret, played by Pierre Renoir (Jean's brother), solved the crime according to his patent method, which exactly corresponds to what the viewers of *film noir* as well as Poetic Realist films are expected to do: soak in the atmosphere, rather than follow a clear, logical narrative. The importance of the

Still: Michel Simon and Janie Marèse in Jean Renoir's La Chienne.

visual definition of this atmosphere was clear to Simenon, who insisted that the covers of his early novels be illustrated with photographs (some of them by Robert Doisneau) rather than the traditional drawings; when seen now, they evoke both Poetic Realist films and *film noir*.

As Simenon rose to prominence in the early 1930s, he was keenly aware of increasing competition from Anglo-American crime literature, particularly since the creation in 1927 of the publishing imprint Le Masque which (anticipating Marcel Duhamel's Série Noire by 20 years) published exclusively British and American writers in translation. A few other publishers started putting out American hard-boiled novels – Dashiell Hammett's *The Glass Key* and *Red Harvest* were published in French in 1932. In this sense Simenon's accumulation of realistic detail,

Frame: claustrophobic motifs – the blind man (Georges Douking) in Le Jour se lève.

as that of the Poetic Realist films, while fitting within a long French tradition, can be seen as a response to the need for a sharpened definition of national specificity. The particularity of the French response to crime literature of whatever origin is also that, from way back in the 1910s when the Surrealists rejoiced in *Fantômas*, it united a mass readership with intellectual legitimacy: André Gide was apparently so impatient to read Simenon's novels that he consumed them in proof form (*see* Francis Lacassin, *Simenon 1931, La naissance de Maigret*, Presses de la Cité, Paris, 1991, p.31). It is thus not surprising that one of the most cultured directors of the 1930s, Pierre Chenal, would not wait for a French translation of James M. Cain's *The Postman Always Rings Twice* but tried to adapt it immediately on reading it in English after its publication in the United States in 1934. That the project was submitted first to Jean Renoir, and then to Marcel Carné, with a proposed cast of Jean Gabin, Viviane Romance and Michel Simon (*see* Pierrette Matalon, Claude Guiguet & Jacques Pinturault, eds, *Pierre Chenal*, Editions Dujarric, Paris, 1987, p.125) also underlined the continuity with Poetic Realism. In the version that Chenal himself succeeded in making, entitled *Le Dernier Tournant* ('the last bend in the road'), shot in early 1939 – the first and usually unacknowledged version of this much remade *noir* story – Michel Simon ended up playing the part of Nick, the husband. Although one may dream of a Renoir version (and of the Gabin-Romance-Simon trio), Chenal's film is excellent, a fascinating and underrated example of 'French *film noir*' in a stricter sense, since it was based on American crime material.

Le Dernier Tournant marks the emblematic intersection of Poetic Realism and *film noir*. Chenal made few changes to the story, judging that he needed only to adapt the legal subtleties to the French system. With Luchino Visconti's *Ossessione* (the second version of the story, made in 1943), this is the most socially anchored of the films. Whereas the two American versions (Tay Garnett, 1946, and Bob Rafelson, 1981) emphasise the erotically charged role of the women (Lana Turner and Jessica Lange respectively), and Visconti's the attraction of the young male hero (Massimo Girotti), Chenal's, following the French cinema's tendency to give prominence to the older man, puts the accent on the husband. This is also the result of the casting. Set beside the weaker Fernand Gravey and Corinne Luchaire, Michel Simon dominates the film, drawing far more sympathy than the husband in other versions. At the same time, the ambiguity of his performance chimes with the greater moral cynicism of French film that I have mentioned, intimating that he is a participant in the 'infernal' trio rather than simply a victim. In line with other Poetic Realist films (e.g. *La Bête Humaine*) too, the issue is not so much of an 'evil' *femme fatale* as of internal conflicts in the male heroes. Chenal's cinematography combined low-key *noir* photography in the night-time interior scenes with open-air shooting, which was unusual for the time, thus anticipating *Ossessione* as well as the Tay Garnett version. Apart from the importance of the night scenes, the tension of *Le Dernier Tournant* comes from tightly controlled camera movements and takes of unusually long duration, the average shot length being twenty-seven seconds compared to twelve to fourteen in most French films of the same period, and seven to eight in Hollywood. An entire study could be devoted to the differences in, say, shot length and editing rhythm, between the French and American films. However, if we agree with Place and Peterson (1974, p.31) that a greater depth of field and 'anti-traditional' *mise-en-scène* are a characteristic of *film noir* as opposed to more classical Hollywood cinema, then the French films of the 1930s are an obvious place to look for antecedents. Renoir's work on staging in depth is famous, but he was not alone in this – many French films of the 1930s, particularly those of Chenal and Duvivier, stage the action in several planes and tend to reframe rather than cut – hence the longer takes.

Whether *Le Dernier Tournant* was seen in Hollywood or not, it amply illustrates the point that all the key elements of *film noir* – low-key, contrasty lighting, narratives of blocked escape and doomed love, and crime source material – were already a vital part of the prewar French cinema. The Hollywood film industry of the 1930s and 1940s was an international one, as was the French: *Le Dernier Tournant*, to name but one example, was made by a French director, based on an American novel adapted by a Belgian scriptwriter (Charles Spaak), in sets designed by a Russian émigré (Georges Wakhévitch). When François Truffaut, Jean-Luc Godard, Jacques Rivette, Borde and Chaumeton and other young French critics of the time 'discovered' *film noir* in the late 1940s at Henri Langlois's Cinémathèque Française, it is a pity that they were not shown Chenal's films. Ironically, at least two of them – *L'Homme de nulle part* (1936) and *L'Alibi* – were among the rare few French films shown in New York in the 1930s. Even though French filmmakers in the 1930s held him in high esteem, even though many of his films were very popular, and even though Orson Welles claimed to have been influenced by him, it was not until 1982 that Chenal was given proper recognition by the Paris Cinémathèque, at the suggestion – another irony – of an American critic working in France (*see* Matalon, Guignet & Pinturault, p.171). All this goes to show how wary we should be of apparently neat national divisions in cinematic identities and influence. It is usually more complicated than that. Equally, and soberingly, the example of Pierre Chenal demonstrates how easily important contributions can be ignored when they do not fit into the established grooves of film history.

HOW HOLLYWOOD DEALS WITH THE DEVIANT MALE

Deborah Thomas

'Amid the seeming confusion of our mysterious world, individuals are so nicely adjusted to a system, and systems to one another and to a whole, that, by stepping aside for a moment, a man exposes himself to a fearful risk of losing his place forever. Like Wakefield, he may become, as it were, the Outcast of the Universe.' Nathaniel Hawthorne, 'Wakefield', from *Twice-Told Tales*.

'I think you're swell, so long as I'm not your husband.' Walter Neff (Fred MacMurray) in *Double Indemnity* (Billy Wilder, 1944).

Most critics and viewers share a sense both of the essential male-centredness of *film noir* and of its pervasive mood of anxiety (whether made manifest in visual or in narrative terms). I shall take this uneasy combination as my starting point. The question I wish to pose is a simple one: if *film noir* is a male fantasy, as has often been claimed (for example by Janey Place, 1978, p.35), then why is anxiety so central to its mood? What does the post-war male have to be anxious *about*?

Is the answer, perhaps, a simple one as well? Janey Place links the disequilibrious emotional texture of the genre to male fears of sexuality, as embodied in the type of the 'spider woman', in contrast to the redeeming woman who 'offers the possibility of integration for the alienated, lost man into the stable world of secure values, roles and identities' (Place, 1978, p.50). Sylvia Harvey, too, makes reference to 'a process of general disillusionment for many of those returning home after the war, in search of those values which they had fought to defend' (Harvey, 1978, pp.25-26). Presumably, on this view, *film noir*'s function would be seen as one of managing anxiety, diminishing it in proportion to the extent to which the 'spider woman' is submitted to male containment and control, and the male reinstated to his 'right' and 'proper' place. It is not so much anxiety, that is, as its dispersal which is seen to characterise *film noir*, and this is surely compatible with the wish-fulfilling function of a fantasy. There are a number of problems with this view, not least of which is the way in which the genre's anxiety pervades the entire fabric of such films, and does not merely accrue to its duplicitous women, appearing to linger on despite the resolutions of the narrative and the frequent restoration of its hero to his 'rightful' place. I wish to suggest that, though *the femme fatale* is indeed a threat,

she is no more so than the so-called redemptive woman who is intent on the hero's domestication and the restoration of the status quo.

The question of how a genre of wish-fulfilment can be simultaneously a genre of anxiety has been addressed by Sigmund Freud in connection with dreams, and his claims may be useful here: he sees the dreamer as an amalgamation of two people, one of whom repudiates and censors the other's wishes and thus derives no pleasure from their fulfilment. However, in anxiety dreams, such wishes are not distorted by the censoring mechanism of the mind, but appear fulfilled in undisguised fashion, resulting in the replacement of censorship by anxiety. Punishment dreams, on the other hand, though wish-fulfilments as well, represent the wishes, not of instinctual impulses but of 'the critical, censoring and punishing agency in the mind' (*New Introductory Lectures on Psychoanalysis*, Pelican Freud Library, vol.2, Penguin, Harmondsworth, 1973, p.57). The protagonist of *film noir*, like the dreamer, is an ambiguous figure (unlike the traditional problem-solving detective, on the one hand, or the gangster, on the other). He is caught between his conscience (which can be seen as an internalised version of American society's expectations of its men) and those desires which violate such norms and find expression, to a greater or lesser extent, in the films. This dividedness may be projected on to other characters who represent the separate aspects of the hero.

But there is a difficulty in determining exactly what 'normal' masculinity entails, particularly in the postwar context of the 1940s and 1950s. Is it best exemplified by the rather pallid figure of the good husband and father in the all-American family? Or is it embodied in the man's man (the adventurer or soldier, say), to whom domestication is a threat? The latter view of masculinity, pushed to an extreme, becomes incompatible with the former, the returning soldier out of place in the family he had left behind. I would argue that much of Hollywood cinema has grappled more or less explicitly with a kind of male schizophrenia which both puts enormous pressure on men to be 'normal' and yet represents such normality in contradictory terms. The war and its conclusion provided crisis points which crystallised the contradiction in America's expectations of its men by imposing sudden and extreme shifts in the norms invoked. What was normal during the war – such as close male companionship, sanctioned killing, and 'easier' and more casual sexual behaviour, all heightened by the constant possibility of one's own sudden death — became deviant in the context of post-war calm, though such elements lingered on in the *film noir* world as the focus both of longing and of dread. Postwar men had much to gain from returning to their previous secure position within society (and identifying with the law, rather than with lingering desires now become explicitly transgressive), but perhaps much to lose as well.

Fritz Lang's American films are exemplary in this context. Consider *While the City Sleeps* (1956) and *Beyond a Reasonable Doubt* (1956). In the former, Ed Mobley (Dana Andrews) gets engaged to his respectable girlfriend Nancy (Sally Forrest), though this turns out to be a ploy on his part in order to set her up as bait for a murderer who will presumably undertake to kill her as a way of getting back at Mobley, a television newscaster. In view of the consistent parallels which the film sets up between Mobley and the murderer, and given the fact that Nancy is shown both to refuse Ed's pre-marital advances while reacting stonily to his relationship with a sexually much more liberal rival Mildred (Ida Lupino), it is easy to read Ed's behaviour in setting Nancy up as expressive of an unacknowledged wish to be rid of her (his alter ego accomplishing the task he can't consciously admit to wanting done). That Ed and Nancy finally marry, after the murderer is confronted by Ed in the subway and caught by the police, is testimony less of Ed's love for Nancy and desire for married life than of the bleakness of Lang's world view. Similarly, in *Beyond a Reasonable Doubt*, it is arguable that Tom Garrett (Dana Andrews again) is threatened by his prosperous fiancée Susan Spencer (Joan Fontaine), who dominates him both visually and by the appropriating of traditionally male prerogatives ('I've never seen your apartment.' 'Isn't that supposed to be my line?' 'But you've never used it.') Again, Tom's killing of Patty can easily be read as a displacement of the desire to kill Susan, despite his conscious wish to climb the ladder of social status through his marriage to her (the headline, 'Dancer Strangled', which announces Patty's death, follows on almost directly from the quirky scene where Susan has asked to 'go dancing' in Tom's apartment). Thus, the film seems to be saying that Tom's desire for respectability, which the marriage to Susan would provide, exists side by side with an unacknowledged but potentially deadly antagonism towards her and her high-class world ('You get engaged to my daughter,' jokes Susan's father, 'and all you can think of is capital punishment'). Ironically, it is Susan who is finally responsible for the fact that, at the end of the film, Tom is about to be executed; Nancy in the earlier film merely condemned Ed to marriage. Both women act in the name of respectability.

It is interesting to note that many of the conflicts over which Lang's protagonists struggle are to do with their internalisation of traditional views on gender which conflict with less hidebound, more amorphous desires. In *While the City Sleeps*, the murderer quite explicitly protests to his mother, 'When you adopted me, you wanted a girl, didn't you? And he wanted a boy. Well, neither one of you was satisfied, were you?' Given the consistent parallels between him and Mobley, this suggests similar conflicts in the latter. In *Beyond a Reasonable Doubt*, Tom seems to feel threatened by Susan's appropriation of 'male' roles, while at the same time being not over-eager to take them on himself. *The Blue Gardenia* (1953), a slightly earlier Lang film of this period, fairly openly foregrounds the way in which female stereotypes are matters of construction rather than nature, but the film also, less obviously perhaps, enacts the difficulties for men of fulfilling traditional male roles. This is especially evident in the character of Prebble (Raymond Burr) – on the surface, the nearest thing the film has to a villain, but also its ultimate victim – who unsuccessfully attempts to live up to his false reputation as a womaniser (when asked whether he's successful in this role, a female character confides, 'He is if you ask *him*'). This fundamental conflict for men between the burdensomeness and the privileges of their ordained position within the social world is perhaps most clearly set forth by Lang in *The Woman in the Window* (1944) and *Scarlet Street* (1945). In a similar way to *While the City Sleeps* and *Beyond a Reasonable Doubt*, these two earlier films can be seen as paired, both in terms of having the same actor as the central protagonist of each (Edward G. Robinson instead of Dana Andrews) and in terms of this protagonist being restored to normality (although only apparently the better off for it) in one film of the pair, but destroyed in the other.

These examples seem to me to typify a tendency in *film noir* to dramatise a particular crisis in male identity which, though it is implicit in other genres and throughout the history of American film, appears with special vehemence in the context of a war which made such issues alive for many men. It is not my intention here to say anything conclusive about all *films noirs*. Instead, I hope to show that a significant number of them share certain conflicts or anxieties, though not univocally, but rather as variations upon a theme. My main concern will be with the central male protagonist and his relationship both to narrative events and to the process of their narration.

The Urban Setting

As many critics have remarked, one of the most salient characteristics of *film noir* is its urban setting. The overwhelmingly negative view of this milieu which *film noir* takes for granted is by no means novel, but belongs to a long American intellectual tradition of antipathy towards the city. I would like to suggest that the characteristic anxiety provoked by the contemporary urban setting of *film noir* has its roots, at least in part, in a response to the waves of immigration of the late nineteenth and early twentieth centuries which seemed to make of the city no longer the locus of American 'civilisation' (a native version of white Anglo-Saxon Protestantism) but rather of antithetical 'otherness.'

American civilisation was linked to Europe in its origins and later development, but was also sharply distinguished from it as a thing of its own, and it was in the cities that a definition of 'American-ness', of 'us-ness' (as opposed to 'them-ness') evolved. For Morton and Lucia White, the Civil War was a turning point. Before the Civil War, 'the American city was between its period of colonial charm and its period of industrial chaos' (*The Intellectual Versus The City: From Thomas Jefferson to Frank Lloyd Wright*, Oxford University Press, 1977, p.44), and criticism of it was by no means as virulent as it would later become or as criticism of the European city had already become. Such criticism as prevailed derived from a romanticism whereby the city was seen as *over*-civilised and inferior to the wilderness beyond it which, at that time, was still a viable alternative. After the Civil War, such romantic love of the wilderness was no longer central to the attacks on the American city made by intellectual anti-urbanites. The city became progressively seen as the place from which civilisation was *absent*, this alleged absence of civilisation largely linked to a sense of the city as an alien place.

Morton and Lucia White are undoubtedly correct in their caution that not all criticism of the American city can be attributed to 'racism, nativism, or anti-Semitism' (p.231) on the part of the critics, but it is nonetheless evident that many post-Civil-War anti-urbanists did link their fears to a sense of displacement or dispossession. Even many of those broad-minded intellectuals who welcomed the diversity which the city's immigrant population provided did not deny the importance of such heterogeneity as a constitutive aspect of the modern American city. In the post-Civil-War period, and in particular those years which followed the massive absorption of immigrants into the urban milieu in the late nineteenth and early twentieth centuries, the American city, whether deplored or extolled, was seen more and more as a contrast to the white Anglo-Saxon Protestantism which underlay earlier definitions of 'American-ness'. Thus, cities were seen either (where criticised) as un-American and alien, or (where praised) as forging a new definition of American civilisation in terms of the very diversity – and no longer homogeneity – of their populations.

In general, to the extent that critics put the emphasis on 'otherness,' the immigrant groups singled out for comment tended to be those most in contrast with the 'us-ness' of American civilisation. Thus, relative to the white Anglo-Saxon Protestant version of 'American-ness', Irish and Italian Catholics, Jews, and, in recent years, blacks and Hispanics, lent theselves more readily to the position of aliens than white Protestant immigrants from northern Europe. It is partly for this reason, presumably, that 'otherness' became largely associated with the cities for, although there was immigration to rural areas as well, it was associated more with groups like the Scandinavians, rather than, say, the Jews (*see* Edward Abramson, *The Immigrant Experience in American Literature*, BAAS Pamphlets in American Studies 10, British Association for American Studies, 1982). Of course, insofar as the immigrants themselves found a voice with which to express their own experiences, a point of view developed in opposition to that of already well-established English-speaking citizens to whom they were a threat. To the immigrants, the city was a threat as well, but from their point of view, what was threatening was the strangeness (to them) of America itself. Strangeness and familiarity are, of course, relative concepts, but the anti-urbanism which *film noir* takes on is generally one from whose vantage point blacks, women and immigrants, among others – and not white male Americans – are strange. One point of view among many has become set up as absolute. A passage from Raymond Chandler's *Farewell, My Lovely* provides a good example:

'Two more swing doors closed off the head of the stairs from whatever was beyond. The big man pushed them open lightly with his thumbs and we went into the room. It was a long narrow room, not very clean, not very bright, not very cheerful. In the corner a group of negroes chanted and chattered in the cone of light over a crap table. There was a bar against the right hand wall. The rest of the room was mostly small round tables. There were a few customers, men and women, all negroes.

'The chanting at the crap table stopped dead and the light over it jerked out. There was a sudden silence as heavy as a waterlogged boat. Eyes looked at us, chestnut coloured eyes, set in faces that ranged from grey to deep black. Heads turned slowly and the eyes in them glistened and stared in the dead alien silence of another race.'

This is despite the fact that it is Marlowe and Malloy who are the strangers encroaching on black territory: it may not be their territory, but it is their narrative.

As the city was seen more and more to be the preserve of 'alien' groups, so 'normality' was seen to move with its exemplars to the suburbs and the Midwest, the latter, for example, more and more seen as 'a place of limited vision, materialism, and conventional morality' (Abramson, p.14). The so-called middle way of earlier pastoralists between corruption and savagery was reduced to the midwestern small town, their cultivated garden to that of the suburban home. Eventually, of course, many Jews and members of other immigrant groups became assimilated to such norms, blacks and Hispanics replacing them as the new urban scapegoats.

Film noir, in taking up this point of view, is defining as 'reality' the world as perceived by the white American male, the genre's usual central protagonist. The world of *film noir*, in other words, is a relative one, filtered through the psychology of such a protagonist. So the fact of mass immigration into the urban milieu lends itself to appropriation by a particular point of view (that of the white American male), transforming such an external datum into a psychological response. Thus, the *film noir* city is not an objective rendition of American cities of the time (such 'objectivity' being incompatible with the relativity of the city's presentation as an alien threat), but is more profitably understood as the projection outward of an internal terrain. The 'real' city is significant less in itself than in the response it elicits. Of course, many classical Hollywood films belonging to genres other than *film noir* presuppose such a point of view. However, such subjectivity is built into the very structure of *film noir* with its frequent first-person narration, its dream-like episodes, and the sense of dispossession so often experienced by the genre's usual protagonist.

I have suggested that changes in the modern city's meaning have taken place in connection with its 'invasion' by immigrant groups. However, although anti-Semitism, say, was certainly extant in the postwar years (Elia Kazan's *Gentleman's Agreement*, 1947, is a liberal-minded film which charts its prevalence), overt hostility to such groups as Jews was in decidedly bad taste in the wake of a war conceptualised, precisely because of the country's stance in opposition to anti-Semitism and related evils, as 'America's one black-and-white, good-versus-evil war of the twentieth century' (Myra MacPherson, *Long Time Passing: Vietnam and the Haunted Generation*, Doubleday, New York, 1984, p.48). Irving Howe describes the resultant 'de-Semitisation' in the popular arts:

'In 1944 Ben Hecht noticed "the almost complete disappearance of the Jew from American fiction, stage, and movies." Eight years later Henry Popkin put together a bundle of evidence showing that in the popular arts "the Jew" had become "the little man who isn't there . . ." When Hitler forced Americans to take anti-Semitism seriously, it was apparently felt that the most eloquent reply that could be made was a dead silence' (Irving Howe, *World of Our Fathers: The Journey of the East European Jews to America and the Life They Found and Made*, Simon & Schuster, New York, 1976, p.567).

The city's negative connotations, though originating in a sense of dispossession linked to its increasingly 'foreign' character, were, by the time of *film noir* and in the context of an anti-fascist war, simply a *given*, a convention of the fast-consolidating genre in the late wartime and postwar years. The 'otherness' of the city was tacitly present in the point of view which the genre took up, as was the sense of dispossession to be found, similarly, in the psychology of its central protagonist. However, the genre's main 'heavies' (its main representatives, that is, of an alien and threatening world) are not so much foreigners per se as women and criminals. Thus, the genre, in its concern with a crisis in male identity in the transitional period from wartime to peace, makes use of the traditional antipathy toward the city and the 'otherness' associated with the urban milieu for its own ends.

The Postwar Context

The perception of the city's 'otherness' in terms of its female and criminal inhabitants need not be understood merely as a displacement of hostility from foreigners on to women and the underworld. There are additional, more important factors in play which make the 'otherness' of women, say, within the genre an issue in its own right. Undoubtedly, as the standard explanation of *film noir*'s hostility to women suggests, 'the temporary but widespread introduction of women into the American labour force during World War II' (Harvey, 1978, p.25), taking over from departing GIs, produced a sense of dispossession when these soldiers returned. But to relate the disaffection of returning GIs to a desire, as has been argued, to recover the world as they had known it provides only part of the explanation of *film noir*'s antagonism to women. This approach makes use of one sense of 'otherness' (women seen as subordinate in order to protect male privilege) at the expense of another (women seen as alien in order to deny aspects of the self). However, an exclusive emphasis on shifts in female roles as a result of the war and its aftermath obscures equally significant shifts in *male* roles during the same period of time. Seeing women's 'otherness' at least partly in terms of projection is a useful strategy in pinpointing *film noir*'s obsession with the male psyche, which defines its point of view.

A film like *The Best Years of Our Lives*, (William Wyler, 1946), though obviously not a *film noir*, may be of interest here. It directly confronts the problems of the returning GIs, making clear the incompatibility of their prewar and wartime roles and the impossibility of a simple return to the former. Consider the following exchange between Al (Frederic March) and his wife Millie (Myrna Loy), after Al has been offered a job at the bank where he used to work:

Al: Last year it was 'kill Japs' and this year it's 'make money.'
Millie: We're all right for the time being.
Al: Why do they have to bother me about problems like that the first day I get home? Why can't they give a fellow time to get used to his own family? Why don't you come over here and sit down?

Millie: The chair's liable to break.

Al: We can't be worrying about chairs. Not when they want me back in a nice fat job in a nice fat bank.

Millie: You don't seem very happy about it.

Al: I'm not.

Millie: Why not, darling?

Al: I can't help thinking about the other guys. All the ones who haven't got you.

Millie: You're crazy.

Al: No, I'm too sane for my own good.

Al's explanation of his discontent is not very convincing, especially in the light of an earlier scene, the night before, when, somewhat drunk, he'd fantasised his marriage away:

Al: You know, you're a bewitching little creature. In a way you remind me of my wife.

Millie: But you never told me you're married.

Al: Oh, yeah, I got a little woman, two kiddies, back there in the States.

Millie: But let's not think of them now.

Al: No, you're so right. This night belongs only to us.

What this film makes clear is not the desire of its GI characters to return to normal, but their reluctance to do so. The explicitness of the subject matter (albeit at odds with the film's surface resolutions) makes this example a useful one; I would claim that such issues are more implicit in, but nonetheless absolutely central to, *film noir*. In the postwar period in particular, the return to normality may well have produced ambivalent feelings in men and women alike, giving rise to both *noir* and melodramatic explorations of such themes, from male and female perspectives respectively. Women are not the only ones whom family life and gender norms may constrain, of course, and many cinematic examples can be given of the oppressiveness to men of family and small-town life (the small town, as I've argued above, being the locus of 'normality' in the years following mass immigration to the cities). I have mentioned that, throughout the history of the American cinema, two incompatible models of maleness coexist, of which the soldier and the family man are respective examples. Insofar as *film noir* takes up a male point of view at a time when so many men were expected to take on and discard these roles in turn, it is reasonable to expect the genre's concerns to reflect this in a concentration upon the crisis in male identity which the war arguably produced and which the genre's style and structure befit. There is not, certainly, an exact symmetry between male and female oppression (whereby *film noir* deals with the former precisely as melodrama, say, confronts the latter), for 'normality' privileges the male. It is by virtue of this fact that such oppression tends to be hidden and the men's desires to escape the constraints of a status quo which nonetheless privileges them tend to be denied, the process of projection providing an element in this denial.

The male protagonist of *film noir is* thus divided to varying degrees. Criminals and women of a certain type, by their aggressiveness and (extramarital) sexuality respectively, represent antisocial (or at least 'anti-normal') aspects of the protagonist himself. Yet at the same time, as I pointed out above, the very 'normality' which oppresses the male also privileges him and is not to be discarded lightly nor rebelled against too openly. Whereas women and criminals may stand in for the protagonist's rebellion, it is quite a common strategy within *film noir* for a figure representing the law (a district attorney, a policeman, an investigator) to stand for the protagonist's desire to punish such transgression (e.g. in *The Woman in the Window, Double Indemnity*). The use of such a figure is generally fairly straightforward, as is the use of criminals as alter egos, though the various ways in which they symbolically cohabit in the protagonist's psyche may be more or less interesting and explicit. But the use of women is more complex, for they may represent not only the projected dangers of rejecting 'normality' but the oppressiveness of embracing it as well. Generally, the two functions are assigned to separate women, but more than one *femme fatale* turns out to be a would-be wife.

In summary, then, the divided protagonist of *film noir* projects deviant aspects of himself on to the genre's main representatives of 'otherness', yet is caught between such deviance and his privileged status (embodied in his point of view which defines the *film noir* world). This reflects the historical reality of the returning GI, so recently licensed to kill, who must now resume

Still: Dead Reckoning – *in her apartment with Rip (Humphrey Bogart), Coral (Lizabeth Scott) seems almost domesticated.*

the incompatible role of the 'normal' family man. ('After World War II, sleepless nights and doubts came to young men once taught "Thou shalt not kill" . . . But everyone was telling them that they were heroes' MacPherson, p.50.) Women function within *film noir* as agents both of prescriptive normality and of its transgression, oppressive in the former role and dangerous in the latter. The films are not predominantly about the misrecognition of women as subordinate (a misrecognition which guarantees male privilege), but, rather, about that of women as alien (thus masking a crisis in *male* identity projected on to women). The films, in other words, are fundamentally about men with women used as decoys in a strategy of denial.

Recurring Patterns

One of the most striking patterns in *film noir*, given the fact that critical attention has tended to focus on the centrality to the genre of the *femme fatale*, is the prominence of the 'marrying woman' who sets her sights on the hero, to his obvious but unavowed discomfiture, an unease of which such a woman is fully aware, even if the hero is not. Thus, Coral (Lizabeth Scott) in *Dead Reckoning* (John Cromwell, 1947) warns Rip (Humphrey Bogart), 'Careful what you say to me, I'm the marrying type,' though she is also the film's *femme fatale*, making her more complex than the following purer examples of the type:

Kathleen (Lucille Ball): What is it, Brad?

Brad (Mark Stevens): I got a feeling something's closing in on me. I don't know what it is.

Kathleen: That's me . . .

Brad: I wouldn't be so jumpy just about you.

Kathleen: Oh, yes, you would, 'cause I'm playing for keeps, remember?

       The Dark Corner (Henry Hathaway, 1946)

Paula (Pamela Britton): Frank, you'll take me with you, won't you? You will, won't you? Or am I crowding you?

Frank (Edmond O'Brien): What do you mean, crowding me?

Paula: Maybe you do need this week away alone. Maybe we both do. I know what's going on inside of you, Frank. You're just like any other man, only a little more so. You have a feeling of being trapped, hemmed in, and you don't know whether or not you like it.

       D.O.A. (Rudolph Maté, 1949)

Still: The Dark Corner. *The marrying kind – Kathleen (Lucille Ball) with Brad (Mark Stevens).*

The dialogue from *The Dark Corner* is particularly interesting in that it echoes a statement which Brad makes elsewhere in the film: 'I feel all dead inside. I'm backed up in a dark corner and I don't know who's hitting me.' He's referring to his uneasy feeling of being framed, but the verbal parallels with the previously quoted dialogue where Kathleen explicitly links his anxiety to *her* are fairly pointed. In some sense, then, the film's focus on crime serves to mask or stand in for his unacknowledged anxieties about marriage (significantly, the crime for which he's being framed, here and typically, is the avenging by a husband of his wife's infidelity). The same pattern is present in *Nightmare* (Maxwell Shane, 1956), though in this instance the main protagonist actually does kill the lover of the errant wife, although admittedly in self-defence *and* under hypnosis (a case of the narrative protesting his innocence a bit too much, perhaps).

A different but related pattern emerges, however, in those films where the central protagonist helps a 'bad wife' to murder her husband (e.g. *Double Indemnity*; *The Postman Always Rings Twice*, Tay Garnett, 1946), rather than his standing in for the husband in his revenge upon her. Here the sense of surrender to the woman and the crime and of the inevitably doomed conclusion suggests that the hero is somehow acquiescing in his own destruction as well, the killing of the husband in order to take his place suggesting or predicting his own eventual demise through his association with the same woman. The relation between such bad wives and the good would-be wives who aim to domesticate the hero is not merely dichotomous, the hero appearing in both contexts as an oddly passive potential victim to whom unforeseen things continually happen as though by chance or fate, or in any event as though beyond his control.

The marrying women seem to know the score, whereas the men they want to marry seem both to resist marriage and to deny that they are doing so, unable to resolve their ambivalence until the dangerous alternatives to a conventional marriage have proved to be dead ends. This happens literally in *D.O.A.*: Frank Bigelow is incurably poisoned and doomed to death before he can – 'safely' – feel sentimental about marriage and family (it is after his condition is confirmed at the hospital – 'I don't think you fully understand, Bigelow. You've been murdered' – that a lingering shot is provided of his looking at a little girl, and then at a young romantic couple). Marriage and family can be idealised only when they are doomed, as in *The Big Heat* (Fritz Lang, 1953), or out of reach.

This pattern finds its rawest and crudest realisation in the novels of Mickey Spillane. Thus, in *I, the Jury*, private detective Mike Hammer's descriptions of Charlotte as a potential wife impossibly idealise her both in domestic terms (fixing his favourite meals, taking a friend's baby for a walk in the park) and as a beautiful blonde. She is seemingly so perfect that, when Hammer returns to her side after making love to another woman (who tells him, 'Oh, but you don't have to marry me. I don't want that. It takes all the fun out of it'), and asks Charlotte, 'You been here all the time?', she replies, 'Yep. Just like a good little wife, I sit home while my husband is out with other women.' What is striking is both the excess of the fantasy and the inappropriateness of his marriage plans (she is a psychiatrist who will give up her job to be a stereotypical wife when they marry). That she turns out to be the killer of the war buddy who saved his life and whom he has vowed to avenge is a foregone conclusion, though his reaction to this knowledge is surprisingly overt in the relief it expresses: 'Happy, happy. How could I be so happy? I had the WHY, but how could I be so happy? It wasn't right.' In *Vengeance Is Mine*, Spillane goes even further in rendering impossible (for Hammer) the relationship with the beloved (here

Still: Out of the Past. *The key relationship – Whit (Kirk Douglas) and Jeff (Robert Mitchum), here with Stefanos (Paul Valentine).*

idealised in metaphors of divinity – her name is Juno). She is not merely the killer, but turns out to be a man, and Hammer is thereby saved from marriage on two counts. Thus Hammer's resistance to marriage is denied by Spillane, with external contingencies replacing internal doubt. In general, as with the examples from the Spillane novels, the regaining of control in those films where the hero ultimately triumphs is linked to a repressive denial of his own 'deviance' and an often nasty rejection of the other characters – often women – held responsible for his fate. The Dick Powell character in *Pitfall* (André de Toth, 1948) provides a particularly unpleasant example, though here the transgressive woman is seen to have tempted him away from an already existing marriage, rather than preserving his bachelorhood through her own deviance, as in Spillane.

The hero's dividedness and his lack of self-knowledge are staples of the genre, played upon in the swing between the presentation of the protagonist as a controlling presence, on the one hand, and his doomed or even explicitly acquiescent surrender to narrative loss of control, on the other, a loss ferociously denied through violent self-assertion in Spillane, but taken on and experienced with equal vehemence elsewhere. In each case, what is being denied is the hero's personal responsibility for his deviant desires. Thus, in *D.O.A.* (a remarkably clear example of the pattern in question), virtually the first words of the film are Frank's 'I'd like to see the man in charge' (at the police station), echoing the 'I'd like to see someone in charge here' which leads into his meeting with Halliday (his own murderer)

in the flashback. That a murderer and a policeman are 'in charge', whereas Frank clearly is not, starkly encapsulates the film's suggestion of his own wished-for abnegation of responsibility both in the expression and suppression of his deviant desires. Significantly, it was while Frank was trying to pick up another woman in a bar that the poisoned drink (which he denied was his even as he drank it) was substituted for his own.

In some cases, the protagonist's surrender to powerlessness (or even self-destruction) rather than his being shown to acknowledge and take responsibility for such 'abnormal' aspects of the self, may be linked to the hero's closeness to another man. Rip, in *Dead Reckoning*, can say of his war buddy, 'I loved him more,' but the avowal is more typically unspoken. *Out of the Past* (Jacques Tourneur, 1947) is perhaps the best example of a hero deliberately turning his back on the prospect of uncomplicated domesticity, even though he knows the alternative to be doomed. This film is in some ways atypical in that the hero, Jeff (Robert Mitchum), seems to have an unusual degree of knowledge. He acquiesces in his betrayal by Kathie (Jane Greer), submitting to it almost willingly and certainly knowingly. One way of making sense of this is by seeing as the film's key relationship not that between Kathie and Jeff but that between Jeff and Whit (Kirk Douglas). Jeff acquiesces in Kathie's betrayal of him, that is, as an unconsciously willed and self-inflicted punishment for his own betrayal of Whit, who had said Jeff was both honest and smart (that is to say, he had trusted him). Jeff's reinvolvement with Whit can be seen as a kind of restitution. So Jeff's knowledge of Kathie's character masks a deeper lack of self-knowledge, linked, perhaps, to his relationship to Whit.

Fritz Lang, with his usual clarity, makes the dark sides of his protagonists overt. Thus, in *Man Hunt* (1941), when Thorndike (Walter Pidgeon) is trapped in a cave by the Nazi Quive-Smith (George Sanders), the latter accuses him of self-deception:

'You've refused to face your secret self, Thorn-dike. From the moment you crossed the frontier, you became an unconscious assassin. I'm going to show you to yourself as you really are, Thorndike. I'm going to break through that civilised English mask you were born with. I'm going to show you what you really are and were, an assassin.'

At this point, he shows Thorndike a hat and brooch belonging to a young girl, Jerry (Joan Bennett), who had helped Thorndike and is now dead. Though the issue in question is whether or not Thorndike had really intended to kill Hitler, the unspoken implication is that he is Jerry's assassin, having used her and endangered her for his own safety. Although Lang insists on the darker side of his protagonists' minds, however, he is equally aware of the ways in which they internalise the law and its dictates as well. Thus, in *Scarlet Street*, a reporter, pointing to his heart, states of a guilty man who escapes punishment:

'The problem's just moved in here, where it can never get out – right here, in solitary. So what? So you go right on punishing yourself. You can't get away with it. Never. I'd rather have the judge give me the works than have to do it to myself.'

In other films, like *Double Indemnity*, punishment is more usually externalised into a friendly but upright father-figure, here Keyes (Edward G. Robinson), though there is a suggestive pun, perhaps, in Walter Neff's 'I always carry my own keys', in reply to the maid who tells him the Dietrichson liquor cabinet is locked when she has him wait in the living room. Such puns and metaphors seem to be sprinkled throughout the dialogue and visual imagery of *film noir* – playing with the medium – almost as symptoms or traces of the aspects of the hero which he is unable consciously to acknowledge (in *D.O.A.*, as Frank Bigelow is taken away, presumably to be killed, his would-be killer taunts, 'Just Bigelow and me and baby makes three,' 'baby' being the gun which threatens Bigelow's life). In this respect, Chandler is of great interest. His private eye, Philip Marlowe, is a man of integrity who resists the temptations of the *femme fatale* and thus seems less divided and interestingly less typical

of the genre than has usually been claimed. Nonetheless, certain recurrences in Chandler's work, such as the omnipresence of verbal play, as well as the sense of the law as corrupt and the way Marlowe's loss of control is often linked to a dive into unconsciousness, are worth further study and, I suspect, might undermine Chandler's apparently clear-cut protagonist. (Chandler himself seems to have been unaware of such possible readings of his work. In his famous essay, 'The Simple Art of Murder', he suggests that the protagonist of serious detective fiction 'must be, to use a rather weathered phrase, a man of honour, by instinct, by inevitability without thought of it, and certainly without saying it. He must be the best man in his world and a good enough man for any world' *Pearls Are a Nuisance*, Penguin, Harmondsworth, 1977, p.198).

The unease with which the male protagonist of *film noir* confronts the expectation that he occupy his allotted place within society is much more overt when such a protagonist is the villain of the piece. Thus, Robert Mannette (Gene Kelly) in *Christmas Holiday* (Robert Siodmak, 1944), describing his highly respectable pedigree to Abigail (Deanna Durbin), tells her:

'Oh, it does something to you from the time you're able to see pretty near, you get standards set for you and ideals and ambitions that, well, you know you're just not up to them. I do what I can but I don't seem to be able to . . . Well, it's just that so much is expected of you because you're a Mannette.'

The desire (seen as predominantly male) to step aside, to deviate, from one's ideologically ordained position and path is a recurring theme of *film noir*, though not exclusive to it (the Henry James story, 'The Jolly Corner', for example, is interesting in this regard, as is Hawthorne's 'Wakefield'), but, because of the privileges of that position, such desires, when not ascribed to the villain in order to be condemned, are often either barely acknowledged or interlaced with doubt. Various strategies, including those indicated in my examples, address themselves to such waverings and hesitations, but the indecisiveness is never fully resolved, at least not in the context of *film noir* when such issues, as I've argued, were particularly alive.

Conclusion

It seems to me that the following characteristics, taken together, mark off for consideration a substantial number of *films noirs*:

1) A central male protagonist whose point of view is privileged through such devices as first-person narration (presented either as diegetic – often in confessional form to a figure of authority such as a policeman or priest – or as extra-diegetic) and subjective framing devices like flashbacks or dreams.

2) An undermining of this point of view a) through labyrinthine plots which seem to elude the protagonist's attempts to give them coherence through his narration, and b) through breaks in the protagonist's consciousness (he's knocked out, drugged, hypnotised, or develops amnesia, say), and thus in his control both over the narrative and within it. This loss of control may to an extent be seen as unconsciously willed (or succumbed to) by the protagonist.

3) A protagonist who is divided, but often lacks self-knowledge, this lack projected on to an enigmatic woman or the intricacies of the plot. Thus, lack of self-knowledge is externalised into lack of knowledge of the world. The *film noir* protagonist may be divided in one of several ways: a) Between a somewhat idealised 'there and then' (most typically represented by the war) and the 'here and now' of the film's present-tense frame. b) Between privilege (which constricts) and deviance (which puts one on the wrong side both of the law and of the marriage bed). c) Between loyalty to buddies and attraction to dames. This conflict is overt if it is the buddy's dame to whom the protagonist is attracted, though the buddy – especially if a war buddy – is typically dead. The close male friend may, in some cases, be a figure representative of the law and thus opposed to the protagonist's attraction to a criminal woman. In other cases, the hero's leaning toward him may have an implicit homo-erotic charge. d) Between *femmes fatales* and domesticating women, *both* types presented as threats. The *film noir* hero is usually unmarried – where he's married (as in *The Woman in the Window* or *Scarlet Street*), the genre veers toward male-centred melodrama – but he is often of an age where the possibilities of marriage and family seem about to pass him by (think of Bogart). The chance of marriage seems to be now or never, such a protagonist teetering on the brink of confirmed bachelorhood. Domestic murders figure prominently in *film noir* plots and may reflect the hero's own anxieties and undermine the distinction between these two female types.

So *film noir* dramatises points of crisis – often implicit – in the life of its protagonist, such as those between wartime and peace, and bachelor-hood and marriage.

4) A mood of pervasive anxiety produced by these conflicts and the struggle to resolve them, both by the protagonist and the film, often sig-nalling on either of their parts particularly sensitive areas of conflict. Various narrative strategies of resolution may include one or more of the fol-lowing: a) The protagonist's death. b) The death of one half of the dichotomous pair (e.g. the buddy or the dame, the *femme fatale* or the domesticating woman). c) The transformation of the *femme fatale* into the domesticating woman (she was really good all along and can be mar-ried, though life won't be dull with such a wife) or vice versa (she was really bad and can be rejected or killed, her guilt letting the hero off the hook). d) The exorcism of the past (e.g. by avenging the war buddy) or the living through of the consequences of a temporary lapse into de-viance. In both cases, imminent domesticity may beckon just the other side of the film's final frame. This mood of anxiety, however, is never fully dispersed insofar as the *film noir* protagonist fails to gain conscious awareness of the nature of the conflicts which underlie it. Such narrative anxi-ety is, further, reflected in the visual style of film noir which provides a continuing disturbance to the apparent reintegration of the hero and reso-lutions of the plot.

Coda: The Man Who Knew Too Much

It seems to me reasonable to expect a broad range of films made in the period during and following World War II to reflect the concerns and anxieties which the adaptation to war and the subsequent return to normal provoked. I have maintained that *film noir* was especially well suited, in its visual style and narrative devices, to explore such concerns (albeit in a disguised and implicit fashion) from the point of view of the white American male. This point of view is constructed through frequent first-person narration and subjective framing devices such as dreams and flashbacks, but the control over nar-rative events which such subjectivity seems to imply is undercut by the bewildering complexi-ties of so many *film noir* plots and the protago-nist's lapses into unconsciousness which punctuate such films. The striving for control (both over events and over their narration), in other words, is met by loss of control, and this pattern of struggle and surrender reflects the ambivalence of the protagonist (and his 'real life' counter-parts) towards society and his place within it, a place which both privileges and constricts him.

In *The Man Who Knew Too Much* (Alfred Hitchcock, 1956), a thriller made late in the *film noir* period, the protagonist's struggle for control has largely been lost, and this loss of power within his life is matched by his lack of narrative privilege over his wife (on the former point, note the play made of the wife having a male-sounding name, Jo, and the way in which, through her fame, she eclipses her husband in London). *The Man Who Knew Too Much* is not *a film noir*, despite *noir* elements within it, but its central male character can be seen as the *film noir* pro-tagonist ten years or so further along in his life. The mood of anxiety of *film noir*, as its protago-nist struggles to nudge out a place for himself in the interstices between deviance and domesticity, has now become a mood of at least partial resig-nation ('*Che sera sera*') to the domesticity finally opted for by both husband and wife.

A number of elements within the film support this reading. Consider the two reasons given by Ben McKenna (James Stewart) as to why he has

taken his family to Morocco (where all the trouble begins):

1) On the bus to Marrakesh:

Louis Bernard (Daniel Gélin): What brings you to Marrakesh?

Ben McKenna: Well, you see, we were attending a medical convention in Paris and I thought as much as we were in Europe I'd come down and see Morocco again.

Hank McKenna (Christopher Olsen): Daddy liberated Africa.

Ben McKenna: Well, I was stationed up in Casablanca at an army field hospital during the war.

2) As Ben and his wife Jo are talking about how the various operations on Ben's patients have paid for their trip:

Jo McKenna (Doris Day): What would they say if they heard us?

Ben McKenna: You know, one of the reasons I came to a place like Marrakesh is so we *could* say things like that without everybody hearing us.

Jo McKenna: Well, I'd like to say something where nobody could hear us.

Ben McKenna: This is the safest place.

Jo McKenna: When are we going to have another baby? You're the doctor, you have all the answers.

Ben McKenna: Yeah, but this is the first time I've ever heard the question.

So, for the Stewart character, Marrakesh, as a place and more symbolically as a state of mind, is associated with the war (and, significantly, with liberation) and opposed to the claustrophobia of Indianapolis society and 'normal' family life

Still: The Man Who Knew Too Much. *In the Marrakesh restaurant, the two couples, Jo and Ben McKenna (Doris Day and James Stewart) and Mr and Mrs Drayton (Bernard Miles and Brenda de Banzie).*

(e.g. Jo's desire for another child, which Ben doesn't seem to share).

Dr and Mrs McKenna are initially presented as cloying stereotypes of the happy all-American couple (their child Hank is particularly unappealing in his self-conscious cuteness), but this is soon revealed as a façade and progressively and consistently demolished (one is reminded of the comparable innocents abroad in Hitchcock's *Rich and Strange*, 1932). Marital tensions emerge in a number of areas. Jo has had to give up a highly successful career as a singer and obviously resents it. Thus (in a conversation which literally gives Ben a pain in the neck, as he and Jo turn to answer the Draytons at an adjoining restaurant table):

Mrs Drayton (Brenda de Banzie): When are you coming back to London?

Jo McKenna: Possibly never again – professionally.

Mrs Drayton: Oh, don't say you're giving up the stage.

Jo McKenna: Well, temporarily.

Ben McKenna: Well, it's just that I'm a doctor, and you know a doctor's wife never has much time.

Jo McKenna: What my husband is trying to say is that Broadway musical shows are not produced in Indianapolis, Indiana.

Ben McKenna: Well, no, I . . .

Jo McKenna: Of course, we *could* live in New York. I hear the doctors aren't starving there, are they?

Ben McKenna: Well, it's not that I have any objection to working in New York. It's just that it'd be kind of hard on my patients to come all the way from Indianapolis for treatment.

Ben does not acknowledge the validity of her resentment, which here erupts so readily, and he attempts to disguise with a weak joke his absence of any real reason to live in Indianapolis rather than New York. He continually challenges her perceptions and behaviour (e.g. her earlier – as it turns out, justified – suspicions of Bernard). Thus, after he has insisted she take sedatives before he reveals that Hank has been kidnapped, she replies, 'Six months ago you told me I took too many pills.' But he continues, 'You've been talking a blue streak, you've been walking around in circles,' to which her response is a simple 'I haven't.'

Most crucial, however, are the parallels built up between the McKennas and the Draytons (the latter couple a distorted and criminal version of the former, the passing of the McKenna child Hank from one couple's custody to the other providing an important link between them). These parallels occur in several places:

1) Bernard mistakes the McKennas for the Draytons.

Ben McKenna: He started to talk to us, and the reason he started to talk to us was 'cause he was on the lookout for a suspicious married couple.

Jo McKenna: There's nothing very suspicious-looking about us, is there?

Ben McKenna: No, because he was wrong. It was a different married couple.

2) When Ben breaks open the door where Mrs Drayton has Hank in the embassy, she – and the film audience – thinks it's her husband arriving to kill the boy.

3) In both couples, conflicts develop between husband and wife. Thus, whereas Mr Drayton is willing to kill Hank to save himself, Mrs Drayton wants to save the boy.

These parallels (and the visual presentation of the Draytons in the restaurant as mirror-images of the McKennas) suggest that Drayton can be read as Ben McKenna's alter ego, with Mrs Drayton as Jo's. So Drayton's willingness to kill Hank can be seen as a projected version of Ben's resentment not just of his marriage, but of his son. Although Ben consciously strives to save Hank, it is Jo to whom the film accords most success in achieving this end (Ben goes to the wrong Ambrose Chapel, unlike Jo who discovers the correct one; Ben is later knocked out just as he's about to reach Hank). That the love of Jo for her son to an extent excludes Ben is made clear by both of the film's renditions of 'Che sera sera'. In the earlier one, mother and

child dance together, with Ben in an adjoining room. At the embassy, near the end of the movie, Hank hears Jo singing as she begins the third verse of the song:

'When I grew up and fell in love,
I asked my sweetheart, what lies ahead?
Will we have rainbows, day after day?
Here's what my sweetheart said . . .'

A verse or two later, she repeats these lines, and it is precisely after the words, 'Here's what my sweetheart said . . .', that she stops and hears Hank's whistled reply. Clearly there are no rainbows with Ben (an earlier verse asking 'should I sing songs?' reminds us of her curtailed career), and Hank has usurped his place in her affections.

So the McKennas' marital history can be reconstructed as a series of mutual resentments in the name of love and destiny, a destiny construed ('What will be will be, the future's not ours to see') as outside one's control and one's knowledge. The film's title and the links between McKenna and Drayton centre the narrative on McKenna's predicament, but neither Ben nor Jo is privileged by the narrative to the extent that Ben would be were the film a typical *film noir*. Ben's status has been eroded both within the marriage and, compared to *film noir*, within the narrative structure of the film. Yet the generic connections remain. The man who knew too much, like so many *noir* protagonists, turns out to be the man who knows too little, at least about himself. His resentment of Hank (and the Stewart character's chilling line, 'Why do we have to have all these kids?' in *It's A Wonderful Life*, Frank Capra, 1946, has resonance here) remains hidden and unacknowledged. Just as Pottersville (the nightmare city) is implicit in Bedford Falls in *It's a Wonderful Life*, and just as the kidnapping of one's child in Marrakesh is an unconsciously willed consequence of married life in Indianapolis in *The Man Who Knew Too Much*, so *film noir* and its concerns stalk so many domestic and small-town films of the postwar years.

Still: The Man Who Knew Too Much – *the killing of Louis Bernard (Daniel Gélin).*

PSYCHOANALYSIS AND FILM NOIR

Deborah Thomas

'The law tells us: You will not marry your mother, and you will not kill your father. And we docile subjects say to ourselves: so *that's* what I wanted!' Gilles Deleuze and Félix Guattari, *Anti-Oedipus: Capitalism and Schizophrenia* (Athlone Press, London 1984).

'It was his story against mine, but of course I told my story better.' Dixon Steele (Humphrey Bogart) in *In a Lonely Place* (Nicholas Ray, 1950).

Classical Hollywood films in all their variety and complexity offer substantial, and sometimes elusive, riches for the viewer and critic, – and it should not be forgotten that every critic is, and should be, a viewer first, assailed by pleasures whose sources are not necessarily obvious from the start. The riches can be mined through a number of critical approaches which, while not falsifying the details of the films, may nonetheless determine the particular emphases of the analyses. In short, what we find of interest in a film depends not only on what is there to be found, but on the choice of which aspects we choose to examine (a function of our critical approach), these combined determinants producing critics who, at their best, are both scrupulous and engaged. A feminist may not find what a Freudian will see, though both may be equally true to selected details of the film in question, and, of course, the two approaches may to an extent be combined. But, even then, possible angles of approach will not be exhausted. Further details may be both amenable to further framings, critical choreographies and elucidations, and also the source of additional (as yet unanalysed) pleasures. One may also rethink details already analysed in one critical context by situating them in a new conceptual frame. All of this is obvious enough, but I say it to make clear that I intend what follows to be necessarily partial, not conclusive, though perhaps facilitating a rethinking of *film noir* in ways which will address some of the real pleasures it provides.

It is often appropriate to dismiss a piece of critical analysis as simply wrong (insofar as it misrepresents a film, seeing camera movements, say, where none exist, or omitting a crucial scene or word or gesture which might undermine one's claims). It is equally possible to find two analyses incompatible (and to be compelled to choose between them) insofar as their conclusions or generalisations cannot simultaneously be the case, particularly with regard to the provenance of the details under discussion and the film's relationship to the world outside it (e.g. to psychic mechanisms in real people). Here what is at issue is not the accuracy of the description provided, but the truth of the explanations. Psychoanalysis, like other critical approaches to film, has both descriptive and explanatory uses, bringing aspects of a film to our notice that we might otherwise miss (insisting, implicitly or explicitly, on their importance, and providing terms in which they may be understood), and providing an explanation from outside the film for their presence within it: 'Look!' on the one hand, 'Because . . .' on the other. Of course, descriptive terms are not objective labels and inevitably involve a degree of interpretation and explanation as well, so the distinction is not a hard and fast one.

Where contradictory explanations are not at issue, it frequently happens that a complementary, mutually compatible set of accounts of the same film or films exist side by side in the literature, even if all of us have our own preferences for the emphases, shadings and perceived depth and skill of some over others. The present account is meant to exist in such a complementary partnership with the preceding article in this book. I will retrace some of the ground covered there, though re-mapping it in broadly psychoanalytic terms, but I shall also look obliquely at the genre as a whole to try to locate the source of its pleasures, not only in the obvious mainstream of its narrative events but in the nooks and crannies of the films' imagery and language. Whereas my earlier piece emphasised the bleakness and anxiety of the genre, I now intend to examine its pleasures and delights, not only for the viewers, but at times, surprisingly, for its protagonists as well.

Why Psychoanalysis? Why Film Noir?

In its broadest sense, psychoanalysis is about bodies in culture (*see* Elizabeth Wright, *Psychoanalytical Criticism: Theory in Practice*, Methuen, London, 1984), and the journey each of us makes from infancy to adulthood, a journey both biological and cultural, with both losses and gains. Unlike other developmental approaches, however, it starts from the premise that appearances are profoundly deceptive. Thus, the cornerstones of a psychoanalytical approach are repression and the unconscious, with Sigmund Freud himself insisting on the Oedipus complex as a third *sine qua non*; more of this below. Psychoanalysis provides an approach to both illness and 'normality' (as well as the continuities between them), and it is largely in the latter guise that it is of use for our present purposes. Psychoanalytical man (and we may as well be gender-specific here, since our present concern is, above all, with men) is the product both of his instincts and of his history (his past). Where neurotic, he is 'trying to dispose of unfinished business' from the past (Peter Gay, *Freud: A Life for Our Time*, Dent, London, 1988, p.146), though other forces are at work to resolve these tensions in compromises below the level of awareness. More generally, 'the desire to recall is countered by the desire to forget' (Gay, p.128). All of this is a fairly apt description of the *film noir* protagonist as well. The frequency of flashback structures in the genre is suggestive of the neurotic's compulsion to repeat, as the *noir* protagonist, too, reworks the past to try to master it through his narration. Yet such narrative coherence is illusory, a denial of needs which spill out elsewhere. All is not what it seems in the *noir* and psychoanalytical worlds alike. Whatever the flaws in a neat equation of psychoanalytical man with his *noir* counterpart, there are enough apparent points of contact to suggest that a psychoanalytical approach might have interesting pay-offs (if pitfalls, too). And yet, psychoanalysis of *film noir*'s men *tout court* is a wrong-headed endeavour. The mood of *film noir* is not delimited by the point of view of its protagonists. Its imagery and language – visual as much as verbal – inhabit all the corners of the frame and all the moments of its events, whether the central protagonist is present or absent, narrating or mute.

A further reason for scrutinising the genre through the lens of psychoanalysis is that *film noir* is openly asking for it. Its characters are constantly and frankly described in Freudian terms. Thus:

'Every night I dream. I read somewhere about a . . . about a kind of a doctor. A psych-something. You tell your dream, you don't have to dream it anymore.' Raven (Alan Ladd) in *This Gun for Hire* (Frank Tuttle, 1942).

'When it was all over, a psychoanalyst said that Robert's relations with his mother were pathological. All I know is that Robert was the only thing in the world she cared about. He wasn't just her son, he was . . . he was her everything.' Abigail (Deanna Durbin) in *Christmas Holiday* (Robert Siodmak, 1944).

'Shame on you, Johnny. Any psychiatrist would tell you that your thought-associations are *very* revealing.' Gilda (Rita Hayworth) in *Gilda* (Charles Vidor, 1946).

However, such obvious Freudianisings are perhaps too overt, allowing the psychoanalytical concerns of the texts to be too easily ascribed to the individual pathology of a specific character (and thus safely dismissed), rather than to the *film noir* world as a whole, as the imagery and stylistic disturbances of these films suggest. There are several problems with such reductive readings: their complacency, which encourages a blindness to the social implications of the films, the over-emphasis on deliberate psychoanalytic dialogue at the expense of visual and narrative complexities, and the vastly oversimplified and misleading version of Freud which we're asked to digest, one which dilutes the more radical implications of a psychoanalytical approach.

At the time of *film noir*'s brief predominance, Freud was 'in the air'. As early as the mid-'twenties, in fact, he 'had become a household name' (Gay, p.454), and the technical terms of psychoanalysis were 'embodied in the popular slang of both America and England' (Gay, p.452). Samuel Goldwyn, not one to miss an opportunity, had even purportedly asked Freud to write or advise on a screenplay; Freud refused (Gay, p.454). With the accession of Hitler in 1933, many European analysts, fleeing a climate now grown hostile to their work, ended up in the United States, to be absorbed (as exiles) into a fully medicalised profession (and one in conflict with Freud over the latter's insistence on the importance of lay analysis and the relevance of psychoanalysis to much broader social and cultural issues), which diminished and ultimately removed their sociological edge (*see* Russell Jacoby, *The Repression of Psychoanalysis: Otto Fenichel and the Political Freudians*, University of Chicago Press, 1986). Popularised versions of Freud – reflected in the capsule commentaries within *film noir* (and other genres as well – including Fred Astaire as a psychiatrist in *Carefree*, Mark Sandrich, 1938) – were cultural currency by the 'forties, but hardly an incisive critical tool.

So we must look not at what the films are *saying* (in terms of overt Freud) but at what they *do* (in terms of a highly complex and varied set of interacting images and concerns): what sorts of body and bodily experience are represented in *film noir*, and what are the metaphors used? Which needs and conflicts are being dramatised and addressed? What is the relationship between the streams of desire that flow through these films and the cultural structures which contain and re-route them? These are questions that psychoanalysis may help us to frame and confront.

Whose Psychoanalysis?

Psychoanalysts, whether extending the boundaries of psychoanalytical theory or applying psychoanalysis to particular case-studies, necessarily go into much greater theoretical depth and detail than do those who apply psychoanalysis to an understanding of literature or film. Whole areas of psychoanalysis (for example, its therapeutic effectiveness and its diagnostics) are of only peripheral interest in an understanding of cultural texts, where 'normal' psychic mechanisms provide the models for the processes at work in literature and film. But even here, psychoanalysis is often rifled in a somewhat random and arbitrary manner to turn up what may be of value. Freud's own accounts of works of art are themselves multifarious. At times he analyses characters precisely as though they were real and accessible to such an approach; at others he reminds us – and himself – that they are not; he does both in his study of J.V. Jensen's 'Gravida', (in *The Pelican Freud Library*, vol.14, Penguin, Harmondsworth 1985, as are the other essays cited in this paragraph), sometimes he focuses, through the work, on the artist (as in his essay on Leonardo Da Vinci), at times on the audience ('Psychopathic Characters on the Stage'). Elsewhere he even produces an account (of Michelangelo's Moses) which, while commendable in its meticulous attention to detail, is barely psychoanalytical at all, if quite convincing. I linger on Freud because he anticipates so many of the difficulties of such endeavours – among them: how do authors come to devise dreams obedient to the rules of 'real' dreams (*see* the study of Jensen's 'Gravida'); how is the experience of life different from that of literature ('The "Uncanny" '); what role is played by the pleasures of aesthetic form ('Creative Writing and Day-Dreaming')? In some ways, his practice is exemplary in its concentration on textual details, hesitating in its conclusions until textual corroboration – or what Freud takes to be textual corroboration – can be found. Nevertheless, the application of psychoanalysis to cultural texts is scarcely straightforward: where are we to look, both in the psychoanalytical literature and in the movies?

Elizabeth Wright has done an excellent job of outlining and distinguishing a multitude of ways in which psychoanalysis, in all its varieties, has been used, and this is not the place to repeat her account, which deserves to be read in full. It is useful, however, to note the general characteristics she argues to be central to any psychoanalytical approach:

1) that psychoanalytical criticism investigates texts 'for the workings of a rhetoric seen as analogous to the mechanisms of the psyche';

2) that it must take into account 'the relationships between author and text, and between reader and text';

3) that these relationships, more generally, are 'to do with the constitution of the self in social systems at given moments in history' (Wright, p.6).

Of course, it remains to be determined precisely which psychic mechanisms are analogous to which rhetorical ones. The later Freud sees the mind's topography in terms of a tripartite id/ego/super-ego structure, and one can certainly apply this in such a way that the functions of these three mental entities are projected on to aspects of films or characters within them: thus, for example, the private eye (ego) can be seen as caught between the demands of criminals (id) and the law (super-ego). To an extent, I have drawn on such a model in the preceding article. However, a Freudian understanding of the id tends to characterise it in negative terms as the locus of the socially unacceptable (Klaus Theweleit, *Male Fantasies I*, Polity Press, 1987, p.213), making it difficult to use it as a means of naming the positive strivings of desire (and their representations in texts). Thus, filmic criminals, Indians, and monsters have been tarred with the same psychoanalytic brush as representations of distorted desires, repressed and re-emergent. Although Freud had a 'generous vision of libido' (Gay, 1988, p.148), which, Gay argues, had democratic and subversive elements, and though his therapeutic practice and educative prescriptions aimed at lifting the burdens of excessive repression, he was ultimately a committed rationalist and an advocate of the well-adjusted ego (thus, the famous dictum: 'where id was, there ego shall be', *The Pelican Freud Library*, vol.2, 1973, p.112).

In contrast, Gilles Deleuze and Félix Guattari, in their influential *Anti-Oedipus*, see the Freudian ego as hopelessly enmeshed in the power relations of society as a whole: thus, in Klaus Theweleit's words, 'as long as domination remains, the hopeless, self-destructive task of trying to comprehend yourself as an "ego", a monad with an identity, will inevitably resemble the colonial African's determined effort to feel French. Compare Fanon's famous case of the Senegalese who was the only Frenchman trying to write like Corneille' (Theweleit, p.416). Not only is the Freudian ego seen as the product of social relations of power, but the inevitability of the whole topographical scheme is itself called into question. Deleuze and Guattari turn Freud on his head, de-Oedipalising the Freudian unconscious. That is, they see the unconscious as unstructured productive force, using the word 'machinic' as a positive term to denote such flowings independent of specific objects. Such terms as 'incest' and 'castration' are impositions from outside. Whereas, for Freud, the unconscious is innately Oedipal and incestuous desire primary, Deleuze and Guattari see such structures as 'a form that Desire assumes because of the repression to which it is subject in society' (Theweleit, p.213). Thus, it is the frustrations of the social world which turn the child back in upon the family, *not* vice versa. Desire aspires to the world, but, frustrated, it falls back upon the family.

As Wright explains, Deleuze and Guattari see unconscious desire as tending to either of two poles, what they call the schizophrenic, 'characterised by multiplicity, proliferation, becoming, flowing, a breaking of boundaries', and what they call the paranoiac, 'marked by its unifying procedures, its search for order' (Wright, p.164). Deleuze and Guattari seek to promote the former and undermine the 'territorialising' tendencies of the latter. The language is political and prescriptive, no mere account of the unconscious, but an advocacy of its positive potentials. Similarly, critics of cultural texts ('schizoanalysts') are enjoined to help liberate the desire implicit in such texts.

I propose to see what such an analysis of *film noir* might look like, while putting aside for now the larger questions of advocacy. Without resolving – or even addressing – questions of whether a Freudian self (understood either as phylogenetically given or as socially constructed) is worth fighting for, and of what degree and mechanisms of repression are required to maintain it, let's provisionally and heuristically adopt the hypothesis that the unconscious is not a seething Freudian cauldron but, rather, the home of positive flowings and desirings which the social world seeks to bind and contain. Does *film noir*'s representation of desire cede any space to such free-floating desiring, as well as to the bound and contained version more familiar to us from Freudian accounts? To what extent are the genre's 'bodies in culture' explicable in such terms?

Male Fantasies

In my summation of Deleuze and Guattari's anti-Freudianism, I have leant heavily on Klaus Theweleit's two-volume *Male Fantasies*, a close look at the language and imagery of German fascism in the period between the two World Wars, which draws on Deleuze and Guattari's ideas. In this immensely ambitious work, Theweleit generates from the specific example of fascist 'soldier males' a European history which is to be understood as the history of the European body, 'its splitting into child and adult, into genders, classes, and fragments of itself' (Theweleit, p.363). He rejects the term 'internalisation' to describe the process whereby cultural prohibitions are absorbed, seeing what is called the super-ego and is seen to inhabit the head, rather, as 'the installation of displeasure and anxiety in the experience of pleasure itself' (Theweleit, p.414). Such corruptions of pleasure need not occur only in the context of an Oedipalised family structure: 'When the guilt-ridden hands of unconsciously violating adults cause the child's body to react in terror, they don't have family names' (Theweleit, p.418). Theweleit decries ideologically-based cultural studies which ignore the body, its experiences and needs: 'They have no category for the desiring-production of the unconscious, from which all reality, "psychic" as well as "social," derives' (Theweleit, p.416). Thus, 'They don't give any thought to the thrills that run through the body of a woman reading a hospital romance; they merely find the errors in her thinking . . . The

real problem isn't that shop-girls have incorrect views about God and doctors. The real problem is that our bodies cramp up when they try to feel pleasure'(Theweleit, pp.416-417).

Theweleit's book is too rich to be susceptible to summary. Its great virtue is its concreteness, its literalness in the descriptions of bodily blockages and flows, which go behind metaphor to the lived experiences of real bodies. The patterns Theweleit finds in the language of the novels and autobiographies of fascist soldiers are convincingly and unremittingly displayed. These soldiers 'freeze up, become icicles in the fact of erotic femininity . . . it isn't enough simply to view this as a defence against the threat of castration; by reacting in that way, in fact, the man holds himself together as an entity, a body with fixed boundaries' (Theweleit, p.244). The working class and communists, as well as women, are seen in terms of floods, streams, oceans, dirt, slime, pulp, against which the body must be tightened lest it dissolve or explode. These men 'want to avoid swimming at all costs, no matter what the stream. They want to stand with both feet and every root firmly anchored in the soil. They want whatever floods may come to rebound against them; they want to stop, and dam up, those floods' (Theweleit, p.230). They are rocks against a raging sea.

For Theweleit, Freudian terms are inadequate: that which, according to Freud, is meant to be unconscious ('incest', 'castration anxiety') is overt in these men; they seem to lack Oedipal forms of 'ego', but are not psychotic insofar as they were 'successful' in their devastating effects upon the world. Barbara Ehrenreich locates the full horror of Theweleit's revelations in the absolute literalness of such a soldier's life:

'What he wants is what he gets, and that is what the Freikorpsmen describe over and over as a "bloody mass": heads with their faces blown off, bodies soaked red in their own blood, rivers clogged with bodies. The reader's impulse is to engage in a kind of mental flight – that is, to "read" the murders as a story about something else, for example sex . . . or the Oedipal triangle . . . or anything to help the mind drift off. But Theweleit insists that we see and not "read" the violence . . . Then the question we have to ask about fascism becomes: How does human desire – or the ceaseless motion of "desiring production", as the radical psychoanalytic theorists Deleuze and Guattari call it – lend itself to the production of death?' (Foreword to Theweleit, pp.xi-xii).

It is important not to conflate these men with the protagonists of *film noir*. Ehrenreich goes on to caution that 'It would be a perverse reading of *Male Fantasies*, and a most slovenly syllogism, which leaps to conclude that "all men are fascists" or that fascism and misogyny are somehow the "same thing" ' (Foreword to Theweleit, p.xv). Whereas Theweleit's subjects were fascists, the protagonists of *film noir* are invented from an

Still: Force of Evil – *Mrs Tucker (Marie Windsor) and Joe (John Garfield).*

anti-fascist standpoint in the context of an anti-fascist war. Whereas these Germans were real (even the novels having a strong autobiographical/biographical edge) and committed real atrocities both before and throughout the Nazi regime, the men in *film noir* are fictions; the central protagonists (if not the villains), and their filmic depictions, are restrained by at least minimal standards of decency.

Nevertheless, Theweleit's central images of floods and dams, flows and blockages, have resonance in the *noir* terrain. Do *noir* men too, like Theweleit's soldier males, seek to ward off perceived chaos through a process of metaphorical and literal solidification? Does the genre's imagery, insofar as it is outside *noir* man's control or awareness, provide a response and commentary on such attempts? Allowing for differences amongst the films and occasional exceptions to the rule, do such patterns, in the main, emerge? It's time to look closely at the films themselves.

The Films

Solidity/softness/fragmentation

'Bet you do push-ups every morning just to keep the belly hard.' Christina (Cloris Leachman) in *Kiss Me, Deadly* (Robert Aldrich, 1955).

'He's a stone, that man.' Mrs Tucker (Marie Windsor) in *Force of Evil* (Abraham Polonsky, 1948).

'All the Penningtons are desperately healthy – real rocks of Gibraltar.' Barby (Rita Johnson) in *Sleep, My Love* (Douglas Sirk, 1947).

'There's not gonna be any slip-up. Nothing sloppy, nothing weak, it's gotta be perfect.' Walter (Fred MacMurray) in *Double Indemnity* (Billy Wilder, 1944).

'Between us, we will make him strong.' Mrs Mannette (Gail Sondergaard) in *Christmas Holiday.*

'I was softening him up for you.' Joe (Brian Donlevy) in *The Big Combo* (Joseph H. Lewis, 1955).

'You're trying to make me go soft.' Raven (Alan Ladd) in *This Gun for Hire.*

'Sometimes, chum, you go soft-headed. I'd like to see any blonde do that to me.' Rip (Humphrey Bogart) in *Dead Reckoning* (John Cromwell, 1947).

'You know, I've always been a little soft in the head where you're concerned.' Wally (Jack Carson) in *Mildred Pierce* (Michael Curtiz, 1945).

'You gotta pull yourself together, fella.' George (Hugh Beaumont) in *The Blue Dahlia* (George Marshall, 1946).

'I tried to hold myself together, but I could feel my nerves pulling me to pieces.' Walter in *Double Indemnity.*

'You're breaking up in little pieces right in front of my eyes, you know . . .' Obregon (Joseph Calleia) in *Gilda.*

'If you need a broken man to love, break your husband.' Joe (John Garfield) in *Force of Evil.*

'Just remember, I'm coming out of this in one piece, Miss Carson.' Jeff (Robert Mitchum) in *Out of the Past* (Jacques Tourneur, 1947).

'I knew I had hold of a red-hot poker, and the time to drop it was before it burned my hand off.' Walter in *Double Indemnity*.

'I felt pretty good – like an amputated leg.' Marlowe (Dick Powell) in *Murder My Sweet* (Edward Dmytryk, 1944).

'I suppose you have to be pretty tough in your line of work, don't you?' Brent (Ward Bond) in *On Dangerous Ground* (Nicholas Ray, 1951).

'What are you getting so tough about?' Clint (Richard Widmark) in *Panic in the Streets* (Elia Kazan, 1950).

'Look, Finlay, this sort of life doesn't bother some soldiers . . . Mitchell isn't like that. Mitchell isn't tough.' Keeley (Robert Mitchum) in *Crossfire* (Dmytryk, 1947).

Bannister: Mike's quite a hero, quite a tough guy. *Jake:* Mister, there ain't no such thing. Bannister (Everett Sloane) and Jake (Louis Merrill) in *The Lady from Shanghai* (Orson Welles, 1948).

'Okay, Marlowe, I said to myself, you're a tough guy – you've been sapped twice, choked, beaten silly with a gun, shot in the arm until you're as crazy as a couple of waltzing mice, now let's see you do something really tough – like putting your pants on.' Marlowe in *Murder My Sweet*.

'Remember, I can get brand-new tough guys for a dime a dozen.' Kathleen (Lucille Ball) in *The Dark Corner* (Henry Hathaway, 1946).

'If you want to play with matches, that's your business. But not in gas-filled rooms.' Frank (Robert Mitchum) in *Angel Face* (Otto Preminger, 1953).

'Gotta be careful how you handle this stuff – they'll pick you up in little pieces.' Ciavelli (Anthony Caruso) in *The Asphalt Jungle* (John Huston, 1950).

'You knew he was dynamite. He has to explode sometimes.' Mel (Art Smith) in *In a Lonely Place* (Ray, 1950).

'Mr Dreyer, the secret you think keeps you safe will blow up in your face.' Leonard (Cornel Wilde) in *The Big Combo*.

Lilly: He'd never been in love before. *Sam:* Poor Ole, when he did fall, it hadda be for dynamite. Lilly (Virginia Christine) and Sam (Sam Levene) in *The Killers* (Siodmak, 1946).

Walter: They give you matches when you buy cigars, you know. All you have to do is ask for 'em. *Keyes:* I don't like them. They always explode in my pocket. Walter (Fred MacMurray) and Keyes (Edward G. Robinson) in *Double Indemnity*.

'They got their hands on the money, then they started shooting. Suddenly out of nowhere the whole crazy thing blew up right in my face.' Steve (Burt Lancaster) in *Criss Cross* (Siodmak, 1948).

'I hate this solidity, the stodginess I'm beginning to feel. To me it's the end of the brightness of life, the end of spirit and adventure.' Wanley (Edward G. Robinson) in *The Woman in the Window* (Fritz Lang, 1944).

Sue: You're John Forbes, average American, backbone of the country. *John:* I don't want to be an average American, backbone of the country. I want somebody else to be the backbone and hold me up. Sue (Jane Wyatt) and John (Dick Powell) in *Pitfall* (André de Toth, 1948).

'You're so darn conscientious you're driving yourself crazy.' Walter in *Double Indemnity*.

'You big boys, what've you got? Front, nothing but front. And when that slips . . .' Brannom (Brad Dexter) in *The Asphalt Jungle*.

The bodies of *film noir* men take a lot of buffeting. The central protagonist is typically tough, his body boundaries firm and well-defined, in contrast to the fat, soft villains who provide cautionary reminders of the body gone bad. The solid is the strong, the fit, yet a degree of irony pervades the self-perceptions of at least some of the men (for example, the way Marlowe humorously pulls in his stomach when Geiger is described to him as 'fattish . . . soft all over' in *The Big Sleep*, Howard Hawks, 1946). Thus, the solid is also the apparently strong, the would-be fit, exceptionally tall men – like Moose Malloy (Mike Mazurki) in *Murder My Sweet* – pointing up the grotesqueness of such solid (and stolid) toughness taken to extremes. The solid is also, in contrast, the respectably bourgeois, reflected in the architectural solidity which on occasion is seen to underpin this world (e.g. the pillars of the men's club in *The Woman in the Window* which are ironic visual correlatives of the 'pillars of society' who frequent the club).

In all its manifestations, however, the solidity of the *noir* world, and of the bodies that inhabit it, invites and displays potential or actual fragmentation (e.g. the bombed-out buildings of Frankfurt and Berlin in Tourneur's *Berlin Express*, 1948), particularly through lighting and visual style, as has often been noted. Façades may crack, selves may shatter, whole worlds may explode. Fragmented men – like those gone soft – surround the central protagonist as further distorting mirrors, especially in the shapes of cripples, men with broken limbs, and little men who may try to stand tall. The twin dangers of softness and fragmentation are avoided either through toughness or respectability or both, involving processes of solidification and control which are antithetical to freely flowing forms of desire.

Boundaries/mergings

'Don't crowd me – I haven't got the answers.' Brad (Mark Stevens) in *The Dark Corner*.

'I hated her. So I couldn't get her out of my mind for a minute. She was in the air I breathed and in the food I ate.' Johnny (Glenn Ford) in *Gilda*.

'Is that you . . . that nice expensive smell?' Marlowe in *Murder My Sweet*.

'What to do in a hot wind smelling of night-blooming jasmine except wait and sweat and prime the body to sweat some more?' Rip in *Dead Reckoning*.

'I could smell that honeysuckle again, only it was even stronger now that it was night.' Walter in *Double Indemnity*.

'If I could only drive it out of my mind . . . and get some . . . sleep.' Mike (John McGuire) in *Stranger on the Third Floor* (Boris Ingster, 1940).

'Of course killing you is killing myself. It's the same thing. But, you know, I'm pretty tired of both of us.' Bannister in *The Lady from Shanghai*.

'Look, angel, I'm tired.' Marlowe (Humphrey Bogart) in *The Big Sleep*.

'You're tired. I'm tireder . . .' Joe in *Force of Evil*.

'Oh, I'm so tired, Charlie. There's an end to the running a man can do. You'll never know what it's like to be so tired.' Uncle Charlie (Joseph Cotten) in *Shadow of a Doubt* (Alfred Hitchcock, 1943).

'Mabel, I'm going to call the doctor. It just isn't natural anyone sleeping like that for 36 hours.' Coral (Lizabeth Scott) in *Dead Reckoning*.

'I'm just afraid if I sit down, the next thing I'll lie down. If I lie down, sure as there're worms in little green apples, I'll fall asleep. If I fall asleep, I'm dead.' Clint in *Panic in the Streets*.

'That's a beautiful bed – Stay off it! – walk!' Marlowe in *Murder My Sweet*.

'I watched it get dark and didn't even turn on the light.' Walter in *Double Indemnity*.

'I used to sit there half-asleep with the beer and the darkness.' Jeff in *Out of the Past*.

'A black pool opened up at my feet. I dived in. It had no bottom.' Marlowe in *Murder My Sweet*.

'Well, you could get wetter if you lay down in the gutter.' Mrs Harwood (Veronica Lake) in *The Blue Dahlia*.

'Get in the water. There you'll find peace.' Belnap (Gage Clark) in *Nightmare* (Maxwell Shane, 1956).

Still: Murder My Sweet – *Moose Malloy (Mike Mazurki) and Philip Marlowe (Dick Powell).*

In the critical literature, much has been made of the stylistic fragmentation of the *film noir* world ('No character can speak authoritatively from a space which is being continually cut into ribbons of light' Schrader, 1972), a fragmentation which I have suggested is not only visually explicit but also thematically implicit behind the masks of solidity – either tough or respectable – worn by the central protagonists of the genre. However, the desperation – whether issuing in violence or quiet unease – which accompanies the maintenance of this defensive solidification implies considerable ambivalence on the part of such men and such films. Along with the pressures to hold tight are equally powerful temptations to let go. *Noir* men are typically tired (or are lured by others wanting or advocating peace and rest) and are easily drawn to the tantalising shapelessness of sleep, forgetfulness, and even death. It is in this connection that the imagery of water often pointed out as so prevalent in *film noir* is important: on the one hand, solidity and potential fragmentation, on the other hand, liquidity and merging, an end to the effort of holding oneself together lest one crack into pieces.

Often the process of loosening one's hold is internal, alcohol providing the liquid oblivion into which the protagonist dives. One's tongue may loosen in the process as well. Merging with darkness – when it is unfragmented and all-enveloping – may be a comfort too. So *noir* protagonists may fight to preserve their faltering sense of bodily integrity by casting away what is felt to be alien both inside and around them, or they may let go and drown, metaphorically or for real.

Still: The Dark Corner – *Kathleen (Lucille Ball) and Brad (Mark Stevens).*

Blockages

'You're bottled up – you can't get out.' Michael (Robert Preston) in *This Gun for Hire.*

'I'm clean as a peeled egg – no debts, no angry husbands, no pay-offs nothing.' Brad in *The Dark Corner.*

'What are you afraid of – to show you're afraid?' Mrs Tucker in *Force of Evil.*

'You're afraid of emotion. You keep your heart in a steel safe.' Kathleen in *The Dark Corner.*

'I grant you the jokes could have been better, but I don't see why the rest should worry you. That is, unless you plan to arrest me for lack of emotion.' Steele in *In a Lonely Place.*

'I feel all dead inside.' Brad in *The Dark Corner.*

'I couldn't hear my own footsteps. It was the walk of a dead man.' Walter in *Double Indemnity.*

'He was dead for a long time, he just didn't know it.' Finlay (Robert Young) in *Crossfire.*

'He's dead now, except he's breathing.' Doctor in *The Killers.*

'You talk as if you were dead.' Doris (Beatrice Pearson) in *Force of Evil.*

'I haven't got time to play games.' Johnny (Alan Ladd) in *The Blue Dahlia.*

'You see, some people say what they mean and they have a happy time, and other people get all tangled up inside, can't talk, can't even feel, and they don't have a happy time.' Alison (Claudette Colbert) in *Sleep, My Love*.

'When people are in trouble, they need to talk.' Christina in *Kiss Me, Deadly*.

'You're so clever, but you talk too much.' Jarnac (Luther Adler) in *Cornered* (Dmytryk, 1945).

'Honey, you talk too much.' Brad (Robert Ryan) in *The Woman on Pier 13* (Robert Stevenson, 1949).

'I'd say you talk too much.' Rocky (Dick Powell) in *Cry Danger* (Robert Parrish, 1951).

'You're very excited about something tonight, my beautiful. Perhaps it's in the air. Perhaps you shouldn't have opened the window. Close it. There. See how quiet it is now? See how easily one can shut away excitement? Just by closing a window. Remember that, Gilda.' Ballin (George Macready) in *Gilda*.

'The window was open, but the smoke didn't move.' Marlowe in *Murder My Sweet*.

Before we go on to consider whether the alternatives of solidity/fragmentation and liquidity/merging leave any room for the free flowings of desire, or whether male desire overwhelmingly exists in these movies in the service of masculine power or its abandonment, a bit more must be said about the specific containments and blockages in the *film noir* world. There is a close relationship between such blockages and the process of solidification. Put most simply, what is blocked no longer flows, it congeals. By looking at the sorts of thing that get blocked, we may gain some idea of the sorts of thing that might otherwise flow.

Film noir is most obviously about the blockage of men's emotions and the structuring of their sexuality by conventional norms of gender (toughness, ambition) and class (respectability, middle-class marriage). Perhaps the film which most strongly conveys a sense of emotional blockage behind a façade of precarious and volatile toughness is Nicholas Ray's *On Dangerous Ground*, where even the landscape of cold, packed snow reinforces (until the final frames) the frozen emotions of its characters. Similarly, the dried-up river bed in which the protagonist of *Roadblock* (Harold Daniels, 1951) is eventually trapped provides a particularly apt image of his fate. Lang's *While the City Sleeps* (1956), on the other hand, shows a central protagonist who, for most of the film, flees the constraints of male ambition and middle-class marriage alike in an illusory drunken release, re-routing emotional flow into drink.

Film noir is also about a range of other containments and controls, some of them literal and concrete, others more metaphorical. Examples include the laying of traps, the keeping of secrets, the catching of criminals, the hiding of bodies, and the containment of women (as well as of men) within marriage and stereotypes. I have argued in the preceding article that *noir* women tend to function as a screen for more fundamental thematic concerns with men and what we may now call male blockages. In fact, each of these examples of containment may be seen to reflect aspects of the genre's primary concern with the emotional and physical defences and anxieties of its men. Consider the hiding of dead bodies, for instance. It is striking that such bodies are so messy in their bloodiness and sprawl (an ultimate letting-go, perhaps), and it is no mere coincidence that they are so often discovered by that staple of the genre, the cleaner. To remain 'clean' himself, the protagonist must hide away the untidiness of corpses, while he himself tightens up his own body and clarifies the boundaries between himself and other men. So *film noir* creates a claustrophobic world which multiplies the dammed-up emotions of its men in a series of metaphorical mirrors.

What we have is not merely a reflective system, but an interactive one, and one not neatly divisible into examples of pure blockage on the one hand and flow on the other. Instead there is a constant re-routing of one sort of (forbidden) flow, which has been stemmed, into another less threatening outlet. It has already been suggested that alcoholic flows may replace blocked up emotional ones. Similarly, a criminal caught on the run may release compensatory floods of words in the shape of a confession, and the strain of a secret or a secret life may be relieved by letting money slip through one's fingers in a never-ending stream (e.g. Uncle Charlie in *Shadow of a Doubt* or the numerous gamblers who populate these films). All *noir* men are prone to release floods of violence as well. In psychoanalytic terms, libido will out, as more and more diversionary objects and activities become energised in a constant striving for release, however illusory that may prove to be.

Flowing/play

'I like to talk.' Spade (Humphrey Bogart) in *The Maltese Falcon* (Huston, 1941).

'I never cried like that before in my whole life.' Abigail in *Christmas Holiday*.

Vivian: I like gambling. *Marlowe:* So do I. Vivian (Lauren Bacall) and Marlowe in *The Big Sleep*.

'I never think when I gamble, I just feel.' Rip in *Dead Reckoning*.

'If I always knew what I meant, I'd be a genius.' Marlowe in *Murder My Sweet*.

What has been suggested so far is that, although *noir* men may swim in a variety of metaphorical streams, they tend to lead either to the defeatist and morbid lettings-go of sleep and death (as release from defensive solidifications and the connected fears of fragmentation) or (as with gambling and booze, say, or violence) provide merely substitute outlets which have the effect of shoring up male emotional blockage all the more firmly. Until now, however, we have concentrated only on those examples of apparent flowing that are motivated in narrative terms. *Noir*'s narrative world is undeniably bleak. Its men are caught between impossible alternatives and often seem ill at ease when trying to be 'men' in any of the available terms (whether toughness or respectability, womanising or marriage). They may 'go through the motions', but with a bodily stiffness or, alternatively, an artificially induced relaxation through booze that is at odds with a genuine unblocking of their desires. So are there any pleasures in *film noir* – for either viewer or protagonist – uncontaminated by the ideological dead-ends of its narrative world?

At this point, what can only be described as the playfulness of the genre must be acknowledged. This may sound odd, in view of the genre's sombre mood, but it is undeniable that *film noir*'s play with language and narration is a major source of its pleasure. The complexities of its narratives make it difficult – for viewers and characters alike – to pin down events in a stable, coherent formation. Rather, there is a constant reshaping of events into ever-changing possible worlds as we reassess and reinterpret what has happened. Guilt and innocence, cause and effect, shift and realign themselves into ever-altering constellations. The narrator himself may take pleasure in such narrative motility (for example, Bogart's Sam Spade in *The Maltese Falcon*). Along with this is a use of language whereby words with apparently solid, stable meanings suddenly loosen and slide into nuances, puns, and suggestiveness to produce a sense of possibility and ambiguity not only in the narrative but in the very stuff of its narration and enactment. A few examples may help reveal this:

In *Murder My Sweet*, a business proposition is turned into the suggestion of something else through what appears to be mere repetition:

Mrs Grayle (Claire Trevor): Shall we call this a retainer? *Marlowe:* . . . let's call it a retainer.

Another example of playful slippage comes from *Double Indemnity*:

Keyes: Well, we're not in Medford now, we're in a hurry.

Such verbal shifts and layerings of meanings on top of meanings are contrasted with the simply repetitive and opaque remarks, again in *Murder My Sweet*, of the humourless and stolid (and all-too-solid) Moose Malloy:

Moose: I'd like you to meet a guy. *Marlowe:* Take it easy . . . *Moose:* I'd like you to meet a guy.

Here there is no play at all, no give, just single-mindedness. Now some more examples of words losing their stability through playful repetition, the first again from *Double Indemnity*:

Phyllis (Barbara Stanwyck): I wonder if I know what you mean. *Walter:* I wonder if you wonder.

And two from *The Big Sleep*:

Eddie Mars (John Ridgeley): You're kidding. *Marlowe:* All right, I'm kidding.

The latter affirmation is clearly intended as a negation ('I'm not kidding, but let's say I am').

Eddie Mars: Is that any of your business? *Marlowe:* I could make it my business. *Eddie Mars:* I could make your business mine. *Marlowe:* You wouldn't like it. The pay's too small.

Here figurative language is suddenly deflated and reduced to the literal. Lest it be thought that only Chandler plays at this game (though he's undoubtedly its most adept practitioner), let's take an example from *Out of the Past*:

Marny (Mary Field): First she's got you, now she's got you *and* Bailey. And the only thing I seem to get is older.

And from *Gilda*, as well:

Johnny: In other words, you've changed the subject. *Ballin:* In other words, I've changed the subject.

These lines occur after Johnny has inquired about a pay-off Ballin has made, and his words are turned by Ballin's intonations into an assertion of power. Elsewhere, Johnny's criticisms of Gilda's supposed infidelities to Ballin are neatly reversed and turned into something quite different:

Johnny: Doesn't it bother you at all that you're married? *Gilda:* What I want to know is, does it bother *you*?

Such almost balletic patterns of repetition and reversal are not the only strategies involved in the play with words. More generally, an interplay between the literal and the figurative –a sort of verbal conjuring – destabilises the language as it veers from one level to the other. Airier worlds are woven out of metaphors and other figures of speech in the spaces between the literal words of the narrative, all by a process of on-going and highly pleasurable play.

Performance
The plays with language and narrative which have just been examined are plays with the medium itself, in which film-makers, protagonists and viewers are jointly complicit, sharing the joke. However, one further source of pleasure whose status is more difficult to define must now be looked at: the pleasure of performance. I don't so much have in mind the enjoyment of stars and of the skills and details of characterisation

deployed in the narratives, for these are pleasures found in a variety of genres and not peculiar to *film noir*. What I wish to focus on instead are the numbers embedded within the films, most usually performed by women (though male musicians – often black – loom large as well), which make of *film noir* a genre second only to the musical in the importance of such moments. The best examples of the pleasures I have in mind are to be found in Veronica Lake's first number in *This Gun for Hire*. Ellen (the Lake character) is a magician, and what we have is a marvellous combination of song, music, magic, Lake's own obvious enjoyment and play with the audience within the film, and – through her sleight-of-hand – a breakdown in the stability of appearances, all complemented by her almost constant movement (and her long flowing hair). To an extent, I am taking issue with Laura Mulvey's influential argument in 'Visual Pleasure and Narrative Cinema' (in *Screen*, vol.16, no.3, Autumn 1975) in which she contends that women function in such numbers to halt the flow of the narrative (unlike men who tend to advance it) in moments of visual containment of the women by viewers within and without the films. It does seem to me that her argument – while convincing up to a point – needs to be modified in view of the repressiveness (the blockages) of *film noir* narratives and the way in which the musical numbers may open up such films and allow them to flow, in partial retaliation,

perhaps, on the part of the female characters, for their very real containments elsewhere in the films; thus, the Lake character's policeman boyfriend asks her elsewhere: 'Look, sugar, what does it take to get you to darn my socks, cook my corned beef and cabbage, and sort of confine your magic to one place and one customer?'

A clearer example of performance as retaliation is to be found in *Gilda*, where Hayworth's numbers involve more and more movement as the narrative and Johnny get increasingly oppressive. I see no reason to view such retaliation in terms of the specificities of a Freudian 'castration threat', as Mulvey does, but – in *film noir* at least – find it more useful to see it as a challenge to male solidity more generally, suggesting a better – and not more 'castrated' – world. (This is consonant with Richard Dyer's analysis of the musical in 'Entertainment and Utopia', *Movie* 24, Spring 1977.) Thus, the numbers seem to be saying, if *noir* men were to cease to contain not only women but themselves so rigidly (within stereotypes, and so on), they too could allow their own blocked-up emotions to flow.

A good example here is Bacall's number in *The Big Sleep* (an unusually playful film – unusual, above all, in the heterosexual arena of much of the play). The words of the song ('And her tears flowed like wine . . .'), about the unkindness of men, combine the imagery of female flow and liquidity with a critique of male behaviour. But what one remembers and delights in most, I think, are the interchanges of looks between Bogart and Bacall – the jokiness and play – and Bacall's ease and relaxation with the audience within the film. It is a moment that feels good, that opens up the film, without making one complicit in an oppressive containment of Bacall (even if, as Mulvey rightly points out, all looking in a sexist society is to an extent contaminated – but the function and feel of this number are of liberation, rather than of a guilty pleasure to be denied). In stark contrast to this, however, are Deanna Durbin's performances in *Christmas Holiday*. When we first hear her sing ('Spring will be a little late this year'), her still, stiff posture and mask-like face are at one with the lyrics about winter and the lateness of a reviving thaw. Even the rendition of 'Always', sung with Robert (Gene Kelly) at the piano when the marriage is still apparently happy, is ominous in its lack of movement (which again reflects the song title and lyrics) and in the way her arms encircle Robert from behind.

Perhaps the crucial difference amongst the various examples lies in the fact that in *Christmas Holiday*, Abigail (Durbin) is very clearly on the side of the law, in opposition to an unsympathetic and criminal husband whose world is so obviously alien to her, whereas the Lake and Bacall characters – though ultimately 'good' and involved with 'good' men – are given much more independence of thought and flexibility in working out their moral positions, aligning themselves, when their sympathies and loyalties require it, against the representatives of the law, in the name of a more generous morality. Thus, Ellen (Lake) doesn't turn in Raven (Ladd), and Vivian (Bacall) lies to Marlowe (Bogart) to protect her sister. Gilda (Hayworth) is less clear-cut, a 'good' woman pretending to be 'bad', the movements of her numbers therefore given a veneer of misleading moral laxity (the last number above all, where she is drunk and sexually suggestive). Where Lake's and Bacall's numbers are liberating in their portrayals of a better world, and Durbin's are oppressive in their fixed adherence to destructive norms, Hayworth's dramatise the misuse of the 'look' of liberation (movement, looseness, flow) for destructive and revengeful ends. In *Gilda*, it's all an act (not in the sense of play, but of deception). Clearly the possibilities of the numbers are inextricably linked to the characterisations and positionings of these women in their respective narrative worlds. Each example has to be looked at in its own terms. It would undoubtedly be interesting (though beyond the scope of this article) to look at camera movement, lighting, and so on in terms of their relation to narrative motivation and whether they too provide any extra-narrative freedoms akin to those provided by the performance details just examined.

The heterosexual arena

'He was trying to act like a soldier. I think he went out to look for a girl.' Keeley in *Crossfire*.

'You're a good man, sister.' Spade in *The Maltese Falcon*.

'She's a good guy.' Steele in *In a Lonely Place*.

'You know something, you're a pretty nice guy . . . for a girl.' Frank in *Angel Face*.

We have seen that, as with Theweleit's 'soldier males', the protagonists of *film noir* ward off both fragmentation and liquidity by a process of actual and metaphorical solidification which is not only characteristic of them, but impinges on the narratives and imagery of the films overall. However, whereas Theweleit's fascists are single-minded in the extremes of their defences, *noir* men are much more divided between an adherence to socially imposed norms (of toughness, ambition, and so on) and a longing for escape. A desire to desire is evidenced by all the give and flow and ambivalences noted so far. The fascist soldiers are an extreme – and pathological – embodiment of a misogyny and a fear of the flows of the body which are only partial factors in the constitution of the more democratic males in *film noir* (at a time when fascism was the enemy).

Noir men – most of them, anyway – are curable, their defences more fragile. What is so striking in these films is not so much an absence of play as the fact that such play is usually situated away from the heterosexual arena. *Noir* men often tense up with women; they relax much more in the margins of the films' plots (in verbal sparring and narrative play). The films' most positive (if not most powerful) representations of desire seep out in flows of words, music, performance and imagery, but not generally in narrative events as such. *Noir* men are not fascist males, denying desire, but they *are* males, the products of a culture which slots women (as well as men) into equally threatening alternatives of deviance and domesticity. Only in the exceptional film, like *The Big Sleep*, perhaps, is there a sense of ease in heterosexual encounters. Here, at every turn, Marlowe meets confident and positively presented women who openly and 'healthily' – and playfully – show their interest in him: the woman (Dorothy Malone) in the bookshop across the street from Geiger's, the taxi driver, the employees at Eddie Mars's club – yet even in this movie, more negative feelings are associated with Carmen (Martha Vickers) and Agnes (Sonia Darrin), who are shown as 'sick' and self-interested respectively. More usually, positive male/female relationships in *film noir* (in cases where the women evade the dichotomous stereotypes of *femme fatale* and would-be wife) may be presented via such narrative strategies as either turning the couple into pals or transforming the woman into a figure of spiritual redemption

(like Lake in *This Gun for Hire* or Ida Lupino in *On Dangerous Ground*), decentring the sexuality of the relationship to an extent, at least in conventional terms.

Let me summarise my argument by relating it to that of my earlier account of *film noir*. I suggested there that the anxieties of *noir* men reflect those of American soldiers of the time, caught between conflicting desires, conflicting models of masculinity, and conflicting female types. Thus:

The Man's Man	The Woman's Man
Adventure	Domesticity
Toughness	Respectability
Deviance	Social status
Womanising	Marriage

and so on. What we have now seen is that neither of these models provides a genuine unblocking of male desires, both equally involving processes of solidification which turn narrative resolutions in their terms into emotional dead-ends. The terms of the conflict themselves, by their stereotypicality, misrepresent and constrain within narrow bounds the potentially more free-flowing needs, desires and bodily experiences of real men and women. These find expression in the films in the various forms of play and opening up suggested earlier, but necessarily at a remove from narrative concerns and directives as such. It is in such asides and parentheses within *film*

Still: Shadow of a Doubt – *Uncle Charlie (Joseph Cotten) ingratiating himself in the small town, watched by Charlie (Teresa Wright).*

noir that its more 'innocent' pleasures are to be found. The genre presents us simultaneously with a bleak and hopeless world and a terrific sense of fun, but is unable to integrate the two fully by releasing the narrative world from its heavily stereotypical (and socially accurate) constraints. The nearest we come to this is in admissions of uncertainty by the characters within the films. As Mrs Harwood asks of Johnny in *The Blue Dahlia*: 'Well, where do we go from here?' And, as Marlowe says in *Murder My Sweet*: 'All I can do is keep guessing.'

Shadows and Doubts: Shadow of a Doubt (1943)

I have chosen to concentrate on the pleasures that most successfully elude the structuring of the narrative world (a world which presents at least a partial analogue to our own social world in attitudes to gender, sexuality, and so on), such pleasures seeping out, as it were, through the seams. But, as I hope to have indicated, this is not to suggest any absence of desire in that narrative world itself: desires multifarious and rich in psychoanalytic complexity make up its very fabric, exerting powerful and ambiguous attractions for any viewer immersed in a comparable moral universe. (Indeed, Victor Perkins has suggested to me that the very fictionality of *film noir* may provide a space within which viewers can enjoy pleasures in which it would be destructive to over-indulge in reality, and can thus enjoy them without guilt.) The protagonists' desires, on the one hand, to be strong and tough, and, on the other hand, to let go (and the anxieties associated with each of these positions) are reflected in struggles to gain and relinquish power in the sexual realm as well, motivating, for example, a range of sadistic and masochistic desires. The positing of an Oedipalised unconscious does not seem to me to be necessary for an understanding of such dynamics. Further, insofar as I've hypothesised an essential ambivalence on the part of the *noir* protagonist towards power and responsibility (their burdens provoking as much anxiety as their loss), a Freudian emphasis on 'castration' anxieties (even if understood less psychoanalytically in terms of a loss of social power at the hands of newly emancipated women) seems inadequate and limiting. Nevertheless, a much more thorough exploration of this material, in whatever terms, would undoubtedly be of interest. I would like to make a tentative start by examining the role of suspense.

I ended the previous article with a brief look at Hitchcock's *The Man Who Knew Too Much* as an example of a movie whose central protagonist can be seen as the protagonist of *film noir* a decade or so later on in his life, the conflicting demands of domesticity and deviance having been dealt with – if not resolved – by a fatalistic opting for marriage and family. There is a certain symmetry in concluding here with a look at another Hitchcock work, perhaps equally eccentric at first sight as an example of *noir* dynamics.

Shadow of a Doubt is a small-town movie with comic as well as sinister aspects, and it might not normally be classified as obviously *noir*. Indeed, Hitchcock's Hollywood work generally, despite a substantial degree of overlap with *film noir* in period and themes, lacks a number of important elements of the genre. Thus, whereas typical *film noir* is structured around a central male consciousness through first-person narration, flashback and other subjective devices, with women seen primarily as functions (usually dichotomous) of the man's point of view, Hitchcock's movies provide a much greater degree of play with viewpoint and a much more even concern with gender in terms of contrasting – and warring – points of view. To some extent this is because generically they are interlaced with doses of melodrama and *film noir* in combination – the kidnapping plot in *The Man Who Knew Too Much* (readable as a projection of Ben's repressed aggressions) and that of Jo's career frustrated in the name of marriage and motherhood exist side by side.

Even more intimately linked, via the device of the doubling of young Charlie (Teresa Wright)

and Uncle Charlie (Joseph Cotten) in *Shadow of a Doubt*, are the melodramatic concerns of the former and the *noir* predicament of the latter. Charlie follows one typical melodramatic trajectory from dissatisfaction with women's role within domesticity through involvement with a romantic but disruptive/dangerous intruder to reinstatement (through a more suitable man) within the very domesticity she'd tried to escape, the resolution being signalled stylistically as a defeat. In contrast, her uncle is a criminal on the run, corrupt and doomed.

The doubling of the two characters in various ways (e.g. name, posture, mutual affinity) suggests, of course, that they are hardly distinct, each possessing clear attributes of the other. It is fairly obvious that Uncle Charlie functions as Charlie's dark side (she, too, is capable of killing, as she warns him), but, in focusing on Uncle Charlie's point of view rather than Charlie's, I wish to call attention to Charlie's function as a repressed side of her uncle. Whereas women in Hollywood melodramas may seek or attain the power and position normally seen as the prerogative of men ('You're the head of your family, Charlie, anyone can see that'), I have argued that the men of *film noir* often seek release from the burdens of male responsibility in defeatism and passivity, even unto death. So Uncle Charlie is both the potent male of melodrama who animates Charlie's dreams and mirrors her own rebellion and, at the same time, the *noir* protagonist at the end of his rope, tired, suicidal, seeking rest and release, and a lost identification with the stereotypically 'feminine'.

Uncle Charlie seeks regression to the world of childhood. On greeting his sister Emmy, he chooses to see her as she was then ('Emma, don't move. Standing there, you don't look like Emma Newton, you look like Emma Spencer Oakley . . . the prettiest girl on the block'); further, to her surprise, he has preserved, through all the errant years of his criminal career, the photographs of their parents which she'd thought lost. In looking for refuge with Emmy's family – a world of weak men and stronger women – he is trying to recreate the lost world of his childhood, albeit a suffocatingly indulgent world from which he had run away as a very young man. So his idealisation of the past is shown up as self-deceived. Although he contrasts women like Emmy with women like the rich widows he murders, the contrast his words assert is undermined in various ways, most notably by the gifts – the spoils of his crimes – which he bestows on Emmy and Charlie, turning them into potential victims of his murderous desires, but also by the fact that it is only a matter of chance that the small-town wives are not yet all widows, as Mrs Potter (Uncle Charlie's admirer in Santa Rosa) has become. The potential of the women – and Emmy in particular – to be widowed is emphasised by Joe and Herb's fantasies of murdering each other, which also hint at a link between

Still: Shadow of a Doubt. *Rigidity - Uncle Charlie with Charlie.*

these ineffectual, dominated men and Uncle Charlie. All of this suggests a strong (if unacknowledged) ambivalence on Uncle Charlie's part, a desire to murder his sister – and Charlie – at the same time as he turns to them for salvation. So Uncle Charlie is caught, like so many *noir* protagonists, between the desire to be a man, which here seems to require the killing of women (as representative of the suffocating world he'd fled) in order to establish his separateness, and the desire to regress to the stage of dreamy childhood ('. . . such a quiet boy, always reading') before gender boundaries were rigidly and irrevocably enforced.

Posture

Uncle Charlie's contrasting desires are reflected in the film's representations of bodily posture: on the one hand, the rigid, on the other, the collapsed. Our first view of him (when he is nearest to despair) is of him lying down on the rooming-house bed, money spread about in careless disarray. The landlady encourages him to rest (pulling down the shade so that a shadow envelops him), but her irritating fussiness and chatter have the opposite effect, arousing in the audience, too, a desire to escape from her and her well-meaning interference, if not to throttle her altogether. She is a latter-day version of the motherly women who provoke this ambivalent response. Once the landlady leaves, he stands up and 'pulls himself together', regaining his power and evading the police.

As a last chance at salvation, he arrives in Santa Rosa, posing as an invalid on the train in order to retreat behind a curtained partition and escape scrutiny. On arrival, as in the opening scene, his

posture changes: here, from that of a cripple ('At first I didn't know you, I thought you were sick,' Charlie tells him, perplexed) to that of a literally and figuratively upright citizen, the identity he will maintain in Santa Rosa. But, of course, his niece is right: he *is* sick, and the erect posture he adopts (potent, respectable) is revealed to us as the deeper pose.

So the movie's use of posture is consistent with that of *film noir* as a whole. Two models of masculinity (the deviant, the respectable) are represented in images of solidity/rigidity/uprightness, yet Uncle Charlie's unhappiness with either model (as hinted at in his refusal to be photographed except as a child) is reflected in his desire to relinquish the power and responsibilities of adult masculinity, a desire represented in his tiredness, his recumbent postures, and his fatal fall from the train, the latter more easily readable as a suicide – a final giving up in the face of untenable alternatives – than as an ultimately unconvincing indication of young Charlie's greater physical strength in their struggle. The nihilism which has been noted in Hitchcock's films (the absence of positive alternatives to both the deviant and the normal) is, in fact, fairly central to *film noir* as a whole. A second, related aspect of Hitchcock's work which links him firmly to the genre is his use of suspense.

Suspense

Suspense (being suspended) is in one sense a spatial term, where one is caught between the postural alternatives of falling and having one's feet planted firmly on the ground, and such literally suspended states recur in Hitchcock's work (*Vertigo*, 1958, *North By Northwest*, 1959, and so on). More figuratively, the alternatives can be seen (in terms of what has been argued above) as representative of ideological positionings: whereas having one's feet on the ground metaphorically implies that one is embedded in the world of 'common sense', one's identity secure, the alternative of falling implies vertiginous dissolution (as well as the possibility of literal death). The state of suspension between the two is a state of uncertainty, the outcome as yet unresolved. It is akin to early childhood, where everything still seems possible: the child's identity is not yet fully formed, the immersion in ideology not yet complete. In relation to *Shadow of a Doubt*, the terror of having no identity at all (no separateness from the mother and her surrogates, say) is balanced against the constraints of a rigid and ideologically pre-determined masculinity with both criminal and 'upright' variants.

The idea of suspense as uncertainty relates to Hitchcock's own well-known formulation of suspense in epistemological terms as an admixture of knowledge and apprehension (in contrast to mere surprise). So suspense is a state of uncertain and anxious expectancy where we try to get our bearings and maintain a precarious equilibrium on the basis of imperfect knowledge; thus, we may know what the alternatives are, but not which of them will happen, or we may know which, but not when or how. In that knowledge is accorded the viewer which is denied to the protagonist, we may experience his suspense *for* him, in some sense, by identifying with his predicament (his 'suspension') even where he's not fully aware of it himself. So the protagonist's suspense is partially displaced on to the viewer in such cases. In this way, the viewer's own childhood may be evoked insofar as it can be understood as a sort of prototype of suspense, not only in terms of the child's unformed identity (a hovering between alternatives), but in the child's attempts, on the basis of partial knowledge, to make sense of a potentially threatening world. The interest children take in repetition and in the safe and predictable frights of such toys as the Jack-in-the-Box – the reassurance they provide of the reliability of the world – is evidence of the need to manage the otherwise unbearable vertigo of sustained suspense.

In *film noir*, the frequent use of flashbacks provides some equivalent reassurance that the story will end as the film began (that is, the film's suspense is attenuated by an extra dollop of privileged knowledge), but Hitchcock's movies generally avoid flashback structures or, worse still – in the famous instance of *Stage Fright* (1950) – employ a false flashback. However, considerable predictability is provided to the audience by a range of other narrative conventions, although – after *Psycho* (1960) – we can't even rely on Hitchcock keeping the heroine alive, a betrayal of the viewer comparable to that by a parent who abuses his child, turning a secure and predictable universe upside down.

Filmic suspense's evocation of the extended suspense of childhood, calling up unconscious memories of a time when our sexual identities were still unformed and poorly understood, may account for or contribute to the success as well as the anxiety of *film noir*: it gives us a second chance to manage this anxiety and to shed temporarily the fixed aspects of our social being. If so, Hitchcock parts company with *film noir* mainly in the extent to which he pushes such concerns. Suspense is important in *film noir* (with the link between anxious expectation and partial knowledge omnipresent as a theme); it is absolutely central to Hitchcock's films, in which the heroes are pushed again and again to summits of anxiety that strip them of their ideologically secure positions and suspend them (and us) over an abyss of despair. The world of childhood to which his protagonists regress is not an innocent nor a liberating place (thus, the utter lack of sentimentality in Hitchcock's work). Uncle Charlie longs to return to an ideal world which never existed ('Everybody was sweet and pretty then, Charlie, the whole world, wonderful world, not like the world today, not like the world now'), calling up his murderous response towards female figures of salvation. In Hitchcock's world

(in our world), desire is so pervasively bound, and at so early a stage, that the alternative to Uncle Charlie's becoming a powerful stereotypical male is not his becoming the site of Deleuze and Guattari's desiring production, uncontaminated and unbound. Rather, the alternative is his suffocation and annihilation by a femininity ('Horrible. Faded, fat, greedy women . . .') that is just as stereotypical and constrained as the available models of maleness.

Pleasures

So *Shadow of a Doubt* is an example of a film which, despite its strong authorial signature and generic mixture, nonetheless relates intimately to the *noir* canon of its time. Like *film noir* generally, Hitchcock's work offers playful pleasures as well as animating those corrupt and dark desires that are more closely bound both by the real social world we inhabit and by its embodiment in the narrative. In looking at the genre as a whole, I have chosen to emphasise the pleasures of verbal legerdemain, of narrative play, and, to an extent, of performance. Such pleasures can be seen as in some sense innocent to the extent that they can be separated from the bleak narrative world and its concerns, within which desire is blocked and re-routed. I chose not to explore the contaminated pleasures of the real social world, as represented by its narrative analogues (a world whose blockages of desire, in Deleuze and Guattari's analysis, turn one back, frustrated, upon the family and its surrogates). However, in Hitchcock's films, it is much more difficult – if not impossible – to extricate the playful from the malign. The comic elements in his work deserve a fuller analysis than can be given here, but a few points can be made. His humour is less a matter of playful complicity between film-maker, protagonist and viewer, and more a critique at the characters' expense (e.g. the humour around Joe's and Herb's fantasies of murder in *Shadow of a Doubt*), thus serving to prise us apart from too close and constant an identification with the narrative world. At the same time as we are drawn into the dark world of Hitchcock's vision, being made to experience the most disturbing fears and desires, we are pulled back from the characters (through humour, through the multiple points of view discussed earlier, and through the greater self-consciousness of our experience of suspense, which simultaneously lures us in and holds us back). We are given a space, a position from which to survey this world.

Conclusions

My ambitions here have been fairly modest. First, to avoid a number of pitfalls which have dogged psychoanalytical approaches to film: above all, I have wanted to let the films speak for themselves, rather than imposing my theoretical expectations too rigidly on the material in advance. The argument which has developed has been modified and qualified in the course of my viewing a wide range of films in the genre, though it must be said that, after a certain point, I found that each subsequent movie served to confirm and provide variations upon aspects of what I had found thus far, giving me growing confidence in what had begun as merely provisional.

Related to my wish to avoid over-theorisation was the wish to avoid the jargon of a particular approach wherever feasible and to be open to the possibilities of non-psychoanalytical readings when they seemed most appropriate and useful. Thus, the presence of overtly neurotic/psychotic protagonists in some of the films could most easily be understood in terms of the widespread currency of Freudian ideas (and misconceptions) at the time. As Peter Gay says in the preface to his recent biography of Freud, 'It is a commonplace that we all speak Freud today whether we recognise it or not.' But 'speaking Freud' self-consciously, as such movies seem to, need not require psychoanalytical interpretations. Such details may demonstrate cultural competence and conscious intention on the part of the film-makers, but don't necessarily pinpoint or dramatise issues of great weight and depth for an overall psychoanalytical reading of a given film. They may be red herrings, diverting attention from the more substantial psychoanalytical interest of these films which – certainly in the case of *film noir* – lies elsewhere.

Beyond the negative aim of avoiding the twin pitfalls of distortion and mystification, I have tried, more positively, to see the films afresh, in the light of certain questions which the concepts of psychoanalysis help us to frame. Although the linked concepts of repression and the unconscious have been implicit in my approach, and, necessarily, in *any* psychoanalytical endeavour, I have used Deleuze and Guattari's anti-Freudianism as ammunition in, at the very least, calling into question the Oedipal unconscious (and related castration anxieties) as a third psychoanalytical and critical given. Feminists have always had difficulty with the concept of an innate psychic apparatus structured around female lack. In the present account, I have scarcely entered into the debate – let alone resolved it – in theoretical terms. I have simply tried to demonstrate (with the support of a range of detailed examples) that an account which construes the unconscious as the place of unlimited and un-Oedipalised flow (Deleuze and Guattari's 'machinic production') is consistent with some of the mechanisms of *film noir* and helps us to see them more clearly. So, I have provisionally adopted an approach which does not take Oedipus for granted, responding, rather, to plentiful evidence in the films of positive and free-flowing desires striving for expression in the interstices of a tight and blocked narrative world. I have taken up the question left unanswered in the previous article: what are the sources of the genre's pleasures? I have found the beginnings of an answer in those strivings of desire within the texts which exist apart from their conscious narrative aims and in opposition to the blockages of both the characters and the films. However, the darker desires of viewers and protagonists which resonate within – and motivate – much of the narrative itself cannot be denied, though Deleuze and Guattari may provide a theoretical frame within which to see them as socially constructed and provisional, rather than innate and absolute. The ways whereby authorial and generic conventions (such as those of suspense) function to relate us to the narrative world would also benefit from further psychoanalytical examination and debate.

Establishing beyond doubt the 'truth' of Deleuze and Guattari's formulation over that of Freud (not to mention Melanie Klein or Jacques Lacan or whomever) is outside the scope of the present discussion. Debates about psychoanalytical theory amongst those within the ranks of psychoanalysis itself, as well as amongst cultural theorists, are well underway and will undoubtedly continue. The ideas I have provisionally appropriated have largely been put to what I earlier called descriptive/interpretative, rather than causally explanatory, ends (insofar as these can be separated). That is, I have used Deleuze and Guattari (by way of Theweleit) as a critical lens through which to examine some widespread and consistent aspects of *film noir*. I have not sought to explain how they came to be there in terms of the 'objective' nature of the film-makers' or viewers' minds, let alone those of the characters who, it need hardly be said, are fictions (even if it is unavoidable and necessary to discuss them as though they were real). However, a degree of historical explanation (particularly in the previous article) has seemed necessary to account for the emergence of the genre as a whole. In any case, there are certainly pleasurable aspects of these movies to which audiences gratefully respond and to many of which, as a feminist, one can respond without a sense of moral compromise. The 'why' of audience response remains a question.

If Deleuze and Guattari are right, then an answer is to hand: we respond to such positive strivings because, in our own unconscious, similar desires are likewise seeking release and meeting comparable blocks. A Freudian might wish to explain the same data in different terms (and might well give these pleasures less weight), seeing them not as primary, but as sublimations or displacements of Oedipal desires within the narratives' often disguised familial constellations. These intra-narrative patterns of desire, in turn, would be recognised by adherents of Deleuze and Guattari, although given less prominence and explained as frustrated re-routings of what, to them, is primary. Whatever explanation is offered – whichever model of desire is given causal primacy – its supporting evidence would have to come, it seems to me, from outside the films, which, in the end, exist as products of a larger human and social world.

TAME WOLVES
AND PHONEY CLAIMS
Paranoia and Film Noir
Jonathan Buchsbaum

A critical term that has been invoked continually in discussions of *film noir* but has not been analysed with any rigour is paranoia. In virtually all cases, commentators assert the presence of paranoia without specifying, examining, or recognising its constituent features. In this article, I will attempt to demonstrate the aptness of the term in approaching a particular type of *film noir* by presenting a more precise definition of paranoia. Such a definition may restrict the scope of the term, but it may also galvanise disparate critical observations into a more coherent analytical tool.

When English-speaking critics rediscovered *film noir* in the early 1970s, not only did they fail to explain what they meant by paranoia, but they also wrote in apparent ignorance of several contemporary critics of the same films. These earlier critics did address specifically some of the paranoid aspects of the films, and their observations can serve as a useful and more perspicuous entrée to the question of paranoia in *film noir* than the allusions to paranoia found in writing since 1970. The assumption throughout this article is that the prevalence of the term paranoia in the critical discourse of *film noir* indicates that paranoia is in some way a relevant term. By taking a closer look at the actual psychoanalytical description of paranoia, however, that relevance can be clarified, for the various films that have been called *film noir* and the consistent failure to specify the meaning of paranoia render the critical value of the term vague. A model approach, by articulating a clear paranoid structure, can ground the use of the term concretely, and perhaps allow the term more discriminatory value when it is invoked. Thus, the strongest instances seem to occur in the private detective films of the mid-1940s, before the theme of corrupt institutions began to displace the centrality of the private detective. In the later films, paranoia takes on a more metaphorical meaning, as institutions and bureaucracies assume a more prominent place in the plots and cannot be assimilated to the more purely subjective construction of the protagonist. Concomitantly, the *femme fatale* recedes in importance, for sexuality is no longer the generative nexus of the films. Discussion of two films, *Double Indemnity* (1944) and *Murder My Sweet* (1944), will illustrate a more fully developed paranoid structure,

and the structure uncovered in those films may help to tame the inflation of the term, if not solve the conundrum of *film noir* and its status as a genre.

But more important than the methodological challenge of *film noir*, what distinguishes the critical interest in *film noir* from that in such accepted genres as the western, the musical, and the gangster film, is the claim that this group of films appears now to embody more coherently than any other group of films the mood and anxieties of the postwar decade. For most critics, this position is founded on a straightforward reflection theory of culture. This theory holds that the deep concerns and contradictions of society will inevitably be reflected in the cultural products of the society. While this idea may sound reasonable enough theoretically, establishing the correlations in a convincing manner is a daunting task, for imposing any kind of rigorous control over the correlations is virtually impossible. As Richard Maltby has pointed out,

'Cultural history is too diffuse to allow of clear causal relationships: the most it can attempt is to establish a chain of plausibility, to suggest that one explanation for a particular representation is the existence of a particular set of circumstances . . . A cultural history of the cinema can do no more than examine a set of synchronic events, and propose a relationship between movies and their historical moments which, however plausibly supported by the empirical evidence of production and consumption, remains essentially metaphorical' (*Journal of American Studies* vol.18, no.1, 1984, pp.50-51).

Thus, *film noir* critics pick out various social tensions that attended postwar readjustment in America, compile a list of films that putatively manifest the same kinds of tension and conclude that these seminal films reflect the general paranoia that afflicted the country during those years. For example, Alain Silver maintains that *film noir* 'is a self-contained reflection of American preoccupations in film form . . . McCarthyism and the spectre of the Bomb became the unspoken inspiration for a leitmotif of fear, or, more specifically, paranoia that resounded through the *noir* cycle after the war . . . The films . . . all reflect a common ethos: they consistently evoke the dark side of the American persona. The central figures in these films . . . are America's stylised vision of itself, a true cultural reflection of the mental dysfunction of a nation in uncertain transition' (Introduction to Silver & Ward, 1979).

Other critics are generally less explicit about the concept of reflection, but they consistently mention paranoia as a central characteristic, either in the film and/or in the society:

'each group felt paranoid about another, and each was sure that those in power were under the enemy's control' (Paul Jensen, 'Paranoia in Hollywood', *Film Comment* 7, Winter 1971-72, p. 37)

'the characteristic *film noir* moods of claustrophobia, paranoia, despair, and nihilism constitute a world view' (Place & Peterson, 1974, p. 30)

'the hallmark of the *film noir* is its sense of people trapped - trapped in webs of paranoia and fear' (Robert Sklar, *Movie-Made America*, Vintage, New York, 1975, p 253).

The social sources of this paranoia are familiar by now. The bomb powerfully marked the national consciousness with its destructive potential, spawning fears of world-wide annihilation. The Cold War only exacerbated these fears by reducing the complexity of international diplomacy to a life and death struggle between democracy and communism. McCarthyism brought these fears to a fever pitch with dire warnings about communism eating away at the body politic from the inside. These tensions extended to the film industry as well. The government reopened its antitrust case in 1946, leading to the first divestiture decision in 1948. When a bitter labour dispute broke out after the war, red-baiting within the Hollywood labour movement shattered the previous labour unity. Shortly afterward, studio heads buckled to the hysteria over the communist menace by instituting a rigidly applied blacklist. These themes recur in the writings about *film noir*, but none of the commentators explains why paranoia is the apposite critical term. In each case, rather than justifying the use of the term as a precise psychoanalytical category, critics apply it casually as a synonym for a sense of fear permeating the hostile environment.

Despite the ubiquity of the references to paranoia in the *film noir* literature, no-one has attempted to use the paradigm adumbrated by Richard Hofstadter in his celebrated essay, 'The Paranoid Style in American Politics' (in *The Paranoid Style in American Politics and Other Essays*, Vintage, New York, 1952). Perhaps the modesty of his study accounts for this neglect in discussions of *film noir*, for Hofstadter chose a relatively circumscribed topic, the political rhetoric of extremist political groups, and refrained from proposing the 'paranoid style' of such discourse as a reflection or symptom of the malaise of postwar America. As Hofstadter explained in his article, written in 1964, his immediate reason for applying the term paranoia to political rhetoric was the rising prominence of right-wing movements in the United States at the time, evidenced by the growth in popularity of Barry Goldwater and by the analyses propounded by people such as McCarthy and John Birch Society leader Robert Welch. Though he noted that the paranoid style is neither unique to America nor peculiar to the postwar period, he obviously was responding to the resurgence of this style in that period.

Hofstadter is careful to specify what he means by a paranoid style. For him, the paranoid style consists of several interrelated characteristics. An oversimplified world view attributes the cause of all events to a massive internal conspiracy. A rigid Manicheism infects this vision, with America forced to defend itself as the last bastion of freedom from the conspiracy of the communist evil. Elaborate pseudo-scholarly analyses, building with footnotes, marshall large amounts of data to reach a conclusion that always depends on a sudden leap of imagination to consolidate the proof. The plethora of evidence demonstrates the pervasiveness of the conspiracy and only confirms the necessity of ever greater vigilance. Concomitantly, the mechanism of projection facilitates the denial of domestic problems of American society by imputing them to the forces of conspiracy.

In contradistinction to writers who bandy the word paranoia in *film noir*, Hofstadter at least does clearly identify some of the salient characteristics of paranoia, but even he did not lay out his use of the term with real precision or rigour in a psychoanalytical sense. Perhaps the most significant omission is the lack of emphasis on homosexual anxieties that Freud noted in 1911: 'what lies at the core of the conflict in cases of paranoia among males is a homosexual wishphantasy of *being a man*' (a problem he addresses in his paper on Dr Schreiber, 'On the Mechanism of Paranoia', reprinted in Philip Rieff, ed., *Three Case Histories*, Collier Books, New York, 1963). This idea correlates easily enough with homosexual anxieties but is more general. According to this account, anxieties over weakness impel the paranoid to overcompensate by mobilising his energies at all times, never relaxing this vigilance for fear of allowing breaches in this armour to signal the manifestation of weakness (in *Neurotic Styles*, Basic Books, New York, 1965).

In this state of total mobilisation, the paranoid scrutinises the environment for confirmation of his suspicions. He does not, cannot, ignore evidence that does not support his suspicions. On the contrary, he actively searches for clues at all times, since any new stimulus will be enlisted in the distorted construction of a proof. Shapiro calls this skewed treatment of evidence 'bias'. The paranoid begins with a bias, and, through often brilliant manipulation can twist the data to conform to the preconceptions. This obsessive accumulation of evidence is what leads psychoanalysts to compare the paranoid to a detective:

' . . . the paranoid engages in solitary observation, searches for hidden meanings, asks leading questions, pondering over the answers like a detective, and listens attentively for clues in others' conversations to help him understand' (Norman Cameron, 'Paranoid Conditions and Paranoia', *American Handbook of Psychiatry*, 1959, p. 517).

Furthermore, the paranoid sees this mass of clues as intimately related to his life. There can be no independent or irrelevant piece of data that does not impinge on him directly, despite the apparent imperviousness of people or things to his existence. He refuses to trust appearances, driven as he is to unearth hidden meanings which no disguise can conceal from his penetrating mind. In short, the paranoid subjectivises the entire world in an incessant chain reaction of projection.

Though it is generally claimed that projection entails the expulsion of unwanted or hostile impulses on to an outside surrogate or surrogates, and this is often true in *film noir*, what is perhaps equally (if not more) important is the subjectivisation of the entire external world. Taking these features as an ensemble – rigid mobilisation, the unending search for clues, anxieties over weakness/homosexuality, projection – one can find this pattern in a number of *films noirs*, particularly during the early phases of private detective films. The often macho detective never relaxes from pursuit of the case. Though he cannot always immediately ascertain the meaning of a wealth of clues, every encounter or situation seems to secrete some clue or clues. He rejects the interpretations of others, who attend only to the most conventional forms of syllogism: he prefers to bumble through the mystery or enigma at his own pace and is often subjected to assaults on his itinerary through the hostile landscape. When he is actually responsible for the narration, the hostile world is a product of his subjectivity, displaying the way in which he viewed that world. An alluring woman may inaugurate the narrative trajectory, but his inability to cope with the sexual demands of the woman gives the lie to his macho pose, revealing the sexual inadequacies lurking beneath the excessively mannered stance of sexual maturity.

Where this more psychoanalytical account goes beyond Hofstadter's description of paranoia is the inclusion of sexuality, specifically the relation between constant mobilisation and anxieties over weakness/homosexuality. The so-called hardboiled protagonists in fact recoil from the threat of mature female sexuality. The ascription of manipulativeness to the woman by the protagonist as an excuse for not pursuing the relationship can be seen as his defensive invention to protect him against the weakening of his protective armour. But on a deeper level, the fear of lowering defences is associated with homosexual anxieties and explains the frequent appearance of homosexual characters, coded as effeminate, in a number of these films.

In fact, there is some limited precedent for a more informed discussion of paranoia and *film noir*, though before the category of *film noir* entered the critical vocabulary (in the United States). In their anthropological study of immediately postwar film (from the years 1946-48), Martha Wolfenstein and Nathan Leites devoted a chapter to 'Killers and Victims', in which they speak of 'persecutory fantasies' in many of these films and attribute these fantasies to projection:

'the hero's moral struggle is overdetermined by a persecutory fantasy in relation to his male opponent. We would guess that in the underlying fantasy this dangerous attacker is loved. Since such a sentiment is inadmissible, the hero's opponent is usually presented as an object of negative feelings only . . . The exclusive application of the persecutory pattern to men in the film melodramas illustrates the well-known finding that persecutory ideas are usually related to homosexual wishes. The unacknowledged wish is attributed to the loved man who appears as a dangerous attacker . . .

'In other words, there is a projection of hostile impulses, which are unacknowledged by the hero and seen as concentrated in his attacker, and a repression of the positive component of mixed feelings in the relation between the two men' (*Movies, A Psychological Study*, Atheneum, New York, 1970 edition, pp.177, 196).

Suggestive as their remarks are, Wolfenstein and Leites were admittedly plumbing the films for evidence of deep cultural themes, which could then be used for speculation about differences among American, French, and British national preoccupations. Wolfenstein and Leites acknowledge their debt to Geoffrey Gorer, who was quite explicit about the importance of homosexuality in his study of American national character (*The American People: A Study in National Character*, W.W. Norton, New York, 1948). For example, after claiming that there is an 'American panic fear of homosexuality' (p.125), Gorer goes on to note that 'the lives of most American men are bounded, and their interests drastically curtailed, by this constant necessity to prove to their fellows, and to themselves, that they are not sissies, not homosexuals . . . It is difficult to exaggerate the prevalence and urgency of this unconscious fear.' Wolfenstein and Leites view the woman in the films they study as 'helping' the hero to ward off persecutory fantasies, not as dangerous *femmes fatales* who incarnate the perceived threat of female sexuality. And finally, their comments on the films themselves are extremely summary, eschewing any form of close reading or textual analysis, so that they allow little heterogeneity to the films and pay no attention at all to stylistic markers and narrative complexity.

Writing slightly earlier than Wolfenstein and Leites, Parker Tyler developed a highly perceptive analysis of one key *film noir*, *Double Indemnity* (Billy Wilder, 1944), concentrating specifically

Still: Double Indemnity – *Phyllis telephones Walter Neff (Fred MacMurray) about the plan to kill her husband; Keyes (Edward G. Robinson) has been trying to persuade Walter to take a desk job.*

on the question of sexuality ('Magic Lantern Metamorphoses III', in *Myth and Magic in the Movies*, Simon & Schuster, New York, 1947, 1970, pp 175-189). Though he does not discuss paranoia or homosexual anxieties per se, his analysis of the sexual structure of the film accords perfectly with the structure of paranoia, and supplies the armature for a more elaborated notion of paranoia. Unlike more recent psychoanalytical critics. Tyler does not begin with a codified psychoanalytical grid through which films are to be read. He begins with a question not answered overtly in the film, which leads him to the issue of sexuality. He does not believe that the insurance salesman Neff's fear of claims adjuster Keyes (Edward G. Robinson) is warranted by the manifest elements of the plot. Neff (Fred MacMurray) knows his business and has every reason to think that his story and alibi are strong. Hence, why does he falter and abandon the scheme?

For Tyler, Neff's sexual bravado is only a façade, and Keyes intuitively senses this deception. Tyler seizes on the motif of the match Neff repeatedly lights for Keyes's cigar as the sign of Neff's supposed 'sexual spark' (surprisingly, Claire Johnston discusses this in her article on *Double Indemnity* – Johnston, 1978 – without

once referring to Parker Tyler's article.) When Keyes pressures Neff to take a desk job instead of remaining a glib, successful insurance salesman, Keyes senses Neff's difficulty with women. The tough talking does not conceal from Keyes Neff's failure to satisfy women. The aggressive sexuality of Phyllis Dietrichson (Barbara Stanwyck) offers Neff the opportunity to demonstrate to Keyes his sexual success, but Tyler maintains that ultimately Neff must turn on Phyllis in the fear that she will expose his sexual inadequacy:

'Even if Neff imagines he will be humiliated later by Phyllis's desertion, he is certainly much overestimating such a humiliation in view of the fact that he is counting on half the money with which to console himself – unless this sexual slap in the face should be the climax of previous less crucial humiliations, casual ones that Keyes is always hinting at even though blindly in his little lectures to Neff. The general psychological situation is such that Neff may have placed some supreme hope on Phyllis as a sexual partner who would inspire him to get and give satisfaction – a hope that is crushed' (Tyler, pp.186-187).

Tyler's incisive comments locate Neff's failure of nerve in his sexual inadequacy, which Keyes 'blindly' guesses at, but does not make certain connections that can cohere into a paranoid structure. Neff's entire manner before the murder is one of sexual confidence and potency. From his first encounter with Phyllis, Neff virtually boasts of his sexual readiness. In the famous dialogue about speeding, Phyllis has to warn him that he is exceeding the speed limit. In their next meeting, Neff makes constant references to virility. When Phyllis offers him some tea, he asks if she has something to get the tea up on its feet. After she speaks of the boredom of her marriage, Neff asks why she married Dietrichson; she says maybe she likes the way his thumbs hold up the world, and Neff rejoins lasciviously that she can call on him any time her husband's thumbs get tired. That is, the fast-talking Neff stalks Phyllis with apparent sexual bravado. Yet immediately after the murder, Neff makes every effort to avoid Phyllis. He reluctantly embraces her in the car after they dump the body of her husband; he tells her not to call him or see him. Phyllis is perplexed by his withdrawal, and she even has to revive his courage by warning him that they cannot go soft inside. Neff seems positively relieved not to have to deal with the demanding Phyllis.

Simultaneously with his flight from Phyllis, Neff begins to court the stepdaughter Lola (Jean Heather). In obvious contrast to the hard Phyllis, Lola offers Neff an idealised romantic relationship unthreatened by sexuality. The sublimated form of this fantasy is dramatically illustrated in the idyllic scene when the unlikely couple reposes in the edenic grass above the Hollywood Bowl during a concert of classical music. Presented like the rest of the film as Neff's flashback, the scene represents Neff's wistful vision of heterosexual love unsullied by the destructive demands of sexuality.

Tyler did not sketch out this pattern in terms of paranoia, but he did isolate the crucial link between the hard-boiled pose of Neff and his failure to indemnify those claims. It is here that the role of Keyes assumes its significance, which Tyler only touched on. In his paper on Dr Schreber, Freud remarked that paranoia had its course in the denial of the male's unacknowledged avowal of 'I (a man) love him (a man)' (Rieff, p.165). In fact, in response to Keyes's invitation to join him in the office and, by implication, to renounce the charade of his sexual posturing, Neff ironically deflects the solicitation with a casual 'I love you, too.' This pressure from Keyes, who has already been shown to be an unerring detector of deception, drives Neff to prove the absence of passive homosexuality. Hence, his fatal involvement with Phyllis functions as an indirect proof of his denial, for he abandons Phyllis to pursue the sexless Lola when Phyllis calls his bluff. Phyllis cannot understand his loss of nerve and demands an explanation. On a manifest level, his fear is inexplicable, for Neff listens (later) to the Dictaphone recording of Keyes which clears him of all suspicion: his alibi has worked perfectly. Yet Neff is still terrified of Keyes as he says to Phyllis that Keyes 'knows nothing.' Keyes may know nothing of Neff's participation in the crime, but Neff realises that Keyes does see through Neff's false sexual claims (in the opening scene of the film, Neff describes Keyes as 'wolf on a phoney claim'). Unable to satisfy the desire of Phyllis, and resigned to the futility of his fantasy with Lola, Neff's only solution is to confess his guilt to Keyes, ostensibly his complicity in the murder, but what forces the confession is Neff's ultimate acceptance of the latent homosexual ties between the two men.

In *Double Indemnity*, then, one can see that various features normally associated with *film noir* do in fact cohere in a structure of paranoia far more specifically than the loose association of paranoia with some general sense of fear or persecution indicates, particularly the core generative anxiety about passive homosexuality (all of which the recent spate of writing on *film noir* strangely ignores). This anxiety creates the need for the *femme fatale*, as the protagonist requires her in order to rehearse an aggressive masculinity, which, in turn, helps him to deny anxieties over weakness – hence the hard-boiled patter of the protagonist. The *femme fatale* and the tough talk, then, are two sides of the same anxiety, as it were. Furthermore, if the anxiety is, as Shapiro suggests, more generally about weakness, the male character can never relax his grim vigil: this accounts for his physical and emotional rigidity. He is impelled to see everything as part of a whole pattern directed at him, even if he cannot always distinguish the figure from the ground, as convoluted plots swirl around him.

This proclivity for personalising everything in the environment corresponds to the mechanism of projection, the single most invariant formal operation in paranoia. In the purest analogy to film, the flashback filters the past through the subjective memories of the protagonist, though the subjectivity of the flashback is usually complemented by other markers of subjectivity, such as assertive visual stylisation and stylised dialogue. Furthermore, the plot structure often suggests an implicit subjectivity by following the protagonist in his attempts to unravel the mystery of confusing events. Thus, for example, though *The Maltese Falcon* (John Huston, 1941) has no flashbacks, the events revolve around a single protagonist who is subjected to a series of assaults which result from his association with an alluring woman, and in perhaps the most stylised visual sequence – when Gutman (Sydney Greenstreet) slips a drug in his drink – the film emphasises his subjectivity by presenting several distorted point-of-view shots as the drug takes effect. The flashback structure, then, may not always be present, but its frequency in the *noir* films of the 1940s illustrates most clearly the importance of subjectivity.

Given that the flashback is prompted by some calamity, the narrator necessarily includes material that has contributed to his present predicament. Unlike earlier mystery plots, which teem with false leads, the most disparate elements in the paranoid's experience all turn out to be imbricated in the web of encirclement that has eventually closed in on him. Again, his inability to divine the interstices of the web only reinforces his suspicions, convinced as he is in advance of some hidden design. The discovery of the pattern is what permits the flashback to begin, and justifies the conviction in the interrelatedness of events. When Neff tells Phyllis that Keyes knows nothing, he is terrified because of his paranoid fear that in fact Keyes knows everything, but in addition, Neff is the one relating the flashback, and he knows that Keyes will tumble to the truth.

Though projection is central to paranoia, it is probably more useful not to apply it too literally as the expulsion of unwanted and perhaps unacknowledged feelings on to external characters. Using clinical evidence, Shapiro argues that the content of projection does not always involve hostile impulses, that the content can take many forms. Occasionally one can find neat instances of projection in the more limited sense, as in *Strangers on a Train* (Alfred Hitchcock, 1951), where Bruno (Robert Walker) does carry out the unconscious wishes of Guy (Farley Granger), and the film (like the book) underlines the motif of doubling throughout. But sifting through the characters as a rule to shake out the projective figures is probably too reductive an operation, particularly if one keeps in mind Shapiro's contention that there may be great diversity in the content of the projection. As projection in any

Still: the original ending of Double Indemnity *(cut by Wilder) – Keyes sees Neff go to the gas chamber.*

event enlists external figures into the protagonist's paranoid scenario, denying them autonomous existence independent of the character's proliferating suspicions, it is this insistent personalising of events that enacts the projective drama. The flashback structure makes this projective drama literal, but need not always appear; it does not in *Strangers on a Train*, for example. Personalisation of events leads to elimination of subplots which could introduce non-subjective elements. Thus, in *Double Indemnity*, the film drops the subplot of Sachetti's father, which provides an independent motivation for Neff to involve himself in Phyllis's life and only subsequently to begin his relationship with Lola. Certainly the removal of subplots in adaptations is common enough, but critics have remarked often on the complexity of plots in *film noir*, so the result, if not the objective of this removal, is not greater simplicity or limpidity of plot. With the complexity, however, all of the apparent centrifugal drive of the narrative turns out to be knotted together in the subjective projection of the main character.

A film that has been called 'one of the quintessential *films noirs*' (Silver & Ward, p.192) provides a more fully developed paranoid structure. Writing during the years of the *film noir* cycle, Parker Tyler did not mention the omnipresence of paranoia in these films in his article on *Double Indemnity* and he did not generalise a model from the single film. *Murder My Sweet* (Edward Dmytryk, 1944), however, does offer a sufficiently supple paranoid structure which could serve as a modal example of paranoia in *film noir*.

Based on a hard-boiled novel, *Farewell, My Lovely*, by Raymond Chandler, *Murder My Sweet* places private investigator Philip Marlowe (Dick Powell) in a bewildering plot of violence, duplicity, and sexual manipulation. There are many changes both in theme and plot which actually strengthen the paranoid structure. First of all, the script eliminates all reference to the criminal Laird Brunette connection, the core of the urban corruption theme. Yet Chandler himself described the theme of the book as the 'corrupt alliance of police racketeers in a small California town, outwardly "fair as the dawn" ' (in the 1939 plan of work taken from Chandler's notebook in Dorothy Gardner & Kathrine Sorley Walker, *Raymond Chandler Speaking*, Hamish Hamilton, London, 1962, p.124). Also, a female counterpart to Marlowe in the book, Anne Riordan, is transformed into the daughter of Mr Grayle in the film and thus becomes the stepdaughter of the *femme fatale* (Claire Trevor), who is married to Grayle. This unstable family arrangement, the same one found in *Double Indemnity*, sexually charges the plot with an Oedipal undercurrent.

The changes remove the social dimensions of the novel that Chandler felt were central. While Chandler wished to present some form of social critique, contrasting Marlowe's integrity with the small-time corruption of a small-town police force, the film suppresses this social resonance.

Still: the opening scene of Murder My Sweet – *Marlowe (Dick Powell) being pressured by the cops.*

Thus, there is no world in the film independent of Marlowe's connection to a single family, and one independent character from the book has been added to the family. In conjunction with the flashback structure, which has personalised the story, the erotic lure of Mrs Grayle's leg arouses the protagonist's desire and projectively initiates an Oedipal drama of a young wife to an elderly husband. It is true that Moose Malloy (Mike Mazurki) and Marriott (Douglas Walton) both approach Marlowe before he encounters Mrs Grayle but both seek out Marlowe through the agency of Mrs Grayle (Moose is searching for her, and Marriott is sent by her in order to eliminate Marlowe).

In addition, the type of corruption portrayed by Chandler in the novel is described as a new type of crime, specifically not a Manichean force constructed by the paranoid. It is essentially non-violent, not morally evil. The secondary characters in the book, such as the Bay City police contingent of Chief Wax, Galbraith, and Blane (who do not appear in the film), are only moderately corrupt. Galbraith tells Marlowe he has no idea what the true situation with Amthor and Sondeborg was. Later, Red (an honest undercover cop) explains to Marlowe that Marriott's murder is alien to this new crime:

'The racketeers are a new type . . . And as for the top men like Brunette – they didn't get there by murdering people. They got there by guts and brains – and they don't have the group courage that cops have either. But above all else they're businessmen. What they do is for money. Just like any other businessmen.'

By eliminating this theme, the film conforms to the paranoid tendency to pose problems in personal and absolute terms through a process akin to projection.

The plot then reinforces the subjectivity of the first-person narration and the figure of the private detective contributes an additional element. The private eye continues investigations that the police cannot solve for solution of the crime is not a personal obsession with them. The private eye is always making feeble excuses for why he remains on a case long after the job he has been hired for is completed, as Marlowe does in both book and film.

As a rule, when an entire film is told in flashback, the status of events related is immediately jeopardised by the inherent subjectivity of the narrator. In *Murder, My Sweet*, however, the flashback is doubly subjective, for it is the product of impaired vision. In the opening sequence, before the flashback begins, we see Marlowe with his eyes bandaged, a detail which announces the specific theme of vision in a literal sense in what follows. Thus, when the flashback opens with

Marlowe sitting at his desk, Moose Malloy appears out of the darkness as a blinking apparition in the window, startling Marlowe. Only after spinning around does he find Malloy standing in front of his desk. In the book, Marlowe meets Malloy entirely by accident in the stairwell of Florian's. Malloy has a presence independent of Marlowe's creation in the book. In the film, Marlowe summons up the image of Malloy in the blinking reflection on the window, making Malloy much more clearly a projection in the film. This change does not mean that the film is a dream in any way, only that the narration is invested with an oneiric quality, a characteristic often noted in *film noir* (e.g. by the first writers on *film noir*, Borde & Chaumeton, 1955). What is interesting in this film, however, is the recurrent instability of visual information, such as this first image of Malloy. In the film, as in the world of the paranoid, appearances cannot be trusted.

Critics have remarked on the subjectivity of Marlowe's drug-distorted perception at the sanatorium, but the thematic motif of unstable appearances is far more effective than the occasional visual flourishes. For one thing, the anamorphic images and superimpositions in the sanatorium can be attributed to the drugs, thus motivated or induced by some agent external to Marlowe's psyche. On the whole, the film does

Still: Murder My Sweet – *Moose Malloy (Mike Mazurki) hires Marlowe.*

not create an ambience of oblique shadows, unstable frame compositions, and threatening environment as found in discussions of *film noir*. In fact, the film fails to exploit the visual possibilities of scenes in the book like the following:

'The room was octagonal, draped in black velvet from floor to ceiling, with a high remote black ceiling that may have been velvet too. In the middle of the coal black lustreless rug stood an octagonal white table, just large enough for two pairs of elbows and in the middle of it a mild white globe on a black stand. The light came from this. How, I couldn't see.'

The scene in the film lacks this sense of danger and menace, for it is flooded with light, although tastefully modelled with shadows.

Instead, the unreliability of appearances is developed through narrative elements. Marlowe cannot see Anne Grayle's face at the scene of Marriott's murder, for his vision is still affected by the blow to the head. He places her at the scene only later when she repeats the same question that she had asked when she discovered him earlier, 'Are you all right?' His hearing is more reliable than his vision. The motif of impaired vision extends to photography as well. Marlowe is given a photograph of the woman he is trying to locate, but we eventually learn that the photograph is a fake. As the photograph is assumed to be an accurate representation of the object of the search (Velma/Mrs Grayle), the actual unreliability of the photograph throws the legitimacy of appearance in the film into question. Once again, this unstable status of appearances is stronger in the film. In the book, in addition to the photograph Marlowe takes from Mrs Florian, Anne (Anne Shirley) produces a newspaper photograph of the real woman from the society page in old newspaper files. In the book, there are two photographs, a real one and a false one: the film eliminates the real one.

With the attrition of the visual sense, the other senses are given greater prominence. It has already been remarked that Marlowe connects Anne to the scene of Marriott's murder with his hearing. Marriott's presence in Marlowe's outer office is announced by the odour of his cologne, as Marlowe stops to sniff the air before actually meeting Marriott. And Amthor's association with Marriott is recalled when Marlowe inhales the aroma of Amthor's carnation upon finding Amthor (Otto Kruger) murdered. Throughout the film, Marlowe runs cigarettes under his nose before putting them in his mouth, and he sniffs liquor before drinking it. Finally, in the cab at the end, Anne's perfume informs Marlowe that Anne is in the car, for he neither sees her (his eyes are bandaged) nor hears her.

The motif of perfume identifies Marriott as effeminate even before Marlowe meets him, for the elevator operator comments on it as Marlowe proceeds to his office, where Marriott is already waiting. In the ensuing conversations,

Still: Murder My Sweet – *Marlowe takes the false photograph from Mrs Florian (Esther Howard).*

Marlowe insults Marriott several times with snide remarks about his effeminacy. As Marriott fondles some object on Marlowe's desk, Marlowe asks derisively if Marriott can pull his flaps in. The film puts slightly more stress on Marriott's affected manner. In the book and the film Marriott finally responds to Marlowe's taunts by asking how Marlowe would like a 'swift punch on the nose'. In the book, Marlowe merely gets up to leave; in the film, Marlowe replies derisively, 'I tremble at the thought of violence.' Despite this attitude, Marlowe agrees to accompany Marriott to retrieve some stolen jewellery, but he bungles the job when Marriott is murdered. At that point, Marlowe no longer has any obligation to Marriott, but he notes in voice-over that he felt responsible for the murder, for he had been hired to protect Marriott. Thus, Marriott's death can be seen to have resulted from Marlowe's undisguised hostility to him, particularly given Marlowe's unsolicited confession of responsibility. The encounter with effeminacy in this sense unleashes a hostility in the aggressively masculine Marlowe which leads to the 'weak' character's death, the only death in the film for which Marlowe could be accused of any responsibility.

A related pattern emerges in his relationship with the seductive and sexually aggressive Mrs Grayle. Marlowe ostentatiously stares at her bare leg when he first meets her and her elderly husband. After the huband excuses himself on account of fatigue, Mrs Grayle immediately proposes getting down to some serious drinking, and Marlowe readily accepts. As Mrs Grayle joins him on the couch and begins to unveil her seductive charms, Anne, the stepdaughter, abruptly interrupts the scene and quickly leaves. This triangle establishes the sexual pattern of the film.

Belying his sexually confident pose, Marlowe consistently repels Mrs Grayle's advances and seeks the domestic shelter of Anne's maternal affection. When a date with Mrs Grayle ends in the sanatorium nightmare, Marlowe escapes to the refuge of Anne's apartment, where she tenderly cares for him. When Mrs Grayle invites Marlowe to the dark and secluded beach house to solicit his help in her troubles, Marlowe agrees (though it is understood that he is lying). Once the plans for the following night have been worked out, Mrs Grayle sits down beside Marlowe on the couch and turns the lights off, plunging the room into darkness. The film immediately cuts to a tense Marlowe stiffening as he senses the danger of her seductiveness: he abruptly disengages himself from her embrace and leaves, offering the lame excuse that he has many things to prepare for the next night.

The point is that Marlowe's sexual bravado is a lie. Fleeing the sexual demands of the mature Mrs Grayle, Marlowe prefers the pre-adult sexuality of the stepdaughter, Anne. The ending neatly captures this sexual ambiguity. After Marlowe finishes telling his story to the police, the gruff Lieutenant Nulty (Paul Phillips) guides the still-bandaged Marlowe to a taxi. Silently, Anne, instead of Nulty, enters the cab with Marlowe. Identifying Anne by her perfume, Marlowe feigns a playful ignorance when he asks 'Nulty' (Anne) if he would kiss him.

Now, in most discussions of *Murder, My Sweet*, the paranoia is dealt with on a superficial level. Marlowe suffers a series of assaults during the course of the film as he navigates through a hostile environment. These unprovoked attacks, which become a comic refrain when the flashback voice-over returns after each loss of consciousness to repeat 'A black pool opened up . . .', serve to justify the use of paranoia as the protagonist appears to be persecuted at every turn. What is being argued here is that the clinical description of paranoia can tie together many threads of this film, and others in the *noir* cycle, uncovering deeper structural relations among

Still: Murder My Sweet – *Moose with the body of Velma/Mrs Grayle (Claire Trevor).*

them than can be revealed by the vague ascription of persecution.

In *Murder, My Sweet*, a tough, outwardly self-confident, sarcastic male protagonist travels through an environment fraught with danger, where he is repeatedly assaulted and apparently unable to put all the pieces of the puzzles together. The temptation of a sexually demanding woman seems to hold the answer, but the character only intuits her complicity until the revelation of the dénouement. Along the way, the detective meets a character who makes no pretences of aggressive masculinity, in contradistinction to himself, and may be presented as effeminate, frequently a coded characterisation for homosexual. This figure will elicit hostile and often violent behaviour from the protagonist. This reaction is caused by the defensive denial and expulsion of such feelings of weakness in the main character and represents the flip side of the excessive masculinity adopted in his relations with women. A non-threatening younger woman mediates between the two defensive postures, defusing the detective's sexual anxieties by occupying a space insulated from sexuality. In the purest case, the detective projects these anxieties on to a single family. He sees the elderly husband as essentially emasculated and withered by the sexual desire of the young wife, and he idealises the stepdaughter as a pre-sexual figure who offers sanctuary from the fatiguing total mobilisation of attention and energy required in his relations with adults. With her, tender feelings can surface, and he can remove the armour donned in the unsuccessful dual struggle against the acknowledgement of interior weakness on the one hand, and the projected feelings of fear and danger from the outside.

The sexual economy of paranoia can link together, then, a number of characteristic features of *film noir*: the macho hero, the *femme fatale*, the convoluted plot structure, the threatening environment, irrational violence, effeminate characters, subjective narration. At the heart of paranoia lies anxiety over a loss of autonomy, which may be directly related to passive homosexual fears, and that anxiety activates the defensive operations that produce rigid mobilisation against internal and external threats at the same time.

Of course, this constellation of features does not necessarily appear in a large number of *films noirs*. But perhaps the search for a concise, overarching conception of *film noir* is futile, given the multiple variations of plots, characters, narrative devices, and sexual relationships. The modal structure discussed above in relation to *Double Indemnity* and *Murder My Sweet* seems to justify critical application of the psychoanalytical term paranoia, against which other films might be measured. If paranoia is a core element in *film noir*, as most critics assert, then male anxieties over loss of autonomy and sexual inadequacy must necessarily inform discussion of *film noir*.

FILM NOIR AND SUPPRESSIVE NARRATIVE
Beyond a Reasonable Doubt
Douglas Pye

In a famous exchange with François Truffaut, Alfred Hitchcock distinguishes between suspense and surprise:

'Let us suppose that there is a bomb underneath this table between us. Nothing happens, and then all of a sudden, "Boom!" There is an explosion. The public is surprised, but prior to this surprise, it has been an absolutely ordinary scene, of no special consequence. Now let us take a suspense situation. The bomb is underneath the table and the public knows it . . . In these conditions this same innocuous conversation becomes fascinating because the public is participating in the scene. The audience is longing to warn the characters on the screen . . .' (François Truffaut, *Hitchcock*, Panther, London, 1969, pp.58-59).

Hitchcock's distinction is based on the control of the flow of narrative information to the spectator and on varying the relationship between characters' knowledge and spectators'. Surprise suppresses narrative information and places the spectator on an equal footing (in Hitchcock's example) with the characters, but, in addition to limiting access to information, it depends, in effect, on misleading the audience in order to spring the surprise. Suspense, on the other hand, privileges the audience, offering more information than the characters have and explaining the real nature of the situation. Hitchcock also introduces a third term, 'mystery', only to dismiss it: 'To my way of thinking, mystery is seldom suspenseful. In a whodunnit, for instance, there is no suspense, only a sort of intellectual puzzle'. In the case of mystery, the audience, like an investigator, knows that there is a puzzle to be solved, but the information that could lead to its solution is withheld.

In practice, crime stories and thrillers, including Hitchcock's, mix all three, creating varying relationships with the audience as the narrative develops. Characteristically, suppression of narrative information plays such a major part in these genres that we come to expect it, so that while specific incidents may surprise us, the effect of surprise, like mystery and suspense, is controlled by our experience of the generic field. On the whole, then, knowledge of the conventions provides us with a large degree of security. In the whodunnit, for instance, we know that there is an enigma and that information about it is being suppressed; equally, we can be confident that the mystery will be cleared up and that what has been withheld will be revealed. If the crime represents a disorder in the world, then the implicit promise of a solution acts as a guarantee that order will be restored. We may be placed in a position of very limited perception and understanding as the narrative unfolds but much of our pleasure in the genre depends on the *frisson* of anxiety which uncertainty and deceptive appearance can provide when they arise from a mystery that we know will finally be solved. As John Cawelti suggests: '. . . the excitement and uncertainty are ultimately controlled and limited by the familiar world of the formulaic structure' (*Adventure, Mystery and Romance*, University of Chicago Press, 1976, p.16).

Michael Walker has outlined *film noir*'s debt to the development of the whodunnit represented by the hard-boiled American crime writers of the 1930s and 1940s. In both the novels and the films, disorder cannot as conclusively be put right by the hero's actions as in the classic detective story. The disturbance in *film noir* goes beyond individual criminal acts to encompass a derangement of familiar social and narrative roles and relationships. Increasingly, writers have associated the troubling of the agency of the hero with doubts about his male power and authority and seen a corresponding uncertainty about traditional female roles. Often, in *film noir*, the hero, rather than standing apart from the corruption, tends to become implicated, often through his involvement with a woman, in the world he enters. Instability, opacity of motivation, deceptive appearances and treachery as pervasive aspects of the fictional world are parallelled by anxiety, neurosis, unstable identity and guilt in the central characters.

Critical interest in *film noir* springs mainly from its representation of fictional worlds, narratives and characters that are so much at odds with the dominant patterns of Hollywood cinema and the affirmative vision of the American Dream. Coupled with characteristic forms of narration, *film noir* seems to promise a much less comfortable experience for the spectator than more traditional crime fiction – a balance between anxiety and security much less reassuringly held. Richard Dyer, for instance, in characterising the structure of *film noir* as labyrinthine, writes of expectations undermined or denied, whole episodes of plot which go nowhere, solutions to mysteries which are incomprehensible and ambiguities which remain unresolved, the heterosexual couple not getting together in the end, and, perhaps most significantly in this context, the way in which dream, flashback and voice-over structures 'cast into doubt the status-as-truth of the events presented' (Dyer, 1977).

Some of the most interesting analyses of *film noir* are those which have pursued the implication of Dyer's last point, that certain forms of narration in *film noir* undermine the reliability of what we see and hear. Christine Gledhill, for instance, suggests that voice-over in *film noir* 'loses some of its control over events' and that one way of looking at plot in *film noir* 'is to see it as a struggle between different voices for control over the telling of the story'. Correspondingly, she argues that there is a proliferation of points of view and a struggle within the text for one viewpoint to gain hegemony' (Gledhill, 1978). Gledhill's argument is part of a wider account of contradictory impulses in *film noir*, and her use of 'voices' is at least partly metaphorical: the sense is of traditional structures – of narration, character, gender – beginning to fracture, rather than (in most cases) of multiple narrative voices. Nevertheless, the distinctly modernist terms ('struggle between different voices', 'proliferation of points of view') are significant in implying unusual formal openness and considerable pressure on the spectator.

J.P. Telotte argues that *film noir* was unusually open to narrative experimentation and that in frequently exposing the problem of viewpoint, particularly by using subjective narration, the films dramatise 'an unprecedented concern with how we see, understand, and describe our world . . .' (Telotte, 1989 p.35). At times, he suggests, subjective narration threatens to destabilise the spectator's traditionally fairly secure position. But he is rightly circumspect about the extent to which the spectator is implicated in the epistemological uncertainty endemic in the films' worlds: ' . . .we should note that even the darkest *noir* visions of American culture usually reserve a stable position from which to speak. Even when it seems to strike at the very foundations of popular film, to lay bare its ideological operations, the *film noir* typically exempted the *spectator's* position from direct scrutiny' (p.21).

Narration which, for instance, uses flashback and voice-over (often considered especially characteristic of *film noir*) does seem to emphasise the labyrinthine nature of the fictional world and to link us closely to the limited perceptions of the protagonist. These are forms of narration which might seem to involve the spectator very directly with the problems of subjectivity and of orientation in the films' worlds, suggesting the impossibility of achieving a secure and detached overview. In practice, though, their effect seems very different. In the first instance, recognition of genre plays a determining role in producing expectations both of narrative and strategies of narration. Although *films noirs* are unconventional in a number of ways, they largely remain within the broad generic band of 'crime story', a category within which, for example, withholding of information from the spectator is a fundamental convention. Moreover, the films characteristically introduce us fairly quickly to worlds in which deceit and uncertainty are pervasive and therefore become part of what we expect in the narrative. Even in *noir*, generic conventions tend to 'naturalise' the films' methods and worlds and, as Cawelti suggests, to control and limit uncertainty.

Rather than subjecting us to the limited perceptions and bewilderment of the protagonist, voice-over and flashback also distance us from the films' worlds. Voice-over may seem to involve us with the experience of the protagonist, but it is experience recollected and the account inevitably removes us from the events themselves. Our access to events is filtered through the act of story-telling – we are privileged observers of a story which is being told, sometimes to another character (*Double Indemnity*, Billy Wilder, 1944; *Out of the Past*, Jacques Tourneur), sometimes directly to us (*The Lady from Shanghai*, Orson Welles, 1948). Flashback further emphasises our distance from events. In these films we also tend to know from the outset, at least in part, what the outcome of the past events has been for the protagonist. The most extreme cases are perhaps *Sunset Boulevard* (Billy Wilder, 1950) and *D.O.A.* (Rudolph Maté, 1949), where the protagonist is dead or dying as the narrative begins, but even where the final outcome is withheld, the voice-over narration and mood of the film are doom-laden enough for us to expect the worst. Foster Hirsch comments on the distance that these devices create between the narrator and his past (Hirsch, 1981, p.75), but the devices also inevitably distance the spectator. At times, we may share the protagonist's bewilderment but the containing narrative framework (voice-over, flashback) requires us to adopt a perspective characteristic of what Northrop Frye calls, in *Anatomy of Criticism* (Princeton University Press, 1957), the 'ironic mode', in which we look down from a superior position on a scene of limitation and struggle.

As Telotte points out, films which use the subjective narration that is commonly held to be particularly characteristic of *film noir* are actually a minority of the films within the cycle (about 40 out of 130 in his survey). Most *films noirs* use the more familiar forms of narration, unmediated by voice-over and undisturbed by flashbacks. In these films the unstable world of *film noir* is still present, but, on the face of it, their less problematical narration and their use of apparently more authoritative views of events, unhindered by intervening voice-over, should produce even less discomfort for the spectator. What is more, it is rare for such films to restrict the spectator to the range of perception of the protagonist –

often our access to events is significantly wider. Here the spectator would seem to be even more removed from the pervasive insecurity of the *noir* world.

However, if the familiar conventions of direct narration seem straightforward and trustworthy, the mode also allows the possibility of challenging the spectator very directly (and without prompting by voice-over narration) to wrestle with the problem of appearances, to penetrate the surfaces characters present to each other and to us, and to make sense of the appearances we are offered. The extent to which the spectator is challenged in such ways depends, of course, on how the film-maker makes use of the conventional means of offering the access to narrative information and to the motives and feelings of the characters. Within the conventions, it is not necessary to resort to voice-over to acquaint the spectator with mental states – a whole rhetoric exists in narrative film-making which can signal 'authentic' access to thought and feeling. What films present us with are characters moving and speaking, the outward marks by means of which inner life must be inferred (Richard Dyer helpfully discusses the relationship of inference to interiority as a problem of the construction of character in movies in *Stars*, British Film Institute, London, 1979, pp.132-139). These processes of inference are as fundamental to movies as to life, and it is a basic convention of narrative film-making, buttressed by various rhetorical devices, that most of the time such inferences may be made without undue caution. We have no choice but to accept this convention, at least as a working hypothesis, but a film-maker may exploit our willingness to trust in it too readily and completely – inferences may be apparently encouraged and then undermined.

There is no necessary link between such probing of the convention and *film noir*, but it is hardly surprising that, within the cycle's recurrent preoccupation with deceptive or ambiguous appearances, some film-makers have exploited these possibilities. Nicholas Ray, for instance, presents his characters and the spectator with the challenge and risk of making judgements of others on what the films show to be inherently insecure grounds (as in *In a Lonely Place* and *On Dangerous Ground*), but without showing any great interest in suppressive narrative as such. More commonly, *films noirs* withhold particular knowledge in order to release it later and resolve the question of, say, the *femme fatale*'s nature.

This restriction of access to reliable information about motive and character is built on the basic conditions of film as a dramatic art. In its more straightforward form, it can also be associated with the other forms of narrative suppression which characterise the crime story and which form part of the expectations we are likely to bring to our viewing of *film noir*. The method I associate with Nicholas Ray is perhaps more challenging to the spectator because it has the potential to undermine expectation and to make conventional assumptions about character problematical. It is the extension of this challenge to the spectator's wider relationship to the narrative and the role played by massively suppressive narrative that are particularly remarkable in Fritz Lang's *Beyond a Reasonable Doubt* (1956).

Strikingly, both Lang and Alfred Hitchcock made unusually extensive use of suppressive narrative in the late *film noir* period (Hitchcock's films sometimes have interesting but rarely straightforward relationships to the cycle – *see*, for instance, the Introduction to this book and 'Psychoanalysis and *Film Noir*'). In both cases, it is plausible to associate the strategy with a desire to engage critically both with narrative conventions and with the spectator's expectations and response: if not to subject the spectator's position to 'direct scrutiny' (Telotte), then, through indirect means, to erode the security represented by conventional ways of seeing. Two of Hitchcock's greatest films, *Vertigo* (1958) and *Psycho* (1960), for instance, depend on suppressive narrative and on the moments of revelation produced by sustained withholding of information from the spectator. Each of the films departs radically from Hitchcock's expressed preference for the methods of suspense, in which the spectator is placed in a position of knowledge, in favour of surprise, in which something previously withheld is suddenly revealed. *Vertigo* is particularly interesting in this context because the complete suppression in the first part of the film of Gavin Elster's (Tom Helmore's) plot to murder his wife and to ensnare Scottie (James Stewart) in the masquerade of Judy's (Kim Novak's) impersonation of Madeline, is associated with a further restriction of the narrative which compels us to a large extent to follow Scottie's experience of events. In another link with *film noir* and its insecure heroes, the film suggests from the outset (if we grasp its significance) the precarious state that Scottie is in, but we have no choice except to become involved in his increasing obsession with Madeline. Correspondingly, we have small chance, because of the narrative suppression, of grasping the significance of what appear in retrospect to be powerful signifiers of fantasy in the visual style of certain sequences.

Crucially, however, narrative suppression is accompanied by a use of generic cues which have the effect of misleading the spectator. In *Vertigo* and *Beyond a Reasonable Doubt*, it is vital for the orientation of the spectator that conventions of the crime story – in particular the expectations of narrative suppression and deceptive appearances during a murder investigation – should be deflected: that it should be impossible to suspect what is being withheld from us. In *Vertigo*, as the rational approach to life which Scottie asserts is undermined by the apparently paranormal elements in the story of Madeline's supposed possession by Carlotta Valdes, so Hitchcock undermines our expectations by seeming to imply a generic shift from his normal territory to the fantastic – a tale of possibly supernatural events. As a number of writers have suggested (*see* Rosemary Jackson, *Fantasy, the Literature of Subversion*, Methuen, London 1981), in fantasy, characters and/or readers are faced with events which may be either naturally or supernaturally caused, and there is a hesitation between incompatible explanations which cannot be resolved. Something similar happens in *Vertigo*, and, in parallel ways, the doubts act to erode both Scottie's sense of himself and the world, and the spectator's orientation. There is a parallel here with the uncertainty often faced (though without the supernatural dimension) by the *film noir* protagonist, but in *Vertigo* the spectator's experience is much more radically disturbed. The apparent generic shift disorientates us and, together with our close involvement with Scottie, forms the basis for the effect of the later revelation that Elster murdered his wife and that Madeline was a charade. Once we know what happened but Scottie does not, we become increasingly distanced from his treatment of Judy and aware of the monstrous implications of an obsession and a way of seeing which, in the earlier parts of the movie, we substantially shared.

Beyond a Reasonable Doubt is the most extreme example of interest in suppressive narrative and in the manipulation of spectator response which span Lang's career (*see*, for instance, George Wilson's analysis of *You Only Live Once* in *Narration in Light*, Johns Hopkins University Press, Baltimore, 1986, and my article on *The Blue Gardenia* in CineAction 13/14, Summer 1988).

Still: Tom (Dana Andrews) inadvertently reveals to Susan (Joan Fontaine) that he killed Patti/Emma.

In ways that are both strikingly parallel to and very different from Hitchcock's in *Vertigo*, Lang maintains an extraordinary level of narrative suppression, tangles our generic expectations and maintains complex systems of visual narration that we are unlikely at first to understand. When we look back from the end of *Beyond a Reasonable Doubt*, the film fairly clearly contains a number of elements that we can associate with the familiar descriptions of *film noir*. It is a crime story in which the hero becomes ensnared and is destroyed. The plot contains abrupt and unpredictable twists and turns – Austin Spencer's (Sydney Blackmer's) sudden accidental death and the destruction of crucial evidence, the last-minute return of his executor and the discovery of Austin's letter describing the conspiracy just in time to save Tom Garrett (Dana Andrews) from execution, then the revelation of Tom's guilt. As in so many earlier films, characters who try to assert control are brought down. Very little in the narrative world is as it seems. Like a number of other *noir* stories, it involves a male protagonist held between two milieus – the respectable, established society of the Spencers and the seedier half-world represented by the Club Zombie – and between two women – Susan (Joan Fontaine), the newspaper proprietor's daughter to whom he aspires but with whom he hardly seems comfortable and Patti/Emma, his wife, whom he murders. It is not difficult to imagine the story told in ways that would more obviously link it to the *noir* tradition – in flashback from Tom's condemned cell, for instance.

Crucially, however, a good deal of what associates the movie with *film noir* is available only in retrospect. As I have argued, in most *films noirs*, the kind of world the film will present is cued fairly decisively from the outset and appropriate expectations evoked. Here the *noir* cues are largely absent. There is no sign that the characters are involved in anything resembling the action of, say, *Double Indemnity*, *Out of the Past* or *The Lady from Shanghai*. In fact, at first – and for some time – the generic cues suggest something more like a social problem movie. At the same time, the visual style is in many scenes quite flat, very different to the chiaroscuro and unstable composition that is thought of as a hallmark of the *noir* cycle. All this is to suggest how massively Lang suppresses narrative information and to what extent he works on our point of view. In the absence of clear cues to evoke 'story of investigation', 'whodunnit, 'mystery', or whatever, we are confronted by the challenge of appearances and thrown back on habitual forms of reading and response.

What that implies for our grip on events is dramatised with extraordinary force in the revelation near the end of the movie that Tom Garrett killed Patti Grey, a crime for which, as part of a conspiracy to expose the judicial system, he has deliberately caused himself to be tried and convicted, but with which, to the audience, he seemed to have had no connection. Tom's guilt is an extreme case of surprise in Hitchcock's sense – there was, as it were, a bomb under the table all the time, but we didn't know it. The suppression of Tom's guilt and its ultimate revelation can, of course, seem like a particularly extreme form of cheating. In a whodunnit it might be possible to get away with producing a murderer who could not have been suspected, but Lang might seem to compound the abuse of the spectator by not even evoking the conventions of the whodunnit. Tom's guilt is a shock as great as the revelation in *Vertigo*.

It is necessary with *Beyond a Reasonable Doubt*, as with *Vertigo*, to rescan the early parts of the film in the light of the revelation in order to establish what is at stake in the use of such extreme narrative suppression. How, for instance, is the suppression of Tom's crime related to what initially seems the film's central thematic and dramatic focus – capital punishment?

The film opens with a man being led to the electric chair, flanked by warders and watched by a number of male observers, including Dana Andrews and Sydney Blackmer (we do not yet know the characters' names). There could be no more dramatic way of pointing up the full implications of the title, *Beyond a Reasonable Doubt* (the credits appear over the execution sequence). The second sequence introduces the characters of Tom Garrett (Andrews) and Austin Spencer (Blackmer) after the execution (a newspaper headline, 'Peters Executed' opens the sequence) and Spencer's position as an editor crusading against the death penalty becomes rapidly clear. But the discussion in the scene centres less on the moral question of whether capital punishment can be justified than on the fallibility of judicial process and the use of circumstantial evidence – conviction on the basis of evidence which, by its nature, is inconclusive. These issues become, some time later, the basis of the plot which Austin and Tom concoct to have a inno- cent man convicted of murder.

When they are joined by District Attorney Thompson (Philip Bourneuf), a further issue emerges – the way 'an able and persuasive pros- ecutor like you can make a jury believe that a thing is a fact when it isn't.' In other words, Spencer is preoccupied not only with the pro- cesses of rational argument leading to proof of guilt but with the rhetoric that complicates that process – the way people can be persuaded to accept something, or, indeed, be dissuaded from accepting it, even though the evidence is incon- clusive. That is, argument may be incomplete but it may also be misleading in that it encour- ages a confidence in the conclusion offered that is unwarranted.

Within the drama, Lang involves the charac- ters in questions of proof and evidence in several ways. The issues are most obviously present in the central plot (evidence of Tom's guilt), but the characters repeatedly address the question

'How do you know?' and its variants to each other as well as at times asserting 'knowledge' that is really belief or assumption (as in Susan's assertion of Tom's innocence). Equally, the problem of rhetorical persuasion is embedded in a range of ways in the film's courtroom drama as the lawyers attempt to sway the jury. Simulta- neously, however, Lang begins to engage the spectator with problems both of knowledge and of persuasion, although their presence as prob- lems is much less clearly foregrounded for us than for the characters. Indeed, they are unlikely to be directly perceived as problems at all because they are embedded both in a suppressive narra- tive (something of which we cannot be aware) and in familiar processes of narration and narra- tive involvement. Our 'evidence' is incomplete because of what Lang withholds, but, at the same time, we are inevitably subject to the whole battery of rhetorical processes that char- acterise popular narrative and to the expectations we bring with us to the act of viewing, and Lang uses both to implicate us in processes which bear closely on the film's more obviously dramatised concerns.

This may begin to suggest that capital punish- ment itself is not the centre of Lang's interest. Locating a trial for murder and the death penalty itself at the centre of the plot provides the most extreme focus for the linked issues of proof and persuasion. Lang, then, dramatises these issues in terms of the processes of perception, selec- tion, interpretation and presentation and makes these processes involve the spectator (although we are unlikely to recognise this) as much as the characters. The final revelation and hence awareness of the preceding suppression of narra- tive information become ways of bringing home our willingness to be persuaded to accept what is apparently but not conclusively the case. Per- haps, in other words, the film plays on the spectator in much the way that Austin Spencer suggests an able and persuasive prosecutor plays on the jury.

In believing that we know the truth (that Tom is framing himself in order to demonstrate the flaws in judicial process), we are placed in a sit- uation similar to that of the characters who are expressing in a variety of ways their confidence in what they 'know'. Yet, in the drama, Lang exposes the emptiness of that confidence and the tenuous basis that it rests on. What passes for knowledge and/or proof is a mixture of instinct, belief, circumstantial and apparently objective but flawed evidence. The film implicitly points to the flimsiness of the evidence against Tom, for instance, by dressing a variety of extras and Thompson himself in overcoats and/or hats simi- lar to those supposedly worn by the killer. Susan asserts that she 'knows' Tom is innocent, but her knowledge is no more than belief. Thompson has no substantial proof, only his instinct that 'beneath his cultivated exterior', Tom was 'moved by brutal impulses'. Ironically, Thomp- son's instinct turns out to be correct, but it has

no more basis and is no more reliable than the other processes by which the characters reach their judgments. In parallel but much less apparent ways in the film's imagery and its narration, Lang challenges us to recognise that our confidence is similarly misplaced.

The processes of perception, selection and presentation that lead to interpretation and judgement are linked to the spectator and to the film's narration at one level by the repeated presence in the drama of forms of visual representation: photographs and television images, press and TV cameras, as well as the Polaroid camera with which Austin records the stages of the conspiracy. Within the film's minimal *mise-en-scène*, their presence takes on considerable force and Lang accentuates them by making photographs and newspaper stories the only things seen consistently in close-up. Once one perceives the pattern, it can become evident that they mark the fact of mediation – both the 'secondhand' nature of the representations and the processes of selection and emphasis that are inevitably involved in making any representation. The visual media can record (and only in part) no more than what is there to be seen. What is represented is at best partial and at worst a falsification. Thus, Austin's photographs, designed to record the stages of the plot and therefore to establish Tom's innocence, establish only that

Still: Thompson (Philip Bourneuf, in overcoat) and Hale (Arthur Franz) with Tom before he is booked for murder.

Tom and Austin planted the evidence which led to Tom's arrest. They do not constitute proof of innocence any more than the trial evidence constitutes proof of guilt.

Even more striking, especially given that television cameras did not have access to American trials in 1956, is the bulky presence of TV cameras in Lang's courtroom. Their presence reminds us repeatedly of the fact of mediation. They record what is there to be seen and heard – the apparent drama of Tom's trial – and from that drama 'highlights' are screened each evening, an event we witness being watched by Susan, Austin and Jonathan, Tom's attorney (Shepperd Strudwick). The recorded highlights emphasise two kinds of selection: from the day's events and from the visual field – selections from the temporal unity of the day to create a condensed narrative with its own imposed emphases ('highlights') and selections from the space of the courtroom to create views for the TV cameras. These are also, as we know, selections from an event which is itself only part of the wider drama to which we have been given apparently privileged access. The striking presence of TV cameras offers us briefly a kind of film within the film which also

*Still: Austin Spencer (Sydney Blackmer) photographs
Tom wiping his car clean of fingerprints..*

presents a model of the relationship between
story, narration and spectator. The cameras in
the courtroom parallel the cameras that present
the drama to us; the edited highlights parallel
the film's narrative organisation; the television
audience parallels our own position as spectators
of the film. The use of television points, though
enigmatically, to the fact that our access to the
story is both partial and controlled.

As this implies then, the suppression of narrative
information is part of a wider set of strategies of
narration by means of which the spectator's perceptions and responses are channelled. I want
now to turn to Lang's control of narration, visual
style and performance.

Perhaps one of the commonest responses to
the film is that, apart from its unusual plot, it
seems conspicuously unremarkable – rather flat
in both its visual style and its performances. In
more positive terms, it might seem functional in
style, to the point of minimalism – all superfluities
stripped away. This is a point made by Jacques
Rivette in a very acute early article (*Cahiers du
Cinéma*, November 1957). He suggests that the
film places the spectator under unusual pressure
because of a series of 'denials': the film seems to
refuse orthodox elaboration of character or incident and to subordinate everything to the most
abstract function, close to the bare minimum
that will allow the narrative to operate. The elements that make up this apparently functional
surface, however, also work very precisely both
to control the spectator's viewpoint and to develop the film's concern with perception and
knowledge. Several strategies can be identified:

l) From its inception, we know about the plan to
have Tom convicted and are therefore likely to
believe that we have privileged access to narrative information. The fact that other characters
remain in the dark and that secrecy is of the

essence if the conspiracy is to succeed tends to
increase our security in the knowledge we possess. In other ways, too, our access to what is
going on does not seem unduly restrictive – in
fact we see and therefore know more even than
the conspirators (as in scenes – like the police
questioning the night club girls – at which they
are not present). Both in terms of our possession
of information and of access to the film's world,
our position seems initially relatively secure and
not subject to significant restriction.

2) In other respects, however, the narration suggests certain limits to our view. The film is made
up of over 40 sequences, most of them very
brief. Many of these are tightly linked so that,
particularly early on, a reference in one scene cues
a transition directly to the next, for instance,
from the club (sequence 2) to Tom's apartment
(3), to Spencer's house (4); from a reference in
sequence 4 to the rarity of murders with no
obvious suspects, to a close-up (sequence 5) of
a newspaper with such a case described. One
effect of this is to produce a sense of very strong
narrative progression – a forward drive which we
experience as almost remorseless. Once the plan
to have Tom framed is put into action, this
powerful narrative drive is heightened by a larger-
scale principle of narrative prolepsis: we know
how the plot is supposed to develop, and each
stage in the manufacturing of evidence and then
in the trial points forward to the next as Tom
and Austin's plan unfolds.

3) At the same time, Lang heightens this strong
forward momentum by showing us only the narrative 'kernels' of each scene: 'topping and tailing'
many scenes so that we come into them after the
characters have entered and move to another

scene before they exit. It is as if we witness only part of the whole scene. Correspondingly, just as there are few entrances and exits to begin and end scenes, there are virtually no transitional sequences: we tend not to see characters en route from one location to another. We could, for instance, follow Tom and Susan (Joan Fontaine) out of the club (sequence 2) or see them in a car on the way to Tom's apartment, but Lang cuts directly from one interior to the next and to a point in the action where the scene in the apartment is not just underway but almost over.

The spectator is placed by these decisions in the grip of a very strong controlling narration. There is no sense here of narration seeming to follow the characters, of characters apparently dictating narrative progression. Rather, we are carried along by the narration itself. This process of narrative shaping could emphasise how selective our access to the narrative is, how schematic the narration. But particularly once the conspiracy is launched, the film's plot naturalises the narrative drive: the selectivity and the schematism can seem little more than ways of showing us what is pertinent to the development of the plot. Any other functions which may be served by these processes are difficult to perceive because they have no clear 'anchor'. When we later rescan the film, it can become clear that

narrative selectivity is a pervasive process, both in the presentation of individual scenes and at the level of the wider story, and that it goes well beyond the selectivity that is indispensable to any narrative, or to the demands of the conspiracy plot. The incompleteness of our access to the narrative is in fact constantly stressed, though we are likely to remain blind to its scale and significance.

4) Our access is also restricted (although, again, we are unlikely to perceive its pertinence) in relation to the characters' thoughts and feelings. In particular, the film seems consciously to avoid many of the conventional ways of signalling access to thought or feeling. For instance, we rarely see characters alone – a situation that conventionally encourages us to accept what we see as signalling the character's 'authentic' self. To take one example when we do – as Tom takes the phone call after Susan leaves his apartment in sequence 3, the scene is cut short before we can know who is calling and before we can interpret Tom's reaction to the call. Later, he says the call was from his publisher, and we have no reason to doubt him (although reading back from the end of the film, we might surmise that it was from Patti/Emma). This connects to the absence of transitional sequences, entrances and exits; we could see characters alone much more than we do.

A related strategy is the very small number of moments when Lang uses methods (such as

Still: Sequence 2 – Tom and Susan in the club.

Still: Susan visits Tom in prison.

cuts into close-up), which conventionally give us privileged access to a character's response or alert us to something that other characters have not observed. Such moments as do exist are not always easy to interpret – Tom on the telephone, the cut to Austin Spencer on Tom's line 'I know what I'd like to do' in response to Susan's question about what they should do after dinner, or the close-up of Tom after Susan's exit from the first prison visit. In the context of the film's visual style, they stand out but seem both to invite and refuse interpretation simultaneously. In the television highlights of the trial, the commentator in a way draws attention to the issue when he remarks over a shot of Tom, 'The defendant didn't seem too concerned with this . . . and maintained the same calm that he has displayed since the trial opened', where it is clear that not only the commentator but Susan, too, watching the broadcast, want to know what lies behind Tom's demeanour. We have on this occasion privileged knowledge which enables us (we believe) to bridge the gap between appearance and what lies behind it; elsewhere in the film we have only the close-up itself.

5) Such decisions are also bound up with other characteristics of Lang's *mise-en-scène*. Much of the time, the visual strategies he adopts seem designed to require us to scrutinise the characters, rather than to encourage empathy or a play of differential response. As striking as the small number of close-ups is the fact that few scenes are built largely on angle/reverse angle cutting, probably the most familiar method of scene dissection for dialogue scenes in Hollywood movies. Where it is used, Lang predominantly favours the over-the-shoulder version in which both characters remain in shot (as, for instance, when Austin first suggests the plot, in the questioning of the dancers, Tom's first visit to the Club Zombie dressing room, Susan's visit to prison, and so on). Equally, there are few point-of-view shots, other than the close-ups of newspapers, photographs and so on, which may be technically point-of-view but tend not to be presented in the conventional manner (a shot of the thing looked at enclosed by two shots of the character looking out of frame).

Instead of these familiar devices, which might take us into the scene and encourage participation, the camera is characteristically at some distance from the characters. Lang also uses other strategies which detach us even further from the action. One repeated method is to cut within a scene to a wide shot with a character in the foreground looking in on the action as an observer. There are several examples: the police interrogation of the dancers, the judge at the trial, the interrogation of Tom, with Lt Kennedy (Edward Binns) in the foreground. In each case we observe a scene being observed. Another related strategy is to cut to a distant view to detach us from the action or to mark particular moments or lines of dialogue. When, for instance, Susan asserts that Tom 'is certainly no murderer', there is a cut from a frontal shot of Susan to one behind her, framing all three characters present. The cut breaks any identification we might have with Susan's faith in Tom and nudges us to question a 'certainty' which can have no firm basis: she cannot know that Tom is innocent any more than we can. When Tom and Austin are planting the lighter as incriminating evidence on the mountain road where Patti's body was found, Lang cuts, as Austin takes the photograph of Tom which will 'prove' that the evidence was planted, to a high-angle, distant shot, looking down on the scene.

6) I suggested earlier that performances in the film tend to be somewhat flat. This isn't universally the case, but for much of the time the 'respectable' characters, at least, act within what seems calculatedly a limited range of performance effect. In the cases of Tom and Austin, performances seem as minimal and functional as they could be without giving up altogether. Their bodies seem almost dead; there is little animation or gesture. This can be associated at the dramatic level with the nature of the 'respectable' social world Lang is creating, a milieu of considerable restraint and control. But for the spectator these restrained performances make the characters even more difficult to 'read'. Together with the lack of rhetorical emphasis within the *mise-en-scène*, this creates not just a kind of opacity of character but a situation in which, even if certain gestures of performance seem odd or awkward, it is difficult to make anything of them.

Sequences 2 to 4 can exemplify some aspects of the processes outlined above, particularly with regard to the presentation of Tom. As scene 2 (the scene after the credits) opens, we still have no indication of Tom's potential narrative role or of why he and Austin were present at the execution. Although Tom is played by the male star, it becomes clear that he is someone who is *with* Austin rather than being an initiator of action. He is also apparently unmoved by the experience of the execution, and his ironic, slightly bantering tone in the opening exchange with Austin suggests a lack of engagement with the issue of capital punishment. What, then, is his position? Why, if he is basically unconcerned, did he go at all? There is no trace of a motive on his part initially – only Austin's wish, apparently unsuccessful, to convince him that capital punishment is wrong. But Austin does not press the matter – there is no polemical pressure, no urgent questioning ('Now, surely you're convinced?' or similar). The motivation is stated but not at all buttressed. Did Tom go, then, just to please Austin? That would suggest a pleasant disposition but hardly a sense of appropriateness or a seriousness of principle. Could his action have to do with the fact that Austin is his future father-in-law and ex-employer? That might indicate a far from admirable desire to please, something more like a humouring of Austin's whims. None of these questions is raised by the film directly; they emerge only if we interrogate what is presented (and what is not presented) rather harder than the sequence seems to encourage. Tom's characterisation is as minimal as Lang's *mise-en-scène*.

Interpretation of Tom when Thompson enters is also difficult. He calls Thompson 'Sir', in itself an unusual form of deference. In the argument between Austin and Thompson, he is mainly silent, but when he speaks it is to ask questions of Austin ('You don't mean that you think Peters was innocent, do you?' 'Would you have Mr Thompson ignore circumstantial evidence?') which imply a position closer to Thompson's than to Austin's. In tone and conversational strategy, they might also suggest someone inserting himself into the conversation less out of conviction than convention, while being careful not to offend either side. The questions could signify alert interest but could equally be conversational gambits that commit Tom to nothing.

There are also slight indications that Tom is less relaxed and involved than he tries to appear. In a number of small ways, he is more mobile than Austin or Thompson, both of whom sit very still and speak with very few gestures. This is most obvious in his fruitless and repeated search through his pockets for matches, but he also has a number of nervous gestures – rapid blinking, moving his cigarette in his hand, stubbing it half-smoked, moving his arms off the table (almost knocking over his glass as he does so), pulling at his sleeve when his hands are out of sight – none of which are either striking in themselves or visually marked (Lang's camera keeps its distance). When he jumps up on Susan's arrival, his movement is cramped and awkward, and his smile seems slightly embarrassed.

There is little to ground these elements. On initial viewing, in fact, they may hardly appear as signifiers at all, subordinating themselves to a more generalised sense of the scene as exposition, to the grave issue of capital punishment, and to the fairly unexceptional contours of Tom's character. We may, then, hardly note or consider the implications of Austin's remark that Tom and Susan are getting serious and that he allowed Tom to leave the paper in order to write his novel because he had no objection to the relationship. Tom has moved, in other words, from journalist to best-selling author, and we may surmise that the society in which he moves has changed. He is not yet at home in this world, his impeccable grooming, gestures of uneasiness, detached and uncommitted stance, all suggesting, perhaps, a determination to control his behaviour, to play an appropriate part.

What Austin says about Tom and Susan is lightly presented as part of the conversational banter following Thompson's exit and covering Austin's business of signing the bill before leaving, but it is also very revealing. It suggests that behind Austin's action is the motive of making Tom fit for Susan and implies, just before her first entrance, that Susan's expensive tastes govern her choice of men: 'I don't think you'd have made much progress on the salary I was paying you.' In its contrast to conventional ideals of romantic love (as being above such considerations) and what it might imply about the basis of Tom and Susan's relationship (she getting a best-selling author, he marrying the boss's daughter?), it is a striking introduction to Susan at a point when all we know of her is that she and Tom are seriously involved. It is again characteristic of the film's method with details of characterisation and performance that what Austin says is relatively unmarked: here, Austin's light tone belies the implication of what he says, and Susan's entrance cuts off any further exchange, while the image remains the relatively distant two-shot that has been held since Thompson's exit. In other words, the organisation of the scene and the performances require the spectator not only to observe what is there, but to create, with rather less textual help than is frequent, a hierarchy of information as a basis for judgement.

Susan's appearance and what follows further engages with expectations of various kinds. Joan Fontaine's appearance confirms Austin's reference to expensive tastes – she is dressed and coiffed in a way that is at once elegant and severe, her clothes and hair style emphasising rather than attempting to conceal Fontaine's angularity. The effect is of calculated elegance, which in some details (her hat) borders on absurdity. As with Tom, there is a sense of the consciousness of role and position. In their responses to each other, neither seems fully at ease.

The final section of the sequence, in fact, turns on expectations associated with roles. There is in the dialogue a tone of playfulness that is at once suggestive of intimacy and of a certain lack of relaxation. Rather than taking the lead, Tom asks Susan what she wants to do, her playfully indirect reply leading to the suggestion that they should go to his apartment. The final lines ('Aren't we a little mixed up? That's supposed to be my line.' 'But you've never used it!') imply that Tom has been sexually reticent within the relationship and that Susan has therefore taken on the conventional man's role. Again, the implications of this reversal remain unexplored. Is Tom's sexual reserve habitual or confined to his relationship with Susan? Later, we can note how at ease he is with Dolly (Barbara Nichols) and in the nightclub, and how readily as he enters that world he engages in sexual innuendo in the exchange with the hat-check girl. Does his reserve with Susan connote, perhaps, lack of desire, or could it be a further sign of his unease in the world to which he is now aspiring? (His situation and behaviour are reminiscent of the aspiring Guy Haynes, Farley Granger, in Hitchcock's *Strangers on a Train*, 1951.)

We might take the enigmatic presentation of motivation as an indication of Lang's lack of concern with psychological density, but it is more profitable to associate it with the range of strategies already noted that gesture towards a fuller reality, while denying us access to it. Thus, rather than taking us with Tom and Susan as they leave the club and travel to the apartment – a transition that would have provided opportunities to clarify the nature of the relationship – Lang

dissolves directly to a close-up of the record player (playing the song 'Beyond a Reasonable Doubt') in Tom's apartment and then to Tom and Susan kissing at what, it becomes clear, is the end of the scene. Given the build-up to the scene, with its suggestion of sexual invitation, the presentation is oddly perfunctory. In the next scene, we learn that a wedding date has been set, presumably since Austin, Tom and Susan were together in the club, but the proposal is not shown.

Sequence 4 accumulates further puzzling details about the relationship. It opens with the gift of the lighter and Austin's observation that a wedding date has been set. What is striking, on reflection, is the absence of obvious celebration, warmth and enthusiasm. Austin's line is almost matter-of-fact. There is also something stilted in Tom's reception of the gift, as indeed there is in his manner throughout the scene – a sense of a role being not quite convincingly played. This emerges in part from the disparity between what we might expect of a character in his apparent situation and how he acts: there is the absence of warmth and excitement but also of apparent regret and of demonstrated feeling for Susan in Tom's manner as he postpones the wedding (the telephone call in his apartment, he claims, was from his publisher insisting on the delivery of his second novel). His manner seems more consistent with postponing a lunch date and Susan's response ('I wouldn't dream of forcing you to do anything you obviously don't want') may seem to a degree petulant, but it can equally be read as an understandable response to Tom's coolness.

Although these things are extremely difficult to define, throughout there seems a disjunction in Dana Andrews's performance between what he says and both how he says it and how he acts. He remains standing, apart from Susan; his head and eyes move constantly; he holds eye contact only briefly. In a number of ways his performance suggests uneasiness, lack of conviction (this is not at all to suggest poor performance – the effect is undoubtedly calculated). Even more curious in the context is the abruptness with which, following the postponement of the wedding and his insistence on finishing his second novel, Tom changes the subject back to capital punishment. Austin, in fact, comments on the change of subject, which Tom explains by saying that he hasn't been able to get it out of his mind. Nothing in the previous sequences supports his explanation – quite the opposite, if we remember sequence 2 – and the awkwardness of the unmotivated change of subject is matched by an expression of interest which perhaps tries rather too hard to seem fully convincing.

This description of performance and the presentation of character may, however, be somewhat misleading in its emphasis on the problematical. In a number of ways, expectations are not realised as we might expect, but the elements of characterisation I have described, although they are there to be perceived and interpreted, are not marked in ways that at all clearly signal that they form part of a significant system. In the absence of such marking, powerful expectations about, for instance, the nature of hero, heroine or star may override or render more difficult a clear response to what is there in the text. We may store the details in the hope that their relevance will emerge, but Lang makes it difficult for us to establish whether particular details are pertinent. Similarly, Lang's visual style seems unremarkable, functional enough to pass unnoticed.

What is involved here is at one level the entirely orthodox set of procedures by means of which we seek to understand character, situation and the significance of style. We construct, in response to signs in the film and in relation to the expectations we have formed, projections of character type and development together with other more local accumulations of qualities, interpretations of situations, and so on. These processes depend on constant interaction of projection and memory, the formulation of new models and modification or rejection of old. Within the dynamics of response and interpretation, the details of the film are not used up at equal rates. We reach for units of sense, for interpretations, that may outrun the evidence we have available or ignore some of what the film has presented. It is characteristic of the process of reading, as Wolfgang Iser makes clear (*The Act of Reading*, Johns Hopkins University Press, Baltimore, 1974, p.126), that selections are constantly made in order that *Gestalten* can be produced. The residue may be ignored or may force itself to the attention later to modify existing *Gestalten*. But initial hypotheses and sometimes whole readings are dependent on expectation, which may produce what Iser calls 'illusions'. In this context he quotes Yuri Lotman:

'The reader is interested in gaining the necessary information with the least trouble to himself . . . And so if the author sets out to increase the number of code systems and the complexity of their structure, the reader will tend to reduce them to what he regards as an acceptable minimum. The tendency to complicate the characters is the author's; the contrastive black and white structure is the reader's' (Iser, p.125).

This tension, Iser suggests, is capable of being exploited in a variety of ways: '. . . if the strategies are so organised that they increase the pressure exerted by the "alien associations" – i.e. the equivalence of the signs represented in a *Gestalt* no longer corresponds to the apparent intention – then we have a text in which the original implications of the signs themselves become the object of critical attention' (Iser, p.127).

In *Beyond a Reasonable Doubt*, the absence of whodunnit cues and the suppression of Tom's guilt and of his relationship with Emma make it difficult, if not impossible, to attach a range of the given character signs satisfactorily to the narrative position Tom appears to occupy. Many aspects of Lang's narration similarly remain stubbornly resistant to interpretation. They therefore either remain puzzling or are in effect discarded as irrelevant. Put in another way, it is difficult, as the film unfolds, to construct a set of apparent intentions which will account for and bind into our reading not only extensive sets of character signs but also a variety of filmic strategies. This may be partly responsible for the puzzlement with which the film is often received. The most available means of providing coherence are offered by the conspiracy narrative and the role Tom apparently occupies within it, to which other elements become subordinate. Expectations at this level provide Lotman's 'acceptable minimum'. But there remain the 'alien associations' which will not correspond to 'the apparent intention'. In effect, partial, elliptical and matter-of-fact presentation provides a mass of material which challenges the spectator to make sense of it, the very point being that what is offered is partial and unexplained. To put this back in the context of judicial process – the film's overt focus – Lang implicitly presents us with a set of questions which a jury might have to weigh: what counts as evidence; how it can be recognised; how it should be weighed.

The film *seems*, then, to cite Telotte once more, to 'reserve a stable position from which to speak' (p.21), and we readily accept the apparently proffered stability. It offers the illusion of security but simultaneously defines our epistemological position as one of severe restriction. It is only the shock with which we are likely to receive the news of Tom's guilt that enables us to recognise the chronically limited view we have been given and the insecure position we have been occupying.

Challenging the power of generic conventions and the expectation of an ultimately secure spectator position is extraordinarily difficult in popular fiction, even in the disruptive field of *film noir*. In most *films noirs*, as I have suggested, the problems confronting the protagonist and the uncertainties of the fictional world are either given from the outset or fit readily enough into the broad expectations triggered by generic recognition. It is striking that both Lang and Hitchcock, in what are perhaps their most radical movies, should seek to unsettle our familiar patterns of response in such parallel ways – by using suppressive narrative and the power of surprise not just to induce shock but, by misleading and *then* shocking us, to challenge our habitual assumptions. *Beyond a Reasonable Doubt* extends to the spectator, if we take on its implications, the chronic insecurity which *film noir* repeatedly dramatises. It is the movie which most fully embodies the implicit promise (or threat) of *film noir* to unsettle or undermine the spectator's security: not just to display a world of chronic uncertainty but to immerse us in it.

ROBERT SIODMAK

Michael Walker

A Jewish refugee from Nazi Germany, Robert Siodmak had directed films in both Germany and France before arriving in Hollywood in 1940. After directing B movies for various studios, he signed a long-term contract in 1943 with Universal, where his brother Curt was already a screenwriter. Mostly at Universal, but occasionally on loan-out to other studios, Siodmak then directed a whole series of what we would now term *films noirs*. *Phantom Lady* (1944), *Christmas Holiday* (1944), *The Killers* (1946), *Criss Cross* (1948) and *The File on Thelma Jordon* (1949) are mainstream examples of the *noir* cycle, while *The Suspect* (1944), *The Strange Affair of Uncle Harry* (1945), *The Spiral Staircase* (1945), *The Dark Mirror* (1946) and *Cry of the City* (1948) all have *noir* elements (and are often listed as *films noirs* in the literature on the cycle.) This makes Siodmak the director who contributed most extensively to *film noir*. His films helped define and shape the preoccupations and development of the cycle: the auteurist elements, both thematic and stylistic, that recur most strongly in his movies are those which we would now consider quintessentially *noir*.

Siodmak's first contribution to *film noir* came before any of these movies. With Alfred Neumann, he co-authored an original story entitled *The Pentacle*, which was sold to Warners in 1943 and directed as *Conflict* by Curtis Bernhardt (for whom Siodmak had been an assistant in Berlin in 1928). The story concerns Richard Mason (Humphrey Bogart), whose 'happy marriage' has been a barely-maintained façade since he fell in love with his wife's younger sister Evelyn (Alexis Smith). Kathryn (Rose Hobart) won't give him a divorce and so he carefully plots and executes her murder, making it seem like a car accident. But when he reports her missing, the police say they can find no trace of her. Then incidents happen which suggest that she is still alive: Mason smells her perfume in the house, then discovers her safe key and, inside the safe, her wedding ring. He tries to pursue his suit with Evelyn, but she declares that Kathryn will always be between them. Further incidents suggest to Mason that he may be hallucinating; fearing that his sanity is threatened, he turns for help to Mark Hamilton (Sidney Greenstreet), a psychiatrist and family friend. Hamilton's unhelpful response causes Mason to drive out to the scene of murder, where he finds both Hamilton and the police waiting

for him. At the time of Kathryn's disappearance, Hamilton had spotted a flaw in Mason's story, and – with the co-operation of the police – had orchestrated the incidents that were designed to cause Mason to return to the scene of the crime and so give evidence of his guilt.

Structurally the film anticipates *The Suspect*, with an unhappily married man falling for a younger woman and killing his wife. But the sympathy we have in that film for Philip Marshall – for all the monstrousness of his crime – is nowhere in evidence here. Mason is simply a cold-blooded killer. Even though he seems like a typically obsessed and tormented Siodmak 'hero' (on the one hand in the grip of a passion for his sister-in-law; on the other, haunted by incidents which suggest that his murdered wife is still alive), we do not feel for him as we do for the heroes in Siodmak's own movies. And this, in turn, considerably diminishes the *noir* sense of paranoia: the feeling that either he's losing his mind or he's 'haunted'. The movie has a *noir* story but lacks a *noir* atmosphere: our relationship to it is clinical and detached. There is the same dilution of effect in the presentation of the police. As in Siodmak's films generally, their role is highly suspect, as they collude in an elaborate plan to fake incidents in order to prey on the mind of a suspected murderer. Together with Hamilton, they are responsible for *creating* Mason's sense of paranoia. But, far from implying that they should be criticised for this, the film implicitly supports them.

Phantom Lady (1944)

Siodmak served his apprenticeship at Universal by directing a vehicle each for the studio's successful B-picture stars, Lon Chaney Jr and Maria Montez. In Autumn 1943, Joan Harrison (previously Alfred Hitchcock's assistant, but by this time an independent producer) then gave him the opportunity to direct an adaptation of Cornell Woolrich's 1942 novel *Phantom Lady*, which was published under the pseudonym of William Irish. The story has a number of obvious similarities to *The Pentacle* (already filmed, but not released until 1945), and Siodmak was immediately enthusiastic.

As the author of more *film noir* source material than anyone else, Woolrich's place as a *noir* writer is as central as Siodmak's as a *noir* director. With chapter headings denoting the steadily decreasing number of days 'before the execution', *Phantom Lady* is a superb example of Woolrich's distinctive inflection of the *noir* form. After a row with his wife Marcella (he wants a divorce; she won't grant one), Scott Henderson goes out in a rage and picks up a 'woman in a hat' in a New York bar. Without learning anything about her, he takes her to dinner and the theatre, then returns home to find the police in occupation and Marcella murdered. No-one can trace the woman in a hat; witnesses who saw the two of them together deny that she was there. She has become the phantom lady. Scott is convicted for murder and sentenced to death.

On the twenty-first day before the execution, Burgess, who arrested Scott, visits him in prison. He now believes Scott innocent and prompts him to contact his best friend, Jack Lombard, in South America, to ask Lombard to come back and help. With Burgess's approval, Lombard seeks out missing witnesses; at the same time, Burgess also motivates Carol Richman, Scott's girlfriend, to pursue another line of investigation, concentrating on the witnesses who denied the existence of the woman in a hat. Both lines of investigation are frustrated. The witnesses Lombard tracks down are either useless or they promptly die (apparently by accident); similarly, Carol's two false witnesses (the barman and Cliff Milburn, the trap drummer at the theatre) also die before she gets concrete evidence, the former by accident, the latter apparently killed by the man who bribed him to keep quiet. Finally, three days before the execution, a last desperate attempt is made by Lombard to track down the phantom lady herself.

The novel is a very clever piece of writing, in which the reader does not discover until the climax – held back until the hour of the execution – that Lombard is the murderer. We realise this when the phantom lady does after all miraculously turn up, and Lombard sets out to kill her. Only after she has been saved at the last minute do we discover that Carol here was impersonating the phantom lady. Then the inner structure of the novel is revealed: Burgess, suspecting Lombard, had been secretly trying to catch him out; Lombard was using the time to find and then cause 'accidents' to happen to potentially dangerous witnesses. Carol's part in the novel is relatively small but, because she and Lombard have never met, Woolrich is able to pull the final twist of her impersonation. The phantom lady remains a phantom: Burgess had found she was in an insane asylum, and was incapable of testifying.

Although it has a happy ending, the novel contains the essential features of Woolrich's world: the sense of a malevolent force determining the outcome of events, the hero's helplessness against this, and the bitterness and despair which overtake him. (For a general consideration of Woolrich's work in relation to *film noir*, see Tony Williams, '*Phantom Lady*, Cornell Woolrich and the Masochistic Aesthetic' in *CineAction* 13/14, Summer 1988.)

In adapting the novel, Bernard Schoenfeld (in his first screen credit) had to contend with two interrelated problems. First, although it is primarily a brooding suspense thriller, the novel has the hidden structure of a whodunnit, a much less popular genre with Hollywood film-makers than with the detective-fiction-reading public. One reason for this is the difficulty a film viewer, as opposed to a novel reader, has in checking back on clues. At least one chapter of *Phantom Lady* has to be re-read very carefully, in the light of the identification of the murderer, to work out what is going on. Second, the whodunnit discourse masks a subversive notion: the idea of the murderer using the police in order to track down and kill potentially dangerous witnesses. Both problems were solved by removing all the scenes featuring Lombard's investigation. However, whilst this dramatically increased Carol's role, it also required a rearticulation of the place of the murderer in the narrative, which was much less satisfactorily handled.

The film was structured by Schoenfeld into three acts, with bridging scenes of Carol (Ella Raines) visiting Scott Henderson (Alan Curtis) in jail between the acts. The first act, condensed from the novel's first seven chapters, ends with Scott being sentenced. The second act is essentially the sections from the novel in which Carol investigates lying witnesses. Only after this does Lombard, retitled Marlowe (Franchot Tone, cast against type) appear: here introduced *as* the murderer, turning up to kill Milburn (Elisha Cook Jr), after the latter has 'talked too much' to Carol. (In the novel Milburn only seemed to be murdered: in fact, crazed with fear, he committed suicide. This exemplifies the deceptiveness inherent in the whodunnit.) And so, throughout the film's third act – Marlowe and Carol searching together for missing witnesses – we know that he is a potential threat, which generates suspense. The switch – from whodunnit to the suspense attendant on knowing whodunnit – is typical of film adaptations. In this instance the result is none too successful, being marred by Tone's mannered performance: 'afflicted with delusions of grandeur, migraine headaches and overly emphatic hand gestures' (Tom Flinn, 'Three Faces of Film Noir' in *Kings of the Bs*, Todd McCarthy & Charles Flynn, eds, Dutton, New York, 1975).

Before this major departure from the novel, however, *Phantom Lady* – in terms of both narrative and imagery – is a commendable example of early *film noir*. The novel's seedy New York locations were recreated by art directors John Goodman and Robert Clatworthy entirely in the studio, a practice that works particularly well for *film noir*, with its pervasive sense of claustrophic menace. The action takes place almost entirely at night, with the German Expressionist influence clearly visible in a number of dramatically lit scenes and chiaroscuro effects. With this movie, Siodmak adopted Woody Bredell as his cameraman. According to Hervé Dumont (*Robert Siodmak: Le Maître du film noir,* L'Age d'Homme, Lausanne, 1981, p.156), Siodmak then initiated Bredell into the secrets of the famous cameraman Eugen Schüfftan, with whom Siodmak had worked in Europe. *Phantom Lady* and subsequent Bredell films (including Michael Curtiz's visually stunning *The Unsuspected,* 1947) show the fruits of this.

The first distinctively *noir* sequence in *Phantom Lady* is the scene in which Scott returns to his apartment to find it occupied by three men who have been waiting in the dark to catch him unawares. Although taken from Woolrich, the scene is a highly typical Siodmak rendering of the cop as heavy. The three men encircle Scott, hemming him in, watching him, each playing a different role: Burgess (Thomas Gomez) in charge, another (Joseph Crehan) needling him, and the third (Regis Toomey) silently detached, casually chewing gum. In the final part of the scene, after Marcella's body has been removed, the three group menacingly around Scott, pressurising him with incongruous observations about his tie, and Siodmak tracks in remorselessly on Scott to convey his sense of entrapment.

In this scene, Scott admits he asked Marcella for a divorce. Thus, in killing her, Marlowe is structurally like Scott's dark double: an implicit version of what is explicit in *Strangers on a Train* (Alfred Hitchcock, 1951). Scott (here) and Marlowe (at the climax) both speak of Marcella laughing at them, goading the former into

storming out, the latter into murder: the violence Scott represses in himself. Although the *noir* world into which Scott is plunged is created by Marlowe, the links between the two men suggest that it arises, at least in part, from Scott's unresolved hostility towards Marcella.

In the film, Carol is Scott's secretary, not his girlfriend. The change leads to a relatively positive representation of a 'forties working woman, a feature absent from the novel. Learning that Scott is being questioned by the police, Carol nevertheless controls her fears, reassures the anxious stenographer and continues with the work of running Scott's business. In her first scene, both her concern for Scott (we learn later that she has loved him for some time) and her professionalism are concisely conveyed. Carol's role is also structurally more important in the film: she dominates the second act and is similarly the most important character during the third act. Scott as hero is on Death Row twenty-five minutes into the film; thereafter, it is up to Carol as heroine to save him.

The narrative shift to Carol occurs during the trial, which is shot in an unusual (and economical) way. We hear the district attorney addressing the court, and some of Scott's replies, but all we see are the clerk's shorthand notes and reaction shots of the audience. In other words, we see none of the participants in the trial, including

Still: Phantom Lady. *The cops as heavies – Burgess (Thomas Gomez) and his sidekicks (Regis Toomey and Joseph Crehan) pressure Scott (Alan Curtis).*

Still: Phantom Lady. *The castrating power of the look – Carol (Ella Raines) unnerves the barman (Andrew Toombes Jr).*

Scott: he becomes a 'structured absence' whose place at the centre of the narrative is assumed by Carol, shown here looking off-screen at the drama at the front of the courtroom.

Also singled out in the audience is Burgess, who keeps looking at Carol. At one point, she returns his look, her expression accusatory. As she does this, Scott is being mocked off-screen for his failure to remember anything about the woman in the hat. The juxtaposition highlights the feminist thrust of the film. In common with other *films noirs* centring on a victim hero, *Phantom Lady* is crucially about male loss of control. Neither Scott nor Marlowe can control Marcella, and the woman in the hat so successfully eludes Scott's control that she becomes the phantom lady. In placing the strength of Carol's look against a public statement of Scott's weakness, the film registers a shift of power from hero to heroine. This is then elaborated in Carol's later use of her look as a weapon to hound the barman (Andrew Toombes Jr).

Although her strength and independence contrast with his weakness, Carol actually loves Scott for 'how soft he really is'. The film is sympathetic to the weak hero, even going so far as to have him cry. The tough male is the villain, and he is coded as insane. Tony Williams points out that the villain's occupation has been changed from engineer in the novel to artist to facilitate this coding, arguing that 'a mad modernist artist is less of a threat to gender stereotypes than a mad, masculine engineer.' But he ignores the fact that Scott's occupation has also been changed: from broker to engineer. This has the reverse effect: a

weak, helpless engineer is *more* of a threat to gender stereotypes than a weak, helpless broker. *Phantom Lady* exemplifies how standard sexual typing so often breaks down in *film noir* – a feature on which Williams's article is illuminating. He argues that the 'masochist aesthetic' of Woolrich's novels – submissive men, phallic women – strongly influenced *film noir*, particularly the films of Siodmak.

Scott and Carol are not seen together until after his conviction, in the bridging scene at the end of the first act. Sentenced to death for a murder he did not commit, Scott is now at the point of despair so often reached by *noir* victim heroes, and doubts his own sanity: 'Maybe there never was such a woman.' It is Carol who reassures him ('You couldn't kill anybody') and – in place of Burgess in the novel – argues for someone to help him: 'someone who just won't be beaten'. But Marlowe is not summoned back from South America; it is Carol who takes on the investigation. In effect, she becomes one of the very few examples in *film noir* of a seeker *heroine*: she goes out alone into the *noir* world, using her skill and determination to unravel the mystery the law has so conspicuously failed to penetrate. During the second act she is on her own: Scott knows nothing of her actions, and it is not until after the death of the barman that Burgess turns up to offer his assistance.

Her technique with the barman is to unnerve him until he gives something away. Sitting at his bar and simply staring at him, Carol appropriates what feminists have termed 'the male prerogative of the look' to the point where her victim becomes nervous and hounded. As she follows him home, he is sufficiently frightened to contemplate killing her (by pushing her under a subway train). When he finally cracks and turns to confront

Still: Phantom Lady. *Burgess turns up in Carol's apartment to offer assistance.*

her, men in the street come to her aid, and the barman, desperately breaking free, runs into the road and is hit by a truck. From the barman's point of view, Carol is a 'phallic woman' who terrifies him by her accusatory power, but from the men's point of view she is a woman being threatened by a man. That they are misperceiving the situation – we feel that Carol could have handled the man – emphasises, again, the film's breaking of gender stereotypes.

Returning home, Carol finds Burgess sitting in the dark in her apartment. The manner of his intrusion is sinister, explicitly evoking the earlier scene in Scott's apartment – as if Siodmak's impulse were to view even an apparently friendly cop with suspicion. In fact, the reintroduction of Burgess as an investigative figure is double-edged. Whilst he provides Carol with valuable assistance, he also oversees her own investigation as if the film were saying that a woman should go only so far alone.

For Cliff Milburn, Carol assumes a very different persona. Wearing a tight-fitting black dress, heavily made up and provocatively chewing gum, she masquerades as a tart, another comment on gender stereotyping. Excited by her, Milburn takes her to a jam session, one of the most remarkable sequences in *film noir*. The scene as described in the novel is vivid enough – Woolrich refers to looming shadows, demonic faces and the frenzy of the men's performance – but Siodmak takes it further. Not only does he find visual correlatives for Woolrich's expressionistic imagery, but he builds to an extraordinary climax in which Carol enacts highly censorable body movements in front of Milburn whilst he himself has an almost explicit orgasm on the drums.

Filmed with harsh, slashing lighting, the scene in the jazz cellar shows *noir* expressionism at its most frenzied and extravagant. The ensuing scene in Milburn's apartment is in the more familiar low-key (both senses) *noir* style, with a single lamp in the room and a flashing neon light outside. By now, Carol has penetrated to the real seediness of the *noir* world, and she has to perform

a delicate balancing act: trying to keep Milburn interested enough to talk (revealing that he was bribed to keep quiet about 'the woman in the hat') whilst at the same time holding his nauseating sexual advances at bay. For all that she seems like a *femme fatale* in relation to Milburn, it is an assumed role and, when he discovers that she has been sent by the police, she has to fight her way out of the apartment. Here the *noir* imagery intensifies: the lamp is knocked over, plunging the room into almost total darkness and, as Carol escapes, the staircase down which she flees is lit so that shadows of the banisters hem her in. She runs across the road to a delicatessen where a Jewish couple anxiously commiserate while she phones Burgess. Back at Milburn's, however, Marlowe makes his entrance. With the lamp now fixed but askew, the harsh lighting of the jazz cellar is evoked. For Milburn, Marlowe is the superego arising to censor the id unleashed in that sequence. In place of the anticipated sex, he encounters death.

The juxtaposition of the friendly Jewish couple with Marlowe as murderer may be related to the film's later identification of him as a Nietzschean villain, a sculptor who considers himself a superman. Whilst it would probably have been too 'obvious' to have Marlowe stalk through the film intoning Nazi ideology, the cultural intimation is clearly there – an addition from novel to film which reflects the times.

In the third act, Carol's sympathetic understanding and her investigative skills are both brought into play. Twice in this act, she and Marlowe encounter a particular situation: an older woman in charge, a younger, vulnerable woman who knows something that will help. This occurs first in the hat shop, then in the Long Island home of Ann Terry (Fay Helm), the phantom lady herself, who is suffering from a nervous breakdown after the death of her fiancé and is under the doctor's care. In both cases, Carol persuades the older woman to let them see her charge, and finds the right words to win over the younger woman. In doing so, she uses tact and sympathy in a way quite foreign to seeker heroes. This is particularly important with Ann Terry, since she possesses the crucial piece of evidence: the hat.

The staging of this second encounter again shows Siodmak's flair. Carol's first meeting with Ann has led nowhere, and she leaves the room apparently defeated. Then she gathers her strength and returns, to be confronted by the sight of Ann sitting on the floor with the hat in front of her. It is a superb visual coup: the hat in its box like a child in its crib, gently lifted out. (Remarkably, one of the scenes in the novel – the one where Lombard traces the hat-shop girl – centres round a real hidden baby, which is produced, in a similar manner, at the end. This is one of the many examples one can find, in novel-to-film adaptations, of psychoanalytical displacements in the narrative.)

Still: Phantom Lady – *Carol (with the hat) about to be menaced by Marlowe (Franchot Tone).*

As one woman to another ('You want to wear it for him'), Ann does in fact surrender the hat. But the rest of the act is disappointing. Earlier in it, when Burgess delivered a monologue about famous mass murderers, describing them all as paranoiacs, Marlowe looked at himself in a mirror and twitched to indicate that he was just like them. (Burgess is dumber than in the novel: he isn't even looking.) The film's climax in Marlowe's studio apartment has the same heavy obviousness. As he tells Carol the story of the murder, Marlowe is moved to declaim, 'What's any life compared to mine?' as he flexes his hands. There follows a 'heroine threatened by villain' scene which is almost banal in its predictability, Carol being saved at the last moment by the timely and improbable arrival of Burgess, whilst Marlowe obligingly jumps out the window. Clearly, the film here is seeking to recuperate the hitherto independent heroine, placing her in a stereotyped situation of threat in order for her to be saved by a man. But the scene is unconvincing, registering Siodmak's unease at the ideological shift forced on his heroine.

The recuperation of Carol at the film's close – returned to her place as Scott's secretary, taking his orders – is more ambiguously handled. Unable to thank her directly for her part in saving his life, Scott signals his thanks by telling her via the dictaphone that she's having dinner with him that night. However, as the message continues 'and the next night and then every night', the machine sticks on the words 'every night', which are repeated over and over as the camera tracks in to show Carol's ecstatic response. What we are supposed to think at this point (and what, I'm sure, Joseph Breen would have assumed), is that Scott is proposing. Carol knows that that's not all: and the clue is in the rhythm and intonation of the words – to say nothing of the way she holds the dictaphone horn. Banished from the diegesis for the duration of the narrative, sex finally returns, albeit in code.

Phantom Lady is unusual in that its *femme fatale*, Marcella, is never seen. We see Scott's reaction shots as he looks at her body, but she is represented visually only by her portrait, which dominates the scene between Scott and the three cops, a reminder of her power, even in death. Ann Terry, whose mysterious disappearance traps Scott in the *noir* world, is Marcella's ghostly companion: wittingly or unwittingly, the two women are 'fatal' to both the hero and the villain. (Just as Ann's disappearance condemned Scott, so her reappearance condemns Marlowe.) Accordingly, the positive characterisation of Carol is an important corrective to the otherwise conventional *noir* position that women are dangerous trouble. On the other hand, the lack of romance between Carol and Scott – in none of their three scenes together does he show any romantic response to her – undoubtedly assists her gutsy independence. Now that Scott has finally claimed her – and his use of the impersonal methods of a boss testifies to unease here – we can be sure that her independence will be sharply curtailed.

Christmas Holiday (1944)

The producer of *Christmas Holiday* was another German refugee, Felix Jackson, who had risen at Universal from scriptwriter (e.g on *Destry Rides Again*, George Marshall, 1939) to producer and was currently also Deanna Durbin's fiancé. He had just produced *His Butler's Sister* (Frank Borzage, 1943), in which both Durbin and Franchot Tone were cast firmly 'in type' and a pre-Siodmak Bredell showed few signs of his later stylishness. Nevertheless – according to Charles Higham (*Film Journal* 9, February 1958) – Durbin herself was seeking a different sort of role from her standard 'sweetness and light' Cinderella story, and she read and liked the property, Somerset Maugham's 1939 novel, *Christmas Holiday*. Moreover, Universal approved. It was a bold move for both star and studio. Maugham's 'heroine' is a prostitute in a Paris brothel, consciously seeking to degrade herself to suffer along with her husband – a convicted murderer on Devil's Island. The story of her obsession for a 'worthless' man is narrated at one remove to the novel's protagonist, Charley Mason, a young Englishman of genteel background visiting Paris over Christmas. The revelation of such a world shatters him: the novel's last line is 'the bottom had fallen out of his world'.

The adaptation of the novel was entrusted to Herman J. Mankiewicz, whose credits since *Citizen Kane* (Orson Welles, 1941) had mostly been unimpressive. He resited the action in New Orleans, and converted Charley Mason into a young American army lieutenant on leave, but otherwise kept the essence of the story. Of course, the film needed to satisfy the Production Code (and so the brothel becomes the Maison Lafitte with 'dance hostesses'), but overall it's remarkable how much Mankiewicz was able to retain – or, at least, preserve in the film's subtext. Not even Maugham's (highly deceptive) title was changed, though the paperback reprint of the novel in 1949 was renamed *Stranger in Paris* (and was a big success). With Gene Kelly borrowed from MGM to play the husband, Robert Manette, the gap between one's expectations of a film with these two stars titled *Christmas Holiday* and the film itself could scarcely be greater: Durbin plays a prostitute, Kelly plays a murderer.

There were problems during filming. According to Higham, Durbin and Jackson were at odds over the interpretation of the novel and, 'out of sympathy with Siodmak's deglamorisation of her', she even took over some of the filming. Whilst one is sceptical of this last (which scenes?), Siodmak himself has said that Durbin was 'difficult: she wanted to play a new part but flinched from looking like a tramp: she always wanted to look like nice, wholesome Deanna Durbin looking like a tramp' (*Sight & Sound*, Summer/Autumn 1959). But Durbin's role as Jackie Lamont, dance hostess, is an assumed persona; the flashbacks show her as Abigail Martin, an innocent and trusting young woman who falls for a charmer. The tension between the two roles, which the casting of Durbin brings out, works extremely well. Kelly's casting, too, is remarkably successful – the smiling, charming Kelly persona serving to mask the weakness and corruption underneath.

Structurally, the film's hero is Charley (Dean Harens), but he is even less significant than Scott Henderson in *Phantom Lady*: he does little more than give us access to the *noir* world. In *Phantom Lady*, Scott is precipitated into this world by the murder of his wife. In *Christmas Holiday* the equivalent narrative movement arises from a psychological stimulus: just as he is about to return home on leave to marry, Charley receives a 'Dear John' telegram from his fiancée Mona, telling him she's going to marry somebody else. Embittered, he nevertheless continues with his plan to fly home to San Francisco, now intending revenge: 'They're not going to get away with this.' But the flight encounters turbulent weather and is diverted to New Orleans. There is a link here with the subtext of *Phantom Lady*: the sense that the hero's unresolved hostility towards a woman precipitates him into the *noir* world. It's as if Charley's inner turmoil is echoed in the weather which carries him, as in a fairy-tale, to 'another kingdom': New Orleans.

Few American cities have such strong associations in the movies as New Orleans: historically, French dandyism, the slave trade, gambling and duelling; in the 20th century, prostitution, black oppression and (eventually) jazz. During the period of the Code, if a woman came from New Orleans it nearly always signalled that she was an (ex-)prostitute: *Red River* (Howard Hawks, 1947), *The Naked Jungle* (Byron Haskin, 1953). (Boston, of course, was the town whose associations were morally the opposite.) Mankiewicz was indubitably familiar with the coding conventions: hence the New Orleans setting for the Maison. At the same time, there is an attempt to keep Jackie/Abigail from being overtly associated with the Maison's activities: she's a singer, and when an elderly man sends a propositioning note, she promptly passes it on to one of the other girls. As so often in movies made under the Code, the film says both 'yes, she is' and 'no, she isn't'. In 'Psychoanalysis and Film Noir' in this book, Deborah Thomas suggests that the 'stiffness' of Durbin's singing in the film arises from her being 'on the side of the law'. I would put it differently: when she sings in the Maison, her body is registering resistance to the degradation she has forced upon herself. Her rendering of 'Spring will be a little late this year' is full of suppressed yearning.

Charley is taken to the Maison by Simon Fenimore (Richard Whorf), a wonderfully slimy portrait of a journalist as part-time pimp. However, before 'passing out' in the room of the Maison's madame, Valerie de Merode (Gladys George), Simon pairs Charley up with Abigail

Still: Christmas Holiday – *Abigail (Deanna Durbin) as Jackie of the Maison Lafitte singing 'Spring will be a little late this year'.*

and then passes over to him an invitation to Midnight Mass in the cathedral. Abigail wants to go; Charley takes her.

The five-minute sequence of Midnight Mass – filmed by Siodmak with a terrific sense of atmosphere – is the film's only unequivocal signifier of 'Christmas'. As such, it offers a glimpse of a world outside the *noir* frame. When Abigail breaks down on the *Mea Culpa*, we see that the emotional experience of the Mass is serving to release the thoughts and feelings she has suppressed in her adopted persona as Jackie Lamont. After the Mass, she launches almost immediately into her story.

In her voice-over introducing the first flashback, Abigail mentions that she had been happily married for six months and that, on this particular night, her husband had murdered Teddy Jordan, a bookmaker. But, within the flashback, she does not yet know this last, and the scene is very disturbing. She is in bed asleep; Robert enters and kisses her. As she wakes, he lies down beside her and comes out with a series of reasons for his late return that are obviously just excuses, but produced with a calculated, ingratiating appeal. In particular, he puts on a little boy voice to say that he won't do it again and coyly hides his face. Then, when he sees the performance has worked, he bestows a flash of the Kelly smile. From the beginning, Kelly's 'boyish charm' is presented as manipulative, a mask for a murderer.

Robert is characterised as a 'mama's boy', completely indulged by a doting mother (Gale Sondergaard). Although we see the two of them

together only when Abigail is present (the film is rigorous about sticking to flashback scenes Abigail herself witnessed), we soon discover that Mrs Manette already knows about the murder: Robert seems to have returned home and 'confessed'. And her reflex is to protect him: when a 'stain' is found on his trousers, she quickly gets rid of the evidence, at the same time trying to conceal from Abigail the implications of her actions.

It is not until the second flashback – which returns to the first meeting of Abigail and Robert – that the film begins to explore the details of the mother/son relationship. Robert is the last in the line of an extremely influential Louisiana family and, feeling intimidated by the onus this puts on him to be a success, he has turned to gambling and 'bad company'. His mother is disturbed by this, and seeks in Abigail a wife who will make Robert 'strong'. Abigail's

Still: Christmas Holiday – *Robert (Gene Kelly) and his mother (Gale Sondergaard) try to hide from Abigail the significance of the stain on the trousers.*

voice-over, however, quotes a psychoanalyst who later claimed, 'Robert's relations with his mother were pathological.'

Nothing on the surface suggests anything this extreme. Certainly, Mrs Manette is not Oedipally possessive: after she has met Abigail, she is delighted at the impending marriage. It seems that we are being alerted to something else about the relationship. In the novel, there is a clear subtext: Teddy Jordan is explicitly gay, and explicitly attracted to Robert. Although we are told that Robert does not reciprocate, it is not difficult to read his killing Jordan as an attempt to deny his own sexual ambivalence; Maugham finds a precise image for the murder – Robert literally stabs Jordan in the back. He then returns home from the murder and makes love to his wife as never before. She even becomes pregnant: a remarkable link with *Experiment Perilous* (Jacques Tourneur, 1944), in which sexual potency is also achieved through murder. Here it is as if, with his homosexual impulses 'repressed' through murder, Robert can now prove himself sexually with a woman – a specifically Maugham subtext which, consciously or unconsciously, bears testament to the 'problem' that so personally preoccupied him.

This subtext is far less in evidence in the film. Nevertheless Mankiewicz has, I think, preserved it. Just before Abigail quotes the psychoanalyst, she says of Robert: 'He was so gay, so charming, so' – pause – 'different'. And 'gay' was already in currency within gay (and showbiz?) subculture with its now well-known meaning, as *Bringing Up Baby* (Hawks, 1938) testifies. Similarly, the phrasing Mrs Manette uses when she rounds on Abigail after Robert's arrest is pointedly ambiguous: 'You should have known. You weren't blind because you had to be; you wanted to be. It might have hurt to know that [pause] Robert is what he is.' And, finally, there is her insistence that what Robert needed was to be made 'strong' through the combined efforts of both Abigail and herself. These examples indicate that the subtext is speaking of gayness in negative terms ('pathological'; 'weak'). But other examples are different: the sense of excitement with which Robert speaks of Teddy Jordan when he points him out to Abigail in the 'den of iniquity' he used to patronise; the (belatedly revealed) information that, as in the novel, Robert killed him when his back was turned.

Simon, too, seems implicated in the gay subtext. In the novel, this does not seem to be the case: he is an old schoolfriend of Charley's who has become an ice-cold political extremist. In the film, he is a much more ambiguous character, and the manner in which he first ingratiates himself with Charley could just as easily suggest pick-up as pimp. (In the Maison, the way he moves his chair to sit shoulder to shoulder with Charley – and then moves it back for Abigail to sit in – is a delicate little hint.) We see Teddy Jordan only for a few seconds, but shortly afterwards Simon makes his first (chronological) appearance. He acts not a little piqued that he hasn't seen Robert recently, and is suitably snide about the relationship with Abigail: 'Bad boy meets good girl: damage estimated at $10,000.' Robert himself describes Simon as 'One of those fellows I've been getting myself mixed up with,' and then asks Abigail earnestly: 'You do believe me, don't you, that I'm through with all this?' In a brilliant touch, Siodmak dissolves from her reply ('I do') straight into the wedding scene, so that the reply stands in for the ceremonial 'I do'. In other words, Robert's question replaces the priest's. The effect of this is to make the question of his giving up 'all this' the premise of the marriage. Clearly, this, too, may be linked with the gay subtext.

The wedding is rendered unusual in another way, however: Abigail's voice-over says of Mrs Manette 'she was radiant' – as if she were the bride. This gives an alternative twist to the mother/son relationship. Abigail herself has already noted that '(Robert) wasn't just her son; he was her everything.' And whilst a mother seeking to rival a daughter-in-law in her son's affections is virtually a commonplace, *Christmas Holiday* does seem to take it a stage further: as if Mrs Manette sees herself, in fantasy, as 'like' Robert's wife. On the morning after the murder, as Robert comes down stairs, he makes a point of addressing each of the women in turn as 'Mrs Manette'.

Christmas Holiday is a highly coded film, in which tiny details can be as important as explicitly signalled elements. For example, the song that is used to signify the Abigail-Robert romance is Irving Berlin's 'Always'. But, before this, the last word of Mona's telegram to Charley was 'Always'. Whilst this could have just been a conceit, it draws a specific parallel between the irony of Mona's 'always' and the use of the Berlin song: both are false in their promise. When, in a scene which is almost a parody of domestic harmony, Robert plays the piano, Abigail sings the song and Mrs Manette in her rocking-chair knits and looks on indulgently, we are aware of the deceptiveness of the appearance. In the very next shot, with Abigail's voice-over noting that 'overnight everything changed', the narrative has moved on past the murder and Robert's arrest, and the real *noir* imagery begins. Earlier, when a policeman called, the staircase and hallway were evenly lit. Now everything is heavily shadowed, with a network of criss-cross patterns on the stairs and an enveloping darkness at the top. As first Mrs Manette and then Abigail go up the winding staircase, visually it is as if they are entering a maze: the 'happy home' has become a cage.

This is just one example of Bredell's work in the film: there are many other stunning *noir* images. But another vital contribution to the film's imagery comes from the set design (again by Goodman and Clatworthy). When, on the first morning, Abigail becomes disturbed by the give-away behaviour of Robert and his mother (*very*

give-away: the scene is awkwardly scripted and acted), she is dismissed to her room. But the house has been designed with an external landing across the large kitchen window: from this, Abigail sees Robert watching his mother strive to remove the stain on his trousers. Her bedroom also overlooks the courtyard; shortly afterwards she sees Mrs Manette at the furnace burning the trousers. The design helps Siodmak develop a sophisticated up/down pattern in the movie. In both these instances, Abigail's positioning above mother and son suggests her moral superiority. Then, when the film returns to her first meeting with Robert, both are sitting in the gods listening to Wagner's *Liebestod* at a concert. But Robert brings her down, first to the stalls, then, in a subsequent scene in a tea-garden, from the second floor balcony to the ground. (The crane shot that follows the two of them all the way down here is superb – almost Ophulsian.) Apart from movements up and down the stairs in the house – these, now, invariably charged with *noir* imagery – subsequently in the narrative Abigail remains 'grounded'. In the Maison Lafitte, she is only ever seen on the ground floor; in the cathedral (the Mass obviously 'pairs' with Wagner at the concert) she is in the nave.

Having narrated her two flashbacks, Abigail returns to the Maison Lafitte and Charley changes his mind about seeking revenge, deciding to return to camp. In sharp contrast to his predecessor in the novel, he has found her story 'therapeutic'.

Still: Christmas Holiday – *Valerie (Gladys George) looks on while Simon (Richard Whorf) shows his interest in Charley (Dean Harens).*

The film then takes a totally different direction from the novel: Robert escapes from jail. As soon as Abigail has left Charley, he receives a phone call from Simon, and we see that Robert is with Simon in the latter's room. Robert's being with him here (with an unmade bed in the background) is yet another sign that Simon should be included in the gay subtext. And, from the way that Robert accosts Abigail when he tracks her down to the Maison, it seems fairly obvious that Simon – present throughout this scene – has been describing her activities there in a way which has goaded Robert into hating her. (It is even likely that it was Simon's stories about Abigail that led to Robert breaking jail.) When Abigail protests to Robert that she loves him, and that she works at the Maison only in order to share his suffering, he still refuses to believe her, and ends by threatening her with murder. At this point, Charley and the madame, Valerie, burst into the room.

The power that Simon exercises over Robert here – goading him into violence – echoes that of Marcella as *femme fatale* in *Phantom Lady*. Moreover, it is Simon who provokes Robert's death, repeating his name loudly so that the cop prowling outside the Maison overhears, challenges Robert and shoots him through the open window. What strengthens the link is the sense that both Marcella and Simon taunt the male figures with their sexual inadequacies. And this, in turn, reintroduces Charley into the structure: after all, the revenge Robert was planning to take on Abigail also echoes the revenge that Charley had planned on Mona. Thus both 'hero' and 'villain' in each film are implicated in a structure of anxiety about masculinity, which Richard Dyer has suggested is a general feature of *film noir* ('Resistance Through Charisma: Rita Hayworth and *Gilda*' in Kaplan, ed., 1978, p.91).

Whilst it is necessary for Charley to be included in the film's ending, there is no sense – contrary to the assertion in *Time* magazine's review at the time – that he and Abigail 'get together' at the end. In delivering the film's final words, Charley is merely echoing Robert's last words as he dies in Abigail's arms: 'You can let go now, Abigail.' It is Abigail alone that the camera then shows as she stands up and walks to the window, the *Liebestod* swelling up on the soundtrack. The film, here, is seeking transcendence: with her head haloed by backlighting, Abigail looks up at the night sky, and clouds part to reveal stars. The religious experience of the mass – a mere twenty-four hours earlier – here blends with the uplift of Wagner's music to suggest Abigail has finally achieved a release from her past obsession. (If Durbin did film any of the scenes, this seems the most likely candidate.)

In following the novel and seeking to share Robert's suffering by becoming a dance hostess, Abigail is masochistically choosing a sexual degradation, as if to mark, specifically, her own sexual 'failure': 'I can still hear them call you guilty, guilty, guilty, and every time they said it, I knew it was meant for me, too.' It's as if the trauma of 'sexual deviance' resonates through the text, always escaping precise definition, but pushing the narrative in strange ways. Siodmak's place in this is to hold together the different discourses – Maugham filtered through Mankiewicz and the Production Code; Bredell being brilliant; Durbin being 'difficult'; Kelly taking on a highly risky part in terms of his star following (particularly in view of all the fuss over the casting of Fred MacMurray in *Double Indemnity* a few months earlier). The result is a sometimes uneasy, but for the most part a challenging, rich, suggestive film.

Melodrama & Film Noir: from The Suspect (1944) to The Dark Mirror (1946)

Siodmak's next four films are essentially melodramas with *noir* elements. James Ronald's British novel *This Way Out* (1939), from which *The Suspect* was adapted, is a highly sympathetic account of an ordinary middle-aged man driven into committing murder, which could have made an effective *film noir*. However, Universal (perhaps

Still: The Suspect – *Philip (Charles Laughton) declares that he will no longer sleep in the same room as Cora (Rosalind Ivan).*

struck by the potentially exploitable echoes in the story of the Crippen murder case) took the decision to set the film at the turn of the century. The effect is to dilute the *noir* ambience of the story: the period iconography – ornate Victorian interiors, horse-drawn carriages, sett-paved streets, gaslight, fog – grants an aesthetic distance. The casting of Charles Laughton compounds the effect: his performance is theatrical, almost enjoying the game he is required to play with the police rather than becoming guilt-ridden and hounded like a true *noir* hero – and, indeed, like his prototype in the novel. The cameraman was Paul Ivano, a less distinctive talent than Bredell, and visually only one sequence is unmistakably *noir*. Nevertheless, the film's plot structurally anticipates that of Lang's *Scarlet Street* a year later – by common consent, one of the key *films noirs*. Accordingly, comparison of the two films indicates to what extent *The Suspect* may be considered *noir*.

In each film, an unhappily married middle-aged man in a routine white-collar job – Philip Marshall (Laughton) is a London tobacco shop manager; Chris Cross (Edward G. Robinson) is a New York clothing-store cashier – falls for a much younger woman who offers him the fantasy of escape from his shrewish wife (both Cora and Adele are played by Rosalind Ivan with unremitting irascibility). In meeting the young woman, the hero 'rescues' her – Mary (Ella Raines) from the misery of fruitless job-hunting; Kitty (Joan Bennett) from an attack by a man – enacting a male fantasy of saving a damsel-in-distress. *Scarlet Street*, of course, ironises this rescue – the man attacking Kitty was her 'pimp', Johnny (Dan Duryea) – just as it goes on to ironise the relationship between Chris and Kitty herself. She remains in love with Johnny, and Chris becomes their dupe, exploited for money. When

Chris finally discovers all this, he kills Kitty in a rage, and then ensures that Johnny – the obvious suspect – is convicted for the crime. Legally Chris remains unpunished, but he is taken into a *noir* world of madness and despair which is extraordinarily bleak. The film ends, some years later, at Christmas, with Chris now a shuffling tramp, still haunted by the voices of the two people he killed.

Although Philip also kills two people, *The Suspect* has little of the darkness and despair of *Scarlet Street*. Here, Mary genuinely comes to love Philip for his gentleness and kindness. However, Cora refuses to grant him a divorce. It is only after this that Philip tells Mary he's married – he also has an adult son, John (Dean Harens) – and says he must give her up. But Cora has already found out, and threatens to ruin Mary as well as Philip. This scene is also set at Christmas, and begins with Cora mocking Philip's attempts to be festive with seasonal decorations. Although it lacks the powerful irony of the use of Christmas in Lang's movie, it is typical of the *noir* tendency to subvert such 'hallowed' institutions. As soon as Cora has uttered her threat, Philip decides to kill her, taking hold of one of his walking-sticks with obviously murderous intent. There is then an ellipsis to two old women in the street gossiping about Cora's 'accidental death' by falling downstairs.

The coroner is satisfied, but Scotland Yard is not, and the remainder of the film depicts a cat-and-mouse game between Philip and a smooth, creepy detective, Inspector Huxley (Stanley Ridges), another of Siodmak's sinister policemen. Here the film moves more obviously into *noir* territory. Huxley makes his first appearance the night after Cora's funeral. In front of Philip, he then restages Cora's death the way he imagines

Still: The Suspect – *Philip meets Mary (Ella Raines) in a Chinese restaurant.*

it – as murder. As he goes through the various stages – selecting a weapon, turning down the gaslight, unfastening the stair carpet, hiding on the landing, calling to Cora – Siodmak films his actions so that his face remains hidden. Just as Huxley is restaging the crime to disturb Philip, so Siodmak is restaging it to disturb us: we suddenly see Philip the way Huxley does, as a ruthless murderer. It is here that the chiaroscuro of *film noir* is brought dramatically into play; in particular as Huxley hides on the landing, merging into the shadows so that he becomes invisible, a disembodied voice calling a woman out to her death. In effect, Huxley puts on a piece of theatre which, as with *'The Mousetrap'* in *Hamlet*, he hopes will disturb the conscience of the murderer.

At first, Philip is equal to Huxley's manoeuvres. He refutes this version of Cora's death and, by the time Huxley has tracked down Mary, Philip has married her, eliminating her as a possible witness against him. And so, Huxley tries another tack, activating the suspicions of Philip's neighbour, Simmons (Henry Daniell). A drunkard who refuses to work and who beats up his wife, Edith (Molly Lamont), Simmons is only too receptive to the idea that Philip may have murdered Cora. Immediately he sets out to blackmail Philip, telling him that he is quite prepared to testify that he heard sounds of violence on the night of Cora's death.

Philip pretends to accede to the blackmail and, whilst Simmons gloats, quietly poisons him, watching tensely whilst the poison takes effect. Once more, Huxley suspects Philip of the murder (indeed, it is as if Huxley acted as *agent provocateur* and set up the murder) but, once more, can find no evidence. And so, in the manner of other Siodmak policemen, he sets out (again) to trap the hero. Philip has decided that Mary and he should emigrate with John to Canada. Huxley catches him just before the boat sails and tells

him that Edith has been identified as Simmons's murderer. It is a lie, but this time Huxley does disturb the conscience of the murderer. As Huxley had predicted, Philip cannot allow Edith to take the blame. The film ends with Philip returning ashore, leaving John and Mary to sail alone together to a fresh start in Canada.

This second murder reconnects the film with *Scarlet Street*. Like Johnny, Simmons is a sponger who beats up women and, in killing him, Philip is also rescuing Edith from him; that morning he had seen the black eye Simmons had just given her. A similar notion occurs in *Scarlet Street*, although rendered, once more, ironic. When Chris realises that Johnny is Kitty's lover, he believes he can rescue her, but she mocks him, goading him into killing her. And his motive in ensuring that Johnny is convicted for the murder is only secondarily to escape the chair himself; primarily it is to punish Johnny for the way he treated Kitty. In both films, the meek hero defies expectations and disposes of the arrogant bully. But, as in the other comparisons, *Scarlet Street* is again more subversive, since it is through the law that the hero enacts his murder of the bully.

At the same time, it is as if the hero here were also killing his own dark side. In each case, the way that the bully beats up women may be seen to express the suppressed violence in the hero. In *The Suspect*, if Huxley's restaging is correct, Philip really does attack and kill his wife in such a manner. (Huxley assumes that the fall would not have been sufficient, and so Philip would have needed to 'finish her off' with his cane. In the novel, this is indeed the case.) In *Scarlet Street*, when Chris kills Kitty with savagely sexual thrusts from an ice-pick, we can see that he is enacting as murder the sort of violent sado-masochistic sexual relationship Johnny had with her. What takes the hero into the *noir* world is a release of his own latent violence; that which is repressed under the civilised manner of the bourgeois. And yet both heroes retain a great deal of audience sympathy. Rosalind Ivan makes the wives genuinely appalling: the opening of *The Suspect* shows John leaving home, driven out by his mother's behaviour towards him; Chris is henpecked and emasculated to a humiliating degree. Equally, Simmons and Johnny are thoroughly nasty pieces of work; it is hard to regret their deaths. But, unlike Chris, whose conscience punishes him to such an extent that the Breen Office let him get away with a double murder, Philip has no guilt for his crimes. And so, he never really becomes a genuine *noir* hero.

Thomas Job's 1942 play *Uncle Harry* is in the form of a confession, narrated by middle-aged Harry Quincey to a stranger and dramatised in flashback. Resentful at the way his sisters, Lettie and Hester, have blocked his relationship with a younger woman, Harry decides to get rid of both of them: he poisons Hester and frames Lettie for the murder. But, when the young woman still declines to marry him, he regrets his actions and tries to save Lettie from the gallows. She refuses, accepting her own death and preferring to punish him with his guilt.

As adapted by Keith Winter and Stephen Longstreet – and retitled *The Strange Affair of Uncle Harry* (1945) – the film is much more interesting. A crucial change is that Lettie (Geraldine Fitzgerald) is now incestuously possessive of Harry (George Sanders), whilst Hester (Moyra MacGill, the mother of Angela Lansbury), although always squabbling with Lettie, is basically a sympathetic figure. It is Lettie alone who sabotages Harry's engagement to city girl Deborah (Ella Raines, once again called upon to fall in love with a mild-mannered, middle-aged man), provoking Harry to contemplate revenge. But here the poisoning plot goes dramatically wrong, Hester becoming the unintended victim. The maid Nona (Sara Allgood) immediately assumes that Lettie did it, and Harry opportunistically goes along with this. Lettie is tried, convicted and sentenced to death. Here the film returns to the substance of the play. Just before the execution, Harry tries to confess, but the prison warden (Holmes Herbert) won't believe him unless Lettie confirms his story. And she herself prefers to die and let Harry suffer the consequential guilt: 'You'll not be good company for yourself all the long years that stretch ahead, when you can't think or sleep or eat or read.'

As originally conceived – and, according to Hervé Dumont, as actually filmed by Siodmak – the film kept the play's flashback structure. It began after Letty's execution with Harry, on his way to a psychiatric clinic, meeting Deborah in mourning: her husband has died. Although she is now free to marry Harry, he declines; the flashback tells us why. But this means that Harry gets away with murder – which the Breen Office refused to sanction. The solution Universal finally came up with – leading Joan Harrison, the film's producer, to quit the studio – was to remove the flashback structure and recast the poison plot as Harry's fantasy, imagined whilst he sits brooding, the poison bottle in his hand. Critics have tended to follow Joan Harrison and condemn this solution, but at one level it works brilliantly. Just as the events of Fritz Lang's *The Woman in the Window* (1944) make *more* sense when recast as the hero's dream, so this sequence expresses both the contradictoriness of Harry's wishes *and* his inability to carry these out. The *noir* world is *inside himself*: we see him veer from a sadistic attack on Lettie to a masochistic surrender to her greater power; even in his fantasy, she triumphs over him. What spoils the film is what happens after this sequence, when Harry is improbably rewarded with the return of Deborah.

Again photographed by Ivano, *The Strange Affair of Uncle Harry* is again visually *noir* only occasionally, for example when Harry is in his darkened observatory just before the fantasy sequence, and in the final shot of Lettie walking

away down the shadowy prison corridor as she returns to her cell and imminent execution. Nevertheless, for twenty minutes or so, the narrative is genuinely *noir*, with the hero caught in a web of murder and guilt from which he simply cannot escape. When Harry goes to the prison to confess, the warden asks him what motive he could possibly have had for wanting to kill Lettie. He replies, 'I hated her; I wanted to be free of her.' The warden comments, 'And now you want to save her: it doesn't make sense.' Lettie is even more resistant to his confession, at first torturing him by acting as if he had imagined the whole thing and, when he repeats 'I just wanted to be free', scornfully pointing out 'You *are* free.' The sense of the hero confronted with an impenetrable resistance to his desperate attempt to free himself of his burden of guilt is highly characteristic of *film noir*. At the same time, what Harry had wished to be free from is the claustrophobic attachment of an incestuously possessive sister. But that, of course, cannot be mentioned. And so, the web in which he is caught is rendered even more potent by the impossibility of acknowledging its source.

The Spiral Staircase (1945) was the first film made at RKO under a co-production deal between David O. Selznick's Vanguard Films and the studio. Selznick assembled the package – Dore Schary as producer, Siodmak as director, Dorothy McGuire and Ethel Barrymore as stars,

and Mel Dinelli's script (from Ethel Lina White's novel *Some Must Watch*) – and RKO provided the remaining personnel and made the movie. (Later films made under the same deal include Hitchcock's *Notorious* and Edward Dmytryk's *Till the End of Time*, both the following year.) A major RKO contribution was Nicholas Musuraca, one of the cameramen who worked most distinctively in the *noir* cycle. Although *The Spiral Staircase* is more Gothic melodrama (disabled heroine menaced in large house by psychotic villain) than *film noir*, it is a superb example of Musuraca's artistry: shot after shot makes striking use of darkness and shadows.

The film is set in New England in 1906. In the brilliant (wordless) opening sequence, Helen (McGuire) is watching a silent movie (*The Kiss*) in a hotel hall, whilst upstairs an unidentified male eye spies on a lame young woman getting dressed in her room. We then see a shot of the young woman from the man's point of view: distorted with a fish-eye lens, it has been taken by some critics to represent the reflection of the woman on the eye itself. I read it much more as an expressionist device, expressing the man's insanity: the way he *sees* the girl. Seconds later, he kills her, and, shortly afterwards, we learn that

Still: The Spiral Staircase – *Blanche (Rhonda Fleming), Albert (George Brent), Helen (Dorothy McGuire) and Stephen (Gordon Oliver, foreground) with the bedridden Mrs Warren (Ethel Barrymore).*

she is his third female victim, and, like the others, disabled in some way. Back at the Warren mansion where she works as a maid, Helen, who is mute, is marked as the next victim. She has already been shadowed home by a sinister figure and now, as she looks at herself in a mirror on the stairs, a figure on the landing above watches her and again we see a huge close-up of the eye followed by a distorted 'subjective' shot. But in Helen's case the distortion includes the erasure of her mouth: a visual expression of the defect which psychotically obsesses the murderer. At the film's climax, when the murderer Albert Warren (George Brent) finally identifies himself to Helen, he says 'There's no room in the whole world for imperfection.' Again, as with Marlowe in *Phantom Lady*, one senses the Nazi overtones.

As Helen enters the house (about twelve minutes into the film), darkness is falling and a storm begins. The rest of the action takes place in the house on the same night. With the classical unities thus preserved, Siodmak and his collaborators have fashioned a film which is oddly dream-like in its narrative and *mise-en-scène*. Hervé Dumont quotes an interview in which Siodmak has said, 'Mel Dinelli and I tried to create a sort of surrealist film which put the audience into a trance, a state of hypnosis, so that they would accept

the unfolding of events without asking themselves questions. Helen's thoughts were expressed through gestures . . . and Dorothy McGuire conceived her silent role as a sort of ballet. Her choreographic expression enabled us to regain some of the elements of the best silent cinema' (p .181).

All elements of the film combine to produce the 'hypnotic' effect:

1) The Warren mansion has been designed by Albert S. D'Agostino and Jack Okey as a complex of inter-connecting rooms, corridors and staircases, decorated with rich period furnishings. As we follow the characters around it, it seems to be a coherent whole, but analysis reveals a crucial mismatch in the location of the spiral staircase itself between the ground and first floors. Such a discrepancy – an apparent spatial continuity which masks a discontinuity – is typical of dream narratives.

2) With the whole house as its terrain, Dinelli's screenplay is structured theatrically, weaving together the interactions and tensions between the eight occupants (and two visitors) with considerable skill. It also makes effective use of repetition. Almost all the characters are paired (two doctors; two brothers; two young, attractive women; two middle-aged servant women) and key events are repeated: three subjective (distorted) close-ups of the intended victims; three visits to the cellar; four warnings from Mrs Warren (Ethel Barrymore) telling Helen to leave; four unexpected arrivals/ entrances which surprise/disturb, etc. The effect

is similar to that characterised by Leslie Fiedler in *Love and Death in the American Novel* (Paladin, 1970, p.120) as the 'compulsive repetitiveness' of the Gothic novel, which he likens to 'a self-duplicating nightmare from which it is impossible to wake.'

3) In the main body of the house, Musuraca uses wide-angle, deep-focus photography to capture the characters' interactions in depth; in the servants' quarters, and on the spiral staircase which runs both up and down from them, he uses low-key photography which darkens markedly as the action descends to the cellar. In all zones of the house, the *mise-en-scène* is detailed and complex, and even the editing is exactly the way Siodmak wanted: he has pointed out (quoted in *Films in Review*, April 1969) that a technicians' strike in Hollywood prevented the studio from interfering. The result is not only a superbly executed melodrama of steadily mounting suspense, but a stream of elements which speak the psychoanalytical language of the unconscious: stairs, corridors, mirrors, portraits, unexpected entrances and exits, a dark cellar, staring eyes, deceptive shadows, a raging thunderstorm, a psychic bedridden woman and, of course, Helen's

Still: The Spiral Staircase – *Helen makes her way down the spiral staircase.*

muteness, which expresses the terror of the nightmare in which one cannot scream.

Highly effective though it is, *The Spiral Staircase* is not a *film noir* in the usual sense of the term. Although the persecuted-wife cycle may be related closely to *film noir*, expressing for women fears equivalent to those which *film noir* expresses for men, *The Spiral Staircase* is peripheral to that cycle. Its main generic elements derive from the Gothic novels of the eighteenth and nineteenth centuries: setting (the sprawling mansion), themes (the perverted legacy of the dead patriarch, fraternal rivalry and jealousy), characters (a physically vulnerable heroine, an almost useless hero, a psychotic villain), together with a dream-like narrative which dramatises persecuted innocence and threatened violation (both murders we see are filmed to suggest they are a displacement for rape). Like *The Strange Affair of Uncle Harry*, the film contains a fantasy sequence: Helen imagines herself marrying the ineffectual hero, Dr Parry (Kent Smith). And, when she can't say 'I do', her fantasy, too, turns to nightmare, conveyed by a swift darkening of the image and reaction shots of the horrified guests. It's a fascinating link with the corresponding disturbance to the wedding in *Christmas Holiday*, but its nature illustrates how the film's concerns are with melodrama and the Gothic rather than *film noir*.

The Dark Mirror (1946) shares several crucial production features with *The Woman in the Window*. Both films were written and produced by Nunnally Johnson for his own production company at International Pictures, and both were photographed by Milton Krasner and designed by Duncan Cramer. Release of *The Dark Mirror* was delayed until after Universal and International had merged, and it was the first film to be shown under the new Universal-International logo. It became the studio's biggest hit of the year; *The Killers* (made after, but released before *The Dark Mirror*) and Lang's independently made *Scarlet Street* tied for second place.

Both *The Dark Mirror* (in which Olivia de Havilland plays twins) and Bernhardt's *A Stolen Life* (in which Bette Davis plays twins) were filmed in March 1946. *A Stolen Life* is a classic Davis women's film, with the two sisters – their characters polarised along standard good woman versus sexual woman lines – rivalling each other for the love of the hero. *The Dark Mirror* is very different. The most *noir* of Siodmak's four *noir* melodramas, it begins as a murder mystery. The opening sequence shot (a 60-second take around an apartment) ends by revealing a man's body; the second sequence shows Lt Stevenson (Thomas Mitchell) – one of Siodmak's rare likeable cops – questioning witnesses. But, with the discovery that the chief suspect, Terry Collins, has an identical twin sister, Ruth, and with neither sister admitting which of them was with the victim, Dr Peralta, on the night in question, the

Still: The Dark Mirror – *Scott (Lew Ayres) with good twin Ruth (Olivia de Havilland).*

film changes direction. Through the agency of Scott Elliott (Lew Ayres), another doctor who – like Peralta – had been fooled into thinking there was only one of them, and who 'just happens' to be an expert on twins, a psychological investigation is opened up. This not only replaces the traditional police investigation but provides a background against which to read the interaction of the twins themselves, which forms the dramatic core of the film. Scott's tests reveal that Ruth is normal, Terry insane. And, as each of them falls in love with him, Terry (who is indeed the murderer) sets out to dispose of her rival by driving her to a suicidal breakdown.

Up to a point, the film can be seen as a typical *noir* narrative in which the hero, Scott, is caught between a sexually dangerous *femme fatale*, Terry, and a loving, good woman, Ruth. Because they are twins, the question of the deceptiveness of women and the susceptibility of men is foregrounded. From Scott's point of view, a crucial issue is can he *really* tell the twins apart? But the film is more centrally concerned with the relationship between the two women. In this respect, it belongs with other psychological melodramas in which a character's mental disturbance creates the *noir* world for someone else, as in *The Locket* (John Brahm, 1946) and *Secret beyond the Door* (Lang, 1948). As Terry's designs on Ruth become more terrifying, the film becomes more *noir* – the imagery more low key and the narrative more paranoid. Unable to comprehend what

is happening to her, Ruth begins to crack up: the effect is similar to what happens to the heroine in a number of the persecuted-wife films, such as *Gaslight* (George Cukor, 1944).

As a narrative about twins, *The Dark Mirror* is reactionary. The film itself admits that the notion of the sane twin and the insane twin derives from an old superstition, but it nevertheless reinstates the idea, making things worse by dressing it up with 'scientific' credentials (Rorschach tests, word associations, etc.). As a dramatisation of the story of the double, however, the film becomes much more interesting. It may be related to the stories about doubles analysed by Otto Rank in *The Double: a Psychoanalytical Study* (Meridian Books, New York, 1971). The narratives Rank investigates – in literature, myths, even the cinema: his prime example is the 1913 version of *Der Student von Prag* (Stellan Rye) – are similar in that they deal with the double as a *threat* to the hero (all the protagonists in Rank's examples are male), regularly driving him to madness and suicide. This is not the case with most Hollywood versions of 'the story of the double', which range from the double as 'saviour' (*The Prisoner of Zenda*, John Cromwell, 1937, and Richard Thorpe, 1952; *The Masquerader*, Richard Wallace, 1933) to the twin as dangerous usurper (*The Black Room*, Roy William Neill, 1935; *A Stolen Life*). In all these cases, the threat is different in nature from that in Rank's examples. (A rare instance of a film which does dramatise the Rank version of the double is *The Man Who Haunted Himself*, Basil Dearden, UK, 1970.)

Nevertheless, *The Dark Mirror* fits Rank's thesis. Rank argues that the narratives he analyses arise psychoanalytically from a corpus of material, at the heart of which are paranoia and narcissism. *The Dark Mirror* presents both twins in a paranoid framework. Like Rank's heroes, Ruth suffers from a persecution which seems irrational, and which may be read as a dramatisation of paranoia with the double acting as persecutor. Terry, however, is *clinically* paranoid. The film indicates that this has arisen from her intense jealousy that people respond to Ruth much more affectionately than to her. Above all, she resents Ruth's greater success with men. However, there is a clear subtext here. Terry's actions (pursuing Ruth's boyfriends rather than finding her own; disposing of them rather than Ruth) and Ruth's complicity (she tacitly accepts all this) hint at an unacknowledged homosexual attachment which, in Terry's case, shows strong signs of becoming conscious: 'We'll never be separated. You and I are going to be together as long as we live.' Again, this conforms to Rank's thesis: 'the stage of development from which paranoids regress to their original narcissism is sublimated homosexuality, against . . . which they defend themselves with the characteristic mechanism of projection' (p.74). In particular, the strategy that the twins have adopted of pretending that there is only one of them seems to

Still: The Dark Mirror – *the bedroom. Terry (right) shows her hostility to Ruth.*

have been designed by Terry, both to use Ruth and to keep her from gaining independence.

Another of Rank's arguments is that narcissism generates a fear of becoming old (horror at the ageing features in the mirror), 'a fear which is really the fear of death' (p.77). Thus, the double (the embodiment of the mirror reflection) comes to represent death. *The Dark Mirror* confirms this quite remarkably: during her word-association session, Ruth responds to Scott's 'Mirror' with 'Death'. Hearing about this afterwards, Terry recognises that the response refers to her and interprets it as Ruth letting slip that she, Terry, killed Peralta. But Rank's analysis leads us to interpret the response more directly: to Ruth, Terry (her mirror image) represents death. Previously, the twins wore matching clothes; now Terry wears black, which contrasts sharply with Ruth's lighter clothes.

In *The Dark Mirror* the bedroom is the *noir* world and the mirror (as the film's title hints) is the site of disturbance which focuses the tensions between the twins. It is in the bedroom that Terry insidiously seeks to undermine Ruth's sanity and where low-key lighting is most extensively employed. And it is when Terry is reflected in the bedroom mirror that she seems most successful in imposing her paranoid vision on her sister. This occurs in two scenes, and, on both occasions, just after Terry has forced Ruth into a lie about Scott. And so, when Terry – through the mirror – then begins to undermine Ruth's

sense of her own sanity, Ruth's submission seems tied in with her knowledge that she has just lied. She accepts Terry's authority.

At the film's climax, believing Ruth to be dead from the overdose she wished on her, Terry in her madness now declares that she is Ruth. Then Ruth reappears, significantly, out of the bedroom. But it is her reflection that Terry attacks, smashing the mirror. Afterwards Scott says to Ruth that *she* was the reflection and, although this doesn't make sense, it points, again, to the mirror as the place where confusion over separate identities is focused. The most frequent ending to the narratives Rank discusses is the destruction of the double, which immediately results in the death of the hero. (He analyses this as a 'suicide wish'; the paradoxical desire to escape death *through* death.) What *The Dark Mirror* seems to be groping towards is a similar paradox: in attacking Ruth-in-reflection, Terry is symbolically attacking herself (as is spelled out in Scott's 'That's what twins are, reflections of each other.') The film's use of mirrors began in the first shot, when one of the details singled out in Peralta's apartment was a mirror which had been shattered by a sharp impact. In retrospect, it's as if Terry had attacked her own reflection, the mirror image ambiguously representing both Ruth and her own psychotic side. (The latter feature is quite common in films, e.g. in *The Eyes of Laura Mars*, Irvin Kershner, 1978, when, having revealed his 'split personality', Neville/Tommy Lee Jones stabs his mirror reflection. The most powerful recent example of the device is in the scene which finally identifies

Laura Palmer's murderer in David Lynch's TV serial *Twin Peaks*.) Ultimately, Terry projects all her psychotic side on to Ruth, only to find it returning to confront her in the mirror.

The complexity in the film's use of mirrors suggests that *The Dark Mirror*, like *The Spiral Staircase*, would be analysed most productively in non-realist, psychoanalytical terms. It is the peculiarly symbiotic relationship between the twins, and the darkness of the *noir* world into which this takes them, that constitutes the film's primary interest. In some ways a rather confused film, it nevertheless has resonances which make it consistently intriguing.

The Killers (1946)

The Killers was Mark Hellinger's first project as an independent producer working out of Universal. For some time, he had wanted to use Ernest Hemingway's 1927 short story (published in *Men without Women*, Penguin, 1955) as a dramatic beginning for a film; Universal acquired the property for him and gave him the go-ahead. Having been very impressed with *Phantom Lady*, he reunited Siodmak and Bredell for the production, and encouraged them to offer ideas. In an article by Herb A. Lightman on the making of the film in *American Cinematographer* (December 1946), Hellinger is quoted as saying: 'Siodmak deserves special credit for his contributions to the screen treatment. Usually, when you hand a director a script, you are happy if he can bring out 85% of the potential dramatic values it contains. But when you give the script to a director like Siodmak, and he gives you back 125% – well, you've really got something there.' Hellinger was similarly skilful in selecting the two leads, neither of whom were well known at the time. Newly under contract to Paramount, Burt Lancaster had yet to appear in his first film; after four years at MGM, Ava Gardner had yet to be given a major role in an A film. *The Killers* made both of them into stars.

As is well known, Hemingway's story supplies only the first two scenes of the film: the two hoods waiting at the lunch counter and Nick warning the Swede (an ex-boxer) of their intention to kill him. The script was extrapolated from there. It is credited to Anthony Veiller but, in the *Sight & Sound* interview, Siodmak says that it was in fact by John Huston: 'His name didn't appear in the credits because he was under contract to another studio [Warners] . . . but he wrote the script for us in his spare afternoons (with Tony Veiller cracking the whip occasionally).' In his autobiography, *An Open Book* (Alfred A. Knopf, 1980), Huston says (modestly?) that he and Veiller wrote the script together.

From all points of view – characters, narrative, imagery – *The Killers* marks Siodmak's return to mainstream *film noir*. It possesses not only a deceiving *femme fatale*, Kitty Collins (Gardner), but also both sorts of *noir* hero: Reardon (Edmond

O'Brien), an insurance agent, the seeker hero, and the Swede (Lancaster) the victim hero. Its convoluted narrative contains no fewer than eleven flashbacks, not even in chronological order. And it includes some of the finest low-key photography in the whole cycle. Lightman praises Bredell's work on the film, citing the 'realism' created by his technique of dramatically reducing the number of lights on the set. He also refers to what Bredell calls '*out-of-balance* lighting', achieved by 'purposely discarding fill illumination', resulting in a 'sharp contrast between crystal white and velvet black' – what critics would later call chiaroscuro. In an article on Bredell ('Speed Cameraman') in a later issue of *American Cinematographer* (October, 1948), Fred Banker is even more excited by Bredell's work, and says that *The Killers* 'made him the town's most sought-after cameraman.'

When it was made, *The Killers* was seen as a gangster film, as it was in retrospect by Siodmak himself (*see* 'Hoodlums, the Myth . . .' in *Films & Filming*, June 1959). Lightman says that Hellinger actually previewed the film to 'members of the underworld', and that they responded even more enthusiastically than the ordinary preview audience. Nevertheless, although the gangster elements are strong in certain sequences – for example, the beginning – overall, they are subsumed in a classic *noir* double narrative: the story of a murder investigation which leads to other murders, and the story of a loser, destroyed by his obsession for a dangerous woman.

The Killers begins with two hoods, Al (Charles McGraw) and Max (William Conrad) arriving at night in Brentwood, New Jersey, and entering Henry's Diner. They are marked as hoods by their appearance (fedoras, hard faces and tightly buttoned overcoats), mannerisms and patterns of speech – all details from the story, which was written before the Hollywood hood really existed. In other words, Hemingway established in advance of Hollywood the deliberate manner, the posturing, the verbal play, the heavily stressed menace. (However, the Production Code does eliminate Hemingway's casual racism: in the story, the cook, Sam, is automatically referred to as 'the nigger'.) The diner is narrow and confined, the lighting muted and low key, with the camera sufficiently low to show the ceiling, which furthers the sense of enclosure. Siodmak films the scene with long takes, deep focus and with tightly framed group shots, this last reflecting both the tension of the situation and the tightness of the hoods' control. In effect, they 'secure' the diner in the military sense: Sam (Bill Walker) and Nick (Phil Brown), a customer, are tied up in the kitchen; George (Harry Hayden), the proprietor, is kept on the lunch counter as a front. Sure of themselves, they even tell George that they're waiting to kill the Swede.

So, when Swede fails to turn up, and the hoods leave, George sends Nick to warn him. As Nick runs through the back gardens, a fast lateral track expresses the urgency of his mission. Miklos Rosza's pounding music carries this sense of urgency over into the next shot, which begins with a view from the window of Swede's first-floor room. Nick appears in the gardens below, still running; the camera then dollies back and pans across the room, past Swede lying on the bed in the shadows, to the door. As Nick bursts in, the music abruptly stops. Siodmak continues to film with the same long (80-second) take, but Swede's response to Nick's warning and Nick's growing sense of helplessness completely change the mood. Again the dialogue closely follows Hemingway, but the fatalism of the scene is typically *noir*. Hearing that two men are coming to kill him, Swede continues to lie in the darkness, saying that there's nothing he can do about it. Even Nick's offer to call the cops is refused: 'That wouldn't do any good.' In effect, Swede is simply waiting to be killed: 'I did something wrong – once.' We are now at the heart of the *noir* world, where a man so lacks the will to live that he just waits for the end.

Unable to do anything, Nick leaves. Only then does Siodmak cut to a close-up so that we can see Swede's face in the shadows. He hears a creak downstairs and half rises to look at his door. Cut to a wide-angle shot from the top of the stairs as the killers quickly come up and position themselves outside the door. Cut to Swede, waiting. The cross-cutting continues, building tension, until the killers burst in and blast away at Swede. Here the gangster and *noir* elements merge. The scene depicts a typical gangland murder, but Siodmak films it expressionistically and elliptically: the flashes of light from the killers' gun-shots illuminating their faces; Swede's hand sliding down the bedhead signalling his death.

A number of *films noirs* begin with a murder which sets up the enigma of whodunnit: *Laura* (Otto Preminger, 1944), *Mildred Pierce* (Michael Curtiz, 1945), *The Dark Mirror, Crossfire* (Dmytryk, 1947). (Although it isn't discovered until later, the murder in *Phantom Lady* would also have been committed at the point when the film begins.) *The Killers* is quite different: the enigmas posed by Swede's murder concern why he is being killed and why he is so passive. In setting out to answer these questions, the film adopts a complex flashback structure which not only seems modelled on that of *Citizen Kane* but, in a couple of details, seems to acknowledge the influence. (The narrative is unravelled, with only minor errors, in David Bordwell: *Narrative in the Fiction Film*, Methuen, London, 1985, pp.193-198.)

The next sequence introduces Reardon, an agent for Atlantic Casualty, which holds Swede's life-insurance policy. Tying the investigation to an insurance agent requires a certain extension of his professional interest: the film shows him becoming obsessed with seeking out the truth in much the same way that Marlowe becomes obsessed in *The Big Sleep* (Hawks, 1946). From Swede's effects, he takes his first clue: a large

green silk handkerchief, decorated with a harp surrounded by shamrocks (a Freudian design whose import is later apparent). He then goes with Nick to see Swede's body in the morgue. The morgue sequence is filmed with the figures backlit to create a striking silhouette effect. This evokes the imagery Welles used for the shadowy investigator Thompson (William Alland) in *Citizen Kane*, but in context links the beginning of Reardon's investigation with the darkness of the *noir* world: it is from the morgue that Nick narrates the first flashback. Located a few days before the murder, it shows a man – later identified as Colfax (Albert Dekker) – drive up to the gas station; he and Swede recognise each other. Immediately after the man leaves, Swede becomes 'sick' and goes home.

Over the next few days, Reardon uncovers more witnesses: Queenie (Queenie Smith), Swede's beneficiary (in Atlantic City – another reference to *Citizen Kane*); Lt Sam Lubinsky (Sam Levene), Swede's boyhood pal who, as a cop, watched him move from a failed boxing career to involvement with crooks; Lilly (Virginia Christine), once Swede's girlfriend, now Lubinsky's wife, and Charleston (Vince Barnett), who shared a cell with Swede in jail. Narrating six further flashbacks between them, they provide additional pieces of the jigsaw for Reardon, leading up to Swede's involvement in preparations for a payroll heist.

By this stage, however, the film has exposed a major problem with the flashback structure. The narrators themselves do not always identify who they're talking about, but the flashbacks do: an almost inevitable consequence of the story being filmed rather than written. For example, although Nick can describe Colfax, he cannot name him, but the organiser of the heist in Charleston's flashback – whom Charleston is *refusing* to name – is the same man. This sets up a tension: we are repeatedly being provided with more information than Reardon. Although, theoretically, this tension should always be present in film flashbacks (how much of the mass of detail that we can see in a flashback is being communicated to the listener?), few films draw attention to it. In fact, two conflicting narrative impulses are at work here. On the one hand, the flashbacks *are* marked by who narrates them: Lubinsky signals his retrospective detachment from Swede by speaking of his friend as a loser ('seems like I was always in there when he was losing'), whereas Lilly's and Charleston's flashbacks register their own sense of loss as Swede, in effect, leaves each of them in turn for Kitty. On the other hand, the flashbacks function primarily to give the audience the narrative information necessary to further the plot, an operation which is independent of the narrator/listener structure.

The mood of defeatism that marks Swede's death is echoed in the endings of the first three flashbacks. In Nick's, he goes off 'sick' to wait for death. In Queenie's, crying, 'She's gone' (the film's first reference to the *femme fatale*) and smashing up

the furniture, he is only prevented from throwing himself out the window by Queenie's intervention. He ends by falling back on the bed in a position that precisely duplicates the way we first see him in his darkened room. In Lubinsky's (first) flashback, he is badly beaten in a boxing match, and, after the fight, it is revealed that his right hand is broken. His boxing career finished, he declines the companionship of both Lubinsky and Lilly and walks off alone into the night. It is effectively here that he goes into the *noir* world: unable to settle for low-paid legitimate work (he turns down Lubinsky's suggestion that he should join the police), he drifts into crime.

In this recurring pattern, Swede is characterised as a casualty: of his past, of a woman and of a failed career. In his excellent article on the film, Jack Shadoian points out how Swede's death haunts these early flashbacks. During the boxing match, 'A spectator tells Lubinsky that Swede is "getting murdered", that he "can't last" . . . When he gets knocked out, he *looks* dead . . . More to the point is that he is treated as though he were dead. For his manager and trainer, he no longer exists as a person . . . His manager departs with "I never did like wakes". . .' (*Dreams and Deadends,* MIT Press, 1977, p.85). Equally, if we consider the scenes chronologically, we can see that Swede's knockout in the ring (the earliest scene) is echoed in the shots of him supine on the bed, as if Kitty ('she') had knocked the fight out of him. We see nothing of

Swede's life in the years between the Atlantic City scene in 1940 and his chance meeting with Colfax in 1946, but it is clear in retrospect that, having lost Kitty, he considered there was little worth living for. Although Queenie saved him from suicide, he moved into limbo.

Kitty is finally introduced in Lilly's flashback, in which Swede takes Lilly to a party populated with underworld figures, including Blinky Franklin (Jeff Corey), held in the luxury apartment of Big Jim Colfax. With Colfax himself currently in jail, Kitty is their host, a detail which tells us that she is his expensively kept mistress. But, if Lilly grasps the situation, Swede does not; he is instantly mesmerised by Kitty. As she sings 'The more I know of love,' he moves to stand next to her, and the flashback ends with a two-shot with a pointedly phallic light on the piano between them. When we next see Swede – in Lubinsky's second flashback – the consequences of his involvement with Kitty are made clear: he is already engaged in small-time crime (the numbers racket). Then, when Lubinsky moves to arrest Kitty for possession of some stolen jewellery, Swede steps in and takes the blame, socking Lubinsky and getting three years in jail.

In Charleston's two flashbacks, the bed motif is articulated in terms of Swede's loss of and desire for Kitty. In jail, again lying on the bed, Swede plays compulsively with the silk handkerchief Kitty gave him (a clear Hollywood signifier of masturbation) and wonders why she hasn't written. A concerned father-figure, Charleston gently tries to hint at the real reason: 'A girl don't write, that don't mean she's sick . . . not necessarily.' In the scene in which Colfax organises the gang for the payroll heist, it is Kitty who is on the bed, and Swede (just out of jail) is reduced to sitting at the end of it and again playing with the handkerchief. Even though he will finally recognise Kitty's unfaithfulness (at the end of Queenie's flashback, he cries 'Charleston was right'), Swede never grasps just how completely he has been set up. As Colfax entices the other members of the gang – Blinky and Dum-Dum Clark (Jack Lambert) – with the value of the heist, it is Kitty's provocative presence which is designed to ensure Swede's involvement. Here, too, gangster and *noir* elements combine. Assembling a gang for a caper is a familiar gangster scene, and the interplay of barbed suspicion and hostility between the gang members is almost ritualistic. But underlying this is a *noir* plot, in which Swede's desire for Kitty is used to set him up as the patsy.

The silk handkerchief leads Reardon back to a 1940 robbery of the Prentiss Hat Company in which one of the robbers wore such a handkerchief over his face. Siodmak films the robbery (the eighth flashback) with a newspaper account of it as voice-over. With the camera mounted on a crane outside the factory gates, the whole robbery sequence – its moves synchronised with the events described in the voice-over – is shown in one superbly executed two-minute take. Here the inflection given to the flashback is 'documentary': the objectively recording camera. Again, however, we are supplied with information not contained in the newpaper account: some of the gang members are recognisable.

The liberties the film has taken with its flashbacks thus far are, however, minor compared with the next two examples. Summoned by Lubinsky to a hospital, Reardon arrives to find Blinky dying from a bullet wound. Feverishly rambling to himself, Blinky conveniently chooses to talk about what happened the night before the robbery and at the share-out meeting afterwards. The ensuing flashbacks, however, are perfectly coherent. The first shows Swede and Colfax at loggerheads, with an incident – Kitty provoking a row with Colfax and Swede springing to her defence – which, in retrospect, we realise has been staged by Kitty and Colfax. The second shows Swede arriving at the rendezvous

Still: The Killers. *The gang members wait for the arrival of Swede – Charleston (Vince Barnett), Dum-Dum (Jack Lambert), Colfax (Albert Dekker), Blinky (Jeff Corey) and Kitty.*

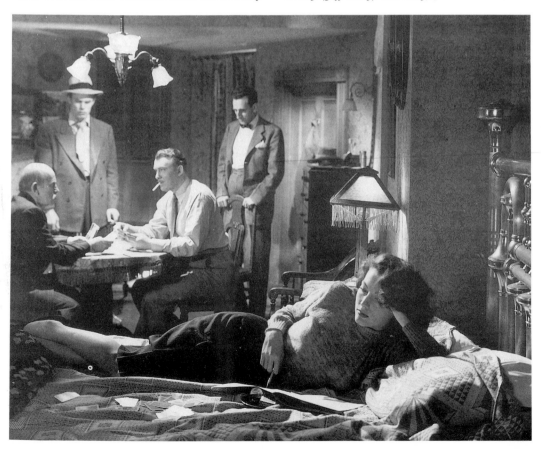

where the share-out is to take place and, claiming he's been double-crossed (they've switched rendezvous), holding the others up and making off with all the money.

Blinky dies. Items in his pockets direct Reardon back to Brentwood, where he anticipates that Blinky's killer will go to seek the stolen money. It is his return to Swede's room – the site of the initial murder – that takes Reardon into the *noir* world. Until this point merely an investigator into past events, he now becomes an active participant. Scarred with holes from the bullets which killed Swede, the room is a space of danger, and Reardon's entry into it releases a series of violent events that echo those experienced by Swede. First, he witnesses Dum-Dum tearing the room apart, an act that duplicates Swede's frenzied assault on the furniture of the Atlantic City hotel room. The parallel reinforces the link between the missing money and the missing Kitty. After Reardon has held Dum-Dum at gunpoint and questioned him, Dum-Dum fights back, kicking the gun from Reardon's hand and cross-questioning him in turn. As the cops gather outside (the assistance that Nick was unable to provide for Swede), Dum-Dum kicks Reardon unconscious, and escapes through the window and over the roof. The scene thus climaxes with an echo of the initial shooting, with Reardon unconscious on the floor and the hood making good his escape.

To grasp the full significance of this scene, it is necessary to unravel a major theme in the film: the issue of male potency. The theme is developed with different inflections in three separate narrative threads: Swede's, the gangsters' and Reardon's. In Swede's case, he was once a virile boxer, but a broken hand cut short his career. His scarred hand (emphasised in big close-up in the morgue) is his 'mark of castration', and chronologically the flashbacks begin with the revelation of this. Among other things, Swede's broken hand makes him passively dependent on Lubinsky, who dresses him after the fight as one would a child; equally, it causes him to lose interest in Lilly, as if he sees himself as no longer worthy of her esteem. (In an unusual variation on the standard *femme fatale*/domestic woman distinction, it is the domestic woman who enjoys the fights and the *femme fatale* who is squeamish: 'I could never bear to see a man I really cared for being hurt.')

Having lost his potency as a boxer, Swede seeks to recover it by entering the criminal world. In the scene in which Lubinsky is about to arrest Kitty, Swede's flashy dress signals his success as a rising gangster, and the punch with which he floors Lubinsky marks his regained potency. The consequence is, of course, ironic: Swede is sent to jail and has to console himself with Kitty's handkerchief. When he comes out of jail, Kitty allows him to have sex with her (her flashback, which contains the film's only kiss) only in order to dupe him. Equally, when he

seemingly reasserts his potency by sticking up the other gangsters and making off with the money, he is again being duped: the theft is part of Colfax's plan. Two days later, Kitty repossesses the money for Colfax. And, as we discover at the end of the movie, the two of them then retire to bourgeois respectability: marriage and (for Colfax) legitimate business.

In this narrative thread, Swede is between two father-figures: Lubinsky, who represents the law, and Colfax, who represents the criminal world. (A third father-figure, Charleston, is present essentially to emphasise Swede's dependence on such figures even in jail.) And so, the three interlocking triangles of *film noir* (*see* Introduction) here receive an unusual inflection. In the Colfax/Kitty/Swede/Lilly/Lubinsky configuration, both triangles involving Swede and another man are potentially Oedipal. In fact, this is played down with Lilly and Lubinsky: it was only after Swede had left her that she turned to Lubinsky, and there seems to have been no animosity between the two men as a result. But with Kitty and Colfax, the Oedipal overtones are correspondingly exaggerated: here the *femme fatale* actually prefers the older husband-figure to the hero. As a consequence, Swede experiences in full Colfax's revenge: not only the loss of Kitty and the money (a loss of potency so severe that he attempts suicide), but a death sentence. Swede knew that any gang member who caught up with him would kill him; the fact that it was Colfax confirms his submission to death as a masochistic surrender to the father-figure's wrath. 'I did something wrong – once' refers to the Oedipal crime: sexual possession of the father-figure's woman.

With the gangsters, male potency finds expression in shooting, a characteristic feature of the genre. Chronologically, the first shots in the narrative are fired during the robbery, when Dum-Dum shoots a security guard in the groin. This implicit sexualisation of shooting then echoes through the narrative. Swede is shot lying on his bed. Dum-Dum gets his name from the 'special type of bullet' he uses: a very nasty type which violently expands upon entering the body. The sexual displacement is very clear, and Blinky, babbling to himself, is registering the trauma of a shooting in which Dum-Dum's bullet has exploded inside him.

With Reardon, played with cocky assertiveness by Edmond O'Brien, the theme finds yet another inflection. Shadoian discusses at length Reardon's desire to take on the gangsters, to enjoy the excitement of their dangerous lifestyle. In effect, he seeks to prove himself in their world, to assert his potency through manly prowess. When Swede's hand is emphasised in big close-up, it is Reardon who is holding and looking at it. His making off with the vaginal handkerchief can be seen as his wish not simply to identify with Swede but to supplant him, to demonstrate that, whereas Swede was 'castrated', he himself is potent.

Still: The Killers – *Reardon (Edmond O'Brien) and Kitty in The Green Cat.*

Accordingly, the scene in which Reardon and Dum-Dum confront each other in Swede's room is crucial. First, as Reardon waits outside the door, we can see him preparing to go in and play his tough-guy scene: the way he juggles around uncertainly with a cigarette and his gun suggests his simultaneous fear and excitement. In fact, when it comes, he is very bad at it: Dum-Dum has little difficulty in turning the tables on him. Then, at the moment when Dum-Dum kicks the gun from his hand, the sexualised undercurrents return. The two men dive on to the already devastated mattress, fighting to get control of the gun. At stake in their struggle is information about Kitty, so that assertion of male potency once more revolves around her. It is Dum-Dum who succeeds in grabbing the gun, and he forces Reardon to divulge the information. (That it concerns her theft of the money, i.e. her power as 'castrating woman', is another issue. Both Reardon and Dum-Dum assume they can deal with this, but it leads to both of them being shot at, Dum-Dum fatally.) Dum-Dum then cocks Reardon's 45, turns him over on his front and retrieves his own gun from Reardon's pocket. Unmanned, Reardon lies there passively – like Swede, accepting his fate – but, at the last second, Dum-Dum does not deliver another sexually charged bullet; instead he kicks Reardon unconscious.

For Reardon, the scene functions in two ways. The alignment of his fate with Swede's generates a melodramatic structure in which, for Colfax and Kitty, Reardon becomes 'the return of the repressed'. He emerges out of Swede's room like a resurrected Swede, bent on revenge. But, for Reardon himself, the experience is cautionary. When he seeks out Colfax and Kitty, he is far more circumspect in his approach.

In implicit response to Lubinsky's earlier request to be 'in on' any revenge, he and Reardon now team up together. This relocates Lubinsky as a good father-figure, first helping restore Reardon's potency by providing him with another gun and, later, saving him from the killers. Correspondingly, when Reardon meets Colfax, the latter is wielding a large hunting rifle, a reflection of his phallic power as bad father-figure. But, unlike Swede, Reardon is canny enough to play Colfax at his own game. A retrospective reading of the scene suggests that he already knows about Colfax and Kitty's marriage, and that he pretends ignorance merely to give Colfax time to set him up and thereby betray his own complicity – in the robbery, the double-cross and Swede's murder.

And so, when Reardon meets Kitty, the killers reappear: now he is their target. He and Kitty go to the Green Cat nightclub, where she narrates the final flashback, describing the way in which she fooled Swede into thinking he was being double-crossed and thus provoked him to double-cross the others. In the flashback, Swede is again shown lying supine on a bed. Hearing Kitty's knock at the door, he is immediately suspicious, but when she enters and tells her duplicitous story, he believes her, and is seduced by her kiss. Coming out of the flashback, Siodmak dissolves to a two-shot of Reardon and Kitty, with a candle burning on the table between them: momentarily, the candle is superimposed over the kiss. Although lacking the intensity of the light bulb which marked her impact on Swede, the candle suggests that Kitty's power is not yet exhausted. Admiring the way she double-crossed Swede, Reardon comments, 'I'd like to have known the old Kitty Collins.'

Before the flashback, Reardon produces the green silk handkerchief when Kitty refers to it. With this comment, he takes his identification with Swede a stage further, cueing the arrival of the killers. As Kitty excuses herself and goes to the powder room, they enter the club. They position themselves at the bar, and Siodmak builds the suspense masterfully, dollying back from Max to reveal Lubinsky further down the bar waiting for them to act. The shoot-out that ensues is dynamically choreographed. The killers rush towards Reardon and start blasting; simultaneously Reardon overturns a table to provide cover, and Lubinsky shoots the killers from the side, bringing both of them down and scooping up Al's gun before Reardon is back on his feet. The sequence is an excellent example of the brutal concision of Siodmak's scenes of violence: the shoot-out is over in a matter of seconds, and Reardon heads at once to the powder room. But Kitty (like Dum-Dum from Swede's room) has already escaped through a window.

It is this scene that refers most explicitly to the gangster genre: a shoot-out in a public place, complete with suspenseful build-up (aided by a deliberately dissonant boogie-woogie on the piano), explosive violence and panic-stricken patrons screaming and running for cover. And

Still: The Killers – *Lubinsky (Sam Levene) and Reardon look on as Kitty arrives to find Colfax dying.*

yet it, too, occurs within a *noir* frame. In the taxi *en route* to the Green Cat, the faces of Reardon and Kitty are intermittently lit by the passing streetlights, a slow-motion replay of the way the killers' faces were illuminated as they shot Swede. Reardon here is journeying deeper into the *noir* world, choosing to go to the very spot which Kitty had suggested in her phone call to him. Whereas his earlier alignment with the fate of Swede was unintentional, here he deliberately sets himself up as a target for the same killers, inviting the violence as if to force the events to a conclusion.

Another *noir* feature of the film is the implicit incompetence of the police. Not only did they fail to track down any of the four original robbers in 1940, but the local chief in Brentwood washes his hands of investigative reponsibility for Swede's killers and, even when his men later surround a building, they let Dum-Dum slip away. It is true that Lubinsky is able, eventually, to shoot the killers and that the master-criminal behind both the Prentiss robbery and Swede's murder is finally exposed, but all these are primarily thanks to Reardon; without him, Lubinsky would have got nowhere. The irrelevance of the police is underlined at the beginning of the penultimate scene. As Reardon and the cops cautiously enter Colfax's house, shots are heard: they assume that they are the ones being fired at and scramble for cover. But it is Dum-Dum and Colfax, the last two members of the gang, shooting it out with each other. Thanks to Reardon,

Dum-Dum now knows enough to work out Colfax and Kitty's double-cross; here he attempts a settling of accounts. He is killed; Colfax mortally wounded. Colfax does live long enough to answer some questions, but otherwise all the police can do is telephone for an ambulance. It arrives too late.

Before Colfax dies, Kitty arrives and begs him to clear her: 'Say "Kitty is innocent!".' This parallels her begging Swede to save her when Lubinsky set out to arrest her, and Swede didn't hesitate, even going to jail for her. But Colfax is not Swede: he dies without speaking further. In Siodmak's versions of the *noir* Oedipal triangles (also in *Criss Cross* and *The File on Thelma Jordon*), it is the hero who is enamoured and who sacrifices himself for the *femme fatale*; the powerful gangster-figure who looks upon her as his is more detached. Just as Colfax played innocent to Reardon about his relationship with Kitty (and hence his part in the double-cross), so Kitty until now has continued to protect Colfax, telling Reardon that the double-cross to get the money was all her own idea. Whilst Kitty's duplicity is repeatedly stressed, the machinations of the dominant male behind her are kept hidden until the end. In the flashbacks, the relationship between Colfax and Kitty is deceptive; in the present, it is masked until this final meeting between them. The effect is to foreground Kitty as *femme fatale*, whereas she is one of the many heroines of *film noir* who (so far as we see) is really only *fatale* to the hero. Her motives are enigmatic: why does she go along with Colfax's plans to double-cross Swede? In her flashback, she makes a speech to Swede describing herself as 'poison', and this has a ring of authenticity, as if she really does feel that she is harmful to someone she cares for. (In *Criss Cross*, which is in many ways a companion film, this notion is developed in the Anna-Steve relationship in terms of the destructive nature of desire.) We simply do not know what the relationship between Colfax and Kitty has been like, but everything that we do see, including his refusal to lie for her at the end, suggests a power relationship in which she has been subservient.

The Killers is one of the most 'complete' *films noirs*: it contains significant elements from all three of the *noir* structures discussed in the Introduction (the seeker-hero structure, the Cain paradigm, the paranoid *noir* story) as well as possessing the three interlocking sexual triangles, which seems to me the key *noir* character-relationship pattern. And yet it has a gap at its centre: the six-year period from 1940 to 1946. The gap neatly avoids the 'problem' of the war, but one nevertheless feels a nagging sense that the presence of the war should somehow have been registered; that the characters should have been

marked by it in some way. As it is, only Colfax's success as a building contractor can be (indirectly) related to the war; the other gangsters, like Swede, disappeared into limbo during those years. Is the war the *film's* repressed? If so, the strategically planned shoot-outs, the daring raid on the hat factory and the bloody deaths could also be seen as the return of the repressed, and Colfax as the ruthless commander who sends his men out to kill and be killed.

Cry of the City (1948)

Siodmak's next film was *Time out of Mind* (1947), adapted from Rachel Field's novel. Another fading dynastic family/weak son story, it has links with all Siodmak's earlier versions: *Christmas Holiday* (the son surrounded by protective women), *The Strange Affair of Uncle Harry* (an incestuously possessive sister) and *The Spiral Staircase* (the setting of the huge mansion, with the castrating patriarch here made flesh), but the film is generically a melodrama, with no *film noir* elements.

Siodmak was then loaned out to Twentieth Century-Fox for *Cry of the City*, one of the studio's

Still: Cry of the City – *Martin Rome (Richard Conte, with gun) as intruder in the Rome household, with Lt Candella (Victor Mature), Tony (Tommy Cook) and Mama Rome (Mimi Aguglia).*

location-based crime thrillers made in the wake of the success of the 'semi-documentaries' pioneered by producer Louis de Rochemont. Although the semi-documentaries seem to me to be materially different from *films noirs* (*see* Introduction) they nevertheless exerted a strong influence over crime thrillers of the era, particularly cop movies, and some films, e.g. Anthony Mann's *T-Men* (1947), seem like hybrids of *film noir* and semi-documentary.

Cry of the City was filmed on location in New York, scripted (from Henry Edward Helseth's *The Chair for Martin Rome)* by Richard Murphy, who scripted the de Rochemont-produced *Boomerang* (Elia Kazan, 1947), and directed by Siodmak. One would have expected it to have been another hybrid, but this is not really the case. It is not completely lacking in *noir* elements, but these are marginalised or displaced, only emerging when the film is analysed more closely. For all the narrative focus on Martin Rome (Richard Conte), the gangster hero, the film basically follows the reactionary cop movie line of privileging the cop Lt Candella (Victor Mature), who hunts Rome down. Visually it lacks the expressionistic flair of the other Siodmak movies: with one or two exceptions, the lighting is much more conventional. (The cameraman, Lloyd Ahern, is no Woody Bredell or Nicholas Musuraca.) Siodmak has said that he didn't enjoy working on location and, for all the skill with which he directs, the film lacks the bite of the *films noirs* which preceded and succeeded it.

Nevertheless, *Cry of the City* has strong structural links with *The Killers* and *Criss Cross*. In each, the male protagonist has grown up with someone who becomes a cop. As adults, the two men come into moral (and legal) conflict, and the different ways in which this is worked through illustrate the ideological conservatism of *Cry of the City* in relation to the other movies. In *The Killers,* both men are presented sympathetically, and the film conspicuously lacks any moralising about the hero 'going to the bad' which so afflicts *Cry of the City*. In *Criss Cross*, the cop is a thundering superego heavy: all our sympathies are with the hero. Having agreed with the hero's family that the hero's ex-wife is bad for him, the cop threatens to frame her: he and the family are partners in repression. In *Cry of the City,* there is a similar closeness between the hero's family and the cop, but in this case the family and the cop are 'good' and the son Martin is 'bad'; when Candella ingratiates himself with the family in order to hunt Martin down, this is not really criticised. Indeed, as Candella takes in hand Martin's kid brother Tony (Tommy Cook) to stop him from following Martin's route into crime, the film clearly supports him.

Cry of the City begins with Martin Rome apparently receiving the last rites from a priest, with his grieving family gathered at his hospital bedside. Even though he does not die from his bullet wounds, he is still a condemned man: he killed the policeman who shot him. This biases the film. For *Cry of the City* to have been a genuine *film noir*, it would have needed to construct Rome as a victim, hounded by an obsessive cop. Candella does become obsessive, but the film is stuck with its project. He and Rome represent alternative role models for kids growing up in the Italian quarter, and Rome, whom Candella fears at one point is being looked upon as a Robin Hood, is a cop-killer. However much we may sympathise with the character Conte creates, he has to be discredited.

The project is enacted through two young people who love Rome and who begin the movie under his charismatic sway: his brother Tony and his girlfriend Tina (Debra Paget). By the end of the movie, both are necessarily 'educated' into seeing the evil of his ways. In Tina's case, this is effected, symbolically, in a church. At the end of the film, Candella tracks Rome down to the church where he is meeting Tina and, forcing her to see Rome the way he does, drives her away. In Tony's, the education occurs under the sign of the law. Before entering the church, Rome orders Tony to go and steal money from their parents. That this seems in context a forced action, inserted to discredit Rome, bears testament to the film's problems. Tony then reappears just after Candella has shot Rome and says that he was going to tell his brother he couldn't go through with the theft. He is then rewarded for rejecting Rome by Candella taking over Rome's place as his big-brother figure. The last shot shows Candella through the back window of a police car comforting the boy whose brother he has just shot: above them, on the vehicle, is inscribed the word POLICE. Tony is recuperated, literally, into the arms of the law.

Such moralising has nothing in common with *film noir*, which is fundamentally subversive of American ideology and institutions. However, the film does have elements that go against the grain of the moralising. Its most sinister character is a lawyer, Niles (Berry Kroeger), who repeatedly tries to persuade Rome to admit to the de Grazia murder and robbery, a vicious case in which an old lady was tortured to reveal the whereabouts of her jewels and then killed. On the surface, Niles is seeking a sneaky way out for his client, who has been arrested for the crime, but it eventually transpires that Niles himself set up the robbery – which became murder – and possesses the stolen jewels. It is his sadism that aligns him most obviously with similar villains in *film noir*. On one occasion, he stands behind the headboard of Rome's bed and, looking down on him, suggests that he'll find Rome's girl and work her over. Provoked beyond endurance, Rome grabs him by the throat and almost strangles him before hospital staff separate them. Our sympathies in the scene are entirely with Rome, and it is at this point that Nurse Pruett (Betty Garde) decides that she'll do as Rome has asked her and hide Tina in her apartment.

Tina appears at the beginning of the film to see Rome in hospital: she emerges out of the shadows and is associated with the iconography of crucifixes surrounding the bed at this point. She then 'resurrects' Rome: after her kiss he says, 'Can't die – now,' and proceeds to live, despite having been given the last rites. Both an angel (Rome's expression) and a phantom, Tina then disappears until the end of the film, when she appears in the church looking remarkably like a madonna. A very different kind of female character from the norm in Siodmak's movies, she lacks the presence of a *noir* heroine, and functions in the film more as a symbol of innocence and purity.

Even though he doesn't know who she is, Candella becomes preoccupied with tracking Tina down. Ostensibly, this is because Rome is a potential suspect in the de Grazia case – one of the stolen rings was found in his possession – and the police know that both a man and a woman were involved in the case. But the obsessiveness of Candella's pursuit seems to go beyond this. In one scene he, like Niles, positions himself behind Rome's headboard and tries to needle him. He doesn't adopt the same leering sadism as Niles, but the staging of the scene is significant. Rome's anxiety for Tina – which prompted him to ask Nurse Pruett to hide her – seems excessive: why should the police want to harm her? But the way Candella keeps returning to the question of the girl who visited Rome in the opening scene fuels Rome's anxiety. Tina's identity becomes such an issue between the two men that one feels strongly that the film is implying something else: something which emerges at the end of the film as a genuinely *noir* subtext.

After Candella has casually dropped Tina's name as one of the women they're looking for, Rome becomes desperate to escape from prison hospital. A trustee, Orvy (Walter Baldwin), has already shown him how it can be done and, in a suspenseful set-piece, Rome follows Orvy's plan and then sets out to track down the real woman in the de Grazia case. This takes him to Niles, and a confrontation which climaxes with one of Siodmak's highly compressed scenes of violence. As Rome holds Niles at knife-point, forcing him to name the woman, Niles's terrified secretary listens at the door. Then, as both men see the shadow of the secretary through the glass in the door, a rapid scuffle ensues: Niles seizes a gun and fires at the same time as Rome wrenches him backwards in his chair. The shot goes wide, but Rome nevertheless stabs Niles in the back, and the secretary falls on the floor as if shot – she has fainted. As Rome hastily takes possession of the de Grazia jewels, the scene ends with Niles's body slumping on to the floor, leaving his chair revolving eerily on its pedestal.

Remarkably, it is almost as if Siodmak were restaging the killing of Teddy Jordan from *Christmas Holiday* – a murder we did not see because of the restriction in the flashbacks to scenes witnessed by Abigail. But, whereas Niles could be gay (certain mannerisms suggest such a coding), Rome's killing him seems motivated purely by revenge and contempt: Niles had threatened Tina. Any further intimations are for the moment held in check.

Rome's plan is to use the jewels to buy his passage out of the country from Rose Given, who stole them, and then tip off the police as to

Still: Cry of the City – *Brenda (Shelley Winters) gets a doctor (Konstantin Shayne) for Martin.*

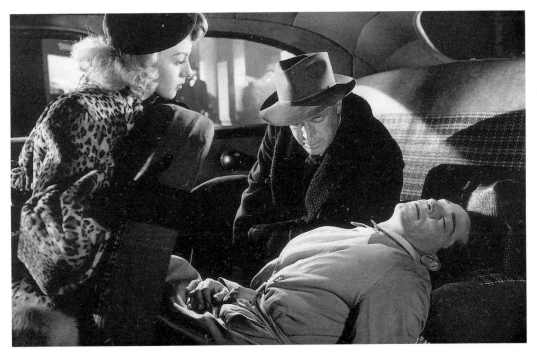

their whereabouts. But, before he can put this into action, his wounds re-open, leading to the film's most explicitly *noir* sequence. Brenda (Shelley Winters), an ex-girlfriend, finds him an unlicensed doctor (Konstantin Shayne), and the man is forced to operate in the back of her car whilst she drives round the city at night. Her fear that Rome will be spotted if they stop is given tension by the doctor saying that he needs more light, a tension which captures a very *noir* anxiety, in which any action is fraught with danger.

Rose (Hope Emerson) is given the film's most striking entrance. Watched by Rome through the glass in her front door, she walks from the back of the building towards him, her massive bulk filling a succession of door frames. Like Tina, Rose is first seen in distant silhouette: she is Tina's underworld counterpart: the real woman in the de Grazia case. When she opens the door, she towers over Rome, an effect emphasised by his being partly hidden in the shadows, so that he seems to cower before her. After the *noir* journey in the back of the car, this scene should have been the *noir* climax, with Rome confronting and doing battle with the female dragon. Unfortunately, it doesn't work like this, both because the scene is shot in conventional high-key lighting and because Rome can so obviously handle Rose. He flirts with her, and, even when she transforms her massage of him into a stranglehold, he deflects the danger with little trouble. At the end of the scene, the film dissolves to Candella and his colleague Lt Collins (Fred Clark), still on the job at 4 a.m. To fortify himself, Candella muses about Rome: 'He's out there somewhere: in an alley, on a roof, looking for a way out – he's not asleep.' Here, explicitly, Candella is undermined: Rome is indeed asleep, safe with the woman who could have been his most dangerous enemy.

Nevertheless, Rose is dangerous, as Rome finds out when she discovers his double-cross as he collects the jewels the next day at a subway station. Two policemen wrestle with her, but she still manages to take a shot at him. At this instant, Candella is leaping over the subway barrier to seize Rome; Rose's bullet misses Rome and hits Candella. Again, Siodmak choreographs and edits brilliantly: as Candella is shot, he rises up on top of the barrier to tower over Rome like an avenging angel, and Rome actually recoils from the sight. In a film full of Christian imagery, it is an emblematic moment.

The wounding of Candella sets up a crucial link between him and Rome. Like Rome before him, he, too, leaves his hospital bed before his wounds are healed. But whereas Rome left to save Tina, Candella leaves to hunt down Rome. It is here that he seems completely obsessed: when he turns up at Nurse Pruett's apartment, he insists to her that Rome might murder Tina. Then, when he confronts Rome and Tina in the church, the film hints – very subversively – at the nature of his obsession. Earlier, when Candella warned Nurse Pruett about Rome's way

with women, or when he read out the list of Rome's ex-girlfriends that he'd been tracking down, one sensed a strong wish to disparage Rome's sexual successes. And now, as Candella insists to Tina that Rome hasn't told her the whole story about the people he has used in his flight from the law, he makes a revealing comment: 'He used them and brushed them aside, just like he uses everybody he's ever known.' Suddenly one sees that he could very well be talking about himself. Throughout the film, the intimacy with which Candella addresses Rome (like Niles, he calls him 'Marty') contrasts oddly with the more formal way Rome addresses him, and the scenes with Rome's parents suggest that he's been to their apartment many times. There is no reference whatever to Candella's own home, or to any women in his life. If we take it that all along Candella has been harbouring an unrequited love for Rome, everything falls into place. And so, the film's ending, so reactionary on the surface, turns out to be highly subversive in the subtext. What we see is Candella embracing the adolescent brother of the man he loved and lost.

Leaping to seize hold of Rome, Candella was shot in the left shoulder, 'over the heart'. The wound may thus be seen as a physical expression of the pain of his unrequited love. When he confronts Rome in the church, he is momentarily triumphant: he 'wins him' from Tina and bluffs him into surrendering by threatening to shoot. (In fact, he has no gun.) But, outside the church, as he persuades Rome to hand over his gun, blood from his wound appears on his palm. Hitherto he has concealed from Rome the extent of his 'wound'; this gives it away. And so, when Rome strikes the wound (in order to incapacitate him), the film finds a vivid action to express his final rejection of Candella. Candella slumps to the ground; Rome bends down to repossess the gun from under his body. But then, in a hauntingly *noir* moment, Rome is caught in the headlights of an approaching car, which causes him to abandon the search and move off quickly down the sidewalk. Candella rises to a sitting position, takes aim and, invoking the law, calls for Rome to stop. Rome carries on; Candella shoots him in the back. As Rome lies on his back on the sidewalk, his body suddenly rises to a sitting position, facing towards Candella, and he releases the blade of his flick-knife. Then he falls back, dead. He answers Candella's bullet with a gangster's reflex that is also an erection, as if acknowledging, at the moment of death, his own repressed desire.

Cry of the City is a problematical film. One feels strongly that with a subtle change of emphasis in the narrative, and with a *noir* cameraman, it could have been a superb example of the cycle. Nevertheless, its *noir* elements are not absent, merely repressed, and they return in one of the most fascinating subtexts of the 'forties. The gun that Candella takes from Rome belongs to Niles; the knife that Rome flicks open in his dying reflex is the one that killed Niles. The weapons, charged with potential Freudian meaning, circulate between the moralistic cop, the sadistic villain and the gangster hero in a highly suggestive way.

Criss Cross (1948)

Mark Hellinger was in the process of setting up a film adaptation of Don Tracy's 1936 novel *Criss Cross* when he died, aged 44, in December 1947. (The film's poster still used his name: 'Mark Hellinger's choice to follow his *Killers* and *Naked City'*.) The project – for which Siodmak and Lancaster had already been contracted – was taken over by Universal and, according to Hervé Dumont, production head William Goetz simply handed it to Siodmak, who thus had a great deal of creative control. Siodmak wrote the script in collaboration with Daniel Fuchs, who had already scripted two little-known contributions to the *noir* cycle: *The Gangster* (Gordon Wiles, 1947), from his own novel, and *Hollow Triumph* (Steve Sekely, 1948). Opposite Lancaster, he cast Yvonne De Carlo, more typically found at the time in Universal's series of exotic Easterns (from *Salome Where She Danced*, Charles Lamont, 1945, to *Cashbah*, John Berry, 1948). Whereas Ava Gardner in *The Killers* seems rather too sophisticated a heroine for a Lancaster hero (which is part of the film's point), De Carlo, with her working-class sexiness, matches him perfectly, and Siodmak exploits their affinity with great success. As his cameraman, Siodmak obtained Frank (Franz) Planer, another highly talented refugee from Germany, who had photographed Max Ophuls's *Liebelei* (1933), *The Exile* (1947) and *Letter from an Unknown Woman* (1948).

Although *Criss Cross* was filmed on location in Los Angeles with a fair number of daytime exteriors, the plot and characters are mainstream *noir*. Like *The Killers*, the film begins dramatically, deep in the *noir* world, and then moves into flashback to trace the events which have led to this situation. The credits occur over a helicopter shot travelling over Los Angeles at night, the dark mass of the city a powerful visual presence. As the credits end, the camera moves down, dissolving smoothly to a high-angle shot of a car park, the rows of cars glistening with reflected light. A car drives into the shot, and a cut takes us to ground level, the camera panning with the car, which travels across the screen, halts, and backs out of shot. The effect of this last manoeuvre is to move a black shape across the image like a curtain being pulled aside; in the background, we now see a kissing couple. As the camera tracks towards them, they are caught in the headlights of the turning car and nervously separate. Cut to a two-shot of the couple, Steve (Lancaster) and Anna (De Carlo), who, in the space of seventy seconds, provide us with an astonishing wealth of information, conveyed through brilliant scripting and tense, concentrated playing. We learn that they are meeting secretly, that Anna has a very suspicious male partner

waiting inside, that they are planning some sort of double-cross on him tomorrow, that this requires them separating, maybe for weeks, after its execution, that Anna is terrified for Steve's safety, that they're desperately in love, that they've had a turbulent history ('all those things that happened to us'), but that 'after it's all over, it'll be just you and me . . . the way it should have been all along . . .' Whilst it seems unlikely that we can grasp all of this on first viewing, the intensity with which the scene is played (assisted by the tightness of Siodmak's shot/reverse shot *découpage*) creates a powerful bond with the couple so that, from this opening scene, we share their anxieties. At the same time, the scene also suggests the excitement of the danger they're in: the thrill of the forbidden. The mixture of fear and excitement is crucial to our subsequent understanding of their relationship.

From Anna leaving Steve, Siodmak cuts to the interior of the Rondo night-club, where Slim Dundee (Dan Duryea) is indeed suspicious about the whereabouts of his wife: his bullying interrogation of a waiter shows his insecurity. The film's sexual triangle is thus established in the first few minutes. The plot of *Criss Cross* relates closely to the heist and double-cross section of *The Killers*, the parallel enhanced by the casting of Lancaster and his rivalry with the gangster boss over the *femme fatale*. But, on this occasion, it is Slim as the gangster boss who is to be double-crossed. It is now the night before the planned robbery, and the gang are assembling to stage an act for police lieutenant Pete Ramirez (Steve McNally) as part of their plan. At a publicised farewell party for Slim and Anna – who, as part of Slim's alibi, are leaving for Detroit – Steve will pick a fight. The fight will confirm the hostility between Steve and Slim, and so side-track the cops from linking them over the robbery. The fight thus echoes the act that Colfax and Kitty stage for the Swede and the other gang members on the eve of their robbery. But here the fight gets out of control: suspecting that Anna and Steve may have met in the parking-lot, Slim pulls a knife.

Tipped off, Ramirez bursts into the room as the knife slides across the floor. Steve has knocked Slim down: another echo of *The Killers*, in which the Swede, fooled by Colfax and Kitty's act, floors Colfax. But here the implicit power structure is reversed: whereas in *The Killers* the gang members (as intended) see the Swede as 'out of line', here the offender is Slim, risking their enterprise by pulling a knife. In retrospect, we realise that Ramirez's arrival in time to see the knife offers Steve a way out of his predicament (hitherto an honest man, he is about to commit a major crime), but he declines it: 'This is just between me and Dundee.' He is referring to their dispute over Anna; all three men know this. But what is crucial is that he chooses to resolve the dispute through crime: the heist and double-cross. As he says that he won't swear out a complaint against Slim, he

139

and Slim are framed in a two-shot facing Ramirez: morally, he has joined the gangsters.

As in other Siodmak movies, however, the subtext suggests that rather more is going on in the scene. It ends with Ramirez, holding the knife in front of him, standing behind Steve and saying, 'If you should happen to change your mind before he leaves . . .' Steve replies, 'I'll let you know, Lieutenant.' Ramirez closes the knife, says 'Chump' and turns and leaves, tossing the knife aside. Subtextually, the exchange can be seen as a sexual invitation which Steve declines. In the frame, Anna is behind and to the left of Ramirez, but her reflected face in a circular mirror is positioned precisely between the two men, as if she is symbolically between them. Like the cops in *The Killers* and *Cry of the City*, Ramirez is an old boyhood friend. But he has also appointed himself as Steve's moral guardian. As the film continues, and Ramirez's hatred of Anna and what he considers she's doing to Steve is made clear, we can discern behind the hatred another unresolved homoerotic attraction. Ramirez is given a wife, but we never see her; indeed, we see nothing of his life outside his relationship with Steve. But here there is no ambivalence: Ramirez is explicitly a nasty piece of work, as subsequent events show.

Steve is employed by an armoured car firm, transporting consignments of money. The following day, as he makes the drive to the factory where the robbery is to take place, an extended

Still: Criss Cross – *Ramirez (Steve McNally) confronts Slim (Dan Duryea) and Steve (Burt Lancaster) over the knife fight. Vincent (Tom Pedi) and Anna (Yvonne de Carlo) in the background.*

flashback shows how he came to be involved. At one point married to Anna, he broke up with her after seven months, left Los Angeles and drifted from job to job. The flashback begins with his return home, his voice-over insisting that it was not on her account that he had returned, whilst making it clear that it was. Steve's ability to deceive himself over his motivations finds particular expression in his repeated tendency to refer to 'fate' as deciding the outcome of events – 'It all went one way . . . it was in the cards,' etc. – when it is obvious that fate had nothing to do with it; back in Los Angeles, he cannot wait to see Anna again.

Before meeting Anna again, however, he meets Ramirez. Ramirez's uncanny ability to read Steve's thoughts (somehow he knew Steve was back in town) suggests that the film is promoting him as Steve's conscience, for example, when he turns up in the hospital after the robbery and accuses Steve (to everybody else, a hero) of complicity. But Siodmak goes further. He makes Ramirez into a punishing superego figure who, at the request of Steve's mother, actually tells Anna that he'll frame her if she doesn't leave Steve alone: a highly subversive link between the family as a repressive institution and the abuse of police

140

powers. This links Ramirez with one of *film noir*'s most monstrous villains: Grant Callum (Dean Jagger) in *Pursued* (Raoul Walsh, 1947). Discussing the psychopathology of Grant, and relating him to Montgomery (Robert Ryan) in *Crossfire*, Andrew Britton argues that the implications of his characterisation 'are a key strategy in *film noir*, where, again and again, the "villain" is there to suggest that American ideology gives birth to monsters' (*Framework* 4, Summer 1976). But in *Criss Cross*, Ramirez is not supposed to be the villain: he's supposed to be the figure who points out the error of the hero's ways. The implications are doubly subversive.

In 'Woman's Place: the Absent Family in *Film Noir*' (in Kaplan, 1978), Sylvia Harvey discusses the negative representation of the family in *film noir*. *Criss Cross* is a good example of her thesis. On the surface, we see a happy family. Although Steve's father is dead, his place has been assumed at meal-times by Steve's colleague from work, whom Steve even calls Pop (Griff Barnett). Steve's brother Slade (Richard Long) has a steady girlfriend Helen (Meg Randall). But undercurrents are apparent from the first evening: Pop has to speak up for Steve with his mother, trying to reassure her Steve has not returned home on Anna's account; Slade pushes Helen around, jokingly, but with an undertow of threat (he'll belt her if she doesn't kiss him). And, later, Mrs Thompson (Edna M. Holland) makes clear to Steve her feelings about Anna, even warning him that she's already spoken to Pete Ramirez about her. The claustrophobic decor of the family home adds to the tensions; each time we see Steve inside with members of the family, he is patently itching to get out of the house.

Steve and Anna are almost certainly Siodmak's most interesting and complex heterosexual couple. The structure of *The Killers* – the Swede can't talk, Kitty does so only briefly – frustrates our access to its central relationship; there is no such obstacle here. Repeatedly we are shown that it is a highly physical relationship; that they should be kissing when first seen is symptomatic. In the flashback, Steve first sees Anna as she is dancing (with Tony Curtis, no less, in his first film role). Anna's dance is the equivalent of Kitty's song: each serves to express the impact the heroine has on the hero. But, whereas the Swede was seduced by the wistful yearning of a song, Steve is captivated by Anna's body. The Latin American music makes her dance rhythmic and sensual (De Carlo trained as a dancer), whilst the way the camera stays close to her, moving with her, emphasises the carnal nature of the attraction she holds for Steve.

As they sit and talk about their past relationship, they remember the way they used to fight. Anna: 'Then we'd make up; that was the best part.' From the looks that she and Steve then exchange, it is clear that 'making up' meant sex, and that was what bound them together. *Criss Cross* comes close to being explicit about the sexual excitement of an intense, violent, physical relationship. At this point, Slim's voice is heard addressing Steve: 'Excuse me, you're sitting in my chair.' The hero and heroine's desire for each other conjures up the gangster, a Hollywood figure whose relationship with women is defined in terms of sex and violence. Steve leaves, abruptly. But Anna then contacts him, leading to another tightly scripted scene. Unlike the opening, however, the messages they signal to each other here are more confused. Anna plays down her relationship with Slim, but Steve is cynical about her motives: 'Half the time you don't what you're doing. The trouble is you always know what you want.' Contradictorily, he then pretends not to know why she wants to see him, leading to her exasperated 'Do you have to ask?' In both his statement and her question, sex is clearly implied. But they then remember the other side to their marriage: his mother's hostility to her; the way they would always fight with each other. Even so, the scene ends with him (aggressively) asking her out and her (aggressively) accepting. The physical attraction between them is so strong that their squabbling is merely postponing the moment when they will begin to resume their affair.

Ideologically, Anna is too sexual to be accommodated as 'wife' in the petit-bourgeois home: 'In some ways she knows more than Einstein' is Mrs Thompson's suitably veiled reference to the problem. And so, Mrs Thompson enlists Ramirez to 'get rid of her'. Although we never see Ramirez with Steve's family, a similar relationship to that between Candella and Rome's family is implied. But here Siodmak is far more critical of the relationship. It is Ramirez's threat to frame her that leads Anna to marry Slim. Superficially, this is a victory for bourgeois repressiveness: Anna is 'where she belongs', married to a gangster. But desire is not so easily repressed: it is only a matter of time before she and Steve meet again and begin what is now a highly dangerous adulterous affair. The effect of the intervention of Mrs Thompson and Ramirez is to set Steve up in a sexual triangle which ultimately proves fatal. At the same time, Steve and Anna are reckless, heedless of anything but their own desires. *Criss Cross* dramatises a crucial contradiction in bourgeois ideology: powerful sexual desire is too disruptive to be accommodated within marriage and family, and outside marriage and family it becomes positively dangerous because it is transgressive.

When Steve hears that Anna has married Slim, his initial reaction is 'good riddance'. But, almost immediately, his voice-over returns, declaring, 'but it was in the cards and there was no way of stopping it' – he and Anna were destined to meet up again. Once more, fate had little to do with it: Steve was simply waiting to see her again. When they do meet, Anna's immediate response is to be cagey. Vincent (Tom Pedi), one of Slim's hoods who has been appointed to

Still: Criss Cross – *caught with Anna, Steve proposes a payroll heist to Slim to cover up. Vincent in the background.*

take her home, may see them together. But Vincent has to deliver the car to Slim in Las Vegas; he drives off, leaving her marooned on the opposite side of the road from Steve. She turns slowly to look across at him. On this, Siodmak dissolves to the interior of Slim's house: Steve and Anna are together in the room which, within the coding of the time, tells us they have resumed their affair. Siodmak offers no explanation: we can only conclude that they merely had to meet again for their desire for each other to be reactivated.

It is not until this scene that Steve hears about Ramirez's threat to frame Anna and send her up to the women's prison at Tehachapi, 'my hair cut short, wearing striped cotton, digging potatoes.' Shortly afterwards, she shows him the marks on her back where Slim has beaten her; implicitly, Slim's physical violence against her is being equated with Ramirez's threatened violence. Representing the id and the superego respectively, the two men are equally vicious. Indeed, Ramirez is the nastiest of all Siodmak's nasty cops, because he has convinced himself he's acting in

the best interests of the hero. Anna's description of his threat is not an exaggeration; he himself later confirms it.

Inevitably, Slim gets wind of Anna and Steve's affair. In the company of Vincent and Mort (Marc Krah), he turns up in Steve's house to confront them, mildly observing, as first Steve and then Anna comes downstairs, that 'It don't look right.' Steve rapidly invents an excuse for her being there: he really wanted to contact Slim, because he wants to do a job and 'You're the only crooks I know.' He suggests they rob one of the armoured trucks, with him as the inside man. Slim seems sufficiently taken with the idea to set aside the question of Anna's fidelity. Structurally, the robbery is like an unacknowledged duel, in which Steve and Slim fight it out for Anna. Just as Steve and Anna plan to double-cross Slim, so Steve knows that Slim will try to double-cross him.

By now, Steve is inextricably in the *noir* world. The repressiveness of his mother and Ramirez, his own susceptibility to Anna and his attempt to deflect Slim's vengeance by proposing a joint criminal venture have all combined to set him on the path which will lead, inexorably, to his death. At the meeting where the gang members plan the execution of the robbery, Anna and Steve snatch a brief moment together in the back kitchen. Steve rapidly runs through their plans for the double-cross, but all Anna does is utter doom-laden statements: 'I wish we'd never met . . . I wish you'd never seen me.' It is as if she is insisting on seeing them as doomed lovers. Even here, where fear is uppermost, she registers the excitement of their transgression.

The planning meeting, directed by criminal mastermind Finchley (Alan Napier), goes on into the night. Far more than the equivalent meeting in *The Killers*, it is filmed in *noir* low-key style: a journey into deeper darkness for all the main characters. As it ends, Anna is asleep on the bed: another explicit echo of *The Killers*. Steve wants two matters settled: that there will be no shooting (he knows Pop will be with him on the run), and the question of who will handle the pay-off. Slim proposes Anna. This, of course, fits in perfectly with Steve's plan, but Slim seems no longer worried about Anna, declaring that he can handle her – a *noir* example of hubris. Siodmak ends the sequence on a close-up of the sleeping Anna; behind the elaborately planned caper, she is the real prize.

The flashback lasts the length of Steve's drive to the factory. Since there is no addressee, it is as if he is justifying his involvement to himself, which would account for his repeated attempts to blame what happened on 'fate'. Certainly, he declines to blame his mother ('Never mind my mother!' he says to Ramirez, when the latter

starts to explain) and is self-pitying in his blame of Ramirez, getting drunk before confronting the man and allowing him to sustain his sense of moral superiority. He is not as masochistic in his attitude as the Swede, but he is still a relatively weak figure. Across Siodmak's films – and across much of *film noir* – is the sense that a man who loves a woman is weak. When, at the end of *Criss Cross,* Slim tells Steve that he, too, loved Anna, he accounts for his own weakness.

But Steve also belongs to another group of Siodmak male protagonists – those who are still living at home with their mothers/families: Robert Manette, Albert Warren, Harry Quincey. Dominated by his mother (sister in *The Strange Affair of Uncle Harry*), the central male character in these films is also implicitly weak in his inability to break away from home. Even though Steve has left home twice – to marry Anna, to travel the country – he has still returned, to complain in one scene that his mother is watching him as if he were a ten year-old.

Under the cover of smoke bombs (an expression of Steve's moral confusion), the robbery begins. Nobody had told Pop that there was to be no shooting; attacked by one of the gang, he shoots the man, provoking Slim to step in and shoot him in turn. Hearing the shots, Steve does a moral

Still: Criss Cross – *Anna and Steve in the back kitchen during the planning of the heist.*

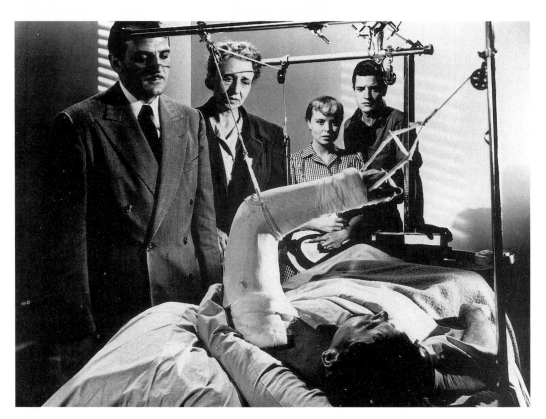

about-turn and starts to attack the gangsters, shooting Slim in the leg before being shot himself and collapsing.

When he recovers consciousness in hospital, he's a hero. Pop is dead, but so are three of the robbers, and Steve has saved half the payroll. But, with his arm and shoulder in traction, he's helpless. Siodmak uses a number of subjective shots during this sequence, partly to mark Steve's drifting in and out of consciousness, but also to emphasise his enforced immobility. The second time he comes to, there is a man on the other side of the room, looking at him. The process work used to suggest Steve's slow emergence to consciousness recreates the fog-like effect of the smoke bombs; the man is Ramirez, but he emerges out of this fog like Slim's alter ego. Lurking in a corner, shadowed by the familiar *noir* motif of Venetian blinds, he is at his most sinister: almost like the Devil, waiting to claim Steve's soul. He comes forward spitting accusations: 'You were in with them.' He then ensures that Steve will have no peace by telling him that, if Anna *has* double-crossed Slim, Slim will take revenge: 'he'll send a gunman for you . . . right through that door, and he'll get you.' He then dismisses the idea of putting policemen to guard Steve, implying that it's unnecessary: it's Steve that Anna will have double-crossed – she'll have gone to Slim.

As Ramirez leaves the hospital room, Siodmak cuts so that, in the mirror, we can see the shadow of a man waiting in the corridor outside. The man is Nelson (Robert Osterloh), who is indeed

Still: Criss Cross – *Steve in hospital, with a doctor (Stephen Roberts), his mother (Edna M. Holland), Helen (Meg Randall) and Slade (Richard Long).*

one of Slim's men, patiently waiting for the opportunity to kidnap Steve. Just as Ramirez first appeared in the hospital linked visually to Slim, so here it is as if he leaves behind a shadow which enacts the punishment of Steve he feels is fitting. Siodmak uses mirrors in a number of ways, but an important one is to suggest psychosis: Marlowe looking at himself during Burgess's monologue about paranoiacs (*Phantom Lady*); Albert Warren 'seeing' Helen's face reflected without a mouth (*The Spiral Staircase*); the elaborate use of mirrors to signify Terry's insanity in *The Dark Mirror*. And, although Ramirez is not insane, the film strongly implies that he, too, has a dark side, and that secretly he wants Slim to kill Steve. There are three pieces of evidence. 1) After his confrontation with Ramirez over Anna, Steve says defiantly that he's going to continue to see her, 'and you and Dundee and nobody else is gonna tell me what to do.' In the very next scene, we discover that 'somehow' Slim has found out about the affair. 2) Ramirez refuses to put a police guard on Steve in hospital, and Nelson seems to have no difficulty in kidnapping Steve. 3) Reunited with Anna for the last scene, Steve isn't worried about Slim: 'I talked to Pete (Ramirez); the cops'll pick him up the moment he shows his face.' Now, this could simply have been wishful thinking on Steve's part, but the cops arrive *immediately* after Slim has shot Steve and Anna. It's as if Slim was given time to enact his vengeance. Unlike *The Killers* or *Cry of the City*, *Criss Cross* has little sense of the cop as an investigative figure. Instead, he is punitive; that he should secretly wish Steve's death is entirely consistent with his character. As the film continues, Nelson does indeed seem like Ramirez's shadow, delivering Steve to Slim.

A common feature of *film noir* is the enigma of strangers: the problem of whether or not the hero or heroine can trust someone he/she meets. The scene between Nelson and Steve has all the features of this characteristically *noir* anxiety. Steve suspects Nelson, hears his story, decides he can trust him and falls asleep, only to wake and find that Nelson has after all been sent by Slim to 'deal with' him. This leads to a brutal kidnapping: Nelson severs the traction wires, producing 'a paroxysm of pain' (Tom Flinn, 'Three Faces of Film Noir'). Once more, Steve passes out.

Recovering consciousness in the back of Nelson's car, Steve bribes him to go to Anna's hideout, a beachhouse at Palos Verdes. When he arrives, Anna becomes uneasy, suspecting that the man will immediately contact Slim. Now, for the first time, she displays the emotional fickleness of the *femme fatale*, hurriedly packing and declaring that 'you have to watch out for yourself . . . what do you want me to do, throw away all this money?' On the one hand, her panic and concern for self-preservation are motivated by a perfectly reasonable fear of Slim's imminent arrival and vengeance. On the other, the film is hastily discrediting the heroine at the last minute so that her death will seem less poignant. Before she can get away, Slim does indeed arrive.

Still: Criss Cross. *The final sequence – Anna and Steve wait for Slim's arrival.*

As Anna and Steve wait fearfully for Slim's entrance, they look towards the blackness of the open door. Evoking the *découpage* as the Swede waited for the arrival of the killers, the link strengthens the sense that Steve, too, now submits to his fate. As Slim enters, he's limping and walking with a stick – the consequence of Steve's bullet – and Steve's left arm and shoulder are in plaster. The two men thus have precisely the same injuries as Rome and Candella at the climax of *Cry of the City*, almost as if Siodmak were also re-staging the end of that movie. But the confrontation here is explicitly over a woman, over who 'wins' her. And to win her is to die with her.

Slim enters like a 'figure of destiny' (Tom Flinn), but, before shooting them, he forces Anna into Steve's arms: 'Hold her; hold her tight.' And so Anna and Steve die as if they really were romantic lovers, in each other's arms. Explicitly echoing their opening words, the last thing each says is the other's name. Siodmak then repeats the effect which revealed the couple at the beginning. As Slim turns to leave, police sirens are heard. The camera tilts from a close-up of his face to his body, blacking out the image. He then moves aside, so that again the effect is like a curtain being drawn across the screen. In the background now are the dead bodies of Anna and Steve, arranged like a tableau: he is slumped back, she is lying across his body. The two 'curtain' shots are not merely flourishes in which Siodmak self-consciously displays his artistry. The link between the opening kiss and the final carefully composed death tableau resonates with the irony of a failed romantic passion. It is one of the great dramatic endings of *film noir*.

The File on Thelma Jordon (1949)

After directing *The Great Sinner* (1949), a version of Dostoyevsky's *The Gambler*, at MGM, Siodmak was invited by Hal Wallis to Paramount to make *The File on Thelma Jordon*. Since Barbara Stanwyck was to star, Wallis no doubt saw the project, like his production of *The Strange Love of Martha Ivers* (Lewis Milestone, 1946), as another 'follow-up' to the hugely influential *Double Indemnity* (Billy Wilder, 1944). The film was based on an unpublished story by Marty Holland, the author of the novel of *Fallen Angel* (Preminger, 1945), and scripted by Ketti Frings, the author of the novel of *Hold Back the Dawn* (Mitchell Leisen, 1941) – two films which, although in different genres, have astonishingly similar plots – but has closer links with Wilder's movie. The cameraman was George Barnes who, although not a *noir* specialist, was indubitably talented (he won an Oscar for Hitchcock's *Rebecca*, 1940, and had just photographed Abe Polonsky's *noir* gangster movie *Force of Evil*, 1949), and one feels that he provided Siodmak with just what he wanted. The result is one of Siodmak's best, and most underrated, films.

In the opening scene of *The File on Thelma Jordon*, Cleve Marshall (Wendell Corey), an assistant district attorney, 'bares his soul' to his friend Miles Scott (Paul Kelly), the DA's chief investigator. He has refused to go home for his fifth wedding anniversary celebration with his wife Pamela (Joan Tetzel) because he resents the intrusion of his father-in-law, ex-Judge Blackwell (Minor Watson), into his married life. Instead, he seeks solace in drink. After Miles has left, Thelma Jordon (Barbara Stanwyck) enters and, mistaking Cleve for Miles, begins to report some attempted burglaries at the home of her elderly Aunt Vera Edwards, where she is currently living. Cleve drunkenly chats her up, and they end by going out for a drink.

The situation is familiar: a lonely man with marital problems, an attractive woman who walks in out of the night and seems available. It is a situation which, given the title of the film, the casting, the director and the mood of the opening scene, we would expect to lead to trouble. Nevertheless, whereas Phyllis Dietrichson in *Double Indemnity* signals her malevolent intent virtually from the start, and Martha Ivers murdered her aunt when she was still a teenager, Stanwyck's Thelma is a more ambiguous figure. As Cleve starts to date her, she seems genuinely attracted to him, and even the subsequent introduction of Tony Laredo (Richard Rober) – a rather sinister boyfriend – does not entirely undermine her

Still: The File on Thelma Jordon – *the first meeting between Thelma (Barbara Stanwyck) and a drunken Cleve (Wendell Corey).*

credibility. Thelma could belong with Stanwyck's early 'forties roles, in which she starts out on the wrong side of the law/respectability – a shoplifter on parole in *Remember the Night* (Leisen, 1940), a professional card sharp in *The Lady Eve* (Preston Sturges, 1941), a gangster's moll in *Ball of Fire* (Hawks, 1941) – but falls for the mild-mannered hero and 'reforms'.

Some 35 minutes into the movie, however, an extended night-time sequence plunges Cleve

Still: The File on Thelma Jordon – *Thelma, Cleve and the body of Aunt Vera (Gertrude Hoffman).*

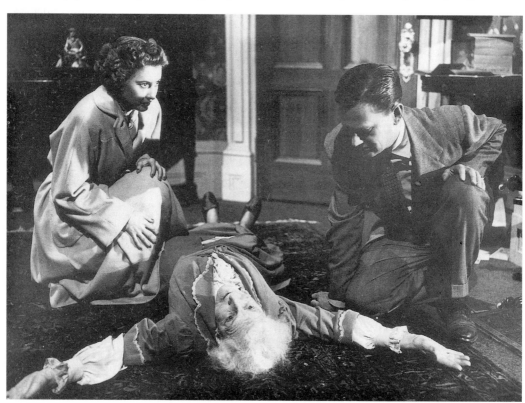

into the *noir* world. He and Thelma have decided to go away together for the weekend. In the Edwards house on the Friday night, we see Aunt Vera (Gertrude Hoffman) wake and, hearing noises, go downstairs, take a gun and enter the library. A shot is fired and we hear a body slump to the floor. The phone rings: Cleve is trying to contact Thelma. Sidney (Harry Antrim), the butler who lives in a cottage in the grounds, takes the call on the cottage extension. At his second attempt, Cleve gets Thelma. She tells him to come at once, 'Something's happened.' We then see that Sidney has overheard. Cleve arrives and is told by Thelma that her aunt has been murdered and the safe burgled. She says she suspects Tony and, to his horror, Cleve hears that she has removed all the fingerprints, including her own. He insists that she put hers back and then call the police. Before she completes this, the phone rings again. Sidney takes the call, Thelma listens in and realises he'll be coming up to the house. This triggers another change of plan: Thelma will return to bed and pretend to be asleep. But Cleve suddenly realises that Sidney could have overheard his second phone call. He begins to panic. Then he notices that his pencil, which he gave to Thelma when he lifted up Aunt Vera's gun, is missing. As they search desperately to find it, Sidney makes his way across to the house. He enters as Cleve makes his getaway through the window. Siodmak sustains the sequence brilliantly, with a whole repertoire of *noir* imagery: expressionistic shadow effects as Aunt Vera peers nervously over the banisters; Cleve framed behind iron railings as he arrives and embraces Thelma; above all, the sense, at the end, of two people caught in a trap, running round desperately trying to find a way out. The sequence illustrates the nightmare quality of the *noir* world: in particular, the sense of destiny contriving to turn Sidney into a highly damaging witness, and Cleve's increasing loss of control, climaxing with him leaving his footprints outside the library window.

The window, like the mirror, is one of the most complex elements in Siodmak's films. Marlowe's suicide, the Swede's attempted suicide and Robert Manette's death, each through a window, mark it as a site of danger. In *The Spiral Staircase*, windows are discovered deceptively open (the murderer doesn't need to enter the house surreptitiously, he lives there) and, at the film's climax, Helen desperately smashes a window in a futile attempt to attract the attention of the policeman outside. Twice in *The Killers*, villains make their escape through windows, but in each case the escape is also futile: both go straight to Colfax, where Dum-Dum is killed and Kitty walks into the arms of the police. Accordingly, the authorial discourse emphasises the precariousness of Cleve's escape.

Up to this point almost all the film has been set at night. Now, with the narrative shift to the murder investigation, it moves into the opposing world of daytime, the law and patriarchal authority. As Miles investigates the robbery and murder, he soon suspects Thelma. Not only did Sidney overhear her panicky summons over the phone, but he knew about her series of night-time rendezvous with a man, dubbed 'Mr X'. Realising that she'll be arrested, Thelma asks Cleve if he could contrive to prosecute the case himself. In love with her, Cleve complies; rather than work with the investigation, he surreptitiously works against it. Anonymously, he hires Thelma a powerful defence lawyer, Kingsley Willis (Stanley Ridges, just as creepy as in *The Suspect*) and then, likewise anonymously, advises Willis of helpful strategies, beginning with a method of disqualifying the District Attorney (Barry Kelley) from prosecuting the case. Even more crucially, Cleve then prosecutes the case himself in such a way as to *help the defence*. It is relatively common in Hollywood court-room sequences for the prosecutor to use manipulative tactics to turn the jury against an accused with whom we are sympathetic: *They Won't Forget* (Mervyn LeRoy, 1937), *Johnny Belinda* (Jean Negulesco, 1948) and *I Confess* (Hitchcock, 1952) provide three typical examples. Here, by contrast, Cleve plays up features which will turn the jury against himself, beginning by stressing the inevitability of capital punishment should Thelma be found guilty. His tactics work, and Thelma is acquitted.

Still: The File on Thelma Jordon – *about to be arrested for murder, Thelma wants Cleve himself to prosecute her.*

147

Although many Hollywood films criticise the judicial process, *film noir* tends to go further than the norm. It is in *film noir* in particular that those guilty of murder are freed (*The Postman Always Rings Twice*, Tay Garnett, 1946; *Angel Face*, Preminger, 1953) and those innocent of murder convicted and executed (*Scarlet Street*; *The Locket*; *The Strange Love of Martha Ivers*; *Nora Prentiss*, Vincent Sherman, 1947). Likewise, Cleve's tactics of undermining his own case in order to secure Thelma's acquittal are balanced by those of Bannister (Everett Sloane) in *The Lady from Shanghai* (Welles, 1947), who defends the hero in such a way as to secure his conviction. How much further a *film noir* may go may be illustrated by comparing the court case in *The File on Thelma Jordon* with those in *The Kiss* (Jacques Feyder, 1928) and *Jagged Edge* (Richard Marquand, 1985). All three films depict a subversive notion: the accused is guilty of murder, but, defended (or, in Thelma's case, prosecuted) by her/his lover, is acquitted. However, in the other two films, the lover genuinely believes the accused to be innocent, and so retains his/her integrity. Cleve, by contrast, is doubly compromised. He admits later that he must, at some level, have been aware of Thelma's guilt but he suppresses acknowledgment of this. (Sidney alerts him to her plot when he tells him about Thelma pretending there were burglary attempts, 'like she was setting up for this one.') And he betrays his professional integrity: the anonymous assistance he gives Willis is deliberately designed to undermine the case for the prosecution. In addition, Cleve risks so much more than the lawyers in the other movies. He introduces Mr X into the case because he knows this will help the defence (they'll have someone else to blame), but, of course, he is Mr X, capable of being identified from his footprints outside as easily as Thelma was identified from her fingerprints inside. And he has to mishandle the case publicly. Indeed, he has a very difficult balancing act to sustain: to convince everyone, but especially Miles and the DA, that he's really doing his best and that his 'blunders' can be put down to inexperience, but at the same time to discredit his own case in the eyes of the jury.

A major *noir* theme which is highly developed throughout *The File on Thelma Jordon* is anxiety about male potency. 1) In the opening scene, Cleve tells Miles that he's been down to The Pike. When Miles sounds interested, Cleve says 'Not that part of The Pike [clearly, the red light district of town]: there are some respectable sections . . . in the other part . . . I wouldn't know what to do.' 2) Cleve was going to The Pike to buy Pamela a whatnot for her anniversary present. He finds that her father has already bought it for her. At the end of the evening, Cleve arrives home drunk to find the whatnot, beribboned, dominating the living-room. He plonks his whisky bottle on top of it in defiance but, of course, Daddy's phallic symbol is much bigger.

To Miles, Cleve had also said, 'He can take his big car out of my driveway and his big fat [pause] windbag out of my living-room': two displacements from the real thing that threatens him. 3) When Cleve first meets Thelma, he says that, when he was a boy, her aunt switched him with an orange branch: 'I've still got the scars; ruined my legs permanently.' Moments later, running out of the office after Thelma, he's hit at thigh height by a low swing door.

All of these references are on the first evening, during which Cleve also pointedly holds his whisky bottle in a way which suggests that it is a phallus substitute. From its beginning the film obsessively stresses the hero's sexual anxieties. Cleve is married to a Daddy's girl who is still clingingly dependent. Pamela knows that being 'father's little girl' ('hair-ribbon, shorts') is her problem, but the way she continues to act like a little girl for Cleve ('I'm trying to be very grown up about this') emphasises its appeal for him, too: sexually, it's undemanding. Thelma, by contrast, is a 'real woman', and it is not difficult to see Cleve's dating her as an attempt to prove his manhood. However, things do not work out this way.

Although Code restrictions necessitated that any film of the era had to be circumspect in suggesting illicit sexual activity, film-makers readily made use of veiled suggestions that audiences could decode. In *The File on Thelma Jordon*, however, all the evidence points to Cleve not having sex with Thelma. Although Pamela is away on holiday with the children when Cleve and Thelma begin dating, the dates nevertheless end with Cleve taking Thelma home. There, Tony is waiting for her, materialising out of the garden bushes to assert sexual proprietorship. On their dates, Cleve and Thelma are repeatedly forced to move on, afraid of being spotted. (One of the people who causes them to move on is in fact a private detective, hired by Cleve's suspicious father-in-law.) And when Cleve hears about her past with Tony ('wherever he is, there's money, gambling, beautiful women'), he clearly feels threatened, even though she says it's over. He insists that they go away together for the weekend. But, in place of a romantic weekend, he's projected into a *noir* nightmare.

In flight from the castrating figure of the judge, Cleve tries to prove his manhood with Thelma, only to run into the double obstacle of a murder case and a highly sexual boyfriend. Like Steve Thompson in *Criss Cross*, he is between a superego figure (the Judge) and an id figure (Tony), and again both serve to 'castrate' him, the former – through the agency of the private detective – even when he isn't there. Cleve's loss of his pencil (Thelma leaves it under the body) is yet another castration-symbol. It projects him into the role of Mr X (searching for it, he leaves at the last second and is seen) but mockingly signals his failure in the role: everyone naturally assumes that Mr X was Thelma's lover. With ruthless logic, the theme of sexual anxiety is followed right through the film. After the trial, when Cleve must think that he can at last claim Thelma, she confronts him with Tony. After she has explained what a sucker he has been, Tony knocks him out, leaving him lying on the library floor where Aunt Vera's body lay. He, too, is their victim.

However, when Thelma tells Cleve that he was the fall guy, and that she's always loved Tony, she is doing this in order to protect Cleve, whom she now loves. This leads to a precisely worked-out sequence of events whereby the film effects closure. Thelma, clearly, has to die, but she is allowed to kill Tony first: as he drives, she blinds him with the car's cigar lighter, causing an accident in which he is killed and she is mortally wounded. Thelma then lives long enough to confess to Miles that she was the murderer of both her aunt and Tony. She declines to identify Mr X ('I love him'), but, in the meantime, Cleve himself has confessed to the DA. This enables Miles to be sympathetic, and point out that, although Cleve will necessarily be disbarred, he has spoken to Pamela and she'd like Cleve to get in touch, 'later'. As in many *films noirs*, the confessions of the heroine and hero function as a moral cleansing. Cleve will do his penance, after which Pamela will no doubt forgivingly welcome him back. The problem of the judge, however, remains unresolved.

The care with which these narrative moves are worked out indicates the extent to which the ideological order in the movie has been under threat. (*Hold Back the Dawn* has a similar series of moves, including a convenient car crash.) Like *Double Indemnity*, *The File on Thelma Jordon* has a hero who is corrupted in his official capacity and who uses his insider's knowledge to further the *femme fatale*'s plans. But, although Cleve is

Still: The File on Thelma Jordon – *Thelma blinds Tony (Richard Rober), causing the car crash.*

less corrupted than Walter Neff (he doesn't commit murder), a corrupted assistant district attorney is inherently more subversive than a corrupted salesman. And so, the film pulls back from the real bleakness of *Double Indemnity*. The final confrontation between Thelma and Cleve in the house seems consciously modelled on the equivalent confrontation in Wilder's movie, but the relationship here has not degenerated to the same point of murderous self-destruction. Further, whereas Keyes, Miles's equivalent in *Double Indemnity*, was unable to see that it was Walter who was that film's Mr X, here Miles solves the enigma of Mr X, and thereby identifies the corruption. Structurally, Mr X (Thelma's alleged lover) is mirrored in the narrative by 'Miss X' (Cleve's alleged lover). And, when Thelma is brought into hospital after the car crash, Miles finally puts the two together: Thelma's sequined scarf fits the private detective's description of the one worn by 'Miss X'.

Miles is another version of the ambiguous figure of the cop in the last three *noir* Siodmak movies. But, unlike the previous two representations, Miles, like Lubinsky in *The Killers*, is essentially sympathetic. The link is suggestive. Lubinsky married the hero's ex-girlfriend and Miles is particularly close to Pamela; the film's first conversation is between the two of them over Cleve's whereabouts. In place of the homoerotic overtones of *Cry of the City* and *Criss Cross*, these two films suggest another paradigm: that the friendship of the cop is somehow cemented through the figure of the 'good woman'. Miles actually says at one point, 'I'm like Pamela – I can't help you if you won't give me a chance.'

Thelma is a *femme fatale* who falls in love with her intended victim. But at the same time she is physically dominated by Tony in much the same way as Kitty is dominated by Johnny in *Scarlet Street*. Here, for the first time, Siodmak depicts the nature of the relationship between the gangster and his woman. In a few short scenes, Richard Rober projects a powerful sexuality that is quite exceptional in Hollywood films of the era. Even though Stanwyck at this point in her career was repeatedly cast in sexual triangles in which one of the men was highly physical – Lyle Bettger in *No Man of Her Own* (Leisen, 1950) and *All I Desire* (Douglas Sirk, 1953), Robert Ryan in *Clash by Night* (Lang, 1952) – Tony still stands out. When Cleve phones Thelma after the trial, Tony, lying on the bed, forces her on top of him and kisses her. He asserts his mastery over her in no uncertain terms. It is not surprising that the film should choose blinding – another symbol of castration – as his nemesis.

Like *The Killers*, *The File on Thelma Jordon* has a double-cross plot which is not revealed until the end of the movie. As worked out with Tony, the original plan was for Thelma to seduce or compromise the unmarried Miles, steal Aunt Vera's emeralds and then ensure that Miles got rid of the incriminating evidence. What is not explained is the successive modifications to this plan that Thelma evolves as a response to rapidly changing events. Even though she is falling in love with Cleve, she continues to go through with the theft part of the plan: is she hoping that the emeralds will buy Tony off? Her killing Aunt Vera is another mystery. We can put it down to panic, but why is she carrying a gun? Even her removal of all the prints, although signalling her guilt (as Cleve should have realised) is hard to explain rationally, although it is hinted that she is hoping she can frame Tony. But Tony has placed himself in Chicago: he has provided himself with a cast-iron alibi.

Thelma's own motives and actions remain a mystery. She cannot explain them to Cleve, because she knows that it would destroy his trust in her. The blockage between them is articulated in a fine scene in which he visits her in jail, before she appears on the witness stand, to test how far she can stand up to cross-examination. As he pressures her about her real past with Tony, we see the cross-examination rehearsal turn into a lover's quarrel. At the same time, in showing Cleve that she cannot withstand hostile questioning, Thelma is protecting her secrets from him. He ensures that she doesn't take the stand.

Although we do not see events from Thelma's point of view, on the night of the murder, she, too, is plunged into the *noir* world. Her entrapment comes home to her at the moment when Cleve speculates that she could be her aunt's heir. This genuinely seems not to have occurred to her but, of course, it provides Miles with a motive to arrest her and Tony with a motive to

Still: Cry of the City – *Martin Rome (Richard Conte) in bed; Lt Candella (Victor Mature) wants to know where he got his ring.*

stick around. *The File on Thelma Jordon* is not simply another version of a susceptible man falling for a dangerous woman and paying the penalty, which is the way it is usually (and disparagingly) discussed. Indeed, when one grasps the extent to which Cleve and Thelma genuinely love each other, the film pushes towards a sense of tragedy. On Robert Heilman's model for tragedy (which I discuss in *Movie* 29/30, Summer 1982), both Cleve and Thelma are divided characters. Just before she dies, Thelma actually says: 'All my life, struggling, the good and the bad . . . Willis said I was two people . . .' Cleve is far more divided – between Thelma and Pamela, between love and duty – than the vast majority of *film noir* heroes. Whereas the Swede and Steve Thompson react to events with the blind impulsiveness of the melodramatic hero, Cleve is much more aware of what he's doing: he has the tragic hero's grasp of a moral dilemma. He knows that his love for Thelma clouds his perceptions ('the jury doesn't look at you the way I do'), but at the same time his love for her transforms her and so makes her much more into the woman he sees.

Perhaps one reason why *The File on Thelma Jordon* has been underrated is because it grafts a woman's-film discourse on to a *noir* story (it is the first of Siodmak's *films noirs* to be scripted by a woman). As a result of falling in love with Cleve, Thelma changes from a *femme fatale* into a woman's film heroine. Such actions as lying to Cleve to protect him and sacrificing her own life as a form of redemption belong to the woman's film, in which it is the heroine who carries the burden of understanding and the hero who, kept in the dark 'for his own good', is the simpler figure. By the same token, Pamela, although 'weak', is a genuinely sympathetic character; both she and Thelma are more complex, more novelistic

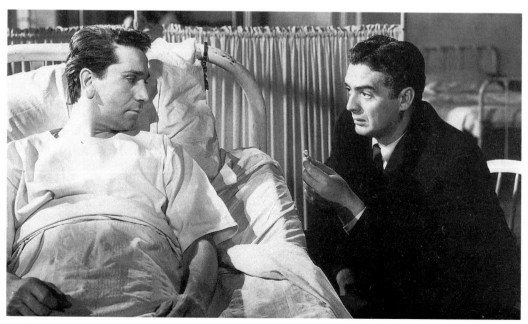

characters than the *noir* norm for women. And so the ending, although downbeat, is not despairing. Cleve walks off alone into the night, the woman he loved dead, his career destroyed, but with at least the promise of a home to return to in the future.

As one traces a path through the eleven films I have discussed, patterns emerge. The first five, including *Conflict*, deal centrally with the male as murderer. What takes the hero into the *noir* world is murder or the threat of murder, invariably directed towards a woman. In *Phantom Lady* and *Christmas Holiday* – in which the hero himself is not a murderer – the villain's murderousness may be seen to express the inner violence the hero feels towards a woman. In killing Marcella in *Phantom Lady*, Marlowe seems like Scott's shadow; in coming to kill Abigail in *Christmas Holiday*, Robert is threatening the vengeance Charley wished on Mona: structurally, the murderers are like the hero's id. In *Conflict*, *The Suspect* and *The Strange Affair of Uncle Harry*, the hero, bourgeois and middle-aged, himself becomes a murderer – if only in fantasy in *The Strange Affair of Uncle Harry* – in order to escape the intolerable chains of marriage/family.

The next two films shift to centre on the heroine and the way in which she is under threat from a psychotic murderer: a man in *The Spiral Staircase*, a woman in *The Dark Mirror*. But, although we are aware of the threat from a relatively early stage, the heroine herself is in the dark until the climax. This 'narrative of suspense' is also found in the third act of *Phantom Lady*. In all three cases, it's as if the heroine conjures up a psychotic figure who homes in on her vulnerability – her role as seeker heroine in the *noir* world in *Phantom Lady*, her physical affliction in *The Spiral Staircase*, her emotional closeness to the murderer in *The Dark Mirror*. Since the murderer is psychotic, he/she represents the dangers of the *noir* world in an extreme form, the equivalent of the monster in the horror genre. But, in *The Dark Mirror*, the sense of her as the protagonist's shadow is again strongly felt.

The last four films may be grouped in two different ways. *The Killers*, *Cry of the City* and *Criss Cross* constitute a *noir* gangster trilogy, in which the hero, as a consequence of past events, is doomed to die. The narrative – predominantly in flashback form in *The Killers* and *Criss Cross* – is essentially a tracing of the events which lead to his death. His journey towards death is marked by a relationship with a cop who was a childhood friend, and who serves structurally to comment on the hero's moral decline. Since it is the hero's criminal activities that ensure his entrapment in the *noir* world, the cop is in part like his alter ego in the legitimate world. But here the alter ego is a (more or less punishing) super-ego figure. Even Lubinsky in *The Killers*, who is basically sympathetic, in effect sends the hero to jail. And the other two cops are highly moralistic figures, each seeming to carry in his condemnation of the hero an unresolved homoerotic attraction. Significantly, both *Cry of the City* and *Criss Cross* have an important scene in which the hero is incapacitated in bed and the cop is trying to get him to confess. And, just as Candella ultimately kills Rome, so it is implied that Ramirez is indirectly responsible for Steve's death, thus linking both men with Simon in *Christmas Holiday*, another figure who, it is implied, is sexually spurned by the criminal protagonist.

Alternatively, *The Killers*, *Criss Cross* and *The File on Thelma Jordon* may be grouped as films dealing with the 'mystery of woman'. It is only in these films that Siodmak deals substantially with the *femme fatale*, and his view becomes increasingly sympathetic. Although, as in most *films noirs*, it is the hero's desire for her that causes his entry into the *noir* world, she herself is not a free agent, but is – to a greater or lesser extent – subject to the tyranny of another man (both the cop and the gangster in *Criss Cross*). She lacks the deadliness of the cycle's most powerful *femmes fatales*, such as Phyllis in *Double Indemnity*, or Kathy in *Out of the Past*, who are explicitly out for themselves alone. Instead, Siodmak captures the sense that, as soon as a woman becomes sexually desirable, a man comes along and seeks to 'colonise' her, to incorporate her into his own (usually criminal) fantasies. Indeed, this would apply to other Siodmak films: *Christmas Holiday* and *Cry of the City*.

In short, Siodmak has dealt with a number of the major issues of the *noir* cycle: a negative view of marriage and the family, a concern with the ways in which ordinary men can be driven to murder, an interest in abnormal psychology and a fascination with the destructive nature of desire. The weakness of his heroes – in particular, their sexual anxieties – contrasts with the resilience of his female characters, who tend to be survivors; only in the last two films does the heroine die. The Freudian overtones to his narratives and character relationships, and the homoerotic subtexts illustrate the sexualised undercurrents characteristic of *film noir*, with its dual preoccupations of crime and desire. Stylistically, his films are smoothly directed, showing equal facility with the long take, classical *découpage* and – when required, as in his scenes of violence – rapid editing. The one uneven feature is his lighting, which seems to be heavily dependent on his cameraman. Nevertheless, with top cameramen – Bredell (*Phantom Lady*, *Christmas Holiday*, *The Killers*), Musuraca (*The Spiral Staircase*), Planer (*Criss Cross*) and Barnes (*The File on Thelma Jordon*) – his films show *noir* cinematography at its best, with richly textured images and superb use of chiaroscuro. Even though he did not make an indisputable masterpiece – however good *The Killers* and *Criss Cross* are, they are not of the same status as *Scarlet Street* or *In a Lonely Place* (Nicholas Ray, 1950) – Siodmak can be placed alongside Fritz Lang as an outstanding *film noir* director.

THE MAN'S MELODRAMA
The Woman in the Window
& Scarlet Street
Florence Jacobowitz

Fritz Lang's *The Woman in the Window* (1944) and *Scarlet Street* (1945) emerged from the specific crossroads of historical and cultural conditions that was Hollywood during and immediately after World War II. They remain valuable in the manner in which Edith Wharton describes significant literature: there is a 'vital radiation' beyond art to social experience. They treat 'subjects in which some phase of our common plight stands forth dramatically and typically' (Edith Wharton, *The Writing of Fiction*, Scribners, New York, 1924). The comparison of a Wharton novel to these *noir* melodramas is not as irresponsibly founded as one might initially think. Both ground the individual narrative within the strict confines of a precise social and psychic network which bears down oppressively upon the protagonists. Thomas Elsaesser's description of the characteristics of the melodrama ('Tales of Sound and Fury' in Bill Nichols, ed., *Movies and Methods II*, University of California Press, Berkeley, 1985) typifies a diverse cross-section of American art:

'. . . alienation is recognised as a basic condition, fate is secularised into the prison of social conformity and psychological neurosis, and the linear trajectory of self-fulfilment so potent in American ideology is twisted into the downward spiral of a self-destructive urge seemingly possessing a whole social class' (p.188).

The efficacy of these cultural works depends upon the participating adult reader/spectator who has enough awareness and experience to appreciate these parallels.

This theoretical premise, of the awake and participating spectator, underpins the following discussion. *The Woman in the Window* and *Scarlet Street* foreground and *place* the narrative's relationship to social determinants through various stylistic strategies. They specifically rely upon narrative devices such as irony, humour, parody, and excessive, heightened modes of dramatisation, as well the performances of their principal stars, to produce a qualified engagement with the protagonists and the unfolding story. The audience is privileged to various levels of awareness and a kind of multiple layering is achieved whereby the spectator can profoundly feel for and identify with a protagonist's predicament or the conditions within which she/he finds her/

himself or the tone and the atmosphere underlying those conditions, but can see beyond the characters' limited points-of-view to the social contradictions which shape their desires.

The audience's pleasure in these films is dependent upon the activity of spectating. Fritz Lang, Joan Bennett and Walter Wanger, the principals behind Diana Productions whose first film release was *Scarlet Street*, were not unaware of this. Their goal was to produce films for a mature, adult audience. Lang considered *Scarlet Street*, surely one of the most extravagantly stylised films of the period, to be 'a realistic film of the people and for the people.' The minutes of a publicity meeting for Diana Productions confirm and elaborate on this: 'Mr Lang believes his direction reflects this respect for audiences, for he depends on audience collaboration to a very large extent to give full meaning to his work' (Matthew Bernstein, 'Fritz Lang Incorporated' in *The Velvet Light Trap* 22, 1986, p.37). Lang specified that 'audience collaboration' included judgments film-viewers make about characters and about the consistency and reliability of narration in his films. The respect for an intelligent, discerning spectator is not only evident in the planning but is relied upon in the production of meaning and worked in as a structuring principle. The films invite and depend upon this participation.

One cannot totally ignore authorial intention in Lang's case (even in the post-Barthesian era of the death-of-the-author) or discount the profound influence of Brechtian dramatic theory in his work. (Lang had collaborated with Bertolt Brecht on the script of *Hangmen Also Die* two years before the making of *The Woman in the Window*.) Perhaps what is most conveniently forgotten of Brecht's theories was his commitment to social reality. 'The task of the artist is to render reality to men in a form they can master' (Sylvia Harvey, 'Whose Brecht? Memories For the Eighties' in *Screen*, vol.231, May-June 1982, p.50). As Sylvia Harvey notes, for Brecht, the term realism involved questions of epistemology beyond questions of style; there is 'a tripartite relationship between textual properties, contemporary social reality and historically formed readers' (p.51). Brecht's work was also deeply committed to pleasure and entertainment, utilising popular forms of dramatic art. Hollywood products are clearly limited in the degree to which they can advocate a transformation of social reality, but they can make ideologically familiar notions of gender and identity within the family and/or workplace strange and foreboding, linking the curtailment of human potential and vitality to socially prescribed demands of normative masculinity and femininity in an inequitable class-structured society. (Although neither film makes any direct reference to notions of class consciousness, they certainly show an awareness of hierarchical social strata wherein power and domination are linked to money and the male sex.) Both films' political significance lies in their ability to situate the individual crisis within social terms, without taking away the pleasures of the audiences familiar with the conventions of popular cinema.

If melodrama can be described (as Andrew Britton has done) as the genre wherein compulsory heterosexuality is presented as a nightmare, one might describe *film noir* as the genre wherein compulsory *masculinity* is presented as a nightmare, and, in this and other senses, the genres are not as far apart as is often suggested. In fact, both share the overriding principle of constriction and entrapment as a defining motif, whether it be within the family or within patriarchal social organisations and demands of gender ideals. The anxiety which *film noir* desperately tries to lay to rest revolves around the male protagonist's crisis of identity and fears of not living up to the responsibilities of domination, power and achievement so central to masculinity. The fears realised in the *femme fatale* are often symptomatic of the hero's doubts and fears of his own feminised inadequacies. Masochistic tendencies of punishment and self-denial significantly cross both genres; the violence may be directed inwardly and be expressed emotionally in melodrama, or directed outwardly and expressed physically in *noir* or gangster films. Masochism is not specific to a particular sex, just as the containment which so vividly characterises melodrama is not specific to women.

The Woman in the Window introduces the central protagonist through the motif of confinement in the workplace, in the family and in a leisure/social setting – the masculine world of the club. The opening long shot of Professor Wanley (Edward G. Robinson) with horizontal bars of light and shadow cast across his face shows him lecturing on the psychological aspects of homicide. He explains how injunctions against murder demand qualification as there are various degrees of culpability. 'The man who kills in self-defence should not be judged by the same standards as the man who kills for gain.' The film immediately links the professor with entrapment and the potential to kill. The following scene at the station introduces Richard Wanley in his role as husband and father within another context of confinement. His wife (Dorothy Peterson) comments on her fears of her husband's being 'cooped up' after he mentions that he will be having dinner at the club. Wanley's remarks to his wife about being sorry that he cannot join her and

Still: The Woman in the Window – *Wanley (Edward G. Robinson) says goodbye to his wife (Dorothy Peterson) and children.*

their two children on the vacation, and his exaggerated declaration that he will miss them 'every minute of the day and every second of the night' is heavily undermined by his cheery monotone, the lack of contact, emotional, erotic or otherwise between any members of the family, and his farewell to his children, 'Goodbye to you little (b)rats,' which ironically links them to the enemies of the gangster, Little Caesar (Edward G. Robinson's most celebrated role, in the 1930 Mervyn LeRoy film). The gangster connotations associated with this star are crucial to the casting of Robinson as Professor Wanley (and Chris Cross in *Scarlet Street*). The masculine potency and physical violence attributed to this genre seem antithetical to his casting as the soft-spoken, emasculated Chris Cross and the assistant professor. His stature and mannerisms in Lang's films connote an almost child-like naiveté and gentleness, precisely those characteristics repressed in the masculine gangster world. In both *The Woman in the Window* and *Scarlet Street*, Robinson's characters feel uncomfortable and displaced in the male world in which they move. As in melodrama, both characters share a limited access to money and hence power, both yearn for a release through romance or creative expression, both suffer a 'mid-life' crisis which activates their desires.

Elsaesser describes a form of melodrama which, on the surface, seems to characterise both films. He calls them melodramas in the *Série Noire* tradition:

'where the hero is egged on or blackmailed by the *femme fatale* . . . into a course of action which pushes him further and further in one direction, opening a narrowing wedge of equally ineluctable consequences, that usually lead the hero to wishing his own death as the ultimate act of liberation, but where the mechanism of fate at least allows him to express his existential revolt in strong and strongly antisocial behaviour' (p.177).

Both *The Woman in the Window* and *Scarlet Street* have been discussed in this way (*see* Kaplan, 1978). In the absence of the family or in response to the suffocating presence of the oppressive, castrating wife (both equally devoid of sexuality), the protagonist meets up with the embodiment of his repressed desires in the form of Joan Bennett. She promises her illicit and forthright sexuality in typical *femme fatale* tradition, but delivers a nightmare of murder, blackmail and deceit. The hero is destroyed, losing his respectability, his social position, his money, his dream girl. Both male protagonists move towards a release through suicide, though Professor Wanley is saved by the *deus-ex-machina* dream ending which abruptly reburies the overwhelming anxiety and frustration that have been unwillingly dredged up (in a similar way to the rebirth of George Bailey, the James Stewart character, at the end of Frank Capra's *It's a Wonderful Life*, 1946). The problem with simpli-

fying either film, particularly *The Woman in the Window*, in this way, is that the dangerous Other in Professor Wanley's safe armchair existence is the only empathetic character who cares for the protagonist and is finally the only one in whom the protagonist can confide. The intruder's significance to the central protagonist in these films extends beyond the sexual – answering needs and listening to admissions which cannot be voiced legitimately elsewhere.

The real threat in *The Woman in the Window* (as in *Scarlet Street*) is the male system, here enshrined in the Burghers' Club, led by the supreme figures of patriarchal law – the District Attorney, Frank Lalor (Raymond Massey), and the physician, Dr Michael Barkstane (Edmund Breon), the male who regulates the body, holding the power of life and death (the supplier of the medication that will kill Wanley). The emphasis on the men's club as the arena where the masochistic wish-fulfilment fantasy is played out is critical, as it supplies a frame of reference, a setting for the nightmare as well as a cast of characters. Chris Cross's adventure is similarly framed by another private boys' club – the dinner party J.J. Hogarth (Russell Hicks) hosts for his employees. The men envy and admire the masculine ideal J.J. embodies. His 'freedom' and 'power' act as a catalyst, setting off Chris's dreams and desires.

The masculine system of competition, power and domination linked to money and social privilege brackets both narratives. The critical shot introducing Wanley's fascination with the portrait of the woman in the window connects his desire to his two friends: Lang cuts from Wanley looking, to the two men at the left of the composition watching Wanley looking, followed by the camera panning back to Wanley. 'Flirting with our sweetheart? We've decided she's our dream girl, just from that picture . . . We saw her first . . .' A layering of the narrative is immediately produced. The spectator sees that Wanley's responses and actions are always monitored and judged against the demands of masculine law. This is made evident in the conversation that follows in the club. The men ask Wanley if he is planning to take advantage of his freedom as a summer bachelor by going to the Stork Club or taking in a burlesque show.

What follows is a treatise on middle-aged death-in-life wherein Wanley complains of feeling the end of 'the brightness of life'. There is great pathos in his painful admission of life ending at forty. 'I hate this solidity, the stodginess I'm beginning to feel. To me, it's the end of . . . spirit and adventure . . .' The DA immediately warns of the consequences for middle-aged men 'who act like colts . . . I'm not joking when I tell you that I've seen genuine tragedy issuing out of pure carelessness, out of mere trifles; a casual impulse, idle flirtation, one drink too many . . .' The system of censorship is firmly in place, enacted by the DA, the watchdog for the law he

Still: The Woman in the Window – *Wanley meets Alice (Joan Bennett) at the gallery window.*

defends, and backed up by the doctor. 'Do you think it's quite safe to leave me alone in this rebellious state of mind?' Wanley asks. The doctor answers him as one would a child, 'You'll be all right – just run along to bed like a good fellow.' Wanley internalises this repression, as is evidenced in his complaint, 'The flesh is still strong but the spirit grows weaker . . . Even if the spirit of adventure should rise up before me and beckon – even in the form of that alluring young woman in the window next door . . . All I'd do is clutch my coat a little tighter, mutter something idiotic and run like the devil.'

The introduction of the Joan Bennett character, to both Wanley and Chris Cross, is the summoning forth of rebellion, the release of the desire to recapture 'the brightness of life', the 'spirit' and 'adventure' extinguished by the demands of gender and emphasised through the passing of time. The evidence of the woman in the window's existence as the embodiment of a wish fulfilment is made clear in the way she appears – her face is imaged over the portrait – in her overstated attire (the sequinned and feathered hat, the cigarette, the sheer chiffon dress which suggests her nudity), and in her over-determined slow-paced speech: '. . . Can I help you? I'm not married, I have no designs on you and one drink is all I care for . . . Is that right?' Wanley's desire is closely related to the masculine response without which it has no meaning, 'I'm thinking of their faces tomorrow when I tell them about this . . .'

Wanley's evening remains devoid of any expression of sexuality. It is the little things he

was warned against – lingering over the extra drink – the 'mere trifles' which initiate a chain of events. Wanley's seemingly innocent 'rebellious state' manifests its darker, more desperate side in the repeated stabbing of Claude Mazard (Arthur Loft), the boyfriend who suddenly appears and claims ownership, parallelling and echoing the earlier moments ('flirting with our dream girl? . . . We saw her first'). The narrative rolls along an erratic path of emotional or dream logic. Mazard's murder is abrupt and sudden, a violent and extreme response to a stereotypical situation, as is common in melodrama.

'Just as in dreams certain gestures and incidents mean something by their structure and sequence, rather than by what they literally represent, the melodrama often works by a displaced emphasis, by substitute acts, by parallel situations and metaphoric connections. In dreams one tends to "use" as dream material, incidents and circumstances from one's waking experience during the previous day in order to "code" them, while nevertheless keeping a kind of emotional logic going, and even condensing their images into what, during the dream at least, seems an inevitable sequence. Melodramas often use middle-class American society, its iconography and the family experience in just this way as their manifest "material" but "displace" it into quite different patterns, juxtaposing stereotyped situations in strange configurations, provoking clashes and

ruptures which not only open up new associations, but also redistribute the emotional energies, which suspense and tensions have accumulated, in disturbingly different directions' (Elsaesser p.180).

The murder of Mazard is the coded murder of the father and patriarchal law as epitomised by the DA. His stature and importance become evident when the DA divulges that Mazard is a powerful industrialist whose disappearance alone will incite severe economic repercussions. When attempting to calm Alice (Joan Bennett) and justify the murder as self-defence, Wanley claims coolly and without regret, 'I have no feeling about him . . . He was trying to kill me, there's no question about that. If I hadn't killed him he would have killed me. If you hadn't given me the scissors I'd be dead,' and proceeds to try and usurp the role of the masculine authority figure who is methodical and in control. Later in the film, when Wanley is on his way to revisit the scene of the crime, he comments, 'This is quite an adventure for me.' Wanley's 'adventure' is not in the promise of eroticism but in the challenge of assuming a position for which he has little experience. (The irony of the restrictions imposed by this overly regulated system is evident in the sign located near the site where Mazard's body was dumped: 'No parking, no picnicking, no bicycles, no walking . . .')

One can encapsulate the entire film in the words of the DA, in the scene in the club when he invites Wanley to accompany him to the woods where Mazard's body was discovered by

Still: The Woman in the Window – *after the murder, Alice and Wanley, who is cleaning the murder wapon.*

a patriotic boy scout: 'We'll show you how the law operates to nail a man.' Nail him, in fact, to his coffin. Professor Wanley's feeble attempts to cover up the murder and get rid of the body, followed by his inability to conceal the endless trail of clues implicating him in the crime, place him in a position, as the DA says, of having continually to 'account for yourself.' The movement of the narrative towards Wanley's increasing self-implication is played out against the subtle rituals of the club, which are precise and complex. Who pays for dinner, where coffee and brandy are

Frame: The Woman in the Window – *Wanley puts Mazard's body in the back of his car.*

156

served, codes of dress and appropriate protocol are examples of a highly codified and regimented system where the rules are absolute. The DA's position in the legal world awards him the privilege of gaining access to confidential disclosures concerning the crime with which he then regales his buddies in the club. Wanley's perpetration of the crime ironically gives him the same powerful knowledge as the DA. Unconsciously, at least, the murder becomes another adventure which Wanley can't wait to divulge to his friends. At one point the DA 'jokingly' accuses Wanley of being eaten up with envy: 'You see my name on the front page of every paper, so you make a desperate effort to elbow your way into my case by insinuating that you're the guilty man,' correctly placing the crime within the masculine world of competition, success and performance.

Alice Reed, who begins her existence as a conjured-up ghost of desire, manages to become a character as the film progresses (evidenced by the change from glamorous costume to everyday clothes) because of Joan Bennett's performance and of the role Alice plays in Wanley's life. She is a helpful, controlled partner – the only moments in the story where credibility is strained are those when Alice is supposedly hysterical. One cannot convincingly argue from the film that the image of femininity is safe when locked within a frame and threatening when let loose. Alice willingly carries out Wanley's plans and instructions and props up his new-found importance. He is happy to hear from her when she calls, 'I'm rather glad that I've heard from you . . .' (she is the only friend who congratulates him on his promotion) and never blames her for having held back his pen or for her unsuccessful attempt to kill Heidt, the blackmailer (Dan

Still: The Woman in the Window – *Wanley becomes faint and retreats to the car. DA Lalor (Raymond Massey) is concerned.*

Duryea) – 'You're very fair, Alice . . . quite generous.' The DA's suspicions that the man and woman who performed the crime live hating and fearing each other, worrying who will 'blab' first, is the only supposition which is entirely incorrect: Alice is the only one Wanley trusts and confides in.

In fact, Alice is less a feared Other than a mirror image (and the proliferation of mirrors in her apartment confirms this: in one shot, Alice and Wanley are parallelled in mirror reflections on either side of Alice's fireplace – they are also of the same height); she represents an inversion of the classic notion of *the femme fatale*. She is a projection of what Wanley wishes for himself (youth, spirit, adventure). Alice is youthful, independent (her apartment is more luxurious than the Professor's) and is associated with creativity (the artist's drawings), glamour and 'class'. One can argue that the blackmailing episodes, apparently beyond Wanley's consciousness, are still 'dreamt' by him, as he and Alice are identified and similarly aligned. Heidt's links to the DA and the powerful masculinist Law of the Father are evidenced in his final lines to Alice, 'How could you lie to Pappy like that? How did you think you could get away with it? . . . since you've been such a smart doublecrosser I'll let you dig up some more dough for Pappy . . .'

Although Alice is sympathetic and more of a double to Professor Wanley, she does not represent a woman's voice or position. Bennett breathes life and a certain autonomy into Alice, but Alice remains a dream symbol – a collection of accumulated emotional energies redistributed and projected on to a character. She remains a portrait briefly animated and laid to rest with the central protagonist.

The expressionist *Weltanschauung* within which the Langian nightmare operates is not life-affirming or rebellious in any positive way. Wanley doesn't want to overthrow the system; he wants to fit in and play a more active role, but his frustration is finally overwhelming. Wanley's wishes, which first lead him to a murder in self-defence and then to a failed attempt to plan and knowingly kill, exhaust him. The film indicts a world where death seems preferable to life, and again veers into melodrama. All Wanley's attempts outwardly to express his frustrations in the social world (even if contained safely within the dream form) ultimately turn inward. As in melodrama, illness becomes a metaphor for the internal implosion taking place. Wanley manifests a variety of symptoms of his illness from stomach upsets, poison ivy, infected cuts, tension headaches, feeling faint in the country, mopping his brow and taking refuge in the car (a classically female position) to finally killing himself by simulating a heart attack (the solution to many a heroine's unanswerable agony in life).

Scarlet Street can be paired with *The Woman in the Window* in the way it articulates similar thematic

Still: Scarlet Street. *Kitty (Joan Bennett) and Chris (Edward G. Robinson) – 'paint me, Chris.'*

material: compulsory masculinity is a nightmare which can be best escaped through death; however, the excess which thoroughly permeates and characterises its vision produces a significantly different product, demanding a different kind of participation and response from the audience.

Scarlet Street, like many of the Marlene Dietrich/ Josef von Sternberg collaborations, defies the simplistic theorisation of the spectator's response to realist art (the magical powers of the mesmerising, sutured narrative, the notion of identification as being and becoming the protagonists, the overriding principle of manipulation and spectator passivity, etc.) in its reliance on overstatement, performance, excess, irony and parody. Although far less outrageously celebrative than any Sternberg work, *Scarlet Street* communicates in a manner significantly different from the dream-like atmosphere of *The Woman in the Window*, manifesting a deliberate awareness of the critique presented through its detached, cynical humour, heavily ironic tone, and layering of perspective. One of my favourite moments which illustrates this tone and the spectator's 'distance' from the narrative is in a scene in Kitty's apartment. Chris is 'tormenting' Kitty, suspecting her of having had another lover who might have been Johnny. Kitty responds by storming to her bedroom and slamming the door. As she changes to go out, she worries about alienating Chris and insists that he remain and paint. Chris tries to mollify her, asking her to marry him, suggesting vaguely that something might happen to his wife, and finally asks to paint her portrait. Kitty answers with the comment, 'I was gonna do it myself, but . . . paint me Chris,' and places her foot regally in Chris's lap as she hands

him the nail polish. Chris kneels down and begins painting; Lang cuts to a close-up of Kitty looking down on Chris as she says, 'They'll be masterpieces.' The scene defies a close reading but elucidates perfectly the demands the film makes for a detached, analytical response (or positioning) from the spectator.

The aesthetic emphasis on artifice, stylisation and all that is not natural is crucial to its meaning. The metaphor of acting as role-playing and deception highlights the unnaturalness of gender roles and of behaviour as social construction. However psychologically motivated, the protagonist's actions are informed by social demands and Chris's adventure, like that of Professor Wanley, is precisely situated within a hierarchical masculine system of power and exploitation. Neither protagonist ever achieves an awareness of this. As in melodrama, the audience is privileged to a perspective and a context which the characters lack. Chris's big problem (one which he shares with all the main characters) is, precisely, his lack of perspective – 'One thing I never could master . . .' This layering of perspective and the disjuncture between audience and character point-of-view is established right at the beginning and structures each scene. Although Chris is introduced as an empathetic character, achieved through his position of being the benign underdog, one's identification with the character is called into question because he quickly becomes an active participant in the system of exploitation in which *all* the characters participate – this reaches its crowning moment in the

Still: Scarlet Street. *J.J. Hogarth (Russell Hicks) has discovered the embezzlement – 'Chris, it was a woman, wasn't it?'*

flashlight signal Chris gives Homer (Charles Kemper) to assure him that the coast is clear: a double-cross. As a spectator, one is implicated in the system to the degree that one's cultural conditioning establishes a bias for Chris against Kitty; the film exposes one's willingness to forgive Chris in the scene where J.J. abruptly forgives Chris's theft without any explanation in his one line, 'Chris, it was a woman, wasn't it? I thought so . . .' In fact, the film has meticulously established otherwise, placing Chris's fall within his struggle to be a 'real' man like J.J. or Johnny.

Scarlet Street obsessively connects the power and freedom, and all the seductive possibilities open to a man like J.J., to the notion of time and ageing, and the combination acts as a catalyst for releasing Chris's desire. The 'idea' of Kitty is born on the night of the dinner party when J.J.'s mistress is discreetly announced by a male butler, which leads J.J. into a rushed presentation of Chris's gift. 'I hate to break up a good party, but you can't keep a woman waiting . . . I see you understand . . . Believe me I've had the time of my life tonight . . . and speaking of time . . .' The scene exposes the false conviviality underlying an event calculated to ensure the devotion and inflate the importance of an objectified worker (a fourteen-carat, seventeen-jewel cashier) and mystify an employer/employee relationship. The engraving on the watch reads, 'to my friend Christopher Cross, in token of twenty-five years of faithful service . . . ' – as a cashier. (The irony of this is emphasised in later shots of Chris in his cage-like cashier booth and in Kitty's surprise at learning that Chris is a painter: 'To think I took you for a cashier!') J.J. is clearly an ideal for Chris – the camera privileges J.J. in the

opening shots over the back of Chris's head – and J.J.'s desired effect is achieved and painfully evidenced in Chris's modest, stammering remark, '. . . All I can say is, we've got the best boss in New York.' J.J.'s ability to buy services and loyalty is displaced as 'generosity'. He imposes one of his specially made-up cigars on Chris, who accepts while objecting 'I, I, don't usually . . .' (the gesture is repeated later when J.J. buys off the police with a box of his cigars) and announces that 'everything is charged to J.J.' (He also challenges Chris's superstition of being the third on a match: Chris denies his belief while the camera privileges the audience to a close-up of Chris's crossed fingers.) As J.J. exits, his employees comment on what a 'great guy' he is and then rush over to the window to watch him, admiring and envious of the 'dame' with whom he departs.

Chris and his fellow employee, Charlie, are set apart from the group and slip out at this point. Although Chris has been the focus of attention and has received a gold watch for his efforts, J.J.'s successes in the masculine world expose his misery and alienation: 'I feel kind of lonely tonight.' Chris mistakes J.J.'s social privilege of buying and owning his mistress for a romantic notion of love, just as the employees attribute their devotion to their boss to his being a 'great guy'. Chris's naive comments, 'Do you suppose J.J. is running around? . . . I wonder what it's like to be loved by a young girl like that . . .', are not shared by the spectator, who is aware that the 'young girl' is an object bought like the cigars. (The opening scene's strains of the romantic 'Santa Lucia' act as ironic counterpoint.) Chris compares his position to J.J.'s – he admits he has never been loved like that, even as a young man. After Charlie's 'When we're young, we have dreams that never pan out . . .', Chris continues, 'When I was young . . . I dreamt I was going to be a great painter.' The notion of lost time, misused time, 'killing time,' and the burden of leisure time, which allows one time to reflect, is raised when Charlie comments that he hates Sundays, 'I never know what to do with myself.' Chris's dreams and his submerged identity as a painter are regulated by his one leisure day a week and are confined to the washroom, and even this privilege is soon threatened when his wife Adèle (Rosalind Ivan) promises to give his paintings to the junk man. The scene between Chris and Charlie outlines the characters' feelings of loss and profound social alienation with great pathos. Chris's sense of his inadequacies measured against an established system of masculinity parallels that of Professor Wanley. The latter's recognition that time has passed him by and that 'life ends at forty' leads him to sublimate his sexuality through the reading of the poetically erotic 'Song of Songs' and to dream up an adventure that will allow him entry into the masculine world of 'spirit and adventure.' Chris's meeting Kitty after wandering around lost in the Village (a place associated with his youthful dream of being an artist) is comparable to Wanley's meeting his 'dream girl' but is heavily tinged with an irony lacking in the earlier film. The audience sees Kitty for what she is – a prostitute wrapped in plastic so that her wares can be displayed, being beaten by a customer or a pimp. Chris's misreading (he has 'saved' and met a 'young girl' who might love him as J.J.'s girl loves J.J.) continues the strategy of a split perspective established in the opening sequence.

Chris's attraction to Kitty is to the image he constructs for himself, one which she willingly reflects back to him. He sees in her the opportunity to be desired, to regain lost time and again be young, and to be acknowledged as the painter he has always wished he was. Chris's fears of being too old emerge in his opening conversation with Kitty, 'Since I'm old enough to be your father . . .' which she senses and wisely parries: 'You're not so old – you're mature . . .' The next day Chris happily reports to Charlie, 'I haven't been to bed . . . I'm not as old as I thought.'

When Chris again meets Kitty in the cafe, he tells her, 'I feel like a kid myself today,' and confesses how 'You walk around with everything bottled up.' The *mise-en-scène* turns the cafe into a pastoral, spring-like setting (beginning with a high-angle shot through the sun-dappled trees, suggesting Chris's feelings of rebirth). With Kitty, Chris can take on the persona of the young artist, a creative disguise which allows him to be defined outside his two disempowering roles – his domestic position as the feminised, aproned husband/housewife who is not a provider and has no-one he cares to possess or provide for, and his alienated position in the workplace, visualised in the literal cage in which he is doomed to count someone else's money while having no access to his own. (This is brilliantly

Still: Scarlet Street. *Chris takes Kitty for a drink in Tiny's bar; Tiny (Lou Lubin) serves them.*

expressed in the scene where Chris is about to steal money from the safe of Hogarth and Company and J.J. approaches with the comment, 'Caught you in time. Cash this for me . . . it's personal.') One of Adèle's generally perceptive, biting remarks to Chris is that he demand a raise ('Homer made a good salary'). The scene follows the one where Chris has attempted to borrow $500 legitimately, but is powerless in the social world where class and ownership, in addition to gender, determine access to money.

Chris's commitment to Kitty is intimately bound to his needs and his identity as much as it is to his being exploited by her and Johnny. The apartment he provides serves as a setting for his new identity, a space where he can both maintain his romance and paint. The scene when Chris agrees to supply the money for the apartment/studio follows the one when Adèle threatens to throw out his work. Kitty is aware of Chris's narcissistic motives and clinches the second, larger, sum of $1,000 by threatening to borrow it from Johnny, 'he's got plenty of money . . .' Chris has just met Johnny – who Kitty pretends is the boyfriend of her friend Millie (Margaret Lindsay) – and dislikes him instantly, sensing that he is a threat (he is young, attractive and condescending). This, coupled with the implicit undermining of his image of himself as provider for his love object, leads to his decision to get Kitty the $1,000, which he steals from J.J.

The limited awareness Chris does exhibit relates to his perception of his marriage as a failure. He

Still: Scarlet Street – *Johnny (Dan Duryea) and Kitty in Tiny's bar.*

tells Charlie openly that he needed a cheap room and, 'Well . . . you know how these things go . . .' The marriage is defined as being sexless ('I never saw a woman without any clothes'), and both he and Adèle confess to being stuck (before Adèle departs to listen to the 'Happy Household Hour'). Chris later explains to Kitty that he got married because 'I was lonely . . . I couldn't stand my loneliness.' In keeping with the style of excess, Chris fantasises about the possibility of murdering Adèle, identifying with the murderers in the newspaper, like the man in Queens who killed his wife. (A version of the male petit-bourgeois obsession with murder is a major theme in Alfred Hitchcock's *Shadow of a Doubt*, 1943). Adèle, clearly picking up the innuendo, quickly counters, 'He didn't get away with it did he? He'll go to the chair, as he should,' and Chris admits, disappointed, that a man hasn't got a chance with New York detectives. (Ironically, Adèle's former husband is an ex-detective who gives Chris his chance.) The most obvious display of Chris's desire and potential to kill emasculating women takes place in the scene where Chris, in his apron, is slicing the liver Adèle has asked him to buy. When Adèle asks about his relationship with Katherine March, Chris responds by raising the butcher knife, moving towards her with the offer to help her off with her coat while Adèle backs away, demanding,

'Get away with that knife . . . you want to cut my throat.' Chris often alludes vaguely to something happening that may free him so that he can marry Kitty, well before the return of Adèle's first husband, Homer.

Thoroughly feminised in his day-to-day identity, Chris releases his repressed potency through his paintings, which Mr Janeway (Jess Barker), the perceptive art critic, describes as possessing a strong 'masculine force'. One of the paintings prominently displays a snake wrapped around a support of the El – the elevated railway. However, Lang links the phallic threat of the snake explicitly to Johnny: he dissolves from a shot of Johnny, hiding from Chris, to the snake in the painting. Given that the painting also includes a young woman standing under a lamp-post and that its setting is where Chris first saw Kitty and Johnny, it can be seen to suggest Chris's unconscious perception of Kitty as a prostitute and Johnny as sexual threat. The perception regarding Kitty never becomes conscious: even after Chris has killed her in a rage, he continues to see her as pure and innocent.

Chris is also aware of the precise rules of power and privilege governing the art world, as he attributes his being a failure as a painter to the fact that, had he brought his works to Dellarowe's gallery, they would never have been accepted. Chris is pleased to have Kitty sign his work because he feels it symbolises a marriage (one that is more successful than his own) and moreover gives him 'a little authority around here.' This newly established authority moves Chris to request that he paint Kitty; his desire to paint her reflects his wishes to establish ownership and to confine Kitty within his image of her – one of illicit sexuality, partly uncovered, in black lace, and of mother/Madonna with exaggeratedly round prominent breasts.

Chris's title for the painting, 'Self-portrait,' foregrounds an additional meaning which is beyond him. Like the woman in the window, Kitty is partly a mirror reflection of Chris, sharing with him a number of affinities. (As Janeway notes, 'Sometimes it's as if she were two people . . .') Kitty, like Chris, subscribes to a complex system of gender and sex definition and depends upon self-deception to give meaning to an otherwise unfulfilling identity. Both she and Chris see themselves as creative artists (Kitty has aspirations to being an actress), however frustrated by their current situations. Both prove to be successful when given the opportunity; Chris's work is lauded and Kitty gives a convincing performance as a painter (Kitty is as much implicated as Chris in her fantasy that Chris is a wealthy painter, as he is in believing that she is a young, fresh-faced actress instead of a prostitute). Kitty uses Johnny's over-inflated opinion of himself to define her importance (despite his belittling her and his condescension) just as Chris tries to use Kitty (despite her lack of interest in anything beyond his money). Both Chris and Kitty are imprisoned in romantic notions of *'l'amour fou'*, stuck in the same groove as Kitty's recording of 'Melancholy Baby' (it sticks on the words 'in love'), and both revere the same ideals of masculinity, valuing masculine authority and power as the criteria for a 'real' man.

Kitty's masochistic commitment to Johnny is based, in part, on the belief that men stake their territory and express their ownership and control through violence. This idea is one supported by popular culture and the film alludes to this when Johnny claims he could be an actor in Hollywood easily because he, too, acts tough and can push girls in the face. Kitty tries to arouse Johnny's jealousy so that he will express his love for her through a claim to ownership when she complains to him of how she dislikes Chris's attempts to kiss her. At least, 'if he were mean or vicious or he bawled me out, I'd like him better' (ironically anticipating Chris's final frenzied, masculine response to her). Although Kitty supports Johnny financially, she buys his potent masculine sexuality in exchange. When Johnny kisses Kitty, she coyly complains 'Can't you do any better?' to which he retorts 'That's all you ever think about, Lazy Legs.' 'What else is there?' 'If you want more heat . . . call the janitor.' When Kitty comments, 'I don't know why I'm so crazy about you,' Johnny remarks pointedly, 'Oh, yes, you do.' The scene in the film where their wild love-making is alluded to begins with the camera's slow track over the battle scene, taking in articles of clothing, finally focusing on Johnny going through Kitty's purse. Chris's attempts at this kind of masculine, passionate kissing are met with Kitty's objection, 'Chris, you're a caveman! I like you to like me, but there's a limit!'

Both Kitty and Chris inadvertently validate their low self-esteem by remaining with partners who exacerbate their deficiencies. Johnny, like Adèle with Chris, constantly deprecates Kitty's creativity ('You've no imagination'), importance ('You've always wanted to be an actress, now's your chance'), and intelligence ('I'm gonna make a monkey out of you'). Like Chris, Kitty deceives herself by legitimising her relationship with Johnny through the guise of 'true love' ('I'm in love . . . crazy in love'), exemplified in her exchange with Millie: 'You wouldn't know love if it hit you in the face.' 'If that's where it hits you, you oughta know.' She reassures herself by calling Johnny her 'fiancé' and reminding him to buy her a ring with the money she supplies. Although Johnny exploits Kitty's ability to use her sexuality to earn money (through 'johns', Chris, Janeway or the public who are suddenly interested in her art – as one critic notes, the artist is even more fascinating than her work), Kitty uses Johnny to give her an identity (as Janeway remarks, 'Lucky she has you to make up her mind for her).

The scene where Kitty is murdered is significant because it culminates in the moment where both Kitty's and Chris's carefully built deceptions

Still: Scarlet Street. *Chris proposes marriage; Kitty laughs at him.*

regarding gender roles and identity threaten to be exposed. The scene takes place in Kitty's bedroom with Kitty in bed, and the camera positioning foregrounds the theme of gender and performance by fragmenting her image in the mirrors around her bed. Millie has just called to warn Kitty that Johnny is coming over and has threatened to beat her up. Kitty continues with her self-deceptions of romantic love, commenting, 'He can't live without me any more than I can without him . . . If you were in love you'd understand . . .' When Chris enters, her disappointment can no longer be concealed and she admits finally, 'Can I help it if I'm in love?' Chris denies what he hears, explaining, 'It's just an infatuation. He's evil . . . he wouldn't let you alone . . . I wanted to kill him . . . ,' and ends with his proposal, 'Marry me . . . I'm free.' Kitty convulses with laughter, which Chris misreads persistently as passionate sobs, telling her, 'Don't cry, I know how you feel.' Kitty's enraged outburst is fuelled by the irony which she cannot acknowledge – here is Chris proposing marriage, when it is Johnny she has wanted all along.

In fact, Chris *does* know how she feels in a manner equally beyond his awareness–both he and Kitty masochistically yearn for a reciprocity which is unrealisable, as both use the idea of romance as a cover for their own alienated, unfulfilled identities. Kitty's final speech unwittingly expresses this, '. . . you idiot! How could a man be so dumb? I've wanted to laugh in your face ever since I first met you. You're old and ugly and I'm sick, sick, sick . . . *You* kill Johnny. I'd like to see you try. Why, he'd break every bone in your body. He's a man. . . *You* want to marry me? . . .' Kitty is 'in love' with Johnny, a real man who could show his love and stake his claim for her by breaking every bone in Chris's body (but ironically always aims for hers). Kitty's final words echo Adèle's, pointing out every weakness Chris has painstakingly tried to bury – his physical weakness, his age, his inability to match another man's sexual potency, his not being a real man.

Chris's repeated ice-pick stabs (like Professor Wanley's furious scissors stabs) express a pent-up frustration of never being able to assume the phallus in all of its manifestations in any social space. Significantly, Chris never perceives his violence as being directed at Kitty: 'You were innocent, you were pure, that's what he killed in *you*, *he's* the murderer.' His violence is directed against the embodiment of ideological masculinity – he steals from J.J., 'double crosses' Homer and then frames Johnny, a 'real man' who competitively beats him by possessing Kitty's love.

When Chris, losing his mind, 'hears' Johnny's haunting whisper, 'See Chris, she loves *me,*' he shouts back, 'That's why you had to die . . . You're the one I killed.'

Chris is so determined to punish Johnny for revealing his inadequacies that he rides to Sing Sing to witness Johnny's electrocution. There was a scene filmed, cut for fear of its being misread and laughed at, which encapsulates the excess and ironic heights the film relies upon. At Sing Sing Chris climbs the pole of a power line so that he can watch the voltage drop and know the moment when Johnny dies. A watchman spots him and shouts, 'What are you trying to do, kill yourself?'

Ironically, Chris can't even manage that. Tormented by his hallucinations of the voices of Kitty and Johnny 'reunited' in death, Chris attempts to hang himself, but he is rescued and cut down. Chris never achieves any authority or a respected masculine identity. His trial plays on the believability of his castrated position – both

Still: Scarlet Street. *The cut scene – Chris outside Sing Sing to witness the moment of Johnny's death.*

he and Adèle testify to his lack of originality and his inability to paint. Years later, Chris cannot confess to his crimes – he is seen as a crazy bum seeking shelter. He is doomed to wander the streets, less eaten with remorse (an excuse expressed in the plot to avoid censorship problems arising from the film's allowing a man to get away with murder) than he is haunted by Johnny's supreme claim over Kitty, echoed in her repetitive whisper, 'Jeepers, I love you Johnny.' Chris never gains insight into the determinants of his behaviour or his life, but the spectator does. The ultimate moment of irony is achieved at the end of the film, when Chris sees Kitty's 'Self-portrait' being carried out of Dellarowe's, but the irony is beyond him. Chris gazes uncomprehendingly while the spectator catches the exchange between the dealer and the buyer. 'There goes her masterpiece . . . I hate to part with it.' 'At $10,000 I shouldn't think you'd mind.' Everyone and everything can be commodified and traded, and the death of the artist only serves to bolster the value of her/his product. The masculine/capitalist system of power and exploitation is firmly in place, while Chris, its conniving victim, continues, haunted by his own lack.

The final sequence of *The Woman in the Window* following Professor Wanley's reawakening is a red herring; it is not the woman who threatens the protagonist, now safely exposed as a 'cheap' prostitute selling herself, but the reflection in the glass. It is the male's ambivalence towards gendered notions of his 'self,' coupled with the petit bourgeois's constricting death-in-life existence that sparks the wish-fulfilment fantasies which take on the form and ambience of a nightmare. *The Woman in the Window* incorporates the *noir* stylistic tradition of dreamlike chiaroscuro lighting, wet glistening streets, the *femme fatale's* sophisticated apartment exuding narcissism and sexuality in the multiple mirrors, overstuffed satin pillows and sensuous floral arrangements (contrasted with the masculine world of the club), but plays upon melodrama's themes of entrapment and release through illness and death. Contrary to the traditions of the genre, Alice Reed is not a threatening *femme fatale:* the only glimmer of a positive relationship in the narrative exists between Wanley and his woman in the window. *Scarlet Street* adopts a darker *noir* approach, using heightened cynicism and irony to depict a social order where every relationship is marked by exploitation and deception so that nothing is ultimately redeemable. Joan Bennett's and Edward G. Robinson's incarnations suffer because they share a marginal position in a social order where the divisions of empowerment are precisely defined. Masculinity is revealed to be a complex gender-class system with intricate laws and demands of who may join and inherit. When the consequences of this unnatural social organisation are exposed in all their bitterness, the oppressive blackness of these films becomes uncomfortably clear.

DOUBLE INDEMNITY
(or Bringing Up Baby)

Peter William Evans

Like many examples of *film noir*, Billy Wilder's *Double Indemnity* (1944) relies very largely on a flashback structure that prioritises the point of view of its leading male character, using a confessional mode that aims, in Paul Schrader's words, to emphasise the 'loss, nostalgia, lack of clear priorities, insecurity' of its anti-hero (Kevin Jackson, ed., *Schrader on Schrader*, Faber, London, 1990, p.86). The flashback is framed by non-subjective narration: late at night, an insurance agent, Walter Neff (Fred MacMurray), enters an office building, the Pacific All Risk Company, approaches his desk and begins to confess into a Dictaphone machine his involvement in fraud and murder. At the end, the film returns to omniscient narration, as the arrival of Keyes (Edward G.

Robinson), Neff's immediate boss, to whom he has been making his recorded confession, leads to a short conversation with Neff, after which Keyes rings the police. At this point Neff, who has been shot by the woman he has been describing in his story, collapses.

In the course of Neff's story, it becomes clear that his downfall has been caused by interrelated transgressive desires to have an affair with an attractive married woman, Phyllis Dietrichson (Barbara Stanwyck), and to defraud the insurance company that employs him. Neither urge is fully satisfied for, as he relates, he gets neither

Still: the final shot – Walter (Fred MacMurray) and Keyes (Edward G. Robinson).

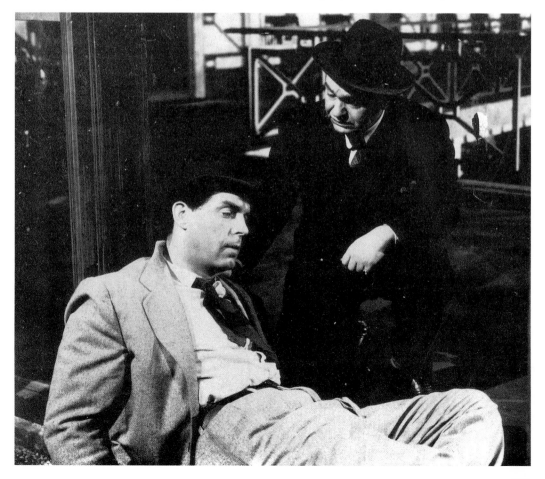

165

the money nor the woman. In preventing Neff from getting the woman, the film repeats the much-rehearsed idea of adultery, not marriage, as the realm of desire; in not allowing him to get the money, it fulfils the pattern of poetic justice demanded by the Production Code that frustrated all attempts by characters in Hollywood *films noirs* to live by ill-gotten gains. The twinning of adulterous desire and criminality not only highlights the indiscriminate power of transgression, but also stresses the quasi-sexual thrills of theft and, concomitantly, the potentially disruptive nature of sexual desire.

In subjective narratives, our knowledge of the characters is limited by refraction through the perceptions, memories and rhetoric of the narrating character. Equally, however, this method of narration has the great advantage of focusing on the inner schisms and contradictions of a mind in crisis struggling to impose coherence on the chaos of self and society. As Deborah Thomas argues (in 'How Hollywood Deals with the Deviant Male'), *film noir* concentrates on the inner divisions of male characters, projecting on to their environment failures of perception and lack of self-knowledge that lead either to ruin or to reintegration into the established order. As the *noir* anti-hero confesses his guilt, the process of self-dissolution and fragmentation on which he embarks leads to the further process of questioning and subverting that quintessentially American cult, the triumph of the enterprising individual, here given its darkest, most despairing perspective.

Like the narration of many heroes and heroines of picaresque fiction, a literary genre with which *film noir* shares certain features, the protagonist's narration depends on rhetorical devices to justify criminal behaviour to a respected, law-abiding father figure; here the father figure is the apparent embodiment of all the dominant social norms from which the hero has been in flight, the super-ego-governed claims man, Keyes, who actually refers to himself lightheartedly at one point as 'poppa'. The name has all the aura of authority and of endorsement of a conformist society. Significantly, it is through Keyes that Neff feels compelled to be shriven, and perhaps the primary enigma of the film concerns the meaning he carries both for Neff specifically and for the doom-laden social and professional milieu in which he moves.

In two crucial scenes, Neff and Mrs Dietrichson each separately refer to keys in ways that cannot avoid echoing the claims man's surname. First, at the beginning of the film, when Neff is ushered somewhat suspiciously and grudgingly into the Dietrichsons' living room by the housemaid, Nettie, he replies to her unprovoked insult about keeping the liquor always locked up by saying that he always carries his own keys with him. Second, when Neff and Mrs Dietrichson meet for the first time after her husband has unwittingly signed the accident insurance form, Neff gives her the policy, insisting that it must be kept in the Dietrichsons' safety deposit box, asking if she has access to it, and she replies 'we both have keys.'

In the first instance, Neff unconsciously declares his willingness to abide by what in a brilliant article on the film Claire Johnston defined as the Law of the Father, 'the symbolic father . . . only imperfectly incarnate in the real father' (Johnston, 1978). If there is, as Johnston argues, an Oedipal relationship between the two men, it would seem only natural that the father leaves his mark on the son. The two men are intimately linked, through friendship, through experience (Keyes discloses that he had once had a terrible liaison with a woman, the consequences of which have left him not far short of out-and-out misogyny) and through ideology (for however much of a transgressor against Pacific All Risk and Mr Dietrichson Neff might be, his behaviour in most other ways marks him out as a conformist, very much in the Keyes mould). This identification between Neff and Keyes is paralleled by Mrs Dietrichson's 'we both have keys', which identifies her husband both with Keyes and also by now with Neff, who carries keys/Keyes around with him.

For all their superficial differences, the three men are in many ways alike. For instance, all three are associated with footballing metaphors: Mr Dietrichson (Tom Powers) almost made 'the Varsity'; Neff also played football and refers to Keyes's initial reactions to Mrs Dietrichson's death and the filed insurance claim by saying 'you were almost playing on our team.' Even Keyes himself challenges the company's president with 'you've got the ball; let's see you run with it . . . you fumbled on the goal line.' So, Mrs Dietrichson's line suggests that she has managed to give herself a double dose of Keyes, the claims man's ideological alter egos, her husband and Neff. The 'double' indemnity she claims – quite apart from the hoped-for $100,000 and release from an inconsiderate and boorish husband – would in reality be, in a variety of unsuspected ways, a second helping of her husband, the reincarnation of the man she has made up her mind to have murdered. The similarities between all three men emerge, unrecognised by Neff, through his narration, the verbal and visual rhetoric of which constantly sharpens the focus on him, revealing his affinity with the system he seems at first glance so desperate to subvert. But the first and perhaps most striking example of the identification occurs at the very beginning of the film. The silhouette of a man on crutches slowly approaches the viewer as the credits roll against Miklos Rozsa's portentous, doom-laden music, its pounding brass chords and slow drum beat emphasising the sombre fate of two men, husband and lover, both victims of a fatal passion.

From what we are allowed to know of him through Neff's narrative, Dietrichson embodies the stereotype of the ideological conformist who treats his wife like a drudge, resorting to dismissive, almost contemptuous language in addressing or referring to her, even in company, and warming to Neff when a mutual interest in manly sports surfaces. Superficially, of course, Dietrichson is set up as the fall-guy not only for his wife, but for Neff too. He is presented as the dour alternative to Neff, everything that Neff promises he will not be. In his relations with his wife, he has created the *ne plus ultra* of what P.L. Berger and H. Kellner have described as modern marriage's progression from the matrix of wider community relationships to a segregated, claustrophobic sub-world of imprisoning intimacy ('Marriage and the Construction of Reality' in Michael Anderson, ed., *Sociology of the Family*, Penguin, Harmondsworth, 1982). Yet, beneath the veneer of Dietrichson's uncouth dismissiveness of his wife lie some of the displaced, alienated tendencies of Neff's own confused and in some ways neurotic identity, where even sporting metaphors conjure up not the aura of confident, upbeat masculinity so characteristic of a nation's psyche under normal circumstances, but a vision of compromise and fallen idols.

The affinities between the two men are further emphasised through use of another sporting metaphor, not football this time, but boxing, a sport notorious for its exposure in Hollywood cinema of the ugly underside of the American Dream. Dietrichson calls his daughter Lola (Jean Heather) a 'great little fighter for her weight', after she pugnaciously answers the charge that she is going to town to meet her boyfriend, Nino Zacchette (Byron Barr). Neff has three prints of boxers hanging on his sitting room wall, a detail hyperbolising both the male ambience of his home and the aggressive nature of his personality.

Now, Dietrichson's coarse, authoritarian attitude in exchanges with his wife is echoed by Neff. For instance, at their first meeting in the supermarket, their conspiratorial meeting-place, he delivers a series of orders, overriding her attempts to speak.

Phyllis: Walter, I want to . . .
Walter: Not so loud.
Phyllis: I wanted to talk to you ever since yesterday.
Walter: Let me talk first. You never saw it [the accident insurance policy], you never even saw it, you understand?
Phyllis: I'm not a fool.

Later, at the railway station, he delivers a stream of orders which, she complains, he has already previously given several times over. Neff has arrogantly assumed a responsibility to take the lead, refusing to listen to the advice of his accomplice, convinced that her female level of competence requires instructions to be constantly repeated if they are to be grasped.

In the first two scenes with Mrs Dietrichson, Neff employs a salesman's ingratiating banter: the remarks about her not being fully covered (by insurance and towels) while she sunbathes, the joke about his name having 'two fs as in *The Philadelphia Story*' (an interesting anachronism: Neff's dated memo shows the film to be set in

1938 – a common way at the time of avoiding reference to the war – but the play was not produced until 1939, while the film appeared in 1940), the refusal to say whether he likes her name, 'Phyllis', until he has 'driven it around the block a couple of times', and the insolent innuendo in his speed metaphors ('How fast was I going officer?'). All of this vanishes beneath the surfacing menace of patronising attitudes after he has decided to go along with the murder.

In many ways, Walter Neff represents the darker side of Philip Marlowe. If Marlowe is a soiled Californian Galahad, tilting at the windmills of individual and corporate wickedness, Neff portrays the knight who has forsaken the defence of a dubious and hypocritical social order, deciding henceforward to strike out for himself. Neff has much of Marlowe's intelligence, determination, initiative and wit, but puts all these attributes to the service of a swelling egocentricity. Like the heroes of ancient myths and classical narratives, he relies on rare qualities, although the divinities with whom he clashes here are the secular upholders of the Law, all patriarchs and corporate men. A downtown Prometheus, moving in the *noir* world, he has stolen the secret of the gods, fire itself. Keyes, most powerful of the divinities in the grubby paradise of insurance salesmen, always has his cigar lit for him, as if magically, by Neff, flicking each match into flame by the click of a thumb. Yet when Walter is on the point of dying at the very end of the film, Keyes, for the first and last time, reverses the action, a fond and reassuring gesture informing us, as if we didn't know, that he knew all along how to light his own cigar, was himself the source of fire, and therefore also, in keeping with the mythic resonances created by these patterns, of knowledge itself. What Walter dared steal, heavenly fire or, in the film's terms, the economic and social potency of the system, Keyes now retrieves. Here, lighting cigars takes on the significance not only of bonding in male friendships, but also of locating the origins of the social, moral and economic order of American society at the very centre of a patriarchal system. Fire, the 'key' to life itself, belongs to the film's most paternalistic, misogynistic father figure, Barton Keyes.

Neff's motivation lies partly in his desire, a common enough feature of *film noir* (e.g. *Scarlet Street*, Fritz Lang, 1945; *Human Desire*, Lang, 1954; *Gilda*, Charles Vidor, 1946), to cheat the system. Neff himself describes this very clearly:

'. . . it was all tied up with something I'd been thinking about for years, since long before I ran into Phyllis Dietrichson. Because, you know how it is, Keyes, in this business you can't sleep for trying to figure out all the tricks they could pull on you. You're like the guy behind the roulette wheel watching the customers to make sure they don't crook the house. And then, one night, you get to thinking how you could crook the house yourself, and do it smart . . .'

Still: Phyllis Dietrichson (Barbara Stanwyck) tells Walter Neff how much she hates her husband.

Testing your wits against men like Keyes, getting your own back on a system that works you hard and pays you not enough, breaking free of obligations to business executives already gorged on profit, striking out against the odds for the sheer hell of it, all this and more prompts Neff into going for the limit.

But cheating the system, or (in keeping with the film's gesture to a traditional metaphor) stealing the fire, or the ideological essence, of the Pacific All Risk, is only a fraction of Neff's motivation. Equally compelling is his desire for Mrs Dietrichson, but, again, he once more unconsciously betrays not only the adult passions but also the regressive neuroses by which he has been gripped. Desire for an attractive married woman unlocks the most virulent of these.

Like most *films noirs*, *Double Indemnity* relies on the disruptive presence of a *femme fatale*. Barbara Stanwyck's Phyllis Dietrichson bristles with the characteristic toughness and resilience of a persona developed in the 'thirties and 'forties through roles ranging from screwball heroines to melodramatic victims, giving as good as she gets in battles of wit or desire. The screwball *femme fatale* of *The Lady Eve*, hopelessly entangling the *ingénu* innocent-abroad, Henry Fonda, in coils of wit and deception, loses her comic aura here as she casts her irresistible spell over Walter Neff, the wise-cracking but shop-soiled and, in her company, ultimately inept novice of love and life. For the greater part of the film, she seems to exemplify the stereotype of the icy, self-absorbed and cruel lady of desire. (Neil Sinyard and Adrian Turner in *Journey Down Sunset Boulevard, The Films of Billy Wilder*, BCW Press, Ryde, 1979, p.261, quite plausibly see in the transformation of the novel's 'Nirdlinger' into

the film's 'Dietrichson' a reference to the queen of all *femmes fatales*, Marlene Dietrich.)

On her first appearance, naked except for a towel, she looks down from the top of the staircase at a drooling Neff, as if from a pinnacle of power and desire, favouring him with a miraculous appearance. From then on, her cool and calculating strategies are designed to cause havoc, as she strives single-mindedly to strike at the male order in the pursuit of unbridled self-gratification. Remote, languidly sensual, she never laughs and rarely shows even the merest flicker of a smile on her ivory-hard face. Stanwyck's streetwise spider lady here finds her definition through association with hot-house blooms. These are not the benign and life-enhancing flowers that create an aura of pastoral idylls, but the cloying, sickly-sweet Sadean emblems of a rotten ('we're both rotten'), fallen world, principally the black orchids decorating her white blouse, which is worn over a black skirt with black tassels that are fingered menacingly at the moment her husband signs his life away, but also the honeysuckle blooms remarked on by Neff after his first visit to her domain of sickly-sweet corruption.

Here, Stanwyck's prototype of *femmes fatales* in *film noir* – a portrayal at first troubling but subsequently pleasing to studio executives – cuts through Chandler and Wilder's placing of her as someone to a large extent projected through Neff's distorted rhetoric, bursting through the constraints of his narration and framing of her, and by her very presence making her own powerful statement of challenge and transgression. A fallen angel, she is a throw-back to the unfeeling, pallid, fatal woman of nineteenth-century literature. In her metallic blondeness, she is not the self-consciously sexual dark lady of her deadly sisters in the genre (Mary Astor, Jane Greer, Joan Bennett), but seems beyond sexuality, an idol of limitless self-engrossed and cruel fatality, rather than of illicit passion. As the lighting, make-up, and costume combine to emphasise the negative ideological rhetoric of the *femme fatale*, Stanwyck's portrayal of ice-cool, self-conscious and calculating evil creates an image of such compelling egocentricity that it all but destroys the viewer's sympathy for Neff, Mr Dietrichson, or any of the other men who may have been her victims. In one scene, at Neff's apartment, as he explains how a woman who tried a similar stunt paid dearly for murdering her husband, she replies, 'perhaps it was worth it to her.' As she speaks the words, softly, ruefully, menacingly, the low-key lighting has only Phyllis's eyes properly lit; the rest of her face remains in darkness. Her eyes move languidly above a faint but unmistakable sneer, and at a stroke the scene is taken from Neff. Despite his nervous prattle about past case histories, the scene belongs to Phyllis, her power, her aura of a resolutely determined woman becoming the image of unnerving and awesome evil.

If, negatively, Barbara Stanwyck's *femme fatale* perpetuates the myth of the female castrator, her involvement in the narrative and the rhetoric of her presentation do at least, more positively, challenge the process of female integration into the established social order. Marrying Dietrichson for his money is, if nothing else, a sign of anti-social predatoriness, but the film leaves one in little doubt that in a 'forties world of male privilege, where a woman's best chance of acquiring status frequently lay most securely in submission to a socially privileged male, Phyllis's manipulation of the system works against the injustices of the legitimising process in the very act of its apparent affirmation. The *femme fatale* here runs even more true to type in her further representation of a self-centred denial of motherhood. By contrast, Dietrichson's first wife – murdered by Phyllis – had been a mother as well as a wife, a union from which the teenage daughter Lola has survived. Phyllis's childlessness represents, like her self-absorbed narcissism, a terrible affront to the bourgeois order. Although, by the end of the film, Phyllis's repressed humanity breaks through to acknowledge the wickedness of her enslavement of Neff in her murderous scheme, the rest of her performance, fulfilling the demands of the stereotyped monstrous castrator, exudes calm under pressure, control and self-possession, with her gestures and language establishing her above all as a ruthless white devil or '*belle dame sans merci*'. Her manipulation of Neff through language shows up in their earliest dialogue exchanges:

Phyllis: There's a speed limit in this state Mr Neff, 45mph.

Walter: How fast was I going officer?
Phyllis: I'd say around 90.
Walter: Suppose you get down off your motorcycle and give me a ticket?
Phyllis: Suppose I let you off with a warning this time?
Walter: Suppose it doesn't take?
Phyllis: Suppose I have to whack you over the knuckles?
Walter: Suppose I burst out crying and rest my head on your shoulder?
Phyllis: Suppose you try putting it on my husband's shoulder?
Walter: That tears it.

Owing nothing here to the original Cain novel, the Chandler/Wilder dialogue stages a three-round verbal contest with a knockout victory for Phyllis. First, Neff takes the initiative and attempts to gain control, with the camera highlighting his bid to gain the upper hand over her by placing his face squarely in medium shot in front of the viewer. Next, Phyllis takes over, responding aggressively by threatening to whack him over the knuckles, a Sadean touch that actually also appeals to him, and then, in the last round, by appropriating his own rhetorical use of anaphora (Suppose etc.), she delivers the linguistic killer punch.

Her embodiment of the sadomasochistic tendencies and provocations of the dragon lady stereotype complements the patterns of Neff's early reactions to the anklet, seen in close-up as she walks down the Dietrichson home's staircase, and then dangled invitingly in front of him as she crosses her legs in the living-room, an anklet he relishes all the more, reminiscing later, for cutting into her flesh. In this further evocation of sadomasochistic desires, where Mrs Dietrichson becomes a *dominatrice* and Neff a cry-baby looking for a mother on whose shoulders to rest his head, Neff's neurosis begins to reveal itself more luridly.

On the surface, Neff's attraction to Mrs Dietrichson is motivated by sexual desire for an attractive, sexually self-conscious woman, her seduction also becoming another transgression against the social order, with Mr Dietrichson's status – embodied in his glamorous wife – accruing to Neff through her act of infidelity. Yet in the language he uses both to describe and address her, he reveals a psychological disturbance inspired as much by a need to rescue her from a loveless marriage as by an unconscious desire to indulge a sexual aberration.

In *A Poetics of Composition* (University of California Press, 1973), Boris Uspensky catalogues the various means available in literary texts for establishing point of view. Of these, terms of address are among the most effective, and in this film, as also later in *The Blue Dahlia* (George Marshall, 1946), Chandler seems obsessed by the revelation, or conversely the concealment, by characters of their own real names. In *The*

Blue Dahlia, the names motif is related to thematic questions about difficulties of communication through the fog of preconceptions and prejudice. Seeing the initials J.M. on his bag, Veronica Lake goes through a playful routine with Alan Ladd, trying to discover his identity. 'Johnny's a nice name, too,' she comments, when he says she should call him by his 'real' name.

In *Double Indemnity*, Neff seems very eager to know the name engraved on Mrs Dietrichson's anklet. Perhaps in part unconsciously disavowing the threat posed by her sexuality, after he has discovered her name, Neff only once calls Mrs Dietrichson 'Phyllis'. Seemingly, Neff is governed by equivocal impulses: on the one hand, attracted to 'Phyllis' because she represents transgression, first, because as a married woman she offers him another opportunity to beat the system, and, second, because she herself epitomises transgression; on the other hand, fearing castration by the transgressive, phallic woman, he prefers to call her 'Baby', which embodies his fundamentally patronising attitude towards her.

Except in the scene in which she is saying goodbye to Neff in the role of her husband as he climbs aboard the train on which the accident is supposed to take place, Phyllis only calls Neff 'Walter'. At the station, she sensibly calls him 'Honey', the term by which she addresses her husband. (In a house reeking with the sweet, cloying smell of honeysuckle, it seems appropriate that the murderous wife should call her husband

Still: Walter disguised as Dietrichson; Phyllis seeing him off at the station.

'Honey'.) But the appellation 'Honey' also suggests a link between the two men, as if Phyllis's feelings for her dead husband are displaced on to Neff, who has lost his own identity and is to be regarded henceforward, whatever his feelings for Mrs Dietrichson, as a double for his own murder victim. Yet honeysuckle, symbol for the atmosphere of destructive sexuality surrounding the Dietrichson home, is also linked indirectly with the way he himself habitually refers to Phyllis as 'Baby'.

Up to their second meeting, even though his muted but unmistakable ribaldry, barely concealed leers, and what she herself calls his 'fresh' behaviour, have reduced her in his mind's eye to the status of desirable and available adulteress, Neff has scrupulously respected middle-class etiquette by addressing Phyllis as 'Mrs Dietrichson'. But as soon as she hints unambiguously at her plan to murder her husband, he discards any remaining shred of courtesy, reducing her to the sex object and infantilised subordinate implied by his use of the word 'Baby' in the remark 'You'll never get away with it Baby.' 'Baby', of course, is common enough as a term of endearment, as capable of expressing genuine, individualised affection as, on this occasion, of signifying the reverse.

The verbal signposting of Neff's attitude towards Phyllis continues right to the end ('Don't be silly, Baby' preludes remarks about why he is going to shoot her). Apart from revealing his unconscious desire to infantilise Phyllis, Neff's use of 'Baby' offers him a route to controlling through language this woman who poses so overwhelming, mature and sophisticated a threat. The point is visually emphasised in the first of the supermarket scenes. As Walter and Phyllis talk, their bodies are framed by cans of baby food, a mother interrupts their conversation to reach for a can (the childless, adulterous and transgressive discourse in collision with the ideology of motherhood), and Walter uses the term 'Baby' twice at the end of the scene.

But if in Walter's confused imagining, Phyllis is infantilised and stripped of her social status through exposure of adulterous and murderous desires, she is also, contradictorily, a helpless, powerless woman, appealing to his chivalrous instincts to rescue her from a life of matrimonial misery. In a way that seems highly relevant to an understanding of *Double Indemnity*, Sigmund Freud, in 'A Special Type of Object Choice', describes neurotic behaviour in love, focusing on a particular form and pursuit of object choice in men, for which he argues that there are four preconditions: first, that the beloved must be attached to someone else, usually a husband, so that there must be an injured third party; second, that the woman in question should be in some way, as Freud puts it, of 'bad repute sexually, whose fidelity and reliability are open to some doubt'; third, fidelity to one love-object is impossible, with the compulsive lover repeating his

obsession with a series of women; fourth, that
lovers of this type are characterised by a desire
to 'rescue the woman they love', such men being
convinced of these women's need of them. All
of these conditions, Freud goes on to argue, are
'derived from the infantile fixation of tender
feelings on the mother, and represent one of the
consequences of that fixation' (*On Sexuality*,
Penguin, Harmondsworth, 1977, pp.227-242).

Walter Neff's behaviour neatly fits into this
category of sexually aberrant or neurotic lover.
First, Phyllis is married, and an underlying identification has already been established between
Mr Dietrichson and Keyes, both father figures,
so, as in the Freudian mould, 'the injured third
party is none other than the father himself'.
Second, her unreliable fidelity and sexual availability are immediately apparent to Neff: the
anklet scene not only draws attention to her
institutionalised enslavement but also suggests
both prostitution (cheap, sexually-aware, fetish-
istic jewellery), and bondage. Walter's obsession
with Phyllis's anklet, especially his recollection
that it 'cuts into her flesh,' points beyond what
Freud calls recognisable links between cruelty and
sexual instinct to an exaggerated aggressiveness
whose twin aims are debasement and subjugation of the love-object, a tendency already noted

Still: Walter shoots Phyllis.

in his variously hectoring, authoritarian or
insinuating language towards her. As Michel
Foucault also notes, 'where there is desire, the
power relation is already present' (*The History of
Sexuality*, vol.1, Peregrine, Harmondsworth, 1984,
p.81). Sex, at least in Walter's conception,
seems to bear out Foucault's view of it as a pivot
of power, a concept of the couple incapable of
formulation without a motivating principle of
inevitable mutual exploitation. Walter's sadism
is primarily generated by transferred Oedipal
neuroses: 'Walter, you're hurting me,' Phyllis
complains when he embraces her after his decision
to murder Dietrichson, his violent intentions
towards the husband confounded now with a
sadistically libidinal embrace of the wife. Additionally, Walter's sadism may not ultimately be
detached from a parallel enslavement to masochistic pleasures, and an unavowed hope that
pleasurable involvement with her will also inevitably bring him pain. Third, Walter's comment
that, as a vaccum-cleaner salesman, he learned a
lot about life, testifies to a series of previous sexual
liaisons – he also wears a wedding ring. Lastly,
like Freud's neurotic, Walter also seeks to rescue
Phyllis from her marriage ('only with me around

171

you wouldn't have to knit'), in the process, at once protecting her from her own taste for sexual transgression and the dangers into which this may lead. Walter's use of the word 'Baby' may thus ultimately be taken as an unconscious expression of the neurotic basis of his displaced Oedipal desires.

In its preoccupation with regression of various types, crime, fragmentation of male identity, female duplicity, urban unease and consumerist excess, *Double Indemnity* falls squarely within *film noir*, providing what Paul Schrader sees as a bridge between its wartime and postwar phases. With its direct (trains, cigars, flowers) and indirect (baby imagery) allusions to the more popular symbols of Freudian psychoanalysis, the film belongs very much to its time – coping with the pressures, anxieties, and self-doubt caused by war, the United States became increasingly introverted and hooked on analysis. Even if – accepting the argument of several writers on the genre – a major consequence of such introversion is the implicit redefinition in many *films noirs* of women's place as again primarily being in the home, it seems clear that in *Double Indemnity*, for Chandler and Wilder at least, these routes lead only to dead ends.

On the evidence of this film, marriage is potentially a recipe for betrayal and murder. American texts on necessary flight from the entrapments of marriage, family and culture are too numerous to catalogue, but there can be no bleaker vision of the ideology of bourgeois marriage than *Double Indemnity*. (Wilder's comedies, such as *The Apartment*, 1960, and *Kiss Me, Stupid*, 1964, make the same point, but more with resignation than with despair.) If such texts as *The Adventures of Huckleberry Finn* are celebrations of regression through flight from the socialising process, *Double Indemnity* shows despairingly that, for men at least, regression can also be a deadly force, especially if provoked by the Oedipally-motivated desire for the sexual conquest of a seductress. The film is, admittedly, guilty of continuing the mythology of the *femme fatale*, but while its attitude to women all too frequently betrays some of the dread and misrepresentation of an elusive 'other' (as also in the Marlowe novels, the Chandler-scripted *Strangers on a Train*, Alfred Hitchcock, 1951, and *The Blue Dahlia*, and Wilder's *Kiss Me Stupid*, *A Foreign Affair*, 1948, *The Seven Year Itch*, 1955, *Sunset Boulevard*, 1950, and so on), its treatment of men cannot be accused of pulling any punches: the husband is a boor, Nino Zachette, Lola's lover, an impetuous, self-regarding adolescent, Keyes a misogynist, Norton (Richard Gaines), the company president, incompetent, and Jackson (Porter Hall), the witness on the train, someone who cheats on his wife. Neff, for all his wisecracking and his ultimate act of philanthropy – with a sentimentalism that fails to mask his deep-rooted conservatism and ideologically motivated endorsement of a potentially disastrous

union, he persuades Zachette to go back to Lola – is mainly an impressionable egoist with sexually aberrant tendencies.

Lola is another character rebelling against the prevailing order, behaving secretly as a transgressor even though she gives the impression of a pert, dutiful daughter, of someone obeying the demands of patriarchal decorum. Pretending to like playing Chinese chequers with a stepmother she loathes, fooling her out-of-touch father into thinking she has a date with a girlfriend and not the boyfriend of whom he disapproves, Lola is, as Neff puts it, 'a nice kid' whose development as a teenager finds no understanding or room for self-expression and honesty in a family loaded with prejudices of one sort or another. Characterised by a natural, dark colouring of hair and complexion, in stark contrast to Phyllis's blonde metallic look, she is everything her stepmother is not: a young woman blossoming naturally, despite all the odds, into maturity, even if restricted by the virginal stereotype that all the nice boys in the audience were expected to go for once the initial excitement but ultimately castrating realities of the *femme fatale* had been worked out of their systems.

So with Lola perhaps leading the way as a counter-influence to the wickedness of other characters, Chandler and Wilder still manage to present the human condition in ways that ultimately escape the facile denials and exasperations of mere pessimism and gloom. Through all the relentless bleakness and despair, the film's humour (especially the exchanges between Walter and Phyllis, or Walter and Keyes) and its stylised portrayal of corrupt sensuality shine through as qualified affirmations of the redemptive potential that makes life worth living even under the most bitter and wretched circumstances of economic, social and psychological confusion.

But overwhelmingly, the film's texture reflects an ambience of darkness, seediness, loneliness and self-centredness. The *mise-en-scène* of office or home interiors, in their Venetian-blind chiaroscuro patterns, or in their night settings, creates a world of relentless gloom and bleakness, and the characters are defined in their solitude or imprisonment. The insurance office where Neff works echoes the nightmarish confines of the workers' underground level in *Metropolis*, a dehumanised world of endless, soul-destroying labour; the railway settings with their impersonal, lonely atmosphere suggest desperate journeys leading nowhere; the supermarket, sign of rampant consumerism, offers only material, not emotional, consolation. The Dietrichson home, with its Venetian blinds, photo frames and fish bowl, always expresses entrapment. It is a space that shuts out the suburban Los Angeles sun, to which Phyllis instinctively turns, her sunbathing becoming a sign of escape from domestic or marital oppression, her outburst of murderous exasperation fittingly defined by Neff as the rain tapping on his window and perhaps taken by the audience as an expression of the film's overall ambience of tragedy. The *mise-en-scène* of twisted desires, primarily of murder but also of the libido – captured in part by Neff's crude talk of 'red hot pokers' – arouses mixed responses in the viewer.

Inevitably, we are repelled by the lovers' killing of Mr Dietrichson. But we are also drawn into partially accepting their behaviour as an understandable even if not ultimately pardonable act of violence against individual or social forms of subjugation. Our mixed responses are perhaps nowhere more teasingly aroused than in the scene immediately after the laying of Dietrichson's body on the railway track. The get-away car fails to start as Phyllis tries to turn the engine over. After a couple of shots at it,

Neff takes over, and the audience breathes a sigh of relief as the car finally starts. The scene demands our complicity, forces us to will their triumph, even if only momentarily, over Dietrichson, the system and our better natures. But, as Neff is identified with Dietrichson, so are we identified with him, forced even if passingly into not only empathising with Phyllis as she rebels both against a tyrant of a husband and the conservative ideology he represents, but also with Walter, regressing, looking in Phyllis for a fusion of dominant mother and complaisant whore, to recognise the 'Baby', perhaps, of our own neurosis-bred fantasies and desires.

Still: Phyllis and Walter dump the body of Dietrichson on the railroad tracks.

DETOUR

Andrew Britton

Edgar G. Ulmer's *Detour* (1945) was filmed in six days on a minimal budget. No-one noticed its existence when it was released, and although it has since acquired what Leonard Maltin calls a 'deserved cult following', its true stature has never really been appreciated, and such critical writing on it as there is tends to misrepresent it. It is also quite scandalously difficult to see if one lives outside North America: at the time of writing, no commercial print exists anywhere in Europe (although it has just become available on tape in Britain). A work can hardly be recognised as a classic if no-one has access to it, and yet there seems to me no doubt that *Detour* deserves classical status. It is not only one of the greatest *films noirs*, but also one of the most demanding and audacious narratives ever produced in Hollywood.

The unreliable narrator

'This is the excellent foppery of the world, that, when we are sick in fortune, often the surfeits of our own behaviour, we make guilty of our disasters the sun, the moon, and stars; as if we were villains on necessity, fools by heavenly compulsion, knaves, thieves, and treachers by spherical predominance, drunkards, liars, and adulterers by an enforc'd obedience of planetary influence; and all that we are evil in, by a divine thrusting on. An admirable evasion of whoremaster man, to lay his goatish disposition to the charge of a star!' William Shakespeare, *King Lear*, I, ii.

It is hardly possible to watch *Detour* without becoming aware that the film seems to attach great importance to the idea of fate, and it has sometimes been argued that the whole work is pervaded by a depressed and nihilistic determinism. (For example: 'Ulmer's films reveal that the director does believe in intangible forces . . . [like] externally imposed fate . . . which circumscribe the free will of his characters. They exercise little or no control over their destinies' John Belton, *Cinema Stylists*, Scarecrow Press, Metuchen, 1983, p.153). Certainly, the film's hero, Al Roberts (Tom Neal), seizes every opportunity to insist that a malicious destiny is responsible for all his troubles. 'From then on,' he tells us, apropos of the death of Haskell (Edmund MacDonald), 'something else stepped in and shunted me off to a different destination than the one I'd picked

for myself.' A few scenes later, fate intervenes once more by introducing Al to Vera (Ann Savage), the only person in the world who is in a position to know that Al must have stolen Haskell's car and disposed of its original owner. 'Just my luck picking *her* up on the road,' he says, and proceeds to complain that this gratuitous calamity is typical of 'life', which delights in giving fate the opportunity to 'stick out a foot to trip you'. His experiences as Vera's travelling companion and putative spouse reinforce Al's conviction that he is the helpless plaything of the gods, and as the police car draws up beside him in the final shot, he leaves us with the warning that 'fate, or some mysterious force, can put the finger on you or me for no good reason at all.' As far as Al is concerned, everything that happens to him is completely arbitrary. He has come to a bad end because providence assigned him one, and, as he surrenders to the inevitable, he has at least the comfort of knowing that things would have turned out much better if he had been left to his own devices.

Vera is neither an impartial nor a sympathetic observer of Al's predicament, but when she tells him, with the lack of feeling which comes to her so naturally, that 'you got yourself into this thing,' she has the film's unqualified support. The whole meaning of *Detour* depends on the fact that Al is incapable of providing the impartial account of the action which convention leads us to expect in first-person narratives, and when we examine the film's detail, we discover that his commentary has a dramatic status quite different from that of O'Hara (Orson Welles) in *The Lady from Shanghai* (Welles, 1948) or Philip Marlowe (Dick Powell) in *Farewell, My Lovely* (Edward Dmytryk, 1944). O'Hara and Marlowe are to be thought of simply as speaking the truth, both about themselves and about the narrative world in general. They may be mistaken, but they never equivocate, and their impersonality is never questioned for a moment. Al's commentary, however, though it is not hypocritical – he plainly believes every word of it – is profoundly self-deceived and systematically unreliable. 'Did you ever want to cut away a piece of your memory and blot it out?' he asks us as the film goes into flashback, implying that the truth of what he is about to say is guaranteed by the pain involved in remembering it. In fact, Al's memory

of the past is in itself a means of blotting it out, and his commentary, far from serving as the clue which leads us infallibly to the meaning of the narrative action, is like a palimpsest beneath which we may glimpse the traces of the history he has felt compelled to rewrite.

Our suspicions are (or ought to be) aroused by the betraying discrepancy between Al's description of his relationship with Sue (Claudia Drake) and what we are shown of their last evening together. According to Al, he himself is 'an ordinary, healthy guy' and Sue is 'an ordinary, healthy girl', and when you 'add those two things together, you get an ordinary, healthy romance' which is 'somehow the most wonderful thing in the world'. It may be thought that Al protests too much, and it is certainly difficult to reconcile this rhetoric with the couple's actual behaviour, the most striking feature of which is the suppressed mutual frustration of partners who want completely different things, both for themselves and for each other. Sue insists that they have 'all the time in the world to settle down,' and wishes to postpone their marriage until each of them has established a successful career. Al wishes to 'make with the ring and licence' at once – not because he is in love, as he wishes retrospectively to believe, but because he has in practice abandoned his expressed ambition to become a concert pianist and decided instead to assume the character of the embittered failure who might have made something of himself if fate

Frame: 'A little bit like working in heaven ' – Al (Tom Neal) and Sue (Claudia Drake) performing in the nightclub.

had not strewn his path with rocks and briars. He has no obvious reason to suppose that he will be incapacitated by arthritis by the time his great chance comes, or that he will be obliged to make his Carnegie Hall debut in the basement, 'as a janitor'. He has simply concluded that this is the way life must be, and the willed (if unconscious) defeatism implicit in his attitude to his blighted career is the first sign of his habitual tendency to attribute his own choices, and their disastrous consequences, to forces external to himself.

Since Al's desire to marry Sue is in fact inseparable from his jaded acquiescence in the necessity of his own failure, it is hardly surprising that his treatment of her is consistently peremptory, and there is no real evidence that he is even fond of her. Indeed, he refuses so much as to listen to, let alone discuss, her plans for their future, even though she makes it clear that she is doing what she thinks is best for both of them, and as soon as he realises that she is not prepared to bow to his wishes, he virtually breaks off the relationship, with calculated churlishness, and walks off on his own in a sulk. However, Al is more than willing to take advantage of Sue's initiative once it has occurred to him that advantage can be taken, and his dramatic change of heart, experienced as the revival of love, is actually inspired by the dawning of a suspicion that a future with Sue might, after all, be a better bet than a future without her. A customer in the nightclub has just rewarded his efforts at the piano with a 'ten-spot' of which he remarks, significantly, that 'it couldn't buy anything *I* want,' and if he now discovers that he is devoted to Sue after all and is even ready to 'crawl' to California to join her, that is because the fantasy of her success, however irrational, at least contrasts favourably with his current prospects. 'It was nice to think of Sue shooting for the top,' he tells us. The ten-dollar bill is a painful reminder of the limits of what he is likely to gain through his own industry (the waiter who hands it to him rubs salt in the wound by remarking that he has 'hit the jack-pot'), and he therefore sets out to gain what he can from Sue's.

Ulmer uses these brief, and extraordinarily elliptical, expository sequences to define his hero as a man who lacks all sense of aim and purpose, who is essentially indifferent to everything but what he takes, at a given moment, to be his own interests, and who, above all, instinctively rationalises his convenience on all occasions, either by absolving himself of responsibility for his actions completely or by providing himself with a spurious but flattering account of his motives. We have thus been carefully prepared to understand why Al behaves as he does when Haskell dies. It is, of course, crucial that Haskell's death is the result either of a genuine accident or of natural causes: we have seen him taking pills regularly, and since his body is already completely inert when it falls from the car, it seems likely that he has simply died in his sleep. The question is never resolved, and is, in fact, immaterial – though it is certainly important that Al, who has noticed the pills, should choose not to become aware at this point that Haskell may have been mortally ill. He opts instead to convince himself that if he tried to tell the truth, no one would believe him; that even Haskell, in the unlikely event of his recovery, 'would swear [Al had] knocked him on the head for his dough,' and that he therefore has no choice but to get rid of Haskell's corpse and appropriate his effects, which is 'just what the police would say [he] did even if [he] didn't.' The necessity of this remarkable course of action is so obviously dubious that Al feels constrained for once to anticipate our incredulity, and refers testily to 'that "Don't-make-me-laugh!" expression on [our] faces.' At some level, he seems to recognise that his actual motive was pure greed, but, unlike Vera, he cannot bring himself frankly to admit that he is primarily interested in money and will go to any lengths to get it. The very fact that he should be driven to prevaricate with us only serves to emphasise the intensity of his need to think well of himself, and he fairly bombards us with far-fetched and superfluous alibis, including the culpable negligence of Emily Post in failing 'to write a book of rules for guys thumbing rides' so that they have some means of knowing 'what's right and what's wrong.' Al is a parasite and an opportunist of the most cynical kind, but he can grasp his opportunities only if he has first disavowed his reasons for doing so.

Given that he has just concealed a dead body in a ditch and is now driving a stolen car, Al has the most compelling of motives not to pick up a hitch-hiker, and Ulmer's treatment of his fatal rendezvous with Vera is the single most astonishing example of the film's oblique and cryptic narrative method. We are not explicitly alerted to the fact that Al's decision to give Vera a lift stands in particular need of an explanation, and Al himself has nothing to say on the subject beyond the simple observation that 'there was a woman . . . ,' as he draws into the gas station. Ulmer merely shows us what happens, just as he showed us the events which precipitated Al's earlier decision to join Sue in California, and we are perfectly at liberty to take both incidents at face value, as if no more were at stake than the hero's realisation that he needs his beloved after all or his honest sympathy for a stranded wanderer. We can perceive that these crucial choices are in any way problematical only by relating them to what Al has said, done or inadvertently revealed in previous scenes, and, while Ulmer makes it *possible* for us to ask the appropriate questions, he also declines to *tell* us that we need to ask questions at all. The only clue we are offered on the present occasion is easily over-looked, for it consists of an apparently innocuous passage of narration in the sequence at the motel where Al spends the night between Haskell's death and the advent of Vera. He tells us that he will have to go on pretending to be Haskell until he gets to 'some city' in which he can be 'swallowed up', and then adds, 'In a city I should be safe enough.' 'Some city' is a vague destination, and the phrasing is significant because it suggests that Al is no longer thinking of joining Sue, of whom we hear no more, indeed, until after Al has realised that picking up Vera was a disastrous mistake which, tragically, has put 'a greater distance between Sue and [himself] than when [he] started out.' It has already been intimated to us that Sue swims in and out of Al's consciousness with the ebb and flow of his financial prospects, and Ulmer now implies that he comes to Vera's rescue because his new-found wealth has given him the sense that he is again a free agent, economically and sexually. He no longer feels a need to bank on the hypothesis that Sue will 'click' in California, and, since Vera seems to be available, he offers her a ride for much the same reasons that Haskell did. Even when Vera has revealed her true colours and Sue has accordingly been restored to favour, Al is still prepared to hedge his bets. He telephones Sue furtively from the apartment which Vera has rented, she herself having at last retired for the night, but decides at the last minute not to speak and hangs up, telling himself: 'Not yet, darling!

Tomorrow, maybe . . .' The operative word is 'maybe'. Al is not yet sure whether or not he will be able to dump Vera and get away with some, at least, of the profits from the sale of Haskell's car, and he refrains from rashly building a bridge which he may not have to cross.

In the brief interlude before Al finds out who Vera is, he recalls his first impressions of her, and they are fascinatingly incongruous. He begins by telling us that 'she looked as if she'd just been thrown off the crummiest freight-train in the world,' but a few moments later he is reflecting on her beauty: 'not the beauty of a movie actress, or the beauty you dream about when you're with your wife,' but a 'natural beauty [which is] almost homely because it's so real.' These contradictions are the residue of the process of rationalisation and revision to which all Al's memories have been subjected: he denies any sexual interest in Vera by portraying her, in opposition to the accredited archetypes of male erotic fantasy, as a generic farmer's daughter, and insists at the same time that he could not possibly have guessed what she was really like from her disarmingly folksy appearance. 'She seemed harmless enough,' he says, and, in the sense that Vera's demeanour does not actually proclaim her identity, this is true, if hardly remarkable. The fact remains, however, that Al's commentary is tellingly silent about the overwhelming impression of Vera's sexual knowingness which Ulmer and Ann Savage communicate to us in the extraordinary reverse tracking shot that accompanies her steady and deliberate progress towards Al's car.

Al misreads the evidence of her sexuality as evidence of an invitation to him, and his opening gambit is the standard observation that Vera reminds him of a girl he once knew in Phoenix. Her response is less than encouraging ('Are the girls in Phoenix that bad?'), but, before he can proceed further, she has discouraged him permanently by raising the subject of Haskell.

Given both the radical influence of psychoanalysis on *film noir* and Ulmer's background in the culture of Weimar Germany, it seems as likely as such things ever can be in the absence of external evidence that the idea of Al's narration in *Detour* was arrived at by way of the concept of 'secondary revision'. Sigmund Freud argues that our recollection of the past is governed by a mechanism of unconscious censorship, such that memories of events which we find too distressing to acknowledge are either repressed completely or reworked by fantasy so as to eliminate their potentially traumatic elements. Between them, repression and secondary revision allow us to remember the past inaccurately but without excessive pain, and the task of the analyst is to restore the memory's true contents to full consciousness by working back from the contradictions, anomalies and silences which invariably characterise the censored materials that the patient currently recalls. While there is not, and cannot be, an exact analogy between reading a film and the procedures of the psychoanalyst,

Frame: Al crosses the state line under the name of Charles Haskell.

Ulmer certainly obliges the spectator of *Detour* to deduce the film's meaning from the discrepancies between two incompatible discourses – the dramatised action and the hero's interpretation of it, the second of which has been distorted in ways, and for reasons, that Freud describes in the theory of censorship.

We should also bear in mind that the undermining of the authority of the narrative voice is a recurrent feature of literary modernism. Many of the late tales and novels of Henry James, for example, present us with a first-person narrator (*The Turn of the Screw*, *The Sacred Fount*) or a central consciousness (*The Ambassadors*, *The Beast in the Jungle*), who fails, or refuses, to understand the significance of the action and who gives an account of it that turns out to be false. James never explicitly warns us that we cannot trust the governess's every word in *The Turn of the Screw*, any more than Ulmer explicitly announces that Al's version of the past is inaccurate and self-serving, although, on the other hand, neither artist misleads us by suppressing or withholding the signs of the narrator's tendentiousness. The information we need in order to distance ourselves from the point of view of the protagonist is always potentially available, and if we fail to notice and make use of it, we cannot blame the author for deceiving us. The whole point of the strategy of unreliable narration is that we cannot gain access to the work until we have discarded the lazy assumptions and preconceptions about narrative which we have derived from other works, and on which we tend inertly to rely in making sense of new ones. The assumption that we can always believe what 'I' says is especially hard to renounce, not only because the only obvious alternative to it seems to be that the narrative is simply nonsense, but also because our instinctive identification with 'I' makes it necessary for us to doubt the reliability of our own perceptions and judgments before we can doubt the narrator's. Unreliable narration undermines the reader's *suffisance* along with the narrator's authority, and the sense of disorientation it induces is so extreme that one is hardly surprised that *Detour* is one of the few movies which have dared to make use of it. (The most extraordinary examples are *The Devil Is a Woman*, Josef von Sternberg, 1935, *Letter from an Unknown Woman*, Max Ophuls, 1948, and *Le Plaisir*, Ophuls, 1951. Elsewhere in this book, Douglas Pye discusses a rather different use of unreliable narration in the work of Fritz Lang.)

Gender

The four protagonists of *Detour* are the products of a single culture, but Ulmer never allows us to forget that this culture (whatever else may be said about it) is permeated by inequalities of sexual power, and that Sue and Vera are oppressed as women. Sue is the only character in the film whose ambitions for herself do not in any way entail the exploitation of others and who is prepared to plan her own future on the assumption that she has interests in common with someone else. The ambitions may be banal and unattainable, and the understanding of common interests entirely conventional – she wishes, in the end, to marry Al and settle down – but she nonetheless retains a capacity for disinterestedness to which her lover is a stranger, and which allows him to use her for his own purposes. Ulmer emphasises, of course, that Sue does not wait on Al's approval or support before leaving for California and that her decision is as much an attempt to escape from the degradation and harassment to which she is routinely exposed by her work in the nightclub as it is an initiative on behalf of the couple. Al fails to comprehend either motive, and, indeed, when Sue tells him that a drunk has made advances to her during the evening, his reaction ('What drunk?') is so peculiar that she takes him up on it: 'What does it matter *what* drunk?' Sue knows that her present situation is intolerable, and she has the independence required to go ahead with her project in the face of Al's opposition, but she does *not* see that the ideal of heterosexual domesticity to which she remains committed makes her vulnerable to forms of masculine predatoriness more insidious than the unwanted attentions of the customers in the club. Both the roles that are available to her – nightclub hostess and girlfriend/wife – are equally oppressive and demeaning, and the material success of which she dreams, even if she were to achieve it, would not spare her the consequences of the *structural* inequalities between the sexes which Al and Haskell take for granted. We cannot hope to understand Vera's role in the film, or the hysterical stridency and excessiveness of Ann Savage's glorious performance, until we have grasped this fact.

Ulmer prepares us carefully for the appearance of a heroine who may be found rebarbative by prefacing it with Haskell's sadistic and lubricious account of his unsuccessful attempt to rape her. As far as Haskell is concerned, Vera was, in a quite literal sense, fair game. 'I was fighting with the most dangerous animal in the world: a woman!', he declares, with the hunter's hyperbole, when Al inquires about the scratches on his hand. If women are wild animals, then it follows virtually by definition that they are also quarry. In any case, Haskell had the right to expect a gratuity for picking her up in the first place: 'Give a lift to a tomato, you expect her to be nice, don't you? What kinds of dames thumb rides? Sunday-school teachers?' Ulmer insists on both the egregious nastiness of the language and the nagging sense of impotence which Haskell's vainglorious bravado conceals, for he at once goes on to add that Vera 'must have thought she was riding with some fall-guy' and then to display the still more impressive scar ('Infection set in later') incurred in the knife fight which obliged him to leave home fifteen years earlier. Haskell recalls

Frame: Strangers When We Meet – Al and Sue in the club after hours.

this scrap as a 'duel', and makes much of the fact that the wound was inflicted by a sabre. Later, in the diner, he goes to great lengths to cut a dashing figure in front of the waitress, and hints broadly that he is a man of means ('Keep the change!'). Haskell plainly feels that he has an image to keep up, and, since Vera (who bears no scars) seems to have been more than a match for him, it may be inferred that his lurid rhetoric is primarily intended to impress himself and other men. (Al, who knows that 'lots of rides have been cut short by a big mouth,' is the perfect audience: 'She must have been Tarzan's mate!') However, Haskell is the more, not the less, dangerous for his suspicion that he is 'some fall-guy' who has a right to use women to compensate him for his failure, and Ulmer offers him, in all his unpleasantness, as a fitting representative of a society in which success is both elusive and a prerequisite for the achievement of a sense of manhood.

Vera takes it as given that all men, with half a chance, will treat her as Haskell treated her. She clearly sets out to 'rook' Al in exactly the same way that he rooked Haskell, who was in turn preparing to rook his own father, but her spontaneous rapaciousness is actually quite different in kind from that of her male antagonists. The most obvious indication of this difference is the hectoring aggressiveness of her manner. Vera is not a trickster like Al and Haskell, and she does not try to deceive, disarm or win the confidence of her chosen victim. On the contrary, she goes straight for the jugular, in order to dispel any illusion that her womanhood makes her susceptible either to physical violence or to seduction. It is not enough for her to present herself as Al's (or any man's) equal, for in the world of *Detour*, where nothing matters but the power to impose one's will on others, the concept of equality has no positive meaning. Vera needs to establish that the inequality of the sexes has been *reversed*, not eliminated, and her every word and action is designed to convince Al that she can do exactly what she likes with him ('I'm not through with you by a long shot!') and to rub his nose in the humiliating fact of his complete subordination to her ('In case there's any doubt in your mind, *I'll* take the bedroom!'). Vera points out, justly, that Al is the author of his own downfall ('Not only don't you have any scruples, you don't have any brains!'), and Ulmer unmistakably invites us to take pleasure in the comeuppance of this obtuse and pusillanimous egotist at the hands of a woman of such formidable wit, energy and intelligence. Indeed, the dialogue of some of their exchanges and the theme of the discomfiture of male presumption and complacency by a female anarchist suggest the direct influence of screwball comedy, and, for all that *Detour* is an unusually bleak *film noir* with a tragic ending, it is very easy to detect within it the makings of a Howard Hawks farce.

Vera, too, believes in fate, but if Al conceives himself to be its passive and blameless victim, she succumbs to necessity in a spirit of self-assertion, on the principle that adversity can and

179

must be turned to advantage. 'That's the trouble with you, Roberts! All you do is bellyache,' she tells him, adding (for reasons of which we are not yet aware) that there are 'plenty of people dying this minute who'd give anything to be where [he is].' Al replies, characteristically, that 'at least they *know* they're done for: they don't have to sweat blood *wondering* if they are.' Vera's contemptuous response – 'Your philosophy stinks, pal' – may be charged with irony by the fact that her own philosophy is no better, but it is a tribute to the complexity and maturity of Ulmer's moral sense that he should wish to give Vera's judgement substantial positive value while enforcing the irony at the same time. Like Al and Haskell, Vera acknowledges no higher imperative than personal gain, but while their acquisitiveness signifies no more than their uncomplaining acceptance of the priorities of their culture, Vera's is also determined by an impulse to resist her oppression by men. She acquiesces in the quotidian brutality of capitalism with exemplary ruthlessness, but, even as she does so, she is struggling against masculine dominance, and Ulmer attributes the appropriate importance to this struggle, and to the pungent critical insights which it has generated, without exonerating or indulging the lack of 'scruples' that Vera shares with Al. Vera has the greater right to her scorn for the Al Roberts world-view because she knows that she is dying of consumption, and she

could easily lay claim, if she wished, to all the alibis for immorality that Al is so anxious to establish in his own pathetic case. She refuses to do so, and Ulmer contrasts Al's habitual self-deception unfavourably with Vera's remorseless honesty. Her values may be despicable, but she never pretends, to herself or anyone else, that they are anything but what they are.

The profound poignancy of Vera's character has less to do with her awareness of the imminence of death than with her desire to cling to the possibility of a relationship with Al which is not based on power, despite the fact that such a relationship is no longer feasible, partly as a result of her own actions. As soon as she has rented an apartment for them in the name of 'Mrs Charles Haskell', her behaviour towards Al becomes startlingly ambivalent. She continues to flaunt her mastery over him while also making it increasingly obvious that she wants to have sex; her invitation to share her whisky, which Al refuses, is intended to encourage not merely intimacy but camaraderie ('If I didn't want to give you a drink, I wouldn't have offered it!'). The clue to the significance of this unexpected development is Vera's insistence, for no apparent reason, that the windows of the apartment must always remain closed. She has no more renounced the

Frame: une maison close – *Vera (Ann Savage), Al and a bottle of whisky.*

Frame: the final argument – Vera and Al in the apartment.

ideal of 'the home' than Sue, her more conventional counterpart, and she wishes to think of the apartment as a place of privacy and seclusion which has no connection whatever with the world outside it and which operates according to completely different principles. Beyond the apartment's walls, the eternal struggle for supremacy continues, and Al, like all men, is a potentially deadly enemy who must be blackmailed and humiliated into total submission, but Vera has only to close the windows to create a new order of things in which power no longer matters and in which, as 'Mrs Charles Haskell', she can enjoy Al's affection and comradeship.

By the time she reads the news about the approaching demise of Haskell's father, she is prepared to surrender her monopoly of all present and future spoils and to offer Al an on-going working partnership based on complete economic equality. Even as she plans to cheat Haskell's family out of a fortune, Vera continues to press the claims of reciprocity and mutual responsibility on her reluctant companion, and she seems to envisage a future of collaborative swindling and chicanery in which she and Al exploit everyone but each other ('We're both alike, born in the same gutter!'). Vera is certainly capable of perceiving the ironies of their situation as a couple, but when she suddenly exclaims, 'You don't like me, do you, Roberts?', her consternation and disappointment are perfectly genuine, and she remains utterly unaware that the fantasy of a

shared domestic refuge from the laws of the jungle by which she herself abides is unrealisable. Al's offended amour propre is a major obstacle in her path, but he has (to do him justice) a certain right to object to being imprisoned, and the harder Vera tries to force him to accept her own distinction between the apartment and the outside world, the more absurdly unreal this distinction becomes. She finds herself in the paradoxical position of seeking to perpetuate her utopia by the coercive methods she wishes to reserve for the road ('I've got the key to that door!'), and the battle for supremacy which began before they reached their haven is inevitably reproduced within it, first as an intensified form of conventional marital bickering, and finally as a lethal game of one-upmanship in which each threatens to betray the other to the police.

They at last come to blows in a struggle for possession of the telephone which will shortly become the instrument of Vera's death, and she tearfully rebukes Al for the violence which her own bluff has helped to provoke by telling him that he is not 'a gentleman'. Vera does not actually believe (when she is sober) that gentlemen exist, and she herself has done nothing to merit consideration as a lady, but it seems sadly appropriate that she has in the end no better model for the kind of heterosexual partnership she wants than an archaic and idealised version of the inequalities with which she is already familiar.

America

'No arts; no letters; no society; and which is worst of all, continual fear and danger of violent death; and the life of man, solitary, poor, nasty, brutish, and short.' Thomas Hobbes, *Leviathan*, Part I, Chapter 13.

None of the central characters in *Detour* has a fixed abode, and even the marginal figures with a settled existence and a role to play in the maintenance and reproduction of what remains of social life are engaged in occupations – running motels and diners, policing highways, buying and selling cars – which relate in some way to the wanderings of others. Ulmer emphasises the protagonists' social rootlessness through their propensity to change their identities. Al becomes Haskell, Vera becomes the new Haskell's wife, and Haskell himself has written a letter to his father in which he pretends to be a salesman of hymnals. We never even know if Vera is the Ann Savage character's real name: she tells Al only that 'you can call me Vera if you like.' The dénouement leaves Al without any viable identity at all: 'Al Roberts' is listed as dead, and 'Haskell' is wanted for murder.

The protagonists have more in common than their mobility. They are all running away from places to which they do not wish to, or cannot, return; they all want to settle down again happily and permanently; and they all believe that this aim can be realised only through the acquisition of wealth. Since none of them has any clear idea about where the wealth is to come from, their journeys have the logic, or illogic, of gambling – literally in Haskell's case, metaphorically in that of the others. They have nothing concrete to lose and no certain prospect of gain, and so they stake their lives on a throw of the dice in the hope that the risks they incur will be rewarded by a fortune. Haskell has set himself the goal of making a killing on the races, and dreams of returning in triumph to Florida, where he has just been swindled, 'with all kinds of jack'. Sue longs for a brilliant career in Hollywood and Al decides, off the cuff, to go along for the proceeds, while reserving the right to play the market until they materialise. Vera, who is coming from 'back there' and going nowhere ('LA's good enough for me, Mister'), seizes the unlooked-for opportunity presented by Al's folly in the same buccaneering spirit that prompted Al to rob Haskell, and she is later willing to improvise her own and Al's future around a newspaper story which she discovers entirely by chance. All four gamblers lose. At the end of the film, Vera and Haskell are dead, Sue is working as a hash-slinger in a cafeteria and Al, who can neither stay where he is nor go back where he came from, is vaguely heading East in a desultory attempt to postpone the evil day when he will be arrested for Vera's murder. The film's title is profoundly ironic: none of the protagonists is in a position to make a detour, for they have no itinerary to depart from.

Al, Vera, Sue and Haskell cannot be seen merely as individuals: the fact that they are travelling towards the West, in the footsteps of the pioneers, suggests plainly enough that we are to think of them in terms of a classical American mythology which represents individual enterprise as heroic and as the means of realising an ideal social project. The ideological connection between individualism and democracy was always willed and tenuous, but in practice it makes no sense to connect them at all, and Ulmer argues in *Detour* that the two terms contradict rather than complement each other. The world he shows us is technically a modern, bourgeois-democratic civil society, but it is actually governed by the principles which obtain in Hobbes's 'state of nature', before the implementation of the social contract, where human beings 'are in that condition which is called war; and such a war as is of every man against every man.'

Ulmer embodies the contradictory concept of the savage, or non-social, society in his use of the metaphor of the road. This metaphor recurs frequently in American narratives, and it is almost invariably used to celebrate individual resistance to the constraints of an intolerably oppressive, conservative and regimented culture. Actually existing American society is seen as an insuperable impediment to the full self-realisation of the individual, and the road becomes the last sanctuary of the true American spirit, which can survive only by taking flight from the social world constructed in its name. This use of the road metaphor turns the mythic American ideals on their head. It employs exactly the same terms of reference – heroic individualism and democratic society – but takes the irreversible debasement of the latter for granted and goes on to affirm the former, through characters whose refusal to participate in social life comes to signify a rebellious vindication of America in spite of itself.

By contrast, Ulmer preserves the connection between individualism and American social institutions established by the original myth, and uses the metaphor of the road to argue that this connection manifests itself in practice, not as a democracy of heroes, but as an exceptionally inhumane and brutal capitalism. Ulmer's road is not a refuge for exiles from a culture in which America's ideals have been degraded, but a place where the real logic of advanced capitalist civil society is acted out by characters who have completely internalised its values, and whose interaction exemplifies the grotesque deformation of all human relationships by the principles of the market. Al, Vera and Haskell are isolated vagabonds whose lives are dedicated to the pursuit of private goals which they set themselves ad hoc, in the light of their own immediate interests, and who collide with one another in a moral vacuum where human contacts are purely contingent, practical social ties have ceased to exist, and other people appear as mere use-values, to be exploited at will. The ambiguous connotations of the image of the road – which can suggest both social and extra-social space, both a planned system of communication between society's parts and a void that separates them – correspond perfectly to Ulmer's view of America as a society which negates society, and it is significant that the only character in *Detour* who is travelling because he has a social task to perform is the long-distance lorry driver who approaches Al in the diner in the opening sequence. The driver is lonely and 'needs to talk to someone,' but Al rebuffs him ('My mother taught me never to speak to strangers'), and he is forced to withdraw, explaining that he was only 'trying to be sociable.' It is a key moment: in *Detour*, the desire to be sociable is doomed to remain unsatisfied.

The corollary of the reduction of society to a loose aggregate of competing individuals is the reduction of culture to the language of sport: when the characters of *Detour* wish to relate their own actions and projects to a larger public world of common values and shared assumptions, they resort at once to a metaphor drawn from baseball. Sue refers to Al and herself as a 'team', says that they have been 'struck out', and describes her move to California as an attempt to get out of 'the Bush League'. Vera tells Al that 'life's like a ball game,' and that you have to 'take a swing at whatever comes along,' or else you'll 'wake up and find it's the ninth inning.'

Frame: Al in the diner.

Later, Al tries to dissuade Vera from going ahead with her plan to acquire Haskell's inheritance by informing her that 'that's how people end up behind the eight ball.' Even the rhetoric of American democracy has evaporated, and the only surviving impersonal warrant for the conduct of private life is a discourse of winning and losing derived from the national team game.

The impression of radical cultural impoverishment which *Detour* communicates so powerfully is fundamental to the film's meaning. Given Al's refusal to admit responsibility for his actions, it is at one level extremely important that the characters should be seen as the makers of their own history, but the fact that Ulmer overrules his hero's appeals to fate does not mean that he fails to take account of the objective determinants of the characters' behaviour. They are free agents in a world which privileges the material wellbeing of the atomised individual above all else and which unofficially encourages the most vicious, unprincipled and irresponsible forms of personal rapacity; they exercise their freedom in exactly the way that these circumstances would lead one to expect. Vera and Haskell know that they are dying, but this knowledge, far from qualifying, actually exacerbates their voraciousness. As Vera says, she is 'on [her] way anyhow', and the approach of death only strengthens her conviction that she is accountable to no-one but herself. She is also intensely aware of the limitations of this kind of detachment from the world, and Ulmer's recognition of the incorrigible survival, in however compromised a form, of the human need for society gives the film's pessimism its tragic character.

FALLEN ANGEL

Bob Baker

The following thoughts are prompted by a film which surfaced at the moment generally agreed to mark either the completion of *film noir*'s gestation period or the birth of the thing itself. They reflect on how the picture skitters in and out of the *noir* mode, pushed and pulled by various circumstances then prevailing, and contrast, as appropriate, some perceptions that were available at the time with others that have emerged since.

What we see first is a bus driver's view of the highway by night. As we speed along, the opening credits swing into view, rendered as road signs: *Fallen Angel*, from Twentieth Century-Fox. Produced and directed by Otto Preminger, of whom we've heard, from a novel by Marty Holland, of whom we probably have not (Robert Siodmak's *The File on Thelma Jordon*, 1949, is also based on one of his stories). Script by Harry Kleiner, then unknown but later to become associated with

various sorts of crime movie (Samuel Fuller's *House of Bamboo*, 1955; Robert Aldrich and Vincent Sherman's *Garment Jungle*, 1957; Peter Yates's *Bullitt*, 1968). Scored by David Raksin, whose pounding rhythms signal the level of intensity the film proposes to sustain. Shot by Joseph LaShelle. Co-starring Alice Faye, a top musical star at the studio, but by then in her mid-thirties and seeking to promote a career as a dramatic actress; Dana Andrews, whose association with Preminger on *Laura* the previous year sets up, now as it did then, a number of anticipations; and Linda Darnell, a beauty. Supporting cast: a mixture of tough guys and eccentrics – Charles Bickford, Bruce Cabot, John Carradine, Percy Kilbride. Copyright MCMXLV, that best

Still: the opening scene – Eric Stanton (Dana Andrews) about to hit town.

and worst of years; released in December (alongside Billy Wilder's *The Lost Weekend*, John Ford's *They Were Expendable*, Leo McCarey's *The Bells of St Mary's*); therefore presumably filmed as the war was ending, conceived while it was still going on. As Raksin diminuendos off the soundtrack, the bus driver, a tough-looking customer, pulls up at the edge of a town and shakes awake a sleeping passenger, Andrews. His ticket has run out, the driver belligerently informs him; if he wants to go on to San Francisco, he has to pay another $2.25. It's obvious Andrews doesn't have $2.25. He and the driver exchange menacing stares, but he gets off the bus, his luggage one scruffy suitcase. And so we begin: a hard man with, we guess, a dubious past and little to lose, alone in the world, deposited by night in a strange town – to find, if this is the sort of movie it promises to be, a pile of trouble, a mystery, a woman who's good for him and a woman who's bad for him, death – or at least four out of the five. We are approaching the heart of the *noir* ethos, and the bus is only just pulling away down the highway, a hundred seconds into the picture.

There is the whisper of a subtext to this opening. It's the only time in the film where what happens can plausibly be seen as standing for something beyond its literal meaning: the idea that the bus and its brutal-faced driver represent fate, destiny, the gods, transporting the hero to whatever mess they've got planned for him. It's the sort of symbolism that would not have been available to, say, the western where the 'stranger in town' motif was most familiar. Had Andrews been ejected from a stagecoach, it would have been minus the implication that, whether at this town or the next one down the trail, things would all work out the same in the end. In 1945, free will still rode the range.

We rejoin Andrews as he's about to explore the town of Walton. So far, everything has had the flavour of exterior shooting: a real bus on a real highway, or at least the make-believe outskirts of a backlot town. Now we go inside the studio, as we cut to a set we're going to be spending some time around. It's *almost* a quintessential *noir* set: Pop's Diner, exterior, night; deserted street, neon on wet paving. Slightly incongruous is the stretch of moonlit shore beyond the buildings, the roaring surf in the background.

Inside Pop's we meet, mainly, Darnell, a waitress. Her first appearance is spectacular: a bell rings, she materialises framed in the doorway, poised for a split-second in mid-stride, broadcasting insolence and provocation. We learn that she's been away for a few days, and her fans have been missing her. Conveniently assembled, these comprise the hearty Cabot, with his friendly bow-tie, doggedly devoted Kilbride (as Pop – is there a Mom? Unlikely), and Bickford, an ex-cop with a famously sinister hat, wide-brimmed, turned down all the way round. He doesn't so much wear it as lurk underneath it. A pleasingly eccentric passage in which Andrews promotes

himself some finance by teaming up with a phoney medium (an avuncular Carradine) also serves to introduce the film's remaining big character – Faye, who is wealthy, single and under the influence of a puritanical elder sister. By the time Carradine's 'spook show' has cleaned up and he's ready to leave town, Andrews has Darnell in his blood. He goes to the bus depot, but can't bring himself to step on board. 'Skip it,' he tells the driver, and a second bus leaves him behind in Walton, California.

By now, all the characters have been introduced, their situations, problems and possibilities clearly laid down in an exceptionally efficient job of exposition. At this point, the narrative might develop in a number of directions, although two points seem reasonably certain: a) someone will be murdered and b) Faye will move to a more central place in the narrative.

We can also note how several of the chief constituents of *noir* have already been marshalled: a hero with a miscarried past, now in the grip of a sexual obsession; its object, an aggressive, potentially fatal *femme*; an authority figure (Bickford) of major malevolence; a wealthy family whose keynote is sexual repression. Several visual motifs have put in a statutory appearance: seedy hotel room, cheap diner, or at least seemingly cheap in contrast with where the rich folk live. Indeed, the subject of money is overriding, even from the opening scene on the bus. On Andrews's first visit to Pop's, there's a wrangle about a bill for a cup of coffee; his second includes the moment when Darnell enquires, was that four beers he had? 'Three beers and a coffee,' he snarls. Clearly, this is a movie where every cent counts – a moment earlier, as if to emphasise the point, Darnell snitched a buck from the cash register when no-one was looking. (This magnificent register is used as the focal point for many of the compositions in these scenes; people talk around it, across it.) The desperation of poverty and the desperation of desire are frequently the twin motors of *noir*.

But cutting across all this are several elements that might be described variously as pre-*noir*, anti-*noir* or extra-*noir*. Arguably (I do argue it) into the middle category falls Preminger's directorial personality. The impulse of his *mise-en-scène* is invariably towards the presentation of events in as plain a manner as possible; the editorialising use of shadow play and precipitous camera angles – arguably (I don't argue it) the essence of *noir* – is present only in the most discreet of measures. Two rhymed dance hall sequences are all that present what LaShelle might have regarded as a challenge, both virtuoso long takes, with camera and dancers choreographed so that Andrews and Darnell dip from medium shot into extreme close-up, emphasising the 'alone in a crowd' world of the clinging couple. Elsewhere, Andrews's second visit to Pop's – early morning sunlight through the slats – looks magnificent enough to be meaningful, but sometimes

mise-en-scène has a mundane message to impart: this is day, this is night.

The presentation of Faye's home makes for, in the nature of things, an interesting confusion. For the purposes of the narrative, we have to feel that it is in effect a prison, from where she must eventually escape. On the other hand, Fox and Preminger would certainly have been alive to the expectations of her fans (extra-*noir*) and the requirement to place her within a certain ambience. So *chez* Faye is shown, quite illogically, as flower-strewn, drenched in brightness, keyed to a whiteness that carries no undertone of sterility. Only the presence of Ann Revere, a sort of female Raymond Massey praying over the breakfast table, nudges the film in the direction it's supposed to take.

It's instructive to speculate as to the ways in which the story might develop at this point, with Andrews simply unable to leave Darnell alone, she only mildly interested in someone so poverty-stricken, and Faye poised to fall for Andrews. A viewer steeped in *noir* might propose, for instance, that Andrews, desperate for money because desperate for Darnell, is persuaded by Cabot, a crook for all his affability, to take part in a hold-up. However, like Burt Lancaster in *The Killers* (Siodmak, 1946), he is actually being set up as a fall guy (as in *The Asphalt Jungle*, John Huston, 1950). He discovers Darnell's treachery and in a drunken quarrel accidentally kills her (as Tom

Still: the Mills sisters, June (Alice Faye) and Clara (Ann Revere), take breakfast.

Neal does Ann Savage in Edgar G. Ulmer's *Detour*, 1945). He goes on the run with faithful Faye, but Bickford relentlessly pursues them. Finally, they are both shot down, like Henry Fonda and Sylvia Sidney in Fritz Lang's *You Only Live Once*, 1937. This incident-packed hybrid is hardly a caricature when set alongside such catalogues of woe as make up, for example, *Out of the Past* (Jacques Tourneur, 1947) or *They Live by Night* (Nicholas Ray, 1948). (A variant, with Faye turning murderously jealous and Darnell opting for Andrews after all, would barely have crossed audiences' minds at the time, being too destructive of Faye's star persona.)

What actually happens is, in telegraphese: Andrews marries Faye for her money; Darnell is murdered; on the run with faithful Faye, Andrews finally responds to her feelings for him and rouses himself to detect the real killer, sadistic Bickford. Happy end. One can see at once that this is a yard or two short of being a wholly *noir* scenario. Apart from anything else, *noir* heroes are required to be destroyed by desire, not to find salvation in love.

I suggest that transactional analysis might offer some illumination at this point, although it can certainly be maintained that the procedure is a somewhat anomalous one to apply to the act of watching movies. Assuming a spectator has taken the trouble to discover the nature of a particular work, one can argue that a transaction of sorts is taking place between film makers (Give me your attention!) and audience (Reassure me! Challenge me! Divert me!). This would seem to posit the involvement of, on the one side, the film maker's Parent ego state and, on the other, the spectator's healthy, adapted Child ego state. But in my fake, composite-*noir* version of *Fallen Angel*, something quite different seems to be going on: one Child ego calling to another to join in a mutually gratifying feature-length game of Ain't it Awful (slogan: look what they're doing to us now).

The distinction I am trying to draw is between Adult-*noir*, where the sense is of being addressed by an objective Adult who has noted that the world can be, among other things, a tricky and dangerous place, and Child-*noir*, where authors and audience find it congenial to linger in an unhappy, rebellious Child ego state, in that voluptuous world of powerlessness and non-responsibility, where punishment is random, affection is transient and liable to be withdrawn without warning. If this concept has any validity, one can see more clearly the forces pulling *Fallen Angel* away from the sort of mental atmosphere I am associating with Child-*noir*. Most notably, Preminger's inclination to present characters non-judgmentally, his insistence that we see them all the way round, implies, to pursue the

notion, an Adult ego state, provoking the spectator to respond in kind. The Darnell character, for instance, might easily have been pigeon-holed as simply the *femme fatale*. But by emphasising the poverty of her background, by implying her narrow horizon of possibilities, above all by undercutting her would-be toughness and sophistication with glimpses of an artless, childlike nature (she has a touching moment of bemusement at Carradine's spook show: 'Gee, that was awful mysterious,' she says wonderingly), Preminger denies us the option of regarding her merely as the agent of the hero's misfortunes; she has her problems too. And as far as Andrews's hero is concerned, perhaps a director with a penchant for melancholy (e.g. Tourneur) might have summoned up the requisite sense of complicity to render uncritically the character's own view of himself. ('Why waste money on a guy like me?', 'Up in smoke, like everything in my life', and so on). But Preminger, one feels, has little patience with such a sorehead; together, director and player contrive not some romantic, wounded soul lurching to damnation, but a rather immature man with a damaging taste for self-pity. Preminger is in effect offering a critique of the *noir* disposition even before its elements have coalesced, let alone been identified.

Photograph: the sadistic cop, Judd (Charles Bickford), and his object of desire, Stella (Linda Darnell), in a publicity shot.

Still: Clara discovers June about to go on the run with Eric.

Rather more problematical but perhaps still worth raising is the historical context. It's no wonder that *film noir* vintage, say, 1945-48, its seeds planted in the Depression-dazed 'thirties, its roots drawing sustenance from the prolonged malignancy of World War II, wants to play Ain't it Awful. (As with many World War II productions, including *Laura* and *Fallen Angel*, it rigorously excludes any reference to the war.) But is it over-slick to suggest that this phase of the *noir* cycle was, if not a reflection, at least a refraction of the grieving process that much of society was undergoing? If not, this brings into focus why the quality most inimical to the *noir* spirit is humour (bitter wisecracks excepted), why a film like *The Big Sleep* (Howard Hawks, 1946), for all its secondary characteristics, simply doesn't *feel* like part of the canon, and why *Fallen Angel*, lacking this dimension of historicity, does so only fitfully.

It's with the scenes following Darnell's murder, however, that the film plunges into the *noir* world at its most savage. The passage begins with Andrews waking up the day after his wedding, to be told by Faye with a massively inappropriate, dreamlike casualness that 'the girl' is dead, and the police are waiting downstairs. His shocked reaction, held for about five seconds, would barely register coming from a Lee J. Cobb;

from a dedicated underplayer like Andrews it's seismic. The daymare builds, with Bickford, in charge of the case, calling out bizarrely, 'Congratulations!' (he's referring to the marriage). At the murder scene, we discover a sheeted corpse being removed, teasing us into recalling *Laura*: there's no mention of any disfiguring shotgun blast, but could it be . . . ? No, no, forget it – *adios*, Linda.

Andrews waits as Bickford questions Cabot in the next room; we hear the sounds of a ferocious beating. The casting here is shrewd. It was Cabot who braved the terrors of Skull Island and Kong to rescue Fay Wray; he projects amiability and strength; he could be, we feel, the hero's chum. When we see him clutching a bloody towel, his chin sunk on his chest, almost sobbing, dismissed by Bickford and slipping quickly away like a man leaving a brothel, the effect is shocking. His function in the narrative (apart from bulking, with Revere and Kilbride, the list of suspects) is to precipitate Andrews's flight. As Bickford confides matter-of-factly that he knew Cabot was innocent but 'happened not to like his face' and intimates that Andrews is actually his chief suspect, this is most convincingly achieved.

At this point, with Andrews on the run and Faye tagging along, one would expect the *noir* overtones of the picture to take control completely: a character in bad trouble, heading for worse. Instead, that side of the movie suddenly falls away as, holed up in a cramped hotel room,

Still: June and Eric go to earth in a cheap hotel.

the two characters wrangle their way, with a tenderness rare in Preminger, towards finally making love, culminating in a shot of them asleep in bed together. (It can be taken as certain that this early example of Preminger's censor-baiting would have had boardrooms full of grown-ups locked in impassioned debate). And as Faye recites what Andrews calls 'something out of a book' – 'We were born to tread the earth as angels,/To seek out heaven this side of the sky,/But they who race alone shall stumble in the dark and fall from grace./Then love alone can make the fallen angel rise/For only two together can enter paradise' – we realise, first, that the fallen angel we've come to see isn't Linda Darnell at all, but Dana Andrews; and second, that the film has decisively severed relations with the *noir* world and shifted to ground properly belonging to the 'woman's picture'. The proceedings are now brought to a perfunctory close. In a showdown at Pop's, Bickford is unmasked and, in the worst traditions of melodrama, hangs around to explain the plot ('Perhaps this might have been the perfect crime if I hadn't dropped the watch.') and then to be overpowered – by Percy Kilbride. Why do we feel that Preminger is not taking this altogether seriously? (Touchingly, Gerald Pratley, in his book on Preminger, offers a synopsis which readjusts this episode into line with convention, by having Bickford 'knocked unconscious by Eric'. This Eric is, of course, the Andrews character, and I hope it's now clear why throughout I have used the players' names rather than their script names.)

The revelation that Walton has a sadistic, murderous policeman attached to its force is also of interest. Bickford stands, in terms of nastiness, at the far end of a line-up which begins with, say, Robert Ryan in Nicholas Ray's *On Dangerous Ground* (1951), Andrews in Preminger's *Where the Sidewalk Ends* (1950), Kirk Douglas in William Wyler's *Detective Story* (1951), characters whose brutality is, at least ostensibly, in the line of duty and who eventually find some measure of redemption; further along is someone like Orson Welles in his *Touch of Evil* (1958), also motivated by the desire for justice but lethally careless of damage to others in pursuit of it. Next would come Laird Cregar in *I Wake Up Screaming* (H. Bruce Humberstone, 1942) where the apparently disinterested investigator is actually hopelessly implicated in the case, to the extent of trying to get an innocent man executed. Finally, we arrive at the unmitigated evil of Bickford, against which we might add, in invisible ink, what might have been the most famous example, the killing cop of *The Mousetrap*, which was due for filming in 1952, as soon as its West End run was over . . .

I suppose, finally, this consideration has to be addressed: just how *noir* is the picture in its representation of the big, amorphous subjects – American society, marriage, the family? It's a banal point to make, but this is a film from half a lifetime away; the majority of the people credited on it are dead, and the preoccupations, assumptions and expectations which informed their work, and those which their audiences brought to it, have all altered with the buffetings of time. We ought therefore to tread with special care around a film like *Fallen Angel*, which concerns itself primarily with the waywardness of human affections, or else we risk misrepresenting the past or being patronising about it.

That said, we quickly become aware of how the film seems unable to find room for any conventional family unit in its scheme. The two sisters who have set up house together are the most the film offers in this respect, and while we are not provided with much data, the arrangement does not seem a particularly happy one. Additionally, we see Bickford with his wife just once, at the spook show. She looks grim-faced, implacable. We don't want to think about their relationship, how they behave when they're alone with each other. Otherwise, the film presents a strictly singles scene, a criss-cross of sexual obsessions – A for B, C for A, D for B – from which finally a couple does emerge, in a 'happy end' that can only be described as ironic. Faye, after all, has essentially used her money to buy the man she wanted, while Andrews's lack of grief over the murder of Darnell underlines the calculating unpleasantness his character demonstrates in the film's first two-thirds. In fact, it's tempting to recast the last scene of *Fallen Angel* into an alternative preliminary to one of the 'heroine marries a rogue' cycle, such as Anatole Litvak's *Sorry, Wrong Number* (1948). Darnell on the other hand, born into circumstances which bend all her relations with men into a search for a way out of them, ends up with Bickford, who is so psychologically misshapen that he is unable to resolve his infatuation in any other way than by beating her to death. Thus, the film offers as comprehensively bleak a commentary on human nature and the sort of society it tends to devise as any in the *noir* portfolio.

Except, except . . . the absence of the family unit is, surely, a reflection of how a town like Walton would have been ordered in a time of total war. Andrews, as already noted, is an actor whose technique 'is to convey feelings in a quiet and reserved way' (interviewed by Lillian Ross in *The Player*); his rendering of the character's grief accords with the rest of his performance, for example, the mingled pleasure and consternation that briefly settle on his features when he first realises that Faye is in love with him. As for Faye, both character and player are acutely problematical. She fell out with Darryl Zanuck during the making of the film and, as a consequence, it seems, her part was much abridged; at any rate, her Fox contract was terminated, and she made no more pictures for seventeen years. There is certainly one raw and bleeding gash in the emotional continuity of the hotel sequence between her and Andrews, and further

Still: Eric watches from across the street as June is picked up by the cops.

hints of excisions in the way Andrews infers a frustrated nature that never manifests itself in anything we see on the screen: a curious omission, since Faye's rendering of 'No Love, No Nothing' in Busby Berkeley's *The Gang's All Here* (1943) is probably the most searing complaint about sexual deprivation to have come out of wartime Hollywood, and would presumably have been her biggest qualification for the role. Be that as it may, the anecdotal evidence all warns against hoping to find much coherence in Faye's side of the movie. The film's ending, it's true, does have an ironic dimension, while the portrayal of Darnell's not very bright waitress desperately trying to promote her physical magnetism into some sort of security could hardly be more uncompromising. In other words, like all the aspects of *Fallen Angel* discussed above, we find a complex, sometimes contradictory picture which, like all good art, resists easy classification. *Fallen Angel* is a neutral title which, like the film itself, evokes various models and encompasses several genres without ever decisively committing itself to any of them – *film noir* shot through with passages of *film gris*, *film rose*, the neon-washed street contained within the same frame as the beach by moonlight.

THE BIG SLEEP
Howard Hawks and Film Noir

Michael Walker

Adapted from Raymond Chandler's 1939 novel, *The Big Sleep* (1946) is probably Howard Hawks's most discussed film, critics returning to it as if to an unsolved mystery, a seemingly inexhaustible source of fascination. And there are, indeed, any number of lines to pursue: as a Bogart-Bacall film, as a Chandler adaptation, as a classic private-eye *film noir*, as a narrative of notorious complexity, as a reflection of contemporary ideological tensions and fears, even as a Hawks movie. The one angle which, to the best of my knowledge, has been ignored is as a film about Hollywood. (The film is set in Hollywood, as Marlowe's visit to the library tells us.) However, whilst I shall pull in whatever seems pertinent from other angles, my focus will primarily be on the dialectic between *auteur* (Hawks) and genre (*film noir*). In *Howard Hawks* (Secker & Warburg, London, 1968), Robin Wood's position is that Hawks was not at home with Chandler, or the genre: 'the Chandler-Hammett atmosphere is too stifling for Hawks to breathe in happily: he lets in what fresh air he can' (p.170). I feel, however, that Hawks's interaction with the *noir* world of Chandler's novel was highly productive. In both text and subtext of the film, one can discern patterns and meanings which are extremely revealing of the director's concerns.

Producer as well as director of *The Big Sleep*, Hawks exercised a great deal of creative control. Asked by Warners to make a Bogart-Bacall follow-up to *To Have and Have Not* (1944), it was he who acquired the property, supervised the scripting (by William Faulkner, Leigh Brackett and Jules Furthman), oversaw the casting and negotiated with the Breen Office over censorship problems. The complexity of the narrative derives in the first instance from the novel, but Hawks took it further. First, although Marlowe (Humphrey Bogart) appears in every scene, Hawks declined to use the flashback and voice-over technique traditionally adopted by *films noirs* adapted from first-person novels. And so, unlike *Murder My Sweet* (Edward Dmytryk, 1944), the film does not provide Marlowe's thoughts and feelings to guide us through the investigative maze. Second, according to Gerald Mast in *Howard Hawks, Storyteller* (Oxford University Press, 1982), Hawks cut out details which would help 'explain' the plot complexities. Clearly he wanted the film the way it is.

Filming was completed in January 1945 and the film was pre-released to the armed forces that summer. Response to Bogart and Bacall was so strong that Warners requested more scenes with the two of them. Hawks shot these (Marlowe bringing Carmen back to the Sternwoods from Geiger's house and the scene in the club with the horse-racing dialogue) and re-edited the film so that the additional scenes are integrated smoothly into the overall narrative. Only a minor detail betrays the time lag in their filming – when Marlowe (in the club) narrates back to Vivian (Lauren Bacall) the story she had already told him of Regan allegedly running off with Eddie Mars's wife. (For details of the long process of scripting and filming, *see* Mast's book and Annette Kuhn's chapter on *The Big Sleep* in *The Power of the Image*, Routledge, London, 1985.)

It is on account of its narrative and characters that *The Big Sleep* qualifies as a key *film noir*: visually, it displays none of the *noir* stylistic features discussed in the Introduction. Even when Marlowe is at the heart of the *noir* world, in his night-time scenes in Geiger's house, we can see all the details in the dimly lit room: the typical *noir* use of chiaroscuro and areas of blackness is conspicuously absent. Instead, the film's visual style is entirely characteristic of Hawks: economical, fluid, smoothly functional, with no unusual camera angles, no 'expressionistic' effects.

The film's plot divides into two halves. This structure goes back to the novel, which was extensively cannibalised (Chandler's own word) from two completely separate *Black Mask* stories Chandler had already published: 'Killer in the Rain' in January 1935 and 'The Curtain' in September 1936. (Both stories are included, together with a discussion of this cannibalising, in the posthumously published collection of Chandler's short stories, *Killer in the Rain*, Penguin 1966.) 'Killer in the Rain' provides most of the plot material of the first half, in which Marlowe is hired by wealthy invalid General Sternwood to rid him of a man, Geiger, who is blackmailing him over his 'wild' younger daughter Carmen (an investigation which rapidly plunges Marlowe into a world of vice, blackmail and murder), and 'The Curtain' provides most of the material of the second half, in which Marlowe investigates the mysterious disappearance of Regan, who was married to the General's other daughter,

Still: Marlowe (Humphrey Bogart) and Vivian (Lauren Bacall) in Marlowe's office.

Vivian. This plot, too, involves blackmail: Carmen killed Regan (allegedly for resisting her sexual advances) and Eddie Mars, a local gambler and racketeer who helped Vivian conceal the crime, is blackmailing her over it.

With two major exceptions (toning down the 'vice' to satisfy the Breen Office and restructuring to provide for a Bogart-Bacall ending), the film follows the novel quite closely. At the same time, it has been very skilfully structured by Hawks and his scriptwriters to provide a commentary on the action. In particular, Hawks uses parallelled scenes. For example, on the first night of his investigation, Marlowe waits in his car outside the house of the first blackmailer, Arthur Gwynn Geiger (Theodore von Eltz), and Carmen (Martha Vickers) drives up and enters. Then, on the second night, he waits in his car outside the apartment block of the second blackmailer, Joe Brody (Louis Jean Heydt), and Vivian drives up and enters. On each occasion, the scenes inside are abruptly terminated by shots, a woman's scream, the corpse of the blackmailer lying on the floor and the murderer fleeing downstairs.

One consequence of the parallelling is that we can see how far Marlowe has gained control over the *noir* world. When Geiger is shot, everything happens too fast. Although alerted by a flash of light and Carmen's scream from inside the house, Marlowe is still outside when the shots are fired and he neither sees the killer nor has the opportunity to give chase. Outside Brody's, he is, for the first time, ahead of the action: playing a hunch, he is anticipating that Vivian will arrive. After she has entered, he follows her to Brody's room and quickly asserts mastery over Brody. He is thus present when Brody is shot and is able to act quickly enough to pursue and catch the murderer. At this point, Hawks strikingly duplicates a shot. The murderer, Carol Lundgren (Thomas Rafferty), makes his getaway on foot; Marlowe follows in his car, overtakes him, and parks ahead, waiting. Hawks then cuts to a shot of Lundgren's legs, briskly walking along the sidewalk. This shot closely echoes the one of the legs of Geiger's murderer, Owen Taylor (the Sternwood family chauffeur) as he runs down the back steps of Geiger's to make his getaway. David Bordwell points out that, on the earlier occasion, the shot is to signify what Marlowe *hears*: 'the shot is a compromise between restriction to Marlowe and suppression of the killer's identity' (*Narration in the Fiction Film*, Methuen, London, 1985, p.65). Hawks repeats the device here to the same end – we can see Marlowe listening as he hunches down in the car seat – but this time Marlowe is in a position of control. As Lundgren passes, he apprehends him.

There are a number of points to note about this. 1) Hawks has returned to a silent movie convention in order to visualise what is heard. 2) He uses the device only on these two occasions, which implicitly links Lundgren and Taylor not simply as young men who have committed murder but as characters who are similar, for example, in their motives for killing. (Both murders are *crimes passionels* enacted on behalf of the murderers' lovers: Taylor 'was sweet on Carmen and didn't like the kind of games Geiger was playing,' Lundgren was avenging Geiger, his gay lover.) 3) It's a pun: they're both 'legging it'. 4) In psychoanalytical terms, the shots are images of male potency.

Still: in Joe Brody's apartment, Marlowe and Vivian are unimpressed when Brody (Louis Jean Heydt) pulls a gun. Agnes (Sonia Darrin) looks on.

Psychoanalytically, this looks remarkably like condensation, a crucial feature of Freudian dream theory. The elements move from the presumably conscious (point 1) to the presumably unconscious (point 4), all telescoped into one image. This leads to the film's subtext, which is not simply Hawks's way of preserving the elements of the novel which needed to be censored (such as explicit references to Geiger and Lundgren's gay relationship), but is an aspect of the film that assumes an energy and meaning which, I would argue, goes beyond Hawks's conscious awareness. There is indeed a dream-like quality to the convolutions of the narrative – as if it were repeatedly seeking to express meanings that lie beneath the surface.

Two other parallelled scenes are the deaths of Brody and of Eddie Mars (John Ridgely). In each case, the man is killed as he opens a door, bullet(s) rip through the door, the killing is the result of mistaken identity (Lundgren thought Brody had killed Geiger; Mars's men assume Mars is Marlowe) and Marlowe is partly (Brody) or mainly (Mars) responsible for the death. In Brody's case, he is responsible in the sense that he refuses to let Brody answer the door with a gun; in Mars's case he fires bullets to drive Mars out the door to be shot by his own men.

In effect, Marlowe sends the villains to their deaths at the hands of their own kind beyond the door. The door is like a threshold between the space Marlowe controls and the dangers of

the *noir* world beyond, but it is also a barrier separating Marlowe from the killing – a device to pretend that he isn't really responsible. But psychoanalytical analysis would identify this as displacement – at a deeper level he is responsible. Each of these villains is killed at a similarly significant moment: Marlowe has just asked Brody what Geiger had on the Sternwoods, and he has been interrogating Mars over Regan's death: was it Carmen or Mars himself who killed him? The effect of the killings is thus to prevent Marlowe from discovering the truth about Carmen's transgressions, a crucial pattern throughout the film. All the men who know (or pretend to know) about her transgressions (including Geiger and Taylor) are killed before they can speak of them. And, given that Marlowe deliberately drives Mars out to be killed *before* he clarifies the issue, the implication is that Marlowe, for all his professed concern (as a private eye) to seek out the truth, no longer wishes to know.

This suggests an uncertainty around Marlowe's powers which is untypical of Hawks's heroes. An obvious question *The Big Sleep* poses is how a Hawks hero would cope in the *noir* world, a world far removed from the (to Hawks) more conventionally manly dangers of driving racing cars, flying planes or fighting Nazis. The hero is still a Hawks professional doing a dangerous job, and his superior powers steer him without too much trouble through a scene such as his confrontation with Joe Brody. He treats Brody's pulling a gun as a joke, pressures him into handing over the blackmail photograph of Carmen without payment, and then interrogates him over Taylor's death in a way which exposes Brody's shiftiness. (A long take as Marlowe circles the seated Brody, who moves around uneasily, trying to avoid Marlowe's look.) This scene is entirely typical of Hawks: Brody is juxtaposed with Marlowe, the hero, defined by virtue of the juxtaposition as 'not good enough' and promptly killed. This happens to Joe (Noah Beery Jr) in *Only Angels Have Wings* (1939), Johnson (Walter Sande) in *To Have and Have Not*, Wheeler (Ward Bond) in *Rio Bravo* (1959) and Luke MacDonald (Johnny Crawford) in *El Dorado* (1966), and the deaths illustrate Hawks's ruthlessness towards those he deems 'not good enough'.

However, the *noir* world also contains dangers which Marlowe is less able to control: Carmen's deviance, Vivian's deceptiveness and her stubborn refusal to talk and, behind this, the powerful figure of Eddie Mars, who is ultimately revealed as the film's master villain. It is Marlowe's very professionalism that is on the line here: can he resolve these problems in a way which protects his client, General Sternwood (Charles Waldron), which is his primary concern? As the film moves towards its climax, he frankly admits to Vivian – who, by this stage, has committed herself to him – that he's scared, that Mars has had the jump on him until now. Highly untypically for a seeker-hero *film noir*, *The Big Sleep* ends with the hero

and heroine still *in* the *noir* world, surrounded by darkness and the threat of violence. And, highly untypically for a Hawks adventure film, it ends with the hero and heroine needing to be rescued – the sirens on the soundtrack signifying the arrival of the police. Finally, the *noir* world is also dangerous in its 'otherness', and this raises more complex issues.

In two respects, *The Big Sleep* does not fit the traditional pattern of Hawks's adventure films: the hero has no best friend and he is not a member of a group. In *To Have and Have Not*, Bogart's separation from a group (the Free French) was only temporary, but here the group, such as it is (the motley crew of blackmailers), has been criminalised. Marlowe is thus obliged, as he notes, to preside over its destruction and, however hard the narrative works to limit the deaths he himself is responsible for, this inversion of a crucial Hawks feature sets up tensions which reverberate through the film. For example, the scene when Marlowe enters Brody's apartment, and both Vivian and Agnes (Sonia Darrin) are hiding in the back, precisely echoes that in *To Have and Have Not* when Renard (Dan Seymour) enters Morgan's (Bogart's) room and Slim (Bacall) and Mme de Bursac (Dolores Moran) are hiding in the back. (In the novel, Vivian is not in this scene, reinforcing the connection as Hawks's.) One could argue that Hawks was simply inverting a structure: in the earlier film, it is the villain who threatens the hero by his unexpected arrival; in the later, it is the other way round. But Renard and Marlowe both force their way into the room intent on similar ends: to pressure the man inside into admitting his 'illegal' activities, which involve one of the hiding women, on whom the intruder considers he has a claim. For all that the scenes then develop along lines which emphasise parallels between Morgan and Marlowe as the films' heroes (each scene has a turning point when Bogart assumes control of the guns), this initial link between Marlowe and the earlier film's would-be destroyer of the heroic group is an indication of the genre/*auteur* tensions in *The Big Sleep*.

The other key Hawks omission is handled rather differently. In Marlowe's relationship with Bernie Ohls (Regis Toomey) from the DA's office, we see a trace of what was perhaps once a close friendship, but it has been set aside in the interests of preserving Chandler's view of Marlowe as a loner. However, there *was* a close male friendship, that between the General and Sean Regan, which was broken when Regan went missing. Severing Regan from Vivian (in the film, she's Mrs Rutledge, not Mrs Regan) accentuates his friendship with the General – who actually says to Marlowe 'Sean has left me,' as if speaking of a lover – and it is not surprising that, over and above the services for which he is hired, Marlowe becomes preoccupied with what happened to Regan. In effect, he is solving the Hawks mystery: what became of the male friendship?

The Hawks male friendship is thus relocated in the past, as a loss – a loss, moreover, which structures the hero's quest. And, crucially, Hawks preserves it as a loss. When Marlowe meets the General in his greenhouse at the beginning of the film, he temporarily takes over Regan's role: drinking the General's brandy and enjoying a man-to-man talk, in this case about the waywardness of the General's daughters. But, although it existed in an earlier version of the script (*see* Mast), a parallel scene at the end of the film – Marlowe tying up the loose ends with both Vivian and the General in the greenhouse – was removed. Presumably, this would have seemed too close to suggesting that Marlowe was replacing Regan as the General's surrogate son. Given Hawks's indifference to the family – amply confirmed in his other films – and the very taintedness of this particular family (the General's reference to its 'corrupt blood'), it becomes necessary, in auteurist terms, for Vivian to be rescued from its contaminations. And so the ending of the film foresees the dissolution of the family: Carmen will be 'sent away', the General will have to live with the fact of Regan's death, and Vivian offers herself to Marlowe to be 'fixed'. The positioning of the heroine as in need of being 'fixed' is significant, and perhaps helps explain why, in this case, Hawks is able unambiguously to end on a celebration of the heterosexual couple. In his other adventure movies, the endings are generally more problematical.

Still: the greenhouse – the butler Norris (Charles D. Brown) delivers Marlowe to see General Sternwood (Charles Waldron).

This is the film's major change from Chandler's novel: building up Vivian's part to move towards a Bogart/Bacall ending. The changes required by the Breen Office were more specific: no pornographic books (Geiger's racket in the novel), no gay relationship (Geiger and Lundgren) and no nudity or drugs (as in the novel's account of Carmen's state when Marlowe breaks into Geiger's house after hearing the shots). Nevertheless, Hawks has deliberately left in most of the evidence of such censorable items – he has just declined to explain them. When Marlowe first visits Geiger's antiquarian bookshop, we see that there is a backroom which a middle-aged gentleman furtively enters, and we later see that the room contains books, which are of sufficient value to be shipped out by Brody immediately after Geiger's death. Although Geiger's racket is now simply specified as blackmail, the film suggests more. Equally, Carmen is of necessity clothed when Marlowe bursts into Geiger's house, but she is coded as drugged (her dopey state, together with the glass Marlowe sniffs), and the camera pointing at her – with its missing film which Brody later uses to blackmail Vivian – hints at unspecified depravities. (We do not see the photograph, but Marlowe's comment, 'She takes a nice picture,' at least hints at nudity. A

well-known still from the film, showing Geiger's body lying at Carmen's feet, seems to have acted as a convenient cover for what Hawks wanted to suggest was in the photograph. The *Hollywood Publications Preview of 1946* says of this still, 'The fight for this photograph gives the screen one of its best melodramas.' But, of course, the blackmail photograph of Carmen – marked by the flash Marlowe sees – was taken before Geiger was shot. He would not be lying at her feet at this point, unless this was part of an interesting game.) As for Geiger and Lundgren, Hawks has retained almost all the indirect references to their gay relationship: their names (Gwynn and Carol), Marlowe's suggestion that Lundgren has a key to Geiger's house, the way in which Lundgren first hides Geiger's body and

The deceptive still: Geiger's house – Geiger (Theodore von Eltz) lying at the feet of Carmen (Martha Vickers).

then later lays it out ceremonially on the bed, the way he kills Brody in (mistaken) revenge for Geiger's murder, and so on.

I believe that, consciously or unconsciously, Hawks was fascinated by the 'decadence and depravity' of the novel, and sought to preserve as much of this as possible as a subtext. The nature of his fascination may be clarified by looking at his other adventure films; critics have often remarked that the films' characteristic triangle of hero, best friend and heroine has gay overtones. Indeed, the 'Hawks triangle' is a highly distinctive (sexual) triangle in which a third person, usually a woman, more rarely a younger man, comes between two men who are close friends. The triangle is present in virtually all Hawks's adventure films from *A Girl in Every Port* (1928) on, reaching its most complete elaboration in *Red River* (1947), where, explicitly or embryonically, it occurs in five or six successive permutations. What is perhaps most remarkable about the triangle is the number of different ways in which Hawks develops and resolves it, expulsion of the woman and reaffirmation of the male friendship occurring explicitly only in *A Girl in Every Port*. Other solutions include the deaths of all three characters (*Scarface*, 1932), the death of the hero (*Tiger Shark*, 1932), the death of the best friend (*Only Angels Have Wings*), all three going off together (*To Have and Have Not*), the heroine serving to reunite the hero and the best friend (*Red River*), and the best friend deserting the hero to settle down with the heroine (*The Big Sky*, 1952). These variations indicate Hawks's ambivalence: the sense that sometimes he was committed more to the male friendship, sometimes more to the 'weaning' of the hero from his best friend, as in *Only Angels Have Wings*. Even so, it should be stressed how difficult the transition from the Kid (Thomas Mitchell) to Bonnie (Jean Arthur) is for Jeff (Cary Grant) in this movie. Each time intimacy with Bonnie threatens – and this includes the ending – he rushes off at top speed.

How conscious Hawks was of such implications in his work is hard to fathom. In Joseph McBride's *Hawks on Hawks* (University of California Press, Berkeley, 1982), after recounting an extraordinary scene – from a film he once planned – in which the hero and the best friend end up in bed together after the heroine has walked out on them, Hawks jokes that the French critics 'are going to think that I've got a couple of homosexuals there.' When McBride then asks what he thinks about critics saying 'that the male characters in [his] films border on homosexuality,' he dismisses the idea: 'It sounds like a homosexual speaking' (p.147). That there are gay overtones to Hawks's male relationships is undeniable – students to whom I have shown the films even insist that they're obvious – but it is hard to accept that a man of Hawks's obvious sophistication would so firmly resist acknowledging this. There is a similar uncertainty with Chandler. In *Western and Hardboiled Detective Fiction in America* (Macmillan, London, 1987), Cynthia Hamilton remarks on Marlowe's 'strange attitude to women which has often been noted in Chandler's work and which has led to much speculation over Marlowe's, and Chandler's, sexual preferences' and adds, 'Chandler was sensitive enough about his portrayal of women to alter Marlowe's celibacy in the books written after *The Little Sister*, probably in response to allegations that Marlowe was a homosexual' (pp.162-163). Other novels may indeed suggest this but, in *The Big Sleep*, scathing remarks about fags and queens clearly register Chandler's homophobia. In the film, though, the issue is handled far more ambiguously.

Lacking the figure of the best friend, *The Big Sleep* has no 'Hawks triangle', but sexual ambiguity resonates through the movie. On the one hand, Hawks's Marlowe can follow Chandler's and, entering Geiger's bookshop, do an imitation of what Chandler (on Marlowe's second visit) and Hawks (in *Hawks on Hawks*) call a 'fairy' – the caricature apparently felt appropriate to such an establishment. On the other hand, Hawks's Marlowe is clearly obsessed with what went on in Geiger's house – he returns to it compulsively, even staging the final confrontation with the villain in it. Analysis of these scenes reveals the source of obsession as the gay relationship.

To the question of how a Hawks hero would cope in the *noir* world, the subtext of the film answers by characterising the world as one of fascination, which takes the hero on a complex journey through variations of sexual desire. At first, secure in his heterosexuality ('I collect blondes in bottles, too' he quips to the blonde librarian), Marlowe sends up Geiger's world with his caricature of a gay and then nips across the road for a bit of hanky-panky with an obliging Dorothy Malone. This is pure Hawksian fantasy (in dream terms, wish fulfilment): that women met casually (a shop-girl, a taxi-driver) would promptly make themselves sexually available to the hero. But these women are not in the *noir* world, and their 'availability' is more than counterbalanced by the very different characterisation of the three major female roles: Vivian, Carmen and Agnes. None of these is a fully-fledged *femme fatale*: Agnes, because she lacks deadliness, Carmen, because she is too uncontrolled, and Vivian, because she is played by Bacall and is guaranteed to be 'redeemed' for Bogart by the end. Nevertheless, they act as significant sources of disturbance for Marlowe in his investigation, and he handles their 'threat' with varying degrees of success. Since he is not attracted to her, he feels safe in patronising Agnes (who works in Geiger's shop, and later turns up as Brody's girlfriend), and he tries to maintain a similar detachment from Carmen, but the trail of male deaths directly or indirectly attributable to them is a measure of their dangerousness. Because he is attracted to her, Vivian is a problem for Marlowe: she makes provocative jokes about his sexual proclivities (speculating that he worked in bed 'like Marcel Proust', wondering if he was a front-runner or whether he came from behind), and her encounters with him repeatedly serve to raise doubts about whether he can trust her. But behind this lies a question that is fundamental to the Hawks authorial discourse: is Marlowe able to purge himself of his obsession with the *noir* world and commit himself to Vivian as heroine?

From the moment Marlowe forces his way into Geiger's house to find Geiger dead and Carmen dopey with drugs, he enters another world. Crucially, he becomes fascinated by it, returning obsessively to the house to explore it further. But it is not until Lundgren makes his dramatic reappearance by killing Brody that the nature of the fascination becomes apparent. As Lundgren flees on foot with Marlowe pursuing by car, we see a subjective shot, from Marlowe's point of view inside the car, of Lundgren walking. Subjective tracking shots are most unusual in Hawks (indeed, I cannot recall another), and this serves to draw attention to what is being visualised – a middle-aged man cruising to pick up a young man, a young man who, within the subtext at least, is coded as gay. (Whether the black leather jacket Lundgren is wearing would signal this more directly to a 'forties audience, I don't know.) Marlowe has been transformed into a resurrection of Geiger. Earlier, when the eye of Dorothy Malone's bookshop girl travels over Marlowe as she describes Geiger, we take this to be a way of contrasting the men. Now, suddenly, all this has changed.

The rest of the sequence continues the implications. The shot of Lundgren's legs as an 'image of male potency' can now be seen to have a specific resonance. Marlowe stops Lundgren with a request for a match – normally, in Hawks, a sign of male bonding or a prelude to intimacy, as in Slim's opening line in *To Have and Have Not*. Police sirens are heard. 'What'll it be, kid, me or the cops?' asks Marlowe, pointing a gun. Raising his hands sharply, Lundgren asks 'What do you want?' By way of response, Marlowe pats Lundgren's body, looking for a gun, and fishes it out of his trouser pocket. He orders Lundgren into the car: 'Soon as this police car goes by, we're going to Geiger's house'. It's as if, the pick-up completed, police activity makes the area unsafe, and so, echoing Geiger and Lundgren's past, they'll go to Geiger's. The nature of Marlowe's obsession with the house suddenly seems clear.

At Geiger's, Marlowe says that Lundgren has a key. (This surely would suggest to a 'forties audience that Lundgren was Geiger's lover.) But it is Marlowe who has the key. At this point – significant in that it concerns crossing the threshold into the house with the pick-up – ambivalence reasserts itself. Lundgren slugs Marlowe and, in response, Marlowe throws down Carmen's small ivory-handled gun and taunts Lundgren into reaching for it. As he does so, Marlowe kicks him unconscious, then drags him inside and ropes his hands behind his back with braided cord.

Ambivalence can be seen in several details. In offering Lundgren Carmen's gun, Marlowe is mocking his gayness – a woman's gun as a response to a weak (woman's) punch. (In the novel at this point, Chandler is characteristically explicit: 'a pansy has no iron in his bones!') He then savagely kicks Lundgren's head, an action which has clear 'gay-bashing' overtones. But the way he ties Lundgren up has, in context, undeniable associations of bondage, an echo of the practices we may assume Marlowe consciously or unconsciously associates with what Geiger and Lundgren did in the house. However, with Marlowe's discovery of Geiger's body laid out religiously on his bed, the gay pick-up overtones abruptly cease: the repressed has returned, to reclaim – if only in death – the bed as *his*.

What are we to make of this extraordinary association of the hero with the sexually 'deviant' Geiger? What is at stake, it seems to me, is the very question of the hero's sexual identity. His journey into the world has aroused a side of himself – a bisexuality – which had hitherto been repressed in a sexual lifestyle of casual encounters with women. Allowing for certain differences of time and place, the subtext of *The Big Sleep* strikingly anticipates a major theme of *Performance* (Nicolas Roeg and Donald Cammell, 1970). The format and characteristics of the seeker-hero *film noir* are vital to the expression of the theme in *The Big Sleep*: both the complexity of the narrative and the nature of the underworld of vice, blackmail and murder serving to generate a surplus of meaning which allows room for such a potentially subversive subtext. It seems to me a theme clearly attributable to Hawks, as if Bogart/Marlowe were his cinematic alter ego, journeying through a dream terrain marked not simply by dangers and obstacles, but also by fantasy and desire.

Carmen, too, is implicated in this: after all, she is the first person Marlowe encounters in Geiger's house. In the novel, her association with the house is used to build up her representation as part delinquent, part *femme fatale*: drugs, pornographic pictures, nymphomania, incipient psychosis, the murder of Regan, the attempted murder of Marlowe. In the film, most of this is necessarily toned down, although her role as source of blackmail material (four counts in all) points to unspecified transgressions. In particular, these are focused in the information in code in Geiger's 'sucker list', which Marlowe takes, along with Carmen, from Geiger's house, but which he is unable to decode. His failure is symptomatic: he never does solve the 'mystery' of Carmen and, by the end of the film, as I have mentioned, it is clear that he doesn't want to. Given the importance, in other *films noirs*, of the hero solving the enigma of the woman, it is worth exploring this further.

The deaths of the men who could speak about Carmen's transgressions have the effect of sealing the details of these away in the film's repressed. Partly this is a censorship ploy: her transgressions are literally unspeakable. At the end of the film, Carmen herself will be similarly sealed away: sent to an institution. However, this ideological repression of the deviant female – which goes back to the novel – is not achieved without difficulty. From her first appearance (when she deposits herself in Marlowe's arms) to her last (biting his hand when he ejects her from his apartment), Carmen's unabashed forwardness makes Marlowe uncomfortable. It is only when she's passive that he feels in control: after her

Still: Brody's apartment – Carmen makes a dramatic entrance.

session at Geiger's, she's so doped-up that, taking her home, he carries her, sleeping like a child, into Vivian's bedroom.

At first, Marlowe attempts to cope with the threat Carmen poses by interrogating her. The scene when the two of them revisit Geiger's together, which could have been highly charged, is largely neutralised by this strategy, and by the unexpected arrival of Eddie Mars. And, although the scene that night in Brody's apartment, when Carmen makes a dramatic entrance, gun in hand, is potentially more sexually charged, Vivian's presence inhibits the interaction between Marlowe and Carmen, and provides a means of getting Carmen home. Nevertheless, Marlowe here keeps Carmen's gun and the blackmail film – symbols of her dangerousness and deviant sexuality. And so, Lundgren's subsequent arrival at the door – like Carmen, gun in hand – is like the return of the repressed dangerousness and deviant sexuality. In each case, the dangerousness (indeed murderousness) is directed towards Brody, but the sexuality implicates Marlowe. The movie links Carmen and Lundgren in a number of ways: association with Geiger, age, dark clothes, deviance. It is as if Marlowe's disavowal of Carmen's sexual attractiveness (and, by implication, the attractiveness of her kinkiness) produces the rather more disturbing threat of Lundgren. The rest of the sequence follows through the implications of this.

In other words, the deviance that, in Carmen's case, is repressed by the film as unspeakable, returns in the form of the homosexual 'deviance' of Lundgren. In effect, this displaces the mystery of the woman that is the hero's more common preoccupation. One senses the same sort of displacement at work in Marlowe's interest in Eddie Mars. When Mars makes his first appearance, walking in on Marlowe and Carmen in Geiger's house, he says, 'I've got two boys outside'. Marlowe's response – 'Oh, it's like that, eh?' – can be seen to register the sexual implications; his next act is to tell Carmen to leave. Whereas Vivian is allowed to be present to witness Marlowe assert mastery over Brody, Carmen is a

complication in Marlowe's confrontation with the far more powerful Mars. As soon as she has gone, Mars confronts Marlowe, swinging his phallic keys (he, too, has keys to Geiger's house), saying, 'Your story didn't sound quite right' – that is, Marlowe has come to Geiger's for a somewhat more suspicious purpose than he claims. It transpires that Mars is Geiger's landlord, and it is fairly obvious he knows what went on in the house. Later, we discover that he has deliberately separated himself from his wife, and seemingly shows no interest in making contact with her. This, together with such details as the two sidekicks he invariably goes around with, suggests that Mars, too, is implicated in the gay subtext. Accordingly, it makes sense that Marlowe should want to stage his final confrontation with Mars in Geiger's house – as if he is finally confronting the unacknowledged demon that has haunted him throughout the movie.

At the point when Marlowe hands Lundgren over to Bernie Ohls, we may feel he has returned to a disavowal of his bisexuality. (It's the cops who take over the investigation of Lundgren's suspect practices: 'What did you hide Geiger's body for?') Certainly the scene which immediately follows, between Vivian and himself in the club, reaffirms heterosexuality in the horse-racing dialogue, when Vivian decides that Marlowe probably is a frontrunner after all. Marlowe now begins the second part of his quest: to discover what has happened to Regan and what Mars has on Vivian. Although this part of the film is less dense and complex than the first part – not least because too many of the colourful characters are dead or locked away – the background threat of Eddie Mars ensures that the subtextual interrogation of Marlowe's sexuality is not yet over.

Marlowe begins the search for Regan by going out to Eddie Mars's nightclub at Las Olindas. The nightclub itself is lively and full of customers but, apart from a brief visit to the roulette table for reasons of plot, Mars remains isolated in his office, with its spare, masculine, sporting decor. In particular, he is isolated from women. From the moment he enters the club, Marlowe, on the other hand, is the subject of attention from miniskirted hostesses, which leads to a very Hawksian little play when Vivian, singing 'Her tears flowed like wine', appraises a hostess's charms as if on Marlowe's behalf and mockingly signals her congratulations. Ben Brewster has suggested to me that the working women in the movie, together with Marlowe's reference, in his two 'phone calls to Bernie Ohls, to 'red points' (meat and dairy rationing, which was stopped at the end of the war), are a reflection of the film's wartime production. There is, nevertheless, a strong sense that Hawks was sufficiently uneasy about the *noir* women to compensate for their threats to Marlowe by interspersing his itinerary with potentially available pickups. All the non-*noir* women given speaking roles – the librarian, the bookshop girl, the taxi-driver, the hostesses –

Still: Geiger's house – Marlowe and the body of Eddie Mars.

show a greater or lesser interest in Marlowe. However, even in the club, the gay subtext momentarily registers: when he leaves Mars's office, Marlowe is immediately approached by two of the hostesses, who simultaneously deliver the message that Mrs Rutledge wants to see him. Seconds later, Mars's two sidekicks likewise approach him and deliver the same message. Psychoanalytically, it's as if the two women are trumped by the two men.

Vivian wanted to see Marlowe so that a) he could witness her winning $28,000 at the roulette wheel and b) he could take her home. However, as he watches Mars smile at Vivian's win, Marlowe becomes suspicious. The scene that follows is another in which the action is closely parallelled later, when Marlowe escapes from Art Huck's, where he has gone to find Mars's wife Mona (Peggy Knudsen). In each scene, anticipating the exit of one of Mars's hoods, Marlowe gets a gun from his car, hides

behind another car and rescues Vivian from the hood, who threatens her with a gun.

In that these scenes deal with Marlowe controlling the *exits* (precisely the area he lacked control over in the first two parallelled scenes), we see that he has gained further mastery over the *noir* world. But the parallels between the two later scenes are also instructive. On the first occasion, Marlowe has foreseen the hold-up and suspects it's a put-up job: Mars has ordered it so that it will look as if he's reclaiming his $28,000. But this requires Vivian's complicity and, in the car drive that follows, despite the signs of a developing romance between her and Marlowe (the kiss; the film's first use of Steiner's love theme), she declines to answer his nagging question: 'What's Eddie Mars got on you?' Subtextually, however, it is established that Mars's hold on her is not sexual: her purse does not contain his $28,000. And, by the time of the second scene, Vivian has changed allegiances. When Canino (Bob Steele) comes out of Huck's house using her as a shield, it is Vivian who fools him into firing off his bullets at a phantom, so enabling

Marlowe to kill him. In the car drive that follows this scene, she and Marlowe acknowledge their love for each other.

In going to Art Huck's, Marlowe is following up the story that Regan ran off with Mona Mars. Structurally, however, his entrance into the house relates most suggestively to his entrance into Geiger's with Lundgren. On the former occasion, he left Agnes and her dead boyfriend Brody, pursued the killer Lundgren, caught him and took him to Geiger's. On the threshold, a fight ensued in which he knocked Lundgren unconscious and tied him up. On this occasion, Marlowe has found out the whereabouts of Mona Mars as a result of an approach by Harry Jones (Elisha Cook Jr), Agnes's new boyfriend, who, like Brody, is promptly killed in front of Marlowe. Agnes then contacts Marlowe and gives him the address. And so, Marlowe again in effect leaves Agnes and her dead boyfriend and, indirectly, follows the killer Canino to Huck's. On the threshold, ambushed by Huck (Trevor Bardette) and Canino, Marlowe is himself knocked unconscious and tied up. He regains consciousness inside the house in the presence of Mona Mars. But it isn't Regan who is with her, it's Vivian.

Symbolically, here, Vivian is being offered in place of Regan. (She even enters the room in response to Marlowe's question to Mona: 'Where's Sean Regan?') The significance of this lies in the relationship the film establishes between Marlowe and Regan. In the novel, Marlowe does not know him. Nevertheless, in his essay comparing novel and film, Roger Shatzkin convincingly argues that, in the novel, Regan is like Marlowe's doppelgänger ('Who cares who killed Owen Taylor?' in Gerald Peary and Roger Shatzkin, *The Modern American Novel and the Movies*, Frederick Ungar, New York, 1978). This, I would maintain, is a typical *noir* motif, relating for example to *films noirs* in which the hero, usually unwittingly, is seeking himself (e.g. *Somewhere in the Night*, Joseph L. Mankiewicz, 1946; *The Black Angel*, Roy William Neill, 1946; *The Big Clock*, John Farrow, 1948) or seeking a close friend whose path he duplicates (e.g. *Dead Reckoning*, John Cromwell, 1947; *Calcutta*, Farrow, 1947). But, in the movie of *The Big Sleep*, Hawks introduces his own inflection. He gives Marlowe and Regan a past in which they met on opposite sides of the law, but in such a way that they became like buddies: 'We used to swap shots between drinks or drinks between shots – whichever you like.' And so, when Vivian appears in place of the dead Regan, it's as if we are seeing a *trace* of a 'Hawks triangle', echoing, for example, Bonnie in place of the dead Kid in *Only Angels Have Wings*. In *The Big Sleep*, the key point is the transference from Regan to Vivian. Regan was not a close friend, like the Kid, but ambivalently both friend and foe, and this ambivalence is duplicated in the way Marlowe, up to this point, has viewed Vivian. But, in this scene, Vivian finally surrenders her suspect persona and becomes a Hawks heroine, helping the hero. At the point when it becomes clear to Marlowe that Regan is dead, making the original male friendship of Regan and the General incapable of restitution, Vivian joins forces with him. The implications for Hawks scholarship are indeed intriguing: in the adventure films, can a woman be acceptable only if she in some sense replaces a man?

At the same time, the 'crossing the threshold' trauma at the beginning of the scene relates to Lundgren at Geiger's. Like Geiger's, Art Huck's is a house belonging to Eddie Mars which is the site of illicit activities and, like Geiger's, it hides a mystery: in this case, what happened to Regan? Mars has ordered the two women to the house to help conceal the fact of Regan's death. (This looks like his attempt to 'screen it off', i.e psychoanalytically, there is a good case for Mars being Regan's murderer.) Like the repressed, Regan's dead body lies behind the two women in the house, a point which the film indirectly reinforces when Marlowe speculates about his own fate: he asks, of Canino and Huck, 'Where are they? Digging a grave?' But, rather than have Marlowe expose this, the scene works to demonstrate his authority as hero.

The two women do not seem to hint at the 'sexual deviance' of the two men at Geiger's; instead their presence in the house is more to do with Mars's power as master villain. On the surface, the scene develops as Marlowe's attack on that power: he enlightens Mona about her husband's gangster-like activities; he gets Vivian to help free him. But, in the subtext, the scene also enacts in heterosexual terms the subtextual intimations of the scene with Lundgren at Geiger's. Here it is Marlowe who is 'in bondage' and who, kissed by Vivian, is the object of desire. And Regan's body does not return to disturb them.

In insisting on a final showdown with Eddie Mars, Marlowe is not so much seeking to solve the mystery of who killed Regan as to find a way in which the various threats to himself and to the Sternwoods can be neutralised. Subtextually, however, more is clearly involved. That Marlowe should take Vivian to Geiger's (the first place he has taken her to, while she is the third person he has taken there) is in itself highly suggestive, as if a) he's making a point of showing Mars the way things are and b) he's answering Vivian's opening gambit in the film, when she invited him into her bedroom. Staging the showdown at Geiger's charges it with echoes of previous scenes in the house, including the one in which Mars walked in on Marlowe and Carmen. But the most telling link relates to the scene with Lundgren. After Mars has entered, the scene moves rapidly to the point where he is killed: far from the traditional detective's explanation of the narrative's mysteries, the final exchange between Mars and Marlowe serves to throw up more uncertainties. Having exposed the crucial flaw in Mars's story that Carmen killed Regan (why didn't he recognise her when he came into

Geiger's house before?), Marlowe doesn't probe further, but loses his temper and starts shooting. Mars is driven out through the door to be shot by his own men.

First, Marlowe shoots Mars in the arms: a symbolic castration. Second, as Mars is killed, he falls, turning as he does so, to lie in the same way (prone) in exactly the same place as Lundgren when Marlowe had him tied up. Marlowe's matching phone call to Bernie Ohls emphasises the connection, which could be taken as simply a symmetrical way of concluding the two parts of the quest, a final duplication. But, subtextually, it is as if Marlowe is repressing the sexual threat of Mars with even greater force than he repressed that of Lundgren. Linked in the *mise-en-scène*, the two bodies on the threshold of the house testify to the violence with which the film treats these ambiguously desired figures. From now on, Marlowe can concentrate on Vivian.

At the same time, the fact that the film ends with Marlowe and Vivian still at Geiger's suggests that, with Mars dead, Marlowe is now the master of the site. The disturbing implications of this are not entirely effaced. The first time that police sirens are heard in the film is when Marlowe is alone in his office, waiting for Vivian's phone-call: the call in which she (in effect) stands him up. (She has decided to go alone to see Brody about Carmen's blackmail photograph.) The second time is later that night, when Marlowe 'picks up' Lundgren – as if this is implicitly a consequence of Vivian standing him up. And, in the film's last shot, as Marlowe pulls Vivian towards him, the sirens are again heard. Although Steiner blends their wail into the film's love theme, they seem, momentarily, to disturb Marlowe, and he and Vivian look away, out into the darkness. It's as if, even at this point, the memory-trace of being with Lundgren in the car is flickering through Marlowe's mind. But he turns back to look at Vivian, and her returning the look reaffirms the sexual charge between them. The shot fades to black.

This essay has been an attempt to show what it is about *The Big Sleep* that is so fascinating. The discussion is far from exhaustive: in particular, I have not analysed the structure of the film's narrative, which can be seen as a series of echoes of the pre-narrative 'traumatic event': the killing of Regan. (The echoes follow a desire-murder-blackmail pattern which is repeated throughout the movie.) Even as a psychoanalytical account, it is partial – three *Wide Angle* articles in the early 'eighties (by Annette Kuhn in vol.4, no.3; Christopher Orr in vol.5, no.2; Judith Mayne in vol.6, no.3) all take other angles on the film. But, unlike other such accounts, this one attempts to relate the psychoanalytical subtext to Hawks as *auteur*. Like all great intuitive artists, Hawks in his works reveals more about himself than he seems able to admit. And, in the darkness of *film noir*, he found a terrain rich in buried meaning.

Still: Marlowe calls Bernie Ohls. Vivian listens.

OUT OF THE PAST

a.k.a. Build My Gallows High

Leighton Grist

Critical writing on Jacques Tourneur's *Out of the Past* (RKO, 1947) has often stressed its generic typicality. Tom Flinn, for example, sees it as 'a veritable motherlode of *noir* themes and stylisations' ('*Out of the Past*', *The Velvet Light Trap* 10, 1973, p.38), while Robert Ottoson notes, '*Out of the Past* is quite simply the *ne plus ultra* of 'forties *film noir*' (Ottoson, 1981, p.132). Produced during what is considered to be the central period of the initial *noir* cycle (1946-48), *Out of the Past* suggests the genre at a point of equilibrium, presenting a stabilisation of conventions developed during wartime *noir* before these underwent more baroque thematic or stylistic elaboration.

To examine this declared typicality, *Out of the Past* will here be measured against three main critical approaches to *film noir*: *noir* as a specific style, *noir* as existentialist drama, and the feminist view of *noir* as an articulation of male sexual paranoia. Through this it will be seen how criticism has engaged in a progressive archaeology of the genre. It is also hoped that, rather than being seen as a 'movement' (Place, 1976, p.36) or a 'period of film history' (Schrader, 1972, p.8), *film noir* will be reinforced as a specific genre, defined by certain visual, narrative, and thematic conventions. This isn't to claim that *noir* elements aren't apparent in films of other genres. But this is perhaps explained not by *noir*'s transgeneric status, but by the fact that, in the words of Steve Neale, 'Hybrids are by no means the rarity in Hollywood many books and articles on genre in the cinema would have us believe' ('Questions of genre', *Screen*, vol.31, no.1, Spring 1990, p.57). In *Out of the Past*, moreover, *noir* fulfils what has been considered genre's mythic function, the aesthetic mediation of irreconcilable cultural contradiction. It is an aspect inextricably linked to the film's industrial and institutional context, to its determination by formal and ideological norms, which make it recognisable as a prime example of 'forties *film noir*.

Out of the Past was shot in a generous 64 working days. Principal photography took place at RKO's Hollywood studio and Pathe's Culver City lot, and on location near Lake Tahoe. There was additional second-unit photography in Acapulco, San Francisco and New York. The film was released on 25th November 1947. Its making involved a number of figures significant in *film noir*. It was produced by Warren Duff

who as a scriptwriter was subsequently responsible for three other *films noirs*: *Chicago Deadline* (Lewis Allen, 1949), *Appointment with Danger* (Lewis Allen, 1951, co-written with Richard Breen) and *The Turning Point* (William Dieterle 1952). The source of *Out of the Past* was Geoffrey Homes's 1946 novel, *Build My Gallows High*, which provided the film's original title, changed when a test poll indicated audience resistance, but retained for the UK release. Geoffrey Homes was a pseudonym of Daniel Mainwaring, who was later to write a number of scripts under his own name. His credits include three Don Siegel movies, *The Big Steal* (1949), *Invasion of the Body Snatchers* (1956) and *Baby Face Nelson* (1957), and *The Lawless* (Joseph Losey, 1950). Mainwaring, however, kept his pseudonym for his initial adaptation of his novel, and 'Geoffrey Homes' eventually received the sole scriptwriting credit for *Out of the Past*, even though further drafts were written by James M. Cain and RKO contract scenarist Frank Fenton. Interestingly, much of Cain's work was discarded before filming (*see* Jeff Schwager, 'The Past Rewritten', *Film Comment*, vol.27, no.1, January-February 1991). *Out of the Past* was shot by Nicholas Musuraca, one of the most important and influential of all *noir* cinematographers, who had also previously worked with director Jacques Tourneur on a pair of typically atmospheric Val Lewton horror films: *Cat People* (1942) and *The Leopard Man* (1943). Composer Roy Webb is likewise worthy of note: he supplied the music for most of RKO's *films noirs*, including *Stranger on the Third Floor* (Boris Ingster, 1940), *Murder My Sweet* (Edward Dmytryk, 1944), *The Locket* (John Brahm, 1946), *Crossfire* (Dmytryk, 1947) and *They Won't Believe Me* (Irving Pichel, 1947). Finally, of the film's three young stars – Robert Mitchum, Jane Greer, and Kirk Douglas – Mitchum is a key *noir* presence. Yet he was cast as Jeff Bailey only after Warner Brothers had refused to loan out Humphrey Bogart and, following Mitchum's success in *The Story of GI Joe* (William Wellman, 1945), his dislodgement of Dick Powell, Philip Marlowe in *Murder My Sweet*, as a box-office attraction.

The plot of *Out of the Past* is quite involved. The film begins in the small town of Bridgeport, California, where Jeff Bailey runs a gas station, assisted by a young mute, the Kid (Dickie

Moore). Jeff also courts Ann Miller (Virginia Huston), a local girl. It is a life disrupted when Joe Stefanos (Paul Valentine) drives into town and informs Jeff that Whit Sterling (Kirk Douglas), a big-time gambler, wants to see him.

That night, Jeff drives with Ann to Whit's house at Lake Tahoe. During the journey, Jeff tells her about his past. His flashbacks recount how Jeff, under his real name of Markham, had been a New York private detective hired by Whit to find his mistress, Kathie Moffat (Jane Greer), who had shot Whit and stolen $40,000. Tracking Kathie to Acapulco, Jeff had fallen in love with her, believing her claim that she hadn't stolen Whit's money. Jeff and Kathie had fled to San Francisco, where they were discovered by Jack Fisher (Steve Brodie), Jeff's ex-partner, who tailed them to a mountain cabin. There, Fisher had threatened blackmail, and he and Jeff had fought, a struggle suddenly ended by Fisher being shot and killed by Kathie. She had then fled, leaving her bank-book, which confirmed her theft of Whit's $40,000.

At Tahoe, Jeff finds that Kathie is once more Whit's mistress. Using Jeff's past deception as leverage, Whit asks him to steal some records from San Francisco attorney Leonard Eels (Ken Niles), who is blackmailing Whit over his non-payment of taxes.

In San Francisco, Meta Carson (Rhonda Fleming), Eels's secretary, arranges for Jeff to meet Eels at the attorney's apartment. Fearing he's being framed, Jeff spies on Meta as she obtains the tax records from Eels's office. He returns to Eels's apartment, only to find the attorney's dead body, and then goes to Meta's apartment, where he unexpectedly discovers Kathie. Confronting her, Jeff learns the details of the frame. An affidavit, signed by Kathie, which states that Jeff, not she, killed Fisher has been placed in Eels's safe. This provides a motive for Eels's murder, and allows Whit to take revenge on Jeff. Kathie also enables Jeff to secure the tax records, which he agrees to trade for the affidavit. But the police turn up at Eels's office, preventing Meta from retrieving the document.

In Bridgeport, Jeff, hunted by the police, hides out in the mountains, dispatching the Kid to Tahoe with a message. With Whit in Reno, Kathie sends Stefanos to follow the Kid, but Stefanos is killed when the Kid pulls him from a bluff with a fishing-line. That night Jeff himself goes to Tahoe, where he tells Whit about Kathie's responsibility for the deaths of Fisher and Stefanos. He also arranges to exchange the tax records for a lifting of the frame, $50,000, and a 'plane out of the country.

Jeff meets Ann outside Bridgeport, and she agrees to join him when he sends for her. Returning to Tahoe, he finds Whit shot dead and Kathie in command. Pointing out that she could betray Jeff to the police, Kathie proposes that they flee the country together. Jeff seems to agree, but telephones the police to tell them of the escape plan. When they come to a road-block, Kathie shoots Jeff before she is killed by police machine-gun fire. Back in Bridgeport, Ann returns to Jim (Richard Webb), the local man who claims a long-standing love.

According to Paul Schrader, 'film noir was first of all a style . . . it worked out its conflicts visually rather than thematically' (Schrader, 1972, p.13). In line with this, Out of the Past stylistically defines contrasting environments. Bridgeport and its environs are generally shot in Hollywood's typical high-key style. Against this the treatment of environments that are exotic (Acapulco) or urban (New York, San Francisco) shows a combination of distinctively noir elements: low-key lighting, unbalanced compositions, claustrophobic and obstructive framing, enclosing shadows, fragmenting verticals. While Musuraca's camera-work eschews the extreme angles and distorting use of wide-angled lenses often seen in noir, the contrast between high-key and low-key sequences is heightened by the harsh brilliance of the sun-drenched Bridgeport scenes. However, in the late scene in which Jeff meets Ann outside Bridgeport, high-key lighting is replaced by noir style – the couple meet in a copse, at night, enclosed by the dark presence of trees and bushes – a suggestion of how Jeff carries the weight of the noir world with him.

The different styles reflect opposed symbolic regimes. On one level they underscore an archetypal country/city opposition. The elements of each style graphically reflect the qualities stereotypically associated with the setting: the country is traditionally linked with openness, honesty and clean living, the city with oppression, dishonesty and corruption. When extended to cover the exotic, noir visuals similarly hint at such notions as dark passions and threatening otherness. All this is reinforced by the mise-en-scène of high-key and low-key scenes. The scenes in the Bridgeport area are marked by location shooting and wide-open vistas. By contrast, the scenes in urban or exotic locales use restricted studio sets and back projection. This adds a further judgmental opposition: naturalness versus artificiality.

Whit's house at Tahoe, however, is the setting of both high-key and low-key scenes. The house is in the country, but is fundamentally of the city; an expression of Whit's corrupt wealth, it is a refuge where he continues his questionable activities. Narratively and symbolically, the location is the interface of country and city, light and darkness.

The suggestion of cultural opposition leads to the concept of genre as myth. Claude Lévi-Strauss claimed that the purpose of mythic narrative in primitive society was 'to provide a logical model capable of overcoming a contradiction' ('The Structural Study of Myth' in Structural Anthropology, Allen Lane, London, 1968, p.229). That is, through the 'ritual condensation' of an irreconcilable cultural dilemma

Still: at Whit's Tahoe house – Joe Stefanos (Paul Valentine), Kathie Moffat (Jane Greer) and the Kid (Dickie Moore).

into a series of thematic oppositions, the problem was temporarily, and aesthetically, worked through and resolved. Such resolution scarcely denied the actuality of the informing contradiction, the narrative structure being repeated with variation as long as the dilemma remained. With its repeated, antinomic thematic structure, historical reference and formalised endings, genre has been seen as analogous to myth, a view which helps to explain the popularity of various genres at different periods.

The dramatisation of the country/city opposition, however, is hardly a constant of *film noir*. Rather, it is the opposition of values associated with each location which reveals a basic thematic structure. The ideological conflicts thus dramatised are the foundation of the existentialist and feminist readings of *film noir*, and part of the generic interest of *Out of the Past* is its ideological clarity.

Bridgeport suggests an almost archaic American dream: the orderly, independent country town built upon non-exploitative capitalism and patriarchal social and sexual relations. Despite this, there are signs of discontent. From the beginning, we note Jim's truculence, Ann's parents' suspicions, and Marny's (Mary Field's) malignant gossip. All this unease, however, is centred upon Jeff: Jim is jealous of his relationship with Ann, Ann's parents want it stopped, while for Marny Jeff has become a locus of sexual frustration. Jeff's disruption of Bridgeport comes to a head with his being accused of murder and

with the resulting manhunt. It is a disruptiveness which can be related to Jeff being a refugee from the urban/*noir* world, to his inability to escape from its malevolent influence. For if Bridgeport implies an American dream, the urban/*noir* world represents an American nightmare. Claustrophobic and menacing, it is an environment ruled by violence and greed, deception and criminality. Independence has been replaced by power and subordination, sexual relationships are transgressive. It is a vision regarded by some early writers on *film noir* (e.g. Schrader, 1972; McArthur, 1972) as a displacement of a number of historically specific influences – postwar disillusion, the beginning of the Cold War, the rise of big business – all of which imply the relegation of the individual. In the light of this, the economic status of Whit Sterling and Jeff Bailey at the beginning of *Out of the Past* becomes noteworthy. Nominally a gambler, Whit seems phenomenally successful. His success and criminality evoke common fears about 'big business' which are underlined by his attempts to circumvent the US tax system and undermine the established, if already corrupt, professional order (the murder of Eels). Against this, Jeff's ownership of the gas station suggests a traditional, smaller scale, more 'humane' capitalism: 'I sell gasoline, I make a small profit. With that I buy

Still: Kathie and Jeff (Robert Mitchum) at the bar in Acapulco.

groceries. The grocer makes a profit. We call it earning a living. You may have heard of it somewhere.'

Jeff, of course, is hiding out in Bridgeport, concealing himself from Whit's vengeance and, possibly, police action over Fisher's death. The opening of *Out of the Past* echoes that of Robert Siodmak's *The Killers* (1946), in which the Swede (Burt Lancaster) hides out in a small town, where he works as a gas station attendant. Jeff has gone a stage further – he owns the gas station. That this supplies cover for Jeff reinforces the gap between *noir* values and those of 'normal' life, a point made explicit by Stefanos: 'Funny racket to find you in Jeff . . . I guess that's because it's respectable.'

The gas station is also the setting for both the film's beginning and end. Such bracketing is part of the narrative's balanced five-act structure. Act One takes place in Bridgeport, and concerns the arrival of Stefanos. Act Two covers the journey to Tahoe and Jeff's flashbacks. The third act is relatively short; taking place in Whit's house, it describes the setting up of the Eels plan. Act Four deals with events in San Francisco, while Act Five cuts between Bridgeport and Tahoe. Opening and closing at Bridgeport, the narrative thus comprises two framing acts, within which there are two parallel and reflective *noir* sections in which Jeff works for and respectively crosses and is double-crossed by Whit. These sections pivot upon the central act at Tahoe, which, in keeping with the setting's intermediate

position in the city/country opposition, is the fulcrum of the whole film.

Developed over the various drafts of the screenplay, this structure represents a major difference between *Out of the Past* and the original novel. In the novel, the first half of the narrative describes the events which become the first four acts of the film. The rest of the book then gradually unravels the plot, with an emphasis on the reactions of various characters to the situation. The restructuring of the story line for the film creates a more compressed narrative effect, with a stress on action rather than reaction. This is partly a consequence of the translation from a literary to a primarily visual medium. Yet there is also a diminished concern with explanation – the San Francisco scenes, in particular, are notable for a seeming confusion that contributes to a typically complex *film noir* narrative.

Such focusing of action is general to the novel's adaptation, even though the film maintains its overall plot outline. The film version of Whit Sterling combines actions and attributes of both his counterpart in the novel and a character called Guy Parker, a corrupt ex-police-chief turned gambler whom Whit controls. Stefanos similarly represents an amalgam of his namesake and a hit-man known as Slats (in the novel it is Slats who suffers death by fishing-line). The shifting of Eels's murder from New York likewise concentrates the 'present time' action in the adjoining states of California and Nevada. Such amendments add to the film's dramatic force. Another improvement is the renaming of the film's central characters. Jeff Bailey avoids the clichéd toughness of Red Bailey, while Kathie

Moffat is undoubtedly an improvement on Mumsie McGonigle. Red might also have been ruled out by its 'Communist' implications (or Mitchum's hair colour).

The novel concludes with Red being shot by Mumsie, whose fate, like the narrative, is left open. The addition to the film of Kathie's death (Fenton's draft) and the Bridgeport coda (Mainwaring's draft) suggests certain institutional influences. The punishment of Kathie aligns the film with the requirements of the Production Code, while the appending of the final scene provides at least a token happy ending for Ann. The narrative's motivating disruption, however, is characteristically *noir*. Jeff's 'new life' is disturbed by the intrusion of his past in the shape of Stefanos and, by association, of his relationship with Kathie. Jeff's former crossing of Whit similarly enables the gambler to trap him in his revenge plot. It is this inability to escape the past that ultimately causes Jeff's downfall, a fate he shares with a number of *noir* protagonists.

Complementing this, Jeff's dominant trait is an almost hopeless lack of will. Fatalistically passive, he is subject both to chance (the closed telegraph office in Acapulco which stops him wiring Whit about Kathie) and the decisions of others. He is hired by Whit, seduced by Kathie, then quiescently accepts their renewed dominance when he is summoned to Tahoe. His inertia is encapsulated in a scene with Kathie on the beach at Acapulco. Asked when he's returning her to Whit, he carelessly tells her, 'There's no hurry.' Then, when she asks if he believes Whit's accusation that she has stolen $40,000, he responds, with ardent abandonment, 'Baby, I don't care.' It is such acceptance of circumstance, as if the protagonist is faced with forces beyond his control, that has led to comparisons being made between *film noir* and, with its ideas on the random indifference of the material world, French existentialism. Philosophically, this is hardly rigorous, but it nevertheless complements the historical fears for the individual claimed for the genre. The suggested futility of struggle is compounded in *Out of the Past* by the way that Jeff's one successfully assertive act is self-sacrificial – telephoning the police to set up the roadblock which indirectly causes his death.

Jeff, in fact, is an archetypal *noir* protagonist. Iconographically, with his trench coat, soft-brimmed hat, and cigarette almost constantly glued to his lower lip, he is a visual exemplar of the hard-boiled private eye. His fatalism is tinged with a witty cynicism that in turn suggests a bruised romantic idealism. These traits, expressed through the snappy *noir* dialogue, point to the genre's literary precursors (Hammett, but especially Chandler) even if many of the film's verbal gems derive from Fenton's draft of the script rather than Mainwaring's novel (*see* Schwager). Jeff's romanticism makes him vulnerable to Kathie and encompasses an implicit honesty which both endears him to Whit and ensnares him in Whit's plans. ('You owe me something. You'll never be happy until you square yourself.') That such moralism is a liability only adds to the darkness of the *noir* world.

Jeff enters the *noir* world as what Michael Walker calls a seeker hero (*see* Introduction), to return Kathie to Whit and thus restore the patriarchal order. Yet while Whit's wealth and power bespeak patriarchal authority, his viciousness and criminality afford his control a negative, illegitimate aspect, which both underscores the genre's nightmare vision of America and exemplifies what a number of critics have considered its potential subversiveness. It is a subversiveness, however, which is usually, if often unconvincingly, recuperated, as in *Out of the Past*. The moment Jeff falls under Kathie's charms he becomes a victim hero, and accordingly pays the price.

This definition of the male protagonist through his relation to the female ties in with the late 'seventies reconsideration of *film noir* by Marxist and psychoanalytically-influenced feminist criticism. Relating their analyses to a more defined historical context – the post-war drive to get women out of the workforce and back into the home, to control their new-found 'independence' – feminist critics have dislodged the centrality of the existential view of *noir*. They have instead recast the genre as primarily an articulation of 'forties male paranoia: in many *films noirs*, the crime or problem to be solved becomes subordinate to an investigation of the threatening or fascinating woman with whom the protagonist comes into contact. Examples can be found throughout the initial *noir* cycle: *The Big Sleep* (Howard Hawks, 1946), *Dead Reckoning* (John Cromwell, 1947), *The Lady from Shanghai* (Orson Welles, 1948), as well as *Out of the Past*, in which Jeff's *initial* quest is to discover the transgressive female.

Typically, feminine transgression is embodied in the *femme fatale*. Although the term is often used loosely to describe decidedly non-deadly women, Kathie Moffat is the genuine article. She is responsible, directly or indirectly, for the deaths of Fisher, Eels, Stefanos, Whit and Jeff. Iconographically, from the moment Jeff sees her enter the Acapulco bar, wearing a close-fitting white dress, she perfectly embodies Janey Place's description of the *femme fatale*, whom she terms the 'spider woman': 'The iconography is explicitly sexual, and often explicitly violent as well: long hair . . . make-up . . . Cigarettes with their wispy trails of smoke can become cues of dark and immoral sensuality, and the iconography of violence (primarily guns) is a specific symbol (as is perhaps the cigarette) of her "unnatural" phallic power' (Place, 1978, pp.43-45). Such power informs Kathie's initial transgression: her shooting of Whit and theft of $40,000 simultaneously implies phallic appropriation and symbolic castration. The overturning of male control continues during her relationship with Jeff, where it is inherently linked to her sexuality. As Jeff admits, 'You're gonna find it very easy to take me anywhere.' Indeed, from the first, Kathie dominates his movements; Jeff's entrapment is symbolised by the omnipresent nets on the Acapulco beach. She arranges where and when they meet ('All I ever had to go on was a place and time to see her again'), while the fact that they lived 'by night' adds to her dark, ineffable force. Kathie even decides when they should, euphemistically, go to 'her place'. Itself an arrogation of male prerogative, Jeff's eager acceptance of his sexual subordination both underlines Kathie's power and supplies a rationale for his later effacement.

Jeff and Kathie's relationship continues when they flee to San Francisco. Its transgressive nature is stressed by the way they have to lie low and are excluded from 'normal' society, as well as by Jeff's utter abasement: 'I opened an office in San Francisco. Cheap little rathole which suited the work I did. Shabby jobs for whatever hire. It was the bottom of the barrel, and I scraped it. But I didn't care. I had her.' Significantly, the moment they surface into mainstream life they are spotted by Jack Fisher, Jeff's ex-partner. While Fisher's death confirms Kathie as 'phallic' and deadly, his killing also looks forward to Jeff's death by the same means. Although he's working for Whit (to restore patriarchal order), Fisher offers to lay off if Jeff gives him a cut of the money that Kathie has stolen. He is willing to accede to their sexual transgression, an ideological 'crime' for which he pays the penalty.

The existential and feminist approaches to *noir* are to an extent parallel in their mutual focus on the diminution of the male protagonist. Stylistically, however, *Out of the Past* lends support to feminist criticism's privileging of male sexual fears as the genre's motive force. Specifically, high-key lighting is used in scenes of patriarchal control, low-key lighting in scenes in which Kathie is in control. This is taken to quite precise lengths. For instance, following Jeff's first meeting with Kathie, which is shot low-key, his abortive visit to the telegraph office (where he seeks to contact Whit and thus reassert male control) is shot high-key. Similarly, when Whit arrives unexpectedly in Acapulco, threatening Jeff and Kathie's relationship, the film again reverts to high-key lighting. By contrast, when Jeff fully commits himself to Kathie the *noir* imagery deepens. The moment occurs at 'her place' when Jeff discards the towel with which they have dried their rain-sodden hair and knocks over the lamp which is the room's only illumination, darkening the already low-key lighting. The door blows open, and there is a tracking shot of the rain outside, images which symbolise coitus. The commentary implicit in the lighting and imagery is emphasised when Jeff closes the door and suggests that they flee from Whit, a denial of patriarchy in the face of Kathie's sexuality.

In this context, the *noir* lighting of the early scenes in which Jeff meets Ann outside her house and drives with her to Tahoe is thematically suggestive. From this point in the film's 'present time' chronology, Kathie can be seen to be in virtual control of the narrative. As much is implied by the plot to kill Leonard Eels. While this allows Whit to revenge himself on both Eels and Jeff, the planting of the affidavit gets Kathie off the hook. Kathie's control extends to the actual events in San Francisco: she oversees the action and gives Stefanos and Meta Carson their orders.

Meta Carson is a secondary *femme fatale*. Reinforcing traits embodied by Kathie, she, too, is represented as explicitly sexual. Dark, voluptuous and cigarette-smoking, she makes a pass at Jeff during their first, brief meeting. She is likewise a threat to the patriarchal order. For while she is Eels's secretary, she toys with his affections and has him under her sexual control. In using her charms to bring about his death, she overturns both sexual and economic hierarchies. Female sexuality is again related to death and transgression: a confirmation of male fears expressed through the figure of the *femme fatale*.

The linkage of Kathie and Meta is at one point made explicit. Kathie pretends to be Meta when, as part of the plot, she telephones Eels's apartment building. She is shown in the chiaroscuro of Meta's apartment; for the only time in the film, she is wearing her hair up, which leads, on a first viewing, to acute confusion over identity. It is a merging of character that stresses the symbolic function of Kathie and Meta.

The pairing of character also emphasises some discrete moments of female justification. When Jeff asks Meta if she isn't sorry to be crossing a 'nice guy' like Eels, she replies sharply: 'Maybe he isn't such a nice guy. Maybe he crosses people too.' This reflects Kathie's more considered vehemence when Jeff tells her that Whit didn't die when she shot him: 'I hate him. I'm sorry he didn't die.' There is also her later admission to Fisher: 'Sure I shot him. I'm not sorry about that.' With the comments uncontested narratively and spoken by strong characters, they stand as a cumulative critique of the already problematical patriarchal order. Another example of *noir*'s potential subversiveness, it is a critique which is again eventually recuperated.

In the San Francisco scenes, the narrative of *Out of the Past* becomes extremely convoluted, with unclear motivation and elliptical, repetitive action. On an existential reading, this complements the sense of anxiety and oppression transmitted by the *noir* visuals. Like Jeff, we are never quite in command of the situation; our timing is just 'a few minutes off'. The section actualises the idea of the *noir* world as nightmare: the confusion of the action mainly suggests dream logic. From this perspective, the symbolic collapsing of Kathie and Meta as they operate the plot suggests the condensation and displacement of a more general male anxiety. This once more validates the feminist view of *film noir*. Indeed, the

Still: Fisher (Steve Brodie) catches up with Kathie and Jeff.

nightmare of San Francisco ends only when Kathie is forced to admit a (temporary) failure of control by her telephoning Whit in Reno. This allows Jeff, and the narrative, to escape the night world of San Francisco for the day world of Bridgeport. It is a metaphorical suggestion underscored by the transition from one locale to the other: a fade to black followed by a shot of dawn breaking.

In common with the film's high-key, male-controlled sequences, motivation and action is generally clearer and more linear in Bridgeport than in San Francisco. A similar imposition of authority is implied by the 'Jeff Bailey' sign which marks the gas station. Emphasised by Stefanos's comment that it's a 'big sign', it reflects Jeff's attempt to achieve normative male control within the patriarchal environment of Bridgeport. Read thus, the sign evokes a desire for accession to the Lacanian Symbolic, 'the order of language and of the Father' (Charles F. Altman, 'Psychoanalysis and Cinema: The Imaginary Discourse' in Bill Nichols, ed., *Movies and Methods II*, University of California Press, Berkeley, 1985, p.520). The fact that Jeff has renamed himself –

Bailey instead of Markham – implies willed male command.

Central to Jeff's reconstructive desire is his relationship with Ann Miller, who is a prime example of a *film noir*'s other main female type, what Michael Walker calls the domestic woman. Fair instead of dark, domestic and dependent rather than sexual and independent (she still lives with her parents), Ann is as submissive as Kathie is assertive: 'Everything you say to me I believe.' She is related to the open and the natural, the lake and the woods – loaded ideological connotations. Ultimately, she is Jeff's last chance for reintegration into and redemption by the patriarchal order. As he says at the lake, 'I'd like to build a house right there, marry you, live in it, and never go anywhere else.' This calls up another, trans-generic cultural opposition played out by Jeff's actions: the wandering versus domesticated male.

For Jeff, however, domesticity can never occur. It is ideologically necessary that he be punished for his failure to uphold patriarchal authority. Even in Bridgeport, he prompts Ann to disobey her parents and is a character of whom they openly disapprove; this is complicated by our sympathy for Jeff against the parents' censure. More damning is Jeff's inability to break Kathie's spell, even when he knows the truth about her. At Meta's apartment, his anger swiftly becomes quiescence as soon as Kathie proclaims a continued love. The same limitation is suggested by his failure to obtain her affidavit. His fascination makes him lie to Ann when, with self-condemning guilt, he denies his renewed attraction towards Kathie in San Francisco: 'I saw her and it was nothing.'

Jeff's domination by Kathie is in turn part of his domination by the past. His voice-over which describes their initial relationship reinforces his passivity and fatalism: 'Mitchum relates his history with such pathetic relish that it is obvious there is no hope for any future: one can only take pleasure in reliving a doomed past' (Schrader, 1972, p.11). Flashbacks with voice-over are another generic commonplace, their often complex manipulation of time adding to the creation of an uncertain fictional world. Predictably a key consideration in existential readings of *noir*, they provide, as Schrader again notes, the sense of 'an irretrievable past, a predetermined fate and an all-enveloping hopelessness'. This also has been recast from a feminist perspective: 'the tendency of the flash-back structure to put a distance between the narrating voice-over and the story narrated also means that a

Still: Whit (Kirk Douglas), Jeff and Stefanos in Acapulco.

distance sometimes appears between the expressed male judgement and the woman who is being investigated and judged – leaving room for the audience to experience at least an ambiguous response to the female image and what is said about her' (Gledhill, 178, pp.16-17).

This gap between male narration and female image is rendered particularly potent in *Out of the Past* by Kathie's duplicity. It is also consistently implied that she is playing a part, acting out a role. Significant here is her delayed, 'star' entrance. Almost too poised and perfect as she walks through the proscenium arch of the bar's doorway, her 'performance' is underlined by both the leading gaze of José Rodriguez (Tony Roux), the guide, who is leaning against the jamb, and Jeff's impossibly romanticised voice-over: 'And then I saw her, coming out of the sun . . .' The suggestion of Kathie's role-playing is later made plain by Jeff's sarcasm when he surprises her in Meta's apartment: 'You're wonderful, Kathie. You're magnificent.' As Tom Flinn notes (Flinn, pp.38-39), this echoes the words of Sam Spade (Humphrey Bogart) to Brigid O'Shaughnessy (Mary Astor) in *The Maltese Falcon* (John Huston, 1941): 'You're good, you're very good.' Indeed, the portrayal of the *femme fatale* as actress is repeated throughout *film noir*, underlining the existential outlook of the male protagonist: 'such characterisations contribute to the instability and uncertainty of the hero's

Still: the final scene at the Tahoe house between Kathie and Jeff.

world . . . In this sense they express a male existential anguish at the failure of masculine desire' (Gledhill, 1978, p.18). They would also seem to be open to consideration in the light of Joan Riviere's concept of the masquerade, concisely summarised by John Fletcher as 'a rebellious or defiant impulse to steal the paternal phallus beneath a mask of feminine compliance' ('Versions of Masquerade', *Screen*, vol.29, no.3, Summer 1988, p.58). The relevance of this to Kathie is plain.

Kathie's centrality to *Out of the Past* is another significant contrast between the film and its source. In Mainwaring's novel, Mumsie McGonigle is a largely peripheral figure, for most of the book the passive mistress of Guy Parker. Mumsie doesn't kill Fisher. He dies when his gun accidentally fires as he fights with Red. It is only at the end that Mumsie becomes deadly and dominant, when she shoots Whit, Stefanos and Red, a development that smacks of narrative expediency. Mumsie also lacks Kathie's sexual power. Red not only doubts her earlier than Jeff doubts Kathie, but is also able to break from her totally. The changes of emphasis that privilege the *femme fatale* not only reinforce the potency of generic convention, but also, following the feminist view of *noir*, suggest how such conventions are themselves loaded with ideological significance. In the words of Andrew Britton, 'the conventions of a genre exist in a *productive* relationship to the essential conflicts and contradictions of a culture: that is, they are both determined as conventions by those conflicts while also acting as a medium in which cultural contradiction can be articulated, dramatised, worked through' ('Blissing Out: The Politics of Reaganite Entertainment', *Movie* 31/32, Winter 1986, p.3).

The ideological 'work' of *Out of the Past* is especially apparent in its later stages. As noted, Jeff's one successful act ensures his eradication. And, even at the end, Jeff's masculine 'failure' is sustained as he is shot (in the groin) by Kathie, to the last the transgressive, 'phallic', castrating female. However, his death, along with that of Kathie at the hands of the law (in all senses of the term), ensures the (violent) restoration of the patriarchal order.

Both deaths relate to the attempt at a closing patriarchal recuperation. The death of Kathie, the dominant figure throughout, is made narratively, as well as ideologically, necessary by her multiplying excesses. In this, her *fatale* aspect is stressed: she sends Stefanos to his death, then kills Whit and Jeff. It is notable that we *see* Whit's avowed violence only near the end, when he turns on Kathie after learning of how she has messed up the Eels plan and, usurping his authority, 'killed' Stefanos. This not only justifies his action, but effectively invalidates the earlier female criticisms of male control. Kathie's enforced punishment and recuperation are complemented by her appearance in her final scenes: her glamorous, sexual look is replaced by a severe, high-buttoned dress and a hat that covers her hair. The effect is a vindictive de-sexing.

Whit's violent reaction to Stefanos's death also invites consideration of the implied homoerotic subtext involving Whit, Stefanos and Jeff. This is introduced early on, when Stefanos suggestively informs Jeff of how much Whit has missed him: 'No-one ever thought more of you than Whit.' It continues during Jeff's first flashback, when he visits Whit in New York. Here, Stefanos's febrile anger at reports of Whit's shooting, his attentive lighting of his boss's cigarette and his grudging agreement to provide Jeff with information, as if he regards him as a rival, all suggest more than an employer/employee relationship. In fact, it is Stefanos's reactions which largely sustain the subtext. We note, for instance, his self-satisfied delight when, leaving Jeff, he departs from Acapulco with Whit, as well as his intent regard, highlighted in close-up, as Whit greets Jeff at Tahoe (during which *Jeff* lights Whit's cigarette).

The presence of homoerotic suggestion is relatively common in *noir*. There is for example, the relationship of Neff (Fred MacMurray) and Keyes (Edward G. Robinson) in *Double Indemnity* (Billy Wilder, 1944), or that of Farrell (Glenn Ford) and Mundson (George Macready) in *Gilda* (Charles Vidor, 1946). It is a feature which can once more be related, historically, to the threat posed by female sexuality and the concomitant breakdown of a stable patriarchal organisation. On one level, with heterosexual relationships dangerous, male characters symptomatically retreat to the safety of homosexual fellowship, an aspect particularly apparent in *Crossfire*, in which the army buddies are almost obsessively reluctant to return to family life. At a deeper level, the prevalence of homoeroticism evokes the contemporary uncertainty of patriarchy, implying a weakening of its sexual regulation.

Ideological recuperation in *Out of the Past* is completed by Ann's acceptance of Jim. Here the positiveness of the ending begins to break apart. A representative of the law – he works as a game warden – Jim is ungraciously jealous of Jeff and also suggested to have violent tendencies. Early on, for instance, Marny tells Stefanos that Jeff had better be careful: 'If he keeps mooning around Jim's girl, nobody'll know him.' Similarly, after Jeff meets Ann towards the end, a meeting Jim spies upon, Jim tells Jeff, 'I was going to kill you . . .' This tends to pair Jim with Whit, the 'legitimate' and 'illegitimate' representatives of patriarchy, and invites a critique of what is superficially commended, as does Ann's parents' attitude toward Jeff, which, while 'correct', seems unnecessarily hostile.

The 'happy ending' is further compromised by being built on a 'saving lie'. The Kid allows Ann to believe that Jeff had intended to flee with Kathie. This releases her from her past, freeing her to 'enjoy' married life with Jim. The Kid's dumbness underlines the notion that he suppresses truths that cannot be spoken: the power of the transgressive female, the failure of male authority. A literary model here would seem to be Joseph Conrad's *Heart of Darkness*. In this, the narrator, Marlow, returns to Brussels from Africa, but is unable to tell Kurtz's fiancée the truth about his death, of his nightmare reversion to the half-light of the primitive. Marlow's rationale is that it would make her life intolerable and reveal the darkness that lies behind the comforting illusion of 'civilisation'.

Ann's uncertain future ends *Out of the Past* on a poignant note which is augmented by the film's final shot, as the Kid walks away from the camera. There is a split in the film's logical and emotional address. Logically, the end marks the restoration of the patriarchal order, but what is memorable is Kathie's strength and sexuality, Jeff's futile struggle and Ann's loss. The ideological tensions dramatised by *Out of the Past* are effectively held in balance, the film's closure undermined by its implicit inadequacy. In existential terms, the assertion of the country-town ideal is forced and unconvincing, and the *noir* world is excluded but hardly denied. In sexual terms, the dominant memory of Kathie, not to mention her violent end, suggests her undiminished threat. Jeff's sign, the signifier of patriarchy, remains, but Jeff himself is dead.

This returns us to genre's mythic function. For while the narrative has worked through and 'resolved' the cultural opposition, the ending presents a formalised, temporary reconciliation of conflict rather than its denial. It essentially articulates the ideological contradictions which inform *film noir*, which in turn relate to certain social and sexual tensions of 'forties America. As with myth, cultural contradiction remains, open to further mediation by subsequent *films noirs*. This mythic suggestion is innately connected to the influence of the film's institutional context. With its 'positive' closure, *Out of the Past* reflects Hollywood's dominant affirmatory tendency. While genre – like myth – expresses social contradiction, it is associated with cultural maintenance, not ideological challenge.

Myth, however, is primarily a social phenomenon, a process whereby society 'deals with' fundamental tensions. Just as generic conventions are ideologically informed, a genre or cycle's life-expectancy is determined by its cultural pertinence: films will continue to be produced as long as people are prepared to pay to see them. Even if one allows for such factors as the influence of publicity and the presence of stars, a genre's longevity is dependent upon the social validity of its preoccupations. With its continuance into the fifties and reappearance in the 'seventies and 'eighties, *film noir* would appear to address a number of recurrent, unresolved ideological conflicts.

Betrayed by Rita Hayworth: Misogyny in
THE LADY FROM SHANGHAI

Andrew Britton

'In *The Lady from Shanghai*, Rita's character dies. It was the only death scene the actress had ever played, and occurs at the climax of the story, when she's been shot and lies struggling on the ground. "I don't want to die!" she cries out. Hedda Hopper was on the set the day the scene was filmed, but her comments weren't concerned with Rita's truly fine acting. "I was there the day Welles wiped up the floor with his wife," the columnist noted, and she went on to say, "That, in my book, is certainly no way to keep a marriage going" ' (Edward Z. Epstein and Joseph Morella, *Rita: The Life of Rita Hayworth*, W.H. Allen, London 1983, p.115).

It has been taken for granted too often in the past that *film noir* is inherently misogynistic, and even if one disagrees, it can hardly be denied that at the heart of the social and moral darkness into which the *noir* hero is drawn there does often lurk an alluring, venal, devious and utterly treacherous woman. In some cases, of which I shall argue that Orson Welles's *The Lady from Shanghai* (1947) is one, it is indeed true that the presence of a female character of this kind is synonymous with

something that has to be called misogyny, but it is all the more important, for this very reason, to bear in mind two points – one about the representation of women and one about genre – before evaluating the sexual politics of any given example of *film noir*.

In the first place, the fact that a work of art contains a female character who is represented as vicious and destructive cannot *in itself* be used as evidence that the work in question is either misogynistic or anti-feminist. One of the greatest feminist dramas ever written, Henrik Ibsen's *Hedda Gabler*, is built around a woman who can only be described as odious, and both *film noir* and the woman's melodrama provide numerous examples of female protagonists whose very monstrousness allows the director to propose a critical analysis of the social conditions which have channelled powerful energies and a formidable intelligence into destructive, and self-destructive, forms. Bette Davis regularly played characters of

Still: the shoot-out in the Hall of Mirrors –
Bannister (Everett Sloane), Elsa (Rita Hayworth)
and O'Hara (Orson Welles).

this kind, most notably in *Beyond the Forest* (1949), where King Vidor derives a critique of women's oppression as audacious as any the cinema has given us from the story of a woman whose values and behaviour are, on the face of it, merely reprehensible. Elsewhere in this book, I suggest that the Ann Savage character in *Detour* (Edgar G. Ulmer, 1945), without doubt the most abrasive fatal woman in the whole of *film noir*, has been conceived along similar lines, by a director and an actress who are prepared to go just as far as Vidor and Davis in defying the audience to find any means of liking the heroine. It is not necessary to formulate 'positive images' of female strength, resistance or independence in order to produce a narrative that criticises patriarchy from a woman's point of view, and many works of the greatest dramatic and ideological power have chosen instead to represent the tragic waste or perversion of a woman's struggle for autonomy and self-definition in the context of an implacably hostile and oppressive culture.

Secondly, generic character types – like all the conventional tropes, motifs and structures associated with a genre – do not have any fixed, definitive dramatic significance or ideological content. The meaning of a convention is primarily determined by the specific narrative context in which it is used, and different directors may well realise the same convention in opposite or contradictory ways, as the comparison between *The Lady from Shanghai* and *Gilda* (Charles Vidor, 1946) later in this essay seeks to demonstrate. Certainly, an artist's leeway with a convention is not infinite, but artistic conventions are at the furthest possible remove from those of mathematics, and they are useful not because of their invariance, but because they conduce to the most complex particularised modifications and inflections of attitude within the general ideological field which they define. This flexibility is always especially marked in the case of generic character types – as it must be if the genre is not to ossify. We may say that a given type becomes conventionalised because it embodies, in rough outline, an individual social destiny which is felt to have a representative significance of such urgent interest that audiences are prepared to see it acted out in concrete detail again and again, with substantive variations that allow the potential ramifications of the basic theme to be thoroughly explored.

From this point of view, the source of the fascination exerted by the '*film noir* woman' is surely clear enough. Like her inverted mirror-image, the persecuted wife, she is the product of an historical situation in which the practical requirements of the US war economy had radically transformed the social position of American women, who were now expected, and encouraged, to abandon their traditional role within the home and to think of themselves instead as workers and wage-earners who were perfectly capable of performing vital social tasks and of taking independent responsibility for their own lives. Where the melodrama of domestic persecution represents male-dominated marriage from the perspective of a woman whose husband seeks to enforce the power-structures of patriarchy through terror and violence, *film noir* produces, in the *femme fatale*, a female type who will stop at nothing to evade, or extricate herself from, the social and economic constraints imposed on women by marriage and domesticity, and who is prepared to use men's desire for her, and men's assumptions about femininity, to achieve ends of her own.

It follows, therefore, that the attitude we are invited to adopt to such a woman will depend entirely on whether her actions are attributed to a specifically feminine, and inherently defective, will, or to the real social pressures which are brought to bear on women in a world where their freedom and their range of action is drastically limited, and where all human relationships are characterised (as those in *film noir* are) by greed, opportunism, self-interest and mutual exploitation. No doubt the *femme fatale* is more readily available for misogynistic appropriation than some other patriarchal stereotypes of women, and the hard-boiled 'thirties detective fiction which so many writers have identified (correctly) as a major source of *film noir* was largely written by men who seem to have needed no encouragement to view her as a castrating bitch. However, the social and generic determinants of *film noir* are very much more complex than those of the novels of James M. Cain and Raymond Chandler, and we need look no further than the film versions of *Mildred Pierce* (Michael Curtiz, 1945), *Double Indemnity* (Billy Wilder 1944) and *The Big Sleep* (Howard Hawks, 1946) to confirm that the sexual politics of these writers is not given in their material. Faced, in *The Big Sleep*, with one of Chandler's poisonous vamps, Hawks simply ignores her existence and encourages Lauren Bacall to develop the persona which they had just created in *To Have and Have Not* (1944), thus reversing the whole meaning of the original text at a stroke. The journey from Gilda to the Rita Hayworth of *The Lady from Shanghai*, which involves an equally spectacular evaluative shift, leads in the opposite direction, but in this case, as in the other, the director, not the genre, is establishing the itinerary.

Women in Welles's Films

One of the most consistent features of Orson Welles's work is his total lack of interest in dramatising the experience of women: there can be few directors with any reputation for being major artists whose treatment of their female characters is more perfunctory. This is not to say that women always play a marginal role in the

Still: Elsa watches Broome (Ted De Corsia) die after he has been shot by Grisby.

films, though they often do. Even when they are theoretically central, however, they are viewed in practice (with one exception) as ancillary to stories about men, and have no more real/dramatic substance than the uncomplicated patriarchal stereotypes on which they have been based; the minimum investment of imaginative energy is expended on them. The point is strikingly exemplified by the film versions of *Macbeth* (1948) and *Othello* (1952), where Welles has inherited two exceptionally vivid and complex female protagonists from the author of the original plays. In both cases, Welles seems hardly to realise that the material has anything to do with heterosexual relationships or the position of women at all. His interpretation of *Othello* – which corresponds exactly to what F.R. Leavis has called 'the sentimentalist's' reading of the play in terms of the destruction of a 'nearly blameless' hero by a diabolically malicious villain ('Diabolic Intellect and the Noble Hero: or The Sentamentalist's Othello' in *The Common Pursuit*, Chatto & Windus, London, 1958, pp.136-159) – reduces Desdemona to being the catalyst for her husband's tortuous encounters with Iago.

The female type with which Welles seems happiest is that version of the Eternal Feminine whose erotic glamour is unsullied by any active participation in the vicissitudes of sexual life and who observes the affairs of men with an ironic but profoundly indulgent eye. This is the part assigned to Tanya (Marlene Dietrich) in *Touch of Evil* (1958), and she is duly equipped with tarot cards and treasures of concession for masculine frailty. The spouses of Welles's male protagonists are treated very differently. The best that can be said is that his realisation of such characters is neutral and external. It might no doubt be claimed that the charm of Loretta Young endows the heroine of *The Stranger* (1946) with a presence of a kind, but Mary Youngstreet is really little more than an ingenuous young woman who has married a Nazi mass-murderer by accident, and she notably lacks the moral and psychological ambivalence which Hitchcock found in an obviously similar character in *Shadow of a Doubt* (1943).

Elsewhere, however, Welles seems to go out of his way to emphasise the shallowness and triviality of his female characters, which is all the more conspicuous for the labyrinthine spiritual complexity imputed to the men he plays himself. The treatment of Susan Alexander (Dorothy Comingore) in *Citizen Kane* (1941) is particularly revealing, in that the section of the film dealing with Kane's second marriage is thematically so close to *Rebecca* (Alfred Hitchcock, 1940) and to the cycle of melodramas about women's domestic persecution which Hitchcock's work inaugurated. The heroine of *Rebecca* is self-abnegating, naively romantic and painfully subservient to her husband, and it would have been easy for a director less sympathetic to her predicament to portray her as a fool, but Hitchcock never allows us to forget that she behaves as she does because she has internalised so completely the fantasies about men and marriage which women are encouraged to have, and he invites us not to feel superior to her, but to share her discovery of the discrepancy between these fantasies and the practical realities of her married life. Welles presents Susan Alexander as a shrill and silly, if pathetic, bimbo whose blighted career is primarily interesting (her personal shortcomings being what they are) as a measure of the scale of her husband's tragic, self-defeating hubris. Her prolonged humiliation and attempted suicide are quickly forgotten, and in the film's final stages it is Kane himself, and not his wife, who is represented as a prisoner of the great patriarchal house, wandering through its corridors haunted by the memory of what he has lost, while Susan sits complacently in the hearth, bitching and making jigsaw puzzles. In *Touch of Evil*, the animus implicit in this mean-minded portrait of a querulous nag erupts in the unmistakable relish with which Welles depicts the ordeal of another mindless blonde, Susan Vargas (Janet Leigh), in Uncle Joe Grandi's motel (Robin Wood draws attention to Welles's undisguised antipathy to the Leigh character in 'Welles, Shakespeare and Webster: *Touch of Evil*' in *Personal Views: Explorations in Film*, Gordon Fraser, London, 1976, pp.134-152).

The great exception to these rules, as to all the rules of Welles's work, is, of course, *The Magnificent Ambersons* (1942), and in attempting to account for the exception we note that the film recounts the tragedy of a family, not the tragedy of a man. The process which culminates in the 'comeuppance' of George (Tim Holt) is certainly poignant, but there is never any danger that George will inspire the narcissistic identification with the decline of a flawed titan which recurs with such obsessional regularity in Welles's other films. What happens to him is more like a spiritual education than a tragic fall, and it takes place in a context of family and social life from which Welles tends, as a rule, to detach his male protagonists. The artistic impersonality which results from this uniquely nuanced and impartial relationship between Welles and his hero is manifested most impressively in the three major female characters, all very different from one another, who play such crucial roles in the film's narrative. In particular, the scenes centred on Agnes Moorehead's staggering performance as Aunt Fanny presuppose a capacity to identify with women and their oppression that is all the more moving for the fact that Welles was never able to recapture it.

The Lady from Shanghai

While *The Lady from Shanghai* is not the only Welles film which is built around a woman (Loretta Young is, ostensibly at least, the protagonist of *The Stranger*), it is certainly the only one in which this woman is represented as being a figure of real power, played by a major star for

Still: Grisby (Glenn Anders) expounds his plot to O'Hara.

whom the film was conceived as a vehicle, and in which heterosexual desire and heterosexual relationships constitute the principal subject matter. This last point is, perhaps, the heart of the matter: *The Lady from Shanghai* portrays heterosexuality as a Byzantine labyrinth into which men are lured by the deceptive but irresistible promise of a culpably glamorous woman who, with malice aforethought, uses her victims' desire, first to exploit, and then to destroy them. The mere sight of Elsa Bannister is sufficient in itself to deprive O'Hara (Orson Welles) of the power of rational thought. 'Once I'd seen her,' he tells us, 'I was not in my right mind for quite some time,' and the point is insisted on repeatedly thereafter, not only in O'Hara's commentary but also in the *mise-en-scène*. Consider, for example, the extraordinary sequence on Bannister's (Everett Sloane's) yacht in which O'Hara, having just turned away in disgust from Bannister's cynical paean to the virtues of money, is compelled despite himself to rejoin the company on the deck by the hypnotic strains of Elsa's song. O'Hara's spontaneous revulsion at everything that Bannister represents is no match for Elsa, who has the capacity to induce a state of moral somnambulism which denies him the guidance of his finer instincts.

The film suggests, indeed, that Elsa's charm is such that the men who succumb to it are thereby absolved of any responsibility for their own actions, however deplorable, and that the blame for any crime or folly which they may commit while under the influence can be laid at the door of the intoxicating siren herself. Even Grisby (Glenn Anders), whose physical and spiritual repulsiveness Welles loses no opportunity to emphasise, eventually takes his place in the roll-call of Elsa's victims as a 'poor, howling idiot'

who, to that extent, has rather more in common with the noble hero than his sweaty upper lip and falsetto giggle would have led one to expect. Bannister himself is viewed sympathetically insofar as his actions can be interpreted as the inevitable corollary of a tragic obsession with a beautiful woman who does not reciprocate his feelings. We are given to understand in the picnic sequence that Bannister has blackmailed Elsa into marrying him, and he thinks nothing either of boasting about it or of asserting his right to humiliate his wife in public ('I don't have to listen to you talk like that!' 'Oh yes you do, lover!'). However, Welles nowhere suggests – as we can imagine a Bette Davis melodrama suggesting – that these facts might go some way to explain Elsa's behaviour and her readiness to resort to murder to regain her freedom. On the contrary, the expedients which Bannister has adopted to secure Elsa's company are portrayed as evidence of the depth and intensity of his desire rather than its selfishness and lack of scruple, and it is quite characteristic of Welles that the only moments of incipient tenderness and affection in the entire film are those in which Bannister ventures, with the awkwardness of a smitten adolescent, to express his hopeless, thwarted passion for his wife. These confessions of vulnerability and unassuaged longing by a man otherwise presented as vicious, corrupt and hypocritical work in very much the same way as Hank Quinlan's professions of devotion to his dead wife in *Touch of Evil*: in both cases, an evil man's surprising capacity to experience what we are invited to see as love is used to invest his evil with a sort of tragic pathos. 'Killing you is killing myself,' Bannister

217

tells Elsa in the Hall of Mirrors, 'but, you know, I'm pretty tired of both of us.' This touching speech bears pondering in relation to Welles's interest in *Othello* – and of course, Elsa has as little say in the matter as Desdemona. Whatever he has done, Bannister is ennobled by his allegiance to a love he would rather die than renounce, and the overall effect of pathos is subtly reinforced by the fact that he is disabled. At one level, of course, his deformed and twisted body can be interpreted, in the light of a familiar convention, as the mirror of his soul, but it also fits him for the mantle of the tragic cripple, condemned by a whim of nature to yearn for the love of Woman in vain. Everett Sloane's performance makes Bannister both credible and moving, but the magisterial authority and subtlety of the actor's art, so admirable in itself, should not distract our attention from the dramatic purposes which the character is used to serve.

Welles tells us what we are to think about Elsa herself on her very first appearance. We see her in medium shot, seated in the hackney cab – cool, poised, elegant, immaculately self-possessed, and smiling directly at O'Hara (and at us) in friendly greeting. 'Some people can smell danger,' O'Hara comments on the soundtrack, 'not me.' On the face of it, there seems no reason why the woman we have seen should inspire a sense of danger, and this is precisely the point the film wishes to make: Elsa is dangerous because it is so terribly difficult to deduce what she is really like from what she appears to be. If we read the film's action retrospectively, it is clear enough that Elsa must have singled out O'Hara as a potential fall-guy more or less at the moment she set eyes on him; not only has she been systematically deceiving him throughout the narrative, but the moments at which she seems to be discouraging his attentions, and even warning him to be on the look-out for 'a trap of some kind', are themselves intended to embroil him all the more deeply. These moments of apparent indecision, when affection or pity for O'Hara seem to compel Elsa to offer him the chance to disengage himself, are especially significant in that it would have been easy to use them to suggest Elsa's genuine ambivalence and the extent of the desperation which has driven her to make use of O'Hara at all. At times, it almost seems as if this is what the film intends to do. Both the content and the tone of her response, in the picnic sequence, to the news that O'Hara is still thinking of leaving Bannister's service ('Why should anyone want to live around us?') convey a sense of helplessness and despair which is amply confirmed in the scenes in Acapulco. After confessing that she has contemplated suicide 'many times', Elsa declares – in what seems to be good faith – her conviction that 'everything's bad' and that 'you can't escape it or fight it.' She goes on to tell O'Hara, gently but firmly, that he is a 'foolish knight errant' who could never take care of her because he cannot even take care of himself.

It is all the more perverse, then, that Welles should invite us to discount the complexities of attitude and motivation implied by details of this kind, and by the minutiae of Hayworth's acting,

Still: Bannister defends O'Hara in his trial for murder.

218

and to conclude that it is in circumstances such as these that the appalling gulf between what Elsa is and what she appears to be yawns widest. The conversation in which she tells O'Hara that she has been tempted to kill herself begins with an innocent inquiry about what Grisby said to him earlier in the day. We will discover later that she already knows the answer, having planned the encounter between the two men with Grisby himself, and the elaborate display of frailty which follows can only be read as yet another stage in the process of duplicitous seduction. This interpretation is confirmed in the very next sequence: Elsa leads O'Hara to believe that she is breaking off the relationship because they have no possible means of support in the full knowledge that Grisby is about to offer him $5,000, baited with the hint that this is just the sum O'Hara needs to make life with Elsa a practical possibility. Elsa is at her most treacherous when she seems to be most vulnerable, and at her most unscrupulously calculating when she seems to take O'Hara's welfare most to heart: the dire warnings about Grisby and Bannister with which she is so lavish in the aquarium sequence are primarily designed to convince O'Hara that if he can trust no one else, he can at least trust *her*. The lyrics of Elsa's song proclaim, with teasing frankness, the nature of her methods: 'Please don't love me – but *if* you love me, don't take your arms away.' Every word and every action is studiously and perfidiously ambiguous, and, in case we should fail to take the point, Welles names Bannister's yacht the 'Circe'. Elsa is related by direct descent to the treacherous enchantress who turned heroes into swine.

Welles even goes so far as to construe his heroine's case philosophically. During the cruise, O'Hara, who is at the wheel, asks Elsa if she believes in love. Her immediate response is a peremptory command that she be allowed to steer, and when the wheel is in her hands she tells him that she was 'taught to think about love in Chinese' and that there is a Chinese saying to the effect that 'one who loves passionately is cured of love in the end.' She adds that the saying promulgates a second thesis, 'Human nature is eternal: therefore, one who follows his nature keeps his original nature in the end.' Welles was clearly drawn to the second proposition, which recurs in *Mr Arkadin* (1955) in the famous anecdote about the scorpion that persuades a frog to carry it across a river, after allaying the frog's fears of being stung with the eminently logical observation that this would drown them both. The scorpion stings the frog anyway, and as they sink, it says that while there is no logic to what it has done, 'I can't help it: it's my nature!'

The obvious significance of the parallel between Elsa's Chinese saying and Arkadin's parable is that Elsa is identified with the scorpion. She is what she is, and her destructiveness can be attributed to nothing but itself. In the context of Welles's work as a whole, however, there is a rider to these fables. Welles is fond of claiming, on behalf of the fallen archangels whom he generally plays himself, that they can't help it because it's their nature: they are absolved of the guilt for their crimes, or pardoned for their corruption, on the grounds that they have remained magnificently true to themselves. Tanya's epitaph on Quinlan in *Touch of Evil* – 'He was some kind of a man. What does it matter what you say about people?' – classically exemplifies Welles's conscious decision to exempt his male protagonists from moral judgment and to justify them by reference to their rich, if blemished, humanity. Elsa can hardly be said to have behaved worse than Quinlan, but she gets a very different send-off, and there is certainly no mysterious soothsayer on hand to tell us that she was 'some kind of a woman'. She is obliged to make do with a pompous sermon from her former lover, who, having first inquired whether she has never 'heard of something better to follow' than her own nature, proceeds to impart the edifying (if unhappily belated) message that we only lose in the struggle against evil 'if we quit', before marching off, with an expression signifying righteousness, into the sunrise. It is, indisputably, one of the cinema's most disgraceful endings, but Welles takes it as seriously as he takes anything, and it is certainly not to be explained away as a concession to 'Hollywood morality'. The morality encapsulates, in the form of sententious homily, what the film has said implicitly throughout, and Welles hardly bothers to conceal his satisfaction that O'Hara is at last in a position to put Elsa firmly in her place.

Rita Hayworth

What *The Lady from Shanghai* does to Elsa is inseparable from what it does to Rita Hayworth: the point is so important that one feels the need to approach it with a certain circumspection. Welles's marriage to his leading actress had broken up before the film was made (though they were not yet formally divorced), but their relations on the set appear to have been amicable, and one does not wish to suggest that Welles's animosity towards Elsa as a character is simply continuous with his feelings about his wife as a person, if only because his treatment of Elsa, for all its virulence, is entirely consistent with the attitude to women in his other films. There can be no doubt, however, that Welles deliberately sets out to undermine Rita Hayworth's persona and to eliminate – as far as that is possible – its positive connotations, and this is what concerns the critic. Naturally, the transformation of Hayworth's image has generally been seen as evidence of artistry. Welles was trying to 'extend her range as an actress', and if Harry Cohn had conniptions and the great American public turned up its nose, this is par for the course in encounters between Creative Genius and the Philistine. The trouble with this view is that it takes for granted that

Hayworth's image was no more than a set of constraints, imposed and maintained by some combination of commercial interests and audience conservatism. This really will not do. The image which Welles changed had a meaning, as did the changes which he made, and the contradiction between these meanings is the key to *The Lady from Shanghai*.

The most obvious change is physical: the cutting, bleaching and coifing of Hayworth's long red hair. (In *Rita*, Epstein and Morella remark that the Columbia publicity department extolled this event as 'the most famous haircut since Samson's', and when one recalls that Samson's hair was cut off in order to deprive him of his power, this analogy seems appropriate in ways of which the PR men can hardly have been aware.) It is no less significant, however, that having cast an actress who is supremely remarkable for the apparently unguarded and spontaneous sensuousness of her every movement (Hayworth was, of course, an exceptionally gifted dancer), Welles should have decided not to let her move at all. The two changes go together, and they have the effect of eradicating the impression of uninhibited pleasure in her own body and her own sexuality which Hayworth habitually creates, and of reducing her to an icon, the principal feature of which is its elaborately contrived and calculated artifice. The discarded Hayworth 'image' connotes vitality, exuberance, openness and a carnality which, though self-conscious and sometimes deliberately provocative, also asserts its independence of male desire. Hayworth's Gilda is perfectly aware of her effect on men, but the awareness is ironic in character, and the detachment from male perceptions of her which this irony implies is the source of Hayworth's astonishing ability, in the nightclub sequence, to perform a voluptuous solo dance as if she intended to please herself rather than the men in the audience. It also allows her, in Gilda's exchanges with Johnny (Glenn Ford), to convey an incisive and astringent critical intelligence which is by no means a standard item in the equipment of the sex goddess, and which is more reminiscent of Marlene Dietrich than of Marilyn Monroe. In *The Lady from Shanghai*, Hayworth's ironic lucidity is redefined as Machiavellian cunning, and her erotic energy is confined and immobilised in a succession of sculptured poses which transform her face into a mask of sphinx-like inscrutability. This radical reconception of the very nature of Hayworth's beauty obviously coincides with the film's view of Elsa's character. The beauty is entirely a matter of surface, and its function is to conceal the essential nature of the woman who manufactured it.

The parallels between *Gilda* and *The Lady from Shanghai* are even closer than those between *Shadow of a Doubt* and *The Stranger*, and one suspects (though as far as I know there is no external evidence for this) that Welles borrowed the structure of his film from Vidor's, which he must surely have seen. However that may be, the two trios of protagonists are virtually identical, the only difference being that Gilda has met and had an affair with Johnny in the past, before the film's action begins. From every other point of view, the works are polar opposites: if *The Lady from Shanghai* is a misogynistic film, *Gilda* is a film *about* misogyny. Both Johnny and Ballen (George Macready) desire Gilda and wish to possess her, but her sexuality appals as much as it attracts them because they experience it as an irresistibly powerful, independent force which generates intensities of feeling that they cannot master at will and which is, to that extent, more powerful than they are. *Gilda* argues that images of charismatic female sexuality generally provoke this kind of ambivalence in men, and goes on to suggest that in such cases heterosexual feeling is accompanied by feelings of impotence and inferiority which can only be made good by overpowering, degrading and – logically – destroying the woman. The theme would be a remarkable one even if *Gilda* were not a vehicle for a star with an extensive male following, but the film can undertake it because it draws as heavily on the melodrama of domestic persecution as it does on *film noir*. Like Alicia (Ingrid Bergman) in *Notorious* (Alfred Hitchcock, 1946), Gilda combines elements of both the *femme fatale* and the entrapped wife, and this union of antithetical types enables Vidor and Hitchcock to focus the theme of men's fear of autonomous female sexuality with unusual clarity.

If Welles had deliberately set out to invert the meaning of Hayworth's most famous film, he could not have done so more thoroughly, for *The Lady from Shanghai* methodically rationalises the feelings about women which *Gilda* defines as neurotic. It must be stressed in this connection that while Vidor undermines Johnny's nominal position as the hero right from the start, and shows us how much he has in common with the nominal villain (whose professional and marital obligations he eventually inherits), Welles insists on maintaining the clearest possible distinction between O'Hara and Bannister. In that they are both betrayed by Woman they share a common male fate, but there is no moral likeness, and all traces of one of *Gilda*'s most fascinating themes – the perverse bonding of male sexual rivals united by their common hatred of the woman they both want – are simply eliminated from the material. One has to admit, of course, that *Gilda* discredits Johnny so completely that it is faced with a problem which Welles does not need to confront: the problem of how to end. Dramatic logic seems to entail a conclusion where Gilda is killed in circumstances that allow the analysis of the two men's joint responsibility for her destruction to be clinched, but the film recoils from the prospect of tragedy, and opts instead to renege in the last ten minutes on everything it has done in the first hundred. The resulting happy ending, in which Johnny is suddenly discovered to be at heart a good chap, is offered without a hint of the irony which Douglas Sirk or Hitchcock use to choke the machinery of conventional narrative closure, but although the shoot-out in the Hall of Mirrors is (judged purely as an *action*) infinitely more logical and satisfying than Vidor's botched-up change of heart, its logic is the product of a narrative that leaves no ideological problems to be solved and no subversive criticisms of our culture's sexual values to be recuperated. No doubt Hitchcock would never have allowed the norms of masculine dominance to take over in the way that Vidor does, but the fact remains that it is much easier to produce a satisfactory dénouement if one has no more to say than that nasty people end up by destroying each other and that the wages of female sin are death. (Richard Dyer makes some very valuable comments on Hayworth's star image and, particularly, her performance in *Gilda* in 'Resistance through charisma: Rita Hayworth and *Gilda*' in Kaplan, 1978, pp.91-99. I should add, however, that I disagree with his account of gender in *film noir*, and that his claim that *Gilda* reinstates 'traditional notions of masculinity and normality' by representing the Glenn Ford character as 'in some sense homosexual' seems to me completely untenable).

The Noble Hero

The inadequacy of Welles's performance is the least of the many problems with the hero of *The Lady from Shanghai*. Robert Mitchum would certainly have done it far better, but the entire conception of O'Hara's character is impenetrably anomalous and contradictory. His comments on his encounter with the hoodlums in Central Park in the opening sequence, where he remarks that he is very far from being the hero that his easy victory might make him seem, suggests that Welles intends to distance us from conventional notions of the heroic role, but the latent possibility of irony is emphatically ignored throughout the rest of the film, and we are unfortunately obliged to accept O'Hara, in all his inconsequence, at face value. He introduces himself as an artless, fresh-faced Irish sailor with a line in winning blarney (he christens Elsa 'the Princess Rosalie') whose head is turned by romantic obsession. Indeed, the degree of gullibility required in order to become a party to the convoluted and implausible mechanics of Grisby's plot does seem to warrant the charge of stupidity which O'Hara brings against himself in his final monologue. At the same time, however, he is represented as being an idealistic political activist who fought for the Republicans in Spain and who, according to a radio commentator at his trial, has acquired the reputation of being a 'notorious waterfront agitator'. The O'Hara we glimpse in the seamen's hiring hall where Bannister goes to find him is neither a sailor nor a whimsical boyo, but a crusading, racket-busting journalist akin to Kane in his salad days, and Welles even shows himself at a typewriter composing (one assumes) an inflammatory socialist tract. In later scenes, O'Hara expresses sympathy for the predicament of Elsa's black maid, and he responds to Elsa's first serious attempt to seduce him by asking if 'all rich women play games like this,' but there is otherwise no evidence that his mind has ever been troubled by a political thought, and it is in any case impossible to reconcile his alleged ideological proclivities and imputed personal history with his role in the narrative intrigue.

As if this were not enough, Welles also requires us to accept that O'Hara is equipped to play the part of the Chorus in a mystery play, passing disinterested comment on the limitations of the other characters, deriving pithy maxims from the details of the action, and even pointing the moral at the end. In light of the fact that O'Hara is a merchant seaman, and of Welles's known interest in *Heart of Darkness* (which he had adapted for radio in 1938, and which he had planned to film before *Citizen Kane*), it is legitimate to assume that he thought of O'Hara as a figure equivalent to Conrad's Marlow, and it is certainly possible to read *The Lady from Shanghai* as a whole, like *Touch of Evil*, as a clandestine variation on the theme of Conrad's novella. Neither Welles nor O'Hara emerges from the comparison with much credit. The narrator of *Heart of Darkness* is portrayed as a man who is capable of being profoundly disturbed by the horrors he has witnessed, but it is in a sense the whole point of the tale that, although his experience gives him both the opportunity and the right to tell the truth about imperialism in Africa, he refuses to do so. He decides to lie to Kurtz's fiancée, and this lie, which shores up the myth of colonialism as a 'civilising' process, makes him complicit with what Kurtz has done.

The most indulgent of Welles's admirers would surely be hard-pressed to establish any intelligible connection between this troubled, contradictory figure, tormented by his own collusion with the powers of darkness, and the conceited prig who narrates the story about the sharks, and then actually recycles it in the intervals of Elsa's death-throes. O'Hara is 'big boob', Tiresian sage or besotted lover at Welles's convenience, and, when the film wishes to make desultory critical gestures in the direction of American capitalism, he is even passed off as some kind of working-class hero; the only thing these roles have in common is that they define the hero as an outsider in a wicked world. 'Well, everybody is somebody's fool,' O'Hara says as he strolls off along the prom in the final shot. It seems an odd remark in the circumstances, but then again, it is perhaps appropriate that the director whose catastrophic limitations as a moralist are betrayed by every detail of the preceding action should choose to end his film with this insouciant bromide.

IN A LONELY PLACE

V.F. Perkins

Nicholas Ray's *In a Lonely Place* (1950) is a very strange literary adaptation. From Dorothy Hughes's novel it retains the title, the names of some characters and something of the structure of relationships: the hero, Dixon Steele, has an ex-army buddy called Brub Nicolai who is now a detective working under a Captain Lochner. Nicolai's wife Sylvia dislikes Steele, who falls in love with the actress Laurel Gray while becoming involved in Brub's pursuit of a strangler whose

Still: Lt Barton (William Ching), Laurel Gray (Gloria Grahame), Brub Nicolai (Frank Lovejoy), Captain Lochner (Carl Benton Reid) and Dixon Steele (Humphrey Bogart) – Laurel arrives at Lochner's office to confirm Dix's alibi. Like almost all production stills, this does not exactly represent what is seen in the film itself.

victims include Mildred Atkinson. Beyond this, the film's changes and inventions are so extensive that merely cosmetic action – a new title and a new set of names – would have been enough to secure it from any suspicion of plagiarism if Santana Pictures (Humphrey Bogart's production company) had claimed it as an original story.

In the first place, a Los Angeles setting is important to Hughes's novel mainly in its topography. But the film treats Los Angeles, specifically Beverly Hills, primarily as a social environment, subjecting it to a presentation which is both distinctive and mordant. It forgoes all the spectacle of movie-making and all the glamour of movie promotion. We never see the inside – or even so much as the gates – of a studio, we meet no tycoons and we are taken to no extravagant premieres or anxious previews. In doing without

the familiar façades of the Hollywood picture, *In a Lonely Place* also deprives itself of occasions to bounce expressively between glittering display and the sad or sordid realities below. Nicholas Ray directs the film without reference to the splurged mascara school of movie rhetoric, holding it to a scale that avoids narrative and thematic inflation so as to pursue intimacy and detail.

Modesty and the commitment to chamber drama underlie the film's most drastic switch from the novel's content. Dorothy Hughes's hero is the killer, a serial killer at that, and the tension of her tale is in the tightening of the police net that catches Dix Steele. The film has only one murder victim, Mildred Atkinson, and it is clear that Humphrey Bogart's Dix did not kill her. If Dix had been produced as her murderer at the end of the movie, *In a Lonely Place* would have gone beyond the acceptable deviousness of the murder mystery to indulge in outrageous and probably futile cheating. The film is interested neither in creating mystery nor in following a process of detection. It is but mildly concerned, for reasons of its own, to identify Mildred's killer. Above plot it promotes character and both psychological and social portraiture, using the suspicion of murder as a pressure to dramatise the course of a romance from the discovery of love to its disintegration.

The twists of conspiracy and revelation that convolute so many *noir* narratives and produce the hero as fall guy are not among the pleasures this picture offers. There is no *femme fatale*, and there are no monsters of greed and perversity. The book works much more in the mainstream of *noir* fiction, immersing the reader in the sick consciousness of its haunted hero. A faithful translation to the screen (but please don't bother) would be likely to involve privileging the anti-hero's perspective by means of voice-over. Ray's movie is shaped as, in the first place, the story of Dixon Steele, but its viewpoint is independent of Dix's; it assesses his responses as well as reflecting them. The film conveys the texture and rhythm of his experience while offering us an understanding larger than Dix's own. Far from locking us into Dix's perceptions, the film gives us much information that is deliberately withheld from him and, as a surprising result, presents a world that in many respects validates rather than offsets his paranoia. He disrupts a nightclub performance by walking out when a cop turns up, unreasonably and perhaps incorrectly supposing that the cop has come to spy on him and to keep his relationship with Laurel under surveillance. However inappropriate Dix's reaction – its violence consists in the noticeable crushing of a cigarette – we have been made aware that he is indeed being spied on, by people representing themselves as his friends, and that the police are taking a covert but intrusive interest in his relationship with Laurel. While paranoia can show itself in a conviction of hostile conspiracy, Dix is also right when he comes to fear that

Frames. Top: Lochner to Dix: 'Why didn't you call for a cab? Isn't that what a gentleman usually does under the circumstances?' Above : Lochner and Laurel with Dix offscreen as murder suspect.

he is being deceived and that he is the subject of others' attempts at manipulation.

Lochner, the chief cop, is played (brilliantly) by Carl Benton Reid so as to evoke the image of the studio boss, secure in the corruptibility of his underlings, as free with an insult as with a purely formal apology, yet puritanically quick to take offence and intolerant of detachment from his definitions of necessity and decorum. As a cop, Captain Lochner from the outset treats Dix and Laurel with a disdain that can be supposed to reflect an impatience with the motion picture crowd; he much prefers people who work in banks (like Kessler, the killer).

A sneaky identification of the cops with the film industry establishment is surely involved when Dix tells his friend and agent Mel Lippman (Art Smith) not to worry about the news reports that Mildred Atkinson, a checkroom girl from Paul's Restaurant, was in his apartment to tell him the story of best seller *Althea Bruce*. Mel thinks that Brodie, the producer, will be outraged by this affront to his property and that Dix will lose a much-needed screenwriting job. Dix thinks not, as there is a way for Mel to appease Brodie. He can say that the motive Dix claimed for taking Mildred home was just an excuse for the police. It was more certainly an excuse for the Breen Office: what Dix offers as a convenient lie about Hollywood prostitution, the Production Code Administration would have vetoed for its discomforting frankness on the same subject. The front office/detective squad parallel is reinforced through the documentation of Dix's misdemeanours that Lochner, giving dictation, intones with such zealous distaste; it looks like a cuttings file and it consists largely of the scandal queens' gossip and commissary tittle-tattle that studios compiled to control the employability of the talent. The Frances Randolph that Lochner and others adduce as their only instance of a female victim of Dix's violence is the same Fran (Alice Talton) who twice shows herself happy to recall and eager to renew her one-time affair with Dix. Lochner's note on Dix's fist fight with a producer ('Fired. No charges preferred.') indicates a free exchange of information between the studios and the investigative apparatus of the state. The relevance to the blacklist is clear, and we are invited, though not compelled, to see *In a Lonely Place* as reflecting on suspicion, deceit and hysteria in personal relations under a threat which, of course, it cannot name, that of the Hollywood witch-hunt.

Making Dixon Steele a screenwriter, in the other most significant change from Hughes's novel, gives ironic access to a metaphor of following the book as a measure of conformism. The film echoes the erratic personality of its hero in its own erratic processes, notable among which is the establishment of the murder victim not as an ingratiating figure of pathos but as a figure of grating comedy. Mildred's enthusiastic synopsis of *Althea Bruce* is part of what extinguishes Dix's sexual interest (more important is his first sight of Laurel), and hastening Mildred's exit from his apartment, is an expression of his desire for release from the romance's grotesque narrative. It is an insider's joke that 'what Brodie wants – a faithful adaptation' should be at issue in a film which is itself unconstrained by respect for its literary source. The boldly nonsensical synopsis delivered by Mildred points up the despair that haunts Dix's efforts to do well in a job that it is demeaning to do at all. Dix's ambivalence about his work and its context emerges in the vulnerability not just of his material prospects but also of his self esteem to the opinions of those for whose judgment he has an intelligent contempt. It is one dimension of conflict in Dix that he is alert to the hollowness of success and tormented by the fear of failure.

That aspect of the character embodies a tension widely remarked as a feature of Hollywood life. Beyond this, the film draws on Hollywood lore for detail like the jibe thrown at a loud-mouthed producer; according to Ray, 'You have put the son-in-law business back fifty years' was a crack famously directed at Milton Sperling (father-in-law, Harry Warner). The character of Dix, the trouble-seeking alcoholic screenwriter who has not written a hit since before the war, seems to owe much to the character and legend of Herman J. Mankiewicz, writer of *Citizen Kane*, but also of *A Woman's Secret* (1948), which was derived from a Vicki Baum novel and became, two years before *In a Lonely Place*, the silliest of Nicholas Ray's directorial assignments. In his autobiography, the producer John Houseman gave an account of a car journey across America shared with Mankiewicz and Ray: 'two of the most violently self-destructive men I have ever known – both drinkers and gamblers on different curves of their respective roller-coasters. Herman was on the downslope . . . and his great wild days were behind him . . . Behind a truculent front he was worrying about jobs . . . His teeth were still sharp but the appetite was gone' (*Front and Center*, Simon & Schuster, New York, 1979, p.177). Like Dix again, Mankiewicz was a victim of the gossip columns, with the Hearst press taking regular revenge for *Citizen Kane*.

Many aspects of Dix's character connect him also to the heroes of other Ray movies like *On Dangerous Ground* (1952), *The Lusty Men* (1952), *Johnny Guitar* (1954) and *Rebel without a Cause* (1955) – tortured male romantics looking for redemption from their own ferocities and riven by the contradiction between what they knowingly desire and what they, in fact, pursue or

Frames. Below – at Paul's Restaurant, Dix's 'victim', Fran (Alice Talton), is defeated in her attempt to renew the relationship: 'Do you look down on all women, or just the ones you know?' Right – portrait of a murder victim. Mildred's brief stardom: 'Gee, you make me feel real important.'

provoke. Confirmation of autobiographical relevance here can be found in some further snippets from Houseman's account: 'Nick was a difficult and sometimes disturbing companion . . . The chance to save him from his own self-destructive habits proved an irresistible attraction [to women] of which Nick took full advantage and for which he rarely forgave them . . . [He had] a perfectionism and sense of commitment to his work which were rare in the theatre and even more rare in the film business. But in his personal life he was the victim of irresistible impulses that, finally, left his career and his personal relationships in ruins' (p.178).

Repeatedly, Ray's hero gives, receives and gives himself one simple piece of advice which also sets a goal beyond price or power: 'Take it easy.' Like several of Ray's best pictures, *In a Lonely Place* explores the results of casting a woman in the role of 'warrior's rest' as a figure whose clear sight, calm and commitment are valued to the extent that they seem to enable relaxation and to promise refuge from the stresses in the male world of public competition. This film offers a rebuff to Hollywood's, and most likely Ray's own, desire to believe in romance as a solution rather than a combination of lovers' problems.

The investment in love, doomed here because on both sides excessive, relates the character of Dix to the persona of Bogart whose public image had become that of a hell-raiser brought to a late mellowing, after his notoriously violent marriage to Mayo Methot, through the happy

Still: 'preparing for repose' – Laurel and Dix with Charlie Waterman (Robert Warwick) reciting 'When in disgrace . . .' Laurel waits with hat and handout.

chance that had united him with Lauren Bacall. Ray claimed credit as the director who took the gun out of Bogart's hand, and that is achieved partly by setting contexts of tenderness and sentiment in which Bogart's still guarded, mainly indirect acknowledgement of need and affection can be felt to express a sensitivity and warmth less rigidly encased in smartness than is the case with his regular tough-guy roles. A key instance here is the scene in which his friends collude in 'preparing him for repose', making him the sleepy dedicatee of a Shakespearean avowal of love. It is a prime example of reaction-shot stardom, relieved of the burdens of exposition to become the art of charismatic passivity. The Bogart role had developed as one in which his character knew what he was after and pursued it directly. Hero or villain, his status was guaranteed by his effectiveness in violence. It is here that *In a Lonely Place* marks so impressive an extension of Bogart's range. Dix is introduced to us as a character preoccupied, locked into his own evidently painful turmoil as he drives through the Los Angeles evening traffic. The first words spoken in the film are his own name, called out to him at a traffic light to summon him back into a public world where recognition is a prime concern. ('Dix Steele! . . . Don't you remember me?') The image is cut to show the delay in his reaction, as if he is waking to consciousness but also as if his own name is as obscure to him as the identity of the woman calling it. Showbiz is, of course, a world where unfamiliarity with one's name may be a fact as well as a metaphor.

If Bogart did not like *In a Lonely Place* – his biographer Joe Hyams says so – that may have been through embarrassment at its evocation of witch-hunt Hollywood; he believed himself to have been duped by the victims of the blacklist and he certainly was humbled by its perpetrators, who manoeuvred him into billboarding his 'Americanism' as if he were a friendly witness. It is also possible that he was uneasy with the exposure in Dix of the pain, anxiety and clumsiness that make this role unique in his career. Yet one of his and the film's triumphs is to render the violence in his instability of mood and purpose with full force, taking it to the edge of absurdity without loss of conviction. For instance, it is almost funny – a risk boldly run – that Dix's attack on Laurel in the final scene occurs when he has come to her apartment to declare his regret for an earlier outburst, and closely follows his contrite vow that such things will never happen again.

The reorientation of the Bogart persona is, though, as much a matter of perspective as of performance. The film aligns him with other Ray heroes by making his violence the index of weakness rather than of strength. When he lashes out at 'Junior', the son-in-law producer, his pretext is outrage at the abuse of his friend, the one-time matinée idol Charles Waterman (Robert Warwick). But the image has displayed Dix's growing rage at the meanings for himself in Junior's trumpeted contempt for a drunk and has-been. It is Dix that Junior leans on while addressing the onlookers at Paul's Restaurant; when Junior responds to the son-in-law crack by tapping his cigar ash into Waterman's brandy, this final provocation (the drink was Dix's gift to Charlie) triggers a release of anger that reflects Dix's identification with failure and his vulnerability to a fool's contempt even more clearly than it shows his carelessness of self interest in defence of a friend.

The truly frightening aspect of Dix is not so much his volatility or his capacity for violence as his almost complete blindness to his own actions, either in their impact on others or in their meanings for himself. He seems never to face the implications of his own feelings or fantasies. Sylvia Nicolai (Jeff Donnell) is repelled by the intensity of his involvement in the imagined motives of a woman-strangler, and that's a reflection of her small mindedness But Dix does not pause to think anything about it, which seems to indicate a panic flight from self-knowledge.

The event that dramatises Laurel's recoil from Dix is his attack on a young motorist whose car he crashes into while driving furiously away from what he has read, correctly, as a scene of

Frames: ambiguities of gesture – three shoulder-clasps in Paul's Restaurant at the start of the film.
1) Has-been writer Dix greeted by wealthy hack director Lloyd Barnes (Morris Ankrum) and watched by agent Mel Lippman (Art Smith).
2) Dix greets ex-matinée-idol Charlie Waterman.
3) Dix becomes a pedestal for Junior (Lewis Howard) boasting about preview success in Pasadena.

betrayal. Diverted by Laurel at a moment when he might, rock in hand, have become a murderer, Dix does his best to repair the damage without appreciating what the damage is. He allows Laurel to demolish his attempts at self-justification but once more evades inspection of the sources and likely consequences of his action. In particular, he shows no awareness of the impact on Laurel; he recognises no shock and he offers no apology. His recovery of calm is as abrupt as his swing into rage. When he reaches his arm out to draw her towards him, the image registers Laurel's recognition and Dix's unconsciousness of the similarity between this embrace and the imagined stranglehold of Mildred's killer. Bogart's facility in irony and mockery is redirected to portray Dix's defence against useful introspection.

The casting of Gloria Grahame as Laurel points up one dimension of correspondence between Dix and Bogart which may have been calculated to provoke the actor into drawing on his experience as much as he relied on his skill. Gloria Grahame was just a little younger than Lauren Bacall, but older at the time of filming than Bacall had been when she married Bogart. Just as the word 'starlet' is never explicitly attached to Laurel, so the twenty-five-year gap in age is not mentioned in the film, though it opens Laurel to Lochner's sarcasm and makes her vulnerable to the sneers embedded in questions like 'Were you interested in Mr Steele because he's a celebrity?' and 'Do you receive a salary for your work?'

While the casting of Gloria Grahame has resonance in relation to the star, it is startling in relation to the director. According to Ray (who admitted to being a liar, though not on the John Ford scale), Harry Cohn and Columbia Pictures wanted Ginger Rogers as Laurel. Ray held out for Grahame, his wife, although their brief marriage was in active disintegration. From a director who encouraged actors to make use of their own experiences and emotions, such a role was not only a generous farewell gift but also – as farewell gifts are apt to be – sharply barbed in its reflections on character and motive. Laurel Gray is constructed as a woman well equipped, under the relevant pressures, to confirm the fears that underlie and follow from Dix's misogyny. The role draws on those aspects of the player that gave unaffected conviction in *The Big Heat* (Fritz Lang, 1953) to 'I've been rich and I've been poor. Believe me, rich is better.'

In many accounts of the film, a romance that otherwise promises redemption and fulfilment is

Frame – after the attack on the young motorist, Dix to Laurel: 'I'll take that cigarette now.'

Frame: Laurel witnesses the attack on the young motorist.

destroyed by the pressures of the police investigation and/or as a result of Dix's neurosis. These versions underrate the picture's depth and originality by either imposing the notion that someone has to be at fault when a love affair ends or perceiving it within stock moulds for the 'if only' love story where star-crossed lovers are threatened by external circumstance. They conventionalise it, too, by making Laurel a passive, only reactive figure. The film's insistence on Laurel's active role is marked by a shot worthy of its place in the Nicholas Ray gallery of strange inserts: the viewpoint into the coffee cup tilted in Laurel's hand when she is first brought to Lochner's office. That image signals the definitive entry into the narrative of a new subjectivity.

Before this, she has been seen only in relation to Dix's perspectives. On her first appearance, her indirectness is apparent as well as her pronounced investment in poise. She walks between Dix and Mildred in the courtyard of the apartments where both she and Dix are tenants with an 'Excuse me' that commands attention but also positions her to claim that she was only minding her own business and being polite. Here and later, she is skilfully dressed in costumes so well supplied with edges and angles as to construct the space for movements simultaneously elegant, erotically promising (she passes close enough for Dix to catch her perfume) and – hands pushed forward inside the pockets of her overcoat – held off from any risk of contact. The stiffness that possesses Dix at climaxes of anxiety is always more or less a feature of Laurel's bearing. She is ever so neat. Finding her way through without being touched is one of her prime objectives. She is visibly a woman who hates to be taken by surprise and not to have her performance under control. The strains to which this subjects her are pictured in the close-up of her shoes pressing against the floor of the car during Dix's enraged drive from the beach, all her terror held with great effort out of sight. But once Dix picks up the rock in his attack on the young driver, Laurel's panic can no longer be contained. The image of her distraught face leaning into camera

Still: investments in poise and distance – at Dix's apartment, Laurel is dressed for the meeting she has contrived.

to shriek at Dix contradicts the earlier shot to mark the discovery that attachment to Dix makes it impossible for her to inhabit her preferred posture.

Life with Dix offers excitement at the cost of security, and Laurel's priorities are the opposite. She brings Dix the priceless gift of relaxation, quieting his turmoil and enabling him to direct his energies creatively. But we should not ignore the darker implications of the sequence that characterises the couple's happiness: in it we learn that Laurel is delighted to have Dix 'kind of dopey this morning. I love him that way', she tells Mel. (By contrast, Dix is unsettled by Laurel's dopiness when he discovers her in drug-assisted sleep.) Her avowal of love at the scene's end is spoken in twice-relayed words, from Shakespeare via Charlie Waterman, in the process of putting Dix to sleep. I note the strategy for getting a bedroom scene past the censors, but I take it seriously that it's an inactive, semiconscious Dix in whose love Laurel scorns to change her state with kings.

It is illuminatingly credible that she turns out to have a lot in common with Mrs Nicolai, the Sylvia who is glad that her husband is not like Dix but 'attractive and average'. Visiting Sylvia, ostensibly for reassurance about Dix – immediately after a scene in which Dix has said that if you want information about him you should ask him directly – Laurel states her aspiration to a life like the Nicolais: 'This is what I'd like to have some day [pause, stands], a small cosy house, near the ocean.'

That? With Dix? Laurel is not sure. Known around town as the mistress of 'the real-estate Baker', she has been lucky on the run from that affair ('We were thinking of getting married. It wouldn't have worked.') to find employment with Dix. Laurel's is the ambition of the tender-hearted gold-digger; there is no scheme to sacrifice desire to calculation but a reasonable hope, when love is found, to find it advantageously. That creates room for a deal of self deception and uncertainty.

We have to wonder why Laurel puts such a convenient gloss on the role in her life of Martha, the masseuse, explaining her to Dix as the last remnant of a movie career, but suppressing her function as a pipeline to Mr Baker. So long as Martha is on hand, Baker can be avoided without being discarded or lost. Laurel is conspicuously economical with the truth here. She makes a point of describing Martha, when she is still only a name spoken into the telephone, as a married woman with a grown-up son. That is an alternative to mentioning what will turn out to be her most striking aspect. The film casts Martha within the butch lesbian stereotype and thereby reflects on Laurel's nervous opportunism; she finds comfort in the knowledge that her glamour will keep Martha at her disposal and eager to be of service.

Laurel is upset when Martha relays the gossip about Dix and Frances Randolph; she tells Martha to leave. Martha's response runs: 'I'll get out, angel. But you'll beg me to come back when you're in trouble. You will, angel, because you don't have anybody else.' That is accurate as a summary of Laurel's position and as a prediction. It also confirms (and announces to us) the knowledge that the break can be enacted without cost to Laurel since it has no effect on Martha's availability – 'You haven't anybody else' contains 'You still have me, and you know it.' Chucking Martha out gives Laurel a way of refusing to listen to insinuations against Dix, after having listened to them.

It is a measure of Laurel's uncertainty, well

Frame: the engagement party – Laurel is much better at deception than Mel.

228

before the car incident and at a time when she claims to have found happiness, that here and in her interview with Lochner she can manage only a stiffly formal assertion of her belief in Dix. She cannot produce what would really count – a quick and spontaneous rejoinder, along the lines of 'Don't be silly,' either to Martha or to Lochner's 'He's our most logical suspect.' Inasmuch as Martha speaks the voices in Laurel's mind, throwing her out is an effort at suppression.

Laurel's problem is that it is not enough to know that Dix is innocent of murder. She needs to feel able to deny that he is, in Lochner's words, an erratic, violent man, or that killing has a fascination for him; and these are simple truths. With Dix, Laurel is incapable of sustaining the irrational trust and reckless commitment that would be love. In Ray's work the ready contrast is with Keechie, the heroine of *They Live by Night* (1948): 'Some say he's bad, but I say he's bonny.' Keechie's counterpart in *In a Lonely Place* is not Laurel but Mel, whose first concern, when he imagines Dix to be the murderer, is how to fix his escape across the border. In this role, Art Smith offers a wry and touching portrait of a friendship (no more platonic, surely, than Martha's for Laurel) that, unlike the lovers' love, is without conditions or reservations.

Mel makes Laurel feel ashamed, appropriately, since the route to her betrayal of Dix is prepared largely by her own lies and evasions. Her first really important deception comes when Dix mentions a picnic invitation from the Nicolais and asks if she remembers Brub. Dix does not know that Laurel has been talking to Lochner again and that Brub played a major role in the interview. Not knowing that Laurel is lying when she claims only vaguely to recall the cop in Lochner's office, Dix does not have our reasons for wondering why Laurel is concealing the fact of the interview and withholding the knowledge that she gained there, which any friend would think it important to pass on. Dix is entitled to know that he is under surveillance as Lochner's prime suspect and that any contact with the Nicolais, who are never going to sacrifice Brub's

Frames: Dix directing the murder of Mildred Atkinson as enacted by Brub and Sylvia (Jeff Donell).

Frame: Dix meets Kessler, the killer, and Brub watches Dix.

prospects to friendship, is less a social occasion than an extension of the investigative process.

If Laurel is unable to be open about a meeting which of itself threatened no disloyalty, we have to conclude that her unease has a different source, in doubts that the interview has created in her own mind about the security of her relationship with Dix. At the very least, Laurel's commitment to Dix does not outweigh the authority of Lochner. When, at the beach, Laurel tries to excuse her silence with 'We didn't want to tell you because it would only have upset you,' the thinness of the explanation is evident, but no more striking than the identification that makes Laurel present herself as part of a 'we' with Brub Nicolai. For both Laurel and Dix, friendship with the Nicolais represents an attempted accommodation with the Lochner world, in which you are supposed to affect concern as to whether a cop reckons your behaviour to be that of a gentleman (or, of course, a lady). One side of Laurel is anxiously responsive to any indication of her acceptability in the established world of official decorum – an escape from her identity as 'Baker's girl'.

Laurel's need for security is at odds with her keenness to keep her options open. The conflict makes her unable to leave Dix and it makes her in staying unable to offer him the reassurance that *his* insecurity constantly demands. So it builds the pressure that pushes Laurel by stages into hysterical deviousness and treachery. First, she visits Sylvia Nicolai, the woman who, at the beach, could not fathom her own motives in breaking the secret of Laurel's meeting with Lochner: 'I don't know why I said it. Brub especially asked me not to.' While at the Nicolais' house, ostensibly to seek persuasion of Dix's innocence, she gives Sylvia information that is sure to be passed on to a grateful Lochner, of Dix's assault on the young motorist. Then she accepts Dix's proposal of marriage while intending to leave him in the lurch. In this way, she embarks on a course of attempted manipulation that is certain to enrage Dix and to construct the circumstances which, directing the Nicolais' enactment of the Atkinson murder, he has imagined as the ones in which a man would kill the woman he loved: 'She's telling you she's done nothing wrong . . . You love her and she's deceived you . . . she wants to get rid of you.'

Finally, she uses Mel as an intermediary to deliver Dix's *Althea Bruce* script to Brodie, gambling that it will be greeted with the warmth to divert Dix from her desertion. The scale of this betrayal, and Laurel's awareness of it, is pictured in the two-handed gesture with which Laurel passes the script into Mel's keeping. The script is what she and Dix have made together out of their love – Dix as writer, Laurel as inspiration and typist – and using it to cheat Dix is poignantly shown to be like giving their baby away. A chairback between Laurel and Mel constructs space across which Laurel has to stretch to pass the script, enlarging the gesture to emphasise the responsibility that Laurel is imposing on Mel. The act and the gesture join the several instances in Ray's work of disastrous efforts at disarmament where a well-intentioned deception (like Jim's of Plato in *Rebel without a Cause*) is experienced as a lacerating betrayal.

At this point, the relationship is over. 'I wanted it to last so much, for my own sake,' Laurel tells Mel, recognising the fact. The film is now concerned with the consequences of this way of making the break from a man with an anguished fear of manipulation and abandonment. Dix's attack on Laurel, interrupted by the telephone call from Lochner that concedes his innocence, is not the cause of the rupture. 'Yesterday,'

Frame: Dix and Laurel. Dix: 'I'll never let you go.'

Laurel tells Lochner, 'this would have meant so much to us. Now it doesn't matter at all.' Yesterday, not an hour ago; that is, before Dix's proposal rather than before his assault.

It is probably more unusual in the movies than elsewhere that the marriage proposal is a sign of the relationship's decay rather than of its prosperity. A marriage contract is a poor substitute for the easy warmth and commitment that Dix wants of Laurel. But, failing that, he wants to rush into marriage, which suggests a desire to avoid having time for thought. It seems that the prospect of marriage panics him to different effect but almost as much as it does Laurel. The

Frames: 'Yesterday this would have meant so much to us. Now it doesn't matter at all.'

Frame: Dix and Laurel – 'She promised Lochner what?'

marriage project is repeatedly advanced by others (Lochner, Sylvia, Effie the housekeeper), and it is in the contemplation of marriage that Dix's behaviour becomes most bizarre. Consider the beach scene and its consequences. Sylvia's gaffe is to tell Laurel to marry Dix and to remind her that she promised Lochner an invitation to the wedding. Dix's immediate response picks up the issue of marriage: 'She promised Lochner what?' – not 'Promised who?' Dix's fury and the re-assertion of control implied by his wild drive up the canyon are responses to a context that includes, alongside Brub's treachery and Laurel's lack of candour, the articulation of the marriage prospect. I give this some weight because, in the aftermath of Dix's attack on the crash victim, the topic of marriage remains unmentioned, and, where we might expect it to re-emerge in the apparent restoration of calm and intimacy, Dix's mind instead turns to divorce. He presents his thoughts for the farewell note in the screenplay, where ('I lived a few weeks while she loved me') the focus is on suffering the loss of a woman's love as a kind of death.

Marriage is on his mind again (put there by Effie) when he starts to prepare breakfast in Laurel's kitchen. The celebrated gesture in which he straightens the grapefruit knife betrays his unfamiliarity with domestic routine. By contrast with his earlier readiness to accept or demand Laurel's mothering, his taking the housekeeping role in itself suggests an anxious desire to be of service. But we should not go too far with these common-sense readings: after all, he has picked the utensil correctly. Removing its curve, while thinking about marriage and a dopily distraught Laurel, he turns the tool into a weapon, the knife into something more like a dagger.

In its reconciliation of clarity with depth of suggestion, in its extraordinary mixture of charm, humour and violence, this moment is representative of the film's achievement. Throughout, we find an eloquence and spontaneity of gesture unsurpassed in Ray's work. In the final scene, Dix's fury in his long-avoided recognition of Laurel's betrayal implodes as an attempt to

Frames. Top: Dix prepares grapefruit for a dopey Laurel. Above: Dix tells Laurel, 'Anyone looking at us could tell we were in love.'

crush and subdue her, a terrible counterfeit of a loving embrace. After this, the parting, echoing the courtship, is performed with Lochner as a relay. But where the courtship was a conspiracy to make something else out of a police interrogation, the parting disguises itself as a conversation with the cops. Dix leaves the telephone for Laurel instead of handing it to her; he acknowledges her recoil from contact, and the fact that their space cannot now be shared, by putting the receiver down on a chairback and moving to the door. There he pauses with his hand on the door-knob and makes a tentative turn into the room, looking at Laurel to submit himself to her decision. That means that Dix feels a possibility of forgiving Laurel's deceit and is concerned to know whether she might forgive his violence. Speaking to Lochner but looking at Dix, Laurel affirms with 'Now it doesn't matter' what Dix still needs to be told: that their love has ended in mutual and mutually justified mistrust.

The film's depth and its modesty are both manifest in an ending which is sad and oddly unresolved rather than tragic. Dix and Laurel are left more or less where we found them at the start; only their relationship has reached a conclusion. Even here, inflation is avoided: what has come to an end is not the finest of romances but a briefly creative respite from looking at the world with anger and receiving its glance with shame.

ANGEL FACE

Edward Gallafent

There are a number of ways in which *Angel Face* (1952) can be placed within the contexts that make up *film noir*. There is the fact of direction by Otto Preminger, and thus its relation to *Laura* (1944) and *Fallen Angel* (1945). In the casting of Robert Mitchum, there is the relation to his earlier work in *film noir*. Most common in brief accounts of the film, there is Jean Simmons's role as murderess, and her inclusion in lists of *film noir femmes fatales*. But the ways in which the film redescribes particular *film noir* situations can be made clearer if it is read as a narrative about the couple, and I will try to identify the nature of this narrative by looking at how it resembles, and does not resemble, Billy Wilder's *Double Indemnity* (1944).

Both films feature a central couple consisting of a man who is not a private eye, detective or policeman and a woman who is part of some kind of fractured or unhappy family. The point of departure for the narratives is when the man, in the course of his profession, calls at the house where the woman lives. This meeting initiates a chain of events that invokes the idea of the man and the woman 'escaping' with each other and leads to the murder of a member of the household. The result of the crime is to bind the couple intimately together. The narrative ends with both the man and the woman dead, and in both cases the woman is directly responsible for the death of the man.

One stark difference between the two films is at the level of conscious understanding of motivation in the couple. At the beginning of Walter Neff's (Fred MacMurray's) confession in *Double Indemnity* he tells us why he killed Dietrichson: 'I killed him for money – and for a woman.' Although we might wish to elaborate on this in terms of our view of Neff's relationship to wealth and sexuality, it is true that, at least until the murder is carried out, both Walter and Phyllis (Barbara Stanwyck) seem to be able to give an account of why they are acting as they do. The narrative deals in actualities – the deliberate contemplation of a crime, for the object of specific monetary gain, is undertaken in the awareness of the possibility of exposure and punishment. Add to this the setting of the confession, and it is clear from the opening moment that the result of transgression here is very probably going to be death.

Against this we might place the moment at the very end of *Angel Face* when Diane Tremayne (Jean Simmons) kills herself and Frank Jessup (Robert Mitchum) by driving over a precipice. It is clear that until the second before it happens, Frank, quite unlike many of *film noir*'s doomed heroes, has no idea that he is going to die. He has no vision of himself as worthy of punishment, for in his own eyes he is not a guilty man. Preminger's film proposes a central couple whose motivations are deeply obscure to themselves: they move in a landscape – a mental as well as a physical one – that they do not properly understand and cannot or will not read. It is to this difficulty of reading, specifically of reading what there is in a woman's face, that the title of *Angel Face* refers us.

Consider the opening sequence of the film, when the man and the woman first see each other. An ambulance is called out to a Beverly Hills mansion; its drivers are Frank Jessup and his friend Bill Crompton (Kenneth Tobey). They are to give aid in a case of gas poisoning – the victim is the mistress of the house, Mrs Catherine Tremayne (Barbara O'Neill), who has been nearly asphyxiated in her bedroom. Frank listens as the doctor and police ponder the possibilities: accident, attempted murder, attempted suicide. We learn that the victim's English husband, Charles (Herbert Marshall), does not share this bedroom; his room is on the other side of a corridor. The camera observes this, moving along the balcony so that our gaze passes from Catherine's room, across the dividing hallway to Charles's window, and we hear the piano being played downstairs. At the foot of the staircase, Bill barely glances towards the pianist, but Frank moves slowly across to where Diane is playing the sensuous 'classical' piece that is the film's romantic theme.

What does he see? Obviously that this rich, cultured household is in trouble, in a way that cannot yet be clearly understood, beyond the sense that this trouble might relate to the empty marriage expressed by the separate suites upstairs and the presentation of Charles as an effete bourgeois husband, and that this girl's relation to it all is expressing itself in her playing this music, providing the scene with its soundtrack, which we might think of as a form of control, of direction. The moment seems to make a connection

Still: transgression – Diane (Jean Simmons) and Frank (Robert Mitchum) in the bar.

not unusual in Hollywood cinema between playing the piano and a desire for control that is often less than benign and can be demonic. It is a thread that runs from Charles Boyer's pianist in George Cukor's *Gaslight* (1944) through this film to the Jack Nicholson character in Bob Rafelson's *Five Easy Pieces* (1970).

Frank moves towards Diane – she looks to him to pronounce the words that will declare Catherine to be alive or dead. He tells her that Catherine is alive, and she becomes hysterical. Frank holds her, shakes her and finally slaps her face. Preminger has framed the two of them in medium shot – now he cuts to a close-up of Diane as she registers the slap. She slaps him back, hard. Is it her way of defining why Frank is touching her? It might then be taken as a moment of shift in their relations from kindly father/doctor figure and hysterical girl to something more directly sexual, as if this gesture of refusal of an unauthorised intimacy had actually created such an intimacy. The camera is on Mitchum's face as he registers this irony. His line here about there being nothing in the medical manual about getting slapped back draws an apology, and he presses home his advantage, finding a way of telling her what her slap meant: 'All right – forget it – I've been slapped by dames before.' This gives him a past for her, and before he lets her go he sketches a future: 'Next time, see if you can't remember to pull that punch a little bit.' She promises to remember.

We may compare the quality of this moment with the conversation about speed and driving which occupies the comparable space in *Double Indemnity*. There, we see a couple who clearly know exactly what they are (metaphorically, of course) talking about: a proposal is being made

and accepted in the context of the couple establishing the similarity of their desires. In *Angel Face*, the force of the scene rests in the perception by both parties of the other as the opposite of the familiar, together with the excitement of the idea that such a gap might possibly be bridged.

The strangeness of the couple and their milieus to each other can be felt in several ways. Mitchum's star persona as a hero in Westerns as well as earlier *films noirs* establishes a sharp contrast with the Herbert Marshall figure, in terms of assumptions about masculine potency and social class. The reference to Europe, represented in the casting of Charles and Diane and in her 'classical' piano, is posed against an unmistakably American star. This seems to be a familiar plot, in which the potent American democratic hero arrives to rescue the European heiress from a situation drained of sexual or creative energy. But equally suggestive are the immediate ways in which this scenario is complicated – by the possibly negative elements in Mitchum's persona, and by the quality of dislocation, the heiress to European sensibility found not in Paris or London but Beverly Hills.

Part of the tentativeness of this encounter leads to a question: is Frank captivated by Diane? There is no evidence in his immediately subsequent actions that he thinks of this as much more than a brief encounter on the part of a man whose face has been slapped by women more than once. He returns to the ambulance station, then goes to a bar to telephone his girl Mary (Mona Freeman). When he is followed to the bar by Diane, he casually deceives Mary in

Still: the first dinner together – Diane contemplates Frank.

order to take Diane to dinner, but his interest in her still seems limited, and the next evening he will attempt to resume his relationship with Mary.

Diane's description of herself in the bar to which she follows Frank and the following scenes with him at dinner and in the dance hall fill in a number of significant details. There is her stress on her youth – almost the first thing she tells him is that she is nineteen. Diane's construction of herself as only just leaving childhood is a consistent element throughout the film, and I will return to it. Obviously linked to this is her next subject, her father. We learn that she loves him, and that he represents European artistic achievement – a 'famous novelist' now transplanted to America as a result of the war, his career interrupted but now writing a 'wonderful' new novel that he has been reading to his daughter. (We will learn later that the last part of this story is a lie.) So she speaks of a man associated with the magic of Art, shipwrecked, as it were, on the shores of an alien land, a man who has lost his wife but brings with him a beautiful daughter – this sounds very much like the opening of *The Tempest*. It is not possible to say that Diane knowingly conceives of herself as Miranda, but the only exchange in the dance hall scene, in which she tells Frank that he is the first man she has danced with since she came to America – 'except my father' – echoes the insistence on the lack of knowledge of men, on her virginity as central to her value, that is true of

Miranda's role and is stated in comparable terms to Ferdinand.

I do not wish to press the connection too far, but it is of interest in that it prompts us to consider ways in which *Angel Face* cannot satisfy the conditions for the development of the narrative along the lines of *The Tempest*. It directs us to the weakness of the father, an impotent Prospero with the lineaments of magic but none of its power, cut off from both money and creativity and utterly unable to intervene in Diane's world. Suggestively, he has no relation whatever to Frank, and, after the opening sequence, they never appear again in the same shot. The inadequate father figure is a recurrent role in Preminger's *films noirs* – we can link the figure of Charles with other older men whose relationship to young women is destructive, Waldo Lydecker (Clifton Webb) in *Laura*, Mark Judd (Charles Bickford) in *Fallen Angel*.

Another thread of significant meaning here concerns Diane's car. To Diane, it has the magical power of bringing her to Frank's side, and in the bar she refers to herself as a witch and to the car as her broomstick. In a film entirely without guns, cars become the force which can destroy – the murder weapon in both cases later on. Charles has a dim sense of this destructiveness. Unconsciously associating it with the war, he describes Diane's car as 'that horrible little jet-propelled torpedo' in a family conversation about accidents. In contrast, Frank sees it as simply a means to an end, a technology that can be manipulated into a profitable business, the sports car workshop that he hopes to start when he has saved sufficient money.

But perhaps he is being disingenuous. Diane clearly recognises the role of the car as a tool in her competition – a word given some stress in the film – with Mary for Frank's affections. Consider the dialogue here, when Frank and Diane have been discussing his relationship with Mary:

Frank: Look, I'm a free agent.
Diane: Mary admits that – but – you know what girls are – it's only natural. Look what I found.

She hands him a paper with the details of a race which she wants Frank (a racing driver before the war) to enter, and they discuss it.

Diane: . . . we could take it [the car] out weekends – do you think Mary would mind?
Frank: Mary has nothing to do with this. If we take that race it'll mean a lot of publicity – make it a lot easier for me to get backing for the shop.

The seamless movement between announcing that competition between girls is 'only natural' and the production of the scheme to win him is ignored by Frank, the price of his continuing to assert to himself that he is a 'free agent' and that nothing is really going on here other than a continuation of his earlier life.

Similar issues persist when Frank accepts the job as the Tremayne chauffeur. Outside the house, the competition was between Diane and Mary. When Frank becomes the chauffeur, he implicitly jilts Mary, but a new area of rivalry opens up, this time between Diane and Catherine. Preminger first shows us a scene of Diane's asserting that she now possesses Frank, as she teases him over the intercom before accepting the perfect breakfast prepared by another servant, and we see Frank's uneasy response. This is followed by a long sequence with Catherine in her study, receiving first Frank and then Charles. The contrast here is between the mutual respect of two people in business, as Frank and Catherine discuss the proposal that she invest in the workshop, and the disdain of the married couple for each other's behaviour and values.

Just as, in the earlier scene, Diane drove a wedge between Frank and Mary in the form of the racing proposal, now the same thing is done to Frank and Catherine. Even the gesture rhymes. Earlier, Frank unfolded the announcement of the race; now Diane meets Frank away from the house and hands him another piece of paper to smooth out – his figures for the workshop, supposedly crumpled up and thrown away by Catherine. He is mildly puzzled, but nothing more. Resisting Diane's attempts to describe Catherine as the wicked step-mother and herself as the persecuted child, he responds 'don't be silly' to her fantasy that Catherine will lock her up.

The scene now returns to the house as night falls. The movement into the world of night at first seems benign – a melody on the soundtrack accompanies the dissolve to where, framed by the curtains, a couple is playing chess. The framing underlines the allusion to a famous moment in *The Tempest*, the point in the final act where the magician speaks, and 'the entrance of the cell opens and discovers Ferdinand and Miranda playing at chess'. This might be Preminger's way of assuring us that he at least is Prospero, but also pointing up an irony, for the couple here are not the lovers but father and daughter, and the subsequent sequence is intercut with Frank's unsuccessful attempts to contact Mary by phone. Father and daughter part at the door of his bedroom and Diane retreats dejectedly to her room, where the theme music again dissolves into her playing on the piano. Preminger lets the camera run on as we look into her face, inviting us to try to read the emotion registered there.

The scene is thus set for another attempt at murder, but it is a fantasised rather than an actual one. Preminger dissolves from Diane's face to a clock-face. It is the middle of the night, and she goes to Frank's room, not to make love but to tell him a story, a fantasy of her being the victim of the wicked stepmother. He accuses her of making this up. His metaphor for it connects to the earlier moments – at last she has offered a document that he can read properly, that he can see is a fake: 'I'd say your story was as phoney as a three-dollar bill.' She replies, 'How can you say that to me?', and he offers an irony: 'You mean – after all that we've been to each other?'

There is a delicate subject here. The force of this line can be fully felt only if we consider the careful hints that make up the film's directions to us concerning Frank's sexual relationships with the two women. The background to the opposition is familiar, with the domesticity of Mary set against Diane's links to crime, speed and mendacity. The complication is that the links of domestic partner and *femme fatale* to sexual activity seem to be opposite to those usual in *film noir*. To put it much more crudely than Preminger does, the implication is that Frank has slept with Mary but may never have done so with Diane.

I have already mentioned Diane's continual assertion of her role as a child, both with Frank and with the rest of the family. An exemplary moment would be the detail of her game with Ito, the Chinese servant, over the composition of the soft drink that he has mixed for her, a piece of business which clearly irritates Catherine. The supposed opposition of Catherine seems also to be used as a ruse to avoid acting on her feelings for Frank, and a justification for refusing him when he wants to 'make a big night of it.' Preminger also poses Diane and Frank in public places or in her open car; we do not see her enter his bedroom until the very end of the film.

In contrast, Mary's contact with Frank is focused by Preminger around her apartment, and we know from her opening line that Frank is familiar with the details of its geography – the fact that the phone is inaudible from the shower. Immediately following the night scene with Diane, there is an extended sequence in which Frank arrives at Mary's apartment to find her in the middle of dressing for work. He reacts to her deshabille with the words, 'I've been here before, remember,' and the lack of embarrassment on both sides implies that they are used to seeing each other undressed. As they talk, Mary sits on her bed, finishes dressing, and finally asks Frank to zip her up.

This may suggest modifications in the common opposition between the *femme fatale* and the domestic woman in *film noir*. Here we seem to be in a position where guilt-free and uncomplicated sex is offered as part of the vocabulary of the domestic woman. The negative quality of the eroticism of the dangerous woman seems marked by the possibility that it doesn't offer the satisfaction of more than minimal sexual contact, that the route to sexual fulfilment with such a woman is obscurely blocked.

How can Diane meet Frank's ironic reference to the distance between them, to her metaphorical – or perhaps literal – virginity? She must find a way of giving herself to him, and we now see her arriving in his quarters with a packed suitcase, which she parks out of sight. Frank announces that he is leaving and articulates as his reasons the differences of class and money that were implicit in the first scene. The two appear to be about to part, when in answer to a question about how a man can be sure that he is loved, she produces the suitcase and offers to go away with him. The embraces here are their most passionate in the film and are accompanied by a conversation about being sure of each other. It is twilight as Diane leaves. We see her outside the house, standing by the precipice next to the garage and, as she tosses an old cigarette packet down the slope, evidently imagining the murder of Catherine.

Still: the domestic couple – Bill (Kenneth Tobey) and Mary (Mona Freeman).

A way of clarifying the link between the murder and the previous scene with Frank might be the repeated term 'sure'. It could be argued that Diane believes that the way to be sure of Frank is to kill Catherine and thus control the Tremayne money, but, given his apparent lack of interest in the fortune, this seems unlikely. The form of the murder is possibly more suggestive. In previous scenes, Frank has described Diane's murderous feelings to her and characterised himself as an 'innocent bystander'. Does Diane consciously – or perhaps unconsciously – now conceive of the murder as a way of binding him inextricably to her, a different way of being 'sure' of him? This is certainly the effect of the choice of the 'fixed' car as the murder weapon. The presence of her suitcase, still in Frank's room some time later and found by the police after the deaths of Catherine and (by mischance) Charles in the car, confirms an effect, if not a conscious intention. Both Frank and Diane are charged with the murders.

A final uncomfortable possibility exists: that it is conceivably easier for Diane to murder Catherine than to go through with the business of running away with, and thus giving herself to, Frank. This cannot be made explicit, perhaps because Diane's sexual fears are a subject that the film has no way of directly addressing.

Preminger now uncovers a further area of irony. It emerges that by her act Diane has not delivered herself to moral judgment, but rather put herself into the hands of men engaged in a professional discourse which is largely indifferent to whether she actually committed a crime or not. Social truth here is 'what the jury decides', and her lawyer Frank Barrett (Leon Ames) carefully ignores her protestations of guilt, absorbed in the logistics of ensuring that no jury will convict his client. His manoeuvre is to manipulate the image of the couple, from transgressive illegitimate lovers to that of a 'young girl' giving herself to a 'hard-working ambitious war veteran' by the ruse of having them marry before the case comes to trial. Thus the union is achieved, not as physical sex but as a legal dodge. Marriage treated as negative or ironic is found elsewhere in Preminger's *films noirs*; we might relate the couple's situation here to the marriage undertaken as a form of robbery in *Fallen Angel* or the moment in *Laura* when Mrs Treadwell (Judith Anderson) offers to marry Shelby Carpenter (Vincent Price) and get him a good lawyer when it looks as if he will be accused of murder. In *Angel Face*, what is on trial becomes marriage itself and technology. The mistrust of the technical is embodied in the juror who tells the story of the failure of a part in his child's toy car, and, after a little undermining of the prosecution's technical expert by Barrett, Diane and Frank are acquitted and return to Beverly Hills.

They now take characteristically different attitudes to what has happened. Diane's is to understand it as a child's game gone terribly

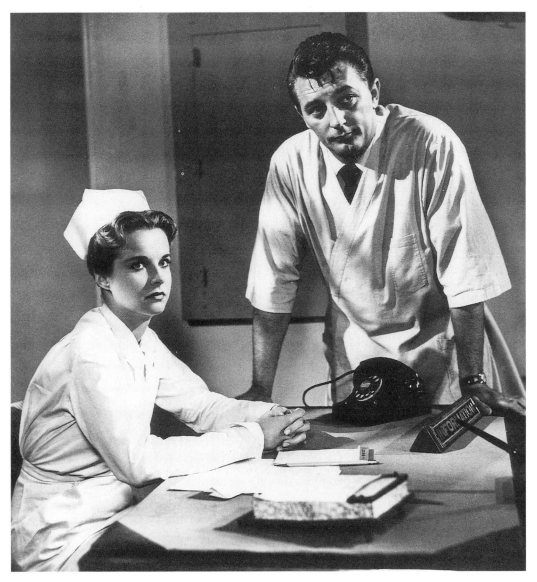

wrong. Her account of waking up to reality only on seeing the bodies both acknowledges her guilt and accepts that the situation cannot be reversed or retrieved. Frank states the simple belief that he can undo it all and be as he was: divorce Diane, go back to Mary and resume his old life. He thus stands at an opposite pole to the *film noir* hero's common position at this point, where the desire to return to or confirm the relationship with the domestic woman is felt in the knowledge that the events of the narrative have made it impossible. He has no response to Diane's suggestion that Mary will not take him back because she would always wonder if he were actually a murderer.

In Frank's final scene with Mary, a crucial difference emerges. He finds her with Bill, but nonetheless asks to be given another chance. When she refuses, Frank puts his defeat down to the randomness of Fate, saying that 'If only it [the call to the Tremayne place] had come five

Still: Frank, Mary and the telephone at the start of the film – 'if only [the call] had come five minutes later.'

minutes later' – he would not have met Diane, and none of this would have happened. But Mary clearly rejects this in favour of an explanation based on character. When Frank, mildly jeering, asks if he is being turned away because Bill is afraid of the 'competition', she replies that it is she who is afraid, of the competition with the series of Dianes that a man like Frank would find. She offers a version of the couple which stands as the end of the film's discourse on competitiveness: 'I want a marriage, not a competition, a husband, not a trophy.' He closes the scene by asking her if she thinks that 'maybe I am guilty, after all,' but she says no. To say this is almost to belittle Frank – to see him as constitutionally faithless, but not corrupt; his lack of a sense of guilt does not seem a positive quality.

We cut from the apartment to the Tremayne house, yet again as darkness falls. Diane dismisses the servants and walks through the house, alone. This is one of the great sequences of *Angel Face*, marking the shift of the centre of attention and meaning in the narrative from the man in the couple to the woman. Preminger is directing us here to contemplate the meaning of 'domestic' space, the messages from the past and fantasies of the future that are inscribed in it, and the relation of objects to human presence and absence. There are a number of parallels – a pertinent one is with the sequence in which Mark MacPherson (Dana Andrews) walks through Laura's apartment in *Laura*, where a similar intensity of yearning seems for a moment to cause a ghost to materialise.

Here the spell does not work. Diane pauses by the piano where she had 'played' the previous murder – for seven notes, out of tune, she plays in synch with the soundtrack, but she can no longer take it over. She moves on, walking along the landing where we have earlier seen her run to her father. Does her costume, white blouse and slacks, as well as the lighting here, emphasise her childlike quality? Certainly her shadow is hugely taller than she is. She looks into Catherine's room, moves across the hall to her father's suite. The camera follows her inside the room, where she stands holding a chess piece and looking at the board set for a game. Behind her in this shot a piece of set – it is literally a shadowy bust on a plinth – offers to our view an enormously magnified image of the piece, which is the white king. From the image of the chess board, and the loss it implies, Preminger dissolves to the exterior of the house, where Diane looks up at the windows of Frank's quarters over the garage. The 'angelic' music on the soundtrack underlines the strain of this moment, the belief that an intensity of longing can magically produce a literal effect. Diane rushes up to the apartment, but Frank has not returned. She touches his possessions – entering his bedroom for the first time in the film, she holds a shirt still in its wrapping from the laundry – objects awaiting an absent human agent to affect them. It is a last irony that she spends the night in Frank's quarters, but he does not return.

Convinced that Frank has left her, she turns to the public sphere, in the form of the lawyer's office, to insist on confessing herself a murderess. Barrett's explanation to her is of the concept of double jeopardy – that now that she has been acquitted of the murder charge, 'confessing' to it would have no effect, would not even give her the reality of an oppositional role in this society, other than that of lunatic. She is now like her father, the blocked writer, a figure with a story than cannot be told. The sequence ends with Barrett tearing up the beginnings of her dictated confession – another dead letter.

The emotional tone of the last scene seems to sum up the weaknesses of the characters, and yet their pathos. Frank, brusque and frozen, returns only to take the western hero's common option of escape – he is headed for Mexico, unable to reply with more than a negative grunt to Diane's plea that he take her with him. Jean Simmons makes Diane's tenseness touching as she plays out the last cards in her hand in an attempt to rescue the romance – the account of the glamour of Acapulco, the sight of a girl and a fast car, finally a romantic cliché from the movies, a bottle of champagne and two glasses.

Why does she jerk the car into reverse and kill them both at the last moment? We may take it that part of what is involved is meeting a Production Code requirement that Diane should not be seen to get away with murder. Dramatically, what we see is an impulse, a last-second response to Frank's shout of complaint at her pulling away before he has poured the champagne, a moment of rage at his indifference.

It could be argued that presenting the murder of Frank as a matter of his passivity and Diane's impulse is appropriate, in that the Mitchum character here takes the *film noir* hero beyond romantic fatalism to a point where he seems almost incapable of any active response to events. Bound up with this is the fact that Frank seems to represent no values, no dreams except for a prosaic desire for success represented by the sports car business. To look back at, say, the scene in *Out of the Past* (Jacques Tourneur, 1947) where the Mitchum character talks to his girl about the house he would like to build suggests the distance between the worlds of the two films. In *Angel Face*, Mitchum is neither able to present such values, nor allowed insight into his loss of them. Richard Dyer in his essay on *Gilda* (in Kaplan, 1978) has raised the question of the difference between the norms embodied by

Still: Barrett (Leon Ames) explains the concept of double jeopardy to Diane.

238

Still: estrangement – Frank and Diane in his quarters.

major and minor stars, and in this context we might recall the striking moment in *Fallen Angel* when Eric Stanton (Dana Andrews) describes himself to his wife as 'a complete washout at thirty'. Does the casting of Mitchum, at least at this stage in his career, move us automatically away from such bleakness, or simply prevent explicit admission of it?

If Mitchum fails to a great degree to embody anything clearly positive beyond his obvious charm, the milieus into which he moves, the replacement of the labyrinthine city common in *film noir* with the 'great house', evokes other anxieties. The image with which Preminger concludes is not of the house burnt to a shell or haunted, but simply empty, like Gatsby's empty house which, after two murders and a suicide, concludes Scott Fitzgerald's novel *The Great Gatsby*. In both cases, the image speaks of the failure of American money successfully to purchase and transplant 'culture', and in a wider context the failure of that money to sustain a functioning life in which sexual desires can be adequately met. It is here that we find the *femme fatale* redescribed as something like a child, an apparent innocent, a descendant of those destructive heroines who 'had never, all along, intended doing anything at all'. The words are Fitzgerald's description of Daisy Fay, the heroine and murderess of *The Great Gatsby*. In both

texts, it is the violence associated with the figure of the beautiful woman, the figure who ought to affirm the best values of the civilisation, that is particularly damning. In *Angel Face*, Preminger places direct expression of this immediately before the murders of Catherine and Charles, in a piece of business which gives the Chinese servant the line: 'The only trouble with America – it spoils the women.'

Angel Face is also about failures of expression and understanding. If the *noir* private-eye hero often survives his films, it may be because he is able to read, to interpret. In the only direct allusion to the film's title, Frank says to Diane, 'I don't pretend to know what goes on behind that pretty little face of yours, and I don't want to.' The unwillingness or inability to read can be linked with the difficulty of writing – a novel or a confession of murder. The image is of a world in which communications fail to function, at the opposite pole from the *film noir* narrative set around the successful act of confession or explication. As Diane's wrecked car comes to rest in the last seconds of *Angel Face*, we see loose papers swirling around it – the last of the series of images that punctuate the film of words torn, crumpled, scattered, unwritten.

KISS ME, DEADLY

Edward Gallafent

The opening shot of Robert Aldrich's *Kiss Me, Deadly* (1955) is of an empty road in the countryside at night. A woman is running down this road – we see her bare feet and hear her gasping breath on the soundtrack. Two cars pass – she waves at them to stop but they drive on. A third car approaches, and she stands directly in its path, forcing it to brake so hard that it skids off the carriageway. There is a shot of the driver, private eye Mike Hammer (Ralph Meeker), and the opening line of the script is: 'You almost wrecked my car . . . Well?' When she does not reply, he says, 'Get in,' and even opens the door for her. He is driving an open sports car, and the radio is already on. As they pull back onto the road, the continuing sound of her sobbing breath is joined by Nat 'King' Cole singing 'Rather Have the Blues'. The camera is now positioned behind the heads of the couple, looking slightly down, so that we look through the windscreen on to the empty road as it passes under the wheels of the car. Against this background the credits roll. The words scroll from top to bottom of the screen, so that we must read them unconventionally, from the bottom upwards. So used is the eye to reading downwards that the effect is difficult and disorienting – we are being taken in a direction in which we are unwilling to follow. Throughout this sequence, the song on the radio competes with the sound of the girl's strained breathing.

Darkness, a moody song, a girl in trouble, and a striking visual style. In this discussion of *Kiss Me, Deadly*, I will not be concerned mainly with that style. What I wish to consider is how, by the mid 1950s, the concerns of the private-eye *film noir* – which is to say the skills of the hero, the pleasures of watching him, and the quality of his relations to women – have shifted away from the earlier versions of Raymond Chandler or Dashiell Hammett texts.

At first, the differences do not seem very obvious. The events which follow the credit sequence show the erotic potential of this uneasy couple. We learn that the girl, Christina Bailey (Cloris Leachman), is naked under the trench coat that she stole in order to escape her unidentified tormentors. When the car is stopped at a police roadblock, she nestles close to Hammer, who lies to the police that she is his wife. When they stop at a filling station to have the car checked

after its spin off the road, the attendant assumes that they pulled into the bushes to make love. Hammer's coolness towards the girl does not contradict any of this – rather, it establishes his status in a familiar way as the hard-boiled private eye, the man who sees a lot of beautiful women, and whose strength is expressed by his ability to resist their seductions. Or at least to resist them until he has identified the good and the corrupt, one point of the narrative often being to dramatise a choice between women.

There is another element in the exposition here. As they drive through the night, Christina criticises her rescuer. She speaks generally, identifying him as a type of man whose 'one lasting love' is himself – his car, his clothes, his physical fitness – these are more important to him than any ability to 'give in a relationship'. The excitement of the rescue and the sexual frisson that goes with it are complicated by her awareness of the inadequacy of her potential partner, summed up in her rhetorical irony: 'And what does woman need to complete her – why, man, of course, wonderful man.' For this terrorised woman, the self-absorbed Hammer is less than satisfactory, but facing the likelihood of her own death, he is all she has got.

The action of the opening is lifted complete from Mickey Spillane's novel of the same title, but Christina's critique of Hammer's narcissism is introduced by Aldrich and his scriptwriter A.I. Bezzerides. To understand the problems of filming Spillane, I want to look briefly at his writing and its contemporary reception. The massively successful series of Spillane novels (twenty-four million copies were in print in June 1954) begins with *I, The Jury* (1947), *One Lonely Night* (1951), *The Long Wait* (1951) and *Kiss Me, Deadly* (1953). Only *The Long Wait* does not feature private eye Mike Hammer as the central character. The popularity of the novels and of Hammer led to several films made by Parklane Pictures and released through United Artists: *I, The Jury* (Harry Essex, 1953), *The Long Wait* (Victor Saville, 1954) and Aldrich's version of *Kiss Me, Deadly*, released by Parklane/UA in April 1955.

In the novels, the figure of Mike Hammer is a right-wing vigilante, a war veteran impatient with the process of law and suspicious about corruption in high, and specifically governmental, circles. The novels are narratives about revenge, and the ability of one man to destroy a corrupt organisation. In each case, the organisation is seen as specifically threatening Hammer and those under his protection, but also more generally as undermining American democracy. The novels reflect the paranoia of their witch-hunting times; in *Kiss Me, Deadly*, the organisation is identified as the Mafia, and in *One Lonely Night*, it is explicitly the Communist party. Perhaps what is most striking about the novel compared to, say, Chandler is the interest in sadism; the destruction of the evil or guilty men enacted by Hammer is presented in terms of the graphic detail of the effects of his violence on these 'soft, pulpy people'.

The perception of the novels as both McCarthyite and pornographic is not new. It was current in the early 'fifties, part of a wider anxiety about pulp fiction and elements of popular culture such as horror comics, which were the subject of investigation by a Congressional committee at the time. Intellectuals were also concerned: in November 1954, Christopher La Farge's piece for *The Saturday Review*, 'Mickey Spillane and his Bloody Hammer', explicitly made the connection between 'Hammerism and McCarthyism' and expressed 'the disgust of all truly liberal minds' at both.

This was the context for Robert Aldrich's treatment of the Spillane material. According in part to the director's own accounts, and certainly according to some critical discussions of the film, Aldrich took it as an opportunity to express his disgust for Hammer and the politics of Spillane. In an interview with François Truffaut shortly after the film was released (*Cahiers du Cinéma*, November 1956), he argued that Spillane was 'anti-democratic'. But we should look at his comments over a period of time. In 1956, he said to Truffaut, 'I regret having accepted the job of making *Kiss Me, Deadly*. Two horrible films had already been made of the Spillane series, and I should have refused.' Interviewed by Joel Greenberg twelve years later (*Sight & Sound*, Winter 1968/69), he said 'I was very proud of the film,' and in answer to the next question (on his debt to Spillane's novel) claimed – inaccurately – 'The book had nothing. We just took the title and threw the rest away.' This seems to accord with current accounts of the film, such as Robin Wood's description of the critique of the hero as 'devastating and uncompromised' (*CineAction* 21/22, Summer/Fall 1990). But in 1956, Aldrich's honesty was disarming: '. . . when I asked my American friends to tell me whether they felt my disgust for that whole mess, they said that between the fights and the kissing scenes they hadn't noticed anything of the sort.'

The problem would seem to be as follows. To film a Spillane novel and attempt to be faithful to the effects evoked in the text would have been very difficult in 1955. Even had it been technically possible to present the smashing of faces, the fascination with female nudity recurrent in the novels would have been impossible to present on screen under prevailing censorship regulations. Equally, it seems unsurprising that a liberal director at this time would want to make a film that appeared critical of author and hero. I would argue that the figure of Hammer created by Aldrich and Bezzerides is actually quite unlike the figure in the novels and owes a lot to their vision of the role of the *film noir* private eye in the mid-'fifties. What they have done is to create a different model of the hero and then offer a critique of that figure, rather than treating Spillane's hero from an oppositional point of view. To establish this, we need to understand the ways in which the central figure – and central couple – of the film are conceived.

The opening exposition of *Kiss Me, Deadly* concludes with Hammer unable to protect Christina. Unidentified hoods again force his car off the road, capturing them both. Christina is tortured to death, but a faked car accident fails to kill Hammer, and he wakes up in hospital. When he recovers, he is questioned by the FBI in the guise of the 'Interstate Crime Commission'. In the novel this scene is treated as a conversation between equals and serves only to establish some facts about the dead girl before Hammer starts on his mission of revenge. Aldrich's version is radically different. In a series of shots which express the alienation of the two sides from each other, Hammer stares away from the investigators as they describe him, starting with his name and moving on to his profession. We are told that the main form of his activity as a private eye is not crime but divorce work. Their account makes it indistinguishable from a seamy blackmail racket, with Hammer seducing the wives, and his secretary and girlfriend Velda (Maxine Cooper) acting as bait for errant husbands.

A simple attack on Hammer might have thrown its weight behind this account of him, but we are not asked to identify with the FBI. The scene suggests that their professed contempt is tinged with envy – Hammer and Velda ('real woo-bait', according to one FBI man) are being attacked precisely because they have found a financially rewarding way of exploiting their sexuality without doing anything that is literally illegal. Behind the censure lie the tensions widely observed in the America of the period, the envy of the individual entrepreneur that was felt by those swallowed up by the relentless expansion of corporations inside and outside Government, and the feeling of those whose success depends on the repression of their sexuality towards the couple who use sexuality to create their success.

The hostility of the FBI is also contrasted with the friendliness of the local cop, Pat Chambers (Wesley Addy), in two scenes with Hammer which frame the interrogation scene, and underlined by the fact that Pat refuses the FBI's invitation to join in the questioning. The quality of Meeker's delivery of Hammer's final line to the FBI - 'All right, you've got me convinced, I'm a real stinker' - makes clear that this is not so much his admission of moral corruption as a piece of weary sarcasm.

Our attitude to Hammer and Velda is refined in a later scene, when he finally returns to his apartment. The set – one of two specially constructed for the film, the other being Velda's apartment – is important here. It speaks of modernity, of precise order, and of money. It is of a piece with Hammer's fast car and his neat suits and ties, the place of a man who has exploited new technologies successfully for gain – one of its most prominent features is a reel-to-reel tape recorder built into the wall as an answering machine. The technology of audio tape, first commercially exploited in the late 'forties, is central to the divorce business; later, we gather that Velda's role has involved the making of 'incriminating' tapes.

Velda arrives, and the ensuing scene is an amalgam of different kinds of work and pleasure. We see the couple's sexual interest in each other, Hammer's desire to investigate Christina's death, and the ongoing detail of the divorce business. These are not sequential – even in a clinch, Hammer is giving Velda instructions. The overall effect of the scene is one of frustration and anxiety, their lovemaking blocked both by the sense that Velda's seductiveness needs to be put to work on her latest 'Mr Friendly' and by the consciousness that Christina's death has inserted Hammer into a mysterious and possibly dangerous world.

How can we sum up an attitude to the couple? The reservations are clear. There is the sordid side to the divorce business, of which Velda is painfully aware – unsurprisingly, given the greater odium heaped on women in these areas. There is the cockiness of Hammer, prepared to brush this aside in the light of the money and success it has brought. More subtle is the sense of stagnation, of the pair trapped in the endless round of the business – it is significant that part of the conversation in the apartment scene is about a piece of seduction that is having to be done over again. But these reservations operate against the fact that as the young, attractive couple at the centre of this narrative, the roles that they occupy – boss and secretary, heterosexual lovers, strong man and beautiful woman – relate clearly to elements that this culture supports, and their success or failure is central to any vision of the strengths and weaknesses of America in 1955.

It is in this context that Hammer's motivation in uncovering what is behind Christina's death can be understood. Unlike the figure in Spillane's novel, he is not interested in vengeance, but rather fascinated by power. He reasons to Pat that when a girl's death 'rings bells all the way to Washington,' whatever is behind it must be 'something big'. His desire to find the treasure that he assumes Christina to have been protecting is that most American fantasy, of fabulous riches, something that will change his and Velda's life entirely.

But his abilities are in question. Velda's exit line in the apartment scene is 'Stay away from the window – somebody might blow you a kiss.' This neatly juxtaposes her anxiety that Hammer may be on a death list with the awareness behind her irony that, given Hammer's specific field of expertise, he is possibly more used to having kisses aimed at him than bullets.

The next sequence appears to answer this, engaging with the question of the kind of power that the *film noir* private eye needs to possess. Night falls, and Hammer leaves his apartment to follow the first of the leads that will hopefully take him to his prize. As he walks the street, he is followed by a small-time hood. In outline, this has the quality of a moment familiar in the genre; the experience of the private eye is to be expressed by the fact that he invariably knows when he is being tailed, and so can turn on his pursuer and despatch him back to his bosses with a message that he is not a man to be trifled with. Add a little violence, and this is exactly how the scene appears in Spillane's novel.

Aldrich presents the landscape of the street as a series of screens and frames – opaque windows, a mirror, the bars of a news-stand outlining a figure – walking these streets is a matter of seeing, of knowing how light falls and how it is reflected. The moment of conflict, when Hammer, watching his assailant's reflection in the mirror on a cigarette machine, turns and blinds him with popcorn thrown into his face, demonstrates his control in this area. As they fight, the position of the knife makes a visual point about phallic power – Hammer emerges as stronger, smarter, even more of a man than his opponent.

The scene does not end with the hood being sent away. Rather, we see Hammer beat the head of the man viciously against a wall. He slumps to the ground but recovers and attacks Hammer again. It now emerges that the fight is effectively taking place at the edge of a precipice, as the hood is sent hurtling down a long, steep set of steps.

What is of interest here is not Hammer's dominance – that is routine – but the excess, the degree to which the frustrations of the earlier scene with Velda are resolved by the release of massive physical violence. The crucial contrast is between the ease with which satisfactions seem to flow from the exercising of physical violence and the visceral pleasures of speed, compared with the relative frustrations associated with the exercise of sexuality. It might sound as if I am describing the situation of the Robert Stack character in Douglas Sirk's *Written on the Wind*, made in the following year – there are many connections, but both the role of the high performance car as a finally unsatisfying form of access to pleasure and the use of the staircase as a central part of the *mise-en-scène* are obvious links.

Still: the modern couple – Mike Hammer (Ralph Meeker) and Velda (Maxine Cooper).

Hammer now follows his one lead, and thereby obtains the address of Christina's apartment. At the apartment, a kindness to the porter earns him another lead, the new address of Christina's flatmate, Lily Carver (Gaby Rodgers). She claims to be frightened of the men who came for Christina, and in a later scene, Hammer rescues her and takes her back to his apartment. These actions conform in part with how we believe a good detective should act. There are familiar virtues, such as the sympathy for the little guy which commonly earns the private eye information denied to others. And again there is rescue of the threatened woman linked with the control of sexuality, his refusal to let Lily seduce him.

In other ways, Hammer is ill-equipped for his detective role. What is perhaps most clearly lacking in him is sympathy for and relation to the past. Narrative in *film noir* is often a disinterring and ordering of information buried in the past, and it is clear that Hammer is a man with no understanding of or response to a world which relates to earlier times. He knows that he should be able to read the clues buried in the past, but is unable to do so, or even to determine if there are hidden meanings at all. This produces a series of anxious gestures. He had never heard of Christina Rossetti before encountering Christina Bailey, but removes the book of poems from Christina's bedside when he visits the apartment. In the same scene, he notices the Tchaikowsky which is playing on her radio.

When he returns to his own apartment, he tunes to the same station in a baffled attempt to gain some access to the dead girl. His visits to his various leads are similar, all pictured in sets that speak of the old city, in contrast to his own modern apartment block. An exemplary case is the sequence in the room of the opera singer Carmen Trivaco (Fortunio Bonanova). Trivaco is playing a recording of Caruso singing Flotow's *Martha*. Hammer moves around the set, poking in the clutter with which Aldrich has filled it, threateningly breaking a record, aware that he has no apparatus for understanding such material.

We may compare this to his competence in the context of modern technologies. When Hammer is offered a bribe in the form of a new car, his unwary mechanic friend Nick (Nick Dennis) is about to kill himself by starting the engine. Hammer instantly locates one booby trap and is accurate in his guess that there will be another one of a different kind, one associated with pleasure, which would have exploded on the highway, 'when you open her up wide'. The reference to sexual pleasure here is obvious, and can be put in context by considering the figure of Nick.

The fact that he is the only character in the narrative who does not appear in Spillane's novel hints at the importance of Nick. He could be

said to represent the kinds of energy and pleasure that the novel gives directly to Hammer. Aldrich links this brio with Hammer indirectly and implies that pleasures are perhaps entirely satisfying only when assigned to the world of the imagination. They exist in Nick not as action but as catch phrases. His memorable 'Va-Va-Voom' and 'Pretty-Pow!' represent the energy of sex and speed free from the confusions and anxieties of status and progress that haunt Hammer, but we never see Nick driving a fast car and never see him with a girl.

Earlier, Aldrich has cut from Hammer's success in locating the bombs in the car to his first visit to Velda's apartment. There he plots his pursuit of something big, telling Velda that they are giving up the 'penny-ante divorce business' for a while. Her research has dug up some more names, but two of these are the names of men who died in 'accidents' like the one that nearly killed Hammer. Her anxiety is clear, but Hammer, at his most cocky and least attractive, remains impervious to it. He goes off to interrogate the leads, even visiting the head of the hoods, Carl Evello (Paul Stewart), in his mansion. Here, Hammer firmly puts off the blonde who offers herself to him and paralyses the hood sent to dispatch him with a trick that reduces the man to unconsciousness in seconds. In this context, and for a moment, the private eye still

appears to have powers that approximate to magic. But Aldrich emphasises the narrowness of his range – his competence extends only to blondes and hoods, as the subsequent frustrating interrogation of Trivaco shows.

When Hammer finds that Nick has been killed, Aldrich again makes a cut which takes Hammer from the garage to Velda's apartment. The shocked reaction to Nick's death is another mark of the distance from the world of Spillane, where death is commonplace, and the death of the good simply stokes the fires of revenge. We may assume that the divorce business does not generally result in bodies; the scene makes clear that this hero is not one who routinely deals with death.

I take this scene to be central to *Kiss Me, Deadly*, and it is difficult to discuss it adequately in a short space. We see the couple first in an erotic encounter, as Hammer wakes Velda in her bedroom. For a moment, they kiss – then, as Hammer gives her the news, the eroticism seeps away and we see repetition of an earlier device, a series of shots in which a couple talk without being able to look each other in the face. Velda offers a scathing critique of the whole undertaking, and her fear and anger touches on the central question: is the object of the search worth dying for? Hammer's 'something Big' now becomes Velda's contemptuous 'the great Whatsit', suggestive of trickery or illusion, and the enemy becomes 'the nameless ones'. The point here is her recognition that they are caught up in something very different from the world of divorce cases or even of ordinary police work, and that the difference is not simply one of scale – as Hammer's name for the prize implies – but one of quality.

Nor is it the case that the old behaviour becomes heroic in this new situation – it is simply dangerous. As the scene develops, Velda tells Hammer of another man related to the case and asks if he wants her to seduce this man. Maxine Cooper makes Velda's depression and self-disgust here delicately evident. Hammer abstractedly replies that he wants revenge on those who killed Nick, and Velda finally turns on him in utter scorn:

'You want to avenge the death of your dear friend. How touching. How sweet. How nicely it justifies your quest for the great Whatsit. [pauses] . . . Why don't you leave, Mike?'

Even after this, she makes an appointment to meet him again later – the insight that Hammer is trapped in a view of his role that will very possibly destroy them coexists for Velda with recognition of her own dependence.

Hammer now visits a nightclub where he hears 'Rather Have the Blues' again. This chance reference to the night of Christina's death leads to the realisation that the one essential clue is the note that she asked the petrol station attendant to post. This in turn leads, via an interlude in which he again bests Evello's thugs, to the morgue, where the doctor (Percy Helton) has extracted a key from Christina's body. The desire to reach the prize now becomes increasingly hysterical; Hammer first tries to bribe and then attacks the doctor, and repeats the process with the desk clerk in charge of the lockers where the prize is kept. We now learn that it is a box of fissionable material, in effect a very small atom bomb.

In the Spillane novel, the object of the search was a large quantity of drugs. There was apparently a straightforward reason for moving away from this. In his interview with Truffaut, Aldrich raised the problem of censorship, that 'up to *The Man With the Golden Arm*, drugs couldn't be mentioned in American films.' This seems likely; the change in Samuel Fuller's *Pickup on South Street* (1953) from Dwight Taylor's original story, which had dealt with drug traffic rather than spying, may have been similarly motivated.

In *Kiss Me Deadly* the effect of the change to atomic material is pervasive. Aldrich said that 'once we made that decision, everything fell into place.' The bomb exists as both a confirmation and an explanation of the view that Velda expressed in her criticism of Hammer, a rationale for the fact that the age in which they are living is beginning to make the hero, whose prowess is founded on the 'fights and the kissing scenes', an anachronism. The bomb itself is a whatsit of massive destructive capacity and no solid, exchangeable matter – what we finally see consists cinematically of almost contentless white light and sound. Similarly, the change from drugs to bomb entails the move from the named ones (the Mafia of the novel) to Velda's 'nameless ones'. Behind the traditional thugs like Evello where the private eye's prowess, or magic, still works is the figure of Doctor Soberin (Albert Dekker), ambiguously scientist and spy, for whom Hammer is just an irrelevant nuisance.

Still: traditional strengths – Hammer escapes his bonds.

Soberin is defeated in this film, but not by the hero. It emerges that Lily Carver's role as Christina's dead flatmate was a masquerade. In fact, she is Soberin's girl, the exact equivalent of Velda, given the task of attempting to seduce Hammer in order to find out what he knows. Now she too turns on her man, demanding half of what is in the sealed box that contains the bomb.

Soberin's indifference to Lily is marked by his self-absorbed game of trying to characterise the bomb through learned references: Pandora's box, Lot's Wife, the head of the Medusa. Lily's reply is, 'Never mind about the evil, what's in it?' He tells her that he is leaving her, adding almost in the same sentence that she is creasing his overcoat by carelessly sitting on it – unsurprisingly, she shoots him. Although it is certainly clear that whatever the box contains is deadly, she now embraces her own death by opening it fully. The ensuing explosion destroys everything, but a gesture to the benign couple remains on some prints – Hammer has arrived at the house to rescue the abducted Velda, and they stand watching the holocaust in the final shot.

To understand *Kiss Me, Deadly*, it is necessary to connect the woman who opens the film and dies at the beginning of it with the one who closes it by dying at the end, and to link them both to Velda. An important part of my pleasure in this film is the performances of these three actors, and an important part of its coherence is the argument that links them together. Christina's initial criticism, that men are absorbed in their own physicality and the status reflected in their possessions and money, becomes Velda's awareness that Hammer's vision of his powers is positively dangerous. The subject concludes with Lily's murderous response to Soberin's abandonment of her, a response which, suggestively, he completely fails to anticipate. What these three women have in common is their frustration in the face of the self-absorbed, indifferent men. The choice faced by the hero between the 'good' and the 'bad' woman common in *film noir* falls away here, where in every case the eroticised woman is now isolated by male unresponsiveness.

Again, elements in *Written on the Wind* present a parallel context. There male anxiety about expressing sexual need is diverted into both a forward and a backward movement, a reliance on the thrills of new technologies and a nostalgia for an age dependent on simpler physical prowess. In the Sirk, at least one half of this movement is interpreted positively, the pioneer values and the country world offering a fragment of the past as benign. In *Kiss Me, Deadly*, the negative past – represented as a high culture that is becoming progressively incomprehensible and a city of dark spaces – is placed next to a vision of modernity that takes us from the high speed car crash to the atomic bomb. It is the women in Aldrich's film – two of them will die horribly – who speak of this bleakness.

Still: 'Never mind about the evil, what's in it?' – Lily, Soberin (Albert Dekker) and the closed box.

THE BIG COMBO
Production Conditions and the Film Text

Chris Hugo

'Under the hegemony of the multinational corporations and their "world system", the very possibility of a progressive bourgeois culture is problematic . . .' Fredric Jameson, *Aesthetics and Politics*, New Left Books, 1977, p.203.

This pessimistic but potentially accurate statement seems as good a place as any to begin a discussion about a film such as Joseph H. Lewis's *The Big Combo* (1955). The film's story of the apparently unequal struggle between the public good (represented by 'honest' policemen) and the legitimate yet criminal Bollemac Corporation appears to bear witness to the veracity of Jameson's insight. However, it is not only the overall content of the film that can be related to this quotation. As an aware spectator, one might also be surprised at the complexity and intelligence of this sort of movie, particularly in view of its attempt to appeal to the mass audience who would have paid to see it and the entirely commercial motivation of the company (Allied Artists), which deemed such a project a potentially profitable piece of entertainment. As with so many *noir* films of the period, one is amazed that so many of such artefacts could have been made within the commercial Hollywood system. One may also be depressed that so little of this sort of product is turned out today, when the channels for the dissemination of media products are so numerous. However, we should probably not be surprised, now that the media industries, including film production, are more than ever simply divisions of multinational conglomerates.

It would be quite false to draw the conclusion that the capitalist enterprises involved in mid 1950s American film production were necessarily any more 'progressive' than the corporations operating today. The 'freedom' to produce a film like *The Big Combo* was derived from industrial practices specific to the period. The individual film needs to be seen in the context of the institutional background to its production.

In an admirably researched article on the B *film noir*, Paul Kerr observes that 'few exhibitors could afford to book a double bill comprising two relatively expensive A films, those typical products financed and distributed by the dominant Hollywood majors' (Kerr, 1986). As cinemas normally showed double feature programmes in the 1950s (although they were to die out in the early 1960s), cheaper, more affordable B features had to be produced. From the 1930s (when B-film production began in earnest), smaller production companies – some with their own distribution systems – were set up to provide low-budget films in quantity. The idea of the B film was also taken on board by the Hollywood majors, which organised B-film units to operate in-house, yet with practices different from those that underpinned A-film production (one such in the 1940s was the B unit supervised by Val Lewton at RKO).

A key economic feature of the B film was the way it was rented to exhibitors. By the 1950s, the rental for A features was based on a percentage of box-office takings (as is the case today) whilst B films played for a fixed or flat rental and were thus not so reliant on audience attendance figures – at least, not in the short term. In the long term, however, as Paul Kerr notes, 'B units would be compelled to carve out identifiable and distinctive styles for themselves, in order to differentiate their products – within generic constraints – for the benefit of audiences in general and exhibitors in particular' (Kerr, 1986, pp.228-229).

The B *film noir* may be perceived as a clearly differentiated product with its own style – which is especially noticeable when it is viewed in tandem with a bright and colourful A feature. These B films were formed not so much out of a desire to produce progressive texts, but rather as the direct result of a particular method of employing production capital.

The concept of the B film (costing anything from $400,000 downwards, at 1950s prices) was inextricably linked to the flat rental system, which ensured budgetary restraint but which also allowed for a certain amount of creative freedom – as audience figures were not the chief concern. This fact may go some way to explaining how a low-budget specialist such as Joseph H. Lewis could make a film like *Gun Crazy* (1949) which – to contemporary eyes – looks more like something out of the French *nouvelle vague* than a product of mainstream Hollywood. The situation with *The Big Combo* (1955) was, however, somewhat different. Although it was a product of a B film studio, its production conditions were not utterly typical.

Set up in 1929, Monogram was (with Republic)

one of the better-known and financially more successful independent studios operating in the heyday of the Hollywood studio system. With its own distribution system, it functioned as a provider of B films, serials and a few modestly budgeted A features, filling the gaps in demand that the major studios left alone. It goes without saying that the relationship between Monogram and the majors was symbiotic. By 1953, the market was no longer almost guaranteed. The effects of the 1946 divorcement decree, parting the major studios from their first-run theatre chains, and the growth of competition from leisure pursuits other than cinema (notably, television) called for a rethink of business strategies.

In 1953, Monogram changed its name to Allied Artists (originally one of its constituent subsidiaries). Perhaps not sufficiently aware of the crippling costs of distributing A pictures, Allied Artists prepared to compete in the temporarily more open feature-film market and signed up prestigious film makers such as John Huston, Billy Wilder and William Wyler to create big-budget films. As with many other organisations that have tried to challenge the major studios' grip on distribution, this strategy eventually failed and Allied Artists sensibly decided to abandon film production in favour of television.

In the year in which *The Big Combo* was produced, Allied Artists was attempting a changed approach which evolved out of pursuing the newly emergent and younger market for exploitation films, which were sold on the strength of their controversial subject matter. However, perhaps with an eye for wider market potential, Allied Artists did not go down the (more successful) road taken by such production outfits as AIP (American International Pictures), which took the exploitation elements in their films as far as censorship would allow and kept budgets to a minimum. Instead, Allied Artists tried to produce what might be called A/B hybrids. In *The Big Combo*, one can isolate three elements which were combined in an attempt to provide a product with a distinctive appeal:

a) The exploitation element: a story tackling the link between sex and violence in a way that the major studios would have shied away from. At the same time, the film incorporated more 'serious' subject matter (A-film material) in the threat to American society of the quasi-criminal yet legitimate corporation.

b) The B *film noir* look: the use of a (by then) well-known visual style, suited to narrating this sort of story and yet also economical in financial terms.

c) Using the money saved on sets and locations (possibly because of the use of the noir style) for a star cast: Cornel Wilde, Richard Conte and Brian Donlevy gave the production an A-film gloss and, of course, were useful selling points in themselves.

The Big Combo was not a big commercial success in Britain or elsewhere. It did not even merit a showing in London's West End – and was overlooked by 'serious' film reviewers; it rated about half a dozen lines of lofty disdain in the *Monthly Film Bulletin* of February 1956. It is perhaps surprising, then, that it is so well thought of nowadays. The London listings magazine *City Limits*, in a general introductory article on *film noir* published in June 1990, put the film in number one position on a top ten scale of *noir*. Ten years earlier, in April 1980, the *Monthly Film Bulletin* had 'rediscovered' the movie in a retrospective review of the career of Joseph H. Lewis and thus confirmed it as a respectable object of 'serious' criticism.

There is an often-quoted remark, attributed to Henry Kissinger, that could almost have been part of the script of *The Big Combo* 'Power . . . power is the ultimate aphrodisiac.' We are never really shown the extent to which the Bollemac Corporation is involved in the everyday life of the American state, and the exact nature of its multifarious operations is not made explicit (as, similarly, in *The Godfather* movie cycle, where Francis Ford Coppola does not show us the day-to-day operation of the Corleone empire, even given a much larger film budget). Instead, we are shown one of the major representatives of this shadowy organisation, a Mr Brown (Richard Conte). It is he who, right from the beginning, seems to pre-echo Kissinger's comment in numerous scenes where he emphasises the control of economic power as a structure with which to dominate men and, even more overtly, to seduce women. Indeed, the film strongly suggests that, at least to the mind of a ruthless ex-gangster, the ability to control beautiful women without effort is the prime motivation behind winning power.

Philip Yordan's script leaves the audience in no doubt that Brown is a callous villain with no apparent redeeming features. Within the terms of conventional film narrative, the audience expectation is that this bad man will be brought down by the actions of the good cop Leonard Diamond (Cornel Wilde), whose function, traditionally, is to represent the intentions of the law-abiding audience. A satisfactory ending, the violent death or capture of Brown, is what is required to restore the equilibrium which is so clearly unbalanced at the film's beginning. In fact, Brown *is* captured by the 'good cop' at the end of the movie but, while a sense of formal closure is realised in the script, the dark, fog-laden *mise-en-scène*, into which the characters fade, contradicts an optimistic reading of the future after the film has ended. Some commentators have suggested that the last scene of *The Big Combo* is reminiscent of the ending of *Casablanca*, as it features an airfield at night. But the superficial resemblance is as far as this notion goes. The ending of *Casablanca* offers the audience hope and inspiration, as Humphrey Bogart's Rick has made a personal sacrifice for the greater good of mankind (or, at least, the Allied war effort). The end of *The Big Combo*

offers only the slim chance of an interlude in what seems to be an ongoing nightmare.

The overall background to the action in *The Big Combo* is suggested by the title itself. In an early scene at police headquarters, Diamond describes the size and extent of the Bollemac Corporation to his friendly and supportive superior, Captain Peterson (Rob Middleton). Peterson is visiting Diamond to warn him about spending so much of the taxpayers' money to pursue one man, Mr Brown. Diamond replies, 'Brown isn't a man, he's an organisation.' Peterson tries to convince Diamond that the battle is unequal and, by implication, not worth fighting: 'The Bollemac Corporation . . . that's the largest pool of illegal money in the world . . . You're fighting a swamp with a teaspoon.'

From the beginning of the film, the size and power of the 'Combination' is outlined, as is the comparative weakness of the representatives of the liberal state (the police) who simply don't have the resources to oppose it. Even though Brown is eventually captured, the information that large, criminally-inspired organisations are a reality will be remembered by the audience. There is no evidence that the set-up which Brown represents is in a state of dissolution just because his particular section is undone.

In the same scene in Diamond's office, it soon becomes obvious that the possibility of a satisfactory outcome to the film is going to be in jeopardy partly because of the nature of the good cop. The story of a decent man fighting a powerful organisation and eventually succeeding

Still: the last scene – Susan Lowell (Jean Wallace) and Leonard Diamond (Cornel Wilde).

– if only partially – in destroying it, is well known and well loved by cinema audiences. If that same man wins the approval or, even better, the love of a beautiful woman along the way, the mass audience is likely to be satisfied. In *The Big Combo*, this archetypal realist fiction is undermined. While the first half of the scene in Diamond's office sets up his character as that of unimpeachable public servant, even willing to spend his own salary in the pursuit of Brown, the second half presents us with a man driven by intense feelings of thwarted love. Captain Peterson sees through to what appears to be the real motivation behind Diamond's obsessive pursuit of Brown: 'Susan Lowell, she's Brown's girl, you are in love with her . . . Try to face facts Leonard; you can't bear to think of her in the arms of that hood.' Most of the scene has been photographed in medium shots, but now the camera closes in on Diamond's tortured expression as Peterson adds: 'She's been with Brown for three and a half years. That's a lot of days – and nights.'

From this moment, until the film's ending (climax is not an appropriate term), *The Big Combo* uses its title story mainly for the purpose of providing a background to what is actually a disturbing meditation on the erotic attraction of power and the intensely patriarchal motivation that drives a public servant to pursue a beautiful woman under the cloak of doing his duty.

Within the opening moments of *The Big Combo*, the film is skewed towards an 'oppositional' position in relation to the functioning of mainstream realist text. While it is a work of realist fiction, *The Big Combo* refuses to deliver a conventional reaffirmation of the status quo. The ending is not entirely happy or satisfactory, and the narrative formation is generally disturbing – and frequently disjointed. For example, as soon as the audience is introduced to Diamond, the potential hero figure, his motives for bringing down a criminal are seen as thoroughly suspect. Philip Yordan's script and Joseph Lewis's direction foreground Diamond as a man who seems to want control of Susan (Jean Wallace, then married to Cornel Wilde) because she is a potent symbol of Brown's power. There is no hint of tenderness or real affection in any of Diamond's dialogue scenes with Susan. Instead there is a suggestion that he is hiding a deep sexual jealousy while bombarding her with rational-sounding lectures as to why she should leave Brown. Rather than admiring her mink coat, Diamond harangues her tormentedly: 'You think this is mink. You think these are the skins of little wild animals sewn together for your pleasure. You're mistaken. These *were* the skins of little wild animals – people who have been beaten, sold, robbed, doped, murdered by Mr Brown.' This is one of several scenes in which Diamond tries to bully a shell-shocked Susan into admitting that being Brown's girl is a perfidious moral choice – not that the film presents the alternative of being Diamond's girl as a particularly attractive proposition.

I have mentioned that the script leaves the audience in no doubt as to the villainy of Mr Brown. In no way is he presented as a sympathetic

Still: Captain Peterson (Robert Middleton) suspects that Diamond's war on the Combo may be motivated by his desire to take Susan from Mr Brown.

character. Yet he does possess a certainty about himself and what he wants which is in marked contrast to Diamond's more hypocritical stance. Brown openly, and repeatedly, expresses the link between power and sex. In an early scene, set in the changing rooms of a boxing club, Brown is telling his dejected boxer Benny (Earl Holliman) about the difference between himself and his ex-boss but now assistant, Joe McClure (Brian Donlevy): 'We breathe the same air, sleep in the same hotel . . . there's only one difference. We don't get the same girls . . . Because, women know the difference. They've got instinct. First is first and second is nobody.' And he adds: 'Hate the man who tries to beat you, and the girls will come tumbling after.'

The fact that possession of the beautiful, blonde Susan is clearly symbolic of Brown's superiority over other men provides Diamond's motivation in trying to get her to leave him. With this as the centrepiece of the unfolding narrative, it appears that *The Big Combo* has reduced the struggle between law and order and organised crime to a more elemental, primitive contest in which the cipher-like Susan is to be awarded to the most potent male.

The Big Combo does not offer the audience a reassuring vision of the human condition, nor does it operate in a self-consciously tragic vein, as do *film noir* examples like *Criss Cross* (Robert Siodmak, 1949) or *Out of the Past* (Jacques Tourneur, 1947) or even Lewis's earlier *Gun Crazy*. It is hard to see any of the leading characters as a focus for audience identification; neither policeman nor villain is designed to function in that way. *The Big Combo* is thus able to break with mainstream convention by, among other things, keeping a clear distance from its audience, which is able to concentrate more on the ideas offered on screen (an approach adopted more self-consciously in Robert Aldrich's *Kiss Me, Deadly* of the same year).

One then has to ask whether this artistic outcome was a deliberate choice on the part of the film's makers. My suspicion is that the particular conditions of production were in large part the determinants of the film's 'oppositional' feel. For example, there is the *film noir* style itself, which many commentators have argued is intrinsically 'progressive' or 'oppositional', in part because of the expressionistic anti-realist visual devices used which seem, in their turn, to insist upon the choice of a certain sort of (usually) subversive story. As *film noir* goes, *The Big Combo* is about as dark and, in terms of sets or action scenes, as minimal as one can get in the commercial cinema. Out-takes from other movies are used to provide the odd link where a shot of a police car or of police headquarters is required, or to show the audience that a boxing match is taking place. Otherwise, all we see are actors in dimly lit rooms – the number of scenes not taking place at night could be counted on the fingers of one hand.

The initial impetus towards using the *noir* style was cost (*see* Kerr, 1986). Low-key lighting meant less electricity used, less lighting kit and less need for expensive sets or costumes. At the same time, especially by the 1950s, the style had evolved (and been accepted, as a style, by mass audiences) as a means to produce striking images on the screen which foregrounded characters and their relationships without having to show much else. It should be remembered that in the 1950s, despite the disparity in budget between A and B films, the same high-quality cameras and other technical equipment were available for use on both sorts of movie. A cinematographer of the standing of John Alton was able to give a film like *The Big Combo* a quality gloss even if there was little to photograph. It is easy to imagine how the film moved away from the mainstream drama that Allied Artists may have wanted for its hybrid A/B format. For instance, in the 'exploitation' element, the story does tackle the links between sex and violence and between sex and power in a fairly direct way but this has to be highlighted mainly in the script. The reasons seem to be cost (action is expensive), fear of censorship and fear of alienating a potential mainstream audience if too much 'shocking' material is shown. (There is one scene, controversial for its time in which Brown kisses Susan 'all over' but, even here, the act of oral sex is only suggested as Brown's head

Still: 'Hate the man who tries to beat you, and the girls will come tumbling after' – Benny (Earl Holliman), Mr Brown (Richard Conte) and Joe McClure (Brian Donlevy).

moves down Susan's body and out of the frame). The *noir* style also puts the emphasis on the script by showing us very little circumstantial detail.

What we have in *The Big Combo* is a recipe for a film where the ideas in the script take over because the economic conditions have meant that the production of a classic realist text was not possible. We cannot see expensive 'action', be it the day-to-day operation of the Bollemac Corporation, car chases, gunfights, fist-fights, crowd scenes, and country or city locations. To make up for this, we have sometimes complicated, often long, speeches. These set out positions designed to be intense and, perhaps, controversial, in an attempt to give the impression of action and because costly talent is available for their delivery. The plot is somewhat convoluted and, at times, improbable, even by *film noir* standards. Even if little is actually seen on film, the movie is surprisingly dense in the quantity of events that occur (frequently offscreen) and in the extent of the interpersonal relationships which are examined (it is possible to identify at least four triangular relationship systems within the film's diegesis).

I have tried to show how a film made back in 1955, with a thoroughly commercial outcome in

Still: Leonard Diamond, a cop in torment.

mind, can appear today as 'ideas-led', 'modern' and 'sophisticated' (in the 'art-house' sense) when compared to much of the current product. Even such a deliberate low-to-medium budget foray into *film après noir* as Stephen Frears's *The Grifters* (1990) seems somehow tame, self-referential and self-conscious in comparison. The reasons for *The Big Combo* looking as it does appear to be bound up with the particular way that a talented director, Joseph Lewis (who made only B movies) got the maximum impact out of a poorly conceived commercial production package. To the Allied Artists Corporation in 1955, the film could only have been viewed as a disappointing money maker. The concentration on cast over other production values appealed neither to mass audiences nor to contemporary

film critics, as witnessed by Howard Thompson's *New York Times* review of 26th March 1955: '*The Big Combo* isn't very big or very good.'

The commercial films of the past which today are seen as 'oppositional' or read as 'progressive texts', were frequently relatively cheap to produce (like *Citizen Kane*), were made in a way that did not have to take audience figures into direct account (as in B features), or were the result of financial miscalculation. The last case seems to cover *The Big Combo*. It would be pleasant to indulge the romantic sentiment that the old film industry was more interested in creativity than profit. It would also be incorrect. Today's film industry is no more or less interested in creativity as opposed to profits, although the marketing operation is much more dominant and much more sophisticated. With hindsight, the A/B concept, which informed the making of *The Big Combo*, seems ludicrous in its attempt to cover many markets while, in fact, satisfying none. That would be a business manager's judgment. From the point of view of the film makers, the financial constraints and the unbalanced package (cast over production values) might have been seen as an interesting creative challenge.

I would suggest that the economic conditions obtaining today would cause a remake of a film such as *The Big Combo* to look completely different from the 1955 model. Low-budget mass-market films of this sort and the relative freedom that went with them are virtually a thing of the past. A remade low-budget version of *The Big Combo* could succeed only as a minority-interest independent feature, with distribution aimed at art houses and with a UK television showing on Channel 4. With such a 'knowing' audience in mind, the movie would be shaped by the sophisticated expectations of relatively wealthy and well-educated consumers. One suspects that the end product might be somewhat mannered and self-consciously referential to *film noir* of the past, as this 'cultural capital' would be its chief selling point. For this reason, it would probably be a less good movie. At the same time, one suspects that it would stand a better chance than its predecessor of making a substantial profit and, of course, pleasing contemporary 'serious' film critics.

Still: after Susan's suicide attempt, Diamond wants her help in trapping Brown.

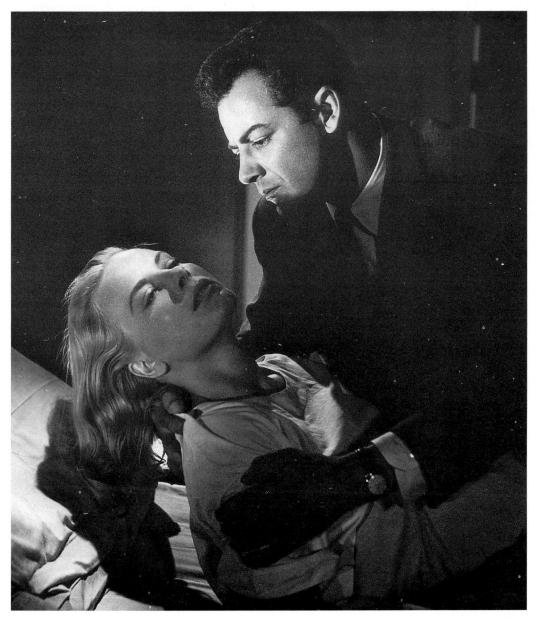

ECHO PARK
Film Noir in the 'Seventies

Edward Gallafent

In the 'seventies, the term *film noir* came increasingly to be used to describe current movies instead of referring to a past period of Hollywood production. By 1978, Christine Gledhill could discuss *Klute* without further ado as 'a contemporary *film noir*' (Gledhill, 1978), supporting the description by identifying the film as part of a cycle – the films cited are *Chinatown* (Roman Polanski, 1974), *The Long Goodbye* (Robert Altman, 1973), *Farewell, My Lovely* (Dick Richards, 1975) and *Marlowe* (Paul Bogart, 1969), all of which explicitly signalled themselves to their audience as contemporary *films noirs*. Three of these four make reference to Raymond Chandler, possibly the best-known writer popularly associated with 'forties and 'fifties *film noir*; all three are versions of Chandler novels. Two use the titles of the original novels, and one of these, *Farewell, My Lovely*, is also a remake of an earlier *film noir*, *Murder My Sweet*, directed by Edward Dmytryk in 1944. The third, *Marlowe*, a version of a lesser known Chandler book (*The Little Sister*), relies on the famous name of the detective as its signal to the audience.

The fourth film is *Chinatown*. The title seems to imply both a connection with 'forties and 'fifties *noir*, and a break from it. There is the reference to a locale which crops up periodically in the fiction of Chandler and Dashiell Hammett – Hammett's story *Dead Yellow Women* is an extended treatment of it – but the reference is a general rather than a specific one, and the screenplay is not based on an earlier story. Yet the film situates itself firmly as *film noir* – obvious components of this are the use of the private investigator as a central character, the setting of the action in California, and the use of a 'period' setting, here 1937.

Of these last three elements, the first two are used (albeit in different ways) by all four films, but the matter of period is more various. *Chinatown* and *Farewell, My Lovely* have period settings, but Altman's *The Long Goodbye* and *Marlowe* take Chandler through time but not space, to the California of the 'seventies.

The relationship to the past is crucial: these films are not attempting to take the devices or moods of *film noir* and apply them, disentangled as far as possible from their historical connections, to the world of the 'seventies. Altman uses the figure of Philip Marlowe and reinterprets Chandler's story – essentially one about crime and loyalty between men – to present his view of the moral worthlessness of contemporary America which the audience is assumed to share. For the film to make sense, the audience must interpret the figure of Marlowe (Elliot Gould) in terms of its distance from Chandler's – or Humphrey Bogart's – Marlowe.

Farewell, My Lovely and *Chinatown* are attempting to characterise the California of the late 'thirties and early 'forties, not simply as a historical 'setting' in the way in which a filmmaker in 1940 might have tried to characterise the turn of the century, but in the consciousness of it being a world which, in the specialised context of this kind of narrative, is a world *already filmed*. One might say in both cases that we are being presented with a new film of this world, a film made in the awareness that the audience has seen 'forties *film noir* and is now being presented with something 'improved', which allows it to be seen more clearly or completely. This relates in part to the most obvious technical 'improvement' compared to the 'forties films: the fact that the 'seventies films are made in colour. Doing again in the 'seventies what had been done in the 'forties suggests a belief in improvement both in technical advances in filmmaking and in changes in the conditions under which films are produced.

The 'seventies *film noir* cycle shares with, say, the Dino De Laurentiis production of *King Kong* (John Guillermin, 1976) the stress on technical improvements and on the relaxation of censorship. (The possible exception to the latter is *Marlowe*, made before the difference in censorship conventions was quite as substantial – or as explicit – as it was later to become.) But alongside the idea that these changes must necessarily lead to better films is another frequent device: the casting of actors who are associated with earlier Hollywood production, and sometimes specifically with *film noir*, as in the use of Robert Mitchum, at that time in his late fifties, as Philip Marlowe in *Farewell, My Lovely*.

Farewell, My Lovely

After an opening shot of an artificial palm tree, the credits sequence of *Farewell, My Lovely* is composed of a series of aerial shots and exteriors of Los Angeles at night; it ends with a low-angle

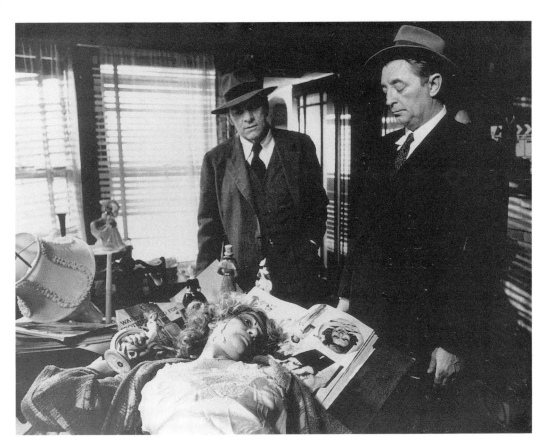

Still: Farewell, My Lovely – *the decent cop, Nulty (John Ireland), and Marlowe (Robert Mitchum) with the body of Jessie Florian (Sylvia Miles).*

shot into a window. The lower part reflects the letters of a scarlet neon 'Hotel' sign; through the upper part we see the figure of Mitchum looking out of the window, and the voice-over begins with his words: 'This past spring was the first that I felt tired, and realised that I was growing old.'

Via his status as a star in the earlier *film noir* canon, Mitchum's presence both establishes *Farewell, My Lovely* as a modern *film noir* and makes clear a shift in meaning. The *noir* hero was commonly an action hero whose physical – and implicitly sexual – prowess was central, often underlined by his being a veteran of World War II. Even in *Angel Face*, made seven years after the war ended, Mitchum is still identified in this way. But in *Farewell, My Lovely*, the stress has shifted from the assertion of physical prowess to the recognition of the inevitability of its passing, which is underlined by another detail of the voice-over. Marlowe is following Joe DiMaggio's winning streak, and DiMaggio's unbroken run is not just a piece of authentic period detail, but also a reference to a peak of physical achievement – like Marlowe's series of sexual conquests, it's a run that must sooner or later come to an end. The point is made again in the final sequence, when the ending of the unbroken run frames the action of the film.

The context in which sexual conquest might take place has also changed. After stressing his age. Marlowe tells us how the story began. He was hired by parents to find a fifteen-year-old runaway girl 'majoring in men', and his meeting with 'Moose' Malloy which initiates the main action is set in the context of finding this girl in a dime-a-dance joint. Her parents collect her, and they are shown as contemptuous of Marlowe, cold and indifferent towards the daughter. As she gets into their car she knees Marlowe in the groin. The scene is representative, expressive of a culture in which the debasement of sexual desire, connected to the failure of the family, is seen as ubiquitous.

Some of these changes in emphasis can be clarified by comparing *Murder My Sweet* and *Farewell, My Lovely*. In both, the central woman is Mrs Grayle, or 'Velma' (Claire Trevor/Charlotte Rampling), the person Marlowe (Dick Powell/ Robert Mitchum) is employed by Moose Malloy (Mike Mazurki/Jack O'Halloran) to find. In both versions, Velma is an alluring woman, married to an older, sexually used-up, but rich and powerful man. She enjoys relationships with other men and is attracted to Marlowe. Both versions use the idea of the instability of success for the woman: coming from lowly origins to marry money, Velma must conceal her past to become the wife of Judge Grayle (Miles Mander/Jim Thompson), and the release of Malloy from prison at the beginning of the film(s) threatens this.

The crucial difference is what Velma's past conceals. In the 'forties version, it is the fact that she is a criminal, and the men she kills are actual or potential blackmailers. The figure of Amthor (Otto Kruger), a 'psychic consultant' who has wormed the truth of the past from Velma and is now blackmailing her, expresses a concern in the film about illegitimate forms of knowledge and authority, but he is not a lover, and Velma's adultery is not the central issue.

In the 1975 version the figure of Amthor is a woman (Kate Murtagh) and is used quite differently. She is now the madam of a brothel, and the matter concealed is that Velma was once one of her whores. Thus the distinction, carefully maintained in the 'forties version, between Velma's criminality and her sexual appetites, has disappeared. In the 'seventies version, now that the sexual past of the woman is identified as the 'crime', her current sexual behaviour can be read as a continuation of her earlier role. At the end of the film Marlowe shoots Velma, and it is implied that what legitimates this is his knowledge that she was really a whore all along.

Farewell, My Lovely places the revelation of Velma's past at the conclusion of a series of negative images of female sexuality. There is Amthor herself, characterised as a sadistic lesbian, jealously possessive of one of her girls. She is duly shot dead in a fight by the heterosexual lover of the girl. Similarly Jessie Florian (Sylvia Miles), the widow of Velma's old employer, to whom Marlowe goes for information, is treated entirely in terms of a negative response to her sexuality. She is a woman of roughly Marlowe's

age, but he treats her fading sexual attractiveness with coolness. Pathetically, she mugs her old stage number for him and begins to cry. Her role is of helpless victim, lost once her body, her only asset, has started to show its age. Later in the film she, like Amthor and Velma, is killed.

In *Murder My Sweet*, Florian is played by Esther Howard, and although the two scenes are similar in their role in the narrative, in the Dymytrk there is no failed seductiveness, and Howard plays the character as a drunk old woman, shrewd and amiable by turns, suddenly galvanised into fear by the mention of Velma and Moose. Her sexuality is never seriously an issue.

Complementary to this insistence in the 'seventies version on the pervasiveness of corrupted female sexuality, is the marginalising of a world in which sexuality and the family can be seen as more benign. In the 1944 version this role is filled by Ann Grayle (Anne Shirley), Velma's stepdaughter. The film poses Marlowe's involvement with Ann against his interest in Mrs Grayle, the child-like monogamous woman against the wicked promiscuous stepmother, and here virtue triumphs: the film ends on the embrace of the good couple in the taxi that is taking Marlowe home.

There is no such character in the later version. Richards's film does have a 'good family', but they are treated as helpless victims. The father is Tommy Ray (Walter McGinn), an ex-bandleader who has married a black woman. The family

Still: Farewell, My Lovely. *The seasoned professional – Marlowe talks to the cops, Rolfe (Harry Dean Stanton) and Nulty.*

lives in the poverty that is the province of the weak – Marlowe comments that their hotel is the kind of place 'I always feared I'd end up in'. When Marlowe interviews the family, Ray's inability to move from his slumped position on the sofa expresses his impotence. He is later killed, unable to provide for his terrorised wife or little boy.

The failure of this family is clearly linked to a failure of masculinity in Tommy Ray. The benign world remains only in the minor male figures, the decent cop, Nulty (John Ireland), or Marlowe's friend, a newsvendor with whom he plays at boxing and discusses baseball. The figure of the good woman is entirely absent.

Several of these features of *Farewell, My Lovely* might be felt to signal 'modernity'. In the 1970s it might have been thought that a film would be more able to confront the pervasiveness of corrupt or commodified sexuality in 'forties California than was possible at the time. Similarly, the 'good' girl can be treated as a sentimental convention and dropped, to be replaced by the ruined Ray family as an indication as to what *really* happens to the virtuous. Finally, the hero's sexual relationship to the *femme fatale* can be franker – outside the restrictions of the Production Code, it is possible to have a plot in which Marlowe actually sleeps with Velma and goes unpunished for it.

This seems to be what the film wants us to feel, that we are now superior to the sentimentality implied in the 'happy' ending, aligning ourselves with Marlowe in weary acceptance of the rottenness of the milieu. But accepting this poses several problems. The first is that the perceived rottenness is so clearly related to gender, with the corruption of the film's women measured against the uprightness of Marlowe, Nulty and even Moose Malloy, who is played in the 'seventies version partly as an amiable sap. The 'forties version, relying heavily on the figure of the huge man whose strength is felt as monstrous, stresses his potentially violent qualities – he attacks Marlowe and kills Judge Grayle.

So what we have is something very unlike earlier *film noir*. The 'seventies Marlowe may be older, but he possesses the power and authority, the uncluttered vision, which we see as enabling him to shoot down the corrupt woman. In Chandler's novel, nobody kills Velma – she flees when her past is discovered. When finally spotted, she commits suicide. In the 1944 film, she is shot by her husband as she prepares to shoot Marlowe. In the subsequent struggle between Grayle and Malloy, the powder flash from a gun temporarily blinds Marlowe. This leads to the framing device of the 'forties narrative – the story is told in flashback while Marlowe is being interrogated by the police, the blindfold over his scorched eyes a simple metaphor for his limited ability to understand and control events.

As for the hero's sexual relationship to the *femme fatale*, rather than using the freedom from the restrictions of the code to explore the complexities of Marlowe's movement between a world perceived as corrupt and one perceived as pure, the 'seventies version extends the corruption to take in almost the whole milieu of the film, and collapses the pure world so that it is almost entirely identified with the figure and consciousness of Marlowe. This divides the two to the point where there are no areas of ambiguity or suggestion that the two worlds might be interdependent.

In contrast, the sexual invitations which are made towards the ending of *Murder My Sweet* preserve the complexities of the question: what sort of woman might be good for a man like this? (And, of course, the related question – for what sort of woman might this man be a good choice?) Dictated by the Production Code, the final choice of Ann is inevitable, but Dmytryk's dénouement scene persistently raises the 'rightness' of Velma and Marlowe, their similarity implied in her line as she prepares to shoot him – 'Just a couple of mugs – we could've got along.'

The ending of *Farewell, My Lovely* has Marlowe taking money to Tommy Ray's baseball-loving little boy. This raises the matter of women only negatively, in that Tommy's wife goes unmentioned, and the point seems to be the transmission of a gift from a man to a male child in the absence of a woman. In 1944, Dmytryk located the benign world at the end of his film in the figure of the couple who must now live with each other's qualities. Here the apparent salvation of the child seems to be a way of asserting a vague belief in the future in the absence of any faith in the film's present.

Marlowe and The Long Goodbye

Some of the qualities of the two films set in contemporary California can be established by consideration of their stars. Paul Bogart's *Marlowe* casts James Garner as the private eye. At this point Garner's career had developed from making serious westerns (John Sturges's *Hour of the Gun*,

Still: Marlowe. *'Does your mother know what you do for a living?'* – Marlowe (James Garner) is beaten.

1967) towards comedy. After two light comedies, he made a successful spoof western, Burt Kennedy's *Support Your Local Sheriff*, in the same year as *Marlowe*. While not a spoof, *Marlowe* makes considerable use of Garner's wit, and one of the ways in which it is unlike *film noir* is that there is very little element of lack of control in the hero's relation to events. The treatment of sex and violence in the film will indicate this sufficiently. Sexually, Marlowe is a figure of stability, provided with a girlfriend who has nothing to do with the detective narrative, and his relation to the other women in the film is relatively undeveloped. Violence in the film is treated as comedy – when he is attacked by hoods Marlowe's line is 'Does your mother know what you do for a living?', and the greatest physical threat to his life, the martial arts of Winslow Wong (Bruce Lee) is treated as farce in a sequence in which Wong is goaded by Marlowe into leaping over a balcony to his death.

It might seem from this that *Marlowe* has no place in a discussion of modern *film noir*, but it is precisely its lack of reference to the material of 'forties *noir* that in some respects exposes one crucial subject which it does have in common with *The Long Goodbye*: its attitude to the California culture of the present and the past.

This is where the film starts, with Marlowe encountering youth/drug culture as he arrives at a cheap hotel in search of a missing person. Narratively this place is a hotel – visually it is a contemporary hippie squat, covered in peace signs and with the name 'The Infinite Pad' written on the wall of the building outside. Marlowe is waved inside, where he finds the proprietor crashed out on drugs, lying asleep. All of this is unambiguously negative, but it is not only youth culture that is worthless. The woman at the centre of the mystery in Chandler's novel was a film star – here she has become the star of a situation comedy, handled by a talent agency. At one point Marlowe stands in the TV studio control room, ostensibly viewing the show but actually watching a clip from a Greta Garbo movie on one of the monitors. Gesturing to it, he says to the star's manager, 'She was great, wasn't she – on film.' The manager's reply – 'Oh, yes, the show we're doing is out there' – draws an unconvinced 'Good' from Marlowe. This is followed by a cut to the two monitor screens, one showing a banal modern dance routine from the show, the other showing Garbo.

These scenes cannot be read as analysis. Rather, they exist as prompts, confirming the audience's assumptions as to the status of the modern. And if the modern is trashy, then a central quality of this modern Marlowe is his old-fashionedness, an adherence to the past that is constantly being reinforced in the film. This is partly a matter of behaviour, such as Marlowe's attitudes to sex and money, but it is also suggested visually. Exteriors for Marlowe's office are not in a modern block, but in an old office building; almost nothing distinguishes the set for the interior of the office from a 'forties counterpart. Marlowe comments on this as an indication of his honest poverty and describes himself to Wong as 'the last of a dying dynasty'. Sometimes the stress on Marlowe's old-fashioned qualities is unlikely. Immediately after the scene with Garbo on the monitor, we are asked to accept that this man does not know the meaning of the term sitcom.

The main action of the plot serves to expose all the central participants apart from Marlowe as more or less representative of the worthlessness of modern times. The only exception to this is the decent police sergeant (Kenneth Tobey), where the connection with tradition is established by casting an actor associated with earlier Hollywood production.

Altman's *The Long Goodbye* operates in not entirely dissimilar, if more pretentious, terms. It shares the strategy of giving as its first *aperçu* on the state of modern times a condemnatory snapshot of youth/drug culture – the apartment opposite Marlowe's is occupied by a group of girls, always seen semi-nude and apparently partly stoned. They continue to appear at intervals throughout the film, the object of voyeurism and speculation. Despite Marlowe's last comment on their state in the film – 'they're not even there' – they are very much present for the audience, as Altman's symbol of the collapse of the younger generation, and specifically of the eclipse of sexual desire by drug culture.

Just as in *Marlowe*, the corruptness of the modern extends beyond the hippie world. Altman's plot turns on the figure of Terry Lennox (Jim Bouton), who brutally murders his wife and ruthlessly uses his old friend Marlowe (Elliot Gould) to make his escape to Mexico. Marlowe covers for him and believes in his innocence, but the narrative slowly confirms his guilt. When finally tracked down by Marlowe, he is indifferent, telling him, 'what the hell, nobody cares'. Marlowe replies that 'nobody cares but me' and shoots him dead.

This modernisation of Chandler radically rewrites the original in order to stress contemporary rottenness. In Chandler's novel, Lennox has the same relationship to Marlowe, but he is innocent – the murder in the novel is committed by a woman for whom Marlowe sees the act as 'a remote kind of suicide', and who does later kill herself. In Altman's version, this woman, Eileen Wade (Nina Van Pallandt), is repositioned as the amoral lover of the murderous Lennox.

Where violence in *Marlowe* tended towards the comic, here it serves as a much more extreme critique of the present. The world in which 'nobody cares' has as its central trope men's violence towards women. This is not only implicit in Lennox's murder of his wife, but is made explicit in the scene in which the gangster Marty Augustine (Mark Rydell) suddenly and for little immediately apparent cause smashes his beautiful girlfriend's face with a coke bottle. This startling moment makes sense read against the wider premise of Altman's film, set up in the opening shots of Marlowe alone except for his cat, and the indifferent, stoned women on the opposite balcony.

Still: The Long Goodbye. *The defeated artist – Roger Wade (Sterling Hayden) with his wife Eileen (Nina Van Pallandt).*

Still: The Long Goodbye. *Not Humphrey Bogart – a characteristic pose from Elliott Gould as Marlowe.*

This is a world in which the idea of the couple has failed completely, and in which the action is punctuated by hysterical and desperate scenes between men. The actual offence for which Augustine's girl is punished with the coke bottle is her daring to intrude uninvited on a male ritual, Augustine's interrogation of Marlowe.

Again, an attitude to the past goes along with this treatment of the present. The difference between *Marlowe* and *The Long Goodbye* here can be expressed as the difference between the Garbo clip and the figure of the gateman at the Malibu Colony in *The Long Goodbye*, who offers at intervals vocal imitations of Barbara Stanwyck, James Stewart, and Walter Brennan. The past is still established by reference to Hollywood, but achieved performance is replaced by party turns.

The exception to this is the character of Roger Wade, the blocked writer played in the film by Sterling Hayden. The use of Hayden represents once more the tendency in *film noir* set in the 'seventies to elevate the past as a complementary gesture to condemning the present. In Chandler's novel Wade is ambiguous, a popular novelist trying to live up to his reputation as a great lover, a figure of pathos finally murdered by his wife. Altman turns him visually into the semblance of Hemingway, and his suicide by drowning represents the artist's Hemingwayesque abandonment of a worthless world that is clearly unworthy of him.

Roger Wade functions very much as the real 'hero' of the film, for Altman's other main device is to offer, via the casting of Elliott Gould, a modernised Marlowe, the point of whose performance is to announce his differences from the private eye of 'forties or 'fifties *film noir*. Partly this

is a matter of Gould's roles up to this point as the star of a number of ironic comedies on modern manners. Another related element is Gould's style of performance: his hesitancy and passivity as Marlowe. The announcement made through the casting of Gould is clearly intended to be unmissable, so that, uniquely in the cycle, one of the offered rewards of the film is the enjoyment on the part of the audience in perceiving how little Gould approximates to its sense of the figure as presented in earlier books and films – how 'modern' he is.

The prominence given to the choice of actor and quality of performance may disguise other differences. The most important of these is the dissociation of the character from the agencies of the society. This is a Marlowe without either an old or a modern office, a Marlowe without any relationship to the police other than one of mutual incomprehension and contempt, a figure who drifts through the film without any ties to places or institutions. Altman's visual expression of it, one of the first things we are shown in the film, is the shot of the wall above Marlowe's bed, disfigured by his habit of striking matches on any convenient surface, a motif throughout the film.

The climax of this is the scene in which Marlowe is taken to hospital after being hit by a car. He wakes up in bed next to a figure who is a familiar element in the satire on the loss of identity in medical institutions – most famously from Joseph Heller's novel *Catch-22* – the man bandaged from head to foot. He tells a nurse that the bandaged man is Marlowe, and discharges himself. After calling at the Wades' house, where he is again mistaken for someone else, he leaves for Mexico to track down and shoot Terry Lennox.

This metaphorical casting off of identity is all simple enough, and it serves to confirm the shift in the conception of Marlowe. Not only does Altman present a world in which nothing has value, but insofar as the modernity of this hero consists of his not having any identity, his final gesture can have almost no point. It is the film's version of the 'happy ending', the destruction of the wicked couple that is Terry Lennox and Eileen Wade.

Of course we wish to see Terry Lennox punished, and Altman seems to wish to say to us that this can now happen only in a place which is nowhere. Mexico is not presented as an alien order – the contrast with *Chinatown* will be instructive – but as an empty stage. Chandler's novel ends with the last meeting between Lennox and Marlowe, in which Lennox is seen as a figure of pathos, a man who has lost his identity. They part, never to meet again, and Chandler reserves his last words for the cops: 'No way has yet been invented to say goodbye to them.' Altman turns Marlowe into a figure with no more identity than Chandler's Lennox, but the subject of irony rather than pathos, dancing off into long shot to the tune of 'Hooray for Hollywood'. We are offered the satisfaction of Lennox's death, but the terms in which the moment is offered insist modishly on its meaninglessness. While the modernity of all this is constantly asserted, the opportunity to ask the question as to whether the kinds of contemporary corruption that produce a Lennox or an Augustine are the same as produce the behaviour of Marlowe is never taken up.

Chinatown

Like every other film in the cycle, *Chinatown* opens with a scene built around its male star, here the private eye J.J. Gittes, played by Jack Nicholson. Again, the meaning of the film is in part accessible if we consider the implications of this casting.

A key moment involving Nicholson in *Five Easy Pieces* (Bob Rafelson, 1970) is the 'chicken sandwich' scene. The setting is a diner, in which the character played by Nicholson becomes increasingly enraged at a waitress who will not accept his order for a particular combination of elements that would make up the simple food that he wants. In Rafelson's film, the moment, ending in a gesture of violence from Nicholson, refers to other frustrations in the narrative, but it has a more general significance as a metaphor for an America in which desire is both pitifully shrunk – to this banal object – and frustrated: even so limited a request can't be met.

Ordering in a restaurant is thus a simple metaphor for getting – or not getting – what you want. The complication of it is when another party is involved and the desire for the right thing is not for yourself but for another – the question becomes: Do you interfere? The subject is then a metaphor for the ability to make the world right for someone else. This is the direction in which the idea moves when it reappears in *The Last Detail* (Hal Ashby, 1973), which immediately preceded *Chinatown* for Nicholson; the two films share the same screenwriter, Robert Towne. The film shows us Nicholson as a 'lifer' in the US Navy. He and another sailor take a young naval convict across country to Portsmouth naval prison, where, as the result of a trivial offence, he is to begin an eight-year sentence. On the journey, struck by the hopelessness of the convict's situation, the two escorts try to show him a good time, or rather to teach him how to have one. The 'chicken sandwich' scene is reprised at two points, a scene in a diner where the Nicholson character makes the convict send his hamburger back, and a later scene in which the convict, unprompted, does the same thing with his badly prepared breakfast.

This looks like a learning process, but within the larger context of the film it is only ironic. The education of the doomed convict, little more than a boy, cannot reverse the social forces within which all three men are trapped. After aborting a pathetic escape attempt, the sailors deliver him to the prison. In *Chinatown*, Gittes will say

of his past: 'I was trying to keep someone from being hurt, and I ended up making sure that she was hurt.' With 'she' altered to 'he' the sentence might stand as an adequate gloss on the action of *The Last Detail*, and as a clue to Nicholson's roles here. *The Last Detail*, a film about American servicemen made between the withdrawal of ground troops from Vietnam in 1972 and the fall of Saigon in 1975, may accurately address the frustrations of an America in which the desire to act is overwhelming, but the conditions in which action is placed are overwhelmingly negative. In Ashby's film, the metaphor for this is the north, much of the action taking place in freezing cold and snow.

In *Chinatown*, Polanski and Towne set this need and the ability to act on it within the context of the *film noir* private eye. Two subjects are stressed from the first. One comes from the film's title and from the dissonant sounds played over the Paramount logo and the names of the stars, before the main theme tune begins. This is the idea of mystery, of a world that operates under a different, inaccessible order. The other is control: the character of the private eye as a successful, competent professional. The latter is strongly established in the opening sequence with Curly (Burt Young), a local tuna fisherman and client of Gittes. The camera moves back from the stills in Curly's hands, which show his wife and another man making love, to include the white-suited Gittes, coolly watching Curly's reaction. This is a world that can reduce passion to black and white stills, smoothly dealing with Curly's grief and anger (Gittes pours him a drink) and anxieties about money (reassuring him about the bill, Gittes shows him out, with a reminder to drive home carefully). This is of a piece with the opening of the main plot that follows it: the fake Mrs Mulwray's request for surveillance of her husband. Again the scene stresses Gittes's control, his flat tones taking all this in as just more business. Control may also mean the ability not to interfere – his advice to 'Mrs Mulwray' is to let sleeping dogs lie.

The Los Angeles – and implicitly the America – that emerges from this is one in which irrational areas, such as adulterous affairs, can be made the subject of rationality through technology: they can be photographed. The scrutiny of Mulwray's public activities that follows is similarly within the capability of Gittes and his 'operatives'. Mulwray can be watched through binoculars, his movements timed via the dollar watches tucked under the wheels of his car, his row with another man again reduced to a set of grainy stills. Even the connection between the private and the public scandals, the idea that Gittes has been manipulated into smearing Mulwray by the latter's enemies in the Water and Power office, can be accepted by Gittes. He tells Mrs Mulwray (Faye Dunaway), 'I'm not in business to be loved, but I am in business,' and treats the problem as an attack on his professional integrity.

But this rationality works only partially or not at all in some contexts, most obviously, at the beginning of the film, in relation to water. If water is power – the linking of the two in the name of the department is an obvious hint – it is an elemental power only partly controlled by technologies. This is the basis of the first scene with Mulwray (Darell Zwerling) in which he opposes the building of a new dam by quoting the number of dead in a previous disaster. Announcing that 'I won't make the same mistake twice,' he leaves the hearing, and Polanski gives us a scene in which Gittes watches him wandering along the bed of a dried up river, trying to put together the details of the chicanery going on in his department. The detail of the image here is important. We see a tall thin figure in a suit and bow tie and wearing glasses stumbling over the awkward terrain. His encounter with a young boy on a horse (Claudio Martinez) simultaneously refers us to the western and emphasises the gap that has opened between pioneer qualities and the world of bureaucrats. He is a man out of place here; he would be at home in the office in which we are never to see him, where the pioneering history of the water company is reduced to the collection of photographs which lines the walls. The next sight of Mulwray is of his dead body being winched up the run-off channel in which he has supposedly drowned – he is still wearing the suit which signifies his unfittedness to deal with the forces aligned against him.

This sounds like a familiar configuration, in which the *film noir* private eye survives because of his greater closeness to western skills – physical strength, skill with a gun – in contrast to the pathos of the 'soft' man, the man who has strayed into the *noir* plot without the apparatus for survival. The contrast is rarely clear cut, and part of its point is to demonstrate the limitations of the private eye's powers. The failure of Marlowe sufficiently to protect his nervous client Lindsay Marriott in either version of *Farewell, My Lovely* is exemplary.

In *Chinatown*, the figures of Mulwray and Gittes are presented in such a way as to stress their similarities. We learn that they are both successful men who have moved from a past with some darkness to it to positions of relative power and success. At the scene of the discovery of Mulwray's body we learn that Gittes was once a policeman in Chinatown. His old colleague Escobar (Perry Lopez) strikes the same note – he is now 'out of there', since his promotion to lieutenant. Escobar's glance at Gittes's suit in this scene expresses his acknowledgement of how far Gittes has come since those days, both in terms of worldly success and perhaps in terms of dandyism. The light suit is a statement that the days of engaging in physical action for a living are apparently over.

The death of Mulwray initiates a movement back into that world. It is at this point that we see Gittes for the first time in a dark suit, wearing it in the scene in which the genuine Mrs Mulwray (Faye Dunaway) identifies the body of her husband. He then repeats Mulwray's walk along the bed of the dried-up Los Angeles river, encounters the same boy and asks him about Mulwray. That night he returns to the run-off channel where Mulwray was found, and is surprised, first by the rush of water which nearly drowns him, and then by the hired gunman Mulvihill (Roy Jenson), and by an unnamed man with a knife – played by Polanski – who slits his nose.

The moment is of great importance in the film, not least to our perception of it as modern *film noir*. Literally it is dependent on effects not present in 'forties and 'fifties *film noir* – on colour, since there is evident blood, and on the technology of special effects, since the slitting of the nostril appears entirely realistic. We may also suppose that so graphic a mutilation might have failed to pass the censor thirty years earlier.

Our understanding of the meaning of the wound depends on a number of related matters. First it is a mutilation of the actor's face; Polanski knows how important this is to photographing Nicholson and has stressed by his frequent use of close-up how vital this asset is to Gittes and his business. His ability to charm and dominate by his gaze is threatened, rendered potentially comic – the film cuts at this point to Gittes talking to his assistant Duffy (Bruce Glover), his face disfigured by the dressing over the wound. It is also the reminder that beneath the new sophistication of clothes and manner lies something older, the threat not only from the gun but from the knife. This takes us back to an earlier exchange. Gittes, teasing Escobar, asks him 'Are you still putting Chinamen in gaol for spitting in the laundry?' Escobar replies 'You're behind the times . . . they use steam irons now and I'm out of Chinatown.' Which is to say, you think that only you have changed, only you have moved on from a more primitive world, but I, too, have moved on, and that world has changed as well as you. The anxiety for Gittes is that in leaving the police and becoming the smooth private eye, he has lost his ability to operate in the world of knives and spit.

Still: Chinatown. *Gittes's bandage.*

It is these elements which play their parts in Gittes's subsequent behaviour. One part of him, back in his office in the next sequence, is the outraged professional, wanting to track down the 'big boys' of the operation so that he can find release by legal process: 'sue the shit out of them.' Another impulse is to return to something like his past life, where crimes were solved by physical confrontation – to fight his way to a resolution. We may see these two impulses as clearly related to his behaviour in interior and exterior sequences in the rest of the film, although in a paradoxical way: inside, he behaves with the impatience of the man of action, and outside, with the ineffectiveness of one who has spent too long behind a desk.

He makes a second visit to Mulwray's office, now occupied by Yelburton (John Hillerman), the former deputy chief. His contempt for Yelburton is expressed by an ironic version of his earlier remark to Duffy. It takes the form of enquiring if Yelburton is a family man, and the suggestion that 'maybe we can put the whole thing off on a few big shots, and you can go on being chief of the department for the next twenty years.' This contempt carries into the sequence in the county's hall of records, where the unhelpful clerk is a 'weasel'. The scenes both seem to promise control, the figure of Gittes successful in uncovering another layer of the scandal surrounding the proposed new dam. Leaving the hall of records, Gittes drives out to inspect the orange groves that are part of the operation, but in this world he is again inept. His car is no match for a man on horseback with a rifle, and he is finally beaten senseless by a farm worker. Again the stress is on his contempt for others. His insult to the farm worker – 'you dumb okie' – recalls the moment he had called the hood with the knife 'midget'.

What happens next is the appearance of Mrs Mulwray, who drives Gittes back to Los Angeles. Further to investigate the water scandal, they pose as husband and wife to gain entry to the old people's home that is a front for the operation. They are surprised there by the same hoods as had attacked Gittes in the nose-slitting scene, but with very different results. Mulvihill is beaten up by Gittes and the hood with the knife is left powerless as Gittes escapes by jumping on the running board of the open Packard driven by Mrs Mulwray. They return to the house, where she bathes his wound, and they make love.

This seems to represent at last a successful return on Gittes's part to his role as man of action. The sexual relationship between the two is clearly prompted by this; when they arrive back at the Mulwray house after the escape from the hoods, Mrs Mulwray asks Gittes how he survives, if the physical perils of the last twenty-four hours are typical. He replies that he hasn't done anything like this for a long time. The linking of the erotic with the ability to act in other ways is made again when, after making love,

Still: Chinatown. *Triumph of the old West – Noah Cross (John Huston).*

Gittes talks of Chinatown, a woman, and a mistake made in the past.

The point of the link being made here is that the impulse to interfere was doomed partly because it was placed in a context of the mysterious order of Chinatown, and possibly because it involved a woman. The film implies the limits of Gittes's understanding of 'other' orders with a script detail of some delicacy. Mrs Mulwray, thinking to be tender, listens to his story and comments, '*cherchez la femme*'. But she has to translate – this is a private eye who does not understand French.

The French that he does understand is one word – earlier he has said to her 'I do matrimonial work, it's my métier'. In subsequent scenes he tries to fit Mrs Mulwray into the categories of such work, first labelling her as the distastefully jealous wife when he thinks she is keeping 'Mulwray's girlfriend' captive, and then as the truly corrupt woman, when he thinks that she murdered her husband. His course of action at this point is dictated by professional imperatives. He telephones the police, and starts to slap Mrs Mulwray into giving the detailed explanation before they arrive, so that he will not lose his licence.

He gets an explanation which falls outside professional categories. Mrs. Mulwray was raped by her father when hardly more than a child – she was fifteen – and the mysterious woman, now seen clearly on the screen as little more than a child herself, is her incestuous daughter. This feels both like a distinctively modern moment – we know that the Production Code would have rendered such an explicit development impossible in 'forties and 'fifties *film noir* – but also an older reference, reaching backwards toward its roots in myth, and ideas of the collapse of dynasties. Its function in the film is decisively to shift our understanding of the source of corruption from the woman to the man, and Polanski has Mrs

Mulwray present almost as an afterthought a plot detail that will confirm that this man was responsible for killing Hollis Mulwray. Thus we have a man who killed his partner – which sounds like a plot from a western – and raped his daughter – which does not. This contradiction may help us to place him.

His name is suggestive – Noah Cross – as is the fact that he is played in the film by John Huston. He thus falls into the group of actors in modern *film noir* whose presence refers us back to earlier Hollywood production. But the differences between the figures is that Mitchum and Hayden, detective and artist in their respective films, play figures rendered marginal by American civilisation, doomed to isolation in one case and suicide in the other. Huston – he will survive the film and even get what he wants – plays a pioneer, a founder of the city that is Los Angeles, a man who comes West and makes his fortune by the successful exploitation of the technical skills and know-how of others. (He is also, of course, John Huston, director of *The Maltese Falcon* and *The Asphalt Jungle*, and we may suspect a play on the idea that a combination of pioneer endurance, technical understanding and intellectual agility make up the attributes of the successful Hollywood director. If so, then by his choice of his own role in this movie, Polanski is engaging in some mockery.)

Before the dénouement in Chinatown, Noah Cross has appeared in two scenes in the film, both interviews with Gittes. In the first of these, he seems to represent a resolution of the conflicts which I have discussed – the setting, a meal on the terrace of the Albacore Club, represents a marriage of inside and outside. Tieless, in white shirt and braces, Cross visually suggests pioneer strengths now old and respectable, successfully poised between the civilisation of the present moment and the wildness of the past. As he and Gittes are served lunch, the sheriff's boys practise riding in the background – the West as harmless side-show.

In the penultimate sequence in the film they meet again in a related setting, the terrace of the Mulwray home. This space is densely emblematic of the subjects of *Chinatown*. Behind them is the interior or rather the 'no home', as the Chinese servant has earlier put it to Gittes, the house where we never saw Mulwray and where the open doors now represent the failure to contain domesticity. Earlier Polanski has accentuated the anonymousness of the space, photographing Gittes and Mrs Mulwray in bed from above so as to show as little of the set as possible.

In the garden of the house is a tide pool, a salt water pool dependent on the tides for its renewal. Cross quotes Hollis Mulwray: 'Hollis was fascinated by tidepools. He used to say, "That's where life begins".' This is linked with Hollis's role as founding father. Twice Cross has said of him, 'He made this city.' The pool in the garden represents a dream of incorporating nature's life-giving qualities into the civilised, the home – a symbol of fertility. But this is not so easily achieved. When Gittes first comes to the house he encounters the oriental gardener, who might make us think of a Shakespearean original, the figure who tends the Duke of York's garden in *Richard II*. Like his renaissance counterpart, this figure expresses the attempt to keep order in an unstable world. He tells Gittes, 'Salt water bad for grass' – only continual replacement of the turf will sustain the illusion of harmony.

Mulwray, builder of the collapsed Vanderlith dam, has recognised this instability. The man who would not make the same mistake twice, he was drowned by Cross in the tide pool when he refused to go ahead with the dam despite the risks. Cross himself represents the desire to civilise – his plan is to make a new Los Angeles by incorporating the newly irrigated land into the city – divorced from any sense of human consequence. The fact of incest represents a related attitude to the family. When he says to Gittes here, 'Given the right circumstances, a man will do anything,' he thinks he is justifying incest – and perhaps murder. What this also makes explicit is the darkening of the benign possibilities implied by a world in which a man might once have done anything: the potential of the West.

Cross's money and political power make him almost impregnable, a perception which would not have seemed strange to a 1974 audience cognisant of the political realities of the Watergate scandal. What is left is the separate peace, the attempt to help the innocent escape, that is the only benign action possible in an America where unsafe dams are unstoppable. The action now moves to Chinatown itself.

The metaphorical meanings of Chinatown must be understood in relation to an American audience that had experienced the greater part of the Vietnam war and was now living through its closing months. One way of expressing this might be to say that the Orient here is not represented by mysterious or wily oriental figures. No oriental has a part of great substance in the film, and none has a speaking part in the Chinatown sequence. Chinatown is a locale rather than a human population, a context in which Americans find themselves in circumstances not of their choosing and in which their actions and dreams are frustrated, but for reasons that cannot be made accessible, because the underlying order cannot be understood or represented. In this respect, we may take *Chinatown* exactly to anticipate the cycle of late 'seventies films overtly set in the Vietnam of the war, with their inability to articulate Vietnamese culture other than as an obscure background to American lives and actions.

The final sequence is as follows. The police (Escobar and Loach) are already present when Gittes arrives in Chinatown with Noah Cross. They have already arrested his operatives, Duffy and Walsh, and Gittes is now arrested and handcuffed to a car when he protests. Mrs Mulwray and her daughter Katherine emerge into the street and attempt to drive away in the Packard. She ignores the police order to stop, and Loach shoots at the car, hitting Mrs Mulwray in the head and killing her. Cross claims the hysterical

Still: Chinatown. *The doomed women – Mrs Mulwray and her daughter Katherine.*

Katherine, and Escobar releases Gittes and his operatives, telling them to take Gittes home.

There are two points here. That this is Chinatown means that it is a world in which Americans in authority – the police – will use guns, and this results in disaster. But it is also a world in which disaster – the death of Mrs Mulwray, the loss of Katherine to Cross – can have no consequences, other, perhaps, than the fact of knowing that such a world exists. The effect of the sequence is both to recognise and give dramatic representation to the fact of there being such a world, and to record, crucial to an American understanding of it in 1974, the necessity of forgetting it, of being able to walk away. To do this is to blame this horror on, or assign it to, the place itself – all these meanings are condensed in the last line of the film when its ordinary man, Duffy, says to Gittes 'Forget it, Jake, it's Chinatown.' Rather than *film noir*, this is like the ending of a horror film – we might be reminded of a massively successful film of this period which ends on a note of forgetting, *The Exorcist* (William Friedkin, 1973).

As Gittes looks at the dead body of Mrs Mulwray, he murmurs to himself 'as little as possible'. He has earlier spoken these words to her in bed, quoting them as the District Attorney's advice to those who worked in Chinatown, in reply to the question, 'What were you doing there?' The point of the reminder to himself seems to underline the hopelessness of intervention in an America determined by on the one hand the obscurities of Chinatown and on the other the power of Cross.

The pessimism of *Chinatown* links it to earlier *films noirs*, but differs in that while the conflict between the acceptance and the refusal of the restraints of civilisation is a shared subject, the suggestion here is that there are areas of American experience beyond the appeal to either side of this division, that must simply be covered by the command to 'forget it'. Polanski gives this idea a human embodiment in Noah Cross, and a geography in Chinatown. Others were later to consider related matters via Vietnam, but this is not to say that Chinatown here is meant to be Vietnam, any more than Vietnam itself can be understood in American culture simply as just another country in south-west Asia.

It is also necessary to add that Polanski and Towne do not claim that this is the whole world. The film follows its stars from initial encounter to bedroom and to Chinatown, where the flaw in Mrs Mulwray's iris is translated into the bloody mess of her shot-out eye. But it also follows Curly, beginning in Gittes office looking at the photographs of his wife, and ending at home eating a meal with his family – though the wife now has a black eye. If these two trajectories are related (and the imagery of eyes and seeing in the film is elaborate and extended), then Curly and his woman, an ambiguously reconciled husband and wife, may have the function of a comment that not all lives end in Chinatown.

I want to return for a moment to the opening sequences of the films that I have been considering. Three of them seem to have one thing in common. The stoned youth outside the hotel in *Marlowe*, and the girls on the balcony of their apartment in *The Long Goodbye*, ask for the same response as the sequence in the dime-a-dance hall in *Farewell, My Lovely*, an acceptance that the atmosphere in which sexuality will function in the movie is one inviting profound cynicism on the part of the audience; we are asked to agree that we all know how hopeless all that is, and to identify with a star who takes the same position. This is a shift from 'forties and 'fifties *film noir* which proceeded from a belief in the importance of sexuality and sexual choice (a belief that clearly doesn't need to depend on the actual choice made in any given case being wrong or right). This is the issue behind a question that I asked earlier: What sort of a man (or woman) might be right for this woman (or man)? I take it that this question – together with the question: Why is this so? – is central to *film noir*, just as it is central to some Hollywood comedy in the 'forties. The problem which the 'seventies films cannot overcome is that having evacuated the area of sexuality of any value, they cannot then cut through cynicism to the point where we can have an investment of any kind in the choices of the principals. This is less damaging in *The Long Goodbye*, where it is part of Altman's thesis not to try, or in *Marlowe* where such matters are gestural, than in *Farewell, My Lovely*, where the relationship between Marlowe and Velma seems only embarrassing.

This leads to a broader question. Given that these are narratives where the subjects have attitudes and loyalties relating to a past world – past cultural material that the audience is assumed broadly to know – how does the sensibility of the 'seventies relate to this knowledge, and to this world? Our reading of these films depends crucially on the positioning of our attitude to earlier *film noir*. At its crudest, this is not much of a difficulty – the superiority of the 'modern' viewer, the one who 'understands' *film noir* – is safely assumed, whether it is inflected towards indulgent tolerance of older loyalties or cynical complicity with their erosion.

Only *Chinatown* resists this. Polanski's trajectory, from Curly's groans over the stills of his wife's love-making to Katherine's screams at the sight of her dead mother, is an insistence on the potential of images to shock, to be hard to forget and to resist categorisation, a powerful point in the America of 1974. In a cultural situation where the danger is of a smooth assimilation of *film noir* narratives into the untroubling category of 'classics', *Chinatown* reprises *film noir*'s role as a vehicle for exploring images that are on the fringes of the permissible. Polanski's witty vision of the artist for the 'seventies is characteristically enlivening – not a grand *auteur*, but a threatening little thug with a knife.

MOVING TARGETS AND BLACK WIDOWS
Film Noir in Modern Hollywood
Leighton Grist

'Every director's favourite genre'
                                    Dennis Hopper, 1990.

Over the past twenty-five years, *film noir* has experienced a critical and industrial renaissance. Critically, it has afforded scope for, and furthered the development of, a number of approaches: formal, historical, feminist, psychoanalytical. Industrially, with its transgressive plots, idiosyncratic character types and distinctive visual style, it has provided fertile ground for very disparate filmmakers. Its darkness and fatalism would seem to be well suited to our stereotypically jaded, cynical modernity. Like critical approaches to *noir,* however, the genre's conventions have undergone various changes. These, in turn, reflect wider cultural, industrial and ideological developments. In dealing with these changes, it is not possible to cover all the films reputed to be modern *films noirs,* the corpus of which is as contested as the original *noir* cycle. Rather there will be a selective attempt to chart and account for what I consider to be the significant trends and cycles of modern *noir*.

I

The most generally accepted starting point for modern *film noir* is *Harper* (Jack Smight, 1966), an adaptation of Ross MacDonald's *The Moving Target*. Its generically typical plot describes private eye Lew Harper's involvement in a complex, sexually charged hunt for a missing husband. In its realisation, however, *Harper* introduces a number of signifiers of modernity, distinguishing marks of industrial and historical context: an updated Californian setting, the use of colour, greater sexual frankness (if not, in this case, openness), the casting of a recognisably contemporary protagonist/star (Paul Newman), the transmission of decidedly modern attitudes and mores. Similar elements are variously apparent in most 'sixties and 'seventies *films noirs,* whether they have contemporary settings (e.g. *Hickey and Boggs,* Robert Culp, 1972) or are period re-creations *(Farewell, My Lovely,* Dick Richards, 1975).

More interesting, perhaps, is a group of films produced approximately from the late 'sixties to the mid 'seventies, which are differentiated by their questioning of the conventions and discourses of *film noir* narrative. Essentially challeng-

ing crucial ideological assumptions embedded in the genre, these films enact a process of formal revision and thematic demystification. Foregrounding generic forms and representation, they are not just modern, but modernist.

Point Blank (John Boorman, 1967) takes the *noir* predilection for elliptical narrative to a self-conscious extreme. Its narrative fragmentation is compounded by occasionally extreme disjunction of space and time and by the constant interruption of 'unmotivated' inserts and flashbacks. Thus, early on an apartment changes from furnished to unfurnished in the time it takes Walker (Lee Marvin) to open a door. Some of the inserts are repeated almost obsessively, especially those of Walker being accosted by Reese (John Vernon) at a reunion and of Walker being shot at Alcatraz. Near the end of the film, displacement of space and time also becomes displacement of character: as Chris (Angie Dickinson) embraces Walker, the film cuts successively to Walker and Chris in bed, Walker and Lynne (Sharon Acker) in bed, Reese and Lynne in bed, Reese and Chris in bed, before returning to the original couple and setting. These manipulations highlight the text's symbolic logic, embodying a characteristically modernist emphasis upon the implication of form in the creation of meaning.

This reflects back upon what *Point Blank* describes. The text's foregrounding of its constructedness declares its status as a fiction. In its denial of linearity before a more fractured, a-temporal progression, the narrative also invites comparison with the operation of subjective fantasy, playing upon the notion of film as dream. Diegetically, the film can be read as Walker's fantasy as he lies, shot by Reese, in Alcatraz. This much is overtly cued by Walker's voice-over just before the main titles: 'Did it happen? A dream?' The nature of the fantasy is central to the text's ideological connotations. It projects Walker as an 'ideal' male protagonist, a potent, unstoppable seeker hero. However, consistent with Sigmund Freud's concept of dream-work, Walker's fantasy equally suggests a working through and re-repression of 'unacceptable' tensions, a condensation and displacement of male fears. This parallels the psychoanalytical implication of classical *noir* narrative, in which the male protagonist repeatedly has to negotiate a series of threats to his personal and sexual identity and

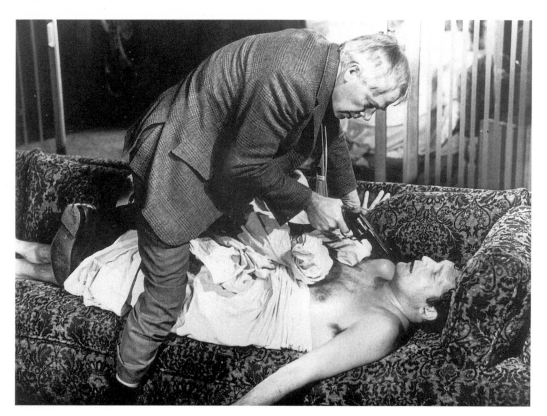

authority. The difference is that in *Point Blank* the process is presented *as* a fantasy, a construct.

Considered thus, Walker's actions during the main body of the film suggest a willed illusion of male heterosexual dominance. Characteristically, for *film noir,* this is in part defined in relation to contrasting female figures. First, Walker revisits his wife, Lynne. Having betrayed Walker for Reese, Lynne represents a sexually transgressive woman, although she is hardly a *femme fatale.* In a projection of Walker's vengeful animus, she not only abases herself before him with admissions of guilt and remorse ('You ought to kill me'), but, in a 'validation' of Walker's rectitude, and an acting out of her compunction (and his subconscious desire), she commits suicide. In a too-convenient, dream-like transference of affection, Walker finds solace in Lynne's 'good' sister, Chris. Despite initially feeding Walker's ego ('You were always the best thing about Lynne'), Chris still requires to be won over. The clichéd manner in which this occurs implies a movie-fuelled masculine fantasy with Chris's struggles suddenly becoming desire as she tussles with Walker on a poolroom floor.

Before this, Walker has to confront Reese – a need explicitly related to Reese's shooting and double-crossing of Walker. The confrontation also implies a denial of homosexual attraction, first hinted at when, after Chris denies any desire for Reese, Walker ambiguously notes, 'I want him.' This is returned to as Walker sets up a decoy to distract the guards of Reese's penthouse: he has two gay men tie themselves up after telephoning

Still: Point Blank – *Walker (Lee Marvin) and Reese (John Vernon).*

the police about his 'assault'. This (narratively gratuitous) figure of coextensive desire and repression is mirrored when Walker confronts Reese as he lies, naked, in bed with Chris (another decoy, whose 'masculine' name here becomes suggestive). Reese asks to be allowed to get dressed, to which Walker equivocally replies, 'I want you this way.' This potential admission of desire is followed by brutal repression. After being questioned by Walker, Reese half-falls, half-throws himself to his death from the terrace of the penthouse. The tacit, 'subjective' motivation for this lies in three quickfire flashbacks which precede Reese's death. In these, Reese demands Walker's friendship as he lies on top of him on the floor during the reunion, their position prefiguring that of Walker and Chris on the poolroom floor. Walker's repression, however, is successful. No further homosexual intimations disturb his 'dream'.

The recuperation of Walker's masculinity is completed by his uncovering of the corruption at the heart of the film's mysterious 'organisation'. During this process, Walker consistently affirms his manhood through violence and intimidation – one fight occurs behind a cinema screen, in a metaphorical dream space, at a club called The Movie House – and the successful termination of his quest permits his apotheosis as a male hero. He refuses to be paid off by Fairfax (Keenan Wynn), the head of the organisation, who has used Walker to kill his rivals. Instead, he holds him in suspense, a position of subordination. Psychoanalytically, this represents a fulfilment of Oedipal desire, a usurpation of the father-figure. Generically, it aligns Walker, who has previously claimed that he just wants the money Reese owed him, with the 'moral' hero epitomised by Philip Marlowe. But Marlowe is a fiction. So is Walker's fantasy, which is diegetically located as a dream. This further underpins the film's critique of the male hero: it is the dream of a dying man, an expiring illusion.

The undermining of the hero is continued in *The Long Goodbye* (Robert Altman, 1973) and *Chinatown* (Roman Polanski, 1974). In the former, Altman and Elliott Gould create a Philip Marlowe who frustrates the expectations that surround Chandler's character. The Marlowe of the novels and their 'forties adaptations is a figure who, through a combination of intelligence, wit, and morality, is able to bring a semblance of order to a corrupt, confusing world. The Marlowe of *The Long Goodbye* is a character who understands little, solves less, and whose wit has degenerated into a mumble of unfunny clichés. More specifically, this Marlowe, as Robert Phillip Kolker notes, 'is a man out of time' *(A Cinema of Loneliness: Penn, Kubrick, Scorsese, Spielberg, Altman*, Oxford University Press, second edition, 1988, p.342). Incongruous, for early 'seventies California, in his black suit and 1948 Lincoln Continental, he seems utterly disconnected from the modern world. Consequently, his residual morality isn't just quaint, like his insistence on 'itemised accounting', but a dangerous liability. It is his old-fashioned trust in friendship, his refusal to believe that Terry Lennox (Jim Bouton) could kill his wife, that leads to his being compromised and threatened. But while all this posits Marlowe's 'mythic' honour and individual prowess as historically inadequate, the film equally criticises contemporary mores. It presents a society dominated by amorality and violence, where people are generally venal or indifferent or stoned, and where the cops who arrest Marlowe are almost indistinguishable from the hoods who

threaten him. This, in outline, suggests an update of the social darkness of much classic *noir*, but in *The Long Goodbye* there is no-one able to achieve even an appearance of order. The only offered alternative would seem to be suicide, the option taken by novelist Roger Wade (Sterling Hayden).

Fittingly, Marlowe's one act of accommodation with the modern world occasions the film's largest break with the Marlowe of Raymond Chandler. At the end of *The Long Goodbye*, Marlowe, finally disabused of illusions, finds Terry Lennox in Mexico and shoots him in cold blood. This would be unthinkable for the 'forties Marlowe. As Michael Walker argues in his article on *The Big Sleep* (Howard Hawks, 1946), even when *de facto* responsible for death, Marlowe's actions are either 'justified' or the act is displaced on to other characters. After killing Lennox, Marlowe walks down a road, away from the camera, eventually breaking into a jig. At this point, a forcedly upbeat version of 'Hooray for Hollywood', taken from *Hollywood Hotel* (Busby Berkeley, 1937), and previously heard at the start of the film, over the United Artists logo, is introduced on the soundtrack. This complicates any narrative satisfaction caused by Marlowe's revenge. On one hand, the music provides a jarring, cynical counterpoint to Marlowe's actions and supplies further commentary on the callousness of modern life. More broadly, it calls attention both to the tendency of Hollywood narrative to celebrate and naturalise such endings and to its frequent validation of the solution of problems through violence.

The reflexivity here complements not only the film's generic revision but also its stylistic approach. *The Long Goodbye* is mainly shot in a series of slow, deliberate zooms, pans and tracks, with the camera rarely static. The sense of uncertainty and instability this conveys, often independent of the narrative, is exacerbated by the de-centring of the action within the Panavision format and by the use of off-hand, overlapping dialogue, which rarely seems to get to the point. These elements are hardly 'invisible' or integrated into the diegesis as a reflection and expression of the protagonist's feelings, as they would be in classic Hollywood *mise-en-scène*. They draw attention to the text as text and need to be negotiated by the spectator as a modernist 'admission' of the text's complicity in its representation of a corrupted world.

While *Chinatown* lacks such formal experimentation – it is realist, if stylised, in approach – it nevertheless continues the deconstruction of generic norms. This again centres upon a critique of the mythic private eye. Its protagonist, Jake Gittes (Jack Nicholson), is a filmic descendant of the Marlowe of *The Long Goodbye*. Hence, inverting a familiar cliché of private eye probity, Gittes's chief source of income is divorce work. His motivation is 'business', not morality. Ironically, the only time he moves outside his *'métier'*

Still: Point Blank – *the fight at The Movie House, a metaphorical dream space.*

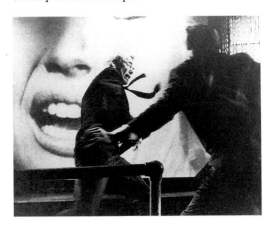

to act personally, with honour, it ends in disaster. For like the Altman/Gould Marlowe, and despite the bluster of his various theories, Gittes is an extremely flawed investigative figure. From the moment he is set up by the fake Mrs Mulwray, Ida Sessions (Diane Ladd), he finds himself in a situation beyond his control.

Gittes is essentially an innocent caught in a dark, violent world beyond his (generically circumscribed) comprehension. A world figured topographically by the setting of Chinatown, 'the symbolic locus of darkness, strangeness and catastrophe' (John G. Cawelti, 'Chinatown and Generic Transformation', in *Film Theory and Criticism: Introductory Readings,* Gerald Mast and Marshall Cohen, eds, Oxford University Press, 3rd ed., 1985, p.509), it obtains personification in the figure of Noah Cross (John Huston). Personally depraved, Cross is the force behind an irresistible complex of political and financial corruption. His ruinous influence is potently underscored by the deep-rooted, mythic connotations of his control of the water supply, his ability to turn Los Angeles into a desert waste land; this degenerative authority is parallelled, on a familial level, by Cross's incestuous relationship with his daughter. Against this, the more limited mythic potency of the private eye is plainly insufficient: the film's main ideological focus is its dethroning of the lone hero. As Cawelti says, 'the image of heroic moral action embedded in the traditional private-eye myth' is progressively shown to be 'totally inadequate to overcome the destructive realities revealed' in the course of the story.

The film ends with the death of the woman, Evelyn Mulwray (Faye Dunaway), whom Gittes had tried to save. The 'contradictory' representation of Evelyn undermines another generic convention, that of the *femme fatale*: the fascinating, sexual woman who lures the hero into criminality, ruin and/or death. For while Evelyn suggests a *femme fatale* visually, and does lead Gittes into corruption and danger, she is a victim rather than a seductress. The daughter and former lover of Noah Cross, she is killed as she attempts to escape her father. The fact that Evelyn's death repeats Gittes's admitted failure to save another woman in Chinatown places her fate within a tacit historical continuum. In a 'correction' of the misogyny inherent in the characterisation of the *femme fatale*, this suggests a comment upon the position of women under patriarchy; it also critically foregrounds the cyclical dominance of patriarchal power, underlined as the narrative ends with Cross in possession of his and Evelyn's daughter, Katherine (Belinda Palmer).

The modernist phase of *film noir* hardly occurred in a vacuum. It typifies a more widespread tendency within American cinema from the late 'sixties to the mid 'seventies which encompassed, for instance, westerns (e.g. *The Wild Bunch,* Sam Peckinpah, 1969; *McCabe and Mrs Miller,* Altman, 1971), gangster movies (*Bonnie and Clyde,* Arthur Penn, 1967), and

musicals (*At Long Last Love,* Peter Bogdanovich, 1975; *New York, New York,* Martin Scorsese, 1977). This was perhaps the only time when parody and reflexivity – long-term, 'innocent' staples of comedy and the musical – have been used in American film with a consistently 'serious' ideological intent. It is a self-conscious, innately critical development that can be located – at the risk of oversimplification – within interactive cultural, ideological/political, and industrial contexts. Culturally, generic revision is part of the reinflection of American film associated with New Hollywood Cinema, a movement marked by the integration of art cinema, especially French New Wave, tropes into Hollywood film-making – most obviously, the use of an elliptical mode of narration and an emphasis on more introspective, ambivalent protagonists. Simultaneously, there is a reworking of the revision and deconstruction of American generic forms undertaken by the New Wave film-makers (e.g. Jean-Luc Godard's *A Bout de souffle,* 1959, and *Alphaville,* 1965; François Truffaut's *Tirez sur le pianiste,* 1960; and Jacques Demy's *Lola,* 1961). In addition, there are specific references, like the way that the fragmented, elliptical narrative of *Point Blank* represents an extended allusion to that of *Hiroshima mon amour* (Alain Resnais, 1959).

It is vital to remember that New Hollywood Cinema was largely financed and distributed by the major studios. This helps to explain the comparative conservatism of New Hollywood Cinema: there was little possibility that the majors would, or could, support a high-modernist or Godardian counter-cinema, as Dennis Hopper discovered to his cost when he made *The Last Movie* (1971). On the other hand, genre provides a framework within which ideological and formal challenge can be both expressed and contained within familiar, commercially acceptable boundaries. As Thomas Elsaesser wrote in 1975, American cinema 'remains an audience-orientated cinema that permits no explicitly intellectual narrative construction. Consequently, the innovatory line in the American cinema can be seen to progress not via conceptual abstraction but by shifting and modifying traditional genres and themes, while never quite shedding their support' ('The Pathos of Failure: American Films of the 'Seventies – Notes on the Unmotivated Hero', *Monogram* 6, October 1975, p.18).

New Hollywood's questioning of generic convention and relative blockage of the linear-affirmative narrative/goal-directed hero implies a response to wider ideological fragmentation. It can be seen to reflect the undermining and the perceived instability of patriarchal norms occasioned by the period's numerous social and political upheavals: racial tension, the rise of counter-culture, the New Left and feminism, the Vietnam War, Watergate. The increasing darkness of 'seventies *film noir* – whether modernist or not – indexes a vision of America where order and justice seem ever more impossible. As much is summarised in the America of *Night Moves* (Penn, 1975), a setting where everyone is implicated, all action is tainted, and 'truth' is impossible to discern.

Related to this is the brief cycle of paranoia films which flourished in the wake of Watergate, a cycle to which *Chinatown*, with Gittes ultimately helpless before personal as well as institutional corruption, tangentially adheres. While this cycle includes such formally contrasting films as *The Conversation* (Francis Ford Coppola, 1974) and *Three Days of the Condor* (Sydney Pollack, 1975), it offers a common, *noir*-inflected structure. The films present a claustrophobic/paranoiac world of threat and mistrust, within which their protagonists seek, but usually fail, to expose the corruption within an all-powerful, oppressive economic or political organisation. It is a pattern perfectly embodied in *The Parallax View* (Alan J. Pakula, 1974), a film which significantly foregrounds its generic antecedents through a self-conscious, chiaroscuro conclusion.

That earlier interrogative and formally innovative films found a ready space in late 'sixties Hollywood can be referred to the industry's state of crisis. The consequence of a number of factors, including surburbanisation and the loss of the majority audience to television, it meant that the studios became prepared to accommodate a new audience, specifically the young, largely college-educated, vaguely left-liberal viewers who, by the end of the 'sixties comprised 'three-quarters of all "frequent moviegoers" ' (Thomas Schatz, *Old Hollywood/New Hollywood: Ritual, Art, and Industry*, UMI Research Press, Ann Arbor, Michigan, 1983, p.190). It was also the demographic group predominantly involved in the various challenges to the dominant ideology. Hence Hollywood's partial – and only partial – encouragement of 'different' subjects and approaches. What we regard as New Hollywood Cinema was never more than a minority of Hollywood production, and the failure of most of the films to turn a profit contributed to the studios' almost total return, by the late 'seventies, to more 'conventional' modes of film-making.

Taxi Driver (Scorsese, 1976) supplies a fitting culmination to the modernist phase of *film noir*. Narratively, *Taxi Driver* is a less direct descendant of classic *noir* than, say, *Chinatown*. Instead, it relocates and critically reworks *noir* elements in a 'seventies New York setting to make a highly developed, reflexive, modernist totality. It contains a plethora of references to various precursors, re-presenting motifs, elements and structures from a variety of films, its most extended, integrated allusions being to *The Searchers* (John Ford, 1956), *Psycho* (Alfred Hitchcock, 1960), *Journal d'un curé de campagne* (Robert Bresson, 1950), and *Peeping Tom* (Michael Powell, 1960). At one level, the film asks to be read via such references as a self-conscious/reflexive artefact. On this level the text achieves a formal homology with the suggested psychology of its protagonist, Travis

Bickle (Robert De Niro). Travis is represented less as a coherent, unified individual than as a radically decentred personality, differentially determined by and acting out such clichéd mythical roles as the gabby cabby, the idiosyncratic romantic and the lone, avenging hero. Given his final violence, it is no coincidence that early in the film his cab is filmed passing a cinema showing *The Texas Chainsaw Massacre* (Tobe Hooper, 1974).

Within this framework, conventional representations are similarly reflexive. Betsy (Cybill Shepherd) – the political campaign worker whom Travis dates once, offending her when he takes her to a porno movie – moves from virgin to whore, 'pure woman' to potential *femme fatale*, but only as a construct of Travis's consciousness. As much is signified by her first appearance. Betsy is first seen in slow-motion as she enters campaign headquarters from the street. Her movements are accompanied by Travis's voice-over: 'She was wearing a white dress. She appeared like an angel, out of this filthy mess.' The awkward rhyme explicitly locates the vision as that of Travis, a connotation confirmed when, as if with mental effort, he hesitantly completes his voice-over, 'They . . . cannot . . . touch . . . her,' and the shot dissolves to the same words uncomfortably written in large, clumsy print in Travis's diary. As in *Pierrot le fou* (Godard, 1965), this slightly disturbs the action's direct address by implying the contingency and constructedness of the given viewpoint. The slow motion not only draws attention to itself as a technical, cinematic effect, but, typically of Scorsese's work, again connotes subjective apprehension. Later, after Betsy has refused his further advances, Travis recasts her as 'corrupt': 'you're gonna die in hell like the rest.' Travis's terms of reference

Still: Taxi Driver – *Travis Bickle (Robert De Niro), a radically decentred personality.*

are significantly those of the misogynistic dualism fundamental to patriarchal culture in general and *film noir* in particular. Compounding the factitiousness of this are the scenes of Betsy without Travis, during which she seems nothing other than an 'ordinary', if somewhat empty, woman.

The perception of Betsy as *femme fatale manquée* implicitly structures Travis's failed assassination attempt. In a tacit re-enactment of the Oedipal revolt of *Double Indemnity* (Billy Wilder, 1944) or *The Postman Always Rings Twice* (Tay Garnett, 1946) – what Frank Krutnik terms the *noir* 'criminal adventure' (Krutnik, 1991, p.136) – he is 'driven' by his failed desire for Betsy to kill the political candidate Charles Palantine (Leonard Harris), who is structurally placed as his father-figure rival. His failure to kill Palantine causes Travis to direct his murderous attention to the pimp Sport (Harvey Keitel). He also exchanges one generic mode of action for another. Instead of an Oedipal rebel, he now becomes the hero of a captivity narrative, an update of Ethan Edwards (John Wayne) in *The Searchers*, as he seeks to 'save' the teenage prostitute Iris (Jodie Foster) – whom he has fallaciously constructed as 'imprisoned' – and to exact vengeance on her captors. The extreme nature of Travis's consequent actions in turn problematises, or rather blasts apart, the myth of justifiable male violence – reverberations that are intensified by the close identification we are encouraged to have with Travis.

Indeed, *Taxi Driver* invites an identification so complicit that much of the text's reflexive self-criticism becomes apparent only in retrospect, after the film's final break in identification – another example of the accommodation/innovation dualism previously seen in New Hollywood's generic revision. Central to our identification with Travis is the film's controlled formal approach. In a successful reworking of *noir* expressionism, *Taxi Driver* presents a dark, claustrophobic world lit by the glare of garish, symbolic reds and greens. We share this vision as Travis's reflected subjectivity, a perspective reinforced by both local, if systematic, perceptual signifiers (slow motion, the use of non-classical editing to imply personal disjunction) and the predominance of the character's often voyeuristic point of view. Once we are in his cab, we invariably enter his perceptual space. Travis's vision is obsessed – fascinated but repulsed – by 'the scum' and 'the filth' that it perceives. As the film proceeds, Travis becomes engulfed by this world of violence and corruption, becoming part of what he sought to destroy. A reprise of the *noir* protagonist's frequently compromised negotiation of the *noir* world, this process is psychoanalytically underscored by a cogent return of the repressed scenario, as Travis's sexual frustration achieves articulation through phallic violence. It also explains his symbolic suicide when, at the end of the closing massacre, he fires an empty pistol into his throat

and holds a bloodied finger to his temple and 'shoots' himself. Yet through our identification with Travis we, too, are drawn into this world, made to 'understand' and give assent to Travis's outlook. As we become locked into Travis's hermetic world view, his actions seem to be the only credible answer to the perceived corruption. Politics, in the shape of Palantine, who seems to be living out a cliché of the populist politician, appear powerless. Ironically, Travis's violence is a literal acting out of Palantine's empty campaign slogan, 'Let the people rule.' Misdirected thus by the film, which plays upon our culturally determined 'need' for heroes, we are proffered a salutary corrective by the resultant massacre. As in *Psycho*, we are punished for our desire for transgression, our indulgence of questionable urges. First, the violence acts as a punitive release for the plot's accumulated tension. Then we are forced to contemplate the implications of our identification with Travis. When three cops enter Iris's room, our sharing of Travis's perception is abruptly broken by a cut to an 'objective' overhead shot, from which the camera proceeds steadily to crane and track, via dissolves, out of the building in a graphic clarification of Travis's carnage, the results of the masculine violence in which we have been complicit. The coda presents Travis as a media hero. As in the conclusion of *The Long Goodbye*, we are asked to consider the condition of a society which champions a killer and sanctions such representations. *Taxi Driver*, however, exceeds the questioning of the hero in previous films through its *active* challenging of our social conditioning. In its encouragement and subsequent undermining of our need for vicarious aggression, it prompts an awareness of our own subjective implication in the sustenance of destructive myths.

II

While *Taxi Driver* represents a culmination of the *noir* revision of the 'sixties and 'seventies *Body Heat* (Lawrence Kasdan, 1981) holds a seminal position in 'eighties *film noir*. Enthusiastically received on its release, *Body Heat* is an entertaining, stylish thriller, with upfront, selfconscious allusions to classic *noir* that serve to legitimise its 'aesthetic' status. Stylistically, with its blue-black darkness, its use of enclosing shadows and framing devices, and the onmipresence of murky, claustrophobic sea-mist, *Body Heat* atmospherically duplicates a familiar *noir* world. Narratively, with a plot overtly culled from *Double Indemnity*, the film exemplifies a *noir* 'criminal adventure'. Ned Racine (William Hurt), a small-town lawyer, becomes passionately involved with Matty Walker (Kathleen Turner), under whose influence he plans to kill her husband. Both characters are clear *noir* types. None too bright, and sexually tempted into transgression, murder and ultimate ruin, Ned is (almost too) obviously a victim hero. Matty, who uses her sexuality and cynical intelligence to trap Ned, is correspondingly (and

Still: Body Heat. *Victim hero and* femme fatale –
Ned (William Hurt) and Matty (Kathleen Turner).

equally hyperbolically) a *femme fatale.* First appearing in white, and always one step ahead of Ned, she especially recalls Kathie Moffat (Jane Greer) in *Out of the Past* (Jacques Tourneur, 1947), one of the most potent *femmes fatales* of the 'forties. Completing the *noir* characterisation is Matty's husband, Edmund (Richard Crenna), a shady businessman. These elements are contained within a context of modish sexual openness, apparent both in the film's *noir*-ish one-liners and its steamy, explicit sex scenes. *Body Heat* shows what classic *noir* could only suggest; the film's title – with its connotations of passion, oppression, and intemperate behaviour – is its dominant metaphor and was a major selling point.

The overall effect of *Body Heat,* however, is justly summed up by Steve Jenkins: 'Ultimately, any response to Kasdan's film involves contradiction. The pleasures it affords are undeniable . . . But with regard to the generic area being plundered, it is equally obvious that nothing new is being offered beneath the gloss' *(Monthly Film Bulletin,* vol.49, no.576, January 1982, p.4). In place of the reflexive interrogation and re-inflection of the New Hollywood period, the generic self-consciousness of *Body Heat* is superficial, and not at all analytical – witness the film's representation of the *femme fatale.* Historically, the figure is changeable and ambiguous, with much of her sexual threat coming from motivations that lie outside stable male delimitation. It is an aspect which has been seen as both potentially 'progressive' and proto-modernist: 'not only

is the hero frequently not sure whether the woman is honest or a deceiver, but the heroine's characterisation is itself fractured so that it is not evident to the audience whether she fills the stereotype or not' (Gledhill, 1978, p.18). In *Body Heat,* any potential ambiguity is reduced to a gestural level. During Matty's last scene with Ned, she finally, and with apparent sincerity, claims: 'No matter what you think, I do love you.' This is somewhat jarring. Up to this point, Matty's love has been neither suggested nor dramatised. Matty has seemed to be in complete control of her situation, with any 'feeling' for Ned manifestly that of lust. The late introduction of ambiguity must be taken on trust, accepted as a 'necessary', if here empty and superficial, generic allusion.

This superficiality underlines *Body Heat's* status as a postmodern artefact. Its generic reference is not that of parody – which in its broadest sense covers the reflexiveness of modernist *noir* – but pastiche. As Frederic Jameson explains, 'Pastiche is, like parody, the imitation of a peculiar mask, speech in a dead language: but it is a neutral practice of such mimicry, without any of parody's ulterior motives, amputated of the satiric impulse' ('Postmodernism, or the Cultural Logic of Late Capitalism', *New Left Review,* no.146, July-August 1984, p.65). We have here what Jameson (p.87) describes as the abolition of 'critical distance', an apparent breakdown of the ability to judge representations against an extraneous 'truth' or 'reality'. The representations of *Body Heat* consequently come across as postmodern simulacra, 'endlessly circulating signifiers or representations that nowhere touch a reality' (Michael Ryan, 'Postmodern Politics', *Theory, Culture, and Society*, vol.5, nos.2-3, 1988, p.566). All this contradicts the ideological impulse at the heart of the earlier modernist revision of *film noir*, with respect to which I would contest Jameson's classification of *Chinatown* as postmodern (p.67). In essence the generic reference of *Body Heat* is no more 'productive' than that of *Dead Men Don't Wear Plaid* (Carl Reiner, 1982), a film in which Steve Martin's comic pastiche of *film noir* is intercut with scenes from classic *noir* movies in an elaborate in-joke.

In a period of ideological retrenchment, Hollywood cinema has preponderantly returned to the comforting affirmation, rather than investigation, of dominant myths and representations. As *Body Heat* suggests, generic conventions may be reprised, but rarely interrogated. The innate conservatism of the postmodern is underlined by its tacit denial of history. Jameson examines this aspect via reference to *Body Heat*, which he terms a 'nostalgia film' (p.66), noting how the film cleverly collapses time. Though set in 'eighties Florida, with contemporary stars, and, one can add, sex, the film uses elements like art deco titles, overt generic reference and the subtle use of a small town setting to elide any sense of high-rise modernity – it seems as if 'it were set in some eternal 'thirties, beyond real historical time' (p.68). This can additionally be read as 'an elaborated symptom of the waning of our historicity, of our lived possibility of experiencing history in some active way.' Representation has

Still: Blade Runner – *Zhora (Joanna Cassidy).*

Still: Blade Runner – *Rachael (Sean Young), the epitome of the* femme fatale.

instead become a process of quotation and combination of past styles, images, and stereotypes, an undifferentiated eclecticism within an ahistorical perceptual present.

As it crosses *film noir* with science fiction, *Blade Runner* (Ridley Scott, 1982) underlines the postmodern inflection of early 'eighties *noir*. As in *Body Heat*, its self-conscious use of *noir* conventions, while extensive and consistent, is superficial rather than analytical, pastiche not parody. Hence we are presented with a recognisably *noir* environment – dark, rain-soaked, steam-filled, claustrophobic city streets, heavily-shadowed interiors – which, while visually stunning, does not so much express classic *noir*'s existential angst and oppression as the fact that the film-makers were well versed in genre stylisation. The same applies to the representation of the film's protagonist. Blade runner Deckard

(Harrison Ford) is an update of the cynical, weary investigative hero, able to move between legal and criminal worlds – his semi-retirement from the police parallels the typical semi-detachment of the traditional private eye. He even wears a trench coat and supplies a pithy voice-over. But, again, the references are gestural rather than operative. Indeed, the status of *noir* allusion in *Blade Runner* is summarised by the initial representation of Rachael (Sean Young). Dressed in a tight black dress and spiked heels, heavily made up, smoking a cigarette, and tantalisingly aggressive towards Deckard, she is the epitome of the *femme fatale*. Rachael, however is a replicant, a copy of the real indistinguishable from the real, although the film seems uninterested in investigating the potential reflexivity of this.

The transgeneric nature of *Blade Runner* is likewise typically postmodern. Exemplifying the 'eclecticism' of postmodern aesthetics, it differs from the hybridisation of classical Hollywood in that the combined generic elements tend toward a lesser narrative and thematic integration. Instead there is a more superficial play of quotation, a *bricolage* of distinct allusions and pleasures. In *Blade Runner*, references to *film noir* (iconography, Deckard's actions and confrontations as a lone investigative figure) tend to stand out against the science fiction elements (foregrounded stress on technology, the 'Frankenstein Theme', etc.). Similar combinations of *noir* signifiers and other generic elements recur throughout the decade. *The Terminator* (James Cameron, 1984) alludes to *noir* in a spurious attempt to add to its oppressiveness (e.g. calling a club the 'Tech Noir'), while *Angel Heart* (Alan Parker, 1987) uneasily, and pretentiously, marries *noir* elements and a horror story. *Blade Runner* also projects a textual collapsing of history. Although it is set in the future, in 2019, the undifferentiated presence of signifiers of past and present (generic conventions, architecture, etc.) results effectively in a temporally indeterminate, mythic narrative space.

For all their postmodern allusiveness, however, *Body Heat* and *Blade Runner* show an ideological complicity with the period in which they were made. On one hand, as it indulges a fallacious liberalism, *Body Heat* suggests a residual 'seventies influence. The 'good' cop is black, while Matty, in a nod to Women's Lib, gets away with the money and fulfils her wish 'to be rich and live in an exotic land', ending up on a beach in Acapulco (compare the failed desire of Kathie in *Out of the Past*). Yet, as if tracking the transition from the 'seventies to the 'eighties, this overlies a more misogynistic discourse. As Judith Williamson has suggested ('Consuming Passions' in *Consuming Passions*, Marion Boyars, London, 1988), while in *Double Indemnity* insurance agent Walter Neff (Fred MacMurray) and Phyllis Dietrichson (Barbara Stanwyck) jointly use Neff's inside knowledge to maximise their returns from the death of Phyllis's husband, in *Body Heat* Matty is distinctly represented as the more active partner.

The aim here seems to be to emphasise Matty's culpability, a project compounded not just by Ned's sexual temptation, but also his passivity and incompetence: Matty's surreptitious amendment of Edmund's will – which renders it legally invalid, ensuring she receives all her husband's estate – is based upon her prior knowledge of Ned's legal ineptitude. Considered thus, the film plainly connects with the reactionary shift in American politics and cultural production during the 'eighties. It doesn't only condemn Matty, but also, through the deficiency of Ned – who ends up in prison – points a warning over the failure of masculine authority. Not that Matty goes unpunished. She may finally be in Acapulco, but seems introspective and unhappy. It is as if she regrets losing Ned and, by extension, is not accepting a more 'proper' female role. Compounding her unbelievable, closing statement of love, and contradicting the single-mindedness of her actions throughout, this smacks of vindictive male revenge.

Even for 'eighties Hollywood, the misogyny of *Blade Runner* is extreme. The female rebel replicants, Zhora (Joanna Cassidy) and Pris (Daryl Hannah), are both coded as sexual, independent and aggressive, for which they are duly punished. Not only are they shot by Deckard's (explicitly phallic) pistol, but their deaths smack of a disturbing, distasteful prurience. Fetishistically dressed in thigh-high boots, black rubber bikini, and PVC raincoat, Zhora is shot in the back as she tries to escape Deckard, her death questionably aestheticised, almost lingered upon, as she crashes through a department store's plate glass windows in slow motion. That she falls among store dummies is indicative of the film's sexual politics, as is her prior, identity-fixing occupation as a snake dancer. Pris is killed after she attempts to throttle Deckard between her legs. When she is shot, her death throes vengefully imply orgasm. Conversely, following her initial aggressiveness, Rachael is 'redeemed' by responding to Deckard's charms and accepting her subordinate role. The scene in which Deckard forces her to kiss and admit her need of him is one of the most brutal dramatisations of the offensive, sexist maxim that 'when a woman says no, she means yes' ever committed to film. In moving from *femme fatale* to 'good woman', Rachael shifts from one pole of womanhood to the other, a diametrical change of role the film is once more uninterested in examining. The contrast between this and the representation of Betsy in *Taxi Driver* encapsulates the differing aesthetic and ideological perspectives of 'seventies and 'eighties modernist and postmodernist *films noirs*.

The relationship between postmodern aesthetics and ideological connotation finds further expression in *Fatal Attraction* (Adrian Lyne, 1987). Another film with self-conscious references to *film noir*, it is overtly structured upon an opposition of day and night, 'normal' and *noir* worlds. These are linked to contrasting women, a good woman/mother figure, Beth Gallagher (Anne Archer), and a potential *femme fatale*, Alex Forrest (Glenn Close). Between is Beth's husband, Dan (Michael Douglas). Seduced by Alex, he functions as a victim hero, as his transgression brings his life, his family, and his stable patriarchal existence into jeopardy. The different realms associated with the opposed women are filmed in contrasting styles. Environments dominated by Alex are frequently shot in a *noir* manner: the dark corridors of her reconditioned apartment building; the barred chiaroscuro of the garage in which she trashes Dan's car; the cage-like lift in which she gives a petrified Dan a blow-job. These 'oppressive' elements are in turn complemented by the barren, sterile white of Alex's apartment. Against this is placed the warm domestic clutter of the Gallagher household, which is occasionally filmed in a literally golden glow. But in all this there is once more a sense of pastiche, of the superficial, even the imposed. The latter is particularly suggested by the placing of Alex's apartment in a *noir*-ish, flame-ridden meat-packing area (to be read as a hellish red-light district). Extending this, the film's *noir* allusions ultimately suggest a validation of 'eighties sexual reaction. The opposition of good woman and *femme fatale* works to naturalise a misogynistic denial of 'transgressive' female (sexual) independence before a championing of woman's 'traditional' subordinate domesticity. The tendentious level at which this operates is indicated by the representation of the main female characters. Alex (note the 'masculine' name) is blonde, assertive, and dresses seductively. Financially independent, with a job in publishing, she is sexually aggressive and insatiable; it is she who initiates and is dominant during the weekend affair with Dan. Beth is brunette, pretty, but hardly a sexual threat. Supportive and loving, housewife and mother, she is financially, mentally and emotionally dependent, needing Dan both to make decisions and to bolster her confidence.

This representational blatancy is matched by the film's dramatic partiality. What could be a potentially complex analysis of the repressions and tensions of patriarchal marriage – a potential briefly highlighted when Alex asks Dan, as he describes his 'happy' marriage, 'So what are you doing here?' – swiftly degenerates into an unequivocal, pernicious attack on the single, 'liberated' working woman. It is a process founded upon a dissimulative, extended double-take. Much of what Alex *says* is unexceptional, even broadly 'feminist', such as her demand that Dan face up to his 'responsibilities' when she finds she's pregnant, or her attacks on Dan's cavalier attitude toward her sexuality. However, her comments, and the views they expound, are utterly undermined by her increasingly psychotic actions, as she moves from sexual aggression through self-mutilation and harassment to acts of violence and open criminality. By contrast, Beth's acceptance of her objectification when Dan 'lovingly'

Still: Fatal Attraction. *Increasingly psychotic – Alex (Glenn Close), with slit wrists, kisses Dan (Michael Douglas).*

gazes at her as she sits, in her underwear, before her dressing-table, is afforded idealised, soft-focus approbation. Alex's 'problems' are related explicitly to her lack of patriarchal control (her father died when she was a child), and we are offered the insidious irony that what Alex really wants is to be Beth, a wife and mother, with the sexist implication that there is no other 'satisfying' female role. Finally, it is Beth, in a rare assertive act, who shoots and kills Alex. The destruction of her 'negative' alter ego, this completes the text's dissimulated misogyny: it is what every woman ought to do.

III

Fatal Attraction belongs to the most interesting *noir* cycle of the 'eighties, the Yuppie Nightmare cycle. This was quite short-lived. It commenced with the apparently unrelated production of *After Hours* (Scorsese) and *Desperately Seeking Susan* (Susan Seidelman) in 1985, before grinding to a halt with the heavy-handed, self-conscious comedy of *Blind Date* (Blake Edwards, 1987) and *Frantic* (Polanski, 1988). Industrially, this quick exhaustion of format reflects the economic rationale of cycles as 'a short-term attempt to rework a proven success' (Krutnik, 1991, p.12). Formally, the cycle's use of *noir* conventions supplies a conduit for the examination of contemporary concerns. As Krutnik puts it, the 'conventions have an affirmatory function in that they provide a consolidatory framework and a channel of comprehensibility whereby the new can be both bonded to, and embodied via, the familiar' (p.13). Mainly produced during the period of right-wing triumphalism which surrounded Reagan's re-election and preceded the 1987 stock-market crash, the cycle moves, like classic *noir*, to disclose a nightmare world of criminality and sexual paranoia, and suggests the presence of significant repressions and tensions beneath the confident, public façade of patriarchal-capitalist USA. In the Yuppie Nightmare cycle, a usually young(-ish), successful male protagonist is drawn through a combination of fascination, desire and chance into an underworld of crime and (in patriarchal terms) threatening sexuality. The character also functions to suggest the two worlds' interaction, their mutual dependence and definition. In *Fatal Attraction*, Dan is drawn into an affair with Alex because of his sexually unfulfilling marriage, but consequently needs to deny her, and all she represents, in order to maintain the parameters of his 'normal' patriarchal existence. The cycle's relationship to *film noir* is constantly underlined as its operations devolve into a series of recognisable iconographical motifs (day versus night worlds, domestic versus sexual woman, etc.). Such self-conscious allusion again tends toward the gestural and is essentially postmodern. The films' interest instead lies in their structural and subtextual modulation of tensions within Reaganite patriarchal capitalism.

Like much of Scorsese's work, *After Hours* focuses on tensions within contemporary masculinity. Computer operator Paul Hackett (Griffin Dunne) enters the night world of New York's SoHo on a date, only to find himself in a threatening environment of criminality, homosexuality, and, especially, of sexually aggressive women. With Paul's lack of male control figured narratively by his inability to control events or return home, the film becomes a self-conscious 'castration' nightmare, which is underlined not only by the film's foregrounded Freudian imagery, but also in the way that the plot's almost impossibly manic logic simulates that of a bad dream. These elements connect both to classic *noir* and to the subsequent films in the cycle. In *After Hours*, they plainly call for Paul's experiences to be considered an articulation or return of repressed fears. By contrast, the obvious boredom of his job and, by extension, his 'normal' masculine status, imply the very repression necessary for its maintenance. The irony is that Paul cannot live comfortably in either world, both of which he seeks to escape from in the course of the film. Aptly, Paul ends the film where he begins it – in his office – albeit marked (literally) by his night-time experiences.

The contrasting use of *noir* allusion in *Taxi Driver* and *After Hours* underlines the shift from modernism to postmodernism in 'eighties Hollywood. Both films bear the marks of Scorsese's authorship, but where *Taxi Driver* provides a reflexive investigation of representation and characterisation, as well as an expressionist development of *noir* stylisation, the generic references of *After Hours* remain at the level of pastiche. In short, the film's dark, rain-slicked city streets and enclosing framing devices (windows, fire-escapes, etc.), not to mention the generic status of its

characters (Paul as a victim hero, the women as *femmes fatales manquées)*, are all presented as mere signifiers of '*noir*-ishness' instead of contingent, historically-informed constructs to be investigated and analysed.

In the directness with which it confronts psycho-sexual repression, as well as its challenge to the authority of the patriarchal order, *Blue Velvet* (David Lynch, 1986) is the most extreme film of the Yuppie Nightmare cycle. Set in the mythical American small town of Lumberton, and on one level an 'eighties companion piece to *Shadow of a Doubt* (Hitchcock, 1943), *Blue Velvet*, like *After Hours*, is structured upon an overt dichotomy of day world and *noir* world. Its protagonist, Jeffrey Beaumont (Kyle MacLachlan), enters the *noir* world with a desire for knowledge plainly inflected by a desire for transgression; he is a seeker hero who quickly becomes a victim hero. Marked by criminality and violent sexuality, the *noir* world of *Blue Velvet* represents another metaphorical nightmare. A dramatisation of the patriarchal unconscious, it specifically, and powerfully, reveals the structures of repression upon which patriarchy is founded. As Jeffrey admits, 'I'm seeing something that was always hidden.'

'Seeing' is in turn a central, implicitly reflexive motif. It underpins the key scene – fundamental to the film's concerns and processes – in which Jeffrey is discovered spying upon nightclub singer Dorothy Vallens (Isabella Rossellini) from inside her closet, a voyeuristic position of masculine dominance analogous to that of the mainstream cinema spectator. Returning 'the Look' and appropriating the phallus in the form of a knife, Dorothy forces Jeffrey out of the closet and orders him to undress, placing him as a sexual object in an explicit overturning of patriarchal sexual roles that undermines the spectator's 'masculine' supremacy.

With the arrival of Frank Booth (Dennis Hopper), a psychotic drug-dealer who has kidnapped Dorothy's husband and son, Jeffrey returns to his role of voyeur in the closet. In a grotesque, primal scene that brutally lays bare Oedipally-related obsession, Frank gets Dorothy to call him 'Daddy' and calls her 'Mommy' before forcing violent, animalistic sex upon her. Again, this is played out with reference to the oppression of the sexual gaze. Frank repeatedly commands Dorothy, 'Don't you fucking look at me,' and twice viciously hits her; he also has her open her legs before his look. Jeffrey looks too, but, like the spectator, with horrified fascination. However, by later becoming Dorothy's lover, he literally takes Frank's place. Younger than Dorothy, Jeffrey also symbolically replaces her son, although the sado-masochism that mars their affair once more foregrounds the dominance and subdomination implicit in patriarchal sexual relations. A disquieting, obverse reflection of Oedipal determination, with Frank as a perverse father-figure, Jeffrey's actions significantly occur during a breakdown of 'normal' patriarchal control, while his father has been hospitalised with a stroke. His obsessive return to Dorothy's apartment, despite the obvious dangers, is testimony to the force of his own previously repressed impulses.

The threat this poses to the established patriarchal order is confirmed through narrative detail. Frank has already broken up one family, and Dorothy's admission of love for Jeffrey threatens Jeffrey's 'proper' romance with Sandy (Laura Dern), the daughter of Detective Williams (George Dickerson), the film's chief representative of the Law. This psycho-sexual challenge finds a socio-economic parallel in the activities of the 'Yellow Man' (Fred Pickler). The yellow-jacketed partner of Detective Williams, who uses his position to further Frank's regime of drug-dealing, murder and extortion, he undermines the legal, as opposed to sexual, stability of patriarchal capitalism.

Before order can be restored, Jeffrey has to negotiate a further threat to his socio-sexual identity, that of homosexuality. Discovered at Dorothy's apartment by Frank, Jeffrey is taken by Frank's gang to 'Ben's'. Explicitly, camply gay, Ben (Dean Stockwell), is the object of Frank's ambiguous desire. The nature of this is clarified when Ben mimes to Roy Orbison's 'In Dreams'. During this, Frank's fascinated but agonised gaze bespeaks mutual desire and repression and places Frank himself as a *victim* of patriarchal sexual determination. The choice of song is significant: Frank's desire can be released only 'in dreams' or, by extension, in the nightmare *noir* world of *Blue Velvet*. The return of the homosexual repressed in turn threatens Jeffrey when the gang take him for a joy-ride. Halting the car in a lumber yard, Frank smears his face with lipstick and kisses Jeffrey, repeatedly and violently, on the lips. An act that again implies both attraction and suppression, its connotations are underscored by Frank's threat of 'love letter, straight from my heart', a term for a bullet that conflates desire and its denial. Then, as Frank looks at Jeffrey, his desire battling with aggressive horror, he quotes 'In Dreams' and he rubs Jeffrey's face with his fetish of Dorothy, the blue velvet sash of her dressing-gown. Psychoanalytically, this connects Frank's ambivalent homosexuality to maternal overvaluation, a condition implicit throughout his relations with Dorothy. This again tacitly links Frank with Jeffrey – Jeffrey enters the *noir* world by leaving the closet. Frank's final, violent repression of his desire completes the sense of sexual ambiguity: he gets his gang to feel and admire his muscles before he knocks Jeffrey out. The scene consequently suggests that Frank's violence and aggressive heterosexuality – not to mention his obsessive sexual language – can be read as an overcompensation for his 'inadmissible' desires.

Jeffrey finally denies and successfully re-represses the physical and psychological threat represented by Frank by shooting him from *within* the closet. This is part of the film's restoration of stable patriarchal order: the 'Yellow Man' is killed; Detective Williams clears up the case; Jeffrey and Sandy are reunited. The efficacy of this, however, is undermined by the film's conclusion. Superficially, this affords an overt reinforcement of 'normality'. Waking in his garden,

Still: Blue Velvet – *Jeffrey (Kyle McLachlan) and Dorothy (Isabella Rossellini).*

Jeffrey sees his father, restored from hospital, in friendly communion with Detective Williams. Their wives, meanwhile, talk together in the living-room, while Sandy, anticipating her subordinate role as wife and mother, prepares lunch. That the scene begins with Jeffrey waking up even implies that the prior disruption has, indeed, been a dream. Yet credibility is forcibly broken when Sandy draws Jeffrey's attention to a patently mechanical bird – previously glimpsed by Jeffrey in a tree – as it sits, eating a bug, on the window-sill. This recalls Sandy's earlier recounting of her naively hopeful, and equally unbelievable, dream about the return of the robins, and with them love and transformation. Consistent with the film's undermining of 'normality', it is a vision that lacks any credibility before the powerfully realised *noir* world.

Something Wild (Jonathan Demme, 1986) supplies a less mordant, more optimistic vision. Yuppie Charlie Driggs (Jeff Daniels), newly promoted vice-president of a stockbroking company, is spotted by Lulu (Melanie Griffith) leaving a restaurant without paying his bill. Confronting him outside the restaurant, Lulu, a Louise Brooks lookalike, decides that Charlie is a closet rebel, and offers him a ride back to his office, only to drive him out of town and co-opt him into a series of transgressive adventures. Functioning as a *femme fatale*, Lulu quickly divests Charlie of his telepager, then gets him to rid himself of his umbrella and newspaper: a symbolic castration. In contrast, as she holds a liquor bottle between her legs, Lulu implicitly has the phallus. Her undermining of the law continues as she robs a liquor store and then handcuffs Charlie to the bed while they have sex in a motel (Lulu has the key). Unlike the protagonists of *After Hours* and *Blue Velvet*, Charlie finds all this liberating rather than threatening, a loosening of his initial, uptight Reaganite-capitalist conformity. As he comes under the influence of Lulu, of the pleasure principle, he moves from the dominance of the super-ego to that of the id. Charlie's exultation increases as Lulu forces him to dodge another restaurant bill, and the pair enjoy a drunken drive which ends when their car crashes into a motel sign. This liberation even takes on an implicit political dimension when, the next day, they pick up a car-load of black and hippy hitch-hikers – a harmonious racial-cultural mix as they sing 'Wild Thing'.

The potential progressiveness of this is not followed through: the film subsequently lapses into liberalism, and calls for a better balance of freedom and repression, id and super-ego, within the existing social/psychological situation. The change of emphasis is centred on Lulu's transformation into Audrey Hankel, her actual small-town identity. Blonde instead of dark, and wearing a simple white dress, like a good small-town girl, instead of the more outlandish black number in which she seduces Charlie, Lulu/Audrey switches identity in order to visit her mother and to go to her high-school reunion,

Still: Something Wild – *Lulu/Audrey (Melanie Griffith) seduces Charlie Driggs (Jeff Daniels).*

recuperating Charlie as her husband in the process. Such changing of identity through a change of clothes is a repeated motif in *Something Wild*: hence Charlie can 'become' Audrey's 'husband' by changing his grey business suit for a more casual blue one. Moreover, Audrey's fantasy 'normal marriage' is an acting out of a suggested unconscious desire. First hinted at by the close-up of a plastic nuclear family on the dashboard of her car, it represents a return of the repressed complementary to that of Charlie's liberation and his rediscovery of the rebellion he channelled 'into the mainstream'. Supporting this are the reciprocal false images they initially project to bolster their apparent personas. Charlie claims that he is happily married with two kids, Lulu that she's divorced. But Charlie's wife has left him, with his kids, for the family dentist, while Lulu/Audrey is married to Ray Sinclair (Ray Liotta), who turns up unexpectedly, on parole, at the reunion.

Psychotic and initially dressed in black, Ray is another id figure. Appearing upon, and complicating, Lulu's change into Audrey, he represents the return of what her transformation seeks to repress. For Audrey's desire to be fulfilled, Charlie has to overcome Ray. This likewise underscores the film's liberal trajectory, as it enables Charlie's new-found freedom to be married to Audrey's wish for patriarchal respectability. Charlie's confronting of Ray suggests the confronting, and embracing, of his own repressed self, his doppelgänger. After Charlie is beaten up and implicated in a convenience-store robbery by Ray, who repossesses Audrey, Charlie's desire to regain Audrey requires that he become more like Ray, more aggressive and unrestrained. Tracking Ray and Audrey, Charlie makes his move in a burger restaurant. With Ray hamstrung by the presence of police, Charlie takes his car-keys and money and acquires the most explicit signifier of his aggressive masculinity, his sports car. Leaving with Audrey, Charlie also pulls the trick Lulu had earlier used on him, leaving Ray in the restaurant unable to pay his bill. Now Ray is forced to steal a station wagon, Charlie's 'conventional' ownership of which he had earlier mocked, in order to track Charlie and Audrey. Nevertheless, in throwing out some plastic figures before he drives off, Ray underscores his incompatability with Audrey's dream of normality. The parallelling of Charlie and Ray comes to a head in their long, violent struggle at Charlie's Long Island house. Dressed in similar – and eventually blood-stained – white T-shirts, they come literally face to face as Charlie inadvertently stabs and kills Ray, a fatal articulation of his long repressed instincts.

The ending of *Something Wild*, like those of *After Hours* and *Blue Velvet*, is implicitly cyclical. But instead of projecting disquieting irresolution, the ending connotes successful reconciliation. Seeking Audrey, Charlie is found by her, where they had first met, outside the restaurant. That this meeting represents their necessary 'coming together' is affirmed by their clothes. Both wear a combination of black and white, of conventional and unconventional styles: Charlie wears a check shirt, patterned tie, and casual trousers; Audrey a smart, but idiosyncratic, polka dot, 'twenties-style dress and a wide-brimmed hat. Audrey asks Charlie if he wants a ride, he accepts, but – consistent with the ending's celebration of the patriarchal couple – this time he drives. This conventional championing of an 'improved' patriarchal order undercuts both the film's initial, joyous transgression and the more immediate intimations of change in Charlie: he gives up his stockbroking job, then sympathises with the new tenant of Lulu's apartment over exploitative landlords. In fact, as Cameron Bailey argues, Charlie's overcoming of Ray and Audrey's suppression of Lulu can both be read in class terms as the triumph of the 'dominant' class over the (archetypally sexual and violent) 'underclass' ('Nigger/ Lover – The Thin Sheen of Race in "Something Wild"?', *Screen*, vol.29, no.4, Autumn 1988, p.39). Audrey's final appearance may be unconventional, but it is hardly progressive – as Cameron Bailey puts it, 'Her final incarnation borrows from the *upper*-class style of another generation; she looks as if she had just stepped from a Scott Fitzgerald novel.'

Like *Something Wild*, *Desperately Seeking Susan* centres upon the figure of the doppelgänger. It is the only female-centred film in the Yuppie Nightmare cycle, and its protagonist, Roberta Glass (Rosanna Arquette), is initially bored and repressed in a materialist, bourgeois marriage to Gary, 'the spa king of New Jersey' (Mark Blum).

Her only release is the vicarious one of charting the movements of Susan (Madonna), a female free spirit, through the messages she exchanges with her boyfriend, Jim (Robert Joy), in the personal column of *The New York Mirror*. The contrasting situations of Roberta and Susan are quickly established as those of patriarchal determination and determination of self: of having a hair-do the way Gary will love against the literal (if narcissistic) self-definition implied by Susan's first act, the Polaroid she takes of herself in the hotel bedroom of a lover in Atlantic City.

The key of a public locker in which Susan has stored her belongings comes into Roberta's possession when, after obsessively following Susan in New York, she buys a jacket that Susan has traded in a clothes store. Roberta's 'becoming' Susan, her alter ego, continues as she changes her fashionable, bourgeois attire and hair style (an index of her oppression) for the alternative, junk-store look popularised by Madonna, both as Susan and through her mid-'eighties pop persona. The transformation is completed when, having arranged to meet Susan and return the key, she knocks herself out while fleeing from Wayne Nolan (Will Patton), the murderous partner of the Atlantic City lover. Suffering from amnesia, she is actually taken for Susan by Jim's friend Dez (Aidan Quinn).

Roberta has entered a realm of indeterminate identity, of fluid self-definition; she finds herself in a disconcerting *noir* universe, summarised by the 'nightmare landscape inside and surrounding the "Magic Club" ' which is 'lit in a foreboding chiaroscuro' (Peter Benson, 'Screening Desire', *Screen*, vol.31, no.4, Winter 1990, p.388). Her unease, however, is matched by that which she causes the men in her life. Simultaneously 'Roberta', 'Susan', and, after she takes a job as a magician's assistant, 'Davina, Queen of the Night', she stands outside stable male fixation. Thus Dez, who is attracted to Roberta, is troubled by her apparent inconsistency, her failure to match Jim's image of Susan. For her husband, Gary, the situation endangers his whole lifestyle. Seeking Roberta, he enlists the help of Susan, who is looking for her possessions. Operating as a metaphorical 'feminine consciousness', Susan reveals a side of Roberta – suggested by her hidden self-help and sex therapy books, and her diary, which is all 'about' Susan, her other self – which has lain dormant behind her masquerade of bourgeois compliance. The challenge to Gary's image of his marriage is heightened when Roberta is arrested on a prostitution charge and his sister, Leslie (Laurie Metcalf), claims that 'four out of five prostitutes are lesbians.' Roberta is constructed as both sexually promiscuous and homosexual, a double threat to the monogamous, heterosexual economy of patriarchy.

The film's concern with female self-definition overtly structures its conclusion. Confronting Gary in her dressing-room, Roberta pleads, 'Look at *me.*' Gary's failure to understand results in Roberta

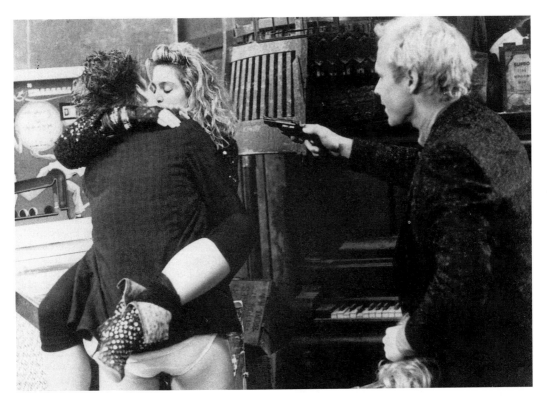

Still: Desperately Seeking Susan – *Jim (Robert Jay), Susan (Madonna) and Nolan (Will Patton)*.

returning to Dez, who is represented throughout as a less bourgeois, more understanding male. This is nevertheless disappointingly, even dissimulatively, recuperative. More significant in *Desperately Seeking Susan*, to paraphrase Laura Mulvey, is the dust the story raises along the road, its demonstration of patriarchy's instability before the implicit threat of the transgressive female.

IV

While the Yuppie Nightmare cycle uses a consistent *noir* structure to articulate a critique of Reaganite patriarchy, the use of *noir* elements in other mid and late 'eighties films varies greatly in form and effect. Among the most formally interesting and ideologically challenging of the films are those that at least partly eschew postmodern pastiche for a more integrated, if no less self-conscious, use of generic convention, with a return to textual depth instead of just a play of surfaces. The films may be compromised ideologically or uneven in effect, but their limitations are as instructive as their successes.

Someone To Watch Over Me (Ridley Scott, 1987) is unusual for an American film in foregrounding class difference. Structurally, it suggests an inverse Yuppie Nightmare movie. In particular, it offers a number of parallels with *Fatal Attraction*. Working-class policeman Mike Keegan (Tom Berenger), newly promoted to detective, is assigned to protect wealthy socialite

Claire Gregory (Mimi Rogers), who has witnessed a murder by psychopath Joey Venza (Andreas Katsulas). Mike and Claire become involved in an affair which not only threatens Mike's marriage but, when Venza targets his wife Ellie (Lorraine Bracco) and son Tommy (Harley Cross) as retributive victims, the lives of his family. While it is clear from the start that Mike is fascinated by Claire and her upmarket lifestyle, Claire functions as a *femme fatale:* more worldly and intelligent than Mike, she seduces him from his wife and class.

In *Someone To Watch Over Me, noir* stylistic features have two specific areas of reference. They provide an implicit commentary on the transgressive relationship of Mike and Claire, and underline the menace of Joey Venza. The two aspects are linked in that, as Mike becomes more involved with Claire the threat represented by Venza gradually encompasses himself, his friends and his family. Another reading, however, is invited by the film: once Mike is on the case, Venza functions as his doppelgänger, and acts out his disturbing, unconscious wishes. As much is exemplified by Venza's initial threatening of Ellie, when she hears him prowling outside her house. A genuinely unsettling scene, shot in a frightening chiaroscuro, it occurs simultaneously with the first consummation of Mike and Claire's affair, and implies the dark obverse of Mike's transgression, a brutal wish to deny his wife. A complementary suggestion occurs when Venza accosts Claire in a washroom at the Guggenheim Museum. Claire has gone alone to the washroom, against Mike's wishes, and

Venza's appearance can be seen as a projection of Mike's need to be considered indispensable by his charge. Another connection between Venza's violence and Mike's desire is suggested by the shooting of Mike's old friend and partner, T.J. (Tony Di Benedetto). Shot by one of Venza's men, who has been despatched to kill Claire, T.J. knows about, and is thus a threat to, the affair with Claire.

The threatening of Ellie and shooting of T.J. reflect Mike's tacit yearning to transcend and break class ties through his relationship with Claire. The fear and pain caused by these incidents augment the anguish and confusion shown by Ellie when she learns of Mike's affair to connote, in an ideological corrective to American cinema's usual, knee-jerk celebration of upward class movement, the negative face of such mobility, the suffering of those left behind. Mike's unconscious wish to kill or at least deny Ellie further relates to the implicit threat she poses to his masculinity. A foul-mouthed ex-cop, usually dressed in practical, asexual clothes, Ellie is a 'masculinised' woman who fixes the car and carries the groceries. By contrast, Mike is comparatively 'feminised': he is seen cooking and preparing food, and much is made of the smart clothes he wears and his blushing. Claire is traditionally feminine: dressed in stylish, 'womanly' clothes, she is someone with whom Mike can 'be a man'. Even when he turns up at her apartment, tired and drained after Ellie has discovered his affair, and abases himself before Claire's gaze, the intrusion of Venza's hit man swiftly enables him to reassert his male authority. Nevertheless, the killer's appearance at the point of Mike's temporary masculine 'failure' asks to be read as another projected response to Mike's 'endangered' manhood. It is similarly suggestive that Venza institutes his plan to kill Claire when Mike's feelings towards her are briefly ambiguous after his confrontation with Ellie.

The film reaches its conclusion when Mike meets Claire at a reception and tells her that their relationship can't work. This is interrupted by a telephone call from Venza, who is holding Ellie and Tommy as hostages, to be exchanged for Claire, a development that suggests a residual hostility by Mike towards his 'restrictive' family. Arriving at his home with Claire, Mike enters alone and tries to bargain with Venza. Getting Venza to hold him instead of Tommy at gunpoint, Mike becomes literally threatened by his doppelgänger, a metaphorical extension of the threat to his class and social identity implicit in his actions throughout. It takes Ellie to save the family, when she shoots Venza with a pistol handed to her by Tommy from its hiding-place under a table. Although this destruction of a threat to the family by a wife and mother replicates the climax of *Fatal Attraction*, its implications are significantly different. Certainly, it reunites the family unit: Claire withdraws after seeing Mike, Ellie, and Tommy in a desperate embrace upon

Still: Someone To Watch Over Me. *The restoration of the family (Tom Berenger, Harley Cross, Lorraine Bracco).*

the living-room floor. But unlike Beth Gallagher, who kills her own 'dangerous' alter ego, Ellie kills that of Mike. This completes Ellie's gradual assumption of familial (and phallic) authority. Her 'masculine' competence has allowed her to punch Mike down when he confesses his adultery; after throwing him out, she goes to a shooting-range, where she shoots out the groin of a male-figured target. This is another direct contrast with *Fatal Attraction,* in which Beth, after Dan briefly moves out, passively mopes. The concluding ideological connotations of *Someone To Watch Over Me,* while not unequivocally progressive, are uncommon for 'eighties mainstream Hollywood. Ellie's actions represent both a successful rearguard action by an embattled working-class and an inversion of gender authority within the patriarchal family, a feature hardly elided by the final, reconciliatory clinch between Ellie and Mike after he has pleaded to be taken back. Like many preceding *film noir* victim heroes, Mike is punished for his actions: he has lost Claire, forfeited familial control to Ellie, and his affair has caused his suspension, leaving his career in tatters. Claire's fate appears more questionable. Ejected empty-handed from the narrative, she is seemingly – and somewhat broadly – punished for her class status and, like a classic *femme fatale,* her sexuality.

The opening third of *No Way Out* (Roger Donaldson, 1987) similarly presents a forceful *noir* vision. A remake of *The Big Clock* (John Farrow, 1948), *No Way Out* begins with a sequence of potent political-sexual transgression. Naval officer Tom Farrell (Kevin Costner) meets Susan Atwell (Sean Young) at a Washington function, and they have sex in the back seat of an official limousine as they cruise past the White House, the Monument and the Capitol Building. Susan is the paid mistress of Defence Secretary David Brice (Gene Hackman), for whom Farrell goes to work as an intelligence officer. We are thus presented with an archetypal *film noir* Oedipal triangle of economically/socially successful older man, kept woman, and virile, younger man. This is given particular piquancy not only by the various personal and political transgressions of all involved (Brice is married), but also by the mutual possessiveness and jealousy of Brice and Farrell, between whom Susan is placed as victim. Much of this opening section is shot in variations of classic *film noir* lighting. A potentially pastiche effect, it is made to work, as in *Someone To Watch Over Me*, by convincing dramatic and thematic contextualisation.

Farrell and Susan return to Washington after a weekend away together, and Brice sees, but doesn't recognise, Farrell leaving Susan's house. Viciously confronting Susan, in a scene with effective low-key lighting, Brice knocks her to her death from an upstairs landing. Personal obsession and patriarchal violence here combine, through the characters' situation, with an intimation of political corruption and exploitation to afford a disturbing and, within the context of 'eighties Hollywood, potentially subversive moment.

It is also quickly nullified. Brice confesses his situation to his personal assistant, Scott Pritchard (Will Patton), who devises a plan to set up a search for the 'other man', to be framed as the killer, on the pretence of looking for a fabled Soviet spy, 'Yuri'. Assigned to head the investigation, Farrell – like his predecessor George Stroud (Ray Milland) in *The Big Clock* – simultaneously becomes a victim and seeker hero as he is instructed to 'find' himself. It is a *noir* situation which is never developed. The film instead devolves into an unconvincing mix of updated police-procedural story and conspiracy thriller. In the former strand, Farrell has to extricate himself from the situation before a computer-generated image, taken from the discarded cover of a Polaroid found at Susan's house, reveals him as the suspect. In the latter, the villain becomes Pritchard, who is gratuitously represented as a homosexual, Nietzschean overreacher and rampant neo-fascist, who hires a couple of ex-Special Forces assassins, fresh from Central America, to 'handle' 'Yuri'. This blatantly overdetermined characterisation, abjectly linking homosexuality and right-wing extremism, is central to the film's recuperation of its earlier 'subversion'. Pritchard is represented as so unregeneratively 'evil' that his suicide, when Brice reasserts himself and states his willingness to sacrifice his assistant, suggests a relieving restoration of 'proper' order. Indeed, despite his violence and transgression, Brice – an old-fashioned 'instinctive' individual for whom 'the normal rules don't apply' – is by the end of the film made to appear morally superior to any other authority figure, be it the clownish Senator Duvall (Howard Duff), his 'poodle', Marshall (Fred Dalton Thompson), the head of the CIA, or Sam Hesselman (George Dzundza), a systems analyst and flawed father-figure, who betrays Farrell to Pritchard. At this,

Pritchard shows just how evil he is by shooting Hesselman dead in order to implicate Farrell. In this context, Farrell's late sending of evidence incriminating Brice to the CIA appears but a gesture. By the conclusion, Susan and her fate are largely forgotten. Even so, lest there be any qualms over Brice's recuperation, the closing revelation that Farrell is, after all, 'Yuri', who had been ordered to engage in an affair with Susan, places her murder as 'instigated'. That at the last Farrell, although a Soviet spy, wants to 'remain' an American, only caps the film's tendentiousness.

As the *noir* vision of the opening of *No Way Out* unravels, so its use of a *noir* visual style – the darkened shots of Pritchard in his office, the chiaroscuro of Hesselman's murder in the gym – becomes gestural rather than operative and approaches pastiche. *No Way Out* is ultimately unable to transcend the limitations of its broader

Still: Black Widow – *Catherine (Theresa Russell).*

cultural context, to follow through its initial challenge to 'eighties patriarchal hegemony.

A similar failure is apparent in *Black Widow* (Bob Rafelson, 1987). In this, Catherine (Theresa Russell) is a fully fledged *femme fatale*, a woman who uses different identities to marry, kill and profit from a series of husbands. She is a figure with whom Alex Barnes (Debra Winger), a researcher in the Justice Department, becomes obsessed. The source of this obsession is ambiguous. What begins as an apparent desire for justice soon implies an equal desire for communion. Alex is represented as rather masculine. Apart from her name, she dresses functionally, refuses to go on dates, and plays poker with the boys. By actively investigating Catherine, she also takes the usual male role of the seeker hero. While her investigation is typically complicated by a growing personal involvement, the nature of this involvement (at first) seems decidedly atypical. When she follows Catherine to Hawaii, a lesbian attraction between the two is strongly signalled. Their first meeting, at a scuba diving class, suggestively moves from them practising mouth-to-mouth resuscitation, through an indulgence in mutual admiration, to Catherine asking Alex back to her hotel room for a 'decent' drink. It is a suggestiveness continued when Catherine saves Alex during a diving 'accident', even though she is aware of Alex's investigation, and reaches a climax when after Catherine's marriage to Paul Nuytten (Sami Frey), she kisses Alex on the lips.

But even before this, the film has begun a process of recuperation, almost as if it doesn't know how to – or is afraid to – develop the inherently oppositional situation it has established. Indeed, the forced, unconvincing and narratively complex plot to trap Catherine implies little beyond a virtually hysterical need to deflect attention away from the film's earlier connotations. Alex, in place of her earlier, implicit challenge to the patriarchal order, reverts to being its agent, as she ensures the arrest of the *femme fatale*. As in *Fatal Attraction,* the final defeat of the transgressive woman by another woman, who accepts the Law, adds to the ending's reactionary force. Catherine, moreover, accepts her capture without protest, as if concurring with the necessity of her punishment. As Teresa de Lauretis has noted, the Catherine-Alex relationship is ultimately reinflected as an Oedipal mother-daughter structure, underlined as Alex becomes more 'feminised' – literally wearing Catherine's clothes – and finds sexual satisfaction with a father-figure in the shape of Paul ('Guerilla in the Midst: Women's Cinema in the 'Eighties', *Screen*, vol.31, no.1, Spring 1990). This is textually underscored by the film's final scene. Having solved the case, Alex retains her more feminine identity, as if she has achieved a balance of career and gender fulfilment *within* patriarchy.

Unlike most modern *films noirs, Black Widow* avoids any pastiche or reworking of *noir* visuals.

Its visual surface is generally realistic, although marked by a symbolic use of colour (the recurrent use of red, green, and blue). An analogous approach is apparent in Rafelson's 1981 remake of *The Postman Always Rings Twice,* which replaces the (admittedly weak) *noir* expressionism of Tay Garnett's 1946 version with naturalistic period re-creation.

Manhunter (Michael Mann, 1986) is one of the most disquieting and formally challenging of all modern *films noirs*, but again generally refrains from using classic *noir* tropes. It transmits a parallel mood of oppression through a stylised, and variously alienating and claustrophobic, use of colour: green, blue, blue-black, even white. For a film concerned with psychopathology and the effects of technology, white affords an apt sense of clinicalness. It also reflects the film's return to a modernist approach by playing against generic expectation. In the scene in which detective Will Graham (William Petersen) visits jailed psychopath Dr Hannibal Lecktor (Brian Cox) at a high-security mental hospital, the white-on-white decor supplies a disorientating, obverse *noir* environment. As Graham and Lecktor sit face to face, shown in reflective reverse shots that place each character 'behind' the white bars of Lecktor's cell, we are graphically presented, once again, with the figure of the doppelgänger. Graham's speciality is entering the mind-set of psychopaths in order to track them down. This has allowed him to arrest Lecktor, to whom he has returned to get the 'scent'. Graham's uncovering of his darker side is underscored by the repeated use of mirror shots and given a jarring dramatic twist when his son Kevin (David Seaman) refuses to leave Graham alone with his mother/Graham's wife, Molly (Kim Greist). *Manhunter* implicates

Still: Manhunter – *Freddie Lounds (Stephen Lang) and Dollarhyde (Tom Noonan).*

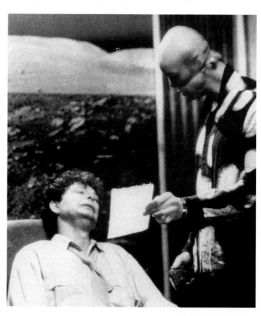

both the spectator and its own textual processes in the mechanics of masculine aggression. As Graham re-enacts the activities of serial killer Francis Dollarhyde (Tom Noonan), also known as the 'Tooth Fairy', we are constantly given Graham's point of view and, as he speaks into a tape recorder or mouths aloud, direct access to his thoughts. As these mirror those of the killer, we are made to share Dollarhyde's unsettling visual and emotional space. This produces a vitally critical, rather than possibly vicarious, perspective through the text's reflexive interrogation of technology, of the cinematic apparatus. *Manhunter* is a film filled with audio-visual technology: cameras, video, tape recorders and computers are the *modus operandi* of its narrative's investigative process. It is through viewing photographs and, especially, videotapes that Graham mainly gets to understand his quarry, to engage with his other self. As we are frequently shown these tapes while Graham views them, this reflects back upon our situation as cinema spectators, and implicitly questions our own position and pleasure in watching a film like *Manhunter* – the more so as it is through the same tapes that Dollarhyde, who works in a photographic laboratory, desires, objectifies, and selects his victims. Further implicated in this is the coded male gaze of mainstream cinema, and its structured and structuring dominance within Western media and society. It is an emphasis on 'the Look' that evokes and replays that of *Peeping Tom;* as Graham says of Dollarhyde, 'Everything with you is seeing.'

The collocation of 'the Look', visual technology, and male violence finds a frightening expression as Graham flies from Atlanta to Birmingham. Falling asleep, he dreams of Molly. She is filmed from his point of view, her image intercut with a reverse close-up of Graham, wearing an expression of ambivalent, possibly threatening desire. From this, we are taken, via three quick shots of photographs of Dollarhyde's mutilated victims, to the anguished reaction of the small girl sitting next to Graham on the 'plane – she has been alarmed by the photographs, which have fallen from Graham's lap. That this occurs upon Graham's dream-objectification of his wife intimates his unconscious potential for sexual violence. Another underscoring of the link between Graham and Dollarhyde, the correlation is again significantly mediated through photographs, the products of visual technology.

While dominating and desiring, Dollarhyde, too, seeks to be wanted and desired. Yet he can stand to be looked at only by his dead victims, who are no threat to his masculine authority, and whom he arranges as an audience to admire his power. It is a self-controlled objectification which, especially given his obsession with becoming God-like, suggests a narcissistic fetishisation of his power. His inability to accept the living female 'Look', however, implies a fear of taking a passive 'feminine' position, no matter how much he desires it. Dollarhyde's criminality

can be read as drastic masculine overdetermination, its implication of tensions within his sexual identity being underlined by his violent reaction to a planted newspaper report that he is gay: he burns the offending journalist alive.

Dollarhyde's preoccupation with visual dominance is only broken, in another nod to *Peeping Tom,* by the affection of a blind fellow-worker, Reba McClane (Joan Allen), who represents no visual threat. Ironically, it is a relationship destroyed when Dollarhyde mistakenly thinks he *sees* Reba kissing another worker. This motivates the film's final shoot-out, in which Graham overcomes Dollarhyde as he attempts to re-establish his dominance by killing Reba.

V

The modernist strategies and achieved seriousness of *Manhunter* have not been built upon in subsequent *films noirs. The Hot Spot* (Dennis Hopper, 1990) ushers the genre into the 'nineties with a full-blown return to a postmodernist aesthetic. An adaptation of Charles Williams's novel *Hell Hath No Fury,* the film was scripted in 1961. It concerns a drifter, Harry Madox (Don Johnson, in a role originally written for Robert Mitchum), who arrives at a small Texas town, where he gets a job as a car salesman and robs a bank. He also gets involved with two archetypal *noir* women: a young good woman, Gloria Harper (Jennifer Connelly), and a *femme fatale,* Dolly Harshaw (Virginia Madsen), who just happens to be married to Madox's boss (Jerry Hardin). Dolly not only tempts Madox into sexual transgression, but, after she sexually induces her husband's fatal heart attack, undermines Madox's relationship with Gloria and blackmails him into dependence. In the course of this, *The Hot Spot* affords a number of local pleasures: Madsen's exuberantly physical performance; the use of stylised colour to replicate *noir* oppressiveness; a fine, original blues soundtrack (Miles Davis, John Lee Hooker, Taj Mahal). Ultimately, however, the film is little more than a superficial exercise in genre pastiche. As in *Body Heat,* there is a subtle blurring of context. Setting, decor and dress place the action in an indeterminate temporal realm, as evocative equally of the 'fifties as of the 'eighties or 'nineties. All this is especially disappointing given Hopper's previous willingness to engage with socio-political actuality, whether in the problems of youth culture (*Easy Rider,* 1969; *Out of the Blue,* 1980), cultural imperialism (*The Last Movie*), or interracial gang warfare (*Colors,* 1988).

The Hot Spot closes on Madox's words, 'I've found my level, and I'm living it.' If this ends the film on a suitably fatalistic, *noir*-ish note, it also implies an elegy for the genre as represented by *The Hot Spot.* For what is vital is not so much the continuation of *film noir,* as the perspective of its re-working: whether its conventions present and analyse social tensions, or just exist as a collection of generic signifiers.

INDEX

Italic numerals indicate illustrations. Page references for directors and actors are restricted to specific information and comment; coverage of the films with which they were associated appears on the pages listed under individual film titles. In director entries, bold numerals indicate extended coverage of a film or films by that director. Literary sources for films are listed by author.